Organized Crime

World Perspectives

Edited by

Jay S. Albanese
Virginia Commonwealth University
Richmond, Virginia

Dilip K. Das
State University of New York
Plattsburgh, New York

Arvind Verma
Indiana University
Bloomington, Indiana

Upper Saddle River, New Jersey 07458

Library of Congress Cataloging-in-Publication Data

Organized crime: world perspectives/ edited by Jay S. Albanese, Dilip K. Das, Arvind Verma.
    p. cm.
  Includes bibliographical references and index.
  ISBN 0-13-048199-8
  1. Organized crime. 2. Organized crime—Cross-cultural studies. I. Albanese, Jay S. II. Das, Dilip K., 1941 - III. Verma, Arvind.
HV6441.O76 2003
364.1'06—dc21

                                                      2002016999

Publisher: Jeff Johnston
Executive Editor: Kim Davies
Assistant Editor: Sarah Holle
Production Editor: Rosie Jones, Clarinda Publication Services
Liaison: Barbara Marttine Cappuccio
Director of Production and Manufacturing: Bruce Johnson
Managing Editor: Mary Carnis
Manufacturing Buyer: Cathleen Petersen
Creative Director: Cheryl Asherman
Cover Design Coordinator: Miguel Ortiz
Cover Designer: Lorraine Castellano
Cover Image: Michael Paraskeras/Stock Illustrated
Marketing Manager: Jessica Pfaff
Editorial Assistant: Korrine Dorsey
Formatting: The Clarinda Company
Printing and Binding: Phoenix Book Tech Park

Pearson Education LTD.
Pearson Education Australia PTY, Limited
Pearson Education Singapore, Pte. Ltd.
Pearson Education North Asia Ltd.
Pearson Education Canada, Ltd.
Pearson Educación de Mexico, S.A. de C.V.
Pearson Education—Japan
Pearson Education Malaysia, Pte. Ltd.

Copyright © 2003 by Pearson Education, Inc., Upper Saddle River, New Jersey 07458. All rights reserved. Printed in the United States of America. This publication is protected by Copyright and permission should be obtained from the publisher prior to any prohibited reproduction, storage in a retrieval system, or transmission in any form or by any means, electronic, mechanical, photocopying, recording, or likewise. For information regarding permission(s), write to: Rights and Permissions Department.

10 9 8 7 6 5 4 3 2 1
ISBN 0-13-048199-8

CONTENTS

Preface

Contributors

Introduction: A Framework for Understanding   1
Jay S. Albanese and Dilip K. Das

PART ONE   PERSPECTIVES FROM NORTH AMERICA   19

Chapter 1   Organized Crime: A U. S. Perspective   22
Harald Otto Schweizer, Castle Nishimoto, Julienne Salzano, and Mike T. Chamberlin

Chapter 2   Organized Crime: A Canadian Perspective   46
Daniel J. Koenig

PART TWO   PERSPECTIVES FROM EUROPE   79

Chapter 3   Mafia and Mafia-type Organizations in Italy   82
Umberto Santino

Chapter 4   Organized Crime: A Perspective from the Netherlands   101
Oon van der Heijden

Chapter 5   Organized Crime: A Perspective from Poland and Eastern Europe   127
Emil W. Plywaczewski

Chapter 6	Organized Crime: A Perspective from Russia *Yakov Gilinskiy*	146
Chapter 7	Organized Crime: A Perspective from Slovenia *Darko Maver*	165
Chapter 8	Organized Crime: A Perspective from Austria *Maximilian Edelbacher*	188
Chapter 9	Organized Crime: A Perspective from the Council of Europe *Peter Csonka*	212

Part Three — Perspectives from Asia — 237

Chapter 10	Organized Crime: A Perspective from India *Arvind Verma and R. K. Tiwari*	240
Chapter 11	Organized Crime: A Perspective from Japan *Ayoka Uchiyama*	267
Chapter 12	Organized Crime: A Perspective from China *He Bingsong*	279

Part Four — Perspectives from South America — 299

| Chapter 13 | Organized Crime: A Perspective from Colombia
Leonardo Jesus Ramirez Rivera, Jorge Cesar Quadro, and Roger Juan Marcelo Tomas Botto | 301 |
| Chapter 14 | Organized Crime: A Perspective from Argentina
Hugo Antolin Almiron | 317 |

Part Five — Perspectives from Australasia — 331

| Chapter 15 | Organized Crime: A Perspective from Australia
John Broome | 333 |
| Chapter 16 | Organized Crime: A Perspective from New Zealand
Greg Newbold | 352 |

Part Six — Perspectives from Africa — 377

| Chapter 17 | Organized Crime: A Perspective from South Africa
C. J. D. Venter | 379 |

Chapter 18	Organized Crime: A Perspective from Tunisia *Rekik Riadh*	392
Chapter 19	Organized Crime: A Perspective from Zambia *Francis K. Ndhlovu*	406
Chapter 20	Organized Crime: A Perspective from Zimbabwe *Augustine Chihuri*	427
	Conclusion: Challenges for the Future *Jay S. Albanese*	438
	Additional Readings	460
	Appendix	469
	Index	472

Preface

Representatives from six continents and more than eighteen nations were assembled from law enforcement, research, and academia to offer the perspectives gained from their study and experience with organized crime. The perspectives were diverse and the approaches to understanding the phenomena varied widely, and their work formed the basis for this book. When we gathered in Yokohama, Japan, at the Third International Police Executive Symposium, it was apparent that organized crime is an issue of enormous concern around the globe, yet its nature and scope remain elusive.

The purpose of the symposium was to highlight the nature and extent of organized crime, the measures being taken to combat it around the world, and to make a comparative evaluation and debate on issues where there was a lack of consensus. It was found that despite obvious differences, organized crime manifests similar forms across borders. The need for cooperation was a resounding theme of the papers presented.

The information presented in this book is significant for several important reasons:

- A number of these national profiles of organized crime describe conditions in countries that are not widely known. The translation of some of these accounts into English and their presentation in this book provides information and insights into the nature of organized crime in locations around the world that previously were not well documented.

- The authors of each chapter are natives or persons greatly experienced in the countries they describe, who have the benefit of long-term experience and exposure to the political, economic, and social roots of organized crime and its control.
- The comparative summaries and analyses offered in the introduction and concluding chapters offer an assessment of common elements in organized crime and its control from a world perspective.

This book is a culmination of revisions of several drafts of the papers first presented at the symposium in Yokohama. The updated and edited versions of these presentations form the various chapters of this book. Nine challenges for the future conclude the manuscript, eliciting nine fundamental themes that cut across the earlier chapters. Suggestions for further readings are included at the end of the book.

The University of Kanagawa provided generous financial assistance and hospitality in hosting the four-day symposium in Yokohama. Professor Madoka Nagai of the Institute of Legal Studies at the University was a wonderful host. One well-known figure from each of the six continents represented selected top experts from their continent for participation in the symposium. These individuals were Obi N.I. Ebbe (Africa), Mangai Natarajan (Asia), Greg Newbold (Australia), Maximilian Edelbacher (Europe), Robert McCormack (North America), and Rubin Ruiz de Olanao (South America). Their work in selecting well-qualified participants for the symposium is responsible for the high quality of this volume. The symposium participants themselves are credited in their respective chapters and they have our gratitude for editing and revising their work as requested. Their work is important, contemporary, and has multinational implications for every country discussed.

Editors Kim Davies and Sarah Holle of Prentice Hall were supportive of the concept behind this volume and we thank them for shepherding the manuscript through the publication process. Thanks are also due to Lindsay Young of Virginia Commonwealth University for her editorial assistance on the manuscript.

The authors would also like to thank the following reviewees: Barry Sherman, Madonna University, Livonia, MI; L. Michael McCartney, Westfield State College, Amherst, MA; Patrick A Mueller, Stephen F. Austin State University, Nacogdoches, TX; Gene L. Scaramella, Western Illinois University, Macomb, IL; Michael Hallett, Middle Tennessee State University, Murfreesboro, TN; Francis H. Schreiner, Mansfield University of

Pennsylvania, Mansfield, PA; and Jerry Loar, Walker State Community College, Morristown, TN. Their comments were very helpful in the development of this book.

Jay S. Albanese
Virginia Commonwealth University, Richmond
jsalbane@vcu.edu

Dilip K. Das
State University of New York, Plattsburgh
dilipkd@aol.com

Arvind Verma
Indiana University, Bloomington
averma@indiana.edu

Contributors

Dr. Jay S. Albanese is a professor and chair of the Department of Criminal Justice, Virginia Commonwealth University, Richmond, USA.

Dr. Hugo Antolin Almiron is the director of the Judicial Police at Cordoba, Republic of Argentina.

He Bingsong is the deputy director of the Criminal Law Center of China University of Political Science and Law, Beijing.

Roger Juan Marcelo Tomas Botto works as an analyst for the State Intelligence of the Republic of Argentina.

John Broome is the chairperson of the National Crime Authority of Australia.

Dr. Mike T. Chamberlin teaches at the Criminal Justice Department of the North Carolina Central University, USA.

Augustine Chihuri is commissioner of police at the National Center Bureau of Criminal Investigation Department of the Republic of Zimbabwe.

Peter Csonka is at the Economic and Organized Crime Unit in the Division of Crime Problems, Directorate of Legal Affairs, Council of Europe.

Dr. Dilip K. Das is a professor in the Department of Sociology/Criminal Justice at the State University of New York, Plattsburgh, USA.

Dr. Obi N.I. Ebbe is a professor in the Department of Criminal Justice at the State University of New York, Brockport, USA.

Mag. Maximilian Edelbacher is chief of the Major Crime Bureau Bundespolizeidirektion Wien in Austria.

Dr. Yakov Gilinskiy is a professor at the Institute of Sociology, St. Petersburg, Russia.

Oon van der Heijden is the head of the Scientific Research Advisory unit in the Criminal Intelligence Division of the National Police Agency, The Netherlands.

Dr. Daniel J. Koenig is a professor in the Department of Sociology at the University of Victoria, British Columbia, Canada.

Darko Maver is a special counselor to the prime minister of the Republic of Slovenia.

Dr. Greg Newbold is a professor in the Department of Sociology at the University of Canterbury, Christchurch, New Zealand.

Francis K. Ndhlovu is a senior police officer in the rank of Inspector General in the Zambian Police Service, Lusaka, Zambia.

Castle Nishimotto is a senior officer working for the FBI.

Dr. Emil W. Plywaczewski is the director of the Department of Criminology and Organized Crime problems at the Faculty of Law, University of Warsaw, Poland.

Jorge Cesar Quadro works as an analyst for the State Intelligence of the Republic of Argentina.

Rekik Riadh is a senior police officer at the Police Headquarters in the Ministry of Interior, Republic of Tunisia.

Leonardo Jesus Ramirez Rivera is an investigator in the Republic of Venezuela.

Dr. Julienne Salzano teaches at St. John's University, Queens, USA.

Dr. Umberto Santino is the director of the Center *Siciliano di Documentazione* at Palermo, Italy.

Dr. Harald Otto Schweizer is an associate professor in the Department of Criminal Justice at the University of Central Oklahoma, USA.

Dr. R.K. Tiwari is the chief forensic scientist and deputy director at the Bureau of Police Research and Development, New Delhi, India.

Dr. Ayoka Uchiyama is a social scientist at the National Research Institute of Police Science, Tokyo, Japan.

C.J.D. Venter is a senior police officer with the South African Police in the Organized Crime Unit.

Dr. Arvind Verma is an assistant professor in the Department of Criminal Justice at Indiana University, Bloomington, USA.

Introduction

A Framework for Understanding

Jay S. Albanese and Dilip K. Das

Organized crime has become a national threat in both developed and developing nations. Individual criminals must work together in groups in order to take advantage of growing criminal opportunities provided by the world economy, the supply and demand of illicit products and services, the ease of international travel, ineffective laws, and weak or corrupt government officials. It is unlikely that organized crime can be vanquished, due to the insatiable appetite for money, power, and influence, which manifests itself in nations of all types. Nevertheless, the pooling of information regarding what is known about organized crime can make a tangible difference in developing a framework for understanding and addressing it, because organized crime is growing in importance as the world economy expands—and is shadowed by a criminal economy.

This sharing of knowledge and experience was the motivation behind the Third International Police Executive Symposium's theme of "Organized Crime: A World Perspective," on November 28 through December 1, 1996, in Yokohama, Japan. Attended by participants from 18 countries, representing six continents, the four-day meeting focused on several major themes:

- The concept of organized crime
- The nature and extent of organized crime
- The methods used in confronting organized crime
- The comparative evaluation of methods (and proposed measures) against organized crime.

It should be recognized that the nations participating in the symposium do not represent *all* organized crime problems around the world. Both the symposium and this book are limited by the number of nations able to be included. Some nations were invited to attend the symposium and submit papers but were not able to do so. The introduction to each section of this book indicates how the events in other nations of each continent continue to shape the nature and extent of organized crime in many different countries. At the same time, this book contains information about organized crime in many nations that has not been reported widely in the past, nor have earlier reports been written by those as experienced in the nation they report on. When reading this book, it is important to understand that many factors influence the perspectives reported here. Some important factors to consider are as follows:

1. A nation's *geographic location* often plays a role in its problems with organized crime. A location between a source country for narcotics, for example, and a demand country can result in organized crime involvement that otherwise would not occur.

2. A nation's *economic circumstances* is a crucial element in its ability to resist the temptations (demand) for illicit profits from drugs, trafficking in women, and other kinds of organized crime activity. National poverty is important for source countries, whereas disposable income is important in maintaining demand in wealthier nations.

3. A nation's *political and governmental situation* is an important determinant in the extent to which it prevents effective response to organized crime through law, enforcement, and concern about stopping official corruption.

4. Understanding a nation's *history* is often central to understanding its beliefs, laws, economy, and government. The incredible decentralization and overlapping government structure and authority in the United States, for example, can only be understood in context of how the nation was formed from a group of independent states joined together by violent revolution from an oppressive government. This history helps to explain, for instance, the apparent sluggishness of the legislative process in the United States.

5. A nation's *social culture, beliefs, and traditions* play a significant role in its susceptibility to certain forms of organized crime. The role of women and children in a society, for example, influences the degree to which social or government action are taken in response to prostitution and the use of children in criminal enterprises. Varying degrees of tolerance around the world for different crimes, such as money laundering, narcotics, bribery,

and official corruption are related to the actions or inaction by societies and their governments.

Thus it is crucial that geography, economy, government, history, cultural beliefs, and traditions of a nation be studied when examining the problem of organized crime. The chapters in this book do not contain all of this background and contextual information due to length considerations, but the serious student of organized crime would do well to study the national context that underlies organized crime and the responses to it.

Pedagogical Uses

There are several interesting ways in which this book can be used effectively in the classroom. Individual country trend analysis, adjacent country examination, product-flow analysis, and group migration studies are four fascinating ways to launch further inquiry into studies of organized crime.

Individual Country Trend Analysis

Crime trends change quickly, and organized crime is influenced significantly by political, economic, and social changes. Students might search for information about crime in a specific country within the past year to see if they can identify any recent political, economic, or social changes that may have influenced crime trends and then attempt to explain the nature of the impact.

Adjacent Country Examination

The circumstances in countries that border other nations can have dramatic effects on a country's problem with organized crime. The transit of illicit goods and services across a territory, status as a supplier or demand destination, and major political or economic changes in one nation often have an impact on bordering nations. A student might research events and incidents occurring in the past year in countries adjacent to a particular country to look for cross-border effects and the reasons for them.

Product-Flow Analysis

Organized crime groups often converge around criminal opportunities. A useful investigative exercise is to examine an actual case where a particular illegal product (e.g., narcotics, trafficking in humans, stolen property, etc.) was transported across a country or across national boundaries. A student can investigate how the supply was created or manufactured, shipped or transported without detection and sold, and then can glean how the illicit proceeds were laundered. This information often is not available in a given case, but several cases of the same type can be examined to see if reasonable estimations can be made of the product-flow of illicit goods and services and how this flow might be interrupted.

Group Migration Studies

Organized crime figures and sometimes entire groups migrate within a country and among countries in order to develop new suppliers, customers, or to evade law enforcement. A student might research all known references, articles, and cases involving a given criminal group over a period of time in an effort to determine how and whether the group has moved, grown, or shrunk, as it responds to criminal opportunities and attempts to evade detection.

These pedagogical exercises help to make clear the connection of organized crime with shifts in both criminal opportunities and in political and economic circumstances within a country and across an entire region of the world. The exercises also show how understanding of organized crime can occur from several different perspectives: the organized crime group, the illicit product, and from the effect of political, economic, and social changes on crime.

THE CONCEPT OF ORGANIZED CRIME

All participants in the symposium were asked to describe the concept of organized crime from the perspective of their countries. This task is an enlightening process, because there are large differences in how organized crime is conceptualized around the world. In some countries, criminal laws do not define organized crime. In these cases, the concept has been derived from perceptions of the characteristics of such crimes and criminals. The official government perspective in the United States—from the Federal Bureau of Investigation—defines an organized crime enterprise as a continuing criminal conspiracy, having an organized structure, fed by fear and corruption and motivated by greed (Nishimotto, 2001). The most important elements in this concept are the existence of an organized structure, an ongoing criminal conspiracy, and the generation of profit (see President's Commission on Organized Crime, 1986). On a transnational level, the International Criminal Police Organization (Interpol) defines organized crime as a "systematically prepared and planned committing of serious criminal acts with a view to gain financial profits and power . . . by more than three accomplices united in hierarchy and job divisions . . . in which the methods of violence, various types of intimidation, corruption and other influences are used" (cited in Edelbacher, 2001). Countries such as Namibia, South Africa, and India use the definition offered by the Interpol. Other countries (Estonia, for example) have combined the Interpol definition of organized crime with their own (Markina, 2001).

Organized crime, as described in Germany, uses "business or business-like structures" and exerts "influence on politics, media, public administration, judicature or economy" (Edelbacher, 2001; see Sielaff, 1988). Some countries (The Netherlands, Poland, and Slovenia) use working definitions of organized crime for police work: "A widely recurrent characteristic of organized groups is the laundering of the proceeds of the criminal activities." This feat is accomplished "by investing in legitimate businesses or heritable property or by channeling money, using routes abroad." Further, "three-quarters of the groups maintain contacts with the upperworld in some fashion or the other." In this context "the police, members of the business world, and lawyers are especially mentioned" (van der Heijden, 2001).

Nations can be viewed to define organized crime in a variety of ways, but they usually employ one of two perspectives: *the activity* or *the group*. In some nations, such as the United States and Germany, the *structure of the group* is central to what is defined as organized crime. The precise illicit product or criminal market is secondary. In others, such as The Netherlands, Poland, Slovenia, the *type of activity conducted* by the group determines whether it is part of organized crime. Illegal narcotics or money laundering may be considered part of the organized crime problem, but illegal prostitution or gambling may not, depending on how the nation views these types of conduct.

Another important difference in definitions of organized crime lies in the *sophistication* of organized crime groups. In some countries, these groups are defined as bureaucratic," "life-long commitment of members," "syndicates"—all connoting sophistication, hierarchy, large groups, and other terms often employed when people speak of "Cosa Nostra" or "Yakuza." In other countries, however, organized crime is defined as comprising less formal groups or gangs that emerge around an illegal product or other criminal opportunity—suggesting that organized crime is somewhat less sophisticated. There is reason to believe, therefore, that organized crime exists in different forms and at different levels of sophistication within and among nations. Even more significant is the fact that a nation's definition of organized crime determines whether or not a problem is considered to be part of organized crime. Juvenile gangs, for example, may or may not be considered part of organized crime, depending on whether a nation views the type of threat they pose as credible. This stance has obvious implications for the degree to which these groups are targeted by laws, enforcement and prosecution, or in prevention efforts.

In some countries organized crime has yet to be defined, but these nations can learn from the approaches of other countries. In China, for instance, "there is no special legal provision . . . no clause defining organized crime," but there is a recognition that organized criminal groups have a "comparatively large, stable membership" (Bingsong, 2001). In New Zealand, there is no "official definition of organized crime" (Newbold, 2001), but the prevailing concept is influenced by the definition used in Australia, which includes criteria such as "continuing activity" (Broome, 2001).

The national perspectives presented in this book indicate general agreement that organized crime has common features, such as:

1. Criminal activities are conducted in a *planned* manner for the purpose of profit.
2. There is a *continuing enterprise* or conspiracy that is based on a pre-existing social, ethnic, or business relationship, or around a particular illegal product or opportunity.
3. *Intimidation, threats, and sometimes violence* are used to obtain access to an illicit opportunity and to maintain it from competing criminal groups.
4. *Corruption* (bribery and extortion) is often used to maintain a degree of immunity from government interference (law enforcement and prosecution).
5. Organized crime groups show tremendous *adaptability* in responding to changes in supply, demand, law enforcement, and competition. They sometimes move geographically, shift to another illicit product, find new partners, or take other measures to ensure profitability and a degree of success in evading law enforcement.

THE NATURE AND EXTENT OF ORGANIZED CRIME

Santino (2001) declares, "the Sicilian Mafia" has not invaded the world, but today's world with its many contradictions of economic, social, and political nature has "produced more and more groups and organizations of the Mafia type." This statement indicates that organized crime emanates directly from economic, social, and political causes. The primary criminal groups reportedly working in Europe are the Italian groups (Mafia, Ndrangheta, and Camorra) as well as Japanese Yakuza, Chinese Triads, Colombian Cartels, Jamaican Posses, Russian criminal networks, West African syndicates, the Turkish Clans, Iranian elements, and other ethnic groups like the Pakistani, Yugoslav, and Polish organizations (Santino, 2001; Plywaczewski, 2001). In The Netherlands about 450 groups are reportedly involved in organized crime, including native Dutch groups and foreign groups. Poland has 290 organized gangs, of which 100 are of foreign origin, mostly from the former communist countries. In Slovenia, gangs of Albanian origin dominate the organized crime scene. Argentina is host to Peruvian, Bolivian, and Chinese criminal organizations. Canada's major organized crime groups are Asian (particularly Southeast Asians), Eastern European, Italian, Aboriginal, outlaw motorcycle gangs, and Colombian in composition. There are also youth gangs, prison gangs, skinheads, and militia-type groups (Koenig, 2001).

It is important to note that although the roots of organized crime lie in economic, social, and political causes, these groups usually are defined in ethnic and national terms as previously mentioned. This has been called the *ethnicity trap*, because ethnicity may help to *describe* a particular person or group, but it does not *explain* that person's or group's behavior (especially when compared with other members of that ethnic group who do not engage in organized crime activity) (Albanese, 1996). Thus, precise description of particular economic, social, and political conditions, opportunities, and influences is more useful in explaining organized crime than are biographical attributes such as ethnicity.

The activities of organized crime are diverse—their only common link is any product or service for which a profit can be made. The most often cited examples of organized crime activity include drug trafficking, money laundering, a variety of financial frauds, extortion, illegal gambling, trafficking in alcohol, tobacco, firearms, people, body parts, endangered species, stolen diamonds/gold and corruption of public officials to thwart apprehension and prosecution efforts. Globally, drug trafficking and the money laundering associated with it are generally regarded as "the economic mainstay of organized crime" (Ryan, 1995). According to a study by the Center of Investigations in Venezuela and the Mexico National University, drug trafficking in the world is a $600 billion dollar business (Ruiz de Olano, 2001). It accounts for "40 percent of organized crime activity in the U.S. and its profits are estimated at about $100 billion per year" (Salzano, 2001). In Canada, it is estimated that the annual revenue of organized crime is $20 billion Canadian dollars, "about half of it from drug trade" (Koenig, 2001). The drugs cartels in Colombia acquired such vast economic power that they "surpass the total government budgets of Peru and Colombia" (Schweizer, 2001). Besides heroin, hashish, marijuana, and synthetic drugs, "tons of cocaine" are sold in the European market. Austria alone faces "an overall economic damage" of $500 million dollars from organized crime activities in drug-related fields (Edelbacher, 2001).

Money laundering involves investment of the illicit proceeds of crime into legitimate banks and other businesses so it appears as if the money was earned legally. This method provides a way to mask the true source of the money and offers a legitimate "front" for the organized crime group. Money laundering impedes the ability of law enforcement authorities to follow the money trail and to determine the income of different organized crime groups. One analyst has observed that ". . .money laundering alone has clearly reached such proportions that it is capable of affecting the economies and governments of some countries" (Broome, 2001). Australia's financial transaction reporting agency, AUSTRAC, indicated ". . .a range of between $1,000 and $4,500 million is likely to be laundered in and through Australia . . . with perhaps some confidence that the most likely figure is around $3,500 million." According to a report from Holland, the Office for the Disclosure of Unusual Transactions (ODUT) received 16,215 reports concerning questionable transactions. Fourteen percent of these were judged suspect and passed on to the police (van der Heijden, 2001). About $16 billion is laundered annually in Austria (Edelbacher, 2001).

There are countries in which money laundering is welcomed. Namibia became independent in 1990, for example, and is a developing third world country in dire need of funds to strengthen its economy. It welcomes investments by foreign countries and companies, but the government admits that it neither has the expertise nor the experience to combat money laundering (Pool, 2001). The same is true in other nations. In Poland, where new laws have been enacted in the recent years, the laws from the communist regime still constitute the major source of prosecution, and nobody has been convicted of money laundering. In Zambia, there are currently companies such as wholesales agencies, bakeries, confectioneries, beer and liquor outlets, public transport services, and commercial banks that are legal fronts for money laundering. In Zimbabwe, there is no law against money laundering. Effective government legislation and enforcement in the area of money laundering is clearly needed.

Organized crime and politics have a relationship of "cohabitation" that allows them to "infiltrate government organizations, judicial, police and local authorities." It has been noted that "the long lasting relationship between Mafia and legitimate authority is almost like two distinct sovereigns." This relationship is illustrated in Italy where 72 city councils have been dissolved for "the presence of Mafia members as counselors, mayors, or aldermen or because of connections (friendships or even relatives) between Mafioso and administrators" (Santino, 2001). The same is true in other countries where organized crime uses the political system for the following two purposes:

1. *Organized crime groups use their influence* to commit bribery, extortion, and corruption to obtain a degree of immunity from enforcement and prosecution.
2. *Government officials use their position* to steal public property, enrich themselves, or extract illicit payments from private companies doing business with the government.

This symbiotic relationship between organized crime and government often involves misuse of power and influence on *both* sides. It is rare for government to be an unwilling victim. More frequently, government officials willingly accept or even solicit corrupt payments from organized crime. According to a Secretary General of the United Nations, "these criminal elements . . . command vast sums of money, which they use to suborn state officials" (cited in Plywaczewski, 2001). In Russia, several leaders of criminal enterprises occupy positions in the executive or legislative branch of the government. In 1995, in Moscow alone, "22 assistants to deputies of the State Duma were arrested . . . for their dealings with the criminal world" (Gilinskiy, 2001, also see Findlay and Zvekic, 1988). Similarly, it is said that the "intrusion organized crime has made in . . . politics of the country" is "the worst aspect of the phenomenon in India" (Verma, 2001). In other words, organized crime in many countries has "deeply rooted alliances with close ties to the political system" (Schatzberg and Kelly, 1996).

Corruption of government officials by organized criminals is mentioned universally as essential for the success of organized criminal enterprises. In South America, international companies have been suspected of involvement in massive corruption of government leaders and bureaucrats, making government contracts in public service projects virtually criminal enterprises (Ruiz de Olano, 2001). In some African countries such as Nigeria, organized crime emerged simultaneously with independence as former colonial contractors converted the business of contracts into criminal enterprises almost crushing Nigeria under foreign debts (Ebbe, 2001). In Australia, Turkey, Poland, Russia, and other nations, police corruption has been a serious problem, which is closely linked with government corruption at higher levels (Broome, 2001; Plywaczewski, 2001; Gilinskiy, 2001).

Methods to Combat Organized Crime

A variety of methods employed to combat organized crime include international and interagency cooperation, legislative initiatives, police enforcement strategies, and nongovernmental prevention efforts. It is crucial that nations learn from the experiences of their peers, and that the ease of international travel, shipping, and fund transfer make international agreements in response to organized crime a pressing issue.

The transnational nature of criminal enterprises requires concerted international efforts such as mutual assistance treaties, joint operations, increased liaison, and assistance in providing advanced training where training opportunities are otherwise somewhat limited (Nicaso and Lamothe, 1995). The presidents of both Russia and the United States have stressed concerted action and increased cooperation against transnational criminality. The president of Colombia has asked for a global strategy to combat trafficking in narcotics. The presidents of Argentina, Brazil, and Paraguay have called for increased cooperation among their countries (Schweizer, 2001). For its part, the Council of Europe has adopted a convention making money laundering a crime in all member states (Csonka, 2001).

One strategy that was praised by representatives from countries in southern Africa (South Africa, Namibia, and Zimbabwe) is the South African Regional Police Commissioners Coordinating Committee (SARPCC) and the Inter-State Defense Security Conference. Both groups have facilitated a multinational approach to the problems of organized crime in this region through better communication about organized crime groups and their movement within and between countries. Holland, South Africa, the United States, Canada, and Australia are making extensive use of assigning police officers to foreign countries to strengthen international police cooperation. In order to address organized crime in the former Soviet Union, the United States has spent $30 million to train police officers there (Schweizer, 2001). Austria has started the Central European Police Academy with a view to increasing cooperation among the police organizations in Central Europe to combat transborder crimes, especially those carried out by organized crime groups.

Agreements among countries for assistance with police training are positive developments. These training initiatives include investigative training, extradition treaties between neighboring countries, guidance and support from the United Nations, collaboration with foreign police forces, and increased joint investigative collaboration with foreign agencies. Canada, for example, has established integrated anti-drug profiteering units (IADP) and proceeds of crime units (IPOC). These task forces include not only police from different jurisdictions with different expertise, but also prosecutors, forensic accountants, taxation investigators, computer and electronic specialists, and multilingual interpreters. Australia's National Crime Authority is an advanced effort in this area, as are cooperative arrangements among policing authorities in India, Zimbabwe, Sudan, and South Africa.

Many laws have been enacted in recent years that target specific manifestations of organized crime. The effectiveness of many of these laws has yet to be established. In Namibia, for example, legislation regulating various aspects of the diamond industry, drugs, and firearms has been implemented. In The Netherlands, provisions to deal with tainted property and suspicious bank accounts are in place. Severe laws relating to drugs, prostitution, trading in human beings (including transportation of people across national borders), and sabotaging the financial order have been enacted in China, where the maximum penalty for manufacturing, trading, or transporting guns without authorization is death (Bingsong, 2001). In India, the Narcotic Drugs and Psychotropic Substance Act (1985) is designed to both deter and punish drug trafficking offenses in India (Tewari, 2001). Crime and anti-money laundering legislation in Australia and New Zealand allows for seizure of assets accumulated as a result of crime (Broome, 2001; Newbold, 2001). Between 1982 and 1992 Italy witnessed the enactment of 114 different statutes regarding organized crime that were largely responses to the criminal challenge (Santino, 2001). More recently, as the menace of organized crime became obvious, "small reforms" of penal legislation incorporating new crimes such as money laundering, drug possessions, extortion, and seizures of assets have been made in Croatia (Vulinec, 2001).

Police are experimenting with proactive initiatives in many different countries. In Namibia, for example, close cooperation exists between diamond-mine security departments and the police (diamonds are stolen from mines and traded by organized crime). Similar efforts have been made for drug investigations. Study of the *modus operandi* of thieves, getting private companies to pay for police equipment, and consultation between the interministerial drug committees and those involved in the rehabilitation of drug addicts have all proven to be useful initiatives. National crime prevention strategies, national integrated databases, destruction of drug-cultivation by chemicals, the use of surveillance, and the profiling of people and cargo have been beneficial in crime prevention and law enforcement in various countries.

Other proactive measures include aggressive collection of intelligence from members of the public (Zimbabwe) and special police units for specific offenses involving economic and organized crimes (Argentina, Austria, Estonia, Hungary, India, Slovenia, and Tunisia). In some countries the effort to motivate investigators includes offering a share of the money recovered from crime (Croatia, India, and Tunisia). Allowing the police greater technological capabilities for surveillance, eavesdropping, and wiretapping is being employed in a growing number of nations (Austria, Canada, Hungary, New Zealand, Slovenia, and the U.S.). Other proactive measures include whistle-blowing (Council of Europe), penalizing membership in criminal gangs (Japan and Estonia), and enabling the police to buy support from criminals through reduction or exemption of penalty (Canada, Estonia, and Slovenia). Witness protection (Canada, the U.S., and Council of Europe), sophisticated intelligence analysis (The Netherlands); and keeping records of large monetary transactions (Australia, Canada, and the U.S.) have enabled police in these nations to better track suspected organized crime activities.

These efforts are usually *offense-specific* and do not address *criminal groups* that may change their focus from one illicit product to another because of changes in demand, competition, or in law enforcement effectiveness. If drug laws in a certain jurisdiction become severe enough and the risk of apprehension increases substantially, it is reasonable to believe that organized crime groups will move to other illicit markets, such as human trafficking, fraud, or gambling. In an effort to target criminal *groups*, the Racketeer Influenced and Corrupt Organizations Statute (RICO) in the United States has provided for the prosecution of criminal enterprises for a course of illegal conduct, rather than only individuals for a specific offense. It provides for enhanced penalties for such systematic criminal behavior, and the law has been imitated in several other countries (Nishimotto, 2001). Civil provisions of RICO also permit the government to seize the assets (homes, cars, boats, etc.) of any business or group that has used them as part of an ongoing criminal enterprise.

Perhaps the most significant efforts to address organized crime are those that do not involve the government. There have been comparatively few efforts in this regard, but their common feature is reducing public tolerance for organized crime—focusing on its deleterious effects on the economy, government, and on the quality of life. In India, for example, judicial activism (judges taking up public interest litigation on written petitions from members of the public) has fortified the efforts against slave and child labor. Croatia, Poland, and Slovenia noted efforts to get academics involved in addressing organized crime and its impact on society. There is broad agreement among nations that cooperation and trust between the police and community is necessary to combat organized criminal activities. This belief was expressed by a United States Senate subcommittee that "open lines of communications must be established between the police and the community" (U.S. Congress Report, 1996; also see Stolberg, 1995; Herbert and Tritt, 1984 and, Kelly, Ching, and Schatzberg, 1994). In Japan, the police claim success in their fight against organized crime because of a change in public attitude toward the Boryokudan, a change brought about by the government and media publicity.

COMPARATIVE EVALUATION OF THE METHODS FOR COMBATING ORGANIZED CRIME AND PROPOSED MEASURES

Effective strategies in combating organized crime remain few, although several tactics have shown promise in certain countries. Laws that make money laundering difficult and that attack criminal enterprises (rather than only individuals) have shown success, as have some innovative policing strategies and police-public partnerships.

Following "the money trail" has proved effective in prosecutions in the United States. Major prosecution successes have resulted from the RICO statute. Conviction and long sentences for more than 25 Cosa Nostra leaders and scores of lesser organized crime figures occurred in the United States during the 1980s and 1990s. This outcome was produced largely by illustrating how these groups of individuals were connected in ongoing criminal enterprises, rather than as individual criminals (Nishimotto, 2001; Albanese, 1996; Moore, 1991; Rebovich, Coyle, and Schaaf, 1993). In Japan, reducing the profit by the Boryokudan also has shown success—eighty groups involving 1,130 members have disintegrated in recent years (Uchiyama, 2001; see Yakoo, 1995).

Although no scientific evaluation study has been done in regard to the effectiveness of various methods over the long term, the anecdotal evidence is encouraging. In India and Sudan, people's movements against organized crime have been effective (Verma, 2001). In Zimbabwe, depoliticizing the police and increased public cooperation in the form of neighborhood watch committees, citizen arrests, dialogue between the community and police officers, and a hotline for citizens to give anonymous information have been effective against organized crime (Chihuri, 2001). Sudan has organized a national crime prevention body to educate the public. Other police strategies that have shown success are criminal intelligence analysis (Holland), collaboration with witnesses (Italy and the U.S.), rewards to informants (one-third of the value of diamonds recovered is paid to the informants in Namibia), professionally trained secret police units for surveillance work (Australia, South Africa, and the U.S.), and following suspicious financial transactions (Australia and Holland).

Cooperation both at domestic and international levels has been found to be effective when it occurs. SARPCC, which comprises Botswana,

Namibia, South Africa, Zambia, and Zimbabwe, has had success in communicating about shared organized crime problems. New Zealand has found it useful to combine strict immigration control measures and continuous surveillance on police corruption to hinder organized crime. There is a realization that "policy makers may broaden their options . . . experiment with methods that do not rely primarily on law enforcement or they may include a better ordering of law enforcement priorities and strategies" (Inciardi and Faupel, 1980). Measures being proposed or considered include a number of legislative proposals that are directed at the correlates of organized crime activity. The assumption is that making it difficult for criminal groups to obtain useful tools to commit crimes will make it difficult for them to organize effectively. Some of these measures are restricting illegal firearms (Sudan and Namibia); increasing enforcement on theft of motor vehicles (Namibia); anti-money laundering legislation (South Africa, Namibia, Estonia, Poland, Slovenia, and Croatia); removing protections from ill-gotten wealth in safe deposits boxes in hotels and profits obtained through front organizations (Slovenia).

Conclusion

Although organized crime control has not yet shown lasting success, the delegates at the conference also rejected the contention that "crime is winning . . . perhaps permanently" (Fremantle, 1995). Part of the difficulty is that "methodologically it is hardly possible to measure organized crime" (van Duyne, 1996; see also U.S. Congress Report, 1984). Even so, there is broad consensus that, although some battles have been won, organized crime remains a significant problem around the world.

The reasons why organized crime flourishes in the face of growing and persistent world-wide attention are not difficult to understand. As noted earlier, organized crime provides products and services that are often in great demand despite legal prohibitions. The fact that it occurs in every society, by groups of all kinds illustrates that "it is not alien, it is not foreign, it is not a conspiracy against the very fabric of society. It is, in fact, very much part of the fabric" (Potter, 1994).

Organized crime is facilitated by corrupt public officials who misuse their position and power for personal benefit. Likewise, some private companies use their influence to similar illicit advantage. In some cases, the law creates criminal opportunities by prohibiting desired behaviors such as gambling. As Bayer (1992) comments, there is a need for "a serious examination of the appropriate role of the state in regulating the behavior of competent adults" to ensure that markets for organized crime are not created unnecessarily (see Shelley, 1981). Politically, governments can worsen organized crime problems through covert government involvement with drug traffickers, as has been alleged both in Indochina and in Latin America (Koenig, 2001). In an analogous way, it is unrealistic to expect to make an impact on organized crime if the targets selected for enforcement and prosecution are low-level individuals and groups. In New Zealand, for example, it has been charged that "measures to deal with elite fraud have been half-hearted and largely ineffective, while there has been an unremitting tendency for law enforcement authorities to look for crime in lower socioeconomic classes" (Newbold and Ivory, 1993).

Finally, organized crime is the price we pay for the opacity of an international financial system characterized by banking secrecy, tax havens, and financial innovations that "favor symbiosis between legal and illegal capital" (Santino, 2001). Along with the fall of socialism and the emergence of global capitalism, the gap between richer and poorer nations of the world has continued to grow. This growth can be expected to increase opportunities for organized crime, as illicit relationships develop among supply countries, transit nations, and consumer nations. In an unbalanced world economy, legal economics tends to get replaced by illegal economies. Thus, there is need for broad, balanced, concerted, and innovative strategies against organized crime that adopt the best examples from the present and learn from the errors of the past.

REFERENCES

Albanese, Jay. 1996. *Organized Crime in America*. 3rd ed. Cincinnati: Anderson Publishing.

Bayer, Ronald. 1992. The Great Drug Policy Debate—What Means This Thing Called Decriminalization. *The Milbank Quarterly*, 69 (3): 341–363.

Bingsong, He. 2001. "Organized Crime: A Perspective from China." (in this volume).

Broome, John. 2001. "Organized Crime: A Perspective from Australia." (in this volume).

Chihuri, Augustine. 2001. "Organized Crime: A Perspective from Zimbabwe." (in this volume).

Csonka, Peter. 2001. "Organized Crime: Perspective from the Council of Europe." (in this volume).

Ebbe, Obi. 2001. "Organized Crime: A Continental Perspective from Africa." (in this volume).

Edelbacher, Maximilian. 2001. "Organized Crime: A Perspective from Austria." (in this volume).

Findlay, Mark, and Zvekic, Ugljesa. 1988. *Analyzing (In)formal Mechanisms of Crime Control: A Cross-Cultural Perspective*. Rome: United Nations Social Defense Institute.

Fremantle, Brian. 1995. *The Octopus: Europe in the Grip of Organized Crime*. London: Orion Books Ltd.

Gilinskiy, Yakov. 2001. "Organized Crime: A Perspective from Russia." (in this volume).

Herbert, David, and Tritt, Howard. 1984. *Corporations of Corruption: A Systematic Study of Organized Crime*. Springfield, Illinois: Charles C. Thomas Publishers.

Inciardi, James A., and Faupel, Charles E. 1980. *History and Crime: Implications for Criminal Justice Policy*, Newbury Park, CA: Sage Publications.

Kelly, Robert J., Ching Ko-lin, and Rufus Schatzberg, eds. 1994. *Handbook of Organized Crime in The United States*. Westport: Greenwood Press.

Koenig, Daniel. 2001. "Organized Crime: A Canadian Perspective." (in this volume).

Markina, Anna. 1996. *Organized Crime: An Estonian Perspective*. Paper presented at Organized Crime Symposium, Yokohama, Japan.

Moore, Mark H. 1991. Drugs, the Criminal Law, and Administration of Justice. *The Milbank Quarterly*. 69 (4): 529–560.

Newbold, Greg. 2001. "Organized Crime: An Australasian Perspective." (in this volume).

Newbold, Greg and Ivory, Robert. 1993. Policing Serious Frauds in New Zealand. *Crime, Law and Social Change*. 20: 233–248.

Nicaso, Antonio, and Lamothe, Lee. 1995. *Global Mafia*. Toronto: Macmillan, Canada.

Nishimotto, Castle. 2001. "Organized Crime: An American Perspective." (in this volume).

Plywaczewski, Emil W. 2001. "Organized Crime: A Perspective from Poland." (in this volume).

Pool, Martin. 1996. "Organized Crime: A Namibian Perspective." Paper presented at Organized Crime Symposium, Yokohama, Japan.

Potter, Gary W. 1994. *Criminal Organizations: Vice, Racketeering and Politics in an American City*. Prospect heights, IL: Waveland Press.

President's Commission on Organized Crime. 1986. *The Impact: Organized Crime Today*. Washington, D.C.: U.S. Government Printing Office.

Rebovich, Donald J., Coyle, Kenneth R., and Schaaf, John C. 1993. *Local Prosecution of Organized Crime: The Use of RICO Statutes*. Washington, DC: Office of Justice Programs.

Ruiz de Olano, Ruben. 1996. "Organized Crime: A South American Perspective." Paper presented at Organized Crime Symposium, Yokohama, Japan.

Ryan, Patrick J. 1995. *Organized Crime*. Santa Barbara: ABC-CLIO.

Salzano, Julienne. 2001. "Organized Crime: An American Perspective." (in this volume).

Santino, Umberto. 2001. "Organized Crime: An Italian Perspective." (in this volume).

Schatzberg, Rufus, and Kelly, Robert J. 1996. *African-American Organized Crime*. New York: Garland Publishing.

Schweizer, Harald Otto. 2001. "Organized Crime: An American Perspective." (in this volume).

Shelley, Louise I. 1981. *Crime and Modernization: The Impact of Industrialization and Urbanization Crime*. Carbondale, IL: Southern Illinois University Press.

Sielaff, Wolfgang. 1988. Organized Criminal Activity in the Federal Republic of Germany. *The Police Chief*. 55 (11): 76–79.

Stolberg, Mary M. 1995. *Fighting Organized Crime*. Boston: Northwestern University Press.

Tewari, R. K. 2001. "Organized Crime: An Indian Perspective." (in this volume).

Uchiyama, A. 2001. "Organized Crime: A Japanese Perspective." (in this volume).

U.S. Congress. 1996. *Russian Organized Crime in the United States*. Washington, D.C.: U.S. Government Printing Office.

U.S. Congress. 1984. *Profile of Organized Crime: Mid Atlantic Region*. Washington, D.C.: U.S. Government Printing Office.

U.S. Department of Justice. Criminal Investigative Division. July 1993. *An Introduction to Organized Crime in the United States.*

van der Heijdan, Don. 2001. "Organized Crime: A Dutch Perspective." (in this volume).

van Duyne, Putrus C. 1996. *Organized Crime in Europe.* New York: Nova Science Publishers.

Verma, Arvind. 2001. "Organized Crime: An Indian Perspective." (in this volume).

Vulinec, Mladen. 1996. "Organized Crime: A Croatian Perspective." Paper presented at Organized Crime Symposium, Yokohama, Japan.

Yakoo, Toshio. 1995. The Japanese Police Campaign against the Boryokudan. *International Criminal Police Review.* 3: 38–45.

PART 1

PERSPECTIVES FROM NORTH AMERICA

The United States and Canada have unique organized crime problems due to a shared border that is 3,000 miles in length and the fact that both nations border on both the Atlantic and Pacific Oceans. The history, legal systems, and economies of these nations differ widely, but their geographic position and large consumer populations (with a higher standard of living than much of the world) make them prime markets for organized crime activity. Demand for drugs, illegal gambling, and prostitution are comparatively high in these countries and despite strong governments and law enforcement agencies, organized crime has thrived in both nations. A long tradition of mafia-related (i.e., Italian-American) crime is shared by both countries as are newer groups of non-Italian criminals and biker gangs (Sallee, 2001; Nathanson Centre, 2001).

Mexico's strategic location linking North America with South and Central America has been a crucial link in trafficking both drugs and humans into the United States. Although a chapter on

Mexico is not included in this book, it is discussed in several places. A student may wish to examine recent references to Mexico in the periodical literature that describes recent governmental changes and Mexico's continuing efforts to battle corruption and reduce the power of organized drug-trafficking gangs there. Major drug enforcement successes in Colombia, for example, may have created a vacuum that has been filled by some Mexican groups. In nations with weak or corrupt governments, organized crime groups have flourished, a situation made worse by struggling economies in developing countries (Penhaul, 2001; Bailey and Godson, 2001).

The extended ocean borders of both Canada and the United States aggravates attempts to control smuggling by boat. Both drug and human trafficking often occur in this fashion because it is not possible to control water borders as it is airports, for example, because boats can dock almost anywhere. A recent case involving a cocaine and marijuana smuggling ring via speedboat from Colombia through the Caribbean islands to North America was stopped only after a four-nation task force (United States, Canada, Jamaica, and the Bahamas) joined together in a three-year investigation (Reuters, 2001). This sort of multinational effort will be increasingly important in the future as organized crime expands transnationally.

In a similar fashion trafficking in humans is growing at an alarming rate with illegal immigrants taken often by force or by trick from their home countries to North America and to other developed countries where they end up as slaves, prostitutes, or drug couriers (Hughes, 2000). During the 1990s immigration prosecutions became the largest category of United States federal criminal prosecutions, with most of these cases involving entry or harboring of illegal aliens and passport or visa fraud (Kalfrin, 1999). Many human smuggling cases originate in developing nations where desperate individuals are exploited by organized crime groups that take their money and in some cases enslave their victims. Here, again, more substantial efforts to improve social and economic conditions, as well as government and law enforcement corruption, will be necessary to begin to address the problem of trafficking at its source. Likewise, greater public awareness and better law enforcement on the consumer end of human trafficking is needed in developed countries to reduce the demand that expands the market for organized crime groups.

REFERENCES

Bailey, John J., and Roy, Godson, eds. 2001. *Organized Crime and Democratic Governability: Mexico and the U.S.* Pittsburgh: University of Pittsburgh Press.

Hughes, Donna M. 2000. "The "Natasha" Trade: The Transnational Shadow Market of Trafficking in Women," *J. International Affairs* (Spring).

Kalfrin, Valerie. 1999. "Feds Top Prosecution: Immigration," *APBnews.com*, July 26.

Nathanson Centre for the Study of Organized Crime. 2001. http://www.yorku.ca/nathanson.

Penhaul, Karl. 2001. "Colombia's Drug War." *U.S. News & World Report*, February 12, 35.

Reuters. 2001. "U.S., Canada, Jamaica, Bahamas Smash Drug Ring," February 2. http://www.wjin.net/html/news/7197.htm

Sallee, Eponine. 2001. "Canadian Organized Crime." http://organizedcrime.about.com.

Chapter 1

Organized Crime: A U.S. Perspective

Harald Otto Schweizer, Castle Nishimotto, Julienne Salzano and Mike T. Chamberlin

Introduction

The United States of America is about one-half the size of Russia and about three-tenths the size of Africa. It is the world's fourth-largest country (after Russia, Canada, and China) and has a population of approximately 266 million. Although there are distinct ethnic divisions comprising white (83.4%), black (12.4%), Asian (3.3%), and Native American (0.8%), the United States is the melting pot of the world and small communities from every nation on earth exist in this country. The United States is a federal republic with a strong democratic tradition symbolized by its Statue of Liberty and Declaration of Independence. The legal system is based on English common law with judicial review of legislative acts. The judicial branch is headed by the Supreme Court, where the justices are appointed for life by the president with confirmation by the Senate.

The United States has the most powerful, diverse, and technologically advanced economy in the world, with a per capita gross domestic product of $27,500, the largest among major industrial nations. In this market-oriented economy, private individuals and business firms make most of the decisions, and government purchases of goods and services are made predominantly in the open marketplace. In all economic sectors, U.S. firms are at or near the forefront in technological advances, especially in computers, medical equipment, and aerospace, although their advantage has steadily narrowed since the end of World War II.

The United States has a decentralized system of governance in which every state and even the local counties enjoy a considerable amount of administrative and political autonomy. The police system is largely under the control of the local government and consequently there are virtually thousands of different autonomous police agencies of every form. In most systems the police chief is appointed by the mayor and in some places it is still an elected office. Although most of the population is served by small, locally managed police departments with only a few sworn officers, a few large police departments in the metropolitan areas such as Los Angeles, New York, and Chicago are projected around the world by Hollywood movies as the image of U.S. police forces. The country also has one of the highest violent crime rates in the world and almost a million people have been incarcerated in its different prison systems.

THE NATURE AND EXTENT OF ORGANIZED CRIME

The nature of organized crime in the United States is varied. Considering the size of the country and the capitalist mode of market economy, organized crime occurs in different manifestations that vary from the dreaded national Mafia or Cosa Nostra to the small time gang that limits itself to a few neighborhoods. In order to keep the attention focused, this chapter will follow the definition adopted by the FBI that defines an organized crime group or enterprise as a continuing criminal conspiracy, having an organized structure, fed by fear and corruption and motivated by greed. The intrusion into economic activities by organized crime is a threat to civil society in the United States. This chapter will first discuss some of the areas in which organized crime has penetrated and then describe some of the prominent organized crime groups and their activities in the United States.

Areas of Operations for Organized Crime in the United States

Testimony before various congressional committees makes it abundantly clear that transnational criminal organizations are expanding rapidly, becoming more resilient, and represent a serious threat to the United States (see the House International Relations Committee on International Organized Crime (January 31, 1996), and a statement by James F. Collins of the Foreign Service before a Senate Select Committee on Intelligence (1996)). Although the actual extent of organized crime is unknown, current information shows that transnational organized crime has become a formidable opponent of large and small nations worldwide. The formidability of this threat became apparent when the presidents of Russia and the United States both noted that concerted action against transnational criminality was imperative. Both pledged increased cooperation in a combined effort to combat the problem (U.S. Dept. of State Dispatch, 1994). President Samper of Colombia echoed the need for greater transnational police efforts, when he pleaded for a global strategy to combat narcotics trafficking in his speech to the United Nations in September of 1996 (*La Estrella Star-Telegram*, 1996). The presidents of Argentina, Brazil, and Paraguay are investigating increased cooperation between their countries, having become alarmed at the influx of Chinese criminal organizations from Taiwan, Hong Kong, and the People's Republic of China (Torres, Oct., 1996). A bulletin of the information center of the United Nations for Mexico, Cuba, and the Dominican Republic, categorized transnational criminal organizations as a threat to government itself and suggested the creation of multilateral agreements to overcome the expansion of international criminal organizations. In Europe, the need for mutual cooperation on an international scale led to the creation of Europol, the new European Police Agency that is presently becoming operational (*El Pais*, 7 September, 1995). The United States is no exception and the threat of organized crime having international tentacles is as serious here as anywhere else.

The activities of international criminal organizations are diverse and encompass both legal and illegal enterprises. A review of information from the U.S. Department of Justice, the Central Intelligence Agency, Congressional bills and resolutions, and academic sources, shows the most pressing threats from international organized crime involve financial fraud, particularly money laundering, narcotics trafficking, the smuggling of illegal aliens, and government corruption. Recent increases in the activities of international criminal organizations have also been facilitated by political upheavals such as the fall of the Iron Curtain. Western Europe was the first to be affected by the rapid expansion of criminal organizations from former Eastern block countries. Of 8,000 suspects in offenses involving criminal organizations in Germany during the year 1995, two-thirds were foreign nationals from 87 different countries. The recent influx of people from the former communist bloc into the United States has also facilitated the organized crime groups from those countries to develop links in the United States. For example, during the past five years the United States has experienced significant growth in Russian-based organized crime activity, with the FBI reporting the existence of fifteen organized crime groups having origins in the former Soviet Union.

Added to this compendium is the problem of criminal organizations increasingly networking with terrorist organizations when it serves a mutually beneficial purpose. The complex arrangements and activities of some organizations can create ambiguity as to the true nature of the organization. Is it primarily a criminal organization or is it a terrorist organization with political objectives?

Financial Crime

It is not uncommon for organized crime groups to engage in more than one illegal activity, and, even if they derive their main profit from an illegal activity that occurs in a fixed or geographical area, they are dependent on international connections to launder their profits, purchase weapons, or obtain drugs. Money laundering is commonly used by organized criminal groups to permit the investment and use of proceeds from illegal activities. This activity has drawn the attention of several U.S. law enforcement agencies, and its investigation is facilitated by new cooperative efforts between these agencies and regulatory agencies.

For instance, Nigerian organized crime operates advance loan schemes that are becoming particularly insidious, with victims all over the world losing millions of dollars and even their lives. Victims are typically advised that Nigerian firms or government officials need to transfer large sums of money to foreign bank accounts and are asked to cover the cost of the transfer with the understanding that they will receive a portion of the transferred money. The offer is bogus, and some of the victims are asked to travel to Nigeria to complete the transaction, where they are then held for ransom and sometimes killed (Singleton, 1995).

Alien Smuggling

According to the Central Intelligence Agency, the smuggling of aliens is a lucrative venture, and criminal organizations interact closely with other smugglers and corrupt government officials. An article in *India Abroad* (12 January, 1996) indicated that Pakistan and India are major sources of illegal immigrants. Connected with this smuggling activity is also large scale document fraud. Ethnic Chinese constitute a major portion of the illegal immigrants transported by sophisticated smuggling organizations. One recent approach to smuggling involved sending thousands of Chinese to Latin America and then via Mexico to the United States, according to this *India Abroad* article, which quoted an unnamed report compiled by the State Department, Justice Department, INS, CIA, FBI, and U.S. Coast Guard.

An article of 4 April, 1995, in the form of an Internet newsletter generated by the *Washington Times*, quoted Robert Perito, the director of the State Department's Office of International Criminal Justice, stating that "Hundreds of thousands of people are being moved globally by highly organized enterprises operating on all continents. Their primary target is the United States." Mr. Perito estimated that 500,000 persons were poised in Russia to be smuggled into the United States, with another 150,000 persons in other European countries. Most were said to be Chinese paying as much as $40,000 to the well-organized, ethnic or family-based criminal organizations generally known as Triads. The Chinese Triads are developing new operations in Europe and the absence of Chinese-speaking police officers seriously hampers the ability of law enforcement to actively investigate the Triads, according to Perito.

A problem tangential to illegal alien smuggling is the sex slavery trade. Criminal organizations lure and often kidnap young females into permanent servitude as sexual slaves. This problem has become an epidemic in India, Pakistan, and Thailand, but also affects Europe and the United States. Blonde females are in particular high demand in Asian countries and are generally lured there under the pretense of being offerred a modeling career (Yoon, 1996). At the Beijing women's conference in 1995, the trafficking in women was identified as a worldwide concern and governments were urged to engage in international collaborative efforts to combat the problem (*Women's Health Weekly*, 1995). Child slavery and the concomitant activity of pedophilia has been increasing since 1970, particularly in Pakistan, Nepal, India, Sudan, Mauritania, and Thailand (*The Economist*, 1996).

Drug Trafficking

Drug trafficking is the most widespread and lucrative organized crime enterprise in the United States, accounting for nearly 40 percent of this country's organized crime activity and generating an annual income estimated as high as $110 billion (President's Commission, 1986). Over the past forty years, La Cosa Nostra has reaped huge profits from trafficking narcotics such as heroin and cocaine. More recent organizations from South America, the Caribbean and America now play a major role in the drug trade. These newer groups' sole source of income is drug-related criminal activity: the manufacturing, refinement, distribution, and sale of illegal narcotics. These traffickers are neither small-time operators nor quasi business persons; they are marked by a significant degree of violence and corruption. During the early 1980s, cocaine replaced marijuana as the major money maker. Different production and transportation requirements for the two drugs encouraged specialization among drug traffickers. Drug lords trafficking in cocaine also develop complex criminal organizations to handle and launder the large sums of money that are generated. They have also become economically and politically active in order to protect their financial holdings and drug activities.

Drug traffickers are also the most powerful crime syndicate today and the Medellin cartel is considered to be the world's major international criminal organization. The economic power of the cartel is so vast that it surpasses the total government budgets of Peru and Colombia combined, and its network of people is large and well coordinated (Godson and Olson, 1995), which cannot always be said of government agencies. Although government efforts continue to combat drug trafficking, the cartels are effectively expanding production and trafficking routes, while becoming more sophisticated and flexible. The Medellin cartel in Colombia has become so powerful that in the early 1990s it was able to reverse a government policy allowing extradition of Colombian drug traffickers to the United States following a series of bombings and kidnappings that nearly brought the government to its knees (Garcia-Marquez, 1996). This cartel supplanted the government in some areas and its leaders were revered by some of the population for their generosity in providing assistance to the poor and for employing a great number of those unable to find employment (Arango, 1988).

Technology Theft

A new trend in technological crime also appears to be emerging. Unfortunately, state and local law enforcement is relatively unprepared for the large scale theft of computer chips and data. According to John O'Loughlin, the corporate security director of Sun Microsystems in Mountain View, California, most investigators "wouldn't know a computer chip from a potato chip." New and developing technology to store, retrieve, and transfer financial data and funds and the rapid growth of systems that permit access from anywhere in the world, has enabled organized criminal groups to expand their operations and increase their profitability (Rasor, 1995).

Government Corruption

The 1967 President's Commission on Law Enforcement and Administration of Justice made it clear that without corrupt officials, organized crime could not exist, and recommended resolute action against government corruption. Corruption of government officials by organized crime was universally mentioned as being essential for organized crime to flourish. Corruption of U.S. officials does not seem to be as widespread a problem as in some of the Caribbean and African nations, but corruption of governmental agencies anywhere in the world poses a threat to the U.S. society. The nature of international trade and the fact that the United States by and large remains the most significant trading partner of most countries and the biggest market for a large volume of goods produced in the world implies that corrupt officials adversely affect the U.S. trade relations. Jonathan Winer, the Deputy Assistant Secretary of State for Law Enforcement and Crime, noted that the money is used to corrupt officials in these tiny nations and there is no question the traffickers are very adept at infiltrating the higher echelons of government.

Types of Criminal Organizations Operating in the United States

The criminal organizations mentioned most frequently in articles or reports on international organized crime were Russian "Mafia," the Chinese Triads, the Medellin cartel and, to a lesser degree, Nigerian criminal cells. While the Italian Mafia is still alive and well, its influence has diminished in the United States after some very successful investigations and subsequent convictions of La Cosa Nostra members. Additional groups such as those of Caribbean, Vietnamese, Laotians, and Cambodian origin, represent a significant portion of the gang problem, particularly in the United States, where Justice Department estimates show the existence of as many as 15,000 Asian gang members. Their offenses are generally of a violent nature, with Vietnamese gangs involved in extortion, firearm violations, home-invasion robberies, witness intimidation, assault, and murder. The Japanese Yakuza, after experiencing some significant losses of support and a weakening of its power, is beginning to expand to the United States and Europe, with investments in legitimate business totaling nearly $10 billion (Johnson, Webster, and Connors, 1995). A brief description of some of the important groups is outlined below:

La Cosa Nostra (LCN)

The LCN is the most well-known domestic organized crime enterprise operating in the United States today and represents a nationwide alliance linked through sinister conspiratorial ties. The LCN has a detrimental effect on businesses, labor organizations, industries, and American society in general. The LCN engages in murder, extortion, illegal gambling, drug trafficking, money laundering, obstruction of justice, corruption of public officials, and a variety of financial fraud schemes, as well as other typical organized crime-type offenses.

The LCN structure consists of a boss, underboss, *consigliere* (advisor), and street crews, each of which is led by a *capodecina*. Currently, FBI intelligence estimates that there are approximately 2,000 LCN members in the United States. For every identified LCN member, there are ten or more associates whose illegal activities are directed by, or are dependent upon, the LCN. From 1981 to the present, FBI investigations have resulted in the conviction of the leadership of 20 of the 25 LCN families. This includes 29 bosses (including John Gotti), 14 underbosses, 7 *consigliere*, and 71 *capodecinas*. There are presently 25 LCN families active, in varying degrees, in the United States.

Italian Criminal Enterprises (ICE)

The Sicilian Mafia, *Camorra*, *'Ndrangheta*, and Sacred Crown are the four major Italian criminal enterprises operating in the United States. They conduct a myriad of criminal activities, including cocaine and heroin trafficking and money laundering. Four core-level Italian drug trafficking organizations have been identified. These are: the Carini Family, the Cinisi Family, and the *'Ndrangheta Siderno* and *Gioisa Ionica* groups.

Colombian/South American Drug-Trafficking Enterprises

The growth of Colombia's illicit drug industry during the last few decades reflects the influence of geography, insurgency, government policies, and foreign demand. Drug traffickers expanded their operations in the late 1960s in response to rising demand in the United States for marijuana. Colombia's vast coastlines, access to international air and sea carriers, historically weak and corruptible government, insurgency and remote rural areas, support the cultivation of illicit drugs, the installation of drug-processing plants, and the development of distribution networks.

Mexican Drug Trafficking Enterprises

Mexico produces one-third of the heroin and 70 percent of the marijuana coming into the United States. In addition, Mexican drug-trafficking organizations now play a major role in smuggling 70 percent of the Colombian cocaine coming into the United States. Of the major drug trafficking groups addressed in the OC/DE National Strategy, the least is known about Mexican drug traffickers. Tracing the drugs to their source is difficult since the Mexican drug lords insulate themselves from smuggling operations. Many of the participants in the smuggling process serve in various capacities such as buyers, mules, traffickers, and storage facilitators, thus making classification of these individuals difficult.

The vast majority of these organizations have family members carrying out the day-to-day operations. Infiltrating these organizations is a formidable task, since outsiders are viewed with suspicion and informants are dealt with unmercifully. These families are also involved in supplying arms to large security forces to finance their drug operations. Their strategy to build schools and health clinics and bring water and electricity to local villages has also facilitated local support, since local residents view the growers and smugglers of drugs as heroes rather than criminals.

Larger-scale planting of opium poppy began in Mexico during World War II. It was subsidized by American gangsters who feared that their overseas smuggling operations would be cut off by the war. By the early 1970s, Mexico was a major exporter of heroin to the United States, a role facilitated by the disruption of the Turkish heroin trade by law enforcement authorities. By 1973, Mexico was providing 80 percent of the United States heroin market. Today, Mexico produces 2 percent of the total world opium production and provides approximately one-third of the United States illicit opiate consumption. The largest market for Mexican heroin has traditionally been in the Southwest.

For the most part, Mexican groups control the majority of the cocaine traffic that goes through Mexico. The collaboration between Colombian cartels and the Mexican drug-trafficking organizations has become so strong that the most reliable of the Mexican organizations are afforded a 50/50 partnership with the Colombian cartels. The overwhelming wealth derived from this partnership has changed the primary focus of the Mexican groups.

Russian/Eastern European Criminal Enterprises

A number of Russian/Eurasian organized criminal groups and criminal enterprises presently operate in the United States. Clearly, these groups and enterprises are not organized or structured to the extent of other traditional organized crime groups. Some of these groups are associations of criminals aligned with specific leaders. Other Russian/Eurasian organized crime groups are comprised primarily of criminals from a particular ethnic background. Still other Russian/Eurasian criminal enterprises are based around a specific criminal activity and appear focused on monopolizing this activity. Russian mafia is becoming increasingly active in North America and with the reported infiltration of KGB into economic joint ventures between Russia and the U.S., its impact on economic and banking crimes is likely to be substantial.

Asian Criminal Enterprises

The Chinese Triads, criminally-influenced Tongs, subordinate Chinese and Vietnamese gangs, Japanese Boryokudan (Yakuza), and Korean organized groups warrant priority investigative attention in the United States due to their domestic and foreign criminal activities and involvement in murder, kidnapping, extortion, drug trafficking, gambling, and prostitution.

Korean organized crime groups are becoming more active in the United States. Their activities have been detected in Honolulu and on both the East and West Coasts. The most significant of the groups are believed to have thirty to fifty members each and include the Korean Power (New York), Korean Fuk Ching (New York), the Magui (Baltimore), and the Korean Killers and Korean Mafia, from the West Coast. These groups are primarily engaged in extortion, prostitution and increasingly, drug (crystal methamphetamine/"ice") trafficking.

Over 600,000 refugees from Vietnam, including ethnic Vietnamese, ethnic Chinese raised in Vietnam, and ethnic Cham (mon-Khmer and Hmong) have been resettled in the United States. A number of ethnic Vietnamese criminal gangs have been identified in Los Angeles, San Francisco, San Jose, and Orange County, California; Houston; New Orleans; Seattle; New York and the Washington, D.C. metropolitan area. There appears to be clear evidence that the more prominent criminal enterprises, at times (when it seems mutually beneficial) work together to facilitate various crimes. Today, we can look to history to tell us what could happen in the future. Just as prohibition developed organized crime in the United States, narcotics could do the same internationally.

Asian drug trafficking enterprises are, by definition, loosely organized networks, often of Thai, Chinese, Vietnamese, or Korean traffickers, who form ad hoc conspiracies to import Southeast Asian heroin into the United States and distribute it to retail street networks, often managed by Italian, Black, and Hispanic criminals. These groups operate primarily in New York and Los Angeles as Tongs, and powerful Chinese subordinate and independent street gangs, but are not readily described with a name or label. Although these Asian drug trafficking groups do not operate within the rigid hierarchical structure of named Asian criminal organizations, they do, in fact, have an equivalent net effect in conducting themselves in the manner of a criminal enterprise. These groups are commodity driven, instead of being driven by a specific geographic or demographic crime pattern base, like criminal Tongs and their turf-conscious, affiliated street gangs.

Such multi-ethnic alliances have enabled these heroin-trafficking groups to be quite efficient and productive by utilizing the services of various individuals and organizations both inside and outside of the United States. FBI investigations into Southeast Asian heroin-trafficking groups have consistently found that these groups generally are loosely organized networks and each element of the network may perform several functions or be responsible for only one aspect. Some of the individuals involved in the trafficking network may be members or past members of traditional Asian criminal enterprises, and their association with these enterprises sometimes facilitates the heroin-trafficking process that they are involved in. There is a pattern of current members of these organizations using criminal associations made in the course of their memberships to facilitate heroin-trafficking activities in ad hoc groups. In other words, portions of loosely associated networks come together at points in time to consummate a specific transaction or series of transactions.

Measures Including Legislation to Combat Organized Crime

The legislative and law enforcement response to organized crime in the United States occurs primarily at the federal level. Specific federal legislation reflects the interstate, national, and international nature of organized crime and its activities. The federal lead in the fight against organized crime is also a reflection of legal reality. State and local law enforcement agencies have limited resources, a local or, at most, statewide mandate, and cannot justify investigating the activities of criminal organizations that take place outside of their jurisdictions. Organized crime poses a significant threat against the economic and political stability of a nation and a local approach to this type of threat is clearly inadequate. Although the American federal government has achieved significant success against traditional organized crime groups like the Mafia and Cosa Nostra, the existence of a vast and lucrative market economy, international conflicts, increased immigration, a porous border, advances in technology and communication systems, and the relatively disorganized nature of global law enforcement have given older criminal organizations new room for expansion and facilitated the genesis of new, more powerful, international criminal organizations (Godson and Olson, 1995).

Combating international organized crime in the United States clearly requires an international and cooperative approach from criminal justice agencies. The universal impact of organized crime mandates joint efforts by both public and private sector organizations and an informed citizenry. These multifaceted approaches to battling organized crime are already occurring.

The appropriate response to organized crime is dictated by the perceived origin and nature of the threat from a particular criminal organization. As such, effective countermeasures take many different forms or consist of a combination of approaches. Primary efforts by U.S. authorities to suppress organized crime take the following forms:

1. Financial, technical, and training support to assist foreign nations in reforming their criminal justice system and to enhance their ability to combat organized crime

2. Increased budgetary support for the investigation of terrorism and organized crime at the federal level

3. Federal grants to enhance the ability of state and local agencies to combat terrorism and organized crime

4. The establishment of task forces or joint agency operations to investigate organized crime, drug trafficking, and terrorism

5. Diplomatic efforts to encourage other countries to strengthen their own laws in areas that affect organized crime

6. Commissions staffed by persons with expertise in diverse fields to study organized crime and explore creative investigative approaches

7. Expanding the powers of the law enforcement community by passing new, and amending existing, legislation to enhance penalties for organized criminality. Providing prosecutors with new tools to dismantle criminal organizations. Enlisting the assistance of the intelligence community in the fight against drug trafficking and terrorism. Utilizing the information gathering and evaluation expertise of the intelligence community to obtain more precise and detailed information on the structure and operations of criminal organizations

8. Strengthening prevention programs and increasing public awareness through the publication of relevant information on the Internet. Permitting citizens to alert appropriate authorities to suspicious activities, particularly those involving various forms of financial fraud, via that medium

9. Development of new and more sophisticated databases and increased information sharing among law enforcement agencies

10. Conferring and cooperating with other agencies, locally and on a worldwide basis, to exchange information and ideas concerning organized crime

11. Enforcing regulatory laws already in place to impede the criminal organization's ability to function

12. Creating combined task forces to focus the resources of different types of law enforcement agencies on a particular organization or crime problem

13. Identifying a particular organized criminal group and focusing all available resources on the investigation of its activities and prosecution of its leaders and members

Of existing federal criminal statutes, 18 USC 1961, Chapter 96, Racketeer Influenced and Corrupt Organizations (RICO), has been the most effective tool in fighting organized crime. The RICO statute has been successfully used against labor union officials, terrorists, investment firms, drug dealers, and other organized crime figures (Greek, 1991). RICO specifically makes unlawful:

1. Using income derived from a pattern of racketeering activity to acquire an interest in an enterprise
2. Acquiring or maintaining an interest in an enterprise through a pattern of racketeering activity
3. Conducting the affairs of an enterprise through a pattern of racketeering activity
4. Conspiring to commit any of these offenses

Among other kinds of measures, for instance, the FBI has developed an Organized Crime/Drug Enterprise (OC/DE) National Strategy to guide its attack against the various OC/DEs. The OC/DE National Strategy states that the FBI will eliminate major domestic and international OC/DEs as significant threats to American society through sustained, multidivisional, coordinated investigations that support successful prosecution actions. The OC/DE National Strategy also lists several investigative priorities that are set forth by specific OC/DE groups/crime problems.

Another methodology for investigation of organized crime via an operational system identified by the acronym LESAOC (Law Enforcement Systems Attack on Organized Crime) and based on the "systems approach" has been proposed by some ex-FBI officers. It suggests that the involved agencies would function as a team pursuing a definite goal (i.e., elimination of an organized crime system). This system proposes the use of abundant resources available in various fields such as investigations, computers, international tracking, electronic monitoring technology, and others by the law enforcement agencies. Further, in order to ensure that this system operates in a concerted manner and is not plagued by individual egos or objectives that overshadow the ultimate goal, the unit responsible for spearheading the activities is suggested to be an entity outside the law enforcement system but an integral part of the criminal justice system (i.e., the Department of Justice).

Most of these approaches work in tandem, since any increased authority must be granted via appropriate laws, and budgetary increases are necessary to address an expanded jurisdiction. A logical outgrowth of these changes is the need for greater coordination and information sharing with other agencies engaged in similar enforcement activities—locally, nationally, and internationally.

Other specific measures to combat specific forms of organized crime have also been taken by the government and enforcement agencies. Some of these are briefly described as follows:

A Multifaceted Response to Russian and Eastern European Organized Crime

At present the United States government is experiencing a substantial threat from organized crime originating in the republics of the former Soviet Union, the New Independent States (NIS), and the countries of Eastern Europe. The instability of the states of the former Soviet Union and Eastern Europe has left a power vacuum in which organized crime has emerged as a new and growing force. The disruptive influence of organized crime and its ability to corrupt and neutralize government institutions is having a devastating effect on the economy of Russia, and, consequently, can affect international relations between Russia and other countries.

An assessment of the problem has led to an ideal example of a multifaceted response—legislative, financial, and operational. Rather than reacting to the growing threat of Russian Organized Crime (ROC) by simply attacking its manifestations here in the United States, the United States government is recognizing the importance of ensuring a stable government and the need for a justice system that meets international standards in the present-day Russia as a prophylactic measure to block Russian organized crime from establishing itself in the United States. To that end, the United States has provided more than $30 million for crime and justice efforts in the NIS and Central Europe. As part of these efforts, a three-pronged approach was developed to provide the following:

  a. Expansion of the Rule of Law program and renewed emphasis on helping the NIS reform its criminal justice system
  b. Law enforcement training that incorporates a focus on human rights and professional integrity
  c. Efforts to institutionalize US-NIS prosecutorial, law enforcement, and crime prevention cooperation, meeting internationally accepted standards (Collins, 1995).

The very nature of these efforts can lead to beneficial results not only for the United States and Eastern Europe, particularly the NIS, but also for Western Europe. The United States is buttressing these efforts by developing tougher visa standards and new countermeasures to keep criminal elements out of the United States. Additionally, a pilot program, the Russian

Business Investigation Initiative (RBII), has been in operation since 1993, and it enhances the detection and identification of foreign organized crime figures attempting to enter the United States.

A Multijurisdictional Response to Organized Drug Trafficking

The U.S. Department of Justice considers drug trafficking to be the root cause of crime and violence in America, and, in addressing this problem, makes note of the disjointed nature of state, local, and federal law enforcement. Recognizing the need to utilize a multijurisdictional effort by agencies at all governmental levels, the Department of Justice created the Organized Crime Narcotics (OCN) Trafficking Enforcement Program to assist law enforcement agencies in forming regional task forces to combat major organized crime and drug trafficking. OCN projects target specific conspirators through a combined effort. Included in the OCN program is specialized training of local law enforcement officers and the prosecution of financial offenses related to narcotics trafficking. OCN projects must be initiated by state or local law enforcement officials, and federal funds are provided for investigative expenses, surveillance costs, necessary travel, and funds to purchase contraband, other evidence, and information.

A variation of an OCN project, the Statewide Integrated Resources Model (SIRM), was utilized at two locations in 1991 and combined the resources of both investigative and regulatory agencies (DOJ, 1996). The inclusion of regulatory agencies is particularly noteworthy since it brings additional pressure on the criminal organization and the opportunity to financially sanction such an organization for regulatory violations.

Directly associated with drug trafficking is the issue of laundering the profits from such activities. The increasing sophistication and interconnectedness of international financial systems is providing criminal organizations with new opportunities to transfer and invest illicit funds and to engage in more complex financial fraud schemes. Money laundering is international in scope, and the United Nations and the Association of American States have encouraged the countries of the world to pass laws that will inhibit its occurrence. The United States has also played a significant part in influencing other countries to adopt relevant legislation to combat the problem. Recently, the senate of Paraguay responded to U.S. encouragement regarding this issue by introducing new money laundering legislation for that country (*Noticias* on Line, 25 October, 1996). Since 1984, the Drug Enforcement Agency (DEA) and the Treasury Department have examined cash transactions with Hong Kong and noted that more overseas dollars flowed into the United States from Hong Kong than from any European country. This pointed to the existence of the Chinese Underground Banking System, which is an ideal vehicle for money laundering. Transactions are likely to increase now, with Hong Kong having been returned to China in July, 1997. The DEA believes that this banking system handles the majority of the profits from the heroin business in Asia (Cassidy, 1994).

To improve the efforts of federal agencies in investigating and prosecuting financial crimes, of which drug money laundering is an integral part, the Department of the Treasury formed the Financial Crimes Enforcement Network (FinCEN) in 1990, under Treasury Order 105–08. Its mission is to classify, examine, and distribute information on financial crimes, particularly money laundering of drug profits, and to serve as an information clearinghouse for field agents. The utilization of advanced computer systems and information databases is a central part of improving the quality and timeliness of the information available to the agents. The FinCEN functions like a multisource intelligence center to support law enforcement and regulatory agencies in combating financial crimes. FinCEN reports combine information from different databases, such as:

1. The Treasury's Financial Database, which lists reports of transactions over $10,000 filed under the Bank Secrecy Act Requirements, and the importation of currency or similar instruments over $10,000
2. Databases owned and administered by Federal law enforcement and regulatory agencies, and
3. Private, nongovernmental databases available to the public, with business and marketing records and demographic information.

The FinCEN has agreements with law enforcement and regulatory agencies to access some of the information from their databases. The FinCEN is a part of the Department of the Treasury, located in Vienna, Virginia, and has a staff of about two hundred employees, with intelligence analysts, computer experts, and roughly forty agents and analysts on loan from fourteen different federal law enforcement and regulatory agencies.

The Florida Department of Law Enforcement (FDLE) uses an integrated approach to combating organized crime that recognizes the importance of including regulatory agencies in the fight against organized crime. The FDLE charges high-level offenders criminally and also attacks them and their enterprises with every civil and regulatory sanction at its disposal. The department seizes illegally obtained assets and proceeds thereof, dissolves their corporations, seeks disbarment for their attorneys, revokes their beverage licenses, and leaves no possible civil or criminal sanction unapplied to criminal individuals and their organizations.

Referring cases to the federal Internal Revenue Service and their state equivalent for tax implications, enlisting the Federal Aviation Administration (FAA) in taking action on pilots' licenses, and alerting comptroller offices to possible banking violations, are just some of the ways in which regulatory agencies can become involved in a total assault on criminal organizations (Dempsey, 1987).

In the area of computer software and hardware theft, federal agencies such as the FBI appear to be more prepared than state and local law enforcement agencies to address this growing phenomenon. While the FBI actively recruits individuals with specialized technical knowledge, a perusal of entry requirements of all large municipal agencies in the United States shows that computer knowledge is not a requirement for entry as a police officer. The oversight in targeting applicants who have the requisite skills to investigate offenses involving sophisticated technology is only compounded by the traditional policy of placing all new officers on patrol. It usually takes several years before those with the requisite knowledge have any opportunity to be reassigned to an area where those skills can be applied.

Private Sector or Nonprofit Organizations

In addition to private sector businesses that fund the dissemination of information concerning financial and other types of fraud as a public service, there are nonprofit research bodies that study and analyze long-term social, political, economic, military, and national security trends as a basis for developing public policy. One such organization is the Center for Strategic and International Studies (CSIS). It has experts on international finance, U.S. domestic and economic policy, and on foreign policy and national security issues. The organization, which can be reached via the Internet, is presently engaged in a major project with seven task forces on information technology security, terrorism, the nuclear black market, financial crimes, the narcotics industry, Russian organized crime, and Asian organized crime. The CSIS reports that organized crime has entrenched itself in the international economic and financial systems, and that the globalization of its operations presents a significant challenge to the intelligence and enforcement capabilities of national and international law enforcement (Global Organized Crime, 10 October 1996, online).

The National Fraud Information Center (NFIC) is another nonprofit organization and it is the result of a partnership between the National Association of Attorneys General, the Federal Trade Commission, and the National Consumers League. The NFIC is active in disseminating fraud prevention information and maintains its own database of incidents of fraud reported by the public. Reports of these incidents are electronically passed on to the National Electronic Fraud Data Base of the Federal Trade Commission and the National Association of Attorneys General. These reports are also forwarded to various federal and state regulatory and enforcement agencies, such as the FBI, Secret Service, U.S. Postal Inspectors, Securities and Exchange Commission (SEC), and U.S. Attorneys. The NFIC maintains updated alerts on its Internet web page on credit card scams, fraud involving investment schemes advertised in the media, fee for loan offers, identity theft, and has now started a campaign to combat fraud on the Internet.

While law enforcement agencies are generally subjected to the shackles of an inflexible bureaucracy, individual law enforcement officers can more readily bridge the absence of formal agreements by informally sharing information on criminal organizations. From 29 April to 3 May, 1996, the members of the International Association of Asian Crime Investigators held an International Asian Organized Crime Conference in Anaheim, California, with an attendance of 1,700 law enforcement officers from Europe, the United States, and many Asian countries (Brongiel and Buitla, 1996). Their promotion of networking among officers, analysts, educators, and private sector persons who come in contact with Asian crime, and the exchange of their experiences, may well accomplish more than formal treaties and high-level telephone calls. The timely contact between individuals who are in the trenches in the war against organized crime can be much more effective than a formal written request that has to travel through the chain of command and may be useless by the time it is fulfilled.

A private organization with an international focus on fraud is the World Business Organization, which has its own Commercial Crime Bureau (CCB). Operations began in January of 1992 and focus on fraud prevention and increased cooperation between commerce and law enforcement agencies in fighting fraud. The Bureau maintains its own database involving all types of commercial fraud and in the spring of 1996 began the process of establishing a consolidated international database for banks. Members of the CCB receive information on fraud schemes and monthly bulletins on International commercial crime.

Government commissions and committees are a common method for pooling the intellectual resources of experts and policy makers with diverse backgrounds to focus on a pressing problem. In 1951 the Kefauver committee found organized crime to be entrenched and a nationwide problem in the United States. The committee findings spurred the creation of the Organized Crime and Racketeering Section (OCR) within the FBI to encourage the prosecution of organized crime figures. Attempts to bring about an institutionalization of an intelligence program to combat racketeering were unsuccessful, however, due to problems in coordinating federal agencies and a lack of interest (President's Commission, 1967).

A lack of adequate funding for the OCR also caused difficulties in gathering and evaluating intelligence data, along with the added factor of corrupt law enforcement and political systems by organized crime. The Commission stated that although the extent of organized crime cannot be readily determined, it can only exist in conjunction with corrupt government officials. The Commission further opined that to successfully combat organized crime it is essential to know in detail the exact structure and operations of these organizations and recommended that:

> The Department of Justice should give financial assistance to encourage the development of efficient systems for regional intelligence gathering, collection and dissemination. By financial assistance and provisions of security clearance, the Department should also sponsor and encourage research by many relevant disciplines regarding the nature, development, activities, and organization of these special criminal groups (President's Commission, 1967).

The Commission additionally proposed that the federal government provide increased technical, operational, financial, and training assistance to state and local law enforcement agencies and encouraged individual states that have organized crime groups to establish their own organized crime commissions. The importance of the news media in informing the public about the nature, extent, and threat of organized crime was highlighted, and the commission believed that only a unified approach by all sectors and the public itself could lead to success in the fight against the insidious problem of organized crime.

The 1986 President's Commission on Organized Crime re-examined many of the same issues addressed by the 1967 Commission, but its focus was exclusively on organized crime and drug trafficking. In summary, recommendations made by this commission are the continuation of criminal sanctions against illegal drug use, a coordinated response by the federal government, the setting of an ultimate objective for the National Drug Enforcement Policy Board and for the enforcement effort generally. The commission advocated military drug-related intelligence gathering outside of the United States and more coordinated drug enforcement strategies of South American countries, with periodic meetings of intelligence and police officials addressing common problems (The President's Commission, 1986).

Comparative Evaluation of the Methods for Combating Organized Crime and Proposed Measures

Among all the measures taken to combat organized crime in the United States, few could be said to be very successful in their efforts. The impact of the statute on Assistance to United States Law Enforcement Agencies has been softened by the provision of Section 814. By a somewhat puzzling component of Section 814, the state and local law enforcement agencies have been excluded by the legislation. The term United States Law Enforcement Agencies applies only to federal agencies. The exclusion of state and local agencies can only imply that they are not considered safe or trustworthy enough to be provided with information gathered by the intelligence community. It is difficult to see how one can speak of a unified effort to combat organized crime under such circumstances. This exclusion may well be symbolic of the disjointed nature of American law enforcement, pointing to a chasm between federal agencies and state and local law enforcement.

Unfortunately, the drive against organized crime expected from the establishment of commissions or committees has been slow and ponderous. The commissions generally issue findings and make recommendations, such as creating new task forces, funding new units, making organizational changes, and utilizing new tactics in the fight against crime. The absence of any authority by these commissions to ensure the implementation of their recommendations, however, attenuated some of their benefit. The result was that successive committees studied essentially the same problem, arrived at similar conclusions, and made recommendations reminiscent of earlier committees. The 1986 President's Commission has criticized agency infighting, the lack of cooperation between intelligence and law enforcement agencies, the absence of a single standard of success, and the modification of data due to political considerations. Although legislation permitting the intelligence community to exchange information with U.S. law enforcement agencies has addressed part of the recommendations made by the 1986 Commission, the infighting between federal law enforcement agencies has not been resolved. The setting of a national policy for the drug enforcement effort addressed by the 1986 Commission may be inadequate, since most law enforcement occurs at the state and local level and any effort overseen by the Attorney General or a "drug Czar" is therefore likely to be fraught with pitfalls, given the sovereignty of individual states.

New legislation has been drafted to bolster existing enforcement and prosecution efforts. Among them is Senate Bill 735, the Anti-terrorism and Effective Death Penalty Act of 1996, expanding the authority for Alien Smuggling Investigations (Sec. 434), the Expansion of Criteria for Deportation for Crimes of Moral Turpitude (Sec. 435), authorizing state and local law enforcement officials to arrest and detain certain illegal aliens (Sec. 439), and Criminal Alien Removal (Sec. 440), which makes a final order of deportation of an alien who has committed certain, including predicate offenses, not subject to review by any court.

Efforts are also underway to add penalty enhancements to existing statutes when their violation involves organized criminality, and to extend additional authority to state and local agencies when encountering certain illegal aliens. The Economic Espionage Act of 1996 provides for penalties of up to fifteen years of imprisonment for the theft of trade secrets in interstate or foreign commerce. This act specifically addresses the downloading of computer data, the transmission of privileged trade and product information, and conspiracies to commit those offenses.

Senate Bill S. 735, Sec. 439, part of the Anti-terrorism and Effective Death Penalty Act of 1996, authorizes state and local law enforcement officials to arrest and detain illegal aliens who have previously been convicted of a felony in the United States and deported or who left the United States after such conviction. Under this bill, the penalties for counterfeiting of U.S. currency outside of the United States are enhanced, and the posting of U.S. Secret Service agents to overseas posts is expedited. Under Section 321 of Senate Bill S. 735, any resident or U.S. citizen engaging in a financial transaction with any foreign government supporting international terrorism may be punished by up to ten years of imprisonment. Section 303 includes a prohibition on fund-raising or providing material support to designated foreign terrorist organizations. Section 435 provides for the deportation of aliens for conviction of a crime for which a sentence of one year or longer may be imposed.

Section 443 provides for the extradition of aliens who have committed a crime or violence against U.S. citizens in foreign countries, even if no extradition treaty is in existence between the country where the offense occurred and the United States. To improve the ability of the FBI to combat terrorism, Section 811 authorizes an additional $468 million for that purpose during the next four years. To patrol the large U.S. border effectively, 1,000 new officers are proposed to be added by the end of this century, and the number of physical barriers at the border are being increased with better equipment and technology. United States Law Enforcement Agencies are given wiretap authority for alien smuggling investigations, and the offense of alien smuggling is now classified under the RICO statutes. Tougher penalties have been provided for alien smuggling and more prosecutors are being hired to check fraudulent use of government-issued documents. Many new restrictions have also been applied to employers.

Other changes described in the U.S. government's annual report include the establishment of the Office of Investigative Agency Policies, which coordinates the activities of law enforcement agencies within the Department of Justice, a Business Anti-Smuggling Coalition led by a private toy manufacturer and the Customs service, the building of an alliance between licensed gun dealers and the Bureau of Alcohol, Tobacco and Firearms, and the redesign of the $100 bill to stay ahead of counterfeiting technology.

Conclusion

Specific and individual anti-organized crime measures cannot be successful if the objective is the total eradication or significant reduction of the problem. Investigative efforts have to be supported by quality intelligence gathering, collating, evaluating, and dissemination to law enforcement, prosecution, related government agencies, the private sector, and the public. Investigation of organized crime in turn has to be a cooperative effort by all affected agencies. It is furthermore imperative that intelligence information and operational command be centralized. National efforts have to be supplemented by assisting and engaging in joint operations with foreign agencies in their efforts to combat organized crime, since criminal organizations do not have to be located here in the United States in order to victimize its residents. The Nigerian advance fee fraud directed from that country and victimizing persons living in the United States and other countries, is one such example (Leach, 1996).

The ability to engage in the necessary interaction between the United States and foreign justice systems is enhanced when officials in affected countries have an understanding of the functions of American law enforcement and are adequately trained to participate in joint investigative and prosecutorial efforts. Since organized crime is a global problem, it is essential that countries help one another in the development of an effective criminal justice system. To that end, the U.S. Department of Justice provides training and assistance to numerous countries through the Criminal Division's International Criminal Investigative Training Assistance Program (ICITAP), but this effort needs to be enhanced.

Similarly, the success of any individual investigation of a criminal organization is affected by multiple factors, some of which cannot be controlled. The geographic relocation of a criminal organization and flight of wanted individuals to foreign countries cannot be stopped unless other governments are willing to take action. The President's Commission in 1986 focused on the need for a nationally directed and unified effort by law enforcement to combat organized crime, but today we must change the term "nationally" to "internationally" to reflect the more global impact of organized crime.

Criminal justice agencies in the United States are confronted with highly adaptive and economically powerful international criminal organizations. Rapid and unexpected political, economic, and technological changes are allowing criminal organizations to exploit newly created opportunities to expand and diversify their activities on a global scale. Criminal Justice agencies are constantly playing catch-up as criminal organizations quickly employ new methods to elude government countermeasures.

At the same time, law enforcement paradoxically points to increased drug seizures and the successful prosecution of organized crime figures as signs of success. The increased focus on intelligence gathering and better coordination of criminal justice agencies on a local, state, national, and international scale, are one step in the right direction. It is also important to supplement enforcement efforts with a greater focus on government corruption at all levels and to increase the education of the public in order to enlist them in the fight against organized crime.

Much of the increased strength of the international criminal organization is due to its ability to network and develop cooperative relationships with other criminal organizations and its skill in exploiting societal and governmental weaknesses. To have any hope of stemming the threat of international organized crime, governments must reach a similar level of national and international cooperation. American efforts are presently under way to accomplish this goal. Missing, however, is a substantial emphasis on forecasting future trends in organized criminality, which would allow governments to become more proactive, rather than waiting for new developments in organized criminality and then developing countermeasures. A unified and resolute attack on organized crime is needed before it overwhelms the ability of governments in general to maintain a stable and safe economic, social, and political environment.

REFERENCES

Arango, M. 1988. "Son el soporte de un pais en crisis." *Semana* (26 Sept.): 34.

Brongiel, J., and J., Buitla. 1996. Asian Crime Investigators "Network into the 21st Century." *CJ International Online*, 11 October.

Cassidy, W.L. 1994. *Fei-Chien, or Flying Money: A Study of Chinese Underground Banking*. Unpublished report.

Center for Strategic and International Studies, *Global Organized Crime*, October 10, 1996.

Dempsey, R. 1987. The Integrated Approach to Combating Organized Crime. *The Police Chief* (April): 47–49.

Department of Justice Release. 1996. "Attorney General Reno Unveils 14-States Midwest Strategy to Stop the Spread of Methamphetamine." *Dept. of Justice Memorandum* (26 Sept.).

Farah, D. 1996. "Tracing Colombia's Nigerian Connection." *The Washington Post* 21 June, via www.washingtonpost.com.

Collins, J.F. 1996. "Crime in the New Independent States: The U.S. Response." Statement before the Senate Select Committee on Intelligence. *U.S. State Department Dispatch* 3 April.

The Economist. 1996. "The Flourishing Business of Slavery" (21 Sept. Online).

Garcia-Marquez, G. 1996. *Noticia de un Secuestro*. New York: Penguin Books.

Godson, R., and J., Olson. 1995. International Organized Crime. *Society-Journal* (Jan/Feb): 18–29.

Greek, C. 1991. "Is this the end of RICO or only the Beginning? Debate over the expanded use of criminal and civil RICO." *Free Inquiry in Creative Sociology* 19 (no. 1): 11–21.

Women's Health Weekly. 1995. "Group Exposes Trans-Border Sex Slavery between Nepal and India." 4 September, 9–10.

ICC Commercial Crime Services (http://www1.usa1.com/~ibnet/iccbhp.html).

Johnson, C., Webster, B., and Connors, E. 1995. "Prosecuting Gangs: A National Assessment." *National Institute of Justice Research in Brief*, February.

El Pais. 1995. *La Europol empezara a funcioar en 1996.* 7 September, 7.

Leach, J. 1996. "Leach to Iowans: Beware Nigerian Organized Crime Scheme." *House Bulletin* 13 October.

Noticias Online. 1996. *Ley Contra "Lavado" De Dinero Ya Cuenta Con Media Sancion.* 25 October.

President's Commission on Law Enforcement and Administration of Justice. 1967. *The Challenge of Crime in a Free Society.* Washington, D.C.: U.S. Government Printing Office.

President's Commission on Organized Crime. 1986. *America's Habit*, September. Chapter III Part 1: Drug Trafficking and Organized Crime.

Promoting the Rule of Law and Combating Crime. 1994. *U.S. Department of State Dispatch.* Joint statement released by the White House, Office of the Press Secretary, Washington, D.C., 28 September, 41.

Reynolds, B. 1995. "Corrupt Criminal Justice System Invites Crime, Chaos." *USA Today*, 8 September, 11 A.

Rasor, R. 1995. *Capitol Hill Hearing Testimony of Robert Rasor*, Deputy Assistant Director of Investigations, United States Secret Service, 11 October.

La Estrella Star-Telegram. 1996. *Samper Niega Tener Vinculos Con Narcotraficantes*, 27 September.

Singleton, L. 1995. "Security Warns of Nigerian Mail Scam." INEL *Quality Security Education and Awareness Team Newsletter*, 12 December.

Torres, C. 1996. "Hay que combatir los apoyos de la delinquencia." *Noticias Online*, 3 October.

Yoon, Y. 1996. "International Sexual Slavery." *International Law Review* 6, part 7.

CHAPTER 2

ORGANIZED CRIME: A CANADIAN PERSPECTIVE

Daniel J. Koenig

INTRODUCTION

With a land area of roughly 3,601,941.41 square miles, Canada is the second-largest country in the world (after Russia). It holds a strategic location between Russia and the United States via a north polar route. It has ten provinces and three territories. The newest territorial government, Nunavat, came into being in the eastern Arctic on April 1, 1999.

Nearly 90 percent of Canada's slightly more than 30 million population is concentrated within 100 miles of the United States/Canada border. The most populous provinces are Ontario and Quebec, followed by British Columbia and Alberta. The country is ethnically diversified: Although British Isles origin accounts for 40 percent of the people, the French constitute 27 percent, other Europeans, 20 percent, indigenous first nations, 1.5 percent, and others (mostly Asians), 11.5 percent, of the total composition.

Canada is an affluent, high-tech, industrial society with a market-oriented economic system and pattern of production. Since World War II the impressive growth of the manufacturing, mining, and service sectors has transformed the nation from a largely rural economy into one that is primarily industrial and urban.

Canada's government is a confederated parliamentary democracy. The federal government was granted its power under the provisions of the Constitution Act of 1867 (now included in the Constitution Act, 1982) to enact criminal law and procedure. However, power to enforce laws and administer criminal justice, including the establishment of law enforcement agencies, courts, and correctional institutions is delegated to the provinces and territories.

The legal system is based on English common law, except in Quebec, where a civil law system based on French law prevails. Canada's public institutions are influenced by the English system. The judiciary is independent of the legislative and executive powers at both federal and provincial levels. The administration of justice at provincial levels encompasses both civil and criminal matters.

The Royal Canadian Mounted Police (RCMP) is Canada's largest police force. In 1994 the RCMP accounted for 28 percent of Canada's police. The RCMP operates under contract as the provincial police force in all provinces and territories except Ontario and Quebec. It also operates under contract as a municipal police force in many jurisdictions, particularly within the province of British Columbia.

Canada maintains separate federal and provincial court systems in Canada. Most criminal cases are handled by provincial courts. Provinces also have additional courts such as justices of the peace, juvenile courts, and family courts. At the federal level there is a Federal Court of Canada, which is divided into a Trial Division and a Court of Appeals. The court of last resort in Canada is the Federal Supreme Court of Canada, although in certain circumstances further appeals are possible to the Privy Council.

There is much talk about organized crime. Often, the image is of a tightly knit international cabal of which criminologists do not find much evidence. For that matter, with few exceptions throughout this century neither the FBI nor the RCMP have found much evidence for such a conceptualization of organized crime. Rather, the evidence would suggest, in the words of Brodeur (1996), that it would be more accurate to speak of associations of criminals *organizing* crime, rather than of organized crime associations.

It is important to be precise about what is being targeted if our strategies are going to be effective in controlling crime. Consequently, the first objective of this chapter is to examine the phrase, "organized crime." Thereafter, some of the major criminal activities perpetrated by associations of criminals in Canada will be examined. Next, various clusters of associations of criminals classified by the Criminal Intelligence Service Canada (CISC) will be identified. A presentation will follow of relevant recent legislation, related judicial decisions and legislative responses thereto, additional concerns of the law enforcement community, and a recounting of what Canada has been doing to contain enterprise crime and illicit substance distribution. In closing, some critical questions will be raised.

The Nature and Extent of Organized Crime

If we are to devise effective strategies for combating organized crime, we should be precise about whom and what we are seeking to target. Definitions of organized crime are too often merely stereotypical descriptions or vague assertions. Definitions often either are not fully inclusive of what we think of as organized crime or they *do* include other crimes that are not what most people consider to be organized crime. As Brodeur (1996) commented in a major presentation at a National Forum on Organized Crime in Canada's capital in September 1996, we should be careful to distinguish between unlawful activities that are essentially organized crime and criminal activities that happen to be prosecuted under laws that are heralded as laws targeting organized crime.

For example, CISC (1996C) cites the RCMP's Criminal Intelligence Directorate's list of characteristics that differentiate organized crime from other crimes, which are corruption for gain or resulting from blackmail; discipline, including threatened or actual violence to enforce obedience; infiltration of legitimate institutions; insulation of the criminal organization's leaders; a monopoly over activities within a geographic area (which does not preclude collusive agreements motivated by profit); motivation to obtain wealth or byproducts of wealth such as power and influence; subversion of society's legal or moral values; a history allowing entrenchment and refinement of criminal activities; the use of violence; sophistication in the use of advanced systems of communication and asset management, as well as entry into political, judicial, and enforcement circles; continuity of profitable criminal enterprises; diversity of activities engaged in for profit and control; bonding of individuals to one another and of individuals to the group, and mobility across any type of boundary.

If the previous descriptive characteristics are accepted as common to all organized crime, then Canada does not have legislation that is specifically targeted at organized crime. Rather, Canada's *Proceeds of Crime* legislation is a very imprecise instrument that targets a wide range of criminal activities that do not fit CISC's portrayal of the RCMP's characterization of organized crime. Brodeur (1996) cites evidence that excessively broad legislation has exposed the fight against organized crime in the United States to the risk of a counterproductive public backlash.

Brodeur accepts that some criminal groups filling the characteristics of organized crime described by CISC may exist. However, he argues that a wide variety of traditional and newer criminal activities are engaged in by a diversity of organizations, which often are *ad hoc* in nature. These organizations are constantly on the verge of internal conflict leading to collapse because of their transitory nature. Brodeur also differentiates between unlawful activities that are inherently organized crime and those criminal activities that may merely be captured as organized crime under various laws.

Brodeur strongly contends that a notion of organized crime groups operating in isolation from the rest of society is inaccurate. Rather, he sees significant relationships between criminal organizations and conventional society. Brodeur prefers the concept of organizing crime to that of organized crime. His reasons for this distinction are that he sees typical criminal enterprises as much more fluid than bureaucratic, constantly evolving and adapting and organizing, not only their own activities, but also those of others through alliances and networks.

Naylor (1996), who presented another major paper at the Canadian National Forum on Organized Crime, identifies a succinct list of assumed characteristics of organized crime to scrutinize for empirical validity. These are a durable hierarchy; a stress on enterprise offenses; the use of violence and corruption; the achievement of very high rates of return; and the penetration of legitimate business. However, Naylor (1996) does not find this model to be empirically verified. Rather, he sees criminals as engaging in actual crimes either as individuals or in small partnerships. Like Brodeur, he suggests that it would be more accurate to conceptualize the issue as *associations of criminals* rather than as *criminal associations*.

CISC, Brodeur, and Naylor *do* agree that there are many linkages of criminal organizations with legitimate institutions, although there is some disagreement about the reasons for, and the nature of, these relationships. Beare (1996), too, has commented about the integration of many criminal organizations with conventional society, as indicated by her two-dimensional classification of such organizations. One of her dimensions is the apparent legitimacy or illegitimacy of the enterprise, while the other classifies whether the activity is predatory toward or symbiotic with the larger society. As an example, Possami (1996) has reported that many Canadian students began to view smoking black-market cigarettes both as a cool behavior and as a way of sending a protest message to the government about excessive levels of taxation. This attitude generated a "me too" snowball momentum.

Possami (1996) has also noted the annual disappearance of billions of "homeless" cigarettes from the world's international trade balance sheets. He cited an estimate that black-market cigarettes accounted for 30 percent of total Canadian sales by 1993. Moreover, he added that 25 percent of the apprehended shipments of contraband tobacco also included contraband alcohol. He contends that enterprise crimes, such as cigarette smuggling, damage society in numerous unforeseen ways, including increasing the burden on law enforcement both directly and indirectly through the facilitation of ancillary criminal activities, undermining legal distribution and retailing networks through unfair competition, and shortfalls in government revenue that result in service reductions and/or increases in levels of general taxation.

Organized Criminal Activities

Nobody knows with any certainty how much of any type of organized criminal activity takes place. Surveying and analyzing estimates of organized crime's revenues and profits for the United States, Naylor (1996) infers that the amount of profit involved in organized crime is often wildly exaggerated. Be that as it may, the CISC (1996C) estimates annual revenues of at least $20 billion Canadian dollars for organized crime, about half of it from the drug trade. While any such estimate is no more than an educated guess, one can conclude with confidence that enterprising associations of criminals will respond to any lucrative opportunity that arises. Naylor observes that such opportunities, historically, have been entrepreneurial in the sense of providing a good or service that was not otherwise being provided (or, perhaps, which was not being provided predictably or at a sufficient level of customer satisfaction). Most such goods and services were illegal and involved contraband goods or outlawed services.

In a sense criminal entrepreneurs filled a void in a marketplace that was created by governments. By outlawing various goods and services, governments minimized competition and ensured a high mark-up for those who provided them (to offset extraordinary overheads in the form of bribes, hired violence, laundering costs, and sundry other risks involved for whomever provided such goods and services). Gambling activities and the sex trade were among the leading services traditionally provided by organized criminal groups, as was the provision of alcohol during the prohibition years. Today, the unlawful trade in various drugs is thought to be the most lucrative organized criminal activity within Canada. Of course, criminal groups continue to be active in the sex trade and illegal gambling—as well as legal gambling for money laundering purposes. Illegal gambling using video lottery terminals (VLTs) made possible by new technologies is particularly troublesome in the provinces of Ontario, British Columbia, and Quebec (CLEU Policy Analysis, 1995B).

There has been a significant revival in the smuggling of contraband tobacco and alcohol. However, recent smuggling has been motivated by the evasion of high levels of taxation rather than by the legal unavailability of the product—as was the case when (alcohol) prohibition existed in various parts of Canada and all of the United States. Smuggling networks are also trafficking in both firearms and illegal migrants. Additionally, there is apprehension about possible smuggling of plutonium and other nuclear materials for terrorist activities. As well as expanding the scope of goods (and people) that smuggling networks bring into Canada, such networks have facilitated smuggling stolen luxury automobiles and other luxury goods out of Canada for resale. The Insurance Office of Canada estimates losses from unrecovered stolen vehicles at $293 million Canadian dollars per year. The majority of these are stolen from the province of Quebec and are linked with the overseas export of stolen autos in export containers.

In addition to automobile thefts for export, a variety of other profit-motivated automobile thefts occur. For example, "chop shops" strip parts from late model stolen automobiles to upgrade older automobiles, or a wrecked vehicle can be purchased for salvage to switch the Vehicle Identification Numbers (VIN) of the wrecked vehicle with that of a similar stolen model. The stolen automobile with its new legitimate VIN is then sold for profit, while the wrecked hulk is abandoned after substituting the stolen vehicle's VIN for its original VIN (CLEU Policy Analysis, 1995B). Fraud and counterfeiting opportunities continue to be seized by criminal entrepreneurs. New telecommunications, computer, and other technologies have created many new opportunities for such illegal activities. The CISC (1996A) reports that in 1994 Canadian banks lost an estimated $143 million Canadian dollars through fraud, while the insurance industry reckons that it also loses $1.5 to $2 billion Canadian dollars a year from various frauds.

CISC also reports an explosion of telecommunication and telephone toll fraud. Losses due to telecommunication theft and cloned cellular telephone operations are estimated by industry sources at approximately $300 million Canadian dollars per year. Seizures of computer equipment, cloned phones, and software to produce cloned phones have become commonplace in organized crime investigations. Cloned cellular phones are particularly attractive targets for criminals because, even more than inexpensive telephone access, they offer anonymous and virtually untraceable communications access. Commercially available scanners allow criminals to scan numbers from the airwaves and then use them to program cloned phones. CISC also reports that organized crime groups are employing computer criminals to gain access to telecommunications systems, data banks, credit profiles, and other personal information. Killam (1996) reports that high-quality counterfeiting of currency, various types of bank and other credit or debit cards, and many other documents are very much a part of the activities of organized crime networks in Canada. Counterfeiting has become much easier and more accessible because of various technological innovations such as sophisticated laser color and ink-jet copiers or printers. Counterfeit documents (for example, counterfeit birth or baptismal certificates) are used to establish identities for obtaining false passports, new driver's licenses, credit cards, and the like; or for those who have a need to establish a new identity for confounding creditors, law enforcement authorities, insurance companies, or others. Such documents can also be used to establish multiple identities for defrauding various government programs that provide income, social or health benefits.

The Composition of Organized Criminal Groups

The CISC (1996A) identifies outlaw motorcycle gangs and associations of criminals of various similar ethnic backgrounds to be the major visible organized groups of criminals within Canada. The association of organized criminal activity with particular ethnic backgrounds does not mean that CISC thinks either that such activities are characteristic of people with such ethnic backgrounds or that the governments and law enforcement agencies of the countries of origin condone or participate in such illegal activities. Rather, such descriptions simply refer to the fact that the majority of the members of specific organized criminal clusters share an ethnic similarity.

CISC identifies the major organized crime groups in Canada as Asian (particularly Southeast Asian), Eastern European, Italian, Aboriginal, outlaw motorcycle gangs (particularly the Hell's Angels), and Colombian in composition. Youth gangs, prison gangs, skinheads and militia-type groups, among others, would be added to the CISC list by other observers, such as Brodeur. Asian groups operate mainly in Toronto and Vancouver, but also in Montreal, Calgary, Edmonton, and, to a lesser extent, in Winnipeg, Ottawa, and Halifax. CISC reports that there is a preponderance of ethnic Asians at every level of the Canadian heroin trade. Asian individuals and groups, particularly those originating in the People's Republic of China (PRC), are responsible for an estimated 80% of large-scale heroin shipments into Canada according to CISC (1996A). Vietnamese street gangs and some Triad members and their associates are also involved. Additionally, criminal organizations based in the Asian community are becoming involved in multi-kilogram amounts of cocaine smuggling and trafficking.

The activities of criminal organizations based in the Asian communities extend beyond those communities to include white-collar crimes like money laundering, counterfeit check schemes, telephone toll and credit card fraud. Asian groups, particularly one with roots in the PRC and known as "Big Circle Boys" (BCB), are thought to be responsible for most counterfeit credit cards, and there are indications that they are distributing counterfeit currency. They are also involved in major theft rings and commercial break and enter. CISC (1996A) reports that a well-organized criminal group operating in Toronto's Vietnamese community has staged auto accidents throughout the province. This group also continues to be active in the contraband tobacco trade, specializing primarily in smuggling American-origin cigarettes. Vietnamese groups including both males and females have been involved in large-scale shoplifting in many centers.

Of particular concern to law enforcement personnel is the frequent tendency of ethnic Asian criminal groups to develop alliances with legitimate business, such as import companies, to facilitate their activities. By doing so, they recruit and involve other individuals who previously were without criminal backgrounds. They have also established links with the Hell's Angels and with other clusters of organized criminals having origins in the Italian, Iranian, Nigerian, Lebanese, and Aboriginal communities.

Perhaps more alarming to the public is that much of the increase in violent criminal activity is attributed to these gangs that exploit others in their own Asian communities. They are quite mobile and quick in resorting to violence, and are frequently armed with semi- or fully automatic weapons. Typical Asian-gang signature crimes are extortion, loan-sharking, witness intimidation, illegal gambling, prostitution, drive-by shootings, home invasions, and commercial robberies.

CISC (1996A) reports that organized criminal activities linked to groups with Eastern European heritage are concentrated in the Toronto metropolitan area, but appear to be spreading to Montreal and Vancouver. Of particular concern is the penetration of organized crime groups from the former Soviet Union (FSU) into Toronto's FSU community. These groups have links with FSU-based criminal organizations operating in Russia, as well as throughout Europe and the United States. There is also an escalating linkage between FSU-organized criminal groups and entrepreneurial class criminals from the FSU who are associated with large international trading companies that move significant amounts of money into and out of the FSU. Organized criminal groups of predominantly Eastern European membership reportedly engage in a potpourri of criminal activities ranging from extortion, murder, and large-scale theft to money laundering, international frauds, and the smuggling of drugs, cigarettes, weapons, or automobiles.

Beare (1996) suggests that the Italian Mafia initially spread up from the United States to the city of Montreal rather than Toronto because of its geographical proximity, preexisting political corruption (in the province of Quebec) during the Duplessis regime, and the mystique of a Parislike underlife. According to CISC (1996A), the preferred activities of ethnic Italian organized crime groups are drug trafficking, money laundering, gambling, smuggling, and extortion, either alone or in association with other criminal groups.

The Italian Mafia also engage in other illegal activities as opportunities arise. Italian criminal groups are attracted to legitimate gaming venues such as casinos. These enterprises provide them with opportunities for money laundering, loan-sharking, prostitution, and other traditional types of organized criminal activities. Increasingly, Italian organized crime members and their associates are entering the legitimate business world. This provides them with good cover for meetings, as well as for money laundering and smuggling activities. It also concerns law enforcement authorities that the unfair competitive advantages of crime-funded businesses may overwhelm legitimate businesses in the marketplace.

CISC (1996A) reports that there are about 35 outlaw motorcycle gangs, with 70 chapters and about 1,200 members, in Canada. With 12 gangs, the province of Ontario has the largest number of members. However, the most powerful and best organized of these "biker" gangs are the Hell's Angels. The Hell's Angels have 11 chapters, of which 5 are in each of the provinces of Quebec and British Columbia; the other is in the province of Nova Scotia. Some other gangs are closely connected with the Hell's Angels, including all three of the other biker gangs in the province of British Columbia. The British Columbia Hell's Angels are regarded as one of the wealthiest outlaw motorcycle gangs in the world. CISC (1996A) states that one of the Quebec chapters, the Nomads, formed with experienced Hell's Angels members in 1995, was founded specifically to expedite expansion and control of the Hell's Angels' drug trafficking networks across Canada.

It is anticipated that the Hell's Angels are about to establish a chapter in the province of Ontario, which is expected to ignite a major turf war in that province. Beginning in July 1995, within the province of Quebec there has been a fierce ongoing conflict pitting the Montreal and Trois Rivieres chapters of the Hell's Angels against another gang called the Rock Machine. As of mid 1996, this conflict has involved 86 violent incidents and resulted in 26 deaths. One of the deaths was that of a child who was a bystander to an explosion.[1] With the support of other motorcycle gangs across the country, the Hell's Angels are increasing their control of the importation, distribution, and sale of illicit drugs such as cocaine, cannabis, methamphetamine, PCP, and LSD. Hell's Angels also appear to be increasing their involvement in the contraband alcohol and tobacco trade.

CISC (1996A) reports that organized aboriginal criminal activities primarily involve contraband smuggling of liquor, tobacco, and firearms. In addition, there is some smuggling of illegal migrants between the United States and Canada, particularly in Eastern Canada, through reserves

---

[1] The resulting public uproar was instrumental in the enactment of new legislation, to be discussed, targeted at outlaw biker gangs. It took a mere eight calendar days following introduction of the legislation in Parliament for this bill to pass through three readings in the House of Commons, three readings in the Senate, assent by the Governor General in Council, and proclamation!

whose territories spill across the boundary into both countries. In Western Canada, aboriginal street gangs are establishing footholds in prostitution, drugs, and crimes against humanity. Such gangs frequently have strong connections with the aboriginal prison population from which they recruit members. There is a growing tendency for legitimate aboriginal leadership to seek to establish gaming venues (open to all people) on their reserves, which may attract various organized criminal groups seeking to infiltrate and develop links with the legitimate leadership of aboriginal reserves.

CISC (1996A) reports that very sophisticated Colombian drug trafficking organizations continue to play a major role both in the Canadian cocaine trade and in multi-million dollar money laundering operations. They are very difficult to detect because they establish legitimate enterprises as commercial cover and blend into existing Latin American business communities in cities like Toronto and Montreal. The Colombians also distance themselves as far as possible from trafficking and other physical proximity to the drug trade, including a separation of drug and money transactions.

It has become clear that the notion of all-powerful cartels (e.g. the Medellin or Cali cartels) is not accurate. Rather, there appear to be a number of unique organizations, each of which has its own distinct head. For this reason, the Colombian cocaine traffic has been only minimally disrupted by the imprisonment of the Cali cartel leaders, or by the massive 5.4 ton seizure in 1994 from a cocaine mothership. Rather, the greatest threat to the Colombian cocaine monopoly arises from the incursion into the cocaine trade of newer arrivals on the trafficking scene, such as Asian criminal groups, motorcycle gangs, Jamaican posses, and FSU groups.

Measures, Including Legislation to Combat Organized Crime

In 1988, the United Nations Economic and Social Council adopted the United Nations Convention Against Illicit Traffic in Narcotic Drugs and Psychotropic Substances. As CLEU Policy Analysis (1995A) reports, this Convention recognized that the illicit drug trade generates large financial profits and wealth. These monies enable transnational alliances of criminals to penetrate, contaminate, and corrupt structures of government, business, and society at all levels. The Convention also identified the seizure of criminal assets as an effective way of fighting narcotics trafficking. The Convention requires signatory states to enact legislation to authorize the seizure and confiscation of proceeds, property, and instrumentalities of drug trafficking and to make money laundering an offense. It also suggests, where possible, a reversal of the usual onus of proof, so that a criminal would have to verify that his or her assets and property are not derived from the illicit drug traffic. To date, at least one hundred and six states, including Canada, have adopted the Convention. Canada was one of the twenty countries that ratified the Convention, allowing it to come into force November 11, 1990 (Beare, 1996:147).

Before the convention was officially ratified, Canada already had adopted a tripartite policy approach of targeting upwards, seizing proceeds, and facilitating international enforcement. In 1988, Canada enacted Bill C-158, known as the Mutual Legal Assistance in Criminal Matters Act (S.C. 1988, c. 37). As of July 1995, Canada had twelve treaties in force under this legislation and had signed four more that were not yet in force. Types of assistance specified in these treaties included executing searches and seizures, taking evidence from witnesses, gathering and transferring information and evidence, and making people available to participate in investigations (Beare, 1996).

In 1988 Canada also enacted Bill C-61, commonly known as the Proceeds of Crime legislation (R.S.C. 1985, c. 42 [4th Supp.]). This Act, which came into force in 1989, created a new section (462.3) of the Criminal Code and amended the Narcotics Control Act (NCA), the Food and Drug Act (FDA), and the Income Tax Act. The amendment to the Income Tax Act frees from criminal or civil liability individuals who disclose to peace officers that money or property is "proceeds of crime," subject to s. 241 of the Income Tax Act. This legislation also created two categories of offenses (enterprise crime offense and designated drug offense[2]), and made it an offense to launder proceeds from either of them. Moreover, it allows police to place a restraining order on assets believed to be proceeds of these offenses, with forfeiture of the assets possible after the trial. If a defendant is convicted, the Court can order the assets forfeited if the Crown can show a relationship between the criminal, one of the crimes listed in the statute, and the assets themselves.

It proved difficult to document the laundering of proceeds from criminal activity. Consequently, in 1991 Canada passed the Proceeds of Crime (money laundering) Act (S.C. 1991, c. 26). This Act and its associated Regulations came into effect in 1993. The Act and its Regulations apply to entities covered by various Acts relating to banks, insurance companies, cooperative credit associations, trust companies, loan companies, securities

---

[2]The definition of designated drug offense was extended and the offense was renamed "designated substance offense" by the Controlled Drug and Substances Act (S.C. 1996, c. 19), which came into force May 14, 1997.

dealers, and foreign currency exchanges, as well as to certain professions and other business people who receive cash to be transferred to another person. They are required to keep record of any cash transaction of $10,000 Canadian dollars or more for a five-year period. (Beare, 1996; CLEU Policy Analysis, 1992B).

Subsequent to 1988, there have been additional amendments to the Criminal Code and to other Canadian legislation that refined and increased the scope of what originally was designated as an "enterprise crime offense" or a "designated drug offense"; eased the burden of proof, linking the proceeds of crime with the associated crime; strengthened the ability of law enforcement officials to prove money laundering; allowed association with or membership in organized crime to be grounds for not being allowed into Canada; introduced an improved Witness Protection Act (S.C. 1996, c. 15) that came into effect June 20, 1996; renamed "designated drug offense" as "designated substance offense" and extended the coverage of prohibited substances, together with their analogues and precursor chemicals; brought up to date and simplified procedural law relating to search and seizure, interception of communications and surreptitious observation; and made participation in a criminal organization an offense.

Currently, the essence of Canada's Proceeds of Crime legislation is found in Section 462.3 (and subsections thereof) of the Criminal Code. Definitions of "designated substance offense[3]," "enterprise crime offense," "judge," and "proceeds of crime" are included under the Interpretations of s. 462.3. Under current legislation, a "designated substance offense" means

(a) an offense under Part I of the Controlled Drugs and Substances Act, except subsection 4(1) of that Act, or

(b) a conspiracy or an attempt to commit, being an accessory after the fact in relation to, or any counseling in relation to, an offense referred to in paragraph (a)[4]

---

[3]Bill C-8 (the Controlled Drugs and Substances Act [S.C., 1996, c. 19]), was passed by Parliament and received Royal Assent on June 20, 1996. It was proclaimed in its entirety on April 22, 1997, and came into force on May 14, 1997. This bill renamed "designated drug offense" as "designated substance offense," and extended the coverage of this offense to include analogues and precursor chemicals. Bill C-8 fulfills Canada's obligations under the Single Convention on Narcotic Drugs, the Convention on Psychotropic Substances, and portions of the United Nations Convention Against Illicit Traffic in Narcotic Drugs and Psychotropic Substances.

[4]The Criminal Code provides the meaning of counseling in s. 22, the meaning of an accessory after the offense in s. 23, and the scope of what is considered an "attempt" in s. 24.

An "enterprise crime offense"[5] means

(a) an offense against any of the following provisions, namely,

- (i) subsection 99(1) (weapons trafficking),
  - (i.1) subsection 100(1) (possession for purpose of weapons trafficking),
  - (i.2) subsection 102(1) (making automatic firearm),
  - (i.3) subsection 103(1) (importing or exporting knowing it is unauthorized),
  - (i.4) subsection 104(1) (unauthorized importing or exporting),
  - (i.5) section 119 (bribery of judicial officers, etc.),
- (ii) section 120 (bribery of officers),
- (iii) section 121 (frauds upon the government),
- (iv) section 122 (breach of trust by public officer),
- (v) section 163 (corrupting morals),
  - (v.1) section 163.1 (child pornography),
- (vi) subsection 201(1) (keeping gaming or betting house),
- (vii) section 202 (betting, pool-selling, book-making, etc.),
- (viii) section 210 (keeping common bawdy-house),
- (ix) section 212 (procuring),
- (x) section 235 (punishment for murder),
- (xi) section 334 (punishment for theft),
- (xii) section 344 (punishment for robbery),
- (xiii) section 346 (extortion),
  - (xiii.1) section 347 (criminal interest rate),
- (xiv) section 367 (punishment for forgery),
- (xv) section 368 (uttering forged documents),

---

[5]The law is defined with reference to the specific sections of the Criminal Code cited. The parenthetical references are merely descriptive, for convenience, of the focus of the sections that define enterprise crime. Paragraph a (i) was replaced [S.C. 1995, c. 39, s. 151 (1)] by subparagraphs (i) to i (5) (to come into force January 1, 2003. While all are not yet in force, the amendments created by the Firearms Act are included herein as proclaimed. The new a (i) (5) is the same as the former a (i).

Paragraphs (a)(xxiv) and (a.1) were added by Bill C-95, An Act to Amend the Criminal Code (Criminal Organizations) and to Amend Other Acts in Consequence, (S.C., 1997, c. 23); paragraphs (b)(i), (b)(ii), and (c) consequentially also received minor modifications by this same legislation.

(xvi) section 380 (fraud),
(xvii) section 382 (fraudulent manipulation of stock exchange transactions),
(xviii) section 426 (secret commissions),
(xix) section 433 (arson),
(xx) section 449 (making counterfeit money),
(xxi) section 450 (possession, etc., of counterfeit money),
(xxii) section 452 (uttering, etc., of counterfeit money),
(xxiii) section 462.31 (laundering proceeds of crime), or
(xxiv) section 467.1 (participation in criminal organization)

(a.1) an indictable offense under this or any other Act of Parliament committed for the benefit of, at the direction of, or in association with a criminal organization for which the maximum punishment is imprisonment for five years or more

(b) an offense against *subsection 96(1) (possession of weapon obtained by commission of offense) or*[6] section 354 (possession of property obtained by crime), committed in relation to any property, thing or proceeds obtained or derived directly or indirectly as a result of

  (i) the commission in Canada of an offense referred to in paragraph (a) or (a.1) or a designated substance offense,[7] or
  (ii) an act or omission anywhere that, if it had occurred in Canada, would have constituted an offense referred to in paragraph (a) or (a.1) or a designated substance offense,

(b.1) an offense against section 126.1 or 126.2 or subsection 233(1) or 240(1) of the Excise Act or section 153, 159, 163.1 or 163.2 of the Customs Act, or

(c) a conspiracy or an attempt to commit, being an accessory after the fact in relation to, or any counseling in relation to, an offense referred to in paragraph (a), (a.1), (b), or (b.1)

---

[6] The italicized section of paragraph (b) was amended by Parliament by the Firearms Act in 1995 {c. 39, s. 151(2)} and has been proclaimed, but it will not come into force until January 1, 2003.

[7] This section originally referred to "designated drug offense." All references to "designated drug offense" were changed to "designated substance offense" by Bill C-8 Controlled Drugs and Substances Act (S.C., 1996, c. 19).

"Proceeds of crime" means any property, benefit or advantage, within or outside Canada, obtained or derived directly or indirectly as a result of:

(a) the commission in Canada of an enterprise crime offense or a designated substance offense, or
(b) an act or omission anywhere that, if it had occurred in Canada, would have constituted an enterprise crime offense or a designated substance offense, or R.S.C. 1985, c. 42 (4th Supp.), s. 2; 1993, c. 25; 1993, c. 37, s. 32; 1993, c. 46, s. 5; 1994, c. 44, s. 29.

Section 462.31 of the Criminal Code defines the offense of "Laundering Proceeds Of Crime." Specifically:

(1) Every one commits an offense who uses, transfers the possession of, sends or delivers to any person or place, transports, transmits, alters, disposes of, or otherwise deals with, in any manner and by any means, any property or any proceeds of property with intent to conceal or convert that property or those proceeds and knowing or believing that all or a part of that property or of those proceeds was obtained directly or indirectly as a result of

(a) the commission in Canada of an enterprise crime offense or a designated substance offense; or
(b) an act or omission anywhere that, if it had occurred in Canada, would have constituted an enterprise crime offense or a designated substance offense.

If there has been a conviction for an enterprise crime offense or a designated substance offense, when a judge determines on a balance of probabilities that property is proceeds of crime and the offense was committed in relation to that property, the judge can order forfeiture. Alternatively, if the evidence does not establish a link between the offense and the property, the judge can still order forfeiture when convinced beyond a reasonable doubt that the property is proceeds of crime. In situations where the court is unable to order forfeiture because the proceeds have dissipated, left the country, or become irreversibly entwined with other property, the court has the power under s. 462.37 (3) and (4) to impose a fine equal to the value of the proceeds. For default (nonpayment), imprisonment of increased duration as the value of default increases is to run consecutively to any other prison sentence. Already executed transfers of proceeds of crime property can be voided by a judge under s. 462.4.

Sections 462.32 through 462.36, and subsections thereof, are concerned with special search warrants related to forfeiture, restraint orders to prohibit ownership transfers, reviews of both special search warrants and restraint orders, and automatic expiry. Provision is made for special search warrants, but such warrants must be brought to a senior judge, in writing, by an Attorney General, who is required to give such undertakings as the judge considers appropriate with respect to the payment of damages or costs, or both, in relation to the issuance and execution of the warrant.

Prior to the recent Proceeds of Crime legislation, Beare (1996) writes that the s. 487 search warrant was the main provision allowing police to search premises involving criminal investigations. However, Proceeds of Crime cases require the police to gain information from third party locations like banks and other organizations. The new s. 462.32 special search warrant is designed to allow the police to search for and then seize or restrain property that may eventually be forfeited as proceeds of crime.

The Criminal Code (s. 462.33) has also been modified by Bill C-123, the Seized Property Management Act (S.C. 1993, C.37) to provide for the planning, managing and oversight of seized property, and for its disposal when forfeiture is ordered. This Act came into force on September 1, 1993; its associated Forfeited Property Sharing Regulations came into force January 31, 1995. Funds received, net of disbursements, are to be shared with other governments, including foreign governments, but are not to be shared directly with police departments.

As previously noted under the new s. 462.47 of the Criminal Code, and subject to s. 241 of the Income Tax Act, a person, free of liability, may disclose to a peace officer or to the Attorney General any reasonable suspicion that a property is proceeds of crime or that a person has committed or is about to commit either an enterprise crime offense or a designated substance offense. Furthermore, under s. 462.48 an Attorney General, or his/her designate, may make application to a judge to order the Deputy Minister of National Revenue for Taxation (or his/her designate) to allow a police officer to examine or remove specified information and documents in "designated substance offense" cases.

There have, however, been police complaints about perceived weaknesses of these s. 462.32 special search warrants because they require an Attorney General to sign an undertaking accepting liability; they can only be authorized by senior judges; the paperwork is excessive; the special warrants are not recognized interprovincially; and the special warrants are required to be renewed every six months under Sections of Bill C-17, Criminal Law Improvement Act, (S.C., 1997, c. 18), which facilitated interprovincial execution of these special search warrants. Now, such warrants need only be endorsed by a judge of the other province in which they are to be executed. Judicial Decisions And Legislative Response: Beare (1996: 178ff) discusses several important recent court decisions that have restricted police practices, particularly in the areas of electronic surveillance[8] and traditional "ownership" of the voluminous documents and evidentiary materials arising, in part, from undercover work.[9] While disclosure by the Crown to permit the accused to make full answer and defense has always been present, Asselin (1996) notes that providing full disclosure is very costly in diverting resources of time and staff from investigations.[10] Concern has also been expressed about having to dismiss or plea bargain charges to avoid disclosures that would identify informants, undercover peace officers, or ongoing investigations and investigative techniques. Prior to 1990, Canadian law allowed the police to use electronic means to intercept communications, provided that one party to the conversation consented to the interception. Such interceptions had been commonplace in undercover investigations in which police wore bodypacks that permitted electronic transmittal of their conversations, in part for protection of their person.

In 1990, the Supreme Court of Canada[11] ruled that interceptions by consent of one party to a conversation were no more acceptable than completely surreptitious interceptions, because in either case an unwitting person was being subjected to state eavesdropping at the sole discretion of agents of the state. The Court wrote that in a free society the threat that such consent interceptions would pose to privacy is wholly unacceptable. Thereafter, such interceptions required prior judicial authorization to be admissible as evidence. In the same year, another decision interpreted video surveillance as a search, for which prior judicial authorization is required.[12] Two years later the interpretation of a search was extended to include the placing by police of a tracking device inside a car.[13] According to Beare (1996), these decisions were particularly problematic to the police for two reasons. First, the Criminal Code of Canada provided no mechanism for the police to obtain authorization to use some of the newer technologies such as beepers and video surveillance. The other was that some of the targets were highly placed lawyers, government officials, and wealthy business people. Beare (1996:180) adds that some concern, unwarranted

---

[8]Deemed to be in violation of the Canadian Charter of Rights and Freedoms, which specifies (s. 8): Everyone has the right to be secure against unreasonable search or seizure.
[9]Deemed to be in violation of the Canadian Charter of Rights and Freedoms, which specifies (s. 7): Everyone has the right to life, liberty, and security of the person and the right not to be deprived thereof except in accordance with the principles of fundamental justice.
[10]Asselin (1996) proposes charging the defense for the cost incurred to supply such documents to the defense, with exceptions being made for accused represented by Legal Aid.
[11]*R. v. Duarte* [1990, 53 C.C.C. (3d) 1, 74 C.R. (3d) 281, [1990] S.C.R. 30.
[12]*R. v. Wong* 1990, 60 C.C.C. (3d) 460, [1990] 3 S.C.R. 36, 1, C.R. (4th).
[13]*R. v. Wise* [1992, 70 C.C.C. (3rd) (S.C.C.).

perhaps, was expressed that the lawyers assisting the police in the warrant requests might discourage the police from targeting one of their colleagues.

Problems raised by the preceding concerns were mitigated in part by Bill C-109, An Act to Amend the Criminal Code, the Crown Liability and Proceedings Act, and the Radio Communications Act (S.C., 1993, c. 40), which came into force in August 1993. This Act amended s. 184 (and subsections thereof) of the Criminal Code to extend the means of acceptable technologies for the interception of private communications to include "any electromagnetic, acoustic, mechanical, or other device." In addition, section 184.5 of the Criminal Code now explicitly provides for the inclusion of radio-based telephone communication. This Act (S.C., 1993, c. 40) allows an agent of the state[14] to engage in such interceptions if either the originator or the intended recipient of the private communication consents to the interception, the agent of the state believes on reasonable grounds that there is a risk of bodily harm to the person who consented to the interception, and the purpose of the interception is to prevent the bodily harm. Following the interception, the contents of the interception must be destroyed and are inadmissible as evidence, except for the purpose of proceedings in which actual, attempted, or threatened bodily harm is alleged (CC, s. 184.1).

The Act (S.C., 1993, c. 40) also makes interception permissible, with the consent of one party to the communication, if there are reasonable grounds to believe that information concerning an offense will be found. Additional amendments to the Criminal Code now make it possible both to obtain telewarrants for interceptions (s. 187.3) and to engage in interception without prior judicial authorization if there are reasonable grounds that urgency precludes obtaining an authorization and is immediately necessary to prevent an unlawful act that would cause serious harm to any person or to property, and there is consent to the interception by either the originator or the intended recipient of the communication (s. 184.4).

The same Act (S.C., 1993, c. 40) also amended the Criminal Code (s. 187.4) to allow a prosecutor to delete from disclosure about an interception-related warrant any part that the prosecutor believes would compromise the identity of a confidential informant, compromise the nature and extent of an ongoing investigation, endanger persons engaged in particular intelligence-gathering techniques and thereby prejudice future investigations in which similar techniques would be used, or prejudice the interests of innocent persons. Of course, it also provides for the accused to petition the judge for disclosure of deletions.

The same exemptions for denying access to information used to obtain a search warrant have been included in Bill C-95, An Act to Amend the

---

[14]"Agent of the state" is the term used in the legislation for a peace officer or for a person acting under the authority of, or in cooperation with, a peace officer.

Criminal Code (Criminal Organizations), and to Amend Other Acts in Consequence, (S.C., 1997, c. 23). Additionally, the Act also allows a judge to exempt disclosure of information "for any other sufficient reason." It also provides for judges to authorize covert searches with disclosure of such searches to be delayed for up to three months (renewable) after the search has taken place.

Furthermore, the Act to Amend the Criminal Code, the Crown Liability and Proceedings Act, and the Radio Communications Act (S.C., 1993, c. 40) modified Criminal Code provisions concerning search warrants to take account of newer technologies. A new section (487.01) permits the use of "any device or investigative technique or procedure or do anything described in the warrant" that would, if not authorized, constitute an unreasonable search and seizure in respect to a person's property, if reasonable grounds exist that an offense against an Act of Parliament is being committed and information will be obtained about such an act. However, a further subsection explicitly qualifies this section as not permitting interference with the bodily integrity of any person.

Other amendments made by the Act to the Criminal Code allow a tracking device to be used for a period of sixty days (s. 492.2), and allow the installation and monitoring of a number recorder to record telephone numbers to which or from which communications are made (s. 492.1). Two other important cases were *R. v. Stinchcombe*[15] and *R. v. Denbigh*.[16] In Stinchcombe, the Court ruled that the Crown must make full disclosure to the defense of anything that might assist the accused, even if the Crown does not propose to adduce such information. Such disclosure is tempered by some reviewable discretion on the part of the Crown subject to privilege, protection of informants, not to impede an ongoing investigation, and the like. In Denbigh, Beare (1996) suggests that the judge seems to imply a model that would see the police as disinterested accumulators of facts rather than as interested parties who have a commitment to apprehending guilty parties and (lawfully and ethically) assisting in seeing that they are found guilty in court.

For Beare (1996:182) the major issue appears to be who "owns" the massive evidence assembled by the police for the Crown. For the judiciary, the answer appeared rather clearly to be "the public," including the accused. However, others [e.g., Asselin (1996) and CISC (1996B)], see the issue as one of huge and unwarranted expense and diversion of scarce staff resources for fishing expeditions that in various ways will impede investigations, prosecutions, and convictions of guilty parties. Three of the most

---

[15][1991] 3 S.C.R., 326, 9 C.R. (4th) 277, 68 C.C.C. (3d) 1, [1992] 1 W.W.R. 97.
[16]1990, 4 C.R.R. (2nd) 141.

recent new Acts affecting organized criminal groups are the Controlled Drugs and Substances Act, the Criminal Law Improvements Act, and An Act to Amend the Criminal Code (criminal organizations) and to Amend Other Acts in Consequence.

The Controlled Drugs and Substances Act (S.C., 1996, c. 19) received Royal Assent on June 20, 1996, was proclaimed by order of the Governor General in Council on April 22, 1997, and came into force on May 14, 1997. As earlier noted, this Act consolidated Canada's drug control policy to fulfill its international obligations. It repealed and replaced the Narcotics Control Act and Parts III and IV of the Food and Drug Act. This legislation replaced "designated drug offense" under s. 462.3 of the Criminal Code with "designated substance offense." The latter includes analogues (substances chemically similar to those designated), and precursor chemicals. As was true for the Narcotic Control Act [s. 4(1)], "substance" includes "or in any substance represented or held out by that person to be a substance" as defined [s. 5(1)]. In various circumstances, peace officers are authorized to submit information for special search warrants by telephone or other telecommunications, to conduct warrantless searches and seizures in exigent circumstances or in other circumstances where it would be impracticable to obtain judicial authorization for a special search warrant.

The Controlled Drugs and Substances Act (S.C., 1996, c. 19) also specifies as aggravating circumstances in sentencing: trafficking when one carried or threatened to use a weapon; trafficking associated with threatened or actual violence; possession for trafficking in or near a school or school grounds; possession for trafficking in or near any other public place usually frequented by persons under the age of 18; sale to those under the age of 18; when the accused has previously been convicted of trafficking; or when the accused has used a person under the age of 18 to assist in trafficking. At sentencing, if an aggravating circumstance is present, a judge must provide reasons if the accused is not imprisoned.

Another important recent piece of legislation is the Criminal Law Improvement Act, 1996, (S.C., 1997, c. 18), which received Royal Assent on April 25, 1997, and was proclaimed to come into force in stages on May 2, May 14, and June 16, 1997. One focus of this bill is counterfeiting. Criminal Intelligence Service Canada (1996A) believes that by dealing with possession of counterfeit credit cards, misuse of account information, misuse of equipment to make counterfeit credit cards, and misuse of passwords, this legislation will facilitate enforcement efforts by thus making the prosecution of counterfeit credit card activities easier.

However, other aspects of the Criminal Law Improvement Act, 1996, may be more far-reaching by adding s. 462.31(3) to the Criminal Code. This Act explicitly provides peace officers (and, in certain circumstances, convicted criminals working under the supervision of and assisting the peace officer) with immunity for criminal acts "if done for the purpose of an investigation or otherwise in the execution of the peace officer's duties" pursuant to the investigation of criminals who receive or conceal proceeds of crime. Peace officers operating under this bill are granted immunity from prosecution for offenses committed in the course of an investigation of certain offenses, and the resulting evidence is admissible in court. This legislation has the effect of accepting a need for specialized enforcement techniques to deal with sophisticated criminal activities, while ensuring that peace officers, and the agents of peace officers, employing such techniques will be doing so within the law.

This Act also amends the Criminal Code to facilitate extending the reach of warrants interprovincially under Proceeds of Crime investigations [Criminal Code s. 462.32(1) and (2)]; to enable authorization of search telewarrants [by adding Criminal Code s. 487.091]; to facilitate searching and gathering information from computers; to make it lawful for police to conduct surveillance "by means of television cameras or sundry electronic devices of activities in circumstances in which persons had reasonable expectations of privacy" under circumstances similar to the interception of private communications [Criminal Code s. 487.01(5)] as also amended by this Act; to allow nighttime execution of search warrants if approved by a judge (Criminal Code s. 488); to allow warrantless searches and seizures for exigency under certain circumstances (Criminal Code s. 487.11); to extend several of the sections (Criminal Code ss. 183–196) concerned with the interception of private communications to apply equally to observations made by peace officers; and to make it also an offense for a person *to believe* that a person is laundering proceeds of crime in addition to knowingly laundering such proceeds (Criminal Code s. 462.31).

A third important recent piece of legislation is Bill C-95, An Act to Amend the Criminal Code (Criminal Organizations) and to Amend Other Acts in Consequence (S.C. 1997, c. 23), which received Royal Assent on April 25, 1997, and is now in force. This Act responded to a wide range of proposals advanced by the police community—for example, the provisions of the Model Anti-Organized Crime Act suggested by Asselin (1996).

As was previously noted, this Act extended the range of offenses considered to be "enterprise crime" to include any indictable offense under any Act of Parliament for which the maximum punishment is imprisonment for five years or more when such an offense is committed for the benefit of, at the direction of, or in association with a criminal organization. A criminal organization is defined as any group of five or more people, whether formally or informally organized, any one or more of which has engaged in a series of offenses subject to a maximum prison sentence of five years or more, and having as one of its primary activities the commission of an indictable offense. As also discussed, it modified the Criminal Code (s. 487.3) to exempt from disclosure and to deny access to information used by authorities to obtain warrants for a wide range of reasons.

Substantively, it also introduced several new provisions to the Criminal Code, which include defining murder by the use of explosives, when committed in relation to a criminal organization, as first degree murder, whether or not it was deliberate; making unlawful possession of explosives in relation to a criminal organization punishable by up to fourteen years imprisonment, which term must be served consecutive to, rather than concurrent with, other prison sentence; treating as an aggravating factor at sentencing or for considering parole eligibility any crime committed in relation to a criminal organization; a provision to require a peace bond from persons who present a risk of committing an offense in relation to a criminal organization (and imprisonment for up to twelve months for a person refusing to provide such a peace bond or violating it); provision for forfeiture of property used to commit offenses when committed in relation to a criminal organization and forfeiture of proceeds of crimes committed in relation to criminal organization offenses.

Canada's legislation against organized criminal activity is still unfolding. Proposals for new or amended legislation to augment the struggle against collusive criminal activities continue to be advanced. Thus, following a "Forum on Organized Crime" in Canada's capital region on September 27–28, 1996, Solicitor General Herb Gray and Minister of Justice and Attorney General Allan Rock reaffirmed Canada's intention to develop new measures to help Canadian law enforcement agencies fight organized crime. Their joint press release identified the following as among the measures recommended to the Government by Forum participants:

- Legislative changes to allow police greater access to income tax information for major criminal investigations and to expand the scope of enterprise crimes so that police can target more forms of criminal profiteering;

- The introduction of mandatory suspicious transaction reporting by financial institutions to facilitate police investigations into organized crime and, in particular, to prevent money laundering;

- The introduction of cross-border currency controls. This measure would provide police and customs officers with the necessary tools to investigate the movement of large sums of money across borders.

- New criminal intelligence arrangements, building on the CISC system. The new system will allow police to make queries about activities of other police forces, helping cooperation and information exchange; and

- Establishment of national and regional coordinating committees to support law enforcement action against organized crime. These committees will help facilitate multi-agency operations and ensure that public policy decisions by governments are sensitive to operational concerns and requirements.

The police community is particularly strong in its proposals to make money laundering and currency transfers more difficult. Some proposed means for doing so are: greater access to income tax information; mandatory suspicious transaction reporting; cross-border currency and monetary instrument reporting and controls; and elimination of the Canadian $1,000 bill as a unit of currency. These changes would facilitate following the money to its ultimate recipient. They may also be effective in reducing the incentive to engage in enterprise or substance crime by making it more and more difficult to realize significant financial benefits from such activities (CLEU Policy Analysis, 1992B; Beare, 1996; Killam, 1996).

Currently, Canadian casinos and other gaming houses provide ready opportunities for money laundering. Beare (1996) suggests that these opportunities be made more difficult by bringing such facilities under mandatory reporting requirements. She notes that for casinos in the United States, rules concerning cash transactions are extended to cash equivalents (chips, tokens, front money deposits, cash bets, purchase of casino checks, and exchanges of currency). Casinos must keep records of customers who have purchased or redeemed slot machine tokens of more than $3,000 in a single gaming day; multiple cash transactions must be treated as a single transaction if they are "by or on behalf of any person"; if a customer's cash in or cash out transactions, when aggregated, exceed $10,000 in a gaming day, the casino must obtain the identification of the customer if it is "reasonably available."

CLEU Policy Analysis (1995A) has proposed that, in addition to Proceeds of Crime forfeiture and prosecution under the Income Tax Act, civil forfeiture be considered as a third option for taking the profit out of crime. CLEU believes that a provincial civil forfeiture statute could probably be constitutionally enacted. They propose that such a statute should limit prosecutions of civil forfeiture actions to the Crown; restrict proceeds of crime and instruments of crime to such forfeiture; apply only to property associated with major crimes; require only a balance of probabilities proof;

require the owner of the property to explain how the property was acquired under certain circumstances; have clauses to protect their party rights; and include appropriate provisions for pre-trial restraining orders to prevent the removal of the property from provincial jurisdiction before the courts rules on the forfeiture issue.

Asselin (1996) has suggested that there also be cost recovery for disclosure of evidence to the defense and that those convicted of an enterprise or designated substance offense be required to pay investigative and trial costs associated with their offenses. Other suggestions include creation of the offense of *misprision of felony*[17], and new provisions affecting sentencing, including harsher sentences to facilitate targeting upward by inducing lower-level offenders to provide information in return for sentencing considerations.

COMPARATIVE EVALUATION OF THE METHODS FOR COMBATING ORGANIZED CRIME AND PROPOSED MEASURES

Canada's evolving law in the area of enterprise crime and designated substance offense is so new that it is premature to judge its efficacy. There has been little jurisprudence involving Proceeds of Crime and related legislation, and there have been few publicly disclosed investigations as of this writing. Nevertheless, the police have been given very powerful tools that appear to be having a significant effect. On August 31, 1994, for instance, the RCMP announced the completion of a three-part, four-year undercover operation code-named "Operation Contrat/Compote/Creditor," that had involved a collaborative working arrangement among the Colombian cartels, the traditional Italian Mafia, and the Hell's Angels. Over two hundred banking accounts in twenty-nine banking institutions were frozen, including all the records and bank accounts of thirty-four companies. Three lawyers were arrested (Beare 1996).

Criminal Intelligence Service Canada (1996A) reports that this operation resulted in sentences of up to fifteen years and asset forfeiture of up to $4.5 million Canadian dollars. The principal lawyer involved, Joseph Lagana, reputedly was the brains behind the criminal operation and was the only man in direct contact with alleged Montreal Mafia chieftain Vito Rizzuto. Lagana's sentence of thirteen years and asset seizure of $2.7 million Canadian dollars are being appealed by the Crown as too lenient. Lagana

---

[17]Misconduct or neglect of duty, especially by a public official, concealment of knowledge of a felony or of treason by a person other than the culprit.

confessed to having laundered $47.4 million Canadian dollars in drug proceeds and having participated in a conspiracy to import 558 kilograms of cocaine. CISC (1996A) also reports the conclusion of another investigation in April, 1996 that resulted in the arrests of more than thirty subjects in Quebec, Ontario, and abroad. Among those arrested, ranging from baggage handlers to a brokerage firm executive, were several high-profile crime targets.

The RCMP created Anti-Drug Profiteering (ADP) units attached to drug investigation sections across Canada in 1982 to use the criminal legislation of the day, but Killam (1996) reports that these units were not very successful. As part of Canada's Drug Strategy, Killam continues, in 1992 an initiative entitled Integrated Anti-Drug Profiteering (IADP) was funded in Vancouver, Toronto, and Montreal. The intent of the units was to bring together an integrated system of enforcement personnel, including RCMP investigators, Justice Crown Counsel, forensic accountants, provincial and municipal police, and Revenue Canada investigators. These IADP units, which essentially were an enhanced Joint Forces Operation and which were to be evaluated annually to measure their effectiveness, received five-year funding totaling $33 million Canadian dollars. These units have been judged to be so successful that the concept of integrated units is also being recommended for the thirteen operational Proceeds of Crime (POC) units.

Indirectly, the POC units had their origin after the offenses of laundering or possessing the proceeds of tobacco and alcohol smuggled into Canada were created in 1993. The RCMP was granted additional resources related to the Anti-Smuggling Initiative announced in April 1994. The intent of the initiative was increased RCMP customs and excise enforcement and also the dismantling of criminal organizations by attacking the proceeds of their activity. As a result of this initiative, the RCMP merged resources previously diffused among anti-drug profiteering, enterprise crime, and proceeds of crime from smuggling, into POC units.

Based upon the success of the IADP units and following a December 1994 evaluation, the RCMP proposed that all thirteen existing POC units across Canada be converted into *Integrated Proceeds of Crime* (IPOC) units. Killam adds that it has been recommended that the three existing IADP units in Vancouver, Toronto, and Montreal also be converted into IPOC units and be continued past their planned expiry of December 31, 1997.

There are also other integrated units fighting crime. For example, CISC (1996A) relates that Toronto's Combined Forces Special Enforcement Unit (CFSEU) and Combined Forces Asian Investigation Unit (CFAIU) have successfully investigated credit card fraud in the last several years. At the same time, Killam (1996) reports that the RCMP has only two hundred four full-time personnel involved in POC enforcement. For that reason, the RCMP has also taken other initiatives to thwart organized criminal activities, which have taken a variety of forms. In 1992, Killam (1996) relates that the RCMP entered into a voluntary agreement with the Canadian Bankers Association, whereby the banks agreed to disclose suspicious transactions to deter money laundering. A similar agreement was made with the Credit Union Central of Canada (CUCC) in January 1996. Negotiations for parallel negotiations are ongoing with other financial institutions and agencies, such as the Canadian Health and Life Assurance Association. These voluntary agreements fill a lacuna because at this time Canadian law does not require mandatory reporting of suspicious transactions, but requires only that records be kept by the institutions.

Killam (1996) recounts that the RCMP has formed strategic partnerships with various interests such as the banking and telecommunications industries, credit card manufacturers, and computer professionals to develop effective enforcement, educational and deterrence strategies, including lobbying the Department of Justice for amendments to the Criminal Code of Canada. Additionally, the RCMP are engaged in a number of other initiatives, such as: distributing warning labels to the manufacturers of color copier equipment to be affixed at the point of distribution to discourage "weekend" counterfeiters; working with manufacturers of color copiers to develop anti-counterfeiting technologies; developing educational initiatives for merchants, banks, and the general public about the recognition of counterfeit currency and credit cards, and producing a "Technological Crime Bulletin" that is distributed to Canadian police agencies and to outside agencies sharing a legitimate interest in law enforcement. The RCMP is also considering the introduction of a computer ethics program in schools and the use of the Internet to post crime-prevention messages related to technological crime.

On a slightly different tack, the Solicitor General Canada has provided funding to Osgoode Hall Law School to establish a Research Center on Organized Crime and Corrections. In addition, many police departments have been seeking to involve the community more in the fight against crime through various community-based and problem-oriented policing initiatives. Such public involvement is essential if the smuggling of drugs, other contraband, people, and illicit transfers of dirty money are to be contained. Canada has tens of thousands of miles of borders, largely undefended and unguarded. Although most of these borders are rugged and sparsely populated on three oceans, there are also 8,893 miles of common border with the United States, including 2,477 miles of extremely rugged terrain bordering Alaska. Such a situation makes Canada a very attractive staging point for the smuggling of money, people, drugs, and other contraband into and out of the United States.

Certainly the public should perceive that it has a stake in increasing its involvement in fighting criminal activities, particularly in the current period of harsh fiscal realities. By way of illustration, in the province of British Columbia, CLEU (1992C) estimated the economic cost of illicit drug use for 1989 to be at least $349 million Canadian dollars (or roughly $100 per every resident in the province). Put differently, this was approximately equal to the cost of highway maintenance across the entire province, or equivalent to the cost of educating more than 78,000 children for a year in British Columbia schools. Most of these costs were justice-related, including drug law enforcement services ($67.9 million) and the policing of non-drug crimes, such as break and enter or crimes of violence, that were related to illicit drug use ($151 million). Drug-related workplace accidents and reduced productivity due to drug-related absenteeism was estimated at $48.3 million Canadian dollars, while the cost of injury claims (including innocent parties) for automobile accidents involving illicit drugs was estimated at $39 million.

In contrast to these huge enforcement and third-party costs, CLEU reckons that British Columbia taxpayers spent only $13.8 million Canadian dollars on provincial programs directed at the prevention of substance abuse, of which a minuscule $1.8 million was directly targeted at the prevention of illicit drug use. Other costs included $20.6 million for social assistance expenditures for drug users; $3.1 million for health care programs involving methadone maintenance, AIDS, needle exchange, and partial cost of infants of substance abusing mothers; and $17 million for federal contributions for treatment, federal and provincial treatment services, and employee assistance programs.

Any new measures or steps cannot be contemplated without reflecting upon the existing state of affairs and evaluation of the existing measures, which demands asking some important questions about what has been done and how well it has achieved its objectives. Recent years have seen efforts at a radical transformation of Canadian law as it relates to profit-motivated substance crimes and an eclectic array of what are defined as enterprise crimes. This transformation has been far-reaching and includes provisions relating to search, seizure, interception of communications, surreptitious observation, and immunity of police from prosecution for crimes they engage in or direct others to commit[18] during the course of

---

[18]When the others have been authorized by a judge to work on an investigation under the supervision of a peace officer.

an investigation into the large and increasing array of offenses included as enterprise crimes or designated substance offenses. No doubt, many Canadians are pleased to see the increasing success of police in gaining convictions against major substance criminals and to see "loopholes and technicalities" being closed in the detection, pursuit, and conviction of a wide range of other criminals.

However, these recent developments raise several issues: (1) that criminal entrepreneurs typically have thrived by providing goods or services for which there is a widespread demand, but that governments have either outlawed or limited; (2) as pointed out by CISC (1996A), Beare (1996), Brodeur (1996), and Naylor (1996), criminal entrepreneurs typically have a variety of mutually rewarding associations with what are considered legitimate companies and institutions; (3) whether organized crime is a rhetoric being used to mobilize public support for a hidden agenda. Other than briefly noting these concerns, this work is not the appropriate place or time to analyze them. Such a task would require an additional chapter.

Naylor (1996:54) succinctly summarizes the first issue by stating that "there has never been a black market in history that has been successfully tamed by a supply-side attack." Brodeur (1996) makes the same point in quoting Albanese and Pursley (1993:66) that "there is a great deal of evidence to suggest that organized crime will exist as long as there is a demand for goods and services that cannot be obtained legally."

Throughout most of this century, Canada has tried to reduce both the supply of and the demand for a variety of illegal goods and services. It gave up on prohibition of alcohol. To oversimplify somewhat, it accepted prostitution provided the solicitation is not pressing. Recently, the extensive smuggling of alcohol and tobacco caused the Canadian government to reduce excise taxes on tobacco products in an attempt to shrink the market for smuggling Canadian cigarettes sold for export back across the border into Canada. In addition to having implications for Canada's national health policy, governments were driven to forego $500 million Canadian dollars per year in revenues as a result of excise tax reductions they felt constrained to make.

Criminals have much interaction with conventional members of society in the course of providing them with illegal goods and services. As has been noted, typically there are significant relationships between alliances of criminal entrepreneurs and what are commonly considered to be law-abiding individuals, organizations, or companies. Brodeur (1996) notes, for example, that corporations are quite prepared to do business with questionable waste treatment companies, "no questions asked."

When the traffic in cigarette smuggling was exploding to evade high excise taxes, Canadian cigarette manufacturers experienced an increase in exports from $222 million in June 1990 to $2.235 *billion* by March 1993. Did Canadian cigarette manufacturers believe that Americans had developed a craze for Canadian cigarettes? Or did they know (and not care) that the exported cigarettes were being smuggled back into Canada to avoid excise taxes, especially when they also know that cigarette consumption increases when the cost of purchasing cigarettes decreases. And have the bankers and others who have been laundering dirty money been unaware of what they have been doing or have they not cared so long as they were making a good profit?

Naylor (1996) asks a slightly different question: whether the real issue is organized crime taking over legitimate businesses or whether it is legitimate businesses using criminal means, and sometimes contracting with criminals, to achieve profit targets. As examples, he cites the widespread insurance fraud of derelict buildings in the 1970s and 1980s with bank cooperation; fly-by-night toxic waste companies that relieve polluters of liability before disappearing; and six large Anglo-American tobacco companies that supplied Latin America with most of its bootleg whiskey and electronics, as well as cigarettes, by many of the same channels that have been reversed now for the export of cocaine.

Conclusion

Calavita and Pontell (1990) have reported that estimates of the costs to bail out insolvent savings and loan associations (S&L) *begin* at $300 billion U.S. dollars, and that government reports suggest that criminal activity was involved in 70 to 80 percent of these insolvencies. In those cases where prosecution occurred, U.S. attorneys complained that convicted criminals typically received very lenient sentences, frequently probation—often without any restitution required.

Similarly, Kappeler et al. (1993) cite the Bank of Commerce and Credit International (BCCI), then the world's seventh largest private financial institution, as a good example of the cozy relationship that may arise among drug traffickers, white collar criminals, the intelligence community, and leading politicians from both parties in the United States. BCCI was in the truest sense a "full service bank." It laundered millions of dollars for the Colombia cocaine cartels, helped Marcos transfer money out of Philippines, and acted as a conduit for CIA funds destined for the Contras to support illegal arms deals and Contra-backed cocaine trafficking.

BCCI also had powerful political allies, including Clark Clifford (former Secretary of Defense and adviser to four presidents); Edwin Meese (Reagan's Attorney General); and Black, Manafort, and Stone (the advertising consultants to the Republican Party). Moreover, it had political connections with Senator D'Amato and Presidents Carter and Bush. Perhaps it is unsurprising that the Justice Department appeared disinterested in beginning an investigation into BCCI's affairs.

In contrast to the mild response to the mind-boggling magnitude of the S&L looting, as far back as 1981, Anderson and Wynn (1981) were criticizing U.S. authorities for politically motivated use of RICO legislation to target a variety of groups, as well as "enterprises" as diverse as the Macon (Georgia) Police Department, a General Motors factory, a nightclub, and a pool hall, among others. More generally, the role of the United States government in the drug trade needs to be assessed. Its involvement is not new information. As Kappeler et al. (1993:235–250) document, United States government involvement with the warlords in Southeast Asia's Golden Triangle goes back to the 1960s. Such involvement included using Air America, a CIA front, for the transport of drugs, and using banks such as the Nugen Hand Bank in Australia and the Castle Bank in Florida for laundering drug money.

Beare (1996:69) makes a similar observation in writing that:

> Any objective discussion of organized crime in South America must at least acknowledge the culpability of the CIA and other U.S. government officials who advance foreign policies at the expense of drug enforcement. According to Senator John Kerry, chairman of the Senate Foreign Relations Subcommittee on Terrorism, Narcotics, and International Operations, the congressional hearings into the Contra drugs and arms scandal showed that stopping drug trafficking to the United States has been a secondary U.S. foreign policy objective. It has been sacrificed repeatedly for other political goals.

In short, throughout this century, how serious has the United States been about its wars on drugs and on organized crime? Has its original 1970 RICO Act and its subsequent use of the United Nations and UN bodies to enlist other countries in the wars against drugs and "organized crime," been genuine? Or has there been a hidden agenda? If the concern were merely to dry up criminal organizations' profits from the sale of illicit drugs, a public health approach to drug users would probably be at least as effective and certainly much less expensive. But as Anderson and Wynn (1981) noted long ago, the U.S. government has used RICO to prosecute political groups as diverse as a Croatian nationalist group, the Black Liberation Army, and the Weather Underground.

Naylor (1996:50–51) summarizes arguments from a variety of sources that claim the new legislation, ostensibly directed against "organized crime," confuses criminal and civil matters; reverses the burden of proof so that the accused must establish the legitimacy of his or her assets, rather than the state prove their illegitimacy; erodes civil liberties; demonstrates a marked disparity between the severity of the laws and the abandon with which the offenses are defined; and because of its vast and inclusive coverage, RICO, according to some observers, gives police in the United States the veritable right to loot. While "the right to loot" may be a provocative and needlessly inflammatory phrase, Beare (1996:172) writes that U.S. "jurisdictions short of resources tend to build the 'expectation' of seizures into the budget process."

Naylor (1996:50) observes:

> Furthermore, the proceeds-of-crime approach reflected particular American ideological and institutional conditions. Just as RICO was strongly influenced by the prevailing concern over industrial concentration, so too the anti-money laundering mania occurred against a general background of fears about the deterioration of the American fiscal and financial situation. It was a time when the American international payments position seemed to be weakening. This was complicated by the budgetary situation. Rather than blaming capital outflows on giant corporations shifting production offshore in search for cheap and non-unionized labour, and rather than pointing out that the rich were 'avoiding' their fair share of the tax burden through domestic shelters and offshore havens, public attention was focused on the drug barons, draining off capital and escaping the grasp of the tax collectors. Tighter regulations on international financial flows were supposed to help solve the first, and asset seizure could help rectify the inequities caused by the second.

Combating organized crime is going to be difficult if governments are not serious about confronting the giant multinational corporations. Moreover, if the governments persist in following their own agenda under the guise of national security and remain soft toward the corporate sector, the probability of implementing strong measures against the dangerous elements lurking behind the shadows of business enterprises is going to be small. The example set by the governments till the present period appears to provide little evidence of sincerity in dealing with the activities of large business houses working unfettered in the name of free enterprise.

REFERENCES

Albanese, Jay and R. D. Pursley. 1993. *Crime in America.* Englewood Cliffs, NJ: Prentice Hall.

Anderson, Nancy and Simon Wynn. 1981. "Organized Crime, RICO and the Media: What We Think We Know." Paper presented at the annual Meeting of the American Society of Criminology, Washington, D.C., November.

Asselin, Denis. 1996. "Legislative Solutions to Combat Organized Crime." Paper presented to the 64th Annual Quebec Chiefs of Police Conference. Quebec City, July 2.

Beare, Margaret E., 1996. *Criminal Conspiracies: Organized Crime in Canada.* Scarborough, Canada: Nelson Canada.

Beare Margaret E., and S. Schneider. 1990. *Tracing of Illicit Funds: Money Laundering in Canada.* No. 1990–05. Ottawa: Solicitor General Canada.

Calavita, Kitty and Henry N. Pontell. 1990. "Heads I Win, Tails You Lose: Deregulation, Crime, and Crisis in the Savings and Loan Industry." *Crime and Delinquency* 55: 309–341.

CLEU Policy Analysis, (British Columbia Ministry of Attorney General, Coordinated Law Enforcement Unit). 1992A. *The Costs Associated with Illicit Drug Use in British Columbia in 1989.* Victoria: The Queen's Printer, September.

———1992B. *Money Laundering: The Need for Currency Transaction/Transportation Reporting in Canada.* Victoria, Canada: The Queen's Printer.

———1992C. *Updates on Drug-Related Projects: April, 1992.* Victoria: The Queen's Printer.

———1995A. *Discussion Paper on Civil Forfeiture Legislation in British Columbia.* Victoria, Canada: The Queen's Printer, July.

———1995B. *VLTs:' Video Lottery Terminal Gaming.* Victoria, Canada: The Queen's Printer, April.

Brodeur, Jean-Paul. 1996. "Organized Crime: Trends in the Literature." Paper presented at the Forum on Organized Crime. Ottawa, Canada, September 27–28.

Criminal Intelligence Service Canada. 1996 *Annual Report on Organized Crime in Canada, 1996.* Ottawa: CISC.

———1996B. "Criminal Intelligence and Information Sharing." A CISC Discussion Paper presented by Tom Burns at the Forum on Organized Crime. Ottawa, Canada, Sept. 27–28.

———1996C. "The Police Perspective on Organized Crime." A CISC Discussion Paper presented by Pierre Sangollo at the Forum on Organized Crime. Ottawa, Canada, September 27–28.

Dubro, James. 1985. *Mob Rule: Inside the Canadian Mafia.* Toronto: Macmillan.

Kappeler, Victor E., Mark Blumberg, and Gary W. Potter. 1993. *The Mythology of Crime and Criminal Justice.* Prospect Heights, IL: Waveland Press Inc.

Killam, T. G. 1996. "Organized Crime and the Business Community: The RCMP Perspective." Paper presented at the Forum on Organized Crime. Ottawa, Canada, September 27–28.

Naylor, R. T. 1996. "The Theory and Practice of Enterprise Crime: Public Perceptions and Legislative Responses." Paper presented at the Forum on Organized Crime. Ottawa, Canada, September 27–28.

Possami, Mario T. 1996. "Organized Crime and Canadian Contraband Tobacco Smuggling." Paper presented at the Third Annual Symposium of the International Police Executive. Yokohama, Japan, November 28–December 1.

Serbia and Montenegro have asserted the formation of a joint independent state, but this entity has not been formally recognized as a state by the United States.
F.Y.R.O.M. - The Former Yugoslav Republic of Macedonia
Greenland (DENMARK)
Jan Mayen (NORWAY)
Greenland Sea
Denmark Strait
Barents Sea
Norwegian Sea
Arctic Circle
Reykjavík
ICELAND
NORWAY
SWEDEN
FINLAND
Gulf of Bothnia
RUSSIA
Hammerfest
Tromsø
Kiruna
Luleå
Oulu
Umeå
Murmansk
White Sea
Arkhangel'sk
Lake Onega
Lake Ladoga
Trondheim
Tampere
Helsinki
Turku
Gävle
St. Petersburg
Gulf of Finland
ALAND ISLANDS
Tórshavn
Faroe Islands (DENMARK)
SHETLAND ISLANDS
ORKNEY ISLANDS
HEBRIDES
Rockall (U.K.)
Bergen
Oslo
Stavanger
Stockholm
Tallinn
ESTONIA
Moscow
North Atlantic Ocean
North Sea
Aberdeen
Glasgow
Edinburgh
UNITED KINGDOM
Göteborg
Gotland
Riga
LATVIA
Baltic Sea
Öland
LITHUANIA
Vilnius
Minsk
BELARUS
Smolensk
DENMARK
Copenhagen
Malmö
Bornholm
Kaliningrad
RUSSIA
Belfast
Dublin
IRELAND
Irish Sea
Isle of Man (U.K.)
Leeds
Manchester
Liverpool
Birmingham
Cardiff
London
Gdańsk
Hrodna
Homyel'
Brest
Hamburg
Bremen
Berlin
Poznań
Warsaw
POLAND
Łódź
Wrocław
Kraków
Amsterdam
Rotterdam
NETH.
Essen
Cologne
Bonn
Leipzig
GERMANY
Kiev
Rivne
UKRAINE
Dnipro
L'viv
Celtic Sea
English Channel
Guernsey (U.K.)
Jersey (U.K.)
Brussels
Lille
BEL.
Frankfurt am Main
Luxembourg
LUX.
Prague
CZECH REPUBLIC
Brno
SLOVAKIA
Bratislava
Chernivtsi
Mykolayiv
Chişinău
MOLDOVA
Iaşi
Odesa
Paris
Stuttgart
Strasbourg
Munich
Vienna
Budapest
Cluj-Napoca
Nantes
FRANCE
LIECH.
Vaduz
Zürich
Bern
SWITZ.
Geneva
AUSTRIA
HUNGARY
ROMANIA
Bay of Biscay
Lyon
Milan
Venice
SLOVENIA
Ljubljana
Zagreb
Bucharest
Constanţa
Black Sea
Turin
Po
CROATIA
BOSNIA AND HERZEGOVINA
Belgrade
Serbia
Varna
Bordeaux
Genoa
SAN MARINO
Florence
Sarajevo
BULGARIA
Bilbao
Toulouse
MONACO
Sofia
Porto
Andorra la Vella
ANDORRA
Marseille
Ligurian Sea
ITALY
Adriatic Sea
Montenegro
Podgorica
Skopje
F.Y.R.O.M.
Istanbul
Zaragoza
Corsica
Rome
Tirana
ALB.
Thessaloniki
PORTUGAL
Madrid
Barcelona
VATICAN CITY
Naples
TURKEY
Tagus
SPAIN
Lisbon
Valencia
Balearic Sea
Sardinia
Tyrrhenian Sea
GREECE
Aegean Sea
İzmir
BALEARIC ISLANDS
Athens
Sevilla
Cagliari
Ionian Sea
Mediterranean Sea
Gibraltar (U.K.)
Málaga
Palermo
Sicily
Rhodes
Strait of Gibraltar
Ceuta (SPAIN)
Alborán Sea
Algiers
Crete
Melilla (SPAIN)
Oran
Tunis
MALTA
Valletta
Rabat
Casablanca
MOROCCO
ALGERIA
TUNISIA
Scale 1: 19,500,000
Lambert Conformal Conic Projection, standard parallels 40°N and 56°N
0 300 Kilometers
0 300 Miles

PART 2

PERSPECTIVES FROM EUROPE

Europe is the second smallest continent in land area (after Australia), yet it contains almost as many sovereign nations as any other continent. It is bordered by water on three sides: by the Arctic Ocean to the north, the Atlantic Ocean to the west, and on the south, by the Mediterranean Sea, the Black Sea, the Kuma-Manych Depression, and the Caspian Sea (moving from west to east). The eastern boundary of Europe (north to south) runs along the eastern Ural Mountains and the Zhem River in Russia and the eastern side of Kazakhstan. The forty countries of Europe constitute one-seventh of the world's population, and its nearly sixty languages are derived from one of three major traditions: Romance, Germanic, and Slavic. Europe also is the second most densely populated continent (after Asia). The combination of many different small countries with different languages and traditions, which are in proximity to one another, has unique implications for organized crime.

Most countries in Europe border on several other nations, which sometimes leads to conflict over ethnicity, immigration, trade, and international relations. Europe's extensive history and many of the battles, wars, and conflicts that occurred long ago are still remembered vividly by Europeans today. This history sometimes contributes to intransigence and poor relations on contemporary issues, which are unrelated to the past.

Six of Europe's nations are considered in this section, although others are included in the chapters on Poland and the Council of Europe. Students are advised to examine the economic, political, and crime situations in the countries that border a nation of interest because conditions in one country often directly affect the situation in neighboring nations. This spillover effect is especially noticeable in Europe, where most nations are small and border multiple countries.

The breakup of the Soviet Union and the emergence of new countries with struggling economies provided many new opportunities for organized crime in Europe. These new nations have switched from a socialist to a capitalist system where government property and businesses have been "privatized," resulting in ownership and control struggles that often have involved bribery, corruption, and extortion of businesspersons and government officials on a large scale. Reports of government corruption and business executives being prosecuted, murdered, or forced to flee are not uncommon (Radio Free Europe, 2000; 2000a; 2001; 2001a; Reuters, 2000). In some cases this situation is the result of government extortion using organized crime elements to carry out threats, and, in other cases, organized crime groups force "protection" on businesses so that they are not damaged by competitors or by other organized crime groups.

High unemployment and underemployment has caused some residents to flee their home countries or be enticed into leaving, with promises of greater financial success elsewhere. Human smuggling from Eastern Europe to the West has become a problem of major international significance (Hughes, 2000). The European Union agreed in 2001 on a policy for curbing illegal immigration and the flow of those seeking political asylum. European governments want "to curb the thriving rackets of those who help smuggle up to 50,000 illegal immigrants a year into Western Europe" (Oakley, 2001).

The ease of movement within Europe has increased dramatically since the fall of the Soviet Union, so international smuggling, drug trafficking, and money laundering are growing problems. Analysis of these problems from the perspective of the product (i.e., how it is produced, transported, and ultimately distributed) requires a multinational analysis, so students should be aware of the ways in which organized crime in Europe is more than ever a transnational enterprise.

REFERENCES

Hughes, Donna M. 2000. "The "Natasha" Trade: The Transnational Shadow Market of Trafficking in Women," *J. International Affairs*, Spring.

Oakley, Robin. 2001. "EU Acts on Illegal Immigrants," *http://www.CNN.com*, February 8.

Radio Free Europe. 2000. "Ukrainian Prosecutors Probe $4.6 Million Bribe Case," November 7. http://www.wjin.net/html/news/6580.htm

Radio Free Europe. 2000a. "Russian Prosecutor Begins New Assault on Oligarchs," November 2. http://www.wjin.net/html/news/6528.htm

Radio Free Europe. 2001. "Businessman Murdered in St. Petersburg," January 29. http://www/wjin.net/html/news/7159/htm

Radio Free Europe. 2001a. "Latvian Shipping Privatization Rocked by Million-Dollar Bribe Charges," January 26. http://www.wjin.net/html/news/7142.htm

Reuters. 2000. "Kazakhstan Blocks Tajikistan-Russia Rail Link to Combat Smuggling," 19 October. http://www.wjin.net/html/news/6372.htm

Chapter 3

Mafia and Mafia-type Organizations in Italy

Umberto Santino

Introduction

Italy occupies an important position in the galaxy of nations. With a population of 57.9 million people (1993), and a density of 75.03 inhabitants per square mile, it is rapidly transforming into an urban society. The present stage of urbanization is 69 percent and life expectancy is around 77.2 years. Italy is a developed nation with a GNP of $1147.1 billion and per capita income of $19,832. Agriculture contributes 3.1 percent, industry 31.5 percent while service industry accounts for almost 65.4 percent to the GNP.

In Italy there are many types of police institutions: *Polizia*, *Carabinieri*, *Guardia di Finanza*. The *Direzione Investigativa Antimafia* (DIA) is a connecting body that also coordinates the work of investigating magistrates (*procuratori o pubblici ministeri*). The Italian police are a highly trained, professional body. They have recently notched several successes against the Italian Mafia.

The term "Mafia," first used only to define a Sicilian phenomenon, is now used to describe any organized criminal group, and it is certainly one of the best known and most internationally used words in the Italian language. The reason for it being so is not only due to the influence of the media, which tends to simplify reality with labels that are often incongruous and misleading. The phenomenon called "Mafia" as developed in Sicily, presents some characteristics that have made it a sort of paradigm, or frame of reference for similar organizations which have developed elsewhere in more recent times.

Mass media represent the Mafia as a sort of universal evil, the "octopus" that controls all criminal activities: from drug to arms trafficking and now even radioactive substances. In reality, the Sicilian Mafia can be considered a "winning model" of organized crime (at least until now) due to its complexity and long-standing role in society, but care must be taken against stereotypes that always see the octopus tentacles everywhere.

The Mafia's strength lies in its capacity to be both local and international and transnational, in the sense that it grew to a worldwide level without losing its roots in Sicilian society. Its strong point has historically been the capacity to combine continuity with innovation: It has never abandoned its traditional activities (extortion, for example), but knew how to choose the most profitable activities and become a part of them.

Immigration to the United States during the end of the nineteenth century has also had a role in the formation of this cultural elasticity and adaptability, even though at first the connections between Sicilian Mafiosi and Sicilian-Americans were rare. Only after the Second World War has the connection between them grown closer and has drug trafficking welded Sicily to the United States, but both groups remain autonomous. In recent decades, the Sicilian Mafia has grown on the national, European, and international levels. It has trafficked heroin with the French Connection, with Turkish, Middle East, and Asiatic clans and now deals cocaine with the Latin-American cartels. International channels are used for money laundering from Switzerland to tax havens worldwide. At first, the Mafia organization was only present in the western part of Sicily, but now it is found throughout Sicily and in many Italian regions, European countries, and in the world. Many criminal organizations similar to the Mafia are present in Italy: the *'Ndrangheta* in Calabria, the *Camorra* in Campania, the *Sacra Corona Unita* in Apulia, and other groups. On the international level, besides historical groups like the Japanese Yakuza and the Chinese Triads, new organizations like the South American cartels and the Russian Mafia have arisen.

The earnings from the activities of organized crime cannot be determined exactly. According to prudent estimates, the amount of illegal capital is between $500 to $700 billion American dollars per year. The largest part of the proceeds arises from drug trafficking. Today the criminal market is complex because the criminal activities are more articulated and the criminal groups have grown in number. Therefore, it is misleading to hold that the Mafia or any other criminal organization has a monopoly on world crime. There is not a monarchy (a "number one") in the organized crime world, but there are many republics that variously interact and are protagonist of the international division of criminal labor.

Today's society produces more organized criminality because of some of its main characteristics—globalization of capitalism has increased the gap between underdeveloped and developed nations, and between social groups. The monetarization of economy and liberalization of the circulation of capitals has opened many possibilities for laundering illegal capitals. Prohibition of drugs has made the traffickers the richest criminals in history. Intertwining of legal and illegal economies as well as of criminal organizations and other social institutions have strengthened criminal enterprises. Drugs and money laundering are the best known aspects of today's criminal activities, but the most devastating is the connection between politics and crime. This mixture between the illegal and the legal, the criminal and the institutional, is the heart of the Mafia's historical model. It has grown and spread independently of the presence of Sicilian Mafiosi or Sicilian-Americans. It is not the Mafia that has invaded the world; it is the world that has produced more and more groups and organizations of the Mafia type.

THE NATURE AND EXTENT OF ORGANIZED CRIME

The Official Definition of Mafia-Type Associations

The Italian anti-Mafia law of September 1982 (No. 646, Art. 416), characterizes the first time Mafia-type association with the following features: the intimidatory power of the bond of association, the condition of subjection and of *omertà* derived from intimidation. Compared to other criminal associations that exist as long as there is a bond of association, an organized structure, and a plan of criminal activity, the Mafia has an extra capacity. It is able to exercise power through systematic intimidation, which is referred to as *omertà*. This is the "law of silence," and it consists in the duty of associates to keep silent about a secret. However, this also applies to everyone else. The Mafia rules over an extensive area, and many citizens, either by habit or out of fear, even if they know where the Mafiosi are to be found or have witnessed a Mafia crime, do not collaborate with the forces of law and order.

The oldest, most numerous and most powerful Mafia organization is the *Cosa Nostra*. Its structure has been disclosed since 1984 through the testimonies of various Mafioso State witnesses, the so-called *pentiti* (repenters), including Buscetta, Contorno, Calderone, and Marino Mannoia. The Cosa Nostra has been described by judges as a pyramidlike, unified organization. It is controlled by a powerful leader. At the bottom there are the *families*, who take the name of the territory that they control. The family comprises the so-called *uomini d'onore* (men of honor) in numbers varying from ten to one hundred. They are organized into groups of ten, with each group controlled by a *capodecina*. At the head of the family there is the *capofamiglia*, who has a deputy and a few advisors. Three or more families with adjoining territories are represented by the *capimandamenti*, who are members of the *cupola* or *commissione*. This is the central direction of the Mafia responsible for supervising all the activities of the whole organization at a provincial level led by a *capocommissione*. For some years, there has been an interprovincial structure that coordinates the activities on Sicilian soil. Within this structure, the *capocommissione* of Palermo dominates (Tribunale di Palermo, 1985; 1987).

The Cosa Nostra is the elite of the Mafia organizations that include external and contrasting groups. For example, there is the *Stidda* in the provinces of Agrigento and Caltanissetta, and there are many groups operating in Catania, but only a few of them are members of the Cosa Nostra. Official reports identified 181 Mafia groups operating in Sicily with 5,487 affiliates (Parlamento Italiano, 1995: 38).

The Mafia-Enterprise—a Sociological Definition

The Mafia phenomenon is much wider and much more complex than the Cosa Nostra. The Mafia is not only a criminal organization. In recent years the idea has been widely accepted that since the 1970s, the Mafia is an *enterprise*. The Mafia criminal activity is conducted in the same way as an enterprise, with a rational combination of the means and the results. There are also legal economic activities that have certain characteristics, identified as such by the anti-Mafia law. They are run by the Mafiosi, they employ illegally earned capital, and they use intimidatory tactics against the competition (Santino and La Fiura, 1991).

The Mafia enterprise is in reality not a recent phenomenon. Since the beginning, it was undertaken according to rational decisions and with the aim of self-enrichment. Neither are legal economic activities of the Mafiosi a new phenomenon. These legal activities existed in the 1920s in the United States and are documented in Palermo as far back as the 1950s. Although the description of the Mafia as an enterprise shows us its economic aims, it does not fully depict the Mafia in all its complexity.

The Paradigm of Complexity

The Mafia is a system of violence and illegality directed to accumulating wealth and power. It also uses a cultural code and enjoys a certain popular support (Santino, 1995). The Mafia has multifarious aspects: criminal, economic, political, cultural, and social. The actual criminal association is part of a network of relationships, which is much vaster: a *social block* with an interclass composition that ranges from the lowest social levels to the highest. Within this system, the dominant function is carried out by the legal-illegal class, which is the richest and most powerful. They are *Mafia bourgeoisie*, consisting of probably tens of thousands of people. For the poorer and more marginalized levels, the criminal activity represents the means of earning a living. It is a criminal career that offers the real possibility of social mobility. The number of people involved and their respective roles is difficult to determine. Nevertheless there are probably hundreds of thousands of people involved in the Mafia activities in Sicily.

The Sicilian society can be considered to be a society-producing Mafia (*società mafiogena*) for several reasons. Many people consider violence and illegality as a form of survival and as a way of acquiring a social role. Violence and illegality usually remain unpunished in the society. The legal economy is also too weak to offer substantial opportunities. The State and the institutions are seen as distant and foreign, approachable only through the mediation of the Mafiosi and their friends. The struggles against the Mafia have been lost and the consequence for many people is the mistrust, the belief that it is impossible to change the situation. The social life is lacking because of a crisis of political parties, the role of trade unions, and civil society is too weak and precarious to stand up.

Mafia is a form of totalitarian State and its peculiarity is the territorial control (*signoria territoriale*), from the economy to politics and to private life. For the Mafia, rights do not exist; there are only favors. This concept of the Mafia goes beyond the ideas popularized by the mass media, which presents the Mafia as an *emergency* (i.e., the Mafia exists only when it shoots someone, particularly important people, and creates a national issue); or as being an *anti-State*. (This stereotype interprets the crimes of the Mafiosi as a war against the State when these crimes have political and institutional representatives as victims.) Too often Mafia violence affects politicians, magistrates, and other institutional representatives. The Mafia is a permanent structural phenomenon. It is not anti-State. As a criminal organization it does not recognize the State's monopoly of power and force. The Mafiosi dispense justice by using crimes, in particular murder, pretending the right to do so. The Mafia operates inside political institutions as far as its economic and political aspects are concerned. It offers tenders for public works, seeks control of voters, and builds the relations with the dominant class and the bureaucratic apparatus, all of which adds to the Mafia phenomenon, distinguishing it from the usual forms of criminal organization.

The present-day Mafia, from the 1970s until today, can be defined as a *financial Mafia*. The Sicilian Mafia, which now controls territory all over the island, is assuming an increasingly important role in the trafficking of drugs and is also accumulating enormous wealth. Its illegal capital is channeled into the financial markets, recycled, and then reinvested in a thousand different ways. Of course some of the money is reinvested in the original illegal activity. Sometimes there is competition within the Mafia itself. When politicians, judges, or the forces of law and order oppose them or do not satisfy their requests, the Mafia gangs unleash a violent offensive.

The financial Mafia has an international range of activities. Its illegal gains annually are estimated to be $45 billion in American dollars. Its infiltration into the financial system is based on taking advantage of the international rule that ensures banking secrecy and proliferation of tax havens. It avoids control on capital, making use of the new forms of the circulation and raising of money, the so-called "financial innovations," such as trust companies (*società fiduciarie*), atypical stocks (*titoli atipici*), and common funds (Santino, 1988).

Mafia as Political Subject

The relationship between Mafia and politics is more complex than this description. The Mafia is a political group, having all the characteristics of that type of group as defined in sociology: a code, territorial extension, physical coercion, and an administrative force capable of ensuring the observance of the rules and effecting coercive measures (Weber, 1981). It contributes as an association and as a social coalition to the production of politics in a comprehensive sense. Its decisions and choices involve manipulation of power and distribution of resources (Santino, 1994).

In its relationship with the State and other institutions, Mafia is two-faced: it is *outside* the State and against it, because it doesn't recognize the State's monopoly of violence by resorting to murder (having death penalty in its code). It is *inside and within* the State, as a series of its activities are connected with the use of public finances (e.g., contracts for public works) and indicative of active participation in public life (elections and control of state institutions).

Until 1982 the Mafia was not considered to be a criminal organization. The impunity may be considered a form of legitimization. Mafia violence that victimized mainly political and social opponents has been useful for the maintaining of power by the dominant classes every time that the direct intervention of the State was impossible due to evident illegality or any other reason. From 1969 to 1984, Italy witnessed several atrocities, which caused 150 deaths and 688 grievous injuries. The guilty parties were punished only for the massacre of Christmas, 1984.

Mafia Today

In 1992 the Mafia killed a member of European Parliament (Salvo Lima), an old Mafia's friend and Mafioso-financier (Ignazio Salvo), and some magistrates engaged in investigation of the Mafia, including Giovanni Falcone, his wife Francesca Morvillo, Paolo Borsellino, and eight of their bodyguards. In 1993 there were ten victims of the Mafia in Rome, Florence, and Milan. These crimes have had many boomerang effects, leading to the arrest of many bosses hiding from justice (Totò Riina, a fugitive for 23 years, was captured in the center of Palermo), new laws, the army in Sicily (essentially a symbolic presence), and the increasing number of *pentiti* (repentants or informants).

Today, the bosses who are still fugitives and the new leaders are thinking that it is more convenient to abandon the bloodline and to return to the classical Mafia model, which favors mediation instead of war, to submerge and not to show off, less violence, and more business. The problem is to find new links with the political world. Italy is living a period of transition between the "first republic" and the "second republic" and instead of old political parties there are new forces and coalitions. Today Andreotti, the most powerful man in Italy for almost half a century, is facing trial for his Mafia connections. Craxi, the former socialist leader does not command power, but sons of Craxi and Andreotti have a role in the present situation.

The 'Ndrangheta from Calabria

The *'Ndrangheta* has rural roots, and like the Sicilian Mafia, has full control of its territory, which includes isolated areas like Aspromonte, the scene of many of the kidnappings that have taken place in Italy. The high number of murders registered every year in Calabria—Reggio Calabria in the 1980s had the highest murder rate in Italy: 48.7 per 100,000 inhabitants—indicates that among the *'ndrine*, the Calabrian criminal groups, which for the most part are divided along family lines, there is a permanent war. It has not resulted in the supremacy of any one family over another. Various *'Ndrangheta* chiefs are said to be affiliated to the Sicilian Mafia, but in Calabria there is no central criminal power. The dispersion of the various groups and the confrontations between them continue. The fact that since October 1991 there have been no Mafia murders in Reggio Calabria has been interpreted as a possible clue that one of the groups has gained predominance.

During the 1970s, the *'Ndrangheta* began to take a greater part in legal entrepreneurial activities and also assumed a significant role in drug trafficking. It has expanded its operations in Northern Italy, moving its members to the North and exploiting family ties. It now exercises control over the heroin route from the Middle East to the United States, as it does in other areas of the world (e.g., Australia). It has links with the Latin American cartels for the trafficking of cocaine in Europe. According to recent official reports, there are 160 criminal organizations operating in Calabria with 5,700 members (Violante, 1994).

The Camorra of Campania

The *Camorra* has urban origins and a notably discontinuous history. At the end of the 1950s, the term *Camorra* was used to describe small criminal groups engaged in illegal activities limited to certain areas. During the 1960s, they grew in size and efficiency due to two factors. First, the Neapolitan area became a center for cigarette smuggling. Second, there was the presence of the Sicilian Mafia bosses who were held under house arrest in the area. These bosses set up criminal groups that acted in support of the Sicilians in their fight for the control of the port and the Neapolitan area. During the 1970s the groups from Campania started to take part in the drug trade and managed to earn themselves large sums of money. At the moment, the *Camorristi* of Campania have an important role in drug trafficking. They have operational bases in Spain and in other European countries as well as in Latin America. According to the DEA, the *Camorra* controls the arrival of one ton of cocaine per week from Colombia. The *Camorristi* seem to have come to an agreement with the Sicilian Mafia about sharing the international market of heroin and cocaine. There are 145 *Camorra* organizations, with 7,000 members (Parlamento Italiano, 1995: 93).

Other Mafia-Type Groups

Mafia-type groups have been formed in other regions of Italy. In Apulia, the best known Mafia-type groups are the *Nuova Camorra Pugliese*, the *Sacra Corona Unita*, *La Nuova Camorra Salentina*, and the *Nuova Famiglia Salentina Libera Leccese*. There are 47 criminal groups, with members totaling 1,755 (Violante, 1994: 123). The formation of such organizations began back in the 1970s when groups of Neapolitan smugglers, to escape the repressive measures being imposed in the Gulf of Naples, transferred their cigarette-smuggling activity to the Apulian coast. They strengthened their ties with the local criminals. During the same period the Sicilian Mafiosi set themselves up in Brindisi. The Apulian organizations became involved in the drug trade, extortion, running gambling houses, and controlling prostitution. Today they control the arms trade and illegal immigration from the Eastern countries in collaboration with new foreign criminal groups.

Persistent Mafia-type organizations have been reported in Lazio, where the Mafia, the *'Ndrangheta*, the *Camorra*, and the local criminal groups operate. There are local groups like the *Centocelles* and the *Magliana*, which have transformed themselves into Mafia-type organizations. They have concentrated on the drug trade. Drug trafficking in the other regions also has undergone an important transformation. In Emilia, Liguria, Lombardy, and in Veneto, drug trafficking is now in the hands of southerners who are working with the locals. In Veneto the best-known criminal group is the *Mafia del Brenta*.[1]

Today, at the international level, many old and new criminal groups are similar to the Sicilian Mafia. Besides specific aspects they have homogeneous characteristics. They are connecting criminal activities with the accumulation of capitals and a political role. They are the American Cosa Nostra, the Japanese Yakuza, the Chinese Triads, the Latin-American Cartels, the Russian Mafia, and the Nigerian Mafia.

Measures, Including Legislation to Combat Organized Crime

The Laws on Mafia and Mafia-type Groups in Italy

Only in recent years has Italian legislation prepared itself to deal with the great increase in the Mafia's activities and with the other forms of organized crime. From 1982 to 1992, 114 laws regarding organized crime were introduced. All of these laws are connected with terrible crimes that shocked both local and international public opinion and are considered the offspring of the emergency situation. These laws are answers to the criminal challenge and not part of a coherent law enforcement program. It is a sort of cycle: the escalation of Mafia violence—the institutional reaction (arrests, trials, condemnations, and seizure of illegal wealth), the weakening of institutional reaction, and the return to cohabitation.

The first general law, the so called Rognoni-La Torre law (named after the backers of the proposal, the Christian-Democrat Minister Virginio Rognoni and the Communist leader, Pio La Torre, assassinated April 30, 1982), or the "anti-Mafia law," was approved on September 13, 1982, after the assassination of General Prefect Dalla Chiesa. The article 416 of the Penal Code, introduced by the new law, defines the Mafia as a specific type of

---

[1]On the criminal groups of the Mafia type operating in many Italian regions, see the reports of *Ministero dell'Interno*, various years.

criminal association. The organization is of the Mafia type when its components use intimidation, subjection, and enforced silence (*omertà*) to commit crimes. Such a criminal group directly or indirectly acquires the management or control of businesses, public contracts and public services to obtain either unjust profits or advantages for the group members or others. Besides the Mafia, the new anti-Mafia law provides measures for controlling the origins of patrimonies, as well as the confiscation of possessions of illicit origin.

During recent years, other provisions have been introduced. The most significant are the measures against money laundering; the provisions for those Mafiosi who collaborate with law enforcement officials; the revision of the Procedure Code for the treatment of Mafiosi and the creation of the Anti-Mafia Investigative Administration (*Direzione Investigativa Antimafia*: DIA); and the National Anti-Mafia Administration (*Direzione Nazionale Antimafia*: DNA). Provisions have been made to deal with Mafia interference with the right to vote.

The crime of laundering money of illicit origin was introduced in Italy in 1978, with article 648 of the Penal Code. It covered the profits obtained from aggravated robbery, aggravated extortion, and kidnapping for extortion. Article 23 of law no. 55 of March 19, 1990, extended the crime to the capital obtained from the production and sale of drugs. Later law no. 197 of July 5, 1991, introduced emergency measures to limit the use of cash and securities in transactions and to prevent the utilization of the financial system in money laundering. These measures provide that sums above 20 million lire must be transferred in cash, through approved mediators or by means explicitly indicated. Law no. 328 of August 28, 1993, repealed in part the European convention on money laundering. This law extends to any case of reinvestment of profits obtained from any type of crime. There are still some problems. A central data bank is lacking and there are no company registries, so it is impossible to follow transactions between firms involving sums under 20 million lire.

After Falcone's and Borsellino's assassinations, new emergency measures were taken. Decree no. 306 of June 8, 1992, converted into law no. 356 of August 7, 1992, introduces significant modifications to the Penal Procedure Code. The proof against the Mafiosi, due to their capacity to intimidate, can be drawn indirectly from other proceedings. The new law introduces further measures for *pentiti* (repentance) and severe prison terms for the Mafiosi. It has two clauses regarding elections. The first clause states that it is organized crime of the Mafia type when intimidation is used to hinder or deny the right to vote or to obtain votes. The second clause stipulates punishment when a member of the Mafia promises to obtain votes for a politician in exchange for money.

On the whole, Italian anti-Mafia legislation is behind the times. Laws were introduced as an emergency response. They are characterized by symbolism. Organized crime of the Mafia type has existed in Sicily since the nineteenth century. It was only with the law of 1982 that the crime of the Mafia type was introduced. From the second half of the 1950s, the Mafiosi became legitimate entrepreneurs. But only the aforementioned law of 1982 made it possible to prosecute Mafia enterprises. Since the 1970s, the financial size of these Mafia groups, both in terms of their capability of accumulating capital and utilization of the financial system for money laundering, is significant, but only with recent measures can the authorities control them.

After the assassination of General Prefect Dalla Chiesa, *maxiprocesso* and other trials have been completed. Many bosses, previously unpunished, have received life sentences. They are being held in a state of "severe imprisonment." Regarding the relationships between the Mafia and local institutions from 1990 to 1995, it should be noted that 83 city councils were dissolved for connection with the Mafia: 36 in Campania, 24 in Sicily, 14 in Calabria, 7 in Apulia, 1 in Basilicata, and 1 in Piemonte. From 1982 to 1995 illegal goods worth almost 9,000 billion lire were seized, but only 967 billion lire worth of goods were confiscated, which represents a very low percentage.

Comparative Evaluation of the Methods for Combating Organized Crime and Proposed Measures

Despite its limitations, the Italian legislation against the Mafia and organized crime of the Mafia type is the most important in Europe. The European Economic Community (EEC) has begun to deal with the problem of organized crime only in very recent years. The member States have diversified situations and there exists a system of variable legality. A few organized crimes of the Mafia type are incorporated in the Italian code. Penal action is obligatory in Italy and Germany but optional in the other nations. The passing of information to other countries is prohibited in Holland if it causes the limitation of liberty of Dutch citizens. It is restricted in Germany.

In September 1986, the European Parliament produced a report on "The drug problem in member States of EEC" (Clark, 1986). During 1991, the European Parliament constituted an investigative committee on the diffusion of organized crime connected with drug trafficking in the member States. The report of this committee (Cooney, 1991) makes a distinction between "organized crime" and "institutionalized crime." Accordingly, organized crime encompasses such crimes that call for special measures. It is also a crime that has the potential to strike not only local areas but also entire nations. Such crimes are undertaken on a large scale by organizations and structured groups whose main motivations are financial profit and the acquisition of power. Those involved in racketeering frequently try to corrupt politicians or other leading figures in order to reduce the risk of criminal prosecution and to facilitate the expansion of their criminal operations. It was added that institutionalized crime can infiltrate into the structure of modern industrialized states in ways not even attempted by organized crime. Given that the trade in narcotics is the most profitable form of criminal activity, it has become the focus of institutionalized and organized crime.

Both institutionalized and organized crime, despite their recent evolution, still follow traditional cultural ways and are based on ethnic identity. By definition, criminal organizations are secret societies and their survival depends on a code of conduct, which is awfully severe. Violating this code inevitably brings about physical punishments, including murder. It is not surprising to discover that the criminal organizations referred to have a family structure, which is as true for the Kray family of the East End of London in the 1960s, as it is for the Corleone family in Sicily. It also goes for the Bonannos of New York City and the Mussululu family from Turkey. The trust that links members of a family often obviates the need to resort to repressive or coercive measures at the highest levels of criminal organizations, even though homicides are not unknown among members of the same family.

The report gives some information on the main criminal groups working in Europe. Besides Italian groups (the Mafia, the *'Ndrangheta*, and the *Camorra*), there are the Japanese Yakuza, the Chinese Triads, the Turkish clan, and other ethnic clans like the Pakistani barons, former Yugoslavian groups, Polish organizations, and others.

In this report, the legal instruments to fight organized crime in Europe are divided into three categories: the signed international conventions, the Community's regulations through the directives, and the national regulations. On the European level, the new Treaty of the Union contains provisions regarding the fight against drugs in the public health sector (Title II, art. 129), regarding penal justice and internal affairs (Title VI), and foreign politics and security (Title V). The first unit that dealt with the drug problem on the European level was the Pompidou Group. Founded in 1971, it has collaborated with the European Council since 1980, sponsoring research on the use and trafficking of drugs and coordinating European politics on drugs.

In 1985, the TREVI group (Terrorism, Radicalism, Extremism, and International Violence) made up of the ministers of the member states of the

EEC, decided to deal with the drug problem. In 1989, the French presidency proposed a seven-point plan, which included common anti-drug policies and also measures against money laundering. In December of the same year, CELAD (European Committee on the Fight Against Drug Abuse) was created, and it proposed a European plan for the fight against drug abuse, which was approved by the European Council of Rome in December 1990, and reviewed and updated by the European Council of Edinburgh in 1992. In June 1994, the EEC Commission presented a proposal for a plan of action, at the European Council and Parliament, in regard to the fight against drugs. The plan has three main points: the reduction of the demand, the fight against illegal trafficking, and international measures.

Recently the Europol and the EMCDDA (European Monitoring Center for Drugs and Drug Addiction) have been constituted. Europol, located in The Hague, has limited employees and inadequate means for its task. The EMCDDA, established in 1995, with headquarters in Lisbon, produced its first report in 1996 (EMCDDA, 1996). In June 1991, the EEC Council approved a directive on the prevention of the use of the financial system for laundering of profits obtained from illegal activities. The European Council directive regards the conversion or transfer of capital with knowledge that it was obtained from serious crimes as money laundering. It includes the production and trade of drugs and other activities by members of organized crime. Since September 1993, the European Council's Convention on laundering and seizure and confiscation of profits of crime have been signed by about twenty states, but ratified by fewer states. With regard to measures against laundering, the actual European scheme is quite confused. In regard to the extension of laundering to all serious crimes, it has not been accepted by the member states. Also, in some countries this legislation is not applied to certain areas that work as tax havens. The islands of Jersey and Guernsey, for example, are not under English laws regarding laundering.

As is evident, Europe is only in the beginning of the battle against organized crime. There have been great delays and many uncertainties. Concern about the utilization of the financial system for money laundering has grown since the Bank of Credit and Commerce International (BCCI) scandal of 1991. One of the expedients used by the BCCI was to take advantage of the difficulties encountered in the collaboration between different countries. They set up headquarters in London and the social seat in Luxembourg (where controls are less restrictive), with bank subsidiaries all over the world. In this manner they could avoid detection of their illegal transactions for a long time. In July 1993, the EEC Commission formulated a proposal that elaborates upon the obligation of a credit institution to have its legal headquarters in the same member state in which it has its administrative headquarters.

These measures try to limit the circulation of capital with the official opening of the European market in 1993. It has yet to be proven how effective these measures will be in light of the fact that there is a trend in transnational markets toward the abolition or reduction in control, which may render the symbiosis between illegal and legal capital easier.

The Activities of the United Nations against Organized Crime

In 1950, the assembly of the United Nations decided the constitution of a committee of experts and the organization of meetings every five years on crime prevention and penal justice. After the Vienna Convention of December 1988, the United Nations, in 1990, created the United Nations Drug Control Program (UNDCP), with responsibilities much wider than those of the United Nations Fund for Drug Abuse Control (UNFDAC). The UNDCP works in four sectors: the reduction of illegal production of drugs, the prevention and reduction of illegal demand, the control of illegal drug trafficking, and the reinforcement of the judicial and legal system to strengthen the fight against drugs. In 1992, the Commission on the Prevention of Crime was established in Vienna with the task to fight money laundering and economic criminality.

In June 1994, the International Scientific and Professional Advisory Council (ISPAC) organized a conference in Courmayeur (Italy) on money laundering, soliciting the creation of a world network to control the crime profits and proposing the limitation of banking secrecy. In November 1995, a ministerial conference on transnational organized crime was held by the United Nations. The conference suggested worldwide legislation to deal with the crime of Mafia-type association like the Italian anti-Mafia law, which is similar to the "conspiracy" law introduced in the United States with the Organized Crime Control Act (OCCA) of 1970.

The Movement against the Mafia— The Sicilian Experience

In Italy the movement against the Mafia consists of social and political programs, public demonstrations, cultural manifestations, and educational activities in the schools. In Sicily particularly, the struggle against the Mafia has played a very important role in the history of the social and political movements as it has engaged itself in a strategy for a radical transformation of society and fighting against a system of power of which the

Mafia has been an important part. The anti-Mafia movement in Sicily is over a century old. The fight against the Mafia was once an aspect of the class struggle in Sicily. In recent years it has become a form of civil engagement. We can distinguish between three phases in this struggle:

1. The first phase, from the last decade of the nineteenth century to the 1950s
2. The second phase, which covered the period between the 1960s and 70s
3. The third phase, which began in the 1980s and continues today.

In the first phase, the protagonist of the anti-Mafia struggle was the peasant movement directed by trade unions and political parties, like the Socialist Party and the Communist Party. The peasants struggled for agrarian reforms and for acquiring the power in local councils against the landowners, the Mafia, and the conservative forces. Casualties were heavy. After every wave of struggle, many peasants were forced to emigrate; in the beginning to the United States and then to Northern and Central Europe. There were one million such emigrants in the early part of this century and one million between the 1950s and the 1970s.

In the second period, the struggle against the Mafia was in the hands of small minorities. The third phase began after the assassination of *prefetto* Dalla Chiesa in 1982. In this phase, new associations have been founded, demonstrations have been organized, and educational work has been held in the schools. There has been indignation against Mafia violence, which is considered an attack on democracy, freedom, civil and human rights, and peaceful coexistence. In 1984, many organizations founded the first *Coordinamento Antimafia*, but this network soon failed. In the last few years, some shopkeepers and small entrepreneurs founded anti-racketeering associations against extortion and usury. This movement is stronger in Eastern Sicily than in Western Sicily, and it is very weak in Palermo.

The Anti-Mafia Movement in Other Italian Regions

Since the 1980s there have been many activities against the Mafia and other forms of organized crime in many Italian regions, especially in the schools. In 1994, there started the *Libera*, a national "association of the associations." The first *Libera*'s initiative was to collect almost one million signatures for the implementation of the law for social use of the confiscated Mafia properties as approved by the Italian Parliament in February 1996. There are many anti-racketeering associations in the Italian territory and a national network of the anti-racketeering associations has been constituted in recent years. Recently, at the European level, some non-governmental organizations (NGOs) are working together in the European NGO Council on Drugs and Development (ENCODD). This informal network's main aims are to increase European public awareness about drug trade and drug control policies. The network promotes coordinated advocacy to ensure that international policies better address the links between drugs and development. An interesting initiative has been the campaign "Coca '95," organized by some European and Latin-American NGOs, to help the coca producers against the manipulations of narcotics traffickers.

In Italy, it is most important to go beyond the "emergency decrees," and attempt to put the various laws in order. The country must build a coherent legislative system against the Mafia and other forms of organized crime. It is necessary to specify exactly the configurations of crimes, like membership in the Mafia-type organization (*associazione mafiosa*) and the complicity in Mafia crime (*concorso esterno in associazione mafiosa*). Some political figures (like the former minister of national government Calogero Mannino) and public servants (like Bruno Contrada) were charged with complicity (*concorso*), but the former Prime Minister Giulio Andreotti has been charged with membership (*associazione mafiosa*).

Another issue that needs attention is the checking of the confessions of the *pentiti*. There are questions like whether it is necessary to have external evidence or whether the court should look for consistency in many confessions of *pentiti*. Earlier, the Supreme Court (*Cassazione*) asserted the first thesis, but in the last few years it has changed its line of approach. I think that the emergency mentality continues to dominate Italian thinking still today. There have not been big Mafia assassinations in recent years. People think that the Mafia is at the end of its long history. The term most used in Italy today is *normale*; Italy is becoming a normal country, without the Mafia, without terrorism, and without massacres. The "emergency" is finished, or at least is finishing. Italy, they say, is now closer to Europe, according to the parameters of the Maastricht treaty.

In this context, the new trend of Italian anti-crime policy is to normalize the legislation produced as the consequence of the emergency. An example is the new treatment of the *pentiti*. In the last few years their number has increased enormously. Until June 1996 they were 1,177 members, (430 from the Mafia, 224 from the *Camorra*, 158 from the *'Ndrangheta*, 101 from the *Sacra Corona Unita*, and 264 from other associations of the Mafia type). The situation produces many problems: protection of *pentiti* and their relatives, the costs for maintenance, and so on.

In the first days of March 1997, the Italian government approved a bill reforming the treatment of the "collaborators of justice" in a restrictive sense. The latter must make their confessions not later than six months from their repentance. The Mafiosi *pentiti* sentenced must serve several years of imprisonment. It appears that earlier there were too many concessions; now there are too many conditions.

Conclusion

In Europe and at the international level the need is to introduce laws against organized crime and to eliminate the conditions that encourage its development. It is necessary to legislate against the crime of Mafia-type association and drugs. Steps must be taken to end the banking secrecy and other forms of opacity of the financial system. All these aspects are linked to the general context of contemporary society. The diffusion of illegal activities and the proliferation of the Mafia-type organizations that unite legal and illegal activities, have a social and economic role, and interact with institutions can be explained by some fundamental contradictions in today's society (Santino, 1993).

Prohibition of drugs was proclaimed at the United Nations Convention of December 1988. Despite measures to reduce the demand and stop drug trafficking, its use has increased. Drug traffickers have accumulated and continue to accumulate huge amounts of capital. Prohibition cannot abolish the Mafia and other forms of organized crime. They have other activities and will dedicate more time to them or find new ones. However, it will certainly hinder their capability to accumulate capital and emancipate drug addicts from the slavery of unscrupulous drug dealers. For many years the debate on prohibition has been dominated by ethical and ideological concerns. Today the discussion is focused mostly on concrete themes like the cost-benefit ratio of repressive measures, overcrowded prisons, paralysis of the judicial system, the diffusion of AIDS among drug addicts, and the policy of harm reduction.[2]

The international financial system is notoriously opaque due to banking secrecy, tax havens, and financial innovations (consisting of new forms of collecting capital and other procedures) that favor the symbiosis between illegal and legal capital. The liberalization of the circulation of capital and the creation of large transnational markets (European Economic Community or North-American NAFTA) demolish borders, abolish

---

[2]See, for instance, the international meeting "Territorial Hells—Tax Havens," for a new International Convention on Drugs, Venice, 11–13 October, 1996, promoted by the Gruppo Abele and the city of Venice with the support of European Parliament.

controls, and favor the circulation of all types of capital, including illegal money. Anti-laundering measures are too weak and inefficacious compared with the use of huge transactions. About $1,000 billion U.S. dollars change hands each day on the world market and a large part of that sum is hot capital looking for more favorable outlets. It is quite probable that in this huge flow of cash, illegal capital may be hidden and laundered.

The capitalistic way of production has extended to the entire world, and, in the last several years, the gap between underdeveloped nations and developed nations has grown (UNDP, 1996). In 1993, the global Gross National Product (GNP) was $23,000 billion U.S. dollars, with $18,000 billion in developed countries, and only $5,000 billion in other countries. The share of the global product among the top 20 percent of the wealthy has increased from 70 percent to 85 percent and that of the bottom 20 percent, the poorest people, has diminished from 2.3 percent to 1.4 percent. Interestingly, 358 millionaires have the yearly income of 45 percent of the world's population. The social gap is also growing in affluent areas, with a great increase in unemployment.

In consequence of the policies of the United Nations' agencies like the World Bank, the International Monetary Fund, and the World Trade Organization, in many areas socialist control over the economies has been dismantled. However, in these nations democratic accountability has not grown with this change. Consequently, illegal accumulation by the powerful sections has increased while the majority has been impoverished. If the poverty of many countries increases, it is impossible to control migrational movements toward the wealthy nations. Such movements can become another channel for organized crime. If in the peripheral areas organized crime represents an answer to the crisis, in the central areas it takes advantage of the convenience offered by the system, such as prohibition, opacity of the financial system, and so on.

FINAL PROPOSALS

If we want to tackle organized crime successfully, we must act in many directions:

- *Knowledge:* We need adequate knowledge of the evolution of organized crime, and for this aim it is necessary to create a network among various subjects: judicial offices, law enforcement agencies, parliamentary committees, and research institutions.

- *International cooperation:* All nations must seek to harmonize their legislation, procedures, and law enforcement activities.

- *Prevention:* Efforts must be made to act on the structural causes of diffusion of organized crime: poverty, conveniences offered by the economy, and connections with institutions.

In this way the fight against Mafia and organized crime can become part of a global policy for democracy, coexistence, and development, ensuring the satisfaction of basic needs for all human beings.

REFERENCES

Clark, Stewart. 1986. *The Drug Problem in Member States of EEC*, September 1986.

Cooney, Patrick. 1991. European Parliament, Investigative Committee on the diffusion of Organized Crime connected with drug trafficking in the member states of European Community, *Project Report*, November.

EMCDDA. 1996. *Annual Report on the State of the Drugs Problem in the European Union 1995*, Lisbon.

Parlamento Italiano, 1995. *Rapporto sul fenomeno della criminalità organizzata*, anno 1994: 38, 93, Roma: Camera dei Deputati, Ministero dell'Interno.

Santino, U and G. La Fiura, 1991. *L'impresa mafiosa*. Milano: Dall'Italia agli Stati Uniti, F. Angeli, 17–53.

Santino, U. 1988. The Financial Mafia: The Illegal Accumulation of Wealth and the Financial-Industrial Complex. *Contemporary Crises*, 12, no. 3 (September): 203–243.

Santino, U. 1993. "La mafia sicilienne et le nouveau marchés des drogues en Europe." In *La planète des drogues*, A. Labrousse et A. Wallon (eds.), 123–143. Paris, Editions du Seul.

Santino, U. 1994. *La mafia come soggetto politico,* Palermo: Centro siciliano di documentazione "Giuseppe Impastato."

Santino, U. 1995. *La mafia interpretata: Dilemmi, stereotipi, paradigmi*, 130. Soveria Mannelli: Rubbettino.

Tribunale di Palermo. 1985. *Ufficio Istruzione processi penali*, 706. *Ordinanza-sentenza contro Abbate Giovanni.*

Tribunale di Palermo. 1987. *Corte d'Assise*, 459. *Sentenza contro Abbate Govanni.*

UNDP (United Nations Development Program). 1996. *Human Development Report 1996*, Oxford University Press.

Violante, L. 1994. *Non è la piovra. Dodici tesi sulle mafie italiane*, 92–93. Torino: Einaudi.

Weber, M. 1981. *Economia e società*, 53–55. Milano: I, Comunità

CHAPTER 4

ORGANIZED CRIME: A PERSPECTIVE FROM THE NETHERLANDS

Oon van der Heijden

INTRODUCTION

The Dutch police organization is made up of twenty-five regional departments and a Department of National Police Services (*Korps Landelijke PolitieDiensten*—KLPD). The criminal justice system of The Netherlands has been influenced by both internal development and, especially since the 1810 annexation, by French developments. A Criminal Code for the Kingdom of Holland was enacted in 1809. A year after the annexation, the French Penal Code of 1810 came into force. It formed the foundation for the theory and practice of substantive criminal law even after The Netherlands regained independence in 1813. In general, the investigation of offenses is dealt with by the police. However, certain specialized authorities, such as those dealing with taxation and customs, also investigate a number of offenses. With regard to petty offenses, classified as transgressions (e.g., traffic violations), the police have the power to utilize a so-called "transaction," which is regarded, in formal legal terms, as a kind of civil agreement between the state agent (the police officer) and the offender. If the offender agrees to pay the "poena" (financial penalty) set by the police officer in accordance with a fixed tariff, this payment ends the case. The results of police investigation in other criminal matters are passed on to the prosecutor. Approximately 20 percent to 25 percent of all police work was reported as having been devoted to criminal investigation duties in 1980. In particular cases, prosecutors are said to investigate actively on their own behalf. The Dutch system of the administration of justice does not adhere to the principle of mandatory prosecution, but follows instead the so-called "opportunity principle". The prosecutor, working in accordance with this principle, may terminate cases in different ways: by technical dismissal if not enough evidence is available; by policy dismissals if the prosecutor believes the case merits no trial; or by a transaction. Since 1983 the prosecutor can offer a transaction in minor cases. In most cases dealt with in this way, this involves a financial obligation. A prosecutor may also transfer a case to another jurisdiction. In 1985, the prosecutors' offices brought to trial 116,492 cases and terminated 95,642 cases.

The Dutch have introduced several innovative measures in their criminal justice system, including the well-known measure to legalize drugs and prostitution. Another innovative measure is dealing with juvenile delinquency, wherein the more important cases involving youth between ages twelve to eighteen are dealt with by a so-called "three party council" (the prosecutor, a police officer, and a representative of the child welfare board). The council quite often moves the dismissal of the case.

Due to its nature, organized crime is not only difficult to combat, it is also a phenomenon not easy to assess. In The Netherlands, criminal intelligence units (CIUs) have been playing an important role in increasing the knowledge and understanding of organized crime in the country and developing measures for combating it. Information about these CIUs and the nature and extent of organized crime in Holland will be presented in this chapter. Next, a series of measures taken in the last ten years will be critically examined. Finally, a new way of analyzing organized crime is proposed as the basis of a more effective approach to dealing with it.

The rationale for the creation and existence of CIUs is that organized crime should be dealt with by the police in a way that differs from the traditional forms of serious crime. In the case of specific crimes, such as fraud and trafficking in drugs, usually no complaint is made by an actual victim. Forensic traces, such as bloodstains and fingerprints, are seldom found, partly because the crime is not perpetrated solely at one location and at one time. Another characteristic of organized crime is the hierarchy of association, secret agreements, and corrupt protection from the enforcement agencies. All these factors make it very difficult to find clues that could provide a sufficient basis for suspicion within the meaning of the Criminal Procedure Act. During their investigation, police officers are then obliged to have recourse to rumors from the criminal fraternity itself as a source of information. If such rumors reach them, they can continue their work in a targeted manner by using informers, tapping telephones, and keeping individuals under surveillance. A large quantity of intelligence is collected in this way, with levels of reliability from *soft* to *hard,* the latter being so reliable that it can be used as evidence at a criminal trial.

In The Netherlands, the collection, collation, and analysis of soft information is the responsibility of special units within the regional police forces: CIUs. There are twenty-five regional CIUs in operation and one National Criminal Intelligence Division (CRI). The task of the CIUs is to promote the detection of crimes that, considering their serious nature, the frequency with which they are committed, or the organized manner in which they are perpetrated, cause serious violation of the legal order. With their intelligence work, CIUs help to investigate persons and legal entities that could be involved in the perpetration of these crimes. The intelligence work of the CIUs is not directed at furnishing evidence. Collecting evidence is the task of the tactical investigation department. The intelligence work, which is for the most part secret, is not intended to be brought up for discussion at the trial, but it has to produce information for guiding the investigation process. This guidance takes shape in the decision as to whether or not a tactical criminal investigation should be instituted, and the direction that a current tactical investigation should take. The CIU functions as an important source for commencing tactical investigations. Crime-pattern analyses of organized crime is also carried out on the basis of CIU information. A national inventory of criminal groups has been made periodically in The Netherlands since 1988. Analysis of CIU intelligence has a great advantage over working with hard information in that intelligence on active criminal groups is obtained at a much earlier stage. Of course, the limited reliability also causes concern about the quality of the results of the analysis.

THE NATURE AND EXTENT OF ORGANIZED CRIME

In 1995, a national inventory on criminal groups was carried out for the fourth time. This survey was based on data collected through a questionnaire format from crime analysts of all the regional criminal activities of every known criminal group. A criminal group was defined as the cooperation of two or more people who are involved in crimes, which, in view of their impact or their frequency or the organized framework within which they are committed, represent a serious violation of the legal order. The questionnaires that were completed were processed at the National CRI. In the analysis of the answers, a number of characteristics were used as selection criteria in order to establish the organizational degree of groups. The following eight criteria were applied:

1. The group has a hierarchic system of leaders and subordinates with a more or less fixed division of tasks between core members;

2. The group has an internal system of sanctions, such as intimidation, acts of violence and sometimes even liquidation;
3. The group concentrates on acquiring income from different forms of crime, depending on the profit opportunities involved in more than one type of serious crime;
4. The group has criminal contacts with the world of trade and industry and/or with corrupt government agents;
5. The group launders criminal earnings by investments in legal enterprises, real estate, movable property, or in foreign money;
6. Business enterprises are being used as a front;
7. The core members have been acting jointly for over three years;
8. The group uses intimidation, acts of violence and sometimes even liquidation against competitors within the criminal world.

In the analysis of the data, the degree of organization of a criminal group is determined simply by counting the characteristics. The group that has more characteristics is placed higher in the degree of criminal organization. The designation "organized" is given to groups that comply with six or more of the eight criteria. The formula of at least six out of eight takes into account both the diversity of organized crime and the fact that the police in the early stages of the investigation process usually do not have complete knowledge of all features of an active criminal group.

In the 1995 inventory on organized crime in The Netherlands, exactly one hundred criminal groups met at least six out of the eight aforementioned criteria and were, therefore, denoted as organized. Ninety-three of the one hundred organized groups have been committing serious crimes for more than three years. Most of the groups (86) traffic in drugs, especially in hard drugs. Other forms of crime frequently perpetrated are illegal trafficking in firearms (by 20 groups) and serious crimes against property (35 groups), such as fraud, robberies, extortions, and vehicle theft.

Almost all organized groups are characterized by a structure of leaders and subordinates and a fixed division of tasks among the core members. Discipline within the groups is usually maintained by violence or threats of violence. Also persons involved do not refrain from violence outside their own circle: almost two-thirds use physical violence against competitors within the criminal milieu. One-fourth of the groups is associated with liquidation.

A widely recurrent characteristic of organized groups is the laundering of the proceeds of criminal activities. Eighty-nine of the one hundred organized groups active in The Netherlands launder the proceeds of crime, which is done by investing in legitimate businesses or heritable property or by channeling money by using routes abroad. Most groups also make use of legitimate firms, which function as a facade to cover up criminal activities. Three-fourths of the groups maintain contacts with the upper world in some other fashion, too. The police, members of the business world, and lawyers are especially mentioned in this context. Almost one half (44) of the organized criminal groups have a core formed completely of persons of Dutch heritage. In the case of one-fifth of the groups, the core members are immigrants or foreigners. Turkey, in particular, scores very high as a country of origin of core members. One-fourth of the groups have a heterogeneously formed core, where, in most cases not only foreigners, but Dutch nationals as well call the shots. The analysis shows that groups with a completely foreign core are more often associated with violence, both against their own members and others, in the criminal milieu. Dutch groups apparently maintain relatively more criminal contacts with the upper world.

Most organized groups are active at the international level. Almost three-fourths not only operate in The Netherlands, but in other Western European countries as well. Almost one-third commit crimes in Central and Eastern Europe. Of the countries outside Europe, Turkey, Morocco and Surinam, Aruba, and The Netherlands Antilles are most frequently mentioned as areas of operation.

The Research Study by the Fijnaut Group

The outcome of the national inventory of 1995 is comparable with another study about the nature, gravity, and magnitude of organized crime in The Netherlands conducted in 1995. This research study was carried out by a group consisting of four Dutch criminologists under the chairmanship of Dr. Cyrille Fijnaut. The study was initiated at the request of a parliamentary commission inquiring into police investigative practices in The Netherlands.

The first priority of the Fijnaut research group was to provide an acceptable definition to guide their further research. They described organized crime as follows:

> There is talk of organized crime when groups of people who are primarily focused on illegal gains systematically commit crimes which have serious consequences for society and are capable of successfully protecting their interests, in particular by being prepared to use corruption or violence to control or neutralize persons (Tweede Kamer, 1996, p. 55).

Several elements of organized crimes from this description correspond with the list of distinguishing characteristics that were used in the national inventory. For example, organized crime is perpetrated by groups; the crimes committed are serious crimes, and corruption and/or violence applied are similar classifications in both. Similarly, the definition also allows for some variation in the form in which organized crime appears (there is, after all, mention of corruption and/or violence), and the description suggests that an activity will be considered as an organized crime if several criteria are simultaneously applicable. Fijnaut and his associates differ from national survey criteria by not including the system of hierarchy, division of tasks, cover firms, and money laundering as typical characteristics of organized criminal groups.

Apart from the definition, the research method of the Fijnaut group is also not the same as the one used in the aforementioned inventory. The group did not only make use of (confirmed) CIU data, but also acquired its information from the files of completed criminal investigations, interviews with representatives of the police, judiciary, economic sectors, and ethnic minorities. In the research report by Fijnaut, few figures are presented and the investigation by the four professors has a qualitative character. Finally, the research group did not restrict its work to one calendar year. The study roughly covers the period 1990 to 1995. The Fijnaut research group further makes a distinction between three main types of criminal groups. Groups of the first type consist of native-born Dutch citizens, those of the second type, of naturalized Dutch individuals who originally came from countries such as Turkey, Morocco, and the former Dutch colony of Surinam, and groups of the third type comprise criminals of foreign extraction.

Domestic Groups

The domestic groups are between thirty and forty criminal organizations engaged predominantly in traditional organized crime, with trafficking in soft drugs as the predominant feature. Apart from the production of amphetamines and other synthetic drugs, the Dutch networks do not have the production in their own hands. The Netherlands, with its Europort in Rotterdam and Schiphol International Airport in Amsterdam, occupies an ideal position as the gateway to Europe. The drugs that enter the country are therefore not only destined for the local market, but flow through the country to other European countries.

Besides drug trafficking, these criminal organizations commit serious property crimes. Only seldom do they have a hierarchical structure. Mostly, there are loose networks of individuals, groups, and networks that sometimes cooperate and sometimes hinder one another. Dutch networks are sometimes quite large; some are made up of more than one hundred persons. In total, the world of the Dutch trade in drugs is more aptly described as an extended network in which thousands of people, often operating in cliques or groups, are connected to each other in either transitory or permanent relationships, or where such relationships can be easily established via a friend of friends if and when the need arises. In these networks, pivotal figures, individuals, and groups with more power than others can be discerned. Many of these relationships are not stable and the interests of various groups or subgroups may be incompatible with the personalities of the leaders, which sometimes clash. Such conflicts are resolved by using avoidance tactics or through unconcealed violence. As a result, new subgroups come into being, either simply to clear up a particular job (e.g., by jointly financing the project or by supplying materials or personnel) or new coalitions of longer duration are also established (Enquêtecommissie Opsporingsmethoden, 1996, p. 317).

According to the Fijnaut research group, Dutch organized crime is a diffuse and constantly changing network of individuals and groups. It has been found that domestic groups increasingly cooperate with criminal groups in countries abroad. In a number of cases, the use of violence by domestic groups is intensive and many of these criminal organizations may also have quite large sums of money. The proceeds of illegal activities are partly channeled in the criminal trade and partly legally invested in The Netherlands and abroad. Little has been found of structural intertwinement of criminal groups and the legal upper world. Only a few make investments in legal sectors such as the catering trade and real estate. The majority of the domestic criminal organizations use the money earned by criminal activities for their own consumptive needs and for the management of their affairs. Nevertheless, a real danger comes from the potential corruption of bona fide businesses as a result of money laundering. The available research suggests that forms of very professional fraud and money-laundering constructions are relatively unknown to the police and justice system, but hold an inordinate amount of financial threat to society.

Naturalized Groups

There are several criminal groups active in The Netherlands whose members live in the country and often hold Dutch passports, but are not ethnically of Dutch origin. These are persons belonging to the three large ethnic communities in The Netherlands: Turks, Moroccans, and Surinamese. Parts of these ethnic communities are involved in the smuggling of narcotic drugs to Europe. The reasons for their involvement in the drug economy relate partly to their easy access to the producers and dealers of the products in their homelands. Furthermore, the socioeconomic position of these ethnic minorities in Dutch society is relatively low, and the increase in their income as a result of the trade and distribution of drugs in their neighborhoods also perhaps influences their decision to become involved and stay involved in the drug world.

The Balkan route makes Turkey an important country for transporting illegal goods, especially heroin. The Turkish Mafia is intensively linked to government services and the business community, and part of organized crime is also carried out by political-criminal groups. These criminal organizations are slowly changing from rigidly led, hierarchical organizations to more loosely-knit networks. Most of the criminal earnings are invested in Turkey, particularly in the tourist industry, though in a few cases, Turkish criminal organizations have been found to invest money in Dutch real estate projects also. The Turkish organizations are extremely violent in comparison with other criminal organizations.

Organized crime from Morocco has focused on the trade in cannabis and increasingly on hard drugs. There are indications that the Moroccan authorities and the judiciary assist the cannabis economy. Moroccan organized crime is not only criminal in nature, but also political. The cannabis sector has become essential for the Moroccan economy, since many Moroccan drug dealers intensively invest their profits in Morocco. Socially speaking, the Moroccan community in The Netherlands finds itself in the lower end of the scale and is becoming a breeding ground for crime. There are signals of large-scale theft of cars, trafficking in humans, and especially cannabis trafficking. Ingenious smuggling methods have also been developed by these groups, and several Moroccan institutions have been deeply affected, but remarkably, Moroccan organized crime is not very violent.

In Surinam, several criminal groups are engaged in cocaine trafficking and have made that country a transit route for the supply of drugs to Europe. There are indications that the former army leadership was also involved in the trafficking and transporting of cocaine. In The Netherlands, there is some involvement of Surinamese subjects in organized crime in drugs, trafficking in stolen vehicles, and prostitution. Drug trafficking partly consists of smuggling large quantities of hard drugs, but couriers and travelers also smuggle small quantities as part of the large distribution network of the Surinamese business community. A certain part of the population group is directly involved in this manner of drug trafficking.

Foreign Groups

There are also several dozen criminal groups of other foreign origin active in The Netherlands. The great variety of organizations, authors, and crimes makes it impossible to give a general assessment. As with the naturalized groups, it is necessary to differentiate between the countries of origin of the various criminal groups. The most important groups come from China, Colombia, Italy, the former Yugoslavia, the CIS republics, and Nigeria.

Chinese organized crime is mostly seen in the form of the Triad structure of which a small number are active in The Netherlands. The power relations between them constantly change, resulting in much violence. However, they are not solely responsible for Chinese organized crime, as investigations in other countries reveal that a sizable Chinese community is a necessary condition for Chinese organized crime to develop. On one hand, the Chinese community in The Netherlands is well-integrated, while at the same time, it is a world on its own in a social and cultural respect. Unlike some other countries, The Netherlands does not have any "Chinatowns" and it remains unclear to what extent the Chinese community is involved in organized crime. It is clear, however, that the active Triads use several Chinese restaurants, gambling houses, and videotheques for their activities.

In recent years, the Colombian drug cartels have grown rapidly. The Colombians have acquired a considerable trading base in Europe in which The Netherlands has a function in a logistical sense. This country simply appears to function as a dropping-off zone for local as well as European markets, and not as an operational center. About 75 percent of the cocaine discovered in The Netherlands has come from Colombia. The cartels operate several active cells in The Netherlands dealing entirely in drugs. Almost all the revenues are repatriated to Colombia through illegal channels.

Since the late 1980s, Italian Mafia like the *Camorra* has been active in cocaine trafficking. The Netherlands is used as a trading place, since it provides good logistical arrangements. Other (non-Mafia) Italians are criminally active in The Netherlands, too, but it is not clear how extensive Italian organized crime is in the country.

In several Dutch cities, violent Yugoslav gangs are active in trafficking in women, in cars, and in burglaries and robberies. They are referred to as the so-called "Yugo Mafia," separate groups that maintain contact, but are not united, due to ethnic differences. The gangs do not shy away from intimidating police and judicial authorities, and their tough stance against the authorities is equally remarkable.

Many opportunities awaited the Russian mob after the fall of the Berlin wall. The Russian mob is becoming increasingly internationally oriented. The presence of Russian troops stationed until recently in Germany and a small Russian community in The Netherlands are their stepping stones. There are indications that Russian criminals are active in Dutch territory to a limited degree in trafficking in women, in cars, extortion, arms, and drugs. However, the Russian Mafia has not as yet established itself in The Netherlands.

Nigerian organized criminals are especially involved in international drug trafficking, illegal car trade, fraud practices, and trafficking in humans. The Nigerian groups active in The Netherlands are the extremes of large criminal organizations. In a number of cases it was also found that Dutch and Nigerian criminal organizations worked together.

Due to its very nature, it is difficult to assess the size of organized crime. According to the Fijnaut research group, exact figures cannot be given. The group estimates that between thirty and forty domestic groups and a few dozen naturalized and foreign groups are active in The Netherlands. This quantification is lower than the figure of a hundred organized crime groups found in the 1995 national inventory. The single most important factor that explains this difference is the use of assumed information in the national inventory, where the Fijnaut research group only uses confirmed information. An analysis of the inventory data in which only answers based on confirmed CIU information was used led to the result that forty-four groups met at least six out of the eight criteria. This leads to the conclusion that when the differences in definitions and research methods are taken into account, the difference in the quantitative results of the two studies is quite plausible. The same is true for the finding that Fijnaut describes of some foreign groups that were not found in the inventory. This can be attributed to the fact that the Fijnaut research describes a period of about five years (1990–1995), while the inventory concentrates on the criminal groups active at one point in time (i.e., the beginning of 1995).

Although the definition and other elements of the research method applied by the Fijnaut group differ from those used in the national inventory of 1995, the qualitative results of both pieces of research work connect up well. The nature of organized crime in The Netherlands is very diverse. What is noticeable is that drug trafficking is the most common type of crime and that it is perpetrated on an organized basis. It is not surprising, therefore, that most organized criminal groups active in The Netherlands also commit crimes in other countries. It can also be seen that most of the naturalized and foreign groups active in The Netherlands do not originate from other member states of the European Union.

The importance of the drug trade for these groups should not be underestimated, which can be illustrated with statistics on seized drugs. Between 1985 and 1995, the quantities of drugs seized every year by the Dutch police have increased considerably for most types of drugs. It applies both to cannabis products and cocaine and amphetamine. As regards heroin, it is concluded that no significant rising trend has been discovered. Another indication of the growth of organized crime is the use of physical violence against (former) members of criminal groups and against competitors on the criminal markets. Liquidations within the criminal world have clearly increased: from eleven in 1989 to twenty-three in 1993 and thirty-one in 1994. Most of these liquidations were related to drug trafficking. The overview of available information can only lead to the conclusion that organized crime is a social problem of the first order in The Netherlands. This problem calls for swift measures to be taken.

Measures, Including Legislation to Combat Organized Crime

Organized crime is a problem that cannot be responded to with the same approach and the same measures as ordinary crime, a fact recognized more than ten years ago by the Dutch Minister of Justice. In a governmental policy plan entitled "Samenleving en criminaliteit" (1985) he noted:

> Although exact figures about this form of crime are scarce, the police and judiciary have the definite impression that this is a great danger threatening Dutch society, against which action should be taken urgently.

Based upon nothing more than this impression, the Minister of Justice took quite a number of measures. CIUs were set up and the instrument of crime analysis was introduced and further developed within the police. Bureaus for financial investigations have been installed, while legislation has been initiated in various fields, such as bills pertaining to the confiscation of illegally acquired financial assets, the reporting by financial institutions of questionable transactions, and the penalization of actions in preparation of a criminal offense. Police forces throughout the country have started the formation of supra-regional teams, comparable with the special task forces that were operational in the United States during the 1980s, for conducting investigations into criminal organizations active on a national or international scale.

As of February 1994, financial institutions are required by law to report questionable transactions to the Office for the Disclosure of Unusual Transactions (ODUT). This new legislation is referred to as Reporting Questionable Transactions (RQT). Transactions are questionable whenever one or more items from a list of indicators, established by a Ministerial Order, are applicable. The ODUT assesses which of the questionable transactions received are considered suspect, which is mainly done by matching personal data of the persons involved in the unusual transaction with the national file on CIU subjects. The information on suspect transactions is then handed over to the Financial Police Unit of the National CRI. When criminal information on the subjects involved is available, it is added to the transaction information. The CRI then disseminates the results among the regional police forces, where they may be used in, or lead to, criminal investigations. The RQT legislation serves a dual purpose: preventing abuse of the financial system for money laundering and fighting money-laundering activities themselves. The ODUT is positioned as a buffer between the financial institutions and the justice system.

Some measures have also been taken that pertain to legal provisions in the field of financial investigations. These concern the obligation of financial institutions to disclose unusual transactions and the increase in legal possibilities of confiscating criminal assets. In 1993 new legislation came into force to increase the statutory powers of the police and the judicial authorities to deprive criminals of their illicit earnings. Both the range of the deprivation order in the Criminal Code, and the scope for seizure were extended considerably. These have also stipulated the way in which CIU information is treated. The order in which the various measures are treated more or less follows the order in the investigation process: first, the collection of CIU information and subsequently, the application of crime analysis and the work of the interregional tactical investigation teams. After that, the prosecution process is given full attention.

Criminal information has in some way been systematically gathered in The Netherlands since the 1970s. Over the years, establishing and maintaining contacts with informers and gathering criminal information in other ways (e.g., by observation) was increasingly becoming a specialist task. Therefore, separate CIUs were set up as early as 1986. There is no standard organization for the CIU in The Netherlands, but there are runners, crime analysts, and administrative staff working in each unit. A runner is the contact person of an informer of the CIU. The number of staff working in a CIU varies from five to over eighty persons, depending on whether a surveillance team or a technical support unit is required.

It is a common experience that the term *organized crime* refers to cooperating entities that are difficult to define and which are responsible for a variety of crimes in different locations. There is no unity of time and location as regards criminal activities. Individual positions are not fixed, but change frequently. Criminal working methods are adjusted in accordance with the circumstances, which results in the police normally having information on organized criminal groups that is far from complete and accurate. There is an estimation that less than 50 percent (and perhaps no more than 10 percent) of the information gathered by CIUs is used in a tactical investigation. In order to make the investigative process as effective and efficient as possible, the police in The Netherlands make extensive use of crime analysis. In actual fact, crime analysts base their right to exist on working professionally with information that is usually incomplete and partly unreliable. Crime analysis has been described as "the identification of, and insight into, the mutual relationships that exist between crime data and other possibly relevant data with a view to strengthening the police and prosecution practices," (van der Heijden, Weimar, and Minnebo, 1991).

The Netherlands has also evolved the concept of core teams. After the "discovery" of organized crime in The Netherlands in the mid 1980s, the idea has spread that this form of crime should not be tackled at a regional level only. Therefore, five supra-regional investigative teams, so-called "core teams," were set up in 1992. Since then, a sixth team and a national investigative team have been formed. The required complement of the teams is predominantly provided by the regional police forces, the CRI, and the Tax Information and Investigation Service. The contribution by regional police departments is the largest; in principle, 1 percent of their complement. The core teams consist of a staff of between sixty and one hundred people. There is a clear relationship between the core teams and the regional forces involved, that is, a core team is placed under a regional force as far as the management is concerned, whereas the authority is vested in a Chief Public Prosecutor. In some cases, the organizational relationship between the team and the managing force is so intensive that the team can hardly be distinguished from a regular investigation unit. The teams utilize the latest views and methods in order to tackle organized crime.

COMPARATIVE EVALUATION OF THE METHODS FOR COMBATING ORGANIZED CRIME AND PROPOSED MEASURES

This evaluation has been facilitated by the fact that new legislation previously described has been subject to a scientific evaluation (Terlouw and Aron, 1996). Central issues in the evaluation of the implementation of the RQT law were the workability and effectiveness of the new legislation. Special attention was given to preventive effects and to the extent to which transaction information was put to use in investigations.

Financial institutions have become more aware of the necessity of public-private collaboration in the fight against money laundering. In 1995 the ODUT received 16,215 reports concerning questionable transactions, 14 percent of which were judged suspect and passed on to police. The amount of money involved in suspect transactions was $165 million U.S.

dollars. Approximately 1,000 individuals were involved in these transactions and about 20 percent of the information on suspect transactions was used in new or current criminal investigations, while the remaining 80 percent was recorded for future references. This transaction information could become relevant at a later time.

Financial institutions are very cautious in giving the police information about financial transactions due to the need to provide adequate protection to their customers. Police investigators consider this a major problem. The computer system of the ODUT is deficient. This generates problems in the process of judging the status of transactions. The financial expertise of the ODUT is still insufficient, quantitatively as well as qualitatively. Due to these difficulties, promising transaction information sometimes does not get enough attention. Important information may therefore remain unused. Problems involving computerization, manpower, and quality were noted in the transaction-information processing chain following the ODUT as well. The lack of financial knowledge is especially pressing at the regional level. The infrastructure of the processing chain has not been tailored to the efficient handling and distribution of the transaction information. Too many organizations are involved, which at their own discretion, add and/or remove data to/from the transaction information. Valuable information can get lost that way. Sometimes transactions get lost completely. All parties involved agree that the almost total lack of feedback in the process is a serious deficiency. The bank representatives hold the opinion that there is not enough interest in the cross-border aspects of money-laundering activities and that the international systems of reporting transactions are poorly geared to one another, which hampers the exchange of information.

It can be concluded that the system of indicators and the obligation to report certain transactions have more or less been accepted by the banks and that the regime is workable. If the system of indicators is maintained adequately and, when necessary, improved, it will largely accommodate the needs of the parties involved. The systems of reporting transactions in Europe should be harmonized. The ODUT computer system needs improving. Also, the infrastructure of the transaction-information processing chain should be adapted. The aim should be for a quantitative and qualitative strengthening of the organizations that process and use transaction information. Fundamental investments are needed in order to enlarge the financial expertise and the knowledge of financial investigation among the police. The structure of communication between the law and financial institutions requires care. Moreover, the feedback of information on the outcome of transactions reported is in urgent need of improvement.

It is clear that the RQT legislation has rendered placement of criminally acquired capital into the financial system more difficult. But displacement effects are apparent. The number of unusual transactions in 1995 was about 30 percent lower than in 1994. The figures for the first half of 1996 show a further decrease of about 15 percent (Annual Report, 1996). There are indications that criminals no longer make use of official financial institutions, but use an informal, underground banking system instead (van Zwam, 1996). As far as is known in 1995, transaction information led to the start of an investigation only a few dozen times. Totally unknown is the number of times that transaction information has led to a successful conclusion of an investigation. Therefore it must be concluded that the RQT legislation did not meet expectations, a conclusion even shared by the Dutch Minister of Justice (1997).

Recently, a scientific evaluation of the effects of the new legislation was also published (Nelen and Sabee, 1996). It appears that the public prosecution service puts in a great effort to set out a policy to stimulate a proceeds-based approach among the public prosecutors. The research has made clear that the policymakers strive to extend the scope of the legislation to all profitable crimes. The latter contradicts the tenor of the political debate in which the legislation was seen primarily as an additional instrument to combat organized crime. Judges are inclined to agree with the political viewpoint and reject the line of the public prosecution department. Consequently, judges are rather ambivalent to the legislation as a whole.

Despite the fact that policymakers within the public prosecution department try hard to encourage the use of the new legal instruments, so far the daily practice has not passed off smoothly. Of course, the required change of mentality toward a proceeds-based approach takes a while. Besides these starting problems, the implementation process has been frustrated by the lack of knowledge within the public prosecution department on financial affairs and civil law. Furthermore, the public prosecutors lack sufficient administrative support.

Within the police force the attitude toward the use of the new legislation is rather indifferent. The police management has adopted a strategy concerning "financial policing" and regards the deprivation of criminal assets as an integral part of this broad concept. However, a specific strategy with regard to the confiscation of illegally acquired income has not been developed. Similar to the public prosecution department, the level of knowledge among police officers on financial affairs and civil law is low. The policymakers with the police have not yet determined how knowledge in financial matters can be increased. There are different views with regard to whether external financial experts should be contracted. An advantage to contracting is that the requisite knowledge becomes quickly available. Disadvantages are the costs involved and the risk that confidential information is treated without the necessary discretion. As a result, the policies of the police and public prosecution departments are hardly geared to one another.

In a number of cases, the police have cooperated closely with the Fiscal Information and Investigation Service (FIOD). This way the police could profit from the financial expertise of FIOD staff. But in some cases it resulted in tensions within the investigative team, because the FIOD staff was primarily interested in tracing confiscatable assets and hardly or not at all in finding proof for the involvement of suspects in the illegal activities.

Since the introduction of the new legislation the instrument is increasingly used. From 1994 to 1995, the number of deprivation orders rose 40 percent, to 969. The majority of cases were related to drug trafficking and serious property crimes. This sounds positive. But the value of the financial assets that were confiscated in 1995 was less than $4 million U.S. dollars, while the Department of Justice had estimated revenues of about $16 million. One of the reasons for this rather poor result, apart from the mixed reception of the legislation by police, public prosecution, and the judicature, is the fact criminals are very creative in hiding their financial assets. One of the most frequently used hiding methods is concluding fake lease contracts for expensive yachts and high-performance cars, which in criminal circles are also status symbols by eminence. To the outside world, these objects are still formally the property of leasing companies. However, often these goods have been secretly paid for and lease contracts are fraudulently drawn up. Another problem is the calculation of the profits that criminals have made with their illegal activities. In a number of court cases, defense lawyers have successfully claimed that the expenses of their clients in running the criminal enterprises were so high, that almost no profits were made. As a result, already seized assets had to be given back. Other reasons for the disappointing results of asset-removal legislation have been the specific problems in seizing objects abroad. They are the result of differences in jurisdiction and cultural factors. Still, at the international level, too, there are positive results. Last year, for instance, a Dutch investigation team successfully appealed to the Turkish judicial authorities for confiscation of four hotels in Istanbul.

Just as with the Disclosure of Unusual Transactions legislation, it has been found that enforcing a new act easily produces problems in practice. Only an integral approach to the problem, with active participation of all social parties involved, will yield positive results. Furthermore, the experience with the two measures evaluated so far points to the importance of intelligence gathering and analyzing, not only regarding criminal activities, but regarding financial aspects as well.

CIUs are playing the principal role in the so-called "proactive phase" of the investigation procedure. In this phase no arrests have yet been made or house searches carried out, and data are collected only about the nature of the criminal activities and the structure of the criminal group. The CIUs gather information by deploying various methods of investigation, such as working with informers, observation, analyzing information from previous investigations, and collecting financial information. CIU investigators consider it their primary task to protect their sources of information. If they leave them unprotected, they run the risk of seeing them dried up soon. Their performance is dominated by finding an answer to the question, "How do we make CIU information operational?" Or, said differently, "How do we inform the tactical CIU without putting the informer at risk?" As a result, the CIU cannot always comply with the need for information that exists with the tactical investigation department. Some information cannot be released for reasons of safety. In practice, CIUs give tips as to the direction in which the tactical investigation should be aimed.

The relationship between the tactical criminal investigation department and the CIU is complicated. Often, the CIU knows more than the tactical investigation department. It is estimated that between 10 and 50 percent of the CIU information is effectively utilized in a tactical investigation (Enquêtecommissie Opsporingsmethoden, 1996, p. 56). This implies that much information is gathered without being used in an actual investigation. It also occurs that the CIU does not have the information that tactical criminal investigators require. Finally, there is the secrecy that the CIU sometimes maintains toward the tactical investigation department, and which sometimes results in troublesome relations.

The aforementioned factors are also active between CIUs themselves. Until recently, the focus of CIUs was on local and regional crime. As a result, they did not feel the need for interregional cooperation. Organized crime, however, is not bothered by national borders and certainly not the borders of police regions. Sometimes, insufficient cooperation results in duplication of running informants and in unavailability of relevant information. Partly, the reservations on the part of CIUs have been based on their desire to keep information for themselves only. The danger of information leakage was considered to be too great. Primarily, the CIU focuses on the traditional criminal world, in which drug trafficking stands out. The CIUs nowadays have insufficient know-how to be able to tackle other areas of crime. CIU informers mostly have information about drug crime and serious property crime (e.g., robberies). CIUs hardly ever have informants in other areas of organized crime, such as fraud and environmental crime. Apparently, the division between upper and underworld also exists with CIUs.

Although crime analysis is becoming an important tool, it is important to distinguish between its various objectives and areas of focus. An understanding of the data on crime is important, both with regard to specific investigations and in determining a certain policy directed toward the prevention and detection of crime. Consequently, there is a distinction between the operational forms of analysis, which specifically focus on resolving a crime or series of crimes, and the strategic forms, which are focused on policymaking.

Strategic analysis aims to provide a helicopter view, to identify trends in crime, and alert the appropriate law enforcement agencies. This allows for the initiation of long-term plans of action directed toward the emergence of crime, rather than a mere reaction to single criminal incidents. In this way, operational activities can be directed and investigation services can determine their targets. The most frequently used strategic form of crime analysis is "crime pattern analysis." The idea is to form a picture of the nature and scale of the crime in a particular area. According to the need, the area may be a country, a police region, or a city. Examples are the national surveys on organized crime in The Netherlands referred to earlier.

Operational forms of crime analysis can help a police officer gain insight and make information collected in concrete investigations accessible; they can also clarify areas in which information is insufficient or indicate if the various bits of information that have been gathered are conflicting. Operational crime analysis can be a very helpful means during the investigation, particularly in complex cases with a lengthy time span, cases that involve a great many subjects, in which the information is rather chaotic, or for whatever other reason, is incomprehensible and not straightforward.

The best known operational form of crime analysis in The Netherlands is "offender group analysis." The general idea is to present with the use of several kinds of charts as clearly as possible the available information regarding the relationships among the probable members of a criminal organization and their contacts. Often the top of a criminal group has stopped its involvement in detectable criminal activities. The top hides behind front companies and other facades and uses the most modern communication techniques to give orders without being recognized or tracked. Therefore, long lines of communication and command must be examined and analyzed.

It is incorrect to regard crime analysis as a new phenomenon that has appeared only recently. In some cases, the way in which the crime analyst looks at data on crime is no different from the perspective of the police officer who has been doing the very same since time immemorial without ever dreaming of calling himself a crime analyst. However, in some aspects, their jobs and methods differ. First, the analyst's job is to analyze the available information, not to collect it (as this would mean moving too much into the field of investigation). The analyst adopts the position of the objective assessor of information and would be hindered if he were to collect the information himself. Second, a crime analyst tries to make intelligence out of raw data. The analyst determines the reliability and value of the information collected as accurately as possible. The analyst does not look at the significance of the separate bits of information only, but composes an overall picture that is as comprehensive as possible.

Crime analysis was introduced in The Netherlands ten years ago. Since then, it has proven to be a useful tool for crime control, especially when organized criminal groups are the subject of investigation. It is now normal to conduct an offender group or case analysis before starting a large crime investigation. Strategic crime analysis is used both at the regional and national levels to determine which criminal groups should be tackled first. Crime analysis has proven to be very successful. Today it is a very significant tool for the police, especially in combating organized crime.

Still, there is criticism from some on the present crime analysis activities carried out in The Netherlands. Criminologists find that crime analysts are one-sidedly oriented to information that is relevant to prosecution. According to some heads of investigative teams, the charting techniques used by analysts result in beautiful images, which leads one to believe evidence can be picked up everywhere. Also, the relational diagram of an offender group would often mistakenly suggest that there is a hierarchical structure. In reality, such a chart has the status of a hypothesis, which, later on in the investigation, may be confirmed or may have to be rejected. In strategic analysis the findings are strongly affected by the way in which information is gathered and recorded. The quality of analysis, be it operational or strategic, is primarily dependent on the availability and quality of the underlying information. Professionally dealing with available data will extract all the intelligence it contains. However, it will not be a guarantee that the only possible solution of the criminal investigation will be found. Crime analysis does not lead to results that meet scientific standards of reliability and validity. Therefore, more information must be supplied to (potential) users of analysis reports, to acquaint them with the possibilities and the limitations of crime analysis.

The Penal Approach

With all the measures taken, one would expect that the combat of organized crime in The Netherlands has been successful. Earlier this year an evaluation was concluded of the repressive approach to organized crime groups (Hesseling and Neefe, 1996). The researchers investigated how many of the organized groups that were recorded with CIUs in 1991 have had dealings with the police and the judiciary in the meantime. Arrests and convictions of 260 core members of the 58 crime groups concerned were considered. Only half of them were arrested on one or more occasions as crime suspects. Not every police booking will lead to a trial in court. Between 1991 and 1995, 78 persons were convicted by a court (i.e., 30 percent of the total number of core members). Considering the data at group level, it is found that some of the core members of most organized groups have been convicted in court. Of the 58 groups, only five saw all of their core members convicted. Of one-third of the organized groups active in The Netherlands in 1991, not a single core member has been convicted in the past five years. This rather poor result appears to contradict the priority that has been given since the mid 1980s to tackling organized crime.

The researchers name a number of possible causes of the apparent insufficiency of the penal approach of organized crime. First, they refer to the fact that the study is based on CIU registers, which mainly contain soft information. Investigations may reveal that registered persons have actually played no role or a less prominent role in criminal activities than had been indicated at the time by the CIU source. Second, it may occur that an investigation fails to make good progress, for instance, in the case of a foreign criminal group. Third, some investigations are unsuccessful in finding legal evidence of someone's involvement in punishable activities. Fourth, the judicial handling of a case may take a very long time. Evaluations have established that this is the case where the matter concerns a charge of membership of an outlawed organization and in drug offenses. So there is always the chance of a number of core members being convicted later. Fifth, it is possible that police forces chose other criminal groups to combat instead of the ones registered in the national survey. It is important to point out that the study dealt with the groups mentioned in the 1991 inventory and that in The Netherlands, national priorities have been set only since 1993. It is unknown which factor is the principal barrier to an effective approach to organized crime. Presumably, it is a combination of these conditions.

In 1994, two years after formal realization of most of the core teams, a first attempt at evaluating them was made; however, it was a failure, since many of the teams were still engaged in their first inquiries. Becoming operational had brought with it bureaucratic growing pains. Apparently the setting up of multi-agency teams tends to lead to problems in the field of responsibilities, competence, and legal position. Moreover, experiences teach that investigations into international organized criminal groups often take more than two years. Some of them have been going on for as many as three years.

Another problem is the manner in which a selection is made of which criminal group will be dealt with. In 1993, a special national council was established to address just this issue: the Coordinating Policy Council (CBO), led by a prosecutor-general and composed of chief public prosecutors responsible for the penal policy of core teams. The decision as to which criminal groupings are targeted is based on the results of the national inventories on organized crime in The Netherlands. The regional police forces oppose the central role of the CBO, which they consider as interfering with matters of regional importance. The competence of the CBO, however, is outweighed by the monopoly the regional police forces have regarding information. Their influence lies in the data they supply to the benefit of the national inventories. Some of the regional forces are reluctant to supply information, as they do not want the results of the inventories to be used for priorities-setting, since they are not in a position to exercise much influence on the outcome of the analyses. The core teams also do not seem to be happy with the role of the CBO. In many cases they do not fulfill their obligation to draw up action plans and inform the CBO on progress made during an investigation. Sometimes an investigation almost automatically passes into another investigation, because the borders of a criminal network can hardly be defined and the investigators simply continue their work by following leads to other suspects. These are the reasons why core teams select investigations rather at random, and their choice is especially determined by previous investigations and by regional preferences. National considerations and the wish for an adequate approach to internationally operating criminal groups play a minor role in the setting of priorities.

In a number of cases, the core teams have been successful. They have found ways to get hold of the leaders of criminal organizations, although great efforts were necessary to achieve results. However, these leaders sometimes continue giving direction to criminal activities from the prisons or penitentiaries they are in. Lower-ranking criminals are often not prosecuted and are detained for a short while only or not at all, allowing them to use their knowledge and experience for starting their own criminal enterprises or for assisting others. The know-how and experience of the dismantled group is thus a seed for another round of criminal organized activities.

Although it is still too early for a final conclusion, it seems that the repressive approach by big, multi-disciplinary teams has not worked very well, due to the dynamics, the network characteristics, and the shields developed by the criminal organizations. Another disadvantage for the core teams is the inadequate organization in the field of investigation. Priorities are not well considered, cooperation between the different disciplines represented in the teams is not always smooth, and the duration of investigations results in fatigue and loss of motivation.

Parliamentary Inquiry Into Investigation Methods

Partly because of the almost complete shielding off of the CIUs from other parts of the police organization, some very serious incidents have occurred in recent times (e.g., the conscious release of drugs into the criminal market with a view to having an undercover agent rise in the hierarchy of a criminal organization). There were other reasons to let drugs pass. If a criminal organization wanted to test a smuggling route before sending off a large consignment, the small quantity used for the test would be allowed to go through. Also, larger consignments have sometimes been allowed through in order to get a better insight into the role of the various members of a criminal organization. In recent years, tons of cannabis products and hundreds of kilograms of cocaine have been taken to the market with the knowledge of the police and the judiciary. In some cases, these methods have achieved the effect desired, and the criminal organizations concerned could be dismantled. But it also happened that the free passage of drugs has not led to the arrest of the top leaders of an organization.

The unsuccessful end to some cases and the disagreement within police and justice circles about the admissibility of this investigation method resulted in the disbandment at the end of 1993 of an interregional investigation team. After investigations into the matter had been held by a specially appointed committee as well as a parliamentary working group, the Dutch parliament requested a special inquiry into police investigative practices. In June 1994, the Minister of Justice instituted such an inquiry to be carried out by a committee consisting of seven members of parliament, under chairmanship of MP Maarten van Traa. In February 1996, the Van Traa committee presented its findings. The general conclusion was that the investigation into organized crime in The Netherlands suffers from a threefold crisis. First, standards are lacking. The legislature and also the judiciary have given too much leeway to the police and the judicial authorities. Second, there is inadequate coordination of the investigation. Investigation agencies often do not work together—they rather tend to work against one another, and the registration of investigation activities often plays a small role. In the opinion of the committee, the crisis within the organization manifests itself mainly in unclear decisions regarding who is responsible for what. The areas of authority and the responsibilities of many of those involved are vague. Third, the public prosecutions department does not exercise sufficient control over the police. Although the public prosecutions department's authority over the police in The Netherlands is explicitly provided for by law, in practice this does not always appear to be taken as a matter of course.

In short, the Van Traa committee came to the general conclusion that the crisis within the Dutch investigation agencies runs deep and even touches upon the legitimacy of law enforcement. Those responsible in the police, the public prosecutions department, and the Ministries of Internal Affairs and Justice have exercised insufficient authority. But the parliamentary committee also recognized that there was a political shortfall in regard to the provision of legislation and in the setting of standards. The parliamentary inquiry led to the dismissal of one of the five prosecutors-general, the secretary general of the Ministry of Justice, and the head of a regional CIU. Furthermore, a number of public prosecutors and chiefs of police were given positions elsewhere. The parliamentary committee justly commented that the crisis in investigation and prosecution could not be solved by some drastic short-term measures. It was stated that a reform was necessary with regard to investigation so that long-term solutions could be sought.

A vision about a future approach to organized crime must, on one hand, be based on an assessment of nature, size, and development of organized crime and, on the other, on a recognition of the possibilities and restrictions of measures taken in the past. Only in this broad perspective will an idea be created of what must happen to arrive at a more effective approach. In recent years, the approach to organized crime has rapidly developed in new directions. It is widely recognized that the approach should be supra-regional, interdisciplinary, and integral. Although the police and judiciary have not succeeded in gaining terrain on organized crime, it can be said that the last few years have seen a stabilization, after the strong rise in the preceding decade.

It has also been seen that dismantling groups of offenders does not automatically lead to a reduction of organized crime. In fact, any vacuum in a dynamic market soon gets filled by new groups. Elimination of a drug gang also entails a temporary shortage of drugs on the market, resulting in a price increase and more profits for other groups. Legislation, too, has limited effect on organized crime. Foreign criminal groups no longer launder their profits through Dutch banking institutions, but take cash money abroad. They use all sorts of property schemes to prevent their criminal assets from being confiscated (Akse, 1996).

It is, therefore, being realized that the traditional penal approach must be altered. Traditional penal law is based on trying separate criminal incidents by individual suspects and is therefore not fitted for tackling organized criminal groups. Furthermore, the criminal prosecution and procedural possibilities always lag behind the latest trends in organized crime. Therefore, there is the need to spend more energy on the preventive aspect of countering crime.

The Netherlands enforcement agencies have understood that the condition for effective prevention measures is insight into the way in which organized crime arises and the conditions that stimulate or slow down its growth. This analysis of the structural opportunities open to organized crime has developed into what is called "phenomenon research." This type of research is focusing on identifying and tackling the criminogenic factors like structural characteristics of an economic branch, a geographical area, a criminal market, or another segment of society that contribute to the rise or growth of organized crime.

This phenomenon research approach has yielded encouraging success in Amsterdam, where investigations revealed that exchange offices in the city center were involved in criminal activities. There were approximately one hundred such offices in the center, and analysis established that the exchange transactions by tourists could not make these offices cost-effective. It was further found that there were a number of clusters of offices, owned by a small number of families. One family was subjected to further investigations. In seven months they had a turnover of $100 million U.S. dollars, while the exchange transactions with tourists only accounted for 10 percent of this amount. The phenomenon research project originated from a law, which provided that a license was needed to run an exchange office and that exchange officers were under the supervision of the Dutch Central Bank. Since the act came into effect, the number of exchange offices in Amsterdam has diminished considerably.

Typical of phenomenon research is the use of information from open sources, such as the press and criminological literature and from restricted sources, such as the databases of the Chambers of Commerce and the Land Registry Office. Data from police investigations also contribute to getting a good picture of the area under study. Authorities are developing a procedure whereby if something is possibly wrong in the area, a draft risk model is quickly drawn up, by means of which a special inventory can be made of possible wrongdoing enterprises and groups.

A draft risk model describes the impact of sector characteristics and social process on the vulnerability of a certain sector to penetration by organized crime groups. An example is the waste processing industry in The Netherlands. With the strict environmental protection regulations drawn up by the central government in recent years, legal processing of all sorts of waste has become much more expensive. As a consequence it has become more lucrative to observe the rules in theory, while in reality, disposing of waste in all sorts of illegal ways. Companies that process waste find it easier to mix waste flows and thereby evade detection. This risk factor analysis has opened the possibility of making new legislation that further criminalizes such practices and which therefore gives clear direction for prosecution.

Another risk modeling project has identified the manner in which an illegal product or service is produced and distributed. This type of "logistics" modeling was developed by the German Federal Criminal Police Office (BKA) a few years ago (Sieber and Bögel, 1993). It is based upon the idea that organized crime shows many businesslike structures as well as economically oriented planning. If it is true that legal and illegal business activities are similar, the logistic processes of organized crime can be analyzed from the point of view of legal business practices. From the end product it can be deduced which activities must be carried out. The following phases have been distinguished in the amphetamine production and trafficking process: acquiring the necessary chemicals, equipment, and knowledge (precursor phase), processing (production phase), smuggling (transport phase), wholesale (distribution phase), and peddling (sales phase). Critical analysis of weak spots in the criminal business process is giving new insight into ways of blocking these criminal actions. In the case of synthetic drugs, the inquiry has focused on the availability of certain chemicals required in the processing. On the basis of a recent phenomenon study, researchers recommended not only the introduction of a licensing system, but also that agreements with the chemical industry should be made requiring the reporting to the police of unusual transactions with certain chemicals. Such a licensing system is now under preparation.

Such examples of phenomenon research are giving an insight into the relation between upper world and underworld and, with that, of society's vulnerability. On the basis of such insight, a structural approach is being developed, both preventive and repressive, that is likely to prove more effective against organized crime. The insight into the vulnerability of (parts of) society is also succeeding in making the public figures, authorities, professional groups, and industrial sectors more aware of the risk and, as a consequence, more able to defend themselves.

Conclusion

Organized crime knows so many ways to manifest itself that it is impossible to develop a blueprint for the strategy to combat it. An integral approach characterized by a smooth and dynamic adjustment to the various and constantly changing manifestations of organized crime is the most obvious solution. Knowledge about the nature and development of organized crime is a basic and primary requirement. This realization has spurred The Netherlands authorities not only to examine the overt criminal activities, the operations of different known organized groups, but also to undertake a deeper look into the sociopolitical and economic factors that promote such crimes. This has assisted in not only developing new crime investigation techniques, creation of specialized units to combat organized crime, but also new legislative measures that prevent loopholes exploited by these groups. A more remarkable measure has been the development of phenomenon research and risk modeling that are empowering the enforcement agencies and bringing together the many other agencies in the fight against organized crime. Such measures have to continue and new ones have to be found, since organized crime by its very nature also keeps changing and attempts to find every loophole to flourish. It is therefore crucial that empirical findings and theoretical insights on the nature of organized crime are constantly exchanged among all who are involved in the combat. This process takes a lot of time and effort, but it does eventually lead to desirable results.

REFERENCES

Akse, T. 1996. "Undergroundbanking in Nederland." (Underground banking in The Netherlands.) *Modus* 4 (Jaargang 5): 14–17.

Annual report of the Office for the Disclosure of Unusual Transactions. 1996, Zoetermeer.

Enquêtecommissie Opsporingsmethoden. 1996. "Inzake opsporing." (Enquiry committee on investigative methods: Concerning investigations). Bijlage VII, Tweede Kamer, vergaderjaar 1995–1996, 24,072 nr. 16: 24–25; 55–56; 317.

Hesseling, R., and M. Neefe. 1996. "Gepakt en gestraft?" (Caught and punished?) Divisie Centrale Recherche Informatie & Ministerie van Justitie, Zoetermeer/Den Haag.

Ministerie van Justitie. 1997. "Begroting." (Budget Plan 1997 of the Ministry of Justice). Tweede Kamer, vergaderjaar 1996–1997, 25,000 hoofdstuk VI, (2): 9.

Nelen, J.M., and V. Sabee. 1996. "Het vermogen te ontnemen." (The power to confiscate.) Arnhem, Gouda Quint.

Samenleving en criminaliteit. 1985. "Een beleidsplan voor de komende jaren." (Society and crime. A policy plan for the coming years.) Tweede Kamer 2 (1984–1985): 46–47.

Sieber, U., and M. Bögel. 1993. "Logistik der Organisierten Kriminalität. (The logistics of organized crime.) BKA Forschungsreihe nr. 28. Bundeskriminalamt, Wiesbaden.

Terlouw, G.J., and U. Aron. 1996. "Twee jaar MOT. Een evaluatie van de uitvoering van de Wet melding ongebruikelijke transacties." (Two years ODUT. An evaluation of the implementation of the Law on Questionable Transactions.) Gouda Quint.

van der Heijden; Weimar, E.C.J., and P. Minnebo. 1991. "Misdaadanalyse in Nederland." (Crime analysis in The Netherlands.) *Justitiële Verkenningen* (1991): 50–69.

van Zwam, Henk. 1996. Personal communication: leader of the Interregional Investigation Team North and East Netherlands, 1 November, 1996.

CHAPTER 5

ORGANIZED CRIME: A PERSPECTIVE FROM POLAND AND EASTERN EUROPE

Emil W. Plywaczewski

INTRODUCTION

Poland is the eighth largest country in Europe, both in size (122,148 square miles) and population (38.6 million), with 62 percent of the population living in urban areas. After the breakdown of the communist system in mid 1989, Poland is in a transition from a centrally planned economy to a market-oriented and democratic system. Political changes and law reforms have been initiated with the amendment of the Polish Constitution made by the parliament in December 1989.

All criminal offenses are classified as either felonies or misdemeanors. Felonies include the violent crimes of homicide, aggravated forcible rape, and robbery; serious crimes can warrant the death penalty, too. Most other crimes are misdemeanor offenses: theft, fraud, embezzlement, burglary, assault, unintentional homicide, bigamy, incest, and breach of a state secret. From 1985 to 1995 Poland has experienced a considerable growth of crime. Police statistics show that the overall number of crimes has increased by 80 percent during that time (from 544,361 in 1985 to 974,941 in 1995). In some categories of hard-core criminality like a homicide, robbery, or burglary, the rate of increase is two or even threefold.

The Minister of Justice exercises the powers of the Attorney General and administers the criminal justice system controlling the police, prosecution, and the prison system. The judiciary is the independent branch of the government. All courts are presided by judges who are appointed by the president on the recommendation of the National Council of Judiciary. The police are centrally organized under the authority of a commander, who works under the Minister of Interior. Police duties, to a limited extent, are also carried out by municipal guards who deal with the maintenance of public order in urban areas. The national police are divided into six basic departments, as stipulated by the Police Act of 1990: criminal police, traffic police, prevention and anti-terrorists squads, special police (e.g., railway and river), local police, and other police agencies appointed by the Minister of the Interior, if necessary.

Organized crime has been identified in various United Nations forums as one of the most pernicious forms of criminality (United Nations Economic and Social Council, 1993 and 1994). Its dimensions are yet to be measured and the full impact is yet to be determined. Such crime constitutes an underground economic system, the gross product and net gain of which perhaps exceeds the gross national product (GNP) of some countries. Organized crime can be described as commissions of criminal actions that are, individually or jointly, of a serious nature and perpetrated in planned manner with a view to profit. It involves a group of two or more persons, each of whom has a specific task to perform and who makes use of business-related structures, as well as violence or other means of intimidation, and exerts influence over politicians, the media, government, criminal justice authorities, or the economy. Organized criminal groups have been engaged in activities such as international car theft, black-market trade in nuclear materials, smuggling of migrants, arms trafficking, trade in human organs, and money laundering (Interpol, 1995).

According to the General Secretariat of the International Criminal Police Organization (Interpol), organized crime is "any enterprise or group of persons engaged in a continuing illegal activity which has as its primary purpose the generation of profits, irrespective of national boundaries." For the purposes of this definition: "enterprise or group of persons" includes any association of criminals, whether working in organizations such as large corporations with internal rules and established hierarchies or operating together for a common purpose. "Activity" means any singular criminal activity or a multiplicity of criminal activities and "Irrespective of national boundaries" means international or ramifications of the activity which are international.

For the purposes of the United Nations documents, organized crime means any offense, committed by a member of a criminal organization which is a part of the criminal activity of such organization. Criminal organization means a permanent group, consisting of three or more persons, and established in order to commit the following offenses:

a. Illicit traffic in drugs or psychotropic substances as defined in Article 1(m) of the United Nations Convention Against Illicit Traffic in Drugs and Psychotropic Substances of 19 December 1988;
b. Counterfeiting currency as defined in the Article 3 of the International Convention for the Suppression of Counterfeiting Currency of 20 April 1929;
c. Terrorist acts as defined in the Article 1 of the European Convention of the Suppression of Terrorism of 27 January 1977;
d. Extortion of money or another material benefit by threat of an attempt against life or health or violent attack against property;
e. Theft of cars and traffic in stolen cars;
f. Illegal traffic in arms, explosive material or devices, or radioactive materials;
g. Money-laundering offenses as defined in Article 6 of the European Convention on Laundering, Search, Seizure, and Confiscation of the Proceeds from Crime of 8 November 1990;
h. Traffic in Persons as defined in the Convention for the Suppression of the Traffic in Persons and the Exploitation of the Prostitution of Others of 2 December 1949;
i. Fraudulent cross-border transportation of goods; and
j. Theft of art objects and traffic in stolen art objects.

According to the Economic and Social Council of the United Nations, five essential common elements in the criminal phenomena of organized crime and terrorism can be identified as:

1. They are usually associative crimes;
2. They invoke the solidarity of associations of persons with a covert link between the individuals for the achievement of the goals of the interested group only;
3. The associative crime involves the development of a criminal organization that sometimes assumes very sophisticated forms of functional integration;
4. The crimes almost always have some connection with power, either economic or political;
5. The crimes have a criminal phenomenology whose methods totally reject every mechanism of democratic consensus.

Each one of these elements has a major social and political importance, has been the focus of scholarly attention, but has not been dealt with from the standpoint of the necessary changes in the methods and approaches for their prevention and control (UN, 1993; UN Commission on Crime Prevention and Criminal Justice, 1994).

THE NATURE AND EXTENT OF ORGANIZED CRIME

The nature and extent of organized crime in Poland and other post-communist countries in Central and Eastern Europe is closely linked to the following groups, most of which are also known internationally. In alphabetical order these are: Chinese Triads, Colombian cartels, Jamaican posses, Japanese Yakuza, Sicilian Mafia, Russian criminal organizations, and West African groups such as Nigerian organized crime groups. Certainly, some other groups could be added, but the seven mentioned are the most widely recognized and perhaps the most dangerous. Some of these groups have long traditions, such as the Asian gangs and the Sicilian Mafia, while others are relatively young, such as Colombian cartels and the Russian criminal organizations. Some others, such as the Nigerian groups, have come to global attention only in the last few years (Savona, Adamoli, Zoffi, and DeFeo, 1995).

Russian Criminal Organizations

Russian organized crime groups are attracting worldwide attention, especially after the breakup of the country, although Russian criminal organizations are not an entirely new phenomenon (Serio, 1993). The underground economy and the pervasive corruption provided the potential for organized crime in the erstwhile Soviet Union, but it was kept under control by the dominance of the communist party. Once the reforms initiated by Gorbachev dismantled the mechanism of social, political, and economic control, these groups came to the forefront. The collapse of the Communist Party and with it the Soviet state has also weakened the system of criminal justice. The new environment is very permissive for organized crime with few laws against criminal associations and continued inefficiencies in the economic system that permit criminal enterprises to flourish (Gilinskiy, 1996). The transition to the market economy is also being carried out without a clear regulatory framework. Russia tried to develop a free market without the system of rules and regulations that are necessary to ensure its integrity, efficiency, and effectiveness. At the same time the end of the Cold War made it easier for the groups in the former Soviet Union to engage in transnational criminal activity. The result has been a consolidation of existing criminal groups, the rise of new organizations, and the diversification of criminal activity (Johnson, 1995).

There are several major kinds of criminal enterprise in which these groups are engaged. In addition to old-style party officials who misused their position, there are also many ethnic-based groups. These include Georgian organized crime groups, which controlled much of the black market under the communist system. Subsequently extending the range of these activities, the Chechens and Azerbaijani groups, and others account for a major upsurge in illicit trafficking, not only in drugs, but also in metals, weapons, nuclear materials, and even body parts. These organizations clearly operate with little regard for national boundaries. In addition to the smuggling of nuclear material from the former USSR, other metals such as magnesium have also been stolen and sold in Western Europe. Moreover, these groups have infiltrated the Russian banking system and have been unscrupulous in their use of intimidation and violence against bankers and businessmen who were not cooperative. As a result, banking in particular has become a high-risk profession in Russia (Ponomarev, 1996).

Furthermore, the top leadership of the criminal world has been spending considerable time and money to infiltrate or influence government structures. It is alleged that several senior officers in the executive or the legislative branches of government are in league with criminal ringleaders. In Moscow alone, twenty-two assistants to deputies of the State Duma have been arrested this year for their dealings with the criminal world. All these facts indicate that the wave of organized crime continues to sweep across Russia. This wave is widening and is penetrating deeper into society as well as government structures. There is widespread belief that almost 70 percent of the country is controlled by the Mafia.

The most productive activities of Russian organized crime groups have been described as the theft of antiques and their smuggling to the West, prostitution, car thefts, the arms trade, and narcotics. Many other activities can also be added to the list. Russian organized crime groups belong to the prototype of "opportunistic organized crime," operating in the domestic and international market. Like the Sicilian Mafia, they concentrate at the local level on keeping control over their territory by excluding criminal rivals. At the transnational level, they use their capabilities in smuggling or any other activity that presents the opportunity of a profit, from cars to arms, medicines, and drugs to raw materials. Many larger Russian organized crime groups have also spread their activities to other countries, including the United States (*Newsweek*, 1993). Among the most important groups are the Odessa organized crime groups (based in Brighton Beach, NY, but also active in California), the Chechens, who typically specialize in contract murder and extortion, and the Malina (Organizatsiay, a multiethnic group in Brighton Beach, NY, which maintains extensive international ties in the areas of drug trafficking, credit card fraud, extortion, and tax fraud). There is evidence of relationship with Colombians and with Italian Mafias, too.

The Situation in Poland

This country is becoming the bridge between western and eastern criminal organizations. Since the disruption created by the war in Bosnia-Herzegovina, Poland has replaced the Balkans as a favored route for heroin, hashish, and other drugs smuggled to the West. Poland's amphetamine industry constitutes the most sophisticated indigenous narcotics enterprise. In Warsaw, the so-called Russian market, located near an old soccer stadium along the Vistula River, has become a major arms bazaar. Poland reportedly loses $38 billion U.S. dollars a year in tax revenue to alcohol and cigarette smuggling. Polish police have reported many attempts at smuggling radioactive materials through Poland to the West. The transport of stolen cars from the West to the former Soviet States occurrs through Poland. Finally, there has been a dramatic rise in intravenous drug abuse in Warsaw. According to the police, there are 293 dangerous gangs with 4,000 members throughout Poland. Many deal in drugs, launder and forge money, falsify documents, and export protection money from legitimate business people. Enforcement agencies too have sounded the alarm that new forms of organized crime are emerging—often as the result of the dramatic political, economic, and technological changes of the 1990s. Criminal groups have been increasingly taking advantage of looser border controls and the movement toward free trade to launch or expand such activities as international car theft, black-market trade in nuclear materials, smuggling of migrants, arms trafficking, trade in human donor organs, environmental crime, computer tampering, and money laundering.

Judging from the extremely high purity of the final product, criminal drug manufacturing groups apparently use first-class laboratory equipment and highly qualified chemists. Like successful trafficking organizations elsewhere, Polish amphetamine gangs are starting to buy in the legal economy. Moreover, outside Poland, especially in Germany and in the Scandinavian countries, they operate through a network of Polish citizens who serve as critical links in the wholesale trade. This network can move any type of drug into Western markets: Central Asian hashish, Afghan heroin, and Colombian cocaine. The Cali cartel recruited Polish couriers to smuggle cocaine across the Polish-German border. An increasing involvement of organized gangs in large-scale car theft and money laundering has also been reported. While Polish authorities reject the use of the term

"Mafia" for Polish gangs, there are well-organized groups that control prostitution, extort protection money from legitimate businesses, smuggle drugs on a large scale, and have infiltrated the criminal justice system. Polish criminals have made their country the fourth largest European producer of illegal amphetamines, after the Netherlands, Great Britain, and Belgium.

According to police data, in the years 1993 and 1994 several highly organized criminal groups specializing in the following activities were recorded:

1. Illegal production of and trafficking in drugs and psychotropic substances—16 groups
2. Internal trafficking in stolen cars—13 groups
3. Forging legal tenders and trafficking in them—7 groups
4. Trafficking in radioactive substances and rare metals—4 groups
5. Trafficking in firearms—2 groups

Many groups from Russia, Ukraine, Lithuania, Yugoslavia, and Albania also act inside Poland. Apart from that, there have been the first signs of criminal activity carried out by Vietnamese groups in Poland. More and more frequent signs that Polish criminal structures are connected with Italian, Asian, and South American organizations speak for the fact that Polish crime is becoming increasingly international. The process of forming criminal structures in Poland has not been finished yet. Most of these groups are young and will undergo different phases of restructuring. However, the existing trends indicate that structural changes within groups functioning in Poland will take place in the oncoming years.

Groups dealing with production of and trafficking in drugs, car theft and smuggling, smuggling of consumer goods, or transfer of people across the border, consist of people of different nationalities, and the scope of activity is international. However, there are groups cooperating internationally that do not form a homogeneous structure. Within each of these groups there are subgroups or teams of criminals specializing in particular activities (e.g., car thieves, document forgers, couriers, receivers of stolen property, or others) (Holyst, 1996). In Poland, the activities that involve money laundering take the external form of legal financial transactions (e.g., banking operations), legal transactions violating particular administrative arrangements (e.g., safety standards in the banking system), or illegal operations forbidden by proper regulations and threatened with economic and penal law sanctions. They constitute methods of money laundering, understood by Polish police as a set of criminal behavior connected with financial operations, and create a model that determines the extent and possibility of using these operations in money laundering (Plywaczewski, 1996).

The Czech Republic

This country, as a part of the Czech and Slovak Federal Republic before January 1993, and separately thereafter, has followed an active privatization program. The news media have given extensive coverage to the alleged presence of organized crime groups from Italy and the former republics of the USSR in the Republic, allegedly investing illegal proceeds or conducting drug trafficking and other illegal activities. Organized crime groups in Prague, the capital, include Russians, Italians, Ukrainians, Yugoslavians, Bulgarians, and even Chinese. There has not been real rivalry between the clans thus far, because they have divided spheres of influence and are cooperating: Russian organized crime focuses on heroin trafficking, while organized crime groups from the former Soviet Union smuggle opiates from Central Asia together with the Balkan organized crime groups. The Arab groups deal in hashish and the Chinese focus on restaurants.

An especially important sphere in which organized crime is finding favorable conditions is the economy. Economic transformation has brought in its wake completely new forms of economic crime added to the conventional forms, linked with operation of state-owned and cooperative companies. At this stage, economic reform in the Czech Republic is still in the process of implementing the theoretical concepts and organized crime in the field of economy has not yet acquired the dimensions and forms that are found in countries with advanced market economies. It should be noted, however, that new types of economic crime had been recorded in the Czech Republic as early as 1990 and that there is clear evidence of their growth both in terms of volume and sophistication. The efforts of the criminal underworld at penetrating all areas of public administration, judiciary and police are expected to further increase with the aim of obtaining a greater influence on the management of the country and its institutions to meet their specific interests. The forms of these efforts are varying, ranging from kidnapping of children and relatives of the rich and the resulting extortion, corruption, defamation, and scandalization to murders of unyielding and incorruptible persons. It may be assumed that the organized character of crime, including international connections, will increase in intensity. It is realistic to expect a struggle of individual gangs for gaining influence through account-settling encounters.

The Slovak Republic

The Slovak Republic is another young country that came into being 1 January 1993, as a result of the division of the former Czech and Slovak Federal Republic. Organized crime taking place in the Slovak Republic has both conventional and new forms. The conventional forms of crime have been here for a long time and they have kept their important position in the crime hierarchy. However, they have "modernized" by adopting foreign models and their scope has been steadily increasing. The conventional forms of organized crime include: loan sharking, organized prostitution, narcotics, illegal trade in antiques, trade in stolen cars and automobile parts, illegal arms trade, counterfeiting money, securities, public papers, sale of stolen goods, and burglary.

New forms of organized crime reflect the current social and economic changes, emerging as a function of the process of transformation from the socialist system to a market economy. Because economic reform in this country has only been undergoing the process of passing from the stage of concept formulation to that of implementation, economic crime has not yet reached the dimensions it has in more economically advanced countries. The majority of new forms of organized crime are economic in character. New forms of organized crime include tax evasion, illegal activities connected with privatization, illegal penetration of foreign entities into state economy, trade with strategic materials, racketeering or extortion of "protection" money, illegal transit and procuring jobs for illegal aliens, violence for hire, environmental crime, computer crime, and kidnapping for ransom (Holdos, 1995).

The Baltic States

The growth of organized criminality in the Baltic region has become international in nature; local and foreign criminal groups use the area as both an operating and transiting zone. Their activities have rapidly expanded across existing national frontiers as both commerce and travel have increased between the countries of Western and Eastern Europe. Countries in Scandinavia and Western Europe have seen criminal groups from the East operate either independently or jointly with local groups. Criminal activities have included smuggling, drug trafficking and distribution, alien smuggling, money laundering, the illegal transfer of capital, prostitution, and illegal trade in stolen vehicles, arms, goods, antiques, strategic metal, and radioactive substances. There has also been an upturn in the degree of violence associated with many crimes.

The Baltic region has become a major transshipment point for the flow of drugs from the cultivation and production areas in central Asia, and Southeast and Southwest Asia to the markets in Scandinavia and Western Europe. Many of the drug shipments find their way into and through the Baltic States from neighboring states such as Russia (including

Kaliningrad), Belarus, Ukraine, and Poland. The war in the former Yugoslavia has also rerouted the drug flow that once went through the Balkans, so that the Baltic States have now become an important route. In addition, the raw materials used to process the various types of lethal drugs have been coming into the region via this route (Skrastnis, 1996). The Baltic States have increased organized crime-sponsored violence and terrorism. Bombings, murders and contract killings, kidnappings and other forms of brutality have taken place since the breakup of the Soviet Union and the growth of criminal activities. The number of bombings has jumped in Estonia, Latvia, and Lithuania. For instance, in Estonia, there were no bomb explosions reported in 1991, but sixty-eight occurred in 1993 (along with more than fifty car bombings). During the early months of 1995, a series of bombings and arson attacks that destroyed kiosks and food stands took place in Tallin, the capital of Estonia, in retaliation for murders between rival criminal groups. In Lithuania, the number of bombings in 1993 was reported at one hundred fifty.

The Baltic States have become a transiting and holding area for persons from developing countries (such as Afghanistan, Somalia, Iraq and Iran, and the former Soviet Union), who are attempting to reach Scandinavia or Western Europe, often illegally. In many cases these persons are being smuggled through Russia, Ukraine, Belarus, Poland, and the Baltic States by criminal networks that also extort large payments from them. Once the persons reach either Estonia or Latvia, for example, they are eventually smuggled by sea to Scandinavia. In the past three years, more than 1,500 people have been illegally transported over the Baltic Sea by criminal groups in fishing boats to Sweden, Denmark, and Norway. In addition to the previously mentioned criminal activities, prostitution, counterfeiting, arms theft and trafficking, extortion and vehicle theft have become common problems. The Baltic States are used as a market and shipment point for stolen vehicles going from the West to the East and vice versa. Estonia, Latvia, and Lithuania have seen vehicle thefts increase domestically. In Estonia in 1993, more than 1,155 vehicles were stolen, while 2,518 were stolen in Lithuania for the same year. In Poland, for instance, vehicle thefts rose from 4,173 in 1988 to 18,620 in 1991, and to more than 58,000 in 1994.

The most common crime in the Baltic States has become smuggling, along with organized criminal violence and drug trafficking. The smuggling of goods, alcohol, raw materials, strategic metals, and radioactive substances is a boom industry in the former Soviet Union and Eastern Europe and has provided quick profits for criminals. In 1992, an estimated $17 billion U.S. dollars worth of profit earned in Russia from the illegal export of strategic material left the country to offshore banking accounts. The Baltic States have become an outlet for a good part of the illegally exported natural resources from Russia, such as oil. For example, the first nine months of 1993, some $35 million U.S. dollars' worth of raw material and metals were exported illegally from Russia to the West through Estonia.

MEASURES, INCLUDING LEGISLATION TO COMBAT ORGANIZED CRIME

The major forms of organized crime in these newly emerging democracies are taking root from the sudden transition to market economy and from the still-evolving legal system to regulate economic activities. It is the failure of the financial institutions and the lack of regulations that are strengthening organized crime syndicates. In this section we will examine a set of initiatives that are attempting to prevent money laundering and control the proceeds from crime.

Control of the Proceeds of Crime

Organized crime, almost without exception, exists and perpetuates itself for the purpose of making money. The concept of greed and the power that money—in vast quantities—ensures, is integral to most manifestations of serious organized crime (Bosworth and Saltmarsh, 1994). Indeed, most criminological definitions of organized crime specify that it is in the business to make money, and thus, where a particular business activity is rendered unattractive, in economic terms, it will move into something else. Organized crime produces enormous amounts of money not for the sake of producing wealth, but to acquire possessions, social standing and respectability, immunity, and other investment opportunities. Sooner or later most criminals are concerned with acquiring legitimacy and thus converting their wealth through a process of obscuring its origins into an index of power and respect (Flood, 1991). The laundering of the proceeds of criminal activity through the financial system is thus vital to the success of these organized criminal operations.

To combat this growing menace, several international initiatives have been undertaken to control money laundering. Some of the more pertinent ones are:

The Vienna Convention

The United Nations Convention against Illicit Traffic in Narcotic Drugs and Psychotropic Substances in December 1998, adopted a number of key proposals (UN, 1988). Specifically, it does the following:

1. Creates an obligation to criminalize the laundering of money derived from drug trafficking

2. Requires international cooperation, thereby facilitating cross-border investigations into money laundering
3. Enables extradition between signatory states in money laundering cases
4. Sets out principles to facilitate cooperative administrative investigations
5. Sets forth the principle that banking secrecy should not interfere with criminal investigations in the context of international cooperation

Ratification of the Vienna Convention by many countries (over sixty) was an important step in establishing contacts and therefore access to external information and expertise essential in countering the international nature of money-laundering activities. Of course, on some questions the Vienna Convention is either completely silent or it has left issues to be resolved or worked out through bilateral or multilateral arrangements between countries.

Basel Statement of Principles, 1988

The Basel Statement of Principles was issued by the Basel Committee on Banking Regulations and Supervisory Practices in December 1988. It signaled the agreement by the representatives of central banks and supervisory authorities of the Group of Ten countries recognizing the dangers posed by money laundering to the stability of the banking system worldwide and acknowledging the need for an international set of principles to overcome differences in the practical implementation of supervisory regimes in each member country.

The basic policies and procedures outlined in the Statement of Principles included:

1. The need for effective procedures to identify customer identification
2. Compliance with laws and regulations pertaining to financial transactions and refusal to assist
3. Transactions which appear to be associated with money laundering
4. Cooperation with law enforcement agencies

The concerns expressed by the Basel Committee are particularly important for countries where the financial services industry is establishing itself in a developing market economy. Public confidence in the new financial arrangements is an important requisite to the growth of these institutions. There is a need to establish an effective money regulation legislation to curb money laundering, otherwise international business with financial institutions in these countries is likely to be significantly hampered by the risks of unaccounted transactions.

Strasbourg Convention

The Council of Europe was the first that, in a "Recommendation of the Committee of Ministers—1980," warned the international community of the dangers that "dirty money" in the financial systems represented to democracy and the rule of law. The approach of the Council has been to make not only laundering of drug proceeds a crime, but also to criminalize the proceeds derived from all kinds of offenses. The idea has been that the criminal should not be permitted to profit from his crime. The work of the Council in the field of money laundering has also been action-oriented. Several international conferences on the subject were held in the 1980s and inspired the work on an international Convention on Laundering, Search Seizure and Confiscation of Proceeds from Crime, the so-called Strasbourg Convention (Council of Europe, 1995).

The Strasbourg Convention came into effect in November 1990. The rules provided for international cooperation against money launderers and the confiscation of criminal gains. The convention recommended criminalization of money laundering not only from drug trafficking, but also from any kind of criminal activity. It also provided for other complementary measures in order to control and confiscate criminal proceeds as well as to reinforce judicial cooperation.

Financial Action Task Force

(FATF) was formed in 1989 by the Group of seven major industrial nations and the President of the Commission of the European Communities to assess the results of cooperation. The task force assessed steps to prevent utilization of the banking system for money-laundering purposes and to consider additional preventative measures in this field, especially the adaptation of the legal and regulatory systems to enhance multilateral judicial action. There are forty measures recommended by the FATF for adoption by countries combating money laundering. These have been grouped as (1) general framework, (2) improvement of national legal systems to combat money laundering, and (3) strengthening of international cooperation. The FATF has an important role in monitoring the effectiveness of the steps taken to counter money laundering and in identifying the increasingly sophisticated methods employed by money launderers (Financial Action Task Force, 1990).

Another, more modest, regional initiative is the Caribbean Financial Action Task Force. As a result of the Caribbean Conference on Drug Money

Laundering, held at Aruba from 8 to 10 June 1990, a series of recommendations for taking action against money laundering was formulated. Some countries, however, have been reluctant to take further action, because of the benefits they receive as tax havens. Progress has generally been slower than was initially anticipated.

Other Initiatives to Counter Money Laundering

In 1988 Interpol formed a working group to pursue international cooperation in gathering and sharing financial information connected with drug trafficking. The working group has developed a model law for identification, tracing, seizure, and confiscation of assets derived from criminal activity and has published and updated a Financial Assets Encyclopedia. In March 1992, Interpol also established an Automated Search Facility (ASF), a system giving access to data held by national systems, but with the provision that members could specify which countries were allowed to receive their information—obviously essential for a body of the size of Interpol, with one hundred thirty-six members, most of whom distrust at least some of the others.

In parallel with these measures, the heads of state of the European Community set up a European Committee to Combat Drugs (CELAD) in December 1989. This aimed to coordinate anti-drug strategies, suppress illicit drug trading, and reduce demand. In 1991 the TREVI group—a regular committee of Eastern Community interior and justice ministers, with associated working groups of their officials, police chiefs, and others established a European Police Organization, EUROPOL, to deal with cross border crime and in December 1993, formed a European Drugs Unit (EDU). In June 1991, the European Union Directive on the prevention of the use of the financial system for the purpose of money laundering was approved by the Council (The European Union, 1991). The EU Directive, which came into force in 1993, requires member states to prohibit money laundering and to introduce by means of legislation a variety of provisions designed to ensure that credit and financial institutions in particular have appropriate procedures for the identification of customers, the reporting of suspicious activities, and other internal control procedures.

COMPARATIVE EVALUATION OF THE METHODS FOR COMBATING ORGANIZED CRIME AND PROPOSED MEASURES

By exploiting the dominant economic trends of the 1990s—globalization and internalization—transnational organized crime has become a major force in world finances, capable of derailing the economic and social development of key countries and undermining international security. In a declaration and Global Action Plan, the Ministers of Justice and the Interior taking part in the Naples (Italy) Conference in November 1994, urged states to move swiftly to counter a rapidly globalizing movement of interlinked organized criminal groups and their spread into new spheres of activity. The plan reflects agreement that if organized crime is not resisted in time, it will undermine political structures, endanger internal peace and development, and threaten not only emerging democracies, but also well-established ones. It calls for improved data gathering and analysis, anti-corruption safeguards, special investigative units, and implementation of existing measures directed against loopholes that allow transborder criminals to circumvent justice (van der Hulst, 1993). It recommends that the Crime Commission of the United Nations begin to solicit states' views on the feasibility of an international convention that would address forms of transnational crime not already covered under existing treaties.

According to past resolutions and decisions of the United Nations, the member states should intensify their efforts to combat more effectively organized crime at the national level. They should carefully consider some of the following measures, keeping in view safeguards of the basic rights under ordinary legal procedures and in conformity with international human right standards:

1. Introduce new offenses directed to novel and sophisticated forms of criminal activity;
2. Provide for the forfeiture of illegally acquired assets;
3. Facilitate the obtaining of evidence abroad for use in criminal proceedings in national courts;
4. Modernize national laws relating to extradition;
5. Conduct national campaigns against drug abuse to develop measures of treatment, rehabilitation, law enforcement, and educational processes to deal with drug abuse;
6. Strengthen law enforcement authorities and the provision to those authorities of increased powers;
7. Establish national institutions, such as national crime authorities or commissions, with appropriate powers, to investigate and obtain evidence for the prosecution of those deeply involved in organized crime activity;
8. Review or adopt laws relating to taxation, the abuse of bank secrecy and gaming houses, in order to ensure that they are adequate to assist in the fight against organized crime, and in particular, the transfer of funds or the proceeds of such crime across national boundaries (Varela et al., 1994).

The member states should also increase their activity at the international level in order to combat organized crime, including, as appropriate, becoming parties to relevant multilateral treaties and entering on extradition and mutual legal assistance. Multilateral cooperation should not be seen as a compromise between various bilateral efforts. Rather, it is something that has significant benefits in its own right, as many regional arrangements have demonstrated. Regional cooperation in judicial and criminal matters is the natural concomitant to efforts to achieve political and economic union. Regional cooperation is also based on the recognition that, although traditional organized crime is a global problem, it takes different forms in different regions and countries. But for more effective and concerted action to combat organized crime it is necessary to work out the United Nations Convention against this phenomenon.

The Secretary-General of the United Nations, Boutros Boutros-Ghali (UN: Department of Public Information, 1995) told the World Ministerial Conference on Organized Transnational Crime at Naples:

> Powerful international criminal groups now work outside national or international law. They include traffickers in drugs, money laundering, the illegal trade in arms—including trade in nuclear materials—and the smuggling of precious metals and other commodities. These criminal elements exploit both the new liberal international economic order and the different approaches and practices of States. They command vast sums of money, which they use to suborn State officials. Some criminal 'empires' are richer than many poor States. These problems demand a concerted, global response.

Organized crime has become predominantly transnational in character, according to recent reports from the United States. But law enforcement worldwide remains predominantly local and national. Although much has been done by governments to affect organized crime, efforts are hampered by lack of knowledge, common orientation, and international cooperation (Kaiser, 1995; Schneider, 1993). A new approach must be sought involving a number of agencies. Success will be achieved by use of a multinational and multidisciplinary approach, which uses preventative as well as control measures applied by the criminal justice system and governments, utilizing the knowledge and resources of industry and science. This new approach to combat organized crime must work alongside an increase in proactive methods. It requires the involvement of public enforcement to provide the solution, but it is clear that crime cannot be tackled successfully unless other sectors of society are involved. One convincing example is the approach by the New York State Organized Crime Task Force to organized fraud, money laundering, and corruption in the New

York construction world. In this field it has proved that only an approach involving the entire enforcement chain together with multidisciplinary and private sector involvement leads to actual results. The application of scientific knowledge as well as industrial methods and techniques to criminal intelligence work will further aid the success. The activities and structures of criminals should be analyzed to identify their weaknesses and appropriate methods taken. The motto for this approach should be, "It concerns us all, let's tackle it together." It is clear that integration of strategies, policies, mechanisms, and their management at the domestic and international level, is the answer to the increasing challenges posed by development of transnational organized crime.

Conclusion

Transnational organized crime has become a major force in the world by exploiting the dominant economic trends of the 1990s: globalization and internationalization. It has developed the capability of derailing the economic and social development of many countries and undermining international security. Although governments have started to take corrective measures and combat the menace of organized crime, their efforts are hampered by lack of knowledge, common orientation, and international cooperation. A new approach must be sought involving a number of agencies before greater success can be achieved (Savona, 1993; The Ninth UN Congress on the Prevention of Crime and the Treatment of Offenders, 1995). If this action is not taken soon the situation may well spiral out of control.

References

Bosworth, Davies and G. Saltmarsh. 1994. *Money Laundering: A Practical Guide to New Legislation.* London, Chapman and Hall.

Council of Europe. 1995. *Convention on Laundering, Search, Seizure and Confiscation of the Proceeds from Crime and Explanatory Report, Treaties and Reports.* Strasbourg Cedex. Council of Europe Publishing.

Financial Action Task Force (FATF). 1990. Money Laundering. Paris, (France), 7 February.

Flood, S. (Ed.). 1991. *Illicit Drugs and Organized Crime. Issues for a United Europe.* Office of International Criminal Justice, The University of Illinois at Chicago, IL: 1–10.

Gilinskiy, Y. 1996. "Crime in Russia During Rapid Social Change." In *Impact of Political, Economic and Social Change on Crime and its Image in Society.* B. Szamota-Saeki and D. Wojcik (eds.). Fifty-first International Course of Criminology, 12–16 September. Warsaw, Poland: Dom Wydawniczy: 87–95.

Holdos, J. 1995. Organized Crime and Terrorism on the Territory of the Slovak Republic. *Europe 2000*, Quarterly Newsletter V (June): 21–26.

Holyst, B. 1996. "Economic Crime in Poland During the Period of Changes in the Social and Economic System (Select Problems)." *EuroCriminol.* 10: 221–225.

International Criminal Police Organization (Interpol). 1995. Report prepared by the Drugs Sub-Division ICPO. Interpol General Secretariat, January, Lyons, France.

Johnson, C. 1995. "Russian Organized Crime." In *Drug Trafficking and National Security*. P. Williams, C. Florez, J. Deal, and J. Furloni, (eds.), Boulder, Colorado, Westview Press.

Kaiser, G. 1995. Criminology at Freiburg Max Planck Institute, Development Review, "Outlook for the Future." *EuroCriminol.* 8–9 (Lodz.): 37–54.

Newsweek. 1993. "Global Mafia: Special Report." 13 December, 16–17.

Plywaczewski, E.W. 1996. "Money Laundering and Financial Systems—Including the Situation in Poland." *EuroCriminol.* 10: 103–120.

Ponomarev, P.G. 1996. Confronting Money Laundering in Russia, Crime and Social Order in Europe. *Crime and Social Order Research Programme*, Newsletter no. 4 (July): 6.

Savona, E. U., S. Adamoli, P. Zoffi, and M. DeFeo. 1995. Organized Crime Across the Borders: Preliminary Results. *Heuni Papers* no. 6, Helsinki: 8.

Savona, E. U. 1993. *Mafia Issues: Analysis and Proposals for Combating Mafia Today*, International Scientific and Professional Advisory Council of the United Nations Crime Prevention and Criminal Justice Program, ISPAC: 33–122.

Schneider, H.J. (ed.). 1993. *Organized Crime in International Criminological Perspective*. United Nations Asia and Far East Institute for the Prevention and the Treatment of Offenders Report for 1992 and Resource Material Series no. 43, Tokyo: 133–148.

Serio, J. 1993. "Organized Crime in the Former Soviet Union: Only the Name is New." *Criminal Justice International* (July–August): 11.

Skrastnis, J. 1996. The Peculiarities of the Organized Crime Development in the Baltic States. *Europe 2000*, Quarterly Newsletter, X (June 5): 22–29.

The European Union. 1991. *Directive on the Prevention of the Use of the Financial System for the Purpose of Money Laundering*. 10 June.

The Ninth United Nations Congress on the Prevention of Crime and the Treatment of Offenders: Cairo, Egypt. 1995. *Less Crime, More Justice: Security for All*. National Statement, Japan: 1–10.

The United Nations. 1988. *Convention Against Illicit Traffic in Narcotic Drugs and Psychotropic Substances*. E/Conf. 82/15/, 19 December, Vienna.

United Nations Commission on Crime Prevention and Criminal Justice. 1994. Report on the Third Session (26 April–6 May 1994). Economic and Social Council, Official Records, Suppl. no. 11.

United Nations Economic and Social Council. 1993. *The Impact of Organized Criminal Activities upon Society at Large*. Commission on Crime Prevention and Criminal Justice. (Report of the Secretary-General), Distr. General, E/CN. 15/1993/3, 11 January.

United Nations Economic and Social Council. 1994. *Problems and Dangers Posed by Organized Transnational Crime in the Various Regions of the World*. World Ministerial Conference on Organized Transnational Crime, 21–23 November, Naples. Distr. General, E/Conf. 88/2. 198, August.

United Nations. 1993. Crime: Special Double Issue on the United Nations Commission on Crime Prevention and Criminal Justice. *Crime Prevention and Criminal Justice Newsletter*, no. 22–23, July.

United Nations: Department of Public Relations. 1995. *Backgrounder, Stop Crime.* The Ninth United Nations Congress on the Prevention of Crime and the Treatment of Offenders, "The United Nations vs. Transnational Crime," April: 1.

van der Hulst, J.W. (ed.). 1993. *EC Fraud, Kluwer,* Deventer-Boston: 11–16.

Varela, Cid E., L. Ferraro, L. Crocce, C. Zin, H. Pelaez, E. Bonino, J. Castro, J. Aguado Zaragoza, and others. 1994. *Narcocriminal.* Latin American Parliament, Brazil, Sao Paulo: 81–100.

Chapter 6

Organized Crime: A Perspective from Russia

Yakov Gilinskiy

Introduction

Russia, even after the breakup of the Soviet Union, remains the largest country in the world in terms of area but is unfavorably situated. It lacks a warm water seaport and most of the regions are either too cold or dry for agricultural purposes. Despite its wealth of natural resources, a well-educated population, and a diverse industrial base, the nation continues to experience formidable difficulties in moving from its socialist, centrally planned economy to a modern market economy. The breakup of the USSR into fifteen successor states in late 1991 destroyed major economic links that have been only partially replaced. Russia still has to make substantial progress in a number of key areas that are needed to provide a solid foundation for the transition to a market economy. The strong showing of the communists and nationalists in the Duma elections in December 1995, further cast a shadow over prospects for future reforms. Moscow has also been slow to develop the new legal framework required in the changed circumstances. For instance, Duma has yet to adopt a land code that would allow development of land markets as sources of needed capital. Most rank-and-file Russians perceive they are worse off because of growing crime and health problems, the drop in real wages, the great rise in wage arrears, and the widespread threat of unemployment (Statistical Review, 1992).

Russia is a federal state and the sources of law include the Russian constitution, federal constitutional law, federal laws, and laws of subjects of federation. Administrative bodies issue decrees that must comply with these laws. The constitution has preeminent force and federal laws cannot contradict federal constitutional law. Although court decisions are not officially accepted as sources of law in Russia, the explanatory rulings of the Supreme Court of Russia can create new legal rules. The penitentiary system and the law-enforcement bodies of Russia are headed by the Ministry of Internal Affairs.

According to Section 71 of the Constitution of Russia, criminal and criminal-procedure laws are under the exclusive jurisdiction of federal bodies. The assurance of public order and safety is a joint duty of the federation and its parts. The most important laws originate from the Criminal Code, the Criminal Procedure Code, the Criminal Punishment Execution Code (in Russian, called the Reforming Labor Code), Law on the Justice System, Law on the Militia, and Law on the Status of Judges. Although the Criminal Code has been amended seven times since 1990, reforms in post-Soviet criminal legislation go rather slowly. For example, the distinction between state and private property was removed from the Criminal Code only in the summer of 1994. Prior to that, the Code called for more serious punishments for crimes against state property.

The following crime statistics were compiled by the Ministry of Internal Affairs for the years 1989 to 1993 on the basis of police reports (Ministry of Internal Affairs of Russia, 1994). In 1993, 2,799,614 crimes were reported; only 1,395,000 of them (50.6 percent) were investigated successfully. Major crimes constitute 17 percent of all reported crimes; crimes against property, more than 50 percent. The definitions of crimes comply with the Criminal Code but are not available in this document.

CRIME STATISTICS—1989–1993

Year	1989	1990	1991	1992	1993
Total	1,620,000	1,890,000	2,200,000	2,700,000	2,800,000
Murder	13,543	15,566	16,122	23,006	29,213
Major injury	36,872	40,962	41,195	53,873	66,902
Rape	14,597	15,010	14,073	13,663	14,400

There were 53,200 drug crimes reported in 1993, which was 1.8 times greater than in 1992.

Russian researchers indicate that certain segments of the population are more victimized by crime than others. For example, youth and senior citizens are victimized more often than other groups. Men are more often the victims of hooliganism, and women more often victims of fraud. In 81 percent of all crime and in 63.2 percent of major bodily injuries, the victims were relatives or friends of the offenders. The occupations of individuals also determine whether or not they will be a victim of crime. Taxi drivers, business people, or bank employees, militia officers, and cashiers are considered more at risk in Russia. In certain cases, some culpability belongs to the victim, too. For example, in 40 percent of all rape cases and 41 percent of all manslaughter cases, alcohol was found present in the victim's bloodstream.

The Militia (police) forms a part of the structure of the Ministry of Internal Affairs. It is subdivided into the Criminal Militia and the Public Security Militia. The Criminal Militia is subordinated to the Ministry of Internal Affairs of Russia and the ministries of internal affairs of the republics that constitute the Russian federation. The Public Security Militia is also subordinated to the local authorities. The Criminal Militia has the task of prevention, suppression, and exposure of criminal offenses that require a preliminary investigation. The Public Security Militia, or local militia, has the task of ensuring the personal security of citizens, protection of public order, and the prevention and suppression of criminal offenses and minor delinquencies. There are other responsibilities, too, like the disclosure of criminal offenses that do not require a preliminary investigation, investigation of criminal offenses in the form of inquiry and the general rendering of assistance to citizens, officials, businesses, establishments, organizations, and public associations. An independent police structure is the Department of Taxation Police, which is charged with the prevention, suppression, and exposure of taxation crimes and infringements, safeguarding taxation inspection, and protection of the department's officers. Annual expenditure on the law-enforcement system in 1994 was approximately 16 trillion rubles ($7 billion U.S. dollars).

The militia is authorized to use firearms, rubber batons, tear gas, and fire hoses. To join the militia, a person is required to pass professional training in specialized higher or secondary educational establishments of the Ministry of Internal Affairs or other state departments. To enter these establishments, a person must be eighteen to thirty-five years old, have a secondary education, and no prior convictions. An officer serves a probation period lasting from three months to one year. A citizen can appeal against the actions of a militia officer to higher officers or militia bodies, to the prosecutor, or to the court.

According to the new Constitution of 1993, a capital sentence may be imposed only for serious violent offenses against human life. There have been sixty executions per year over the past few years. Execution is performed by firing squad.

Russian Gulag has become well known to the world from the writings of Alexander Solzhenitsyn. The penitentiary system consists of 764 reforming labor institutions called *ispravitelno-trudovich colonii*, and 13 prisons. There are 60 educational-labor institutions for juvenile criminals, too. Men and women are confined in separate institutions, as are adult and juvenile criminals. At the beginning of 1994 there were over 600,000 persons in reformatory labor institutions of which 21,600 were women and 19,100, juveniles. Of those in institutions, over half have been convicted of violent crimes and half are either alcoholics or drug addicts. The number of prisoners awaiting trial has also been increasing over the years. There were 233,500 persons in prisons who were being detained while under investigation. In 1993, 437,700 men were detained as alleged offenders in the course of preliminary investigation and two-thirds of them were incarcerated (Nikiforov, 1997).

THE NATURE AND EXTENT OF ORGANIZED CRIME

Despite the virulent media publicity and general impression, the topic of organized crime remains quite latent in the country. Organized crime is constantly expanding into different spheres of influence. Crime organizations are interested in access to state structures to influence a rate of economy and favorable policies. The criminal structures have resources, capital, and they target the businesses, economy, and even the political parties to advance their objectives of making large profits through illegal means. On one hand the organized crime is a serious danger for society, on the other, the stripping of the cloak of mystery and myths of Mafia from organized crime is equally necessary. This topic is particularly important for Russia.

It is impossible to single out any one reason for the extremely serious crisis currently affecting Russian society. Much of it stems from historical roots: the lack of a democratic tradition, Russia's eastern, and therefore marginal, proximity to the West, the nature of Orthodox religious ethics as opposed to Protestant liberalism, and the centuries-long tradition of despotism. The immediate source of today's problems can be traced back to the events of October 1917, when the unique social experiment to forcibly establish a social Utopia was undertaken with a seriousness unmatched anywhere else. (The slogan on the gate of the Solovki labor camp read "Happiness to Everyone through Violence.")

The attempt to build Utopia was accompanied by an unprecedented process of negative selection that saw those most proficient in their fields being repressed, exiled, or destroyed while the gray, mediocre (often criminally minded) elements of society were championed. The repression of the people became nothing short of genocide. This eventually pushed the Soviet state and society into an unavoidable catastrophe, the main symptoms of which have been the disintegration of the economy, the loss of trade skills, and the de-professionalization and de-qualification of the majority of the working population. This has been accompanied by the lumpening of the people, the lack and nondevelopment of a middle class that could provide some kind of stable social base and serious crises in the health, education, transport, communications, and other vital service industries. To further aggravate the situation a number of interethnic conflicts resulting in large numbers of deaths, a series of political crises, lack of spirituality and morality, the increase in various forms of deviant behavior (crime, drug addiction, suicide), and the growth of Mafia-type organized crime has made the country extremely volatile.

Gorbachev's Perestroika was a necessary attempt to save the power structures by way of reform. A similar attempt, the "Thaw" was made by Khrushchev, too. However, every attempt ended with the actual or political death of its propagators and was followed by stagnation. With all due credit to Gorbachev, whose reforms turned out to be the most radical, even these did not turn out to be fully satisfactory. All those aforementioned symptoms of socioeconomic catastrophe have remained untreated. Power has continually been returned to the ruling government; the corruption, usual to Russia, has taken on a monumental stature in all organs of power and establishments while the militarization of economics and politics continues unabated. The interethnic conflicts have given rise to unnecessary, vicious killings in which nationalist, anti-Semitic, and neofascist groups have formed and met with no resistance. The criminal war in Chechnya is terrifying evidence of the neototalitarianism that has taken over Russia. The ever-growing economic polarization of the population, visible in the stark contrast between the poverty-stricken majority and the "New Russians"—a criminalized, nouveau riche minority—has further become a source of very real social conflict. The country has been permitting mass human rights abuses, particularly in the army and penitentiary institutions, where tyranny and torture appear to dominate. Confirmation of these allegations may be found in the international research material compiled by Amnesty International and native researchers (Abramkin, 1996).

The economic reform under way in Russia, the transition from planned state-run economy to market is beyond doubt progressive in nature. Along with it, some "criminogenic" consequences are traceable. Redistribution of property is being carried out not only legally, but also through illegal methods, with bribery, murders, and threats openly being resorted to by the perpetrators. There is a sharp stratification (economic and social) of the population into a pauperized majority and a minority that is growing rich. The differentiation between the incomes of the 10 percent least prosperous and the 10 percent most prosperous stood at 1:4.5 in 1991; 1:8 in 1992; 1:10 in 1993; and 1:15 in 1994.

There is clearly visible in the society an emergence of overt (explicit) unemployment and of partial (incomplete) employment. Technological backwardness and incompatibility of the native production and services spheres have manifested themselves in the course of recent reforms. A consequence of this has been the inferiority complex of the labor force, their disqualification, marginalization, and lumpening. It is well known that unemployed and delinquent people are easy targets for organized crime groups. For instance, people without a permanent income are increasingly forming a larger proportion of the total criminal population (1987, 11.8%; 1990, 17.8%; 1993, 35.9%; 1996, 48.1%).

The disintegration of the services sphere and of the social infrastructure has entailed further difficulties for the population. There is virtual neglect of children and teenagers, whose parents are busy with acquisition of subsistence means, while out-of-school centers for children and teenagers are being closed down because of the lack of state financing. The limited private centers are charging exorbitant fees, which very few can afford. Additionally, the amount of "temptations" (designer clothes, audio and video appliances, junk food) have grown sharply, provoking illegal means for acquiring them. These youth are a "best staff" for criminal organizations. The radical changes in the system of values and norms is now a state of anomie as described by Durkheim. Numerous mistakes and abuses of the country's leadership (authorities) in carrying out economic reforms have also been accompanied by criminogenic processes: corruption, incompetence, and "governmental" privatization. (A privatization in whose course federal and local functionaries—"government"—primarily lay their hands on ex-state-owned property.) In such a situation the extent of organized crime can only be contemplated.

Organized crime is the functioning of stable hierarchical associations, engaged in crime as a business and setting up a system of protection from public control by means of corruption. Criminal associations are a kind of social organization of a "working (labor) collective body" type. The growth of criminal organizations is a natural process. It is a manifestation of the social systems as well as their subsystems guided by economic and political policies, a process seen throughout the world. The high degree of adaptability in many criminal associations (strict selection of the staff, strict labor discipline, and high rate of profit-making) ensures their great vital capacity. "Mafia is immortal!" The members of the criminal gangs, professional criminals, are not heroes, but neither are they scum of the earth, for these are people engaged in their own business like everyone else. Becker, a Nobel Prize winner in the field of economics speaks about it in the following way: "Criminal activity is just the same profession or trade like engineering or teaching to which people devote their time" (Becker, 1987). It is chosen when the profit (the revenues minus the production costs) exceeds that which legal occupations fetch. Certainly, what they do is not in line with moral or juridical laws of society, but their activity is also aimed at satisfying social needs.

In Russia, at present it is hardly possible to draw a distinction between the legal and criminal business abiding by the criteria of morality and legality. The acknowledged three models of organized crime (hierarchical, local or ethnic, and business enterprise) complement each other. "Business enterprise" is the *content* of the organized crime activities, whereas hierarchical, local and ethnic models manifest as *organizational forms* of this activity. The world's literature is more and more often laying emphasis on organized crime as a form of business enterprise (Abadinsky, 1994; Albanese, 1996; Arlacchi, 1986; Block, 1994; Kelly, Chin, and Schatzbery 1994; Mayerhofer and Jehle, 1996).

The criminal syndicate's involvement in the system of organized crime (industry) is defined by the following indispensable traits:

- A stable association of people, designed for long-term activity
- Criminal kind of activity deriving maximum profit as its key goal
- Complex hierarchical structure of the association (organization) with the functions delineated (leaders, groups of supply and security, experts, etc.)
- Corrupting power bodies and law-enforcement agents as the main means of the criminal activity
- Aspiration for monopolization in a certain sphere of activity or on certain territory

Criminal organizations like other social ones strive to exert influence on the state power and to exercise control over it through lobbying, bribery, and infiltration of their representative into power structures. The high efficiency of business enterprise of criminal organizations can be put down to their "professional selection." Their personnel selection is much better, their "labor discipline" is strict, while the youngest, bravest, and most enterprising people with the greatest strength of determination are involved. The system of "will pay for labor" is also more attractive. For instance, in organized crime, the remuneration is several times higher than that in similar structures of the Russian police.

The organized crime in Russia after 1917 existed primarily in the form of gangsterism, and later on, since the 1930s, a peculiar, well-organized association of so-called "thieves-in-law" emerged, professional thieves or swindlers, choosing crime as a permanent way of earning their living. They were well known in the criminal world and obeyed the special code of criminals by keeping silent about associates and cooperating with them. In the 1950s, *Tzechoviki* (groups within professions) and *Tyenyeviki* (shady dealers) merged with the state structures that marked the beginning of institutionalized corruption. This developed into the growth of Mafia-type criminal societies from the 1970s to the 1990s.

In the 1970s, after a number of strikes (which took the character of mini wars), a merger occured between economic "white-collar" crime, committed by big thieves and misappropriators of "socialist property," "shadow economy dealers," corrupted party and state functionaries, and the dangerous penal criminals. Contemporary organized crime is the result of this amalgamation that is working for super profits in a nation besieged by political crisis. Russian organized crime now includes three elements: criminals (old "thieves-in-law" and new "bandits"), "businessmen", and corrupted officials, (policemen, and law-enforcement bodies).

The contemporary *criminal organization* (syndicate) is enterpreneurship in the form of an economic enterprise, criminal syndicates, and virtually a criminal industry. Among all the types of such criminal syndicates, three basic kinds can be identified with respect to their activities: criminal (illegal rackets, narco-business), economic (essentially white-collar crimes), and political (terrorism, striving to seize or wield power). The term "Mafia" is widespread, though cannot be said to be strictly scientific in designation. In a broad sense the word "Mafia" serves as a synonym of criminal organization (association). In a narrower, more specific sense, Mafia means a criminal organization, characterized by a high degree of organization, hierarchy, and resorting to force for attaining its goals.

Apart from the three types of criminal enterprises, there are also three levels of criminal organizations that exist in Russia. First, a criminal group; second, a criminal organization or association; and third, a criminal society or community. For instance, in St. Petersburg there are four criminal Mafia-type communities: the so-called Tambovs, Azerbaijans, Chechens, and Kazans groups: some dozen criminal associations (for example, Komarovs), and hundreds of smaller groups engaged in committing crimes.

The Center of Deviantology at St. Petersburg's branch of the Institute of Sociology of the Russian Academy of Sciences took up a criminological study into black-market economy and organized crime from the period 1993 to the present. The study found that the business sphere of St. Petersburg and other regions of Russia is divided among Mafia groups. Their information system is well organized, which enables them to track and monitor the activities of all commercial enterprises. The moment a new commercial business begins making a profit, it arouses the interest of the Mafia. As the business respondents fearfully asserted, "100% of commercial structures are embraced by racket . . . These [rackets] have penetrated all the enterprises except those of military–industrial complex and some foreign firms." These rackets are essentially a form of extortion and the gangs impose "tributes" on the small kiosks or the large commercial organizations according to their profit margin. In many cases, rather than outright extortion of tributes, the so-called "black racket," the businesses face various indirect, disguised types of demands: for "guarding," for "rendering services in the field of marketing," in compliance with the contract for "joint work," and for "services" (e.g., recovering debts). The Mafia also "takes care" of these businesses by forcing their representatives into the administrative and managerial bodies. One cannot object since the criminals have power, and none can force a debtor to pay, even with the decision of the arbitration court on hand.

Our respondents describe the contemporary situation in shocking detail: "One cannot do without illegal dealing", "legal and illegal methods are interlocked." Heads of the police special units side with them: "The medium of the businessmen is extremely criminalized . . . One has to bribe for everything . . . The debts have to be recovered by resorting to force . . . One cannot deal with taxation inspection without a bribe," "A bribe is an inevitability in the sphere of business . . . The tax inspection system is highly corrupt . . . Mafiosi can even be found among the members of the boards of banks." The research revealed several ways in which situations are created that force businesspeople to commit crimes.

First, one has to bribe in the following situations: when registering the enterprise, when taking lease of premises from state bodies, when acquiring licenses for its utilization with state bodies, for obtaining a low-rate bank credit, when submitting to the tax inspection, and for abiding by the formalities to get customs clearance. Second, one has to conceal income, for with the current taxation rate, amounting to 80 to 85 percent, one cannot survive the competition with other firms by honestly revealing all revenues.

Third, most contemporary non-state-owned enterprises find themselves "under the protection" of gangsters (Mafia): They are "guarded" by some gang against others and have to pay "tribute" for that and render obligatory services. In particular, Mafia include their "representatives" into councils of directors, boards of enterprises, organizations, and banks. Thus legal and criminal business are merging in Russia. Fourth, the rigid normative regulations of economic activity and the absence of such regulations in other fields of business encourage many to ignore the law in some cases and make their own "laws" in others. Fifth, the synthesis of legal and illegal elements in the country's economy has introduced such monsters as faked goods and services, and forged securities.

The main fields of activity of St. Petersburg and Russian criminal organizations are as follows: shady bank transactions with fake letters of advice; fictitious transactions in real estate; hijacking and reselling of cars; illegal export of nonferrous metals; black-market appropriation of food and medicines received for humanitarian aid; production and traffic of hard liquor; arms sale; counterfeiting money; gambling, supplying sexual services, and narco-business.

In 1995 and 1996 the Center of Deviantology conducted a number of interviews with representatives of the criminal world (Ovchinsky, Eminov, and Jablokov, 1996). In the course of interviews the professional skills of criminals became clearly evident. Hi-tech crimes were being committed through computer engineering, bank frauds through financial skullduggery, and new technologies were being pressed to such prosaic areas as falsification of spirits, drinks, drug manufacturing, hijacking of automobiles, development of new weapons, and so on. It can be reliably stated that most new developments in the field of computer engineering are also being utilized by criminal groups. These groups are giving particular attention to the scientific personnel, the chemists, programmers, economists, and lawyers who are being sucked into criminal transactions.

Narco-business is one of the most latent, well-organized forms of criminality in Russia. The police cannot manage to reach the chiefs of Russian narco-mafia and those few arrested by the police thus far have been either drug consumers or ordinary distributors, the lower part of narco-mafia organization. The activity of criminal organization in the sphere of narco-businesses can be judged only indirectly: through the information obtained from the small-time operators arrested by the police or seizures made by custom services and the distribution-consumption centers that reveal drug trafficking routes through Russian territory and so on. The struggle against narco-mafia is complicated by the extensive corruption of law-enforcement agents and even those in authority. The issue is further complicated by the political conflict of Russia with countries that are known exporters of drugs: Azerbaijan, Chechnya, and states of Middle Asia. The data about drug-related crimes in Table 6.1 are very revealing.

TABLE 6.1 DRUG-RELATED CRIMES IN RUSSIA (1987–1995)

	1987	1988	1989	1990	1991	1992	1993	1994	1995
Total	18,534	12,553	13,446	16,255	19,321	29,805	53,152	74,798	79,819
Rate (per 100,000 citizens)	12.7	8.6	9.1	10.9	13.0	20.0	35.7	50.3	54.7
Drug thefts	823	470	439	413	433	315	475	529	691
Manufacture, sale, carriage, trafficking, and acquisition of drugs	15,506	9,527	10,594	13,646	17,036	27,115	49,249	70,420	72,457
Keeping "drug dens"—premises for drug use	444	252	171	206	181	324	499	721	750
Forgery, making forged documents (prescriptions) for drugs	602	248	277	222	296	*	285	162	129
Illegally growing poppies or cannabis	136	74	3	72	76	91	343	593	666
Breaking stock-taking and storage laws	365	776	793	642	488	813	1,066	1,690	1,886
Percentage of drug-related crimes to common crime	1.6	1.0	0.8	0.9	0.9	1.1	1.9	2.8	2.9
Percentage of drug addicts' crimes to common crime	0.2	0.2	0.1	0.1	0.1	0.2	*	*	*
Percentage of crimes committed under drug intoxication	0.3	0.2	0.2	0.2	0.2	0.2	0.7	0.5	0.4

* no data
Sources: *Crime and Delinquency* 7, 1992; *Crime and Delinquency* 8, 1996.

The main body of crimes consists of drug marketing, manufacturing, purchasing and possession for personal use, without intention to sell (pt. 3, 4, art. 224 Criminal Code of the Russian Federation, 1960). Police ("militia") prefer to detain and transfer to court consumers of narcotics, but not their distributors, in view of the comparative ease of identifying the former and complexity of identifying the latter. In 1995 there were 38,560 offenses related to narcotics and strong-action (toxic) substances, of which only 3,734 cases (9.7%) were related to production and purchase with intention to sell.

Mafia displays a keen interest in privatization. As one respondent puts it, "Their goal is to take hold of real estate." They obtain information about forthcoming auctions, come to the auctions with their armed men, and find out who buys what property and at what price. The active rivals from legal business are requested to keep away from the purchase to avoid trouble. The other method for laying hands on real estate is buying up shares from the workers fired from munitions plants and thereby acquiring the controlling parcel of shares. It was established that by 1994 organized crime groups in Russia had acquired around 40 thousand of the privatized enterprises and control of even 400 banks. More and more information is emerging about the intensive lobbying efforts to develop links with some representatives of state bodies by the Mafia. Consequently, Russia is confronting the *criminalization of business* in combination with *economization* and *politicization of the crime*. The official data of organized crime in Russia presented in Table 6.2 is suggestive of such.

MEASURES, INCLUDING LEGISLATION TO COMBAT ORGANIZED CRIME

The manner of combating organized crime has varied simultaneously with the change of the forms of organized crime in Russia. During the years 1918 to 1921, gangs and gangsterism (steady criminal groups committing contract murders, robberies, and other serious crimes) could be ruthlessly suppressed by the revolutionary and military tribunals, and also bodies of VChK (the All-Russian Extreme Commission), which was given the right of direct punishment (including execution). The non-court punishment was applied widely and severely.

In the Criminal Codes of Russian Federation enacted in years 1922 (art. 76), 1926 (art 59), 1960 (art. 77), and 1996 (art. 209), ganging meant organization of armed gangs for committing robberies against residential, commercial establishments, and individuals, too. These codes also prohibited participation in such gangs even if the person did not commit any

TABLE 6.2 SOME DATA ABOUT ORGANIZED CRIME IN RUSSIA (1990–1995)

	1990	1991	1992	1993	1994	1995
Number of known organized criminal groups (OCG)	785	952	4,352	5,691	8,059	8,222
Those OCG with international connections	*	75	174	307	461	363
Crimes committed by OCG	3,515	5,119	10,707	12,431	19,422	19,604
Members of OCG who were prosecuted	*	4,489	8,889	11,351	15,197	14,936
Fire-arms confiscated from OCG	295	371	4,518	11,737	13,808	6,357
Drug substances seized (kg)	46	257	3,297	4,368	3,695	5,841
Foreign money recovered in U.S. dollars (thousand)	*	*	9,700	4,100	31,695	61,074
Money recovered in rubles (mln)	5.5	19	3,100	72,100	171,400	492,526

* no data

Sources: Basis to Combat Organized Crime 12, 172–173.

crimes. In the criminal legislation the most severe measures of punishment for ganging (gangsterism) were provided in the Criminal Code of 1922 (art. 76)—execution with confiscation of property. Even if the circumstantial evidence was not strong, deprivation of freedom for the term of not less three years with strict isolation and confiscation of property could be imposed. Article 59 of the Criminal Code of 1926 provided for the deprivation of freedom for a term of not less than three years with confiscation of property along with the provision of strengthening of punishment if hard evidence could become available, which could even imply execution with confiscation of property. Article 77 of the Criminal Code of 1960 extended these provisions by providing for the deprivation of freedom for from three to fifteen years or execution with confiscation of property. Finally, Article 209 of the Criminal Code of 1996 provided for the deprivation of freedom for from eight to twenty years or (art. 105) deprivation of life through the death penalty. In all criminal codes the increased punishment for crimes was provided to take into account the group nature of these serious offenses. However, the real organized criminality that stemmed from the character, forms of organization, and kinds of crime activity did not fall under formal legal concepts of "gang" or "group."

Unfortunately, judicial punishment and non-court reprisals provided in the aforementioned codes were pursued first of all for political ends of the soviet totalitarian state. On the other hand, from the moment the proclamation of USSR came about, the country where "socialism" has supposedly triumphed, the application of these codes toward nonpolitical crimes virtually stopped. The government proclaimed for its propaganda purposes that "there is no ganging in socialistic state!"

The struggle with "thieves-in-law" was also conducted in nonlegal ways. During the Second World War many thieves-in-law participated in war with fascist Germany under threat of execution or for patriotic reasons. However, after the war, a large number were demobilized and a majority of them again found themselves in penitentiary. Since they were seen as the people who had given "cooperation to the authority," they were dubbed as traitors by their criminal fraternity associates and labeled as the so-called "bitch" and could not gain acceptance into their old groups.

The penitentiary administration also used these differences and provoked the so-called "bitch's war" in all camps of archipelago Gulag. In such bloody wars so many of the very old and new thieves were lost that over a period of time their numbers were sharply reduced. Nevertheless, it could not "liquidate" organized crime in Russia. In the 1960s and 1970s the crime clans steadily increased on the basis of association of these professional "thieves": *Tzechovikis*, *Tyenyevikis* (white-collar crime), and corrupt government officers, including the police got inducted into these associations. Even the highest leadership of the Communist Party of Azerbaijan, Georgia, Kazakh, Moldavia, Uzbekistan, Moscow, and the senior members of the Ministry of Internal Affairs of the Soviet Union reportedly got involved in these criminal organizations.

A serious attempt to combat these newly emerging forms of organized crime was undertaken in the years of government by Andropov (1983–1984) and extended by Gorbachev. The police, prosecutor's office, and courts were authorized to investigate and to consider criminal cases against some of the highest officers. Limited success was achieved: Some were dismissed and some committed suicide to escape the degradation (e.g., former Minister of Internal Affairs, General Schelokov). Radical political, economic, and social reforms, initiated by Gorbachev, the so-called "Perestroika," attempted to remove the secrecy so vital for the operations of organized crime.

Comparative Evaluation of the Methods for Combating Organized Crime and Proposed Measures

Despite efforts by the governments of Andropov and Gorbachev, organized crime in these years could still not be eliminated. From the end of 1980s to the beginning of 1990s, Russian society has become more vigilant against the economic, social, and political dangers of organized crime. However, the struggle to combat it meaningfully has not been easy and is very complex. There are a number of reasons for these failures. First, the discussion "if there is organized crime in Russia," has to be abandoned. There is now sufficient evidence and common perception that syndicates are well-entrenched and growing in power every day.

Second, the legislative base, the criminal laws appear insufficient to successfully counteract these criminal organizations. The proposals for new laws "On Fighting Organized crime," and "On Fighting Corruption" have still not been accepted by the Russian parliament. The decree of the President of Russian Federation (No. 1–226 of 14 June 1994) "About urgent measures on the protection of population from gouging and other displays of organized crime" is incompatible with the Constitution of the Russian Federation. It also conflicts with the provisions and resolution of the State Duma of Federal Assembly passed on June 22, 1994, "About protection of the constitutional rights and freedom of the citizens at realization of measures on struggle with criminality." These legal lacunas obviously need to be rectified.

International experience of struggle with organized crime, for instance, in Italy, the United States, Japan, and other countries shows that the repressive measures of police and criminal justice are not so effective. In present-day Russia it is especially difficult to deal with organized crime for several reasons. First, the laws are insufficient and incompatible with the new emerging system of free-market economy. Necessary regulations have not been enforced—not only due to the shortcomings in the law-enforcement agencies, but also because of the fear of harming the nascent process itself. Second, the continuing apathy and suspicion toward police and other government functionaries is another setback in the struggle against organized crime rackets. Third, the police, judiciary, and lawmakers have yet to learn the new ways of functioning where every action has to be open and accountable to the people. Fourth, technical, financial, and personnel equipment for special police units (e.g., the Regional Board of Organized Crimes—RUOP) is not only insufficient, but also inferior to the technology being used by the organized crime groups. Whereas the police personnel lack sufficient number of communication equipment like wireless sets, the criminals are operating through cellular phones and computers. Fifth, political games and corruption are preventing the development of scientific strategy and effective tactics to struggle with organized crime.

However, the main difficulty is to devise a real and successful counteraction to organized crime in conditions of economic, financial, social, political crisis and instability with total corruption of power structures (federal and regional), police and courts. Unless the macro structures are reformed and the political leadership stirs itself to take the task of administering the country seriously, the struggle to combat organized crime will remain half-hearted.

There are several new laws being contemplated to control the growing criminalization in the country. A new Criminal Code, which was accepted by the Parliament and signed by the President, came into effect on 1 January 1997. In the code many novel features have been introduced that should ensure a legislative basis of struggle with organized crime. This includes for the first time a clear definition of the concepts "organized group," "criminal community," and others. Article 35, for instance, lays down a criterion of the criminal liability for the organization of criminal community and participating in it. Article 210 proposes criminalization of actions sponsored by criminal organizations, like kidnapping of a person and laundering of money. The code also provides for an amplification of the criminal liability for some crimes, such as murder, grievous bodily harm, rape, theft, swindling, robbery, extortion, and others that are usually resorted to by the organized groups. The future will show how these provisions of the new Criminal Code will be utilized by the law enforcement agencies and how effective these will be in practice, but the code certainly provides some hope and determination.

Conclusion

The following are the visible traits of organized crime in Russia:

- A wide extent of its spread (control over 40% to 60% of the country's enterprises and banks);
- A very high profit ("superprofit") derived from criminal activities;
- Declining efficiency of law-enforcement bodies leading to demands like "arbitration," "enforcement of rulings (verdicts)," guarding—so called "krysha" (roof) for organized crime groups;

- Total corruption of power, administrative, and law-enforcement bodies at all the levels;
- A wide social net of support because of the availability of many idle hands among the youth and impossibility of doing legitimate business due to total corruption, high taxes (up to 80% to 85%), growing criminal mentality, social anomie
- A wide extent to which violent methods are spreading
- The criminalization of government policies and economic activities along with the politicization of organized crime.

Russia is going farther and farther along the way of the state's and society's criminalization. The democracy and the economic reforms are jeopardized, which explains the growth of organized crime in the country. What may be done to stem the tide? Apart from the legislative and penal measures strengthening the criminal laws and enhancing the punishments, it seems more important to reform the economical, social, and political institutions in the country. For instance, support and development of legal business enterprises and more involvement of the legal profession in the economical, social, and political activities of the state are urgently needed and will provide a system of objectivity and fairness. It is necessary to remember, that the society is in need of financial and technical knowledge that is still limited to a small section of the society. In many cases it is simply the situation that the legal means are not available or not comprehensible, which forces people to resort to illegal, including criminal, means. The higher the degree of "responsive" societies, the more probable is the conformity to legality and lesser the inclination to illegal behavior of the people. Unfortunately, the degree of "responsiveness" of the modern Russian society is very low and the sudden spurt in criminal or illegal behavior is perhaps a natural outcome of the absence of a well-established and easily understood rule of law. For example, the economic policy of the state should ensure a fair profit for legal businesses, in comparison with illegal enterprises. This requires an imaginative and less cumbersome financial policy, a quick-responding banking system, and easy availability of credit facilities. Since these institutions have not developed in accordance with the needs of the society and are overregulated, the people find it easy to resort to criminal means and approach the loan sharks for their needs.

There is also an urgent need to decrease the unemployment rate. The unemployed, especially the young, form the main social base for organized crime. The share of non-working, able-bodied people among criminals arrested by the authorities has grown in Russia to almost 50 times greater between 1987 and 1996 (Statistical Review, 1996). Undoubtedly, so long as unemployment remains high, the ability of the criminal syndicates to lure young people into its fold cannot be controlled.

Similarly, the reduction of corruption through political methods is a reform that cannot be delayed any longer. "Corruption is global phenomenon" (Transparency International Newsletter, 1996), but it is particularly evil in Russia. The corruption among law enforcement authorities directly affects the capability of the society and government to combat organized crime. The corruption in financial institutions, especially banking, implies that economic crimes will flourish and political corruption acts to destroy the faith of the people in the system itself. Undoubtedly, the main obstacle to combating organized crime in Russia appears to be the widespread corruption in the country at present time.

Moreover, the need for urgent judicial measures and reforms cannot be overstated. For example, the necessity of completing and passing the laws "On Fighting Organized Crime," "On Fighting Corruption," and "On Laundering Money," cannot be postponed much longer. Similarly, the activity of the special police units requires to be enhanced with high professional staff and equipment. Additionally, the information system, operational competence, and international cooperation have to be taken up as a priority. Criminal organizations are an inevitable element of contemporary society and are well adapted to the society. If these are not controlled, then perhaps we may have to adapt ourselves to organized crime.

REFERENCES

Abadinsky, Howard. 1994. *Organized Crime*. 4th ed. Chicago: Nelson-Hall.

Abramkin, V. 1996. *In Search of a Solution: Crime, Criminal Policy and Prison Facilities in the Former Soviet Union*. Moscow: Human Rights Publishers.

Albanese, Jay S. 1996. *Organized Crime in America*. 3d ed. Cincinnati: Anderson Publishing.

Arlacchi, Pino. 1986. *Mafia Business: The Mafia Ethic and the Spirit of Capitalism*. Verso Edition.

Becker G. 1987. *Economic Analysis and Human Behavior: Advances in Behavioral Sciences*. Norwood, NY: Ablex Publ. Corp.

Block, Alan. 1994. *Space, Time and Organized Crime*. Transaction Publishers. New Brunswick, NJ.

Kelly, Robert, Ko-Lin Chin, Schatzbery, Rufus. (eds.). 1994. *Handbook of Organized Crime In the United States*, Greenwood, CT: Greenwood Press.

Mayerhofer, Chr., and J.M. Jehle. 1996. *Organisierte Kriminalitat. Lagebilder und Erscheinungsformen. Bekampfung und rechfliche Bewaltigung*. Heidelberg: Kriminalistik Verlag.

Ministry of Internal Affairs of Russia. 1994. *State of Crime in Russia* (in Russian). Moscow.

Nikiforov, Ilya V. 1997. *Russia Today.* http://www.city.net/countries/russia/. Faculty of Law. St. Petersburg, Russia: Center for Legal Information.

Ovchinsky, V., V. Eminov, and N. Jablokov. 1996. *Basis to Organized Crime* (in Russian). Moscow: JNFRAM.

Statistical Review. 1992. *Crime and Delinquency: 1991* (in Russian). Moscow: Finances and Statistics.

Statistical Review. 1996. *Crime and Delinquency: 1995* (in Russian) Moscow: Ministry of Internal Affairs of Russia.

Chapter 7

Organized Crime: A Perspective from Slovenia

Darko Maver

Introduction

Slovenia is a beautiful small country situated on the Mediterranean Sea. Carved out of the former Yugoslavia, the country has witnessed remarkable socioeconomic progress in the recent years. Bordering Croatia, Austria, Hungary, and Italy, the country has a population of two million and was proclaimed an independent republic on June 25, 1991. The two largest cities are the capital, Ljubljana, and Maribo, where almost one-fourth of the population lives. The highest legislative authority is the National Assembly, which has ninety deputies elected for a four-year term. The president of the country is also the supreme commander while the highest executive body is composed of the prime minister and the council of ministers. The judiciary is independent and obliged only to the constitution, acting as the guardian of civil liberties. The office of the public prosecutor is responsible for bringing cases to trial and initiating and controlling the investigations. The administration of justice is carried out by the ministry of interior, which controls the 6,000 police personnel and other support services. The majority of police officers are high school graduates. Most are members of the Slovenia police union, an independent body, but police are not given the right to strike.

Organized crime is becoming a more important, critical, and controversial issue in many countries of the world. There is no major national or international conference, symposium, or congress on crime that does not include the question of organized crime as its central topic. The phenomenon also gets special attention from social, economic, and even political points of view.

Parliaments, governments, national security councils, ministries of interior, or other state agencies, as well as media, are discussing whether there is a problem of organized crime in their country, and if so, to what extent, which forms it takes, how to tackle it, what methods to use, and how to get the right balance between the powers of the police on one hand and the constitutional rights of the citizens on the other. They look for ways to promote cooperation among the states in the fight against national and transnational organized crime at the investigative, prosecutorial, and judicial levels. They want to find the most efficient legislative measures and other repressive or preventive measures, and implement the best crime policy.

Yet, quite often, there is no consensus about all these very important questions. Some would argue, for example, that the problem does not exist at all, or is only a minor one. Others would put it on the top priority list in the fight against crime. The police ask for more "special measures" (e.g., telephone control, undercover investigations, covert surveillance) and more severe laws, while civil rights activists and some scholars worry about such suggestions and demand a more reasonable approach.

"The truth is out there," one could say. But the question is how to find it and what to do about it. Organized crime is like a cancer: It cannot be seen openly, but it grows and can soon endanger the whole body (society). It grows slowly but continuously, and when the symptoms come out, it is almost too late to react. The problem is not new. Even J. Edgar Hoover, for many years the director of the FBI, one of the most powerful law enforcement agencies in the world, did not acknowledge the existence of the Mafia for a very long time (Kessler, 1993). One can, of course, speculate about the reasons for his attitude, but the fact is that the FBI started to work on organized crime only when it was already widespread throughout the country.

Today, the situation in some other countries is the same. Since there are no convictions, no evident cases of organized crime, no evident money-laundering attempts or public corruption cases, the politicians and some scholars would argue that organized crime does not exist or at least is not a big problem. There are signs (e.g., murders with no evident motive, people with a lot of money but no legal sources) that indicate that the situation might not be so idyllic as it seems. The police may also have information and hints about such activities, but the legal evidence is generally lacking. Undoubtedly, objective empirical research is necessary to get a clearer view of organized criminal activities.

As far as research (theoretical or empirical) is concerned, the problem is evident: Very few countries in Europe have made such efforts so far. There is an important lack of adequate empirical criminological research in most European countries and the reasons for that are either inability of the institutions (e.g., Council of Europe, Interpol, Europol) to prepare meaningful reports on organized crime, or "at least their unwillingness to publish such reports, assuming that they are capable of making them (as is the case in some fields)" (Fijnaut, 1996). According to Fijnaut, especially Middle and Eastern European countries are "not willing or not capable, for all sorts of reasons, to further empirical research and/or to assess on a regular basis the actual development of those problems" (1996:5). The need for empirical research has been stressed also in Slovenian criminological literature (Peèar, 1995).

It is also of utmost importance that despite many conferences and congresses, declarations and conventions, and bilateral or multilateral agreements, there is still not enough action and cooperation among states to fight against national or transnational organized crime, and that state borders too often obstruct efficient investigation or prosecution. There are countries where dirty money is quite welcome since "money doesn't stink." They represent safe havens that are quickly filled with criminal entrepreneurs of different colors and nationalities. Their financial power is enormous and it is not only a threat for corruption of all kinds, but it actually endangers whole economic and political systems—especially in newly founded countries and countries in transition, as well as basic ethical and moral values in these societies (Peèar, 1996a, 1996b). Fighting organized crime is therefore extremely difficult and sometimes seemingly useless. It is like fighting a tornado, a hurricane, or great floods. The problem is global, and the possible solution might be achieved only by joint efforts.

Slovenia is a small country with no tradition of Cosa Nostra, *Cammora*, *'Ndrangheta*, and other Mafia organizations or big, notorious organized crime organizations like cocaine cartels of South America, Chinese Triads, Japanese Yakuza, or Russian Mafia. It cannot be compared with other countries in terms of experience in combating organized crime. Yet, because of its geostrategic position as a crossroad from east to west and from south to north of Europe, the harbor of Koper and many airline connections, it is also open for transit of organized crime activities as well as for the rise of domestic criminal organizations. Slovenia is also a country in transition, with privatization processes going on rapidly. Therefore, it is even more vulnerable to different kinds of organized crime (Peèar, 1995, 325).

The Nature and Extent of Organized Crime in Slovenia

So far there is no clear and commonly used definition of organized crime. Criminologists and representatives of the police or other law enforcement agencies usually agree that organized crime is a phenomenon that represents far greater danger for a given society than other forms of crime. Yet, it cannot be simply defined because of its specifics and diversity (Karakaš, 1996). Therefore, it is easier to talk about the features of organized crime, to name the areas where it appears or to describe its forms, than to give any definitions.

Especially in the last few years, there has been a great increase of interest in organized crime in Slovenia from a criminological (or theoretical) point of view, as well as arising from the practical police work. Peèar (1996), Karakaš (1996), Dobovšek (1996b), Maver (1995), Podbevšek (1993), and others have been writing about the problem and attended national or international conferences or seminars where this topic was discussed. However, so far there has been no empirical research done about the nature, extent, and forms of organized crime in Slovenia. There are only police statistics that may indicate how serious the problem is in this country. There are also estimations and speculations about it made by politicians and writers (Ravnikar, 1995).

The characteristics of organized crime as defined in Slovenian criminological literature include the following:

- special structure (as a corporation, patriarchal, or some other model);
- membership (the individual must feel a part of the group or organization);
- activity for a longer period of time (not only for committing one or several specific offenses);
- activity in different in illegal and legal fields;
- the use of force, corruption, or other illegal means to achieve the goals;
- professionalization and specialization;
- influence on state institutions (either through direct or indirect ways).

This is not the only attempt to describe the most important elements of organized crime but it is probably the most widely accepted one. In the ministry of interior, a criminal offense is classified as "organized crime" when the criminal activity is carried out in an entrepreneurial way by a criminal association, using violence or corruption to achieve profitable or parvenu goals. (This definition is based on the analysis of the definitions used by Interpol, in the United States, and in Germany.)

As such it consists of the following elements:

- The existence of a criminal association or group, which presumes an existence of a hierarchically organized and structured group of at least two perpetrators, connected with a joint plan to reach their goals;
- A criminal activity is carried out in an entrepreneurial way, which means that the execution of criminal deeds represents for a criminal group its basic and most important activity for a longer period of time, performed in a professional way;
- The basic goal of the group is to achieve profit with illegal activities;
- The group uses violence or corruption to achieve its goals.

The police use their own definition to classify criminal offenses as "organized crime," and separate statistics for organized crime were introduced in Slovenia only in 1995. Police statistics show only the tip of the iceberg and point more at their own work than at the actual phenomenon. Still, such statistics are important and provide some indication of the increase of offenses that may be said to be associated with organized crime. Compared with the general crime rate, which shows a clear decrease in the last four years, the number of cases of organized crime indicate the opposite trend.

In 1995 the police in Slovenia investigated 735 offenses resulting from organized criminal activities, which is 1.9 percent of all crimes. Among them were 151 forged documents, 124 burglaries (of this, 41 car thefts), 12 robberies, 10 extortions, 99 drug offenses, 49 cases of currency counterfeiting, 49 cases of illegal border crossings, 45 cases of illicit trafficking with weapons or explosives, 15 cases of formation of a criminal association, 3 cases of criminal conspiracy, and 1 homicide (Svetek, 1996).

In 1996, the increase in crimes with elements of organized crime is obvious. There were 1,263 such offenses with an estimated loss of 1,184,000.000 SIT (approximately $1 million U.S. dollars). The biggest increase was in the field of white-collar crime and in drug offenses (+ 147%). Also, the number of murders connected with organized crime has increased from one to six, as well as money-laundering offenses from zero to five. It is difficult to say how much the increase in the number of organized crime offenses can be attributed to the actual increase of such offenses and how much to the improvements in gathering these statistics by the police (Report of Slovenia, 1996).

Some are part of the so called "classical" criminal offenses and some were committed as economic offenses or "special offenses" (e.g., drug and arms trafficking, counterfeiting of currency). In general, most of the forms of organized crime mentioned in Freemantle's popular book, *Octopus* (1996), have been detected in Slovenia also, either in transit or actually being committed in the country itself.

The statistics show a favorable situation when compared to the general crime rates in many other countries of Central and Eastern Europe. However, there is a possibility that the decreasing number of criminal offenses and better clearance rate is not the result of actual crime situation and better police work, but rather of reorganization of police on local and regional levels. This transformation has been going on since for the last two to three years, and there are some changes in the penal code that have affected the nature of crime statistics in the country. Also, further examination of the changes in the structure of criminality in Slovenia shows less optimistic trends. There has been an important increase in more dangerous and more violent crimes and especially in organized crime. This can also be seen through crime statistics, which are most likely part of the organized crimes.

Even a brief look at the figures in Tables 7.1 and 7.2 shows an increase of the criminal deeds with elements of organization, especially in the field of drug offenses. Apart from this slightly alarming fact, we must consider the following troubling issues, too:

- Increase of armament, violence, and ruthlessness of the criminals;
- Their technical equipment is getting better;
- The number of perpetrators with specific skills is increasing;
- In dealing with these categories, Slovene police officers are being more and more exposed to threats and violence;

TABLE 7.1 CRIMINAL OFFENSES IN SLOVENIA (POLICE STATISTICS)

Year	Number of Offenses	Clearance Rate %
1991	42,250	54%
1992	54,085	56%
1993	44,278	58%
1994	43,635	57%
1995	38,176	60%
1996	36,587	65%

TABLE 7.2 SELECTED REPORTED CRIMES IN SLOVENIA

Type of Crime	1991	1992	1993	1994	1995	1996
kidnapping	5	5	4	10	4	8
loss of freedom	29	52	51	65	67	83
car theft	353	431	485	496	714	713
extortion	53	152	210	269	281	206
drug offenses	95	176	199	407	453	675
illegal border crossings	133	30	83	87	166	113

- The citizens, even the victims, are less likely to cooperate with the police and legal authorities;
- The possibilities of legal argumentation are smaller; that has an influence on the efficiency of the courts, which is declining;
- Criminal investigation by the police is insufficient and uncoordinated.

In the last few years, the formation of true criminal associations has been noticed for the first time. They were mostly active in the field of "forced collection of debts," illicit drug and weapons trafficking, and in forming criminal associations. It is being found that they commit more and more serious criminal offenses, are well prepared, professional, and violent. Recently, in Ljubljana, the capital of Slovenia, the shooting between members of two criminal associations at a gas station took place in the old "Al Capone" style. Both groups were composed of members of foreign nationalities. Another major incident—the killing of four people—was committed in a very professional manner. It has been suspected that this crime was perpetrated by organized crime groups either from Slovenia or Croatia. It is significant that the number of organized crime homicides rose from one in 1995 to six in 1996.

As in most Eastern European countries, criminal organizations from the states of the former Soviet Union have also entered Slovenia. They are involved mostly in prostitution, car thefts, and "business cooperation." Criminal groups from Italy are also active in drug trafficking as well as in money-laundering attempts, especially through casinos. Since Slovenia is close to the former war area in Bosnia, it is facing two possible dangers: that more weapons and explosives will be available to the criminals and that certain groups of ex-soldiers will form new criminal organizations or join the existing ones. They are well trained and ready to use violence, so they will move toward the countries of Central, Eastern, and Western

Europe as well as to the other continents. Therefore, Slovenia expects the increase of criminal activities from different foreign groups, but because of its smallness it will probably serve as a transit country only.

There are some indications of nationally homogeneous criminal associations like the Albanian Montenegro and Serbian Mafia that have emerged from the "criminal influence" of disintegrated Yugoslavia. The investigated cases of these criminal associations suggest that the active and dangerous groups are those in which the roles are shared between domestic perpetrators and the members of ex-Yugoslavian nations. The exception is drug trafficking where the perpetrators are mostly of Albanian origin.

As far as drug trafficking is concerned, it is possible that the old Balkan road, which has changed its route a bit because of the war in Bosnia (it went through Bulgaria, Romania, Hungary, and then through Slovenia or Austria to Western Europe), will become more popular again. So we can expect more heroin being smuggled through Slovenia to the West. Another way in which Slovenia appears as the transit region in the "cocaine connection" is the cocaine route from South America to Europe. The harbors in the Adriatic Sea (e.g., Koper in Slovenia, Trieste in Italy, and Rijeka in Croatia) are intermediate stops for final cocaine destinations in Western Europe. Cocaine comes to Slovenia via the airlines as well. The characteristics of these cocaine roads are more or less unknown to us because we were confronted with these problems only recently. (In 1992 a shipment of 19 kg of cocaine was accidentally found in Koper). The third direction in the international transit of drugs is the "cannabis road" from Morocco through Spain, France, and Italy to Slovenia. It is feared that a part of the merchandise stays in the country and the rest goes to Austria and the countries of Northern and Eastern Europe. The fourth is the road of synthetic drugs, which come to Slovenia from Central and Western European countries.

In 1996, the following quantities of drugs were seized in Slovenia: 24.5 kg of heroin, 0.8 kg of cocaine, 5.4 kg of hashish, 34 kg of marihuana, 18,000 tablets of ecstasy, 622 pills of amphetamines, and 947 pieces of LSD. This is not alarming when compared with the seizures in other countries of this region, but together with increased number of drug addicts in the country, it is an important sign of the growing drug problem. Every year more and more people die of heroin overdose. In 1996, sixteen people died, four more than in 1995. As previously mentioned, there was an increase of 49 percent for offenses connected with drugs in 1996 from the year 1995 (675 compared to 453). There was also an increase in the number of petty offenses connected with drugs (1,174 in 1996 and 702 in 1995). In 1995, of the 675 criminal offenses, 203 were classified as organized crime offenses (Report of Slovenia, 1996).

Offenses connected with illegal arms smuggling decreased in 1996 (by 33.5%). However, there were 183 such offenses and 34 were the result of organized crime. The police have arrested two organized crime groups with 35 and 38 kg of explosives. In 1996, the rising trend of offenses of prostitution continued. There were 29 such offenses and 18 were committed by organized crime groups. The act of prostitution is a petty offense in Slovenian law, but organizing prostitution or maiming people to force them into prostitution is a criminal offense. In Slovenia there are two kinds of prostitution: the so called "mobitel" prostitution, where mostly Slovenian women are involved, and the prostitution of women from Eastern European countries, which occurs in clubs and places of nighttime entertainment.

Among the so called "classical" criminal offenses, Slovenia faces the problem of car theft and organized burglaries. For a number of years a continuing increase in car theft in Slovenia and the smuggling of vehicles stolen in Western European countries has been noticed. The transit of such vehicles through Slovenia into the countries of ex-Yugoslavia, Near East, or in the ex-socialist states has increased. Vehicles are usually taken through Hungary or Croatia, where they are sold by using false registration papers. In 1996, there were 713 such offenses, out of which 47 were done by organized crime groups.

Money laundering should also not be underestimated in Slovenia. Besides a general suspicion that money is laundered in casinos, more evidence exists that there is money laundering going on in the field of economic crimes. The statistics given by the Office for the Prevention of Money Laundering at the Ministry of Finance, suggests that between January 1995 and September 1996, a sum of money in excess of 19,000,000,000 SIT (approximately $123 million U.S. dollars) was involved in suspicious transactions. Of this, it is probable that 1,800,000,000 SIT (approximately $12 million U.S. dollars) is actually "dirty" money. To date, 14 cases, involving 55 Slovenian or foreign nationals and 28 foreign or domestic legal entities, have been tried in the courts, numbers that show this to be a serious problem for a small country. It is also a concern that Slovenia is being targeted by well-organized criminal associations from Western Europe and former Socialist countries that are entering the money-laundering business. Criminal associations from the former Soviet Union launder money made mainly through prostitution, car thefts, and "business cooperation," while dirty money from Western European countries is coming from business frauds and tax evasions. Thus far, the collected information indicates that "dirty" money finds its way mostly into the banking sector and in foreign currency exchanges. There is also some evidence that shows it is also moving into the Slovenian capital market (Report of Slovenia,

1996). There were also some fraudulent attempts from other countries, especially from Nigeria, but without success.

In 1996 there was an important increase (19.6%) of economic crime offenses. There were 4,976 such offenses. The biggest increase was in business fraud (2,455, or 30% more than in 1995). Many of them had all the elements of organized crime as previously described. As the country is in transition from one economic system to the other and the privatization process is going on, a large number of economic offenses are likely to occur in this field.

Corruption is usually also connected with organized crime. It is difficult, however, to give a clear answer to the question of the extent of corruption in Slovenia. Nevertheless, it is possible to give some figures that represent a general estimate of the true situation. For the decade from 1986 to the end of 1996, police statistics show 404 processed criminal cases of corruption on the active side (giving of illegal gifts and bribery) and 229 criminal cases on the passive side (acceptance of illegal gifts and bribes). In 1995 there were 31 offenses of giving gifts or bribes and in 1996, 26 such cases.

Among the most common forms of corruption exposed in Slovenia are the bribery of civil and public officials to carry out or ignore certain measures which are against the interests of the state (particularly police officers, customs officers, and officials within administrative procedures), the bribing of senior staff in commercial organizations to act against the best interests of their company in making business decisions, and the bribing of senior government officials to use their influence to secure the adoption of certain regulations to the benefit of specific individuals or groups (Karakaš, 1996).

Measures Including Legislations to Combat Organized Crime

In general, three major reactions to organized crime can be put forward:

- Penal measures
- Procedural measures
- Organizational measures

Penal Measures

In the field of criminal legislation there are provisions with which the state tries to criminalize different kinds of organizing criminal activities and provisions with which certain activities of organized crime groups might be prevented (e.g., racketeering, extortion, drug trafficking, and money laundering). With both kinds of measures certain problems arise: these might be either too wide or too narrow. In the Slovenian Penal Code, there are two articles that deal directly with organized crime, namely Article 297 (Criminal Association) and Article 298 (Criminal Conspiracy), but equally important is the article on Money Laundering (art. 252).

Criminal Association (art. 297)

1. Whoever establishes a group for the purposes of perpetrating criminal offenses for which a punishment exceeding five years of imprisonment may be applied, shall be sentenced to imprisonment for not more than three years;
2. Whoever joins the group under the preceding article, shall be sentenced to imprisonment for not more than one year;
3. If the perpetrator of the offense under the first or second paragraph of the present article has prevented the committing of criminal offense under the first paragraph or has provided information about it, thus enabling the offense to be prevented, his punishment may be remitted.

Criminal Conspiracy (art. 298)

Whoever agrees to commit a criminal offense with another, for which the punishment exceeding five years of imprisonment may be imposed, shall be sentenced to imprisonment for not more then one year.

Money laundering (art. 252)

1. Whosoever engages in banking, financial, or other economic transactions, accepts, exchanges, disposes of, or otherwise by means of money laundering conceals the true origins of amounts of money or property of a considerable value, which he knows to have been acquired by the organized trafficking of drugs, illicit arms trade, or other unlawful activity, shall be punished by imprisonment for a maximum of five years;
2. Any person abetting an act mentioned in the first paragraph of this article and who should have or could have been aware that the money has been acquired through a prohibited activity mentioned in the first paragraph of this article, shall be punished by imprisonment for not more than two years;
3. Money and property from the first and second paragraph of this article shall be confiscated.

The first Slovenian law on the prevention of money laundering was passed in July 1994, and was further amended in November 1995. This law defined the criminal act of money laundering that is not limited only to selected "classic" criminal acts as predicate offenses—with an obligatory identification of clients and bookkeeping in financial organizations (the principle of "knowing your client"). It also imposes the obligation of informing of a special body in the Ministry of Finance—The Office for Money Laundering Prevention—on cash transactions above a certain limit (approximately $23,000 U.S. dollars) and on any suspicious transactions. Slovenia was relatively quick to implement all the essential international standards in this field.

Procedural Measures

Among procedural measures in the fight against organized crime, the introduction of special investigative measures and techniques is important, since classical techniques of criminal investigation or criminalistics do not suffice. The goal for the use of special measures is clear: to get more information and better quality of evidence on perpetrators. Slovenian Code of Criminal Procedure (art. 150) from 1995 allows the police to use special measures:

Article 150:

1.) The investigating judge may order the following measures to be taken against a person suspected of having been in complicity in the commission of crimes prescribed in Article 151 of the present Code:

   1. controlling and recording of telephone conversations and other forms of communication by technical devices;
   2. secret cooperation of the police, secret surveillance and tracking, as well as visual recording;
   3. apparent purchase of objects;
   4. apparent bribery;
   5. eavesdropping in private places by use of technical devices;
   6. access to the computer system of a bank or any other legal person engaged in financial or other economic activity.

2.) Measures from the preceding paragraph shall be ordered by the investigating judge upon a substantiated motion filed by the state prosecutor, provided either that evidence may not be gathered otherwise or that the gathering of such evidence might entail disproportionate difficulties.

Article 151:

1.) Measures from Provisions 1, 2, and 5 of the first paragraph of the preceding article may be ordered in proceedings involving:

1. criminal offenses against the security of the Republic of Slovenia and its constitutional order and criminal offenses against humanity and international law for which punishment of five years or more of imprisonment is prescribed by statute;
2. criminal offenses of kidnapping under Article 144, unauthorized production and trafficking of drugs under Article 196, enabling the use of drugs under Article 197, extortion under Article 218, unauthorized acceptance of gifts under Article 247, unauthorized giving of gifts under Article 248, making of counterfeit money under Article 249, money laundering under Article 252, smuggling under Article 255, acceptance of bribes under Article 267, giving of bribes under Article 268, criminal association under Article 297, illicit manufacture and trafficking of weapons and explosive materials under Article 310, and hijacking under Article 330 of the Penal Code of Slovenia;
3. other criminal offenses for which punishment of eight years or more of imprisonment is prescribed by the statute;

2.) The measure from Provision 3 of the first paragraph of the preceding article may be ordered for criminal offenses of unauthorized production and trafficking of drugs under Article 196, enabling the use of drugs under Article 197, making of counterfeit money under Article 248, and illicit manufacture and trafficking of weapons and explosive materials under Article 309, provided that these objects might serve as evidence in criminal proceedings;

3.) The purchase of objects and apparent bribery may not constitute criminal activity;

4.) The measure from Provision 6 of the first paragraph of the previous article may be ordered in dealing with the criminal offense of money laundering under Article 252 of the Penal Code of the Republic of Slovenia.

These methods have been used especially in investigation of organized crime and the data for 1996 show the following picture (compared with 1995):

- 191 (144) cases of surveillance and tracking as well as visual recording;
- 132 (99) cases of telephone control;
- 256 (96) cases of secret cooperation of police;
- 45 (41) cases of apparent purchase of objects.

Polygraph testing of the suspects was used in 430 (429) cases. (Polygraph is not considered as a special measure according to Article 150 and cannot be used in criminal procedure as evidence. However, the police can use it for tactical purposes. The written consent of the person being tested is necessary.) In 1995 there were 93 positive results; 226 persons examined through this device were eliminated as suspects; in 46 cases it was not possible to give clear opinion; in 29 cases, suspects refused to be tested, and in 35 cases testing was rejected because the persons were not suitable for testing (Report on Work of Criminal Investigation Service and Crime, 1997).

Also important is Article 156 of Code of Criminal Procedure:

Article 156: If there exist reasons for suspicion that a certain person has committed a criminal offense for which punishment of five or more years of imprisonment is provided by statute, the investigating judge shall, upon substantiated motion from the public prosecutor, order a bank or other legal persons performing financial activities to supply information on the bank accounts of such a person, provided that this information could serve as important proof for the detection of other criminal offenses.

According to Article 159, the State Prosecutor can allow the postponement of some investigative measures if a large-scale criminal activity can be cleared in this way. A controlled delivery of drugs can be allowed through this article.

Organizational Measures

The third kind of measure to fight organized crime is of an organizational nature. Since organized crime is a special kind of crime, the organization of state repressive mechanisms, mainly the police and state prosecution, must be specially organized. With the reorganization of the Slovenian Criminal Investigation Service, which started in 1990, more emphasis was given to the specialization and professionalization of investigators. In the Criminal Investigation Directorate at the Ministry of Interior, a special Sector for Organized Crime was established in 1996, which is divided into three divisions (drugs, anti-terrorism, and general organized crime).

In all the eleven regional police administrations, special units in the Criminal Service Bureau for the fight against organized crime were introduced, while on the level of local police stations, some uniformed police officers were changed to detectives and they joined the newly founded "Local Criminal Investigative Units." In addition to this, special units for "the control of the territory" were set up in Ljubljana, Maribor, and Celje, the three largest cities of Slovenia. Their task is not to investigate criminal offenses but to control the most critical places where the criminals gather or where the offenses most often take place. A lot of emphasis was also given to the establishment of analytical support (both operative and strategic). In this view no major case is investigated without the help of the analyst.

The last important element is the desire to get more knowledge, training, and experience in investigating organized crime cases. Several seminars were organized together with the FBI and DEA in Slovenia, Slovenian police officers have attended FBI National Academy in Quantico, International Law Enforcement Academy (ILEA) in Budapest, Hungary, Middle European Police Academy (MEPA), and seminars that are organized by Interpol or other international organizations.

COMPARATIVE EVALUATION OF THE METHODS FOR COMBATING ORGANIZED CRIME AND PROPOSED MEASURES

Comparative evaluation of anti-organized crime measures can be made from at least two perspectives: from the view of measures used in different countries or from the view of measures used in a certain country. We shall briefly touch upon both views. It is obvious that different countries not only have different situations regarding organized crime, but also different laws (penal and procedural), police organization, and crime policies. Some differences are obvious, but it is difficult to assess all of them without a comprehensive, comparative research and study.

As already pointed out, there is no common definition of organized crime or suitable common criminal offense in the penal code of each country. The criminalization of specific offenses that are covered as the part of organized crime (e.g., drug offenses, trafficking with arms, extortion, illegal gambling, prostitution, pornography, and racketeering) differ considerably. Some countries still don't have special legislation against money laundering, some are working on it, and many others have problems with its practical implementation. The situation is the same about drugs and other precursor laws. The undercover police measures or other procedural measures also differ among countries. It is more or less clear that in order to fight organized crime, special measures must be used. But how far to go is another question.

One of the most important problems is how to find the right balance between the measures that enable efficiency of the police and the protection of the rights of citizens. This is a classical dilemma, yet very important for the fight against organized crime. The other side, that is the criminal, does not face such problems or limitations. There are some basic differences between the states in undercover police activities and measures they can use. This becomes clear when instructors from the FBI or DEA come to Slovenia to teach undercover techniques and face a different legal situation in our country. The RICO statute is a very useful tool to fight organized crime, but unfortunately it is not implemented in our legislation. To perform undercover activities in a big country like the United States is quite different but not so simple in a small one like Slovenia. There are also differences in laws that regulate undercover police work in other European countries. In some places bugging is allowed; elsewhere it is forbidden. In some states certain police measures can lead to valid legal evidence, while in others it can be just informal information.

There are also differences in organization of police and other law enforcement agencies, their professionalism, experiences, technical equipment they can use, and the financial support that is available to them. In Slovenia, "task forces," have been introduced within which special units for fighting organized crime are formed at the state prosecutor's office to work together with special police units. Besides that, investigating magistrates and trial judges are becoming specialized to deal with organized crime. In this respect, the experiences from the United States are very welcome.

Analytical support is very important, too. Crime analyses, both operative and strategic, are of utmost importance. It is impossible to imagine successful work on organized crime groups without analytical support. Yet the situation regarding it is still quite different among the various countries in Europe. In this regard, the support of some countries to Slovenia needs to be emphasized.

While talking about different anti-crime, and especially anti-organized crime measures, it is important to note that there are serious efforts to harmonize legislation as well as crime policy within Europe. In this regard European Union is not only working on harmonization in member countries, but is also helping all associated countries in creating their legislation and policy. Through the PHARE program for the fight against drugs, all eleven beneficiary countries get assistance in creating laws against money laundering, illicit drug trafficking, control of precursors, and also legal drugs, as well as for establishing the common drug information systems, drug demand reduction policy, and drug supply reduction measures.

The Council of Europe (with its different committees) has prepared many recommendations regarding specific fields of crime and the fight against crime. Among them, very important is Recommendation number (96) 8 on crime policy in Europe during this time of change. From the point of view of the fight against organized crime, there is another recommendation, though only in the draft stage, which is very important, namely the recommendation on intimidation of witnesses and the rights of the defense. It deals with measures to be taken in relation to organized crime and crime in the family. What is also very important is the part of the recommendation that suggests international cooperation in this field.

Recently, the Council of Europe has launched a large project to fight against organized crime and corruption in states in transition, called project, "OCTOPUS." Countries had to fill out a comprehensive questionnaire on corruption and organized crime and prepare a national report, which was then discussed at the Conference on "Corruption and organized crime in states in transition," held in Sofia from 12 to 14 December 1996. Participants from fourteen countries (Albania, Bulgaria, Croatia, Czech Republic, Hungary, Latvia, Lithuania, Moldova, Poland, Russian Federation, Slovakia, Slovenia, "the Former Yugoslav Republic of Macedonia," and Ukraine), together with scientific experts, discussed the contents of the national reports and tried to evaluate and make recommendations for legislation against corruption and organized crime existing in their countries, and its implementation. The project was designed to be carried out during a period of eighteen months and will continue with the visit of experts to each country involved.

From a world perspective, the Naples Political Declaration and Global Action Plan (1990) against Organized Transnational Crime is important, as well as the resolutions adopted by the United Nations Congress on the Prevention of Crime and the Treatment of Offenders in Cairo in 1995, and resolutions from the General Assembly of Interpol. All of them have produced many practical guidelines for legislative and organizational measures to fight organized crime more successfully.

The comparative evaluation of various anti-organized crime measures already existing in Slovenia is not an easy task. Slovenia is a relatively young country with brand new legislation. It is difficult to assess its effectiveness in such a short time. However, some evaluation is possible. The new Penal Code, Code of Criminal Procedure, Law on Prevention of Money Laundering, and office for the fight against money laundering, as well as organizational changes in police have contributed to successful measures against organized crime in Slovenia.

The weak point is the "double protection" of suspects in police procedure. According to the Slovenian Code of Criminal Procedure, the police have no right to interrogate people as defendants. They can only collect information from them or hold "interviews." The right to interrogate suspects is given only to the investigating judge. Still, the police, when questioning suspects, must inform them of their rights (the right to remain silent, to have their attorney present, etc.) in almost the same way as the Miranda warning in the United States. The statements that suspects give after such warning, however, cannot be used at the trial. After the investigation is finished these statements must be sealed in a special envelope, so that the trial judge and jurors cannot see them. Only in very special circumstances can such statements be used in court. Generally, they are just information for the investigating judge and state prosecutor. So, even if the suspect confessed the crime in the presence of his lawyer, this cannot be used as evidence, which is rather unusual. There are attempts to change this rule to provide that if all warnings are given to the suspect, the statement can be used as evidence.

Another problem is the use of "special measures," according to Article 150 of the Code of Criminal Procedure. The police can use them only if the criminal offense has already been committed, that is retrospectively. It cannot be used to prevent future offenses, no matter how serious these might be. The proposed new Police Act would introduce such provisions and some new measures to facilitate undercover investigation.

The introduction of "local criminal investigative units," units for the "control of the territory," special anti-organized crime units, as well as specialization of state prosecutors have had positive results so far. So has more frequent analytical (operative and strategic) support to investigators and new forensic methods, especially DNA identification.

Organized crime, be it on the field of "classical" or economic crime, is a global phenomenon that does not recognize any national borders. It has enormous financial power, can use violent and illegal means to achieve its goals, infiltrates into legal political and economic institutions, and is well organized and protected (Maver, 1995). Its basic goal is to get money and power. Therefore, the measures to combat organized crime need to focus on these characteristics. Several preventive and repressive measures are now under consideration.

Measures used to improve the success of fighting organized crime must involve the following:

- The true political will to fight: many politicians have been very aggressively verbally attacking organized crime (especially during pre-election campaigns), but the real action is missing. The reasons might be because some are involved in it, they do not want to lose the money that is being invested in their country, they can feel that there are other priorities, they worry about human rights or the police and law enforcement agencies becoming too powerful, or there is not sufficient public support. At the Naples World Ministerial Conference against Organized Transnational Crime, as well as many other conferences, the political will to fight organized crime was clearly demonstrated, but many decisions written in the Global Action Plan have not been realized. So it is important not only to agree about fighting organized crime, but to start doing so. Many bilateral and multilateral agreements on fighting against organized crime have been signed. (Slovenia has signed seven such agreements with neighboring countries and other countries in Europe.) However, many are not enforced. Some countries are especially reluctant in providing information about bank accounts and financial transactions because of bank secrecy, even if clear evidence of money laundering exists. Therefore, more political will and support to actually fight organized crime are of utmost importance.

- The use of prevention strategies and not only repressive measures: since organized crime often covers fields which are often economically neglected by the state or are illegal (so they provide citizens with goods that are either more expensive or not available on the free market), the economic measures by the state could make such illegal activities unnecessary. The never-ending question about legalization of some drugs will stay open for quite some time. When dealing with money laundering, banks and other financial organizations as well as business enterprises need to know the signs indicating possible money-laundering attempts and receive adequate advice about their conduct. Organized crime, as well as crime in general, has its causes in sociological, economic, and political roots of each society. To fight symptoms and not causation is the result of the relative powerlessness of today's world and its state institutions, and it cannot bring us to successful suppression of organized crime (Peèar, 1996b). It is quite clear that repressive measures are important and necessary, too, but more efforts are needed to be directed toward prevention and stressed at international conferences as well as in national crime policy. As far as Slovenia is concerned, it is rather disappointing that it still does not have a clear concept of fighting organized crime. There is no real strategy to do so, either with repressive or preventive measures. Actions are more or less uncoordinated and left to individual institutions. On the other hand, we sometimes try to copy and implement strategies that are used by larger countries that are simply not appropriate for a small country like Slovenia. They should not be brought in without modifications. Thus the creative integration of foreign concepts is necessary.

- <u>Harmonization of legislation (both substantive and procedural)</u>: There are many differences on the fields of legislation among the states and there is an obvious need to make better attempts to harmonize them. The harmonization of legislative measures in Europe (both within European Union or Council of Europe) need to continue and be coordinated with similar procedures on other continents. There is still more to be achieved in the field of substantive penal law than on procedural criminal law since the differences in approach are too great in the latter. It is encouraging that much has been done recently in Europe to harmonize legislation and its implementation in the fight against organized crime in Central and Eastern European States. The so-called "Octopus" project is an effort among the many countries to develop programs for the fight against drugs. These include implementing legislation on illegal drug control, precursors and legal drug control, as well as building harmonized drug information systems and drug demand reduction strategies. Various committees of the Council of Europe at Strasbourg have also been working on witness protection, crime policy, and so on. Besides some changes in the

Slovenian Penal Code and Code of Criminal Procedure (as mentioned previously), the proposed new Police Act will also be very important. It will enable the police to use undercover investigation and other special methods to prevent serious crimes instead of only investigate them when they have already been committed. This will be one of the most important legislative innovations for the fight against organized crime. Special measures for witness protection are another important field of interest for legislators in which serious work is going on.

- <u>Organizational changes of police and law enforcement agencies and their professionalization</u>: Specialized police units are very important in this regard, as well as "task forces" of different kinds. Well-structured and well-organized criminal groups require to be confronted with well-organized police forces. Centralized units for the fight against organized crime as well as other organizational changes in Slovenian criminal police have proven to be successful. However, better cooperation with uniformed police (especially in gathering intelligence) still needs to be achieved. Also, more analytical support (operational and strategic) is necessary. Success against organized crime demands special training and special skills of everyone involved. Cooperation in education and training among states is very important, especially for those who have less experience in this field. It is clear that organized crime cannot be combated in the ways of classical criminal investigation and evidence gathering. Therefore, new strategies must be developed and introduced. Organized crime is well hidden, well structured, and well protected, so it is hard to detect it. Intelligence and counter intelligence measures, undercover work, use of special methods, and other "non-classical" methods investigation must be used. The indices of organized crime activity are demonstrated by financial gain, so without the help of economic and financial institutions and organizations they are hard to trace. Thus, there is the need to develop better coordination and cooperation between the financial institutions and enforcement agencies.

- <u>Better technical equipment for law enforcement</u>: It is clear that in the fight against organized crime, good, modern equipment is needed, which many countries cannot afford because of high prices. Special equipment for undercover investigation is necessary. Systems for efficient identification of offenders are also required, as well as crime laboratory equipment and high standards of quality in evidence preservation, a must for good prosecution. The same goes for better analytical and communication services, since organized crime groups more often use sophisticated high technology. Criminals have found out the advantages that modern information and telecommunication systems offer and have started using them, either as primary tools for executing criminal offenses (computer crime) or as auxiliary tools for keeping records or for analytical work (Ramo, 1996). The police, too, have introduced new technology but are as usual, one step behind the criminals. Among the first measures to take in this field should be a multilateral agreement on police cooperation in exchanging operational information and data. On such a basis a world police information system can be set up (perhaps called Polinet—Police International Network—like Internet), which would allow exchange of data and information in all forms (e.g., words, pictures, and sound). With proper security measures and precautions such a specialized Internet could become very useful against organized crime, as well as other kinds of criminal activities. In the field of crime intelligence and crime analysis, certain methodological standards also need to be set. The example of the European model, which was introduced at the First International Conference on Crime Analyses held at the Interpol General Secretariat in Lyon in September 1995, should be implemented.

- <u>Better cooperation between different institutions and agencies within each country as well as better international cooperation</u>: It cannot be expected that the police or law enforcement agencies successfully fight organized crime alone; a network of different state institutions and organizations or agencies is necessary. Only then would it be possible to get a comprehensive and clear picture of criminal organization and its operations. The focus should not be on criminal offense or perpetrators, but on the organization, financial transactions, and business connections. The so-called "crime enterprise approach" has to be used. Despite Interpol, Europol, and many multilateral and bilateral agreements among the countries, the cooperation is still not strong enough. The reasons for that appear to be numerous: competition, special parochial interests, fear of being compromised, lack of confidence, and covert operations in other fields that mix organized crime and terrorism (North, 1992). It is evident that due to political reasons and because of the mixture of organized crime and other state activities, cooperation with some countries is not possible at present.

CONCLUSION

There is no doubt that all over the world organized crime has increased in recent years and has become more transnational, more sophisticated, and more powerful. New forms have developed that we are still discovering and getting only a glimpse of. Even for a small part of the world, for Europe, it is difficult to say what the true extent of organized crime is because of the lack of reliable data. No real and comprehensive research has been done about new forms of organized crime, about the structure and organization of new criminal groups, or their full international connections. So the knowledge about traditional Mafia and other criminal organizations is used. Of course, they still exist and represent a problem for society, but even more important is the formation of new groups from countries that in the past had not been burdened with crime. These new groups, from the countries of the former Soviet Union, former Yugoslavia, and other newly born countries in Central and Eastern Europe, are far more ruthless and violent but still somewhat disorganized and in competition with one another. However, they have started cooperating more and more with each other. By acquiring greater financial powers and influence in politics and legal business they have also begun to present a real threat to the communities. Especially for small countries like Slovenia, the consequences of organized crime can be far more damaging and crucial than for other countries (Peèar, 1996a). There is an urgent need to be aware of the dangers from organized crime, since it is very difficult to stamp it out after it penetrates every pore of the society. Once the genie is out of the bottle, it is very difficult to put him back.

Organized crime is hard to detect in all its complexity, too. It can be suspected, but it is difficult to uncover and even harder to prove in a court of law. It is therefore important to know all its manifestations and recognize the indicators when they first appear. It is then possible to prevent it from gaining ground. The mutual efforts of different state institutions, their association and cooperation, exchange of information with other countries, and use of special undercover measures are necessary for the detection as well as for the investigation and prosecution of organized crime. Analytically processed information from the world of business can be of vital importance, a reason why the cooperation of the legally recognized business world is essential for combating organized crime.

It should be taken into account that rules and principles similar to those in the legally recognized business world also govern organized crime. The main objective of criminals is to acquire the greatest possible profit with as little cost as possible, and their modus operandi are geared to achieve this result. If profit is the main motive of organized crime and its raison d'être, the best way to prevent and suppress it is by cutting and blocking profits. The actions of the institutions of prevention and overall control should be focused on that fact.

There is hope for a better and more successful war on organized crime by developing and implementing new legislation, improving the effectiveness of police and law enforcement organizations, introducing new technologies, achieving better national and international cooperation, as well as using preventive strategies. However, as van der Heijden (1996, 322) states, what is important is, "Let's go to work!"

REFERENCES

Abadinsky, Howard. 1994. *Organized Crime*. 4th ed. Chicago: Nelson-Hall.

Dobovšek, B. 1996. Organized crime—can we unify the definition? In *Policing in Central and Eastern Europe*, 323–329. Ljubljana: College of Police and Security Studies.

Fijnaut, C. 1996. "Empirical Criminological Research on Organized Crime: The State of Affairs in Europe." Paper presented at V. European Colloquium on Criminology. Bled, Slovenia, September.

Freemantle, B. 1996. *Hobotnica* (OCTOPUS), Ljubljana: Co Libri.

Karakaš, A. 1996. "Organized crime: Between a Phenomenon and the Notion." (in *Revija za kriminalistiko in kriminologijo*). 3–14. Ljubljana.

Kessler, R. 1993. *The FBI*. New York: Pocket Books.

Maver, D. 1995. "Economics of Crime". Ljubljana: Letnega sreèanja Zveze ekonomistov Slovenije, vol. 3, 158–168.

Naples Political Declaration and Global Plan of Action. 1990. Naples.

North, O. 1992. *Under Fire*. Zondervan: Harper Paperback.

Peèar, J. 1995. "Organized and transnational crime." Ljubljana: *Revija za kriminalistiko in kriminologijo*, vol. 4, 319–329.

Peèar, J. 1996a. "Perception of Organized Crime." Ljubljana: *Revija za kriminalistiko in kriminologijo*, vol. 2, 112–122.

Peèar, J. 1996b. "Social control and organized crime." Ljubljana: *Revija za kriminalistiko in kriminologijo*, vol. 1, 14–25.

Podbevšek, B. 1993. "Organized crime against economy and money laundering." Ljubljana: *Revija Policija*, vol. 1, 7–19.

Ramo, J.C. 1996. "Crime Online." *Newsweek*, 23 September, 16–20.

Ravnikar, E. 1995. *UDBO-MAFIJA*, 493. Ljubljana: Slon.

Report of Slovenia. 1996. Multilateral Conference on Corruption and Organized Crime in States in transition, Sofia, 12–14 December.

Report on Work of Criminal Investigation Service and Crime. 1997. Ljubljana: Ministry of the Interior.

Svetek, S. 1996. "Crime in Slovenia in 1995." Ljubljana: *Revija za kriminalistiko in kriminologijo*, vol. 2, 95–112.

van der Heijden. 1996. Measuring Organized Crime in Western Europe. In *Policing in Central and Eastern Europe*, 313–322. Ljubljana: College of Police and Security Studies.

CHAPTER 8

ORGANIZED CRIME: A PERSPECTIVE FROM AUSTRIA

Maximilian Edelbacher

INTRODUCTION

Austria is a relatively small country situated in the core of Europe. Within its 32,812.5 square-mile area there reside an estimated 8 million inhabitants, 750,000 of whom are foreigners. Austria's capital Vienna is the main city situated in the eastern part of the country. This city has a population of nearly 2 million, of which 350,000 are of foreign origin. Austria is a democratic republic and the citizens have the choice to vote among several parties. At present, the National Assembly consists of five large parties and some independent members. Austria was liberated in 1945 after it had been occupied by Nazi Germany from 1938 to 1945. In 1955 a treaty with former occupying powers France, Great Britain, the Soviet Union, and the United States was signed that restored full sovereignty to its people. Since then Austria has become the tenth wealthiest country in the world and has achieved a high economic growth that has placed it among the best in Europe. Furthermore, the rate of unemployment is relatively low and the majority of Austrians are well off (Burgstaller, Flink, Meier, and Schmitzberger, 1996). The gross national product has also been steadily increasing (Mag. Schuller, 1996).

Austria has assumed a major role in the new European economic affairs. The collapse of the communist dictatorships and the revolutionary transformations in the former Soviet Union have created a completely new situation since 1989. The situation in the countries of the former east bloc is characterized by mass unemployment. There is an average of 16 percent to 18 percent unemployment in Poland, Hungary, Slovakia, former Eastern

Germany, Russia, Romania, and Bulgaria. On the other hand, Western Europe has an average of 7 percent to 9 percent unemployment. The feeling of declining achievement and prosperity as compared with western countries has hastened decay and loss of values. Furthermore, the desire for consumer products has given rise to new expectations that are not being satisfied. Consequently, there is a keen longing to migrate to the Western European countries. It is estimated that over the next few years, Western Europe will have to take up between 300,000 and 600,000 immigrants every year, including 250,000 from the former east bloc. Since the 1980s, the biggest migration since 1945 has been taking place. Already, between 1980 to 1992, about 15 million foreigners have settled in Western Europe, 45 percent of them coming from Africa, Asia, Latin America, and Turkey. A questionnaire, conducted by the United Nations in 1993 shows that about 20 million people of Eastern Europe wish to immigrate to Western Europe (Holyst, 1995). For the population from the East, the target countries in Western Europe are Germany and also Austria. According to some estimates, 1.5 to 2 million Russian citizens have emigrated for economic reasons. An additional 5 to 6 million are considering emigration. These are major demographic challenges, which will have an impact on organized crime. For instance, an estimated 150,000 illegal foreigners are reportedly living in Austria (Holyst, 1995).

The fall of the iron curtain has also affected the crime situation in Austria and the rest of Europe (Edelbacher, 1995a). There is a higher proportion of imported crime due to greater mobility of the criminals. In every Western European country, there is also a higher proportion of foreigners among the criminals. New types of organized crimes are increasing like trafficking in humans, drug trafficking, and stolen car trafficking. Violence is increasing, too, and there is a rise in crimes of murder, extortion, robbery, and blackmail.

Austria's future importance in a newly shaped economic area (Edelbacher, 1995b) is also affecting the crime situation. Since January 1995, Austria has been a member of the European Union. The newly created economic area grants four freedoms: freedom to provide service, freedom of trade, freedom of capital, and freedom of establishment. These freedoms are expected to create strong economic impulses. However, crime experts expect that these freedoms will not only have positive results but will also be abused by the members of organized crime syndicates.

THE NATURE AND EXTENT OF ORGANIZED CRIME

Organized crime has not a been a topic of discussion in Austria for centuries. Although the phenomenon of organized crime existed in Italy, there was hardly any impact felt in other parts of Europe. Until the late 1970s, the existence of organized crime was denied by the officials of the law enforcement forces in nearly all countries of Europe. Organized crime became a matter of interest only through the reports of Al Capone in the United States and brutal killings of the Italian Mafia. Nevertheless, organized crime, like cancer, cannot be seen openly, but grows slowly, continuously, and can endanger the whole society. The European countries, including Austria, are now feeling the effects of this slow-growing cancer.

At present, organized crime can be said to be the number-one challenge to police in Europe as well as a growing problem for Austrian authorities. It is difficult to estimate the extent of organized crime. Since 1989, an enormous change has taken place with the fall of the former Soviet Union. The fall of the iron curtain has led to a higher proportion of crimes by offenders operating from outside. Organized crime gangs are increasingly committing several kinds of offenses and are not hesitating to use violence in pursuit of their objectives of quick profits and power. The large-scale migration of people is further accentuating the problem. The new immigrants are easy targets for organized syndicates who prey upon their weaknesses to settle down in foreign areas. People need money to migrate, loans to start new businesses, and protection from marauders. They also require false identities and useful contacts to establish themselves. This provides easy fodder to the organized crime groups for spreading their tentacles and areas of influence.

Moreover, organized crime is not easy to define in law. In Europe, there is no uniform definition accepted by all nations. Therefore, definitions by Interpol, Bundeskriminalamt Wiesbaden (Germany), and the Federal Bureau of Investigation (FBI) in the United States are used in Austria to describe the nature of organized crimes. According to Interpol, organized crime comprises the systematically prepared and planned commission of serious criminal acts with a view to gain financial profits and power. These acts are committed in long, undefined stretches of time by more than three or more accomplices united in hierarchy and job division. This organized criminal association uses the methods of violence, various types of intimidation, corruption, and other influences with the view to secure the development of its criminal activities.

By this definition, organized crime consists of violence or corruption to achieve profitable goals. The following two elements are symptomatic: the existence of a criminal association or group and a criminal activity that is carried out in an entrepreneurial way. The basic goal of the group is to achieve profit with illegal activities. The group also uses violence or corruption to achieve its goals.

The FBI defines organized crime as "criminal activities committed primarily to make money and generate profit by continuing and self-perpetuating criminal conspiracy fed by fear and corruption and motivated by greed. Organized crime groups show: organizational structure, continuing criminal conspiracy, a purpose for the generation of profits." All definitions point out one important feature—that organized crime is greed driven.

Current Austrian law recognizes the term "organized crime" only in the Security Police Act (Szymanski, 1991): In the third part, Article 16, Section 1 sub-paragraph 2 of the Security Police Act, the term "General danger" that is described is appropriate for describing organized activities. General danger exists:

1. In the event of a dangerous attack (sections 2 and 3) or
2. As soon as three or more persons get together with the intention of repeatedly committing criminal acts punishable by the court (gang or organized crime)

The Code of Criminal Procedure and the Criminal Code do not use the term "organized crime" at all. Only in Article 278 of the Criminal Code in describing the formation of the gangs, the term "organized crime" is used (Serini, 1994). Since the problems involved in combating organized crime are largely the same in Germany and in Austria, crime experts have been relying on the definition used in Germany.

The definition of "organized crime" according to the working groups "Judicature/Police" is: Organized crime is the profit and power-oriented systematic commission of crimes which are of considerable importance. This is said to occur if individually or collectively two or more persons cooperate for a long or an indefinite period—

- By using business or businesslike structures;
- By using violence or other means suitable for intimidation;
- By exerting influence on politics, media, public administration, judicature, or economy.

Even this definition does not cover all areas. In practice, the crimes committed by highly active criminals very often overlap and therefore fit this definition of organized crime only in part (Geiger, 1992).

What factors constitute organized crime? The following indicators appear important in describing organized crime:

Planning—Preparation of the Crime

Accurate planning
Hired labor
Large investments

Utilization of the Spoils
- Highly profit-oriented
- Back flow into legal economic cycle
- Money-laundering measures

Connections of the Crime—Relation of the Criminals
- Supra-regional
- National
- International

Conspiratorial Criminal Behavior
- Counter-observation
- Complete withdrawal
- Code names

Group Structure
- Hierarchical setup
- Dependent and authoritative relationship between several crime suspects
- International sanction system

Help to Gang Members in terms of
- Aiding escape from police custody
- Provision of lawyers
- Threats and intimidation to witnesses
- Getting rid of witnesses
- Silence of key persons involved in investigation and trials
- Tutored testimonies of witnesses for the defense
- Matched testimonies of persons from the scene of crime
- Taking care of prisoners
- Looking after the relatives
- Readmission into the gang after release from prison

Corruption
- Inducing dependence through sex or gambling
- Bribery
- Corruption

Efforts to Create Monopolies
- Control of certain sections of night life
- Offering protection against undue payments

Public Relations
> Controlled, tendentious or other press reports of a trial, which distract from a specific suspicion of a criminal act

If these indicators are considered then one can state that organized crime exists in Austria. The Italian Mafia and the *Camorra* as well as Russian groups have already gained a foothold in Austria. Although Austria is still serving as "rest zone" and organized crime activities as seen in other neighboring countries are not visible here, nobody knows how this is going to develop in the future. These gangs have established themselves and can pose a major challenge. A deterioration of the economic situation might lead to an activation of these known structures of organized crime.

There are already factors that worry the authorities. It is generally known that crime in Austria is on the rise as it is in the rest of Europe. Moreover, organized crime is now forming almost 20 percent to 25 percent of the total crimes in many categories. In 1990, about 457,623 crimes were committed in Austria as compared with 486,433 crimes in 1995. The statistics in Table 8.1 describe the growing crime problem in Austria.

The clearance rate of crime in Austria is generally around 42 percent of the total crimes reported to the police. However, there are large differences among the various types of crimes. The clearance rate for murder is higher than 90 percent. In cases of bodily injuries and robberies the rate is only 30 percent to 40 percent of the reported crimes. The rate of clearance is even lower for thefts and burglaries, a rate below 10 percent. Along with the low rate of clearance, in the last twenty years crime has doubled in the country. In 1975, about 245,000 offenses and in 1995, about 490,000 offenses were committed. Therefore, the amount of crime in Austria is becoming a major problem.

However, it is not only the quantity of crime that causes concern but rather its quality. According to the Director General of Public Security, Sika (1996), the proportion of organized crime is approximately 20 percent to 25 percent of the overall crime rate. The opening of the borders to Eastern Europe has created favorable conditions for the import and the spreading of organized crime. At present, the Russian Mafia is intensifying its efforts to extend its foothold and establish a large presence in Austria. The intrusion of external agents in crimes committed in Austria may be seen from the involvement of foreigners. In 1975, it was estimated to be 8 percent; in 1985 it went up to 12 percent and by 1995 it was around 20 percent. The crimes ascribed to the organized crime syndicates is estimated to be 20 percent of all the reported incidents in 1994. By 1995 it was around 25 percent. In 1995 there were 168 attempted and completed killings in Austria, including 69 in Vienna. In 1994, only 1 murder

TABLE 8.1

	1991	1992	1993	1994	1995
Court Prosecutions	468,832	502,440	493,786	504,568	486,433
Criminal Offenses	104,019	119,214	114,794	107,868	101,545
Misdemeanors	364,813	383,226	378,992	396,700	384,888
Murders	182	191	180	185	168
Assaults	30,812	33,645	32,421	33,478	33,287
Car Thefts	2,584	3,314	2,988	2,538	2,224
Fraud	20,095	23,837	24,389	34,970	33,287
Arson	735	886	812	741	713
Drug Trafficking	2,190	3,226	6,143	2,396	2,058
Drug Consumption	3,632	5,224	7,382	9,567	9,577
Robbery	1,938	2,328	2,054	2,063	1,776
in banks/post offices	99	87	85	81	93
on business premises	139	129	151	153	137
on individuals	1,003	1,276	1,169	1,172	913
on drunken guests	86	100	86	105	87
Residential burglaries	12,127	12,231	10,372	9,138	9,154
Non-residential burglary	4,592	4,753	4,842	5,022	4,567
Burglaries in businesses	13,833	14,133	13,424	12,707	14,062
Burglaries in cars	26,885	31,370	27,429	24,618	23,486
Bodily Injuries	40,441	40,542	38,190	38,828	38,817

Source: Ministry of Interior, Austria.

in Vienna was related to organized crime. In 1995 and 1996 3 murder cases were related to organized crime syndicates (Aahs, 1996). In July 1996, it happened for the first time that a so-called Mafia boss of the Georgian Mafia, was killed in Vienna. This shows that the organized crime groups have established themselves in Austria and the struggles between different groups has started. In all three cases, the victims were executed for failing to comply with terms of payments. In two cases the hired killers were able to escape. In the summer of 1995 the torso of an executed person was found in the New Danube. It could only be established that this man was of eastern origin, probably from Romania or Bulgaria. This crime could not be solved.

In general, the same applies to bank robberies, but here the proportion of organized crime is already considerably higher. Of one hundred bank robberies in Austria every year, about 10 percent can be attributed to organized crime. Criminals from Italy and Eastern European nations carry out robberies of Austrian Banks. Actually, this type of money procurement is not new, since Red Army Faction terrorists have committed bank robberies in Austria in the past. Recently, part of a gang of Italians and Germans operating on an international level committed nine bank robberies mainly in Vienna between 1990 and 1995 (Aahs, 1996).

Organized crime has also established itself in extortion rackets. The demands for protection fees from Yugoslavian and Turkish bars and restaurants is quite common. For example, in Vienna there exist about 1,800 restaurants, bars, and nightclubs. Of this number, around 500 belong to former Yugoslavians, approximately 300 belong to Chinese people, and about 220 brothels and bars belong to other communities. It is believed that protection fees are extorted by the Yugoslavian Mafia, the Chinese Mafia, and different gangs, like PKK—the Kurdish political right wing party. A large number of crimes remain unreported in this field and the police are able to apprehend the offenders only in a few isolated cases. A case was reported where it was learned that a group of criminals had extorted protection fees fifteen times from their victims. At the trial, only one victim appeared initially in the court but he, too, finally, did not testify. This helped secure the acquittal of all the offenders. The existing legal instruments are just not adequate to provide appropriate protection to the victims. The victim has to take into account that the criminals will serve only a short term in prison, and after being released, will again put pressure on the victim or his/her family.

These organized groups try to procure the required capital to operate their organization by extorting protection fees from their compatriots in Vienna, who have already established themselves. In this field, the foreign criminals operate independently of the Austrian criminals. The presence of their countrymen provide the basic logistic requirements like interim storage places for the spoils and even associates (Lesjak, 1995).

In 1995, approximately 13,700 burglaries of apartments and houses, around 14,000 burglaries of shops, about 23,500 burglaries of cars, and 2,224 thefts of cars were committed in Austria. In Vienna, too, the figures speak for themselves. In 1995, approximately 6,200 burglaries of apartments and houses, about 6,400 burglaries of shops, around 13,600 burglaries of cars, and about 1,000 thefts of cars were committed (Edelbacher and Lesjak, 1994). The clearance rate for burglaries of apartments and houses is below 10 percent. It is estimated that more than 80 percent of the burglaries are probably committed by foreign criminal groups. For example, 95 out of 130 burglars arrested by the Major Crime Bureau come from former

Yugoslavia. They are not guest workers but criminals who operate on an international level. The most common methods of breaking in are to force open doors by means of lever tools and to twist off the handles. The method of wall breaking is considered a specialty of criminals from neighboring Eastern European countries. They commit the burglaries by breaking through the wall from the cellar. Goods stolen in these crimes are sold underhand on the black market throughout Europe. The vast market and great demand for these goods further encourage such criminal enterprises.

Gangs from South America, especially from Chile, Peru, and Uruguay are organized in "trick" thefts and pickpocketing. These criminals from South America come to Austria in waves. Whenever the police begin to pursue them, they lie low for a few months but reappear, better organized. Such thefts are often types of procurement crimes for subsequent frauds involving checks and credit cards. These criminals mainly aim at the procurement of money orders, bank checks, credit cards, and identity cards.

Organized crime has found a foothold in vehicle thefts, too. In 1995, approximately one million cars were stolen in Europe, including about 500,000 in the United Kingdom, about 300,000 in France, about 400,000 in Italy, and about 140,000 in Germany. Compared with these figures, the statistics for Austria are low. As already mentioned, exactly 2,224 cars were stolen in 1995. About 50 percent of the stolen cars are taken to eastern countries like Russia or Ukraine. Due to technical countermeasures and an intensive search at the Austrian borders, the number of cars sold underhand could be reduced. The so called "rent" method that is closely linked with insurance fraud is still a popular modus operandi of car thefts in Austria (Edelbacher and Lesjak, 1994). Between 30 percent and 50 percent of the cars reported stolen are assumed to be taken out of the country with the help of the owner. The fact that the thefts increasingly occur abroad serves as an indication for this modus operandi. This phenomenon is not only associated with intensified business relations and increased mobility of the Austrians, but also due to the growing criminal motives in the young generation. Regardless, international car theft is firmly controlled by criminal groups from Poland, Hungary, Bulgaria, Russia, and former Yugoslavia.

Organized syndicates are also increasingly turning toward theft of art objects. Ever since the borders to the East were opened, Vienna has become the hub for handling stolen art commodities. For instance, the art treasures stolen in a spectacular burglary at the Jewish Museum in Budapest in 1994 were offered for sale in Vienna. Those pulling the strings in this criminal case were reportedly Romanian criminals. In cooperation with German and Hungarian special agents the case was finally solved. However, castles and monasteries in the neighboring countries of Eastern Europe still contain valuable art treasures. The demand for these goods on the international art market is very high, so a separate industry in the field of organized crime has developed to procure such items.

According to the Austrian crime statistics, fraud cases are increasing rapidly, too. Between 1992 and 1994 the crime figures have risen from 23,837 to 34,970 offenses, although here, too, a large number of unreported cases can be assumed. Banks and insurance companies for obvious reasons are often not very eager to report frauds (Aahs, 1996). International financial fraud comprises many kinds of economic crimes like bankruptcy offenses, insider trading, insurance fraud, fraudulent accounts, giving false or stolen securities, forged checks and credit cards, paper money, forgery of documents and identities, as well as money laundering. In the field of economic crime, Russian organizations have gained prominence in establishing themselves in Austria. Members of these criminal organizations set up front companies with the assistance of lawyers, notaries, and tax consultants. Tax consultants provide their own addresses to be used as company or registration addresses for these operators. These companies usually do not have business licenses, yet considerable amounts of money, mostly U.S. dollars or deutsche marks, are handled through the company accounts. The people in charge of the company acquire property either directly or through front men. For instance, limited liability companies (LLCs) are formed. An Austrian citizen is used as a "front man" for registering the company in the country. Such companies are then allowed to acquire property. Subsequently, company shares will be sold that are obtained by members of the organized crime groups. In Austria, it is comprehended that through this method there are now several hundred companies with Russian participation (Lesjak, 1995).

The provisions of the Banking Act (art. 40) and the panel provisions on money laundering and criminal organizations (arts. 165 and 278 Criminal Code) have been in effect in Austria since 1993. In 1994, there were 38 legal proceedings and 40 in 1995, instituted by the government prosecutor on suspicion of money laundering. So far only three cases were closed with final and binding effect but which ended in acquittals. Two further actions are still pending. There has been no final conviction for suspicious financial transactions in Austria since Article 165 Criminal Code took effect. This suggests the existence of powerful organizations operating behind these crimes.

According to Josef Dick, head of the Austrian Criminal Investigation Department, five groups from the former Soviet Union are active in Austria (Dick, 1995). Approximately $160 billion Austrian dollars were supposed to be laundered in Austria. In 1994, the banks reported 346 cases of suspicious money transactions totaling $1,595 million Austrian dollars. In

1995, the banks reported another 370 cases of suspicious transactions with about the same amount. Although the largest part of the financial operations was thwarted after intervention by the authorities, according to Dick, $2.6 billion Austrian dollars from questionable transactions were still transferred to the country. Only a small part, (i.e., $ 300 million) could be frozen. With regard to the remaining amount, the suspicion could not be proved.

In the field of money laundering, approximately 40 percent of the reported suspicious transactions are connected to the states of the former east bloc. About 30 percent of this amount is directly linked to the former Soviet Union. Nationals from the former Soviet Union enter Austria in order to open bank accounts. At the same time large amounts of money, mostly millions of U.S. dollars, are transferred. Despite such large amounts it is clear that these operators are not looking for profitable investments, since the returns from the Austrian banks are comparably smaller. However, these accounts are opened largely for gaining legitimacy and laundering the ill-gotten money. These people carry out the so-called "transit" transactions with different countries, where only the money is transferred to Austrian accounts, while a flow of goods, if any, cannot be traced. Moreover, police investigations are complicated by the fact that these groups of people mainly do business with off-shore companies. These companies are represented by boards of directors, and no conclusion can be drawn from the documentation in the register of companies about who is actually behind the company. Therefore, the actual origin of the transferred money amounts are difficult to trace (Lesjak, 1995). The annual turnover in Austria, involving this type of organized crime, is about $200 million Austrian dollars. Breaking into cars, trick thefts, and pickpocketing are ways of procurement of checks and credit cards. The Italian Mafia is known to employ cheap labor from South America, primarily from Chile to procure these financial documents (Edelbacher, 1995b).

In 1995, in Austria exactly 2,058 persons were reported to the police for dealing with drugs and 9,577 persons were reported for abusing drugs. It is estimated that approximately 100,000 people in Austria are drug addicts. More than 350,000 people in Austria are addicted to alcohol, too (Edelbacher, 1995c). The criminal experts of the Major Crime Bureau estimate that in Vienna almost 7,000 people are addicted to heroin; this means that in Vienna nearly 2.5 tons of heroin are consumed annually. The data available on heroin addicts is quite reliable, since the addicts are socially more conspicuous than cocaine or synthetic-drug addicts. About 50 percent of the Austrian drug scene is located in Vienna. Thus, the Austrian market has been strong for decades, and Austria is no longer considered only a transit country. However, due to the geographical position, many illegal drug shipments still pass through Austria. The fall of the Iron Curtain, in particular, has created ideal conditions for drug trade.

Organized drug trade in Austria is controlled by criminal organizations from Turkey, Iran, and the former Yugoslavia. Since the opening of the borders to Eastern European countries, illegal drug deposits have been set up mainly in Bratislava to supply chiefly the eastern part of Austria. In 1993 the *Auratorium Sicheres Österreich*, an official organization, attempted to determine the damage to the economy from these illegal drug transactions. Their estimate was that overall economic damage caused by drug trafficking in Austria alone amounted to $5 billion Austrian dollars (Edelbacher, 1995d).

As everyone knows, prostitution and gambling are traditional pillars of organized crime. These crimes have been perpetrated by organized syndicates because these activities have ready markets and provide them large profits. Here, too, the market has changed since the borders to the East were opened. Vienna alone has about 130 brothels and 100 bars, where girls, mainly from the eastern neighboring countries, are brought in to work in these parlors. Organizations engaged in the smuggling of people often bring these women to Austria and Germany on the pretext of offering them legal employment. Undoubtedly, these women are grossly abused and made completely dependent so that they are unwilling to seek outside assistance. It is very difficult for the police to create confidence and convince these victims to testify against their abusers and against the people who kidnap and bring them into this trade. The turnover in this market is estimated to exceed $10 billion Austrian dollars (Effmayer, 1995).

Gambling is also becoming another major problem. Internationally operating groups first imported slot machines legally to Hungary. The resulting obsession with gambling created serious problems for Hungary. Gambling has now spread to Austria also. An international conference was convened in 1994 for the purpose of working out counter strategies but the problem remains serious.

These examples of crime development show clearly that an international network of crime has gained a foothold in Austria. To some extent Austrian criminals cooperate closely with foreign criminal groups. There is evidence of so called "joint ventures" in the criminal field. Austrian criminal organizations import girls for brothels and bars at low cost. With the currently existing legal instruments it is getting more and more difficult for the Austrian police to develop and employ counter strategies and counter measures to combat organized crime (Szymanski, 1991).

Measures Including Legislation to Combat Organized Crime

In the 1970s, Europe was confronted with the burning phenomenon of terrorism; since the 1980s the new problem was the growth of drug trafficking, and since the 1990s the number one problem has been organized crime. In Austria, as all over Europe, the answers to these problems were very similar. If a new problem arose, a new special unit was created. Therefore, the police forces in Austria have special units against terrorism, drugs, and organized crime. These organizational measures were the first efforts to combat organized crime.

Apart from the executive measures, technical measures were considered to improve the possibilities of combating organized crime. The development of technologies is an enormous support in operating against organized gangs. Computer technologies help to analyze crime structures and records of persons and enterprises. Vast data can be stored in computers and their analysis assists in the assimilation of historical information, review of case files, review of court documents, examination of public documents, and other related information. Besides the intensive analytical methods, monitoring, physical surveillance, electronic surveillance, and wire tapping are some of the technical measures being tried to combat organized crime in Austria.

However, all these new methods need a modern, educated police officer, more of a technocrat than investigator in the traditional sense. Of course, interviews and interrogations are still very important, but the fight against organized crime needs modern concepts, strategies, and techniques. Therefore, education and professional training of the officers is considered the most important issue for policing. To combat organized crime a new profile of police officer is necessary. In the European Community, including Austria, new forms of police cooperation are also being initiated. One of the principal ideas was to form the Europol (European Police). The Europol was seen as a special instrument to fight the problem of drug trafficking.

The Austrian police have also initiated activities in two areas against organized crime that have met with approval throughout Europe. On one hand, the Vienna chief of police invited the chiefs of police from neighboring capitals to pursue joint activities; on the other hand, on Austrian initiative, a Central European Police Academy has been created where top officers from eight European countries are trained in a three-month training course.

The chiefs of police from Vienna, Bern, Bratislava, Budapest, Prague, Munich, and Berlin meet regularly to discuss topical problems and develop counter strategies. Every year at the end of January a course in international training starts in Vienna, where between twenty and twenty-two top officers from Austria, Czech Republic, Germany, Hungary, Poland, Slovakia, Slovenia, and Switzerland receive training in all countries according to the rotation principle. In the beginning of May, the final examinations are held in Budapest, where every participant presents a paper on a specific topic. The specialty of this police academy is that the trainee officers get to travel around and are taught in all member countries. This familiarizes them with the organizational setup of other countries and helps to build personal contacts with fellow officers.

These two approaches have been put into practice since 1990 and have already produced positive results in a practical way. The biggest post office robbery in Austrian criminal history could be cleared quickly due to the cooperation between Slovakia and Austria. Two other important successes concerned the murders of an Austrian film producer and of a Georgian Mafia boss, which could be solved with the assistance of the Hungarian colleagues working at the Central European Police Academy and with assistance from Interpol.

These important changes can only be useful with the development of effective legal measures. In Austria and in all European countries new laws are being discussed earnestly. The Penal Code measures are being modified to control organized crimes. In some European countries provisions were set in the field of criminal legislation by which the state has tried to criminalize different kinds of organized criminal activities or provisions. These attempts have been to prevent criminal activities like racketeering, criminal association, criminal conspiracy, extortion, drug trafficking, and money laundering. The procedural measures are also being improved to empower the enforcement agencies. These include special measures such as:

- Wiretapping—controlling and recording of telephone conversations and other forms of communication by technical devices;
- Secret cooperation of the police—secret surveillance and tracking as visual recording;
- Apparent purchase of objects;
- Apparent bribery;
- Eavesdropping in private places by use of technical devices;
- Access to the computer system of a bank or any other legal person engaged in financial or other economic activity.

Austria has also taken a lead in international initiatives to counter money laundering. Organized crime, almost without exception, exists and perpetuates itself for the purpose of making money. The concept of greed and the power that money in vast quantities assures, is integral to most manifestations of serious organized crime. Today organized crime syndicates have adopted the same structures and modus operandi as legitimate businesses. The laundering of the proceeds of criminal activities through the financial system is vital to the success of criminal operations. Besides putting in jeopardy the soundness and stability of the financial system, money laundering permits organized crime to take root and extend its influence over the different regions of the world. This enormous flood of criminal proceeds involves considerable risk of corruption for administration, judicial authorities, and political parties, as well as private institutions and constitutes a danger for the stability of democracies. Austria and other European countries have taken part in various international initiatives to combat money laundering.

Austria has also taken a lead in establishing international cooperation against organized crime. The Vienna Convention is an example of these efforts. The United Nations Convention Against Illicit Traffic in Narcotic Drugs and Psychotropic Substances in December 1988, ratified by over sixty countries, adopted a number of key proposals (Aahs, 1996). Specifically, it:

- creates an obligation to criminalize the laundering of money derived from drug trafficking;
- deals with international cooperation, thereby facilitating cross-border investigations into money laundering;
- enables extradition between signatory states in money-laundering cases, sets out principles to facilitate cooperative administrative investigations;
- sets forth the principle that banking secrecy should not interfere with criminal investigations in the context of international cooperation.

Another significant example of international cooperation is the so called "Basle Statement of Principles." This was issued by the Basle Committee on Banking Regulations and Supervisory Practices in December 1988. It signaled the agreement by the representatives of the Central Banks and supervisory authorities of the Group of Ten countries to the danger posed by money laundering. The principles point to the threat to the worldwide banking system and of the need for an international set of agreements to implement effective supervision in each member country. The basic policies and procedures outlined in the statement of principles included (Plywaczewski, 1996):

- The need for effective procedures to identify customers' identification;
- Compliance with laws and regulations pertaining to financial transactions;
- Refusal to assist transactions which appear to be associated with money laundering;
- Cooperation with law enforcement agencies.

The concerns expressed by the Basle Committee are particularly important for countries where the financial services industry is being established in an expanding market economy. The Committee has pointed out that:

- public confidence in the new range of services offered by financial institutions is an important requisite to the growth of these institutions;
- without effective money-laundering legislation international business with financial institutions in these countries will be significantly hampered by the risks of exposure to money laundering by financial institutions in countries complying with strict money-laundering regulations.

Another landmark agreement is the Strasbourg Convention. The Council of Europe was the first (1980) that warned the international community of the dangers that dirty money in the financial systems represents to democracy and the rule of law. The approach of the Council is to consider not only laundering of drug proceeds in a crime, but also to criminalize the proceeds derived from all kinds of offenses (Csonka, 1996). The idea is that the criminal should not be permitted to profit from his crime. The work of the Council in the field of money laundering is action-oriented. Several international conferences on the subject were held in the 1980s and inspired the work on an international Convention on Laundering, Search Seizure, and Confiscation of the Proceeds from Crime (Strasbourg Convention).

A Financial Action Task Force (FATF) was formed in 1989 by the Group 7 of major industrial nations and the president of the Commission of the European Communities. This sought to assess the results of cooperation and to prevent utilization of the banking system for money-laundering purposes. It is also considering additional preventive measures like the adoption of the legal and regulatory systems to enhance multilateral judicial assistance. So far forty measures have been recommended by the FATF for adoption by the countries to combat money laundering. These include the improvement of national legal systems and strengthening of international cooperation (Plywaczewski, 1996).

COMPARATIVE EVALUATION OF THE METHODS FOR COMBATING ORGANIZED CRIME AND PROPOSED MEASURES

In Austria, the phenomenon of organized crime has been combated by traditional instruments used in many countries. Enforcement agencies have been given more power and their training and resources are being enhanced. Citizens are being informed about organized crime activities and educated to stand against these evils. Other measures, like international cooperation in fighting organized crime, is difficult because of the variety of laws, penal codes, and penal procedure codes. It has also been difficult to sell the idea to authorities that organized crime is a major threat and to accept that it is a serious problem. For many decades, the existence of organized crime was denied in Austria. Now this attitude is changing and the efforts to create social awareness of these problems appear to be succeeding.

A major hurdle in combating organized crime is the sovereignty of the countries. International police cooperation is limited by this fundamental principle of the constitutions of the states. Individualism was always the strength and the weakness of Europe. Even now in the age of the growing European Economic Community (ECC), individualism of the single members of the ECC creates daily problems. United Kingdom, France, and Germany are very powerful but are seemingly resentful of each other's individual actions. To evolve a joint strategy and find compromises, a lot of diplomacy is needed.

It is also difficult to compare the various anti-organized crime measures, since most are of recent origin. Many measures involve other European nations and a comparative evaluation is nearly impossible for lack of information. The legal measures have been successful, as many penal codes and penal procedure codes have been modified. These legal measures are also being effectively used to combat organized crime. Yet, the feeling remains that in Austria, organized crime is not such a problem like in Italy and Russia except for the phenomenon of money laundering. The examples of Italy show that there is some hope in combating organized crime successfully, a measure that has found support in Austria, too. However, the Russian situation appears dismal. All other European countries more or less are also in a similar situation. Overall, there is a positive feeling that the existing measures are succeeding in fighting organized crime.

To propose measures against organized crime it must be remembered that economical, social, and political measures are more important than legal ones. Today's society is so organized that there are contradictions between:

- legality and reality
- the opacity of the financial system and the fight against laundering
- capitalist restructuring and development politics

Today, 23 percent of the world's population consumes 80 percent of the resources. This constitutes a major explanation for the growth of the illegal economy and the diffusion of criminal groups of the Mafia. Any effective anti-crime measure has to be connected with the cultural goals and social reorganization. The secretary-general of the United Nations, Boutros Boutros-Ghali told the World Ministerial Conference on Organized Transnational Crime in Naples,

> Powerful international criminal groups now work outside national or international law. They include traffickers in drugs, money laundering, the illegal trade in arms—including trade in nuclear materials—and the smuggling of precious metals and other commodities. These criminal elements exploit both the new liberal international economic order and the different approach and practices of states. Some criminal empires are richer than many poor states. These problems demand a concerted, global response. Organized crime has become predominantly transnational in character, but law enforcement worldwide remains predominantly local and national (Santino, 1996).

The ministers of justice and the interior taking part in the Naples (Italy) Conference in November 1994, have also urged the member states to move swiftly to counter a rapid globalizing movement of interlinked organized criminal groups and their penetration into new spheres of activities. They have raised concern that if organized crime is not resisted, in time it will undermine political structures, endanger international peace and development, and threaten not only emerging democracies, but also established ones. The Conference has called for improved data gathering and analysis, anti-corruption safeguards, special investigative units, and implementation of existing measures directed against loopholes that allow transborder criminals to circumvent justice.

Although much has been done by governments to combat organized crime, efforts are still hampered by lack of knowledge, common orientation, and international cooperation. The approach demands an increase in proactive methods. It requires the involvement of public enforcement to provide the solution but is clear that crime cannot be tackled successfully unless other sectors of society are involved. Today, success will be achieved by the use of a multinational and multidisciplinary approach, which uses preventive as well as control measures applied by the criminal justice system and governments, utilizing the knowledge and resources of industry and science. The motto for this approach should be, "It concerns us all, let's tackle it together" (Maver, 1996).

According to past resolutions and decisions of the United Nations, member states should intensify their efforts to combat organized crime more effectively at the national level, including enforcement measures subject to safeguards and maintenance of basic rights under ordinary legal procedures and in conformity with international human rights standards. Two measures form three kinds of strategies to combat organized crime.

Long-Term Counter-Strategies

Analysis of the social, economical, and political development of the European economic area is an obvious starting point. There is an urgent need to understand how the newly emerging democracies are developing their economic policies and what is the nature of their markets. Their laws, enforcement, and market conditions will determine the nature and extent of organized crime in neighboring countries like Austria.

Analysis of the migration movements is also an important factor. Once the borders have been opened there is a large-scale influx of Eastern Europeans into Western European countries. The lure of better economic prospects, living conditions, and opportunities is driving thousands of people to go to these developed countries. If legal channels are blocked in this migration, people resort to illegal ways. This encourages organized crime groups to get involved in smuggling people into these developed regions. This, in turn, gives rise to kidnapping and procurement of women for prostitution purposes. Austria is seriously affected because it is a developed country and is seen as a gateway to Germany, Belgium, the Netherlands, and other Western European nations (Hirschfeld, 1995).

There is the need to increase development aid for the poor regions of the world. So long as large parts of the world remain poor and impoverished, the people living in these regions will attempt to migrate to richer regions. In many cases, the situation is so desperate that people are willing to take any risk to be able to go to regions with better prospects. This creates the conditions where organized crime groups find an easy entry.

Cooperation with the international organizations in planning and developing aid programs is another requirement. Again, this is needed in order to develop conditions that will encourage people to stay in their own regions and improve their situation. It will also assist in the development of these regions and act as an incentive to prevent people from attempting to migrate illegally.

Medium-Term Counter Strategies

Preparation of research, teaching and study projects by universities, state institutions, and people with practical experience is required urgently. To combat organized crime there is the need to develop knowledge about its nature, operations, and weaknesses. Only a good information system can assist in developing effective preventive and investigative strategies. In this process the role of research institutions, scholars, and investigators is crucial. They have to be involved to bring expertise to the prosecution authorities in order to make them combat organized crime effectively.

Sensitization of the population to the serious consequences of organized crime has to be emphasized as well. Organized crime is a matter that concerns all, a point that many people ignore completely. For most people organized crime is a distant feature that happens to "bad" people and which is seen only in movies. However, the violence associated with organized crime operations, the economic fallouts, affect all and mostly innocent people. In the long term, the state is endangered, as can be seen in Italy and Russia. This fact has to be known widely and people have to be educated about the dangers of organized crime.

Intensified preventive work is extremely important in combating organized crime. In many spheres organized crime penetrates in small steps. At first, one business is targeted or a few people are threatened. Drug dealing begins with small distribution network and by targeting a few individuals. Once a foothold is established, the gang begins to claim the territory and spreads its tentacles. Therefore, it is at the initial stage, when the operations are being set up, that firm steps—strong preventive measures—can be effective and show immediate results.

Intensified national and international cooperation between Interpol, Europol, and national police organizations is urgently required to combat organized crime. It is known that organized crime has a transnational character. Its members move quickly from one country to another and its profits, too, are siphoned off in other countries. The gangs know that most police forces are restricted to their jurisdictions and cannot pursue beyond their borders. This gives them the advantage of operating from areas outside a region where police vigilance is strong. Most vehicles stolen in Austria are quickly moved to the Eastern European nations. Similarly, drugs are procured in Afghanistan, processed in Eastern Europe, and then distributed in Austria. Action only in Austria nets the street distributors, who are petty criminals working for the big-time operators. The drug trafficking can be stopped only if the entire chain is broken, and for this to happen, police forces have to cooperate nationally and internationally.

Setup of a computer network with data relevant to organized crime is needed to develop an effective information system. Since organized crime gangs operate in different places, work through a large network of associates, and attempt to combine legitimate businesses into their illegal transactions, a good information system is required. The network of operators, informants, sites and dumps for storing and distributing goods, and the vehicles and couriers used in operation, are factual details required to build evidence against these gangs. A good computer network along with efficient and quick communications systems is an important tool in the hands of enforcement agencies to combat organized crime.

Short-Term Counter Strategies

Implementation of selective measures to combat organized crime, such as stolen car trafficking, smuggling of people, arms/drug trafficking, and money laundering are needed. Organized crime operates through some of these well-known types of crime, and enforcement agencies have to target these specific crimes in order to combat organized crime gangs. These measures range from investigating specific cases to targeting particular gang members and leaders. It is only by working on specific cases and gathering evidence that sufficient information can be constructed to bring big-time operators to justice.

Extension of the legal instruments for the police force by the legislators has to be emphasized. Most of the time, enforcement agencies are hampered in their work due to legal constraints. They have to move slowly, seek permission to search suspected places, gather evidence to make an arrest, and are generally prohibited from tapping the phones and information channels of organized crime syndicates. All these measures hinder police in their actions and end up tying the hands of the justice agencies. The organized gangs take advantage of these police handicaps to operate freely and with impunity. Special legislation empowering the police to intercept mail, make quick searches of warehouses and storage dumps, hold inquiries into the background of suspects, and restrict their movements are measures that can work against organized crime effectively.

Modernization of education and training of the police force, both at the national and international level, is also required. The officers have to be trained to conduct proper investigations, to make effective searches, and to read financial documents. Organized crime groups are multifaceted operations, and in order to gather evidence against them, police officers have to be well trained in many fields. They also have to be trained in handling modern firearms, computers, communication equipment, and legal matters. It is only a well-trained and professional police force that can deal effectively against organized crime gangs.

Conclusion

Austria and Europe are confronted with two phenomena of organized crime. On the one hand there exists the traditional organized crime by the classic Italian gangs of Mafia, *'Ndrangheta* and *Camorra*, or the gangs from former Yugoslavia and Poland. On the other hand, Austria is confronted with new forms of organized crime of the former communist countries, especially from Russia. Besides these forms of crime, numerous traditional gangs from former Yugoslavia or Poland are also very active. In addition, criminal gangs from Africa, South America, and Asia are attempting to gain foothold, too. Some of these are integrated in joint ventures with gangs from the European countries. Criminals from Germany, Austria, France, or the United Kingdom deal with these international gangs and make a lot of money.

The activities of organized crime gangs are primarily trafficking in human beings, drugs, weapons (especially when the war was started in former Yugoslavia), stolen cars from Western Europe to Russia, Poland, and Ukraine, as well as involvement in prostitution and gambling. Apart from these traditional fields of organized crime, international financial crimes like offenses against banks and insurance companies, credit card and check frauds, money laundering, and computer crimes are also coming in the ambit of organized crime syndicates.

If Europe wants to fight organized crime much more effectively, international police cooperation has to be improved. The different laws in European countries have to be harmonized. Special legal provisions will have to be introduced in the penal and procedure codes for law enforcement agencies to enforce. The governments have to provide modern education to all members of law enforcement and work to make them into a professional body.

Nevertheless, combating organized crime will require more than these executive measures. The fifteen members of the European Community are not homogenous. There are large differences between the rich and the less rich members of the European Community. It is also very difficult to predict future developments in the political, sociological, and economic dimensions. A very serious problem will be the growth of the unemployment rate in the different European countries. The existence of organized crime is greed driven and cannot exist without corruption. If we cannot overcome the growing differences between poor and rich, we cannot defeat organized crime. The problems of poverty in Africa, South America, and Asia will have to be addressed. The future developments in these parts of the world will undoubtedly influence the political, sociological, and economic situation in Europe and Austria. At the very least, it will bring a very large number of immigrants to these countries. This human migration alone will have grave consequences for every nation, rich or poor. This will be the breeding ground for organized crime.

REFERENCES

Aahs, Manfred. 1996. Bundesministerium fur Inneres, Abteilung II/16, Polizeiliche Kriminalstatistik, March. (Statistic Data of the Ministry of Interior).

Burgstaller, Johann, Heimo Flink, Elisabeth Meier, and Franz Schmitzberger. 1996. *Die Arbeitsmarktiage.* (The situation of the working market in Austria.) Vienna: Arbeitsmarkt service Osterreich.

Csonka, Peter. 1996. "Council of Europe—Organized Crime: A World Perspective." Paper presented at the Third Annual Symposium on Organized Crime, November–December, Yokohama.

Dick, Josef. 1995. Bundesministerium fur Inneres, Leiter der Gruppe, Der Standard, 4–5 March. (The illegal deals in Vienna—a center of money laundering and illegal economic businesses.)

Edelbacher, Maximilian and Karl Lesjak. 1994. Organisierte Kriminalitat, Lagebericht 1993, (Organized Crime—An Analysis of 1993.) Statistische daten und Erscheinungsformen, in Die Bundespolizei, No. September, 3.

Edelbacher, Maximilian. 1995a. "Serie Angewandte Kriminalistik, Schutz vor Kriminalitat." (Safety against Crime.) *Verlag Staatssicherheit*, June, Vienna, 7.

Edelbacher, Maximilian. 1995b. Serie Angewandte Kriminalistik, Internationaler Finanzbetrug. (International Financial Fraud.) *Verlag Staatssicherheit*, May, Vienna, 6–7.

Edelbacher, Maximilian. 1995c. Schutz vor Drogen. Vienna: Major Crime Bureau, Federal Police Headquarters, July. (Currently available as training script for legal experts of the police.)

Edelbacher, Maximilian. 1995d. "Serie Angewandte Kriminalistik, Versicherungsbetrug kennt keine Grenzen." (No Borders for Insurance fraud.) *Verlag Staatssicherheit*, Vienna April, 29.

Effmayer, Wendelin. 1995. "Muß es immer mehr Verbrechen geben?" (Security and Crime—is it necessary that crime is rising?). Schriftenreihe Standpunkte, Politische Akademie 24; 93.

Geiger, Ernst. 1992. "Organisierte Kriminalitat—eine Herausforderung for Justiz-, Polizei- und VerwaltungsbehOrden." (Organized Crime a Challenge for Justice, Police, and Administration.) In Polizeijuristische Rundschau, no. 3–4.

Hirschfeld, Alexander. 1995. The Federal Ministry of the Interior: Figures and Facts about the working year 1994. 1st ed. Vienna: Austrian Federal Ministry of Interior.

Holyst, Brunon. 1995. "Die neuen Richtungen in der Entwicklung der organisierten Kriminalitikt in Osteuropa." (The New Development of Organized Crime in Eastern Europe.) In MEPA-Lehrbrief 2/1995 des Bundesministeriums for Inneres, Seite 34.

Lesjak, Karl. 1995. Bundesministerium fur Inneres, Leiter der Abt.11/8, "Offnung der Staaten des ehemaligen Ostblocks." (Opening of the new Democratic States of the former Eastern Bloc). In MEPA-Lehrbrief 2/1995 des Bundesministeriums fur Inneres, 31.

Mag. Schuller. 1996. Volkswirtschaftliches Buro der Oesterreichischen. (National Bank, Information dated 7 April). Information by the Federal Bank of Austria.

Maver, Darko. 1996. "Organized Crime: A World Perspective and the View from Slovenia." Paper presented at the Third Annual Symposium on Organized Crime, November–December, Yokohama.

Plywaczewski, Emil W. 1996. "Organized Crime: A World Perspective." Paper presented at the Third Annual Symposium on Organized Crime, November–December, Yokohama.

Santino, Umberto. 1996. "Law Enforcement in Italy and Europe against Mafia and Organized Crime." Paper presented at the Third Annual Symposium on Organized Crime, November–December, Yokohama.

Serini, Foregger. 1994. *Das sterreichische Strafgesetzbuch und wichtige Nebengesetze.* 6th ed. Vienna: Manz Verlag.

Sika, M. Personal Conversation, Vienna, 1996.

Szymanski, Fuchs Funk. 1991. *Das Sicherheitspolizeigesetz.* (The Security Police Act.) Vienna: Manz Verlag.

Chapter 9

Organized Crime: A Perspective from the Council of Europe

Peter Csonka

Introduction

The role of the Council of Europe (40 member states) is essentially to establish and uphold conditions for democracy. These conditions are embodied in the principles for which the Council of Europe stands: human rights, the rule of law, and pluralistic democracy. They find expression in every aspect of life in each member state and, in particular, in the widely defined field of crime problems. Thus, the role of the Council of Europe in relation to crime problems is not only to provide a forum for sharing ideas, experiences, and projects, but also to promote human rights and the conditions for the rule of law as they apply in each particular field of activity. Indeed, the promotion of human rights embraces every aspect of life and should not be confined to the conventional principles and the law of human rights. "Crime problems" in the view of the Council of Europe include social attitudes and reactions, institutionalized procedures, as well as domestic and international legal matters, especially as they pertain to human rights. The same should be said of the rule of law, which is not a legal rule but the statement of an underlying guiding principle in the operation of the legal system. Even though the concept has developed since it was first formulated by Dicey in 1885, its point of departure in the criminal law remains untouched, namely the prohibition to punish unless under the law.

The Council of Europe involvement in dealing with crime problems has traditionally been the domain of the European Committee of Crime Problems (CDPC). The list of its past achievements is quite impressive, not only in number, but also having in mind their political and/or practical importance. They include 20 conventions and their explanatory reports; 160 recommendations and their explanatory memoranda; a number of separate reports, many of which had a great impact on the policy and practice of member states; 21 criminological research conferences. In addition, there have been 11 criminological colloquia organized since 1963, which have produced valuable material published under the authority of the CDPC; 13 conferences of directors of prison administration, and 5 conferences on crime policy.

One of the significant achievements of the organization is a comprehensive network of conventions concluded over the past 50 years which provide for all forms of international cooperation—traditional and modern—between national law enforcement agencies. These include:

- surrender of persons for the purpose of prosecution or enforcement of sentence (extradition—1957), and other forms of assistance between judicial authorities (mutual assistance—1959),
- recognition and enforcement of judgments (international validity of criminal judgments—1970), including the transfer of sentenced persons to their home countries (1983), and
- relinquishing prosecution in favor of another jurisdiction (transfer of proceedings—1972).

These conventions operate on the basis of a high degree of mutual trust, which the contracting States have in each other's criminal justice systems. This trust is founded in a common understanding of the principles governing criminal justice, which in turn conditions and governs international cooperation. Widely accepted by member states, these conventions have created a truly European code of international cooperation. Without them the member states of the Council of Europe would have to conclude five hundred bilateral treaties in each of the areas covered by European conventions.

As the number of member states in the Council of Europe increases, disparities grow. They also grow due to the particular circumstances relating to European integration within the framework of the Fifteen European Union States. Such changes in numbers and differences demand the need for more cooperation, not less. However, cooperation in the future must be of two different kinds. On the one hand it must be carried out within the whole group of forty; on the other, it must be cross-sectional and take into account the increasing complexity of the European geometry. In the near future, consideration must be given to the problems arising from the fact that smaller groups of states within Europe are now devoting considerable efforts to cooperation in criminal matters. Such efforts must be combined and coordinated with those of the larger group of states represented by the Council of Europe. In particular, it is expected that the ongoing Intergovernmental Conference on the reform of the European Union will adopt a formula in the revised Treaty on the European Union (the "Maastrich Treaty") that creates an operational link between the activities of cooperation in criminal matters. This cooperation is led by the fifteen Members of the European Union and those reforms undertaken in the more general framework of the forty Members of the Council of Europe.

One must emphasize that the increasing internationalization of organized crime often creates new difficulties. The rapid internationalization of crime is a fairly recent phenomenon in Europe. This is due to a variety of factors, including the increasing mobility of persons, better and less expensive communications, higher standards of living, the opening up of frontiers in general, and, in particular, the abolition of the internal borders between certain European countries. It is also due to the trend toward global markets and specialization. In view of such internationalization, experience shows that uncoordinated national responses to crime lead to serious imbalances, enhance the criminals' ability to re-route and better organize crime. Therefore, procedures for legal cooperation in criminal matters require a radical revision, while traditional patterns of cooperation—usually diplomatic channels—must follow suit and, in particular, must adapt to the new circumstances. This revision is underway in certain forms of international cooperation established by the Council of Europe conventions on extradition, mutual assistance in criminal matters, and transfer of proceedings, either within the framework of the European Union (EU) or the Council of Europe.

But the heart of the problem lies with criminal law itself: It expresses the requirements of a given society, as they are understood in the light of national values, national history, and the state of its development. Criminal law is the most "national" in character. Criminal law enforcement systems are very much linked to national sovereignty: As soon as the policeman, the prosecutor, or the judge purport to exercise their powers beyond a national frontier, they are bound to collide with the neighbor's sovereignty (Robert, 1996; Gully-Hart, 1992; Bernasconi, 1995). In the present state of organization of the world, having seen the tremendous difficulties that the UN-created international courts have experienced in prosecuting war criminals of the former Yugoslavia and Rwanda, international cooperation in criminal matters is the only viable response. The Council of Europe is constantly striving to adapt its methods and its action to changing circumstances. In particular, the area of cooperation was successfully extended all across Europe and most Central and Eastern European States, members and non-members of the Council of Europe, have now become parties to a number of conventions on legal cooperation in criminal matters.

Attitudes toward international cooperation also change. So do the needs for such cooperation, above all as a result of newly emerging forms of criminality: terrorism, drug trafficking, environmental offenses, computer-related crime, corruption, and money laundering. The need to adapt existing conventions to the challenges of new forms of international crime has been met in two ways: by amending the provisions of existing treaties (e.g., by extending extradition and mutual assistance to fiscal offenses) and by concluding separate agreements for specific kinds of crime. Arguably the most important recent treaty is the Convention on Laundering, Search, Seizure, and Confiscation of the Proceeds from Crime of 8 November 1990, which entered into force on 1 September 1993, and is already binding upon fourteen member states (European Conventions and Agreements, 1994). Other international cooperation treaties are being discussed or are almost ready for adoption: a treaty on offenses causing damage to the environment, on crimes committed with the use of information technology, and on the international aspects of corruption. Besides convention-making activities, every year new issues are taken up by the CDPC with the ultimate objective of elaborating guidelines (so-called "recommendations") and reports. These nonbinding, soft-law instruments also contribute to a large extent to harmonization of national policies in a given field. Current activities include the following topics: corruption, organized crime, offenses related to the cyberspace, mediation, prison matters, statistics, protection of witnesses, the role of the public prosecution, and crime prevention (early psycho-social intervention). Hereafter, the chapter will focus on questions related to economic and organized crime.

NATURE AND EXTENT OF ORGANIZED CRIME

The most widely accessible and widely used data on crime are usually police data (i.e., the crimes known to the police). Interpretation and comparability problems, over time as well as across nations, arising from differences between national criminal laws and statistical systems are well known. Many other types of data sources may often be available, but, for the purposes of general overviews or cross-national comparisons, they are even less useful than police data if the goal is to assess crime as a field phenomenon, since they are even further away from the event. This implies a serious limitation, particularly with regard to crime categories where many relevant events remain beyond the grasp of the criminal justice system and police investigations, as is the case for instance, with economic and business or organized crime (e.g., drug-related crimes). Another difficulty in assessing the magnitude of organized crime is that police statistics often do not use this category but rather group the data under separate headings (e.g., robbery, trafficking offenses, money laundering, etc.) and thus make the link connecting such offenses blurred or difficult to establish.

Drug-related crime, especially trafficking, is of particular concern in all countries. New routes via Central and Eastern European countries as well as the abolition of controls in many borders are important factors in this respect. The patterns of drug trafficking may have changed as a result of the recent developments in Europe. In most Western European countries, crime rates in general are reported to have increased (European Sourcebook, 1995). Even though it is not always easy to establish links between trends in crime and changes in the political, economical, and social spheres, the following offenses are reported as showing a sharp increase in the last decade:

- The expansion of organized crime in general
- Car thefts, probably many committed by gangs, with many cars transferred to Central and Eastern European countries
- Economic crime
- Money laundering
- Arms trafficking
- Corruption
- Illegally exported refuse
- Immigration crimes (including smuggling and illegal crossing of borders)
- Visa and passport forgery
- Crime related to industrial legislation, in particular illegal recruitment of clandestine migrant workers
- Criminality linked with prostitution and other forms of sexual exploitation (European Committee on Crime Problems, 1996)

Increase is reported from countries of Central and Eastern Europe in respect to:

- The expansion of organized crime in general
- Racketeering
- Offenses against property

- Economic crime
- Counterfeiting of money
- Illegal trade in and production and possession of firearms and explosive materials
- Corruption
- Import and production of, as well as trading in, adulterated foodstuffs
- Criminality linked with prostitution and other forms of sexual exploitation. (Savona and Adamoli, 1996).

Economic crime, used here as a generic term, covers all sorts of offenses committed by individuals or public/private companies in the context of their industrial, commercial, financial, or other business-related activities (Council of Europe, 1996a). The term comprises a wide variety of crimes, especially those pertaining to property, but also those endangering the natural environment as well as the state's financial interests (e.g., breach of taxation provisions). The central interests are financial, but the consequences of financially motivated activities may be multiple, including damage to the environment, violation of labor protection rules, and in extreme cases, damage to entire monetary systems, not to mention breaches of public morality and the disruption of democratic decision-making processes. A tendency toward international expansion and more complex organizational structures has been observed, aiming at the maximization of profits by illegal means. This is a primary characteristic of organized crime, but economic and organized crime are extremely difficult to separate, with one merging into the other.

In Central and Eastern Europe, economic criminality is closely related to the establishment of the new economic system and the privatization process, the transition to a market economy, and greater liberalization of foreign trade and foreign investment. Most typical forms of economic crime involve embezzlement of state property, violation of tax laws, production and sale of adulterated products, smuggling, bankruptcy of companies, privatization of companies, business fraud and tax evasion, both corruption and unauthorized use of funds by state officials, currency and check fraud, abuse of special forms of payment to the detriment of banks or export companies, and crimes against intellectual property. In Eastern Europe, notably Russia, a large proportion of crimes are committed by the private sector, usually where there is poor police protection, a tradition of corruption, wide variation and fluctuation in incomes, and an increase in production (Council of Europe, 1996b).

Measures, Including Legislation to Combat Organized Crime

Subject to national legal traditions and constitutional principles, one can identify some general tendencies that emerge at the international level and which indicate possible avenues for making the fight against organized crime more effective. Without any ambition of giving an exhaustive list, one may think of the following group of legislative and law enforcement measures. Some of these measures are contained in existing or draft Council of Europe instruments and will be examined in more detail later.

- Introducing specific offenses such as being a member or participant in some criminal enterprise, or other forms of conspiracy crimes, specially directed at the organizational aspects of the crimes committed;
- Measures that target the ill-gotten proceeds of organized crime by criminalizing money laundering, enhancing financial investigations into criminal assets, and enabling confiscation;
- Measures to protect witnesses and collaborators of justice who provide information and/or give testimony against organized crime groups;
- Measures that enable intrusive investigative techniques to gain insight into the activities of the organized crime groups;
- Improvements in the functioning and structures of the criminal justice system and its various components, including the police and customs, prosecution, and speedy trials in courts;
- Improvements of the necessary legislative and regulatory measures to combat corruption.

The Council of Europe in April 1997 also embarked upon an ambitious project to study organized crime and to prepare proposals to improve national and international responses to it. There was a general concern among member states about the difficulties in ascertaining, not only the existence of criminal organizations, but also their features, including their modus operandi. A better knowledge of how such organizations are operating was considered essential for taking effective counter measures. A committee of experts is analyzing the features of organized crime, with particular emphasis on the political, social (environmental), economic, legal, and regulatory factors that facilitate its emergence and/or unrelenting level in a given context. The experts will look into the offenses committed, including the modus operandi of the organizations committing these offenses (taking into account their national or transnational character), their degree of organization (e.g., ad hoc criminal groups, structured criminal networks, and Mafia-type organizations), and the offenders participating in these groups (young people or adults, nationals or aliens, and legal persons, national or transnational).

In a second stage, the committee will assess the domestic responses to organized crime, implemented or envisaged, the resources necessary for them (material as well as know-how), and the means of information available. Particular attention will be given to legislative, social (prevention) measures, and the working methods of the criminal justice system. National legislation will be studied in order to identify existing solutions that could serve as examples for other countries and, more important, to ascertain the criteria used in national legislation to qualify offenses as "committed in an organized manner," "conspiracy," or "association de malfaiteurs" with a view to overcoming the difficulties arising in international cooperation from the differences in these concepts by establishing common criteria. The committee will also identify the lacunae in international cooperation instruments and possible solutions that could be included in international instruments. It is expected that some common procedural principles, especially in relation to banking secrecy, the admissibility of certain types of evidence, or the length and effect of statutory limitation periods will also be examined by the experts.

The financial investigations into money laundering have generally not been fruitful. Law enforcement strategies aiming to penetrate into organized crime groups by using traditional policing techniques are said to be mostly unsuccessful because of the closed structures and secretive communication methods of group members. Police officials often claim that only special investigative techniques, such as telephone tapping, undercover (sting) operations, and controlled delivery can obtain better results. Examples given to justify this approach refer to U.S. law enforcement experience where from the 1970s law enforcement agencies adopted a new, powerful, and aggressive strategy of investigating the assets of criminal enterprises, in parallel with (or mostly instead of) prosecuting individual members. This aggressive strategy was enabled by extensive law enforcement powers created by statutes such as the 1970 Organized Crime Control Act, incorporating the Racketeer Influenced and Corrupt Organization Act (RICO), the Witness Security Program, and the 1984 Continuing Criminal Enterprise Statute. The Hungarian report presented at the previously mentioned conference stressed the following:

> It should be remembered that the standard methods based on the fundamental principles of the state governed by the rule of law, and in particular the law on criminal procedure, are powerless in dealing with

criminal operations which bear little resemblance to traditional forms of crime. Failure to recognize this new development and the time wasted on theoretical and constitutional debate about the methods to be used against organized crime have meant that states have been slow to react to this phenomenon and have often failed to take action until organized crime has already infiltrated different sectors of society.

One has to keep in mind that criminal organizations need to launder their money in order to conceal their illegal assets, and in this field, organized crime people usually ally with white-collar criminals to choose the best ways to disguise their wealth. Money laundering must be seen as an integral part of the entrepreneurial dimension of organized crime. Drug traffickers, the most typical organized crime entrepreneurs, after producing dirty money, frequently take care of the first steps of the laundering within their own activities, and they apply to external professionals only for further laundering techniques and/or investments. This creates a strong connection between the laundering activities and the predicate trafficking activities.

For the aforementioned reasons, it is necessary that provisions of criminal law be supported by appropriate civil laws providing for transparency of transactions and ownership. Most of the specific anti-money laundering requirements relevant to the banking and financial institutions were recommended by the Council of Europe Recommendation N R (80)10 on measures against the transfer and the safekeeping of funds of criminal origin, the European Community Directive N 91/308/CEE of 10 June 1991, on the prevention of the use of the financial system for the purpose of money laundering, and the 40 Recommendations of the Financial Action Task Force (FATF). It is worthwhile recalling some of the fundamental principles:

- Banking secrecy should not be a ground for objection. Judges and prosecutors may ask for banking or financial information within a criminal procedure and countries can no longer allow anonymous bank accounts (European Financial Services law, 1996).
- Financial transactions over a specified amount of money (namely over 15,000 ECU, according to the European Directive) should not be permitted in cash, except in banks or other authorized financial institutions. In order to satisfy this requirement, in Italy, and in many other countries, no saving deposit to bearer can exceed the provided threshold.
- Banks and financial institutions should be required to keep records in their computers of every operation and to inform police about any

suspicious financial transaction, according to a particular procedure and a determined list of possible suspicious transactions.
- The splitting of operations and those effected by the same person within a given time to avoid the threshold limit shall be treated as if they were one single operation.

This is why Council of Europe member states—and some other countries outside Europe—adopted a legal instrument, the aforementioned 1990 Convention on Laundering, which allows for international investigations of criminal assets, as well as the implementation of their seizure and confiscation on an international scale. The strategy of interconnected asset investigations is exactly the philosophy on which the Strasbourg Convention is based. The aim of this convention is to make this coordination of economic investigations possible on an international scale. Every contracting state is supposed to give assistance to one another, first in investigating and tracing criminal assets, and the final target is their seizure and confiscation on an international scale.

The Council of Europe Convention draws on the 1988 United Nations Convention. As far as possible, it uses its terminology and systematic approach. However, it goes beyond it in many ways, in particular, by expanding the definition of money laundering beyond its traditional association with drug trafficking. Indeed the Convention contemplates all forms of criminality. The purposes of the Convention are primarily:

a. To facilitate international cooperation in investigative assistance, search, seizure, and confiscation of the proceeds from all types of criminality;
b. To complement instruments of international cooperation in criminal matters by providing a complete set of rules, covering all the stages of the procedure;
c. To oblige States to adopt efficient domestic measures: legislative and others.

Thus, under the Convention, parties undertake to:

a. Adopt such legislative and other measures as may be necessary to confiscate property used to commit an offense, proceeds and property the value of which corresponds to proceeds (known as value confiscation);
b. Adopt such legislative and other measures as may be necessary to identify and trace property which is liable to confiscation and also to prevent its transfer and disposal;

c. Adopt such legislative and other measures to ensure that bank, financial, or commercial records be made available for investigation purposes;
d. Adopt such legislative and other measures to use special investigative techniques (e.g., monitoring orders, observation, interception of telecommunications, access to computer systems, and orders to produce specific documents);
e. Enforce, upon request, confiscation orders made by courts in another state;
f. Criminalize money laundering, as defined in the Convention.

The Convention has also taken steps to define money laundering in order to strengthen the measures against organized crime syndicates. The Convention has distinguished three offenses, depending on the action taken by the person with respect to the property:

a. The conversion or transfer of property for the purpose of concealing its origin
b. The concealment of the nature, source, location, ownership of the property
c. The acquisition, possession, or use of property

Money laundering, and economic crime in general have been boosted by the recent information technology revolution and the unprecedented opportunities of communication through computer networks like information superhighways and cellular phones. Rumors suggest that the Colombian drug kingpins use the Internet and dozens of mobile telephones every day to transmit information about their customers and to organize their laundering activities. Undoubtedly, it is becoming obvious that electronic information systems are also being used for committing criminal offenses and that evidence of criminal offenses may be stored and transferred by these systems. Recognizing the need to deal with the problem of misuse of technology by organized crime syndicates, the Council of Europe adopted in 1995, Recommendation N R (95) 13, concerning problems of criminal procedural law connected with information technology (Council of Europe, 1996c). This is a follow-up to Recommendation N R (89) 9 on computer-related crime, an "enabling recommendation" intended to give effect to an eighty-page report that a committee of experts had prepared on the subject. This study was a first attempt at tackling, in a systematic way, the problems arising in connection with this new phenomenon of criminality. It focused on the substantive law issues and concluded that the procedural law aspects require further consideration (European Committee on Crime Problems, 1990).

Recommendation N R (95) 13 aims at providing guidance to national legislators, investigating authorities, and other professional bodies on these procedural law issues. It sets principles on the search and seizure of electronically stored data, on technical surveillance for the purposes of criminal investigations, on obligations to cooperate with the investigating authorities, on electronic evidence, on the use of encryption, on research, statistics and specialized training, and on international cooperation.

The Council of Europe also adopted in 1997 a recommendation on the intimidation of witnesses and the rights of the defense, which devotes special attention to witness intimidation involving organized crime groups. The recommendation is based on the idea that the duty to give testimony implies the responsibility of the state to guarantee that witnesses can indeed comply with such a duty without negative consequences. What can be interpreted as a state responsibility may also be seen as a right for witnesses. The recommendation urges member states to enact laws that clearly establish the status of witnesses, comprising both the duty to give testimony and the right to carry out this duty without any interference, harm, or risk. Over the past ten to fifteen years, the question of witness protection has become a major concern for the justice systems of many countries in Europe. This special attention toward witnesses can be related to several different factors. First of all, a noticeable rise in the criminal activities of terrorist and organized crime groups could be registered during this period at both European level and worldwide. These groups increasingly attempt to corrupt and even destroy the normal functioning of the criminal justice system by all possible means, including threats of violence or bribery of justice officials and the systematic intimidation or elimination of witnesses. The protection of witnesses and of their relatives thus became a necessity going beyond the personal interests of the individuals and becoming a duty of public authorities in order to ensure the integrity and effectiveness of criminal justice (Lemonde, 1996).

The recommendation recognizes that it is still difficult to establish a commonly accepted definition of organized crime and, hence, determine the common features of these groups. But it admits that the rule of silence (i.e., the prohibition against disclosing any information to outsiders, particularly to the police, about the activities of the group) seems a general custom among most groups (Multidisciplinary Group on Corruption, 1996). Law enforcement experience in certain countries demonstrates that those who have reported the activities of these groups, whether as outsiders or reformed or active members of the group, may reasonably fear repression and severe consequences for their own lives and that of their relatives. The testimony of these persons can therefore be obtained only if sufficient protective measures safeguard their lives and personal safety.

Corruption is the bridge between economic and organized crime and is being treated as a major threat (De Ruyver and Vander Beken, 1996). Corruption usually comes together with violence as specific means of organized crime groups to penetrate into legitimate activities. Corruption may often be the cover of other crimes, such as fraud and embezzlement committed by enterprises, the payment of bribes to officials, or money-laundering activities. Increasing public awareness of the internationalization of corruption and the growing interest in anti-corruption measures, should now give rise to a firm commitment of countries to adapt their legislation for combating this crime more effectively. Recent recommendations by the Organization for Economic Cooperation and Development (OECD) provided soft-law guidelines for enacting national legislation on corruption in international business transactions, but the time has come to take concerted international efforts to harmonize domestic corruption laws through an international treaty, providing for an equal criminal treatment of domestic and international corruption. The abolition of fiscal advantages that favor domestic enterprises, corrupting foreign officials for obtaining or retaining business abroad, is certainly one of the main concerns of large exporter countries which exert pressure to criminalize domestically the corruption of foreign public officials.

For these reasons in June 1994, the Nineteenth Conference of the European Ministers of Justice discussed the theme "The administrative, civil, and penal aspects of the fight against corruption, including the role of the judiciary." The conference adopted a resolution establishing a "Multidisciplinary Group on Corruption within the Council of Europe." This group started work in 1995. It prepared a Program of Action against Corruption, an ambitious document covering all the aspects of the international fight against this phenomenon. This program was adopted in November 1996, by the Committee of Ministers, which fixed December 2000, as the deadline for its execution. The Multidisciplinary Group on Corruption (better known by its French acronym GMC), has been working intensely in the preparation of several international instruments against corruption. A Framework Convention against Corruption (hereafter the FC) is in an advanced stage of preparation. Based on a multidisciplinary approach, the FC specifies the principles, including the criminalization of corruption offenses and the prohibition of tax deductibility of bribes, which states will have to include in their national strategies against corruption. In addition, the GMC has undertaken work in several other fields covered by the Program of Action against Corruption. A draft Criminal Law Convention providing for the criminalization of various forms of public and private corruption, including bribery in international transactions, as well as specific provisions on international cooperation in the fight against corruption offenses, is currently under preparation. The GMC has also started the drafting of civil law instruments, providing for specific remedies for victims of corruption and compensation for the damages suffered. In addition, the preparation of a Model Code of Conduct for European public officials is under preparation.

Comparative Evaluation of the Methods for Combating Organized Crime and Proposed Measures

Despite the different measures taken against money laundering, the steps for confiscation of property and financial gains requires in particular:

1. Regulatory measures necessary to obtain maximum transparency in the financial systems and to prevent monopolies.

2. Extending the crime of money laundering to the gains of investing proceeds. Intentionally not reporting suspicious transactions should also be considered a criminal offense committed by financial and non-bank financial institutions.

3. Establishing a new investigative strategy that targets the assets of organized criminals through interconnected financial investigations. Such a strategy requires quick legal mechanisms to lift banking secrecy and provisions under which bankers, fiduciaries, accountants, and lawyers may be compelled by judicial order to breach their duty of loyalty toward clients and produce bank records or other financial statements, or, if necessary, give testimony. Additionally, states should also consider the introduction of provisions for asset sharing among countries participating in the same law enforcement operation.

4. Adopting legislative measures for the confiscation or seizure of illicit assets from drug trafficking and other serious offenses, asset forfeiture, as required, and the availability of provisional arrangements, such as freezing of assets.

The measures to protect witnesses and collaborators also require strengthening.

1. Providing effective protection for individuals who have given or agreed to give information or evidence, or who have agreed to participate

in an investigation or prosecution of an offense (and for the relatives and associates of those individuals who require protection) because of risk to the security of the person.

2. Adopting appropriate measures to ensure the protection of witnesses during criminal proceedings. This might include such methods as testifying via telecommunication links or limiting the disclosure of the address and identifying particulars of witnesses. Consideration should be given to the temporary transfer of witnesses in custody, enlargement of the admissibility of written statements, and the use of modern technology to overcome some of the current difficulties in obtaining testimony from witnesses located outside the prosecuting state.

The measures for intrusive investigative techniques still require additional features. These include:

> Introduction of legislation allowing law enforcement agencies to conduct wiretapping or other forms of electronic surveillance, undercover operations and controlled deliveries.
> Review of domestic arrangements for these techniques and facilitation of international cooperation in these fields, while bearing in mind all human rights implications.
> Provisioning of law enforcement agencies with adequate technological resources for wiretapping and electronic surveillance, together with standardized software for databases to be used for tactical and strategic intelligence.

The measures for the improvement in the functioning and structures of the criminal justice system is a long-term project and requires large-scale restructuring of the existing institutions. However, some short-term measures could be adopted like:

1. Adoption of new rules of evidence concerning certain offenses, such as possession of large amounts of narcotic drugs or "illicit enrichment" (i.e., having no justifiable resource for one's economic wealth of dubious origin). This may imply that the burden of proof is exceptionally placed on the defendant and not on the prosecution.

2. Admitting the intervention of new parties, such as financial institutions or NGOs, in criminal proceedings, thus enabling the prosecution to benefit from external information and to use it as evidence in court.

3. Development of new methods of proactive police methods that include intelligence gathering through community support and better crime analytical techniques.

4. Creating specialized inter-agency teams to investigate and prosecute certain offenses in the domain of economic and organized crime (such as the OKOKRIM in Norway or the Serious Fraud Office in the UK) and identifying within existing national structures central contact points for the purpose of facilitating contacts with foreign operational agencies.

5. Providing law enforcement agencies with specific training activities in the area of financial investigation and encouraging these agencies to exchange their experiences in this field.

Despite the improvements in the legislative and regulatory measures there remains the need for:

1. Establishing standards of good governance and legitimate commercial and financial conduct and developing cooperation mechanisms to curb corrupt practices.
2. Increasing the severity of corruption crimes committed at domestic and international levels.
3. Suppressing all financial and economic advantages to domestic enterprises having obtained businesses through corrupting public officials abroad.
4. Extending the offense of corruption to the corruption of foreign public officials.

The attempt to study the nature of organized crime and to develop effective responses against it is laudable but needs, further work. The requirement for a suitable database cannot be overstated and yet there is little to use in this study. There is the need for common criteria to be established to obtain comparable national data on organized crime. By analyzing these data, an integrated European strategy could be developed, with a view toward overcoming the differences in the legal systems of member states concerning organized crime. This analysis may also result in recommendations regarding law enforcement structures and investigation methods. The committee of experts that has been studying organized crime will have to analyze its features with particular emphasis on the political, social (environmental), economic, legal, and regulatory factors that facilitate its emergence and/or unrelenting level in a given context. It is clear that through the laundering and investment of the proceeds of crime, drug trafficking and organized crime create and strengthen areas of criminal economy around the world and within the legal economic system. It happens quite frequently that criminals use, for their own profit, secrecy in banking transactions, secrecy in financial transactions, and secrecy in ownership of companies in order to gain access to a legal economy on an international scale to launder and invest their illegal assets. Furthermore, the lack of transparency in the ownership of companies often allows criminals to control legal enterprises, such as through the ownership of an anonymous company. Consequently, the measures being taken against financial transactions of organized crime syndicates are not proving to be very successful.

These regulatory measures in the financial sector need to be complemented by appropriate criminal law and procedural law measures that increase law enforcement ability to trace, seize, and confiscate dirty money. To attack the wealth of organized crime, criminal law must above all make the laundering itself of the proceeds of (drug trafficking and at present all serious) crime punishable. Furthermore, the criminalization of money laundering is explicitly required by the 1988 United Nations Convention on illicit traffic in narcotic drugs and psychotropic substances and the Council of Europe Convention on Laundering, Search, Seizure, and Confiscation of the Proceeds from Crime (ETS no. 141). The 1991 EC Directive indirectly does so as well.

Beyond criminalizing laundering activities, an effective investigation strategy to attack directly the economic and entrepreneurial dimension of organized crime needs the ability to take action internationally. It is necessary to emphasize that a strategy of systematic and interconnected economic investigations needs to be allowed to develop beyond national frontiers. In order to reach this goal, new tools of international cooperation are needed, not only at a police level, but also at a judicial level, since organized crime and criminal economy do have an international dimension.

Existing measures to tackle the misuse of technology, especially the Internet-based communication systems by the organized groups, is still in its infancy. Law enforcement agencies in many countries now warn that criminal procedural laws do not yet provide for appropriate powers to search and collect evidence in these systems in the course of criminal investigations and that the lack of appropriate special powers may impair investigating authorities in the proper fulfillment of their tasks (Sieber, 1990; Csonka, 1996a and 1996b).

Another main problem in procedural law is that the methods for collecting evidence are not harmonized. It is therefore vital that domestic legislation make possible the use of modern techniques in tracing criminals and collecting evidence on their operations and the organization itself. A reasonable balance needs to be found between the protection of privacy and the need of the law enforcement agencies to collect evidence by wiretapping and other forms of electronic surveillance. Legislation providing these methods, together with other law enforcement methods, such us undercover operations and controlled delivery, should be passed to enable law enforcement agencies to collect sufficient evidence beyond any reasonable doubt. Concerning "search and seizure," it is recommended that criminal procedural laws permit investigating authorities to search computer systems and seize data under similar conditions as under traditional powers of search and seizure. The person in charge of the system should be informed that the system has been searched and of the kind of data that has been seized. The legal remedies provided for in general against search and seizure should be equally applicable in these cases. Investigating authorities should also have the power, subject to appropriate safeguards, to extend the search to other computer systems within their jurisdiction, which are connected by means of a network and to seize the data stored in these systems.

Laws pertaining to "technical surveillance" for the purposes of criminal investigations, such as interception of telecommunications, should be reviewed and amended, where necessary, to ensure the applicability to new information technology, for instance with regard to the collection of traffic data. Criminal procedural laws should be reviewed with a view to making possible the interception of telecommunications and the collection of traffic data in the investigation of serious offenses against the confidentiality, integrity, and availability of telecommunications or computer systems.

The recommendation of the Council to permit investigating authorities to order persons to hand over objects under their control that are required to serve as evidence also needs to be extended to the case of data in electronic form. Subject to legal privileges or protection, investigating authorities should have the power to order persons who have data in a computer system under their control to provide all necessary information to enable access to a computer system and the data stored in that system. Criminal procedural law should ensure that a similar order can be given to other persons who have knowledge about the functioning of the computer system or the measures applied to secure the data therein. Specific obligations should be imposed on operators of public and private networks offering telecommunications services to the public to avail themselves of all the necessary technical measures that enable the interception of telecommunications by the investigating authorities. Specific obligations should also be imposed on service providers who offer telecommunications services to the public, either through public or through private networks, to provide information to identify the user, when so ordered by the competent investigating authority.

Similarly, the measures to develop procedures and technical guidelines for handling electronic evidence—their collection, preservation, and presentation—should be further developed and their compatibility between states should be ensured. Criminal procedural law provisions on evidence relating to traditional documents should similarly apply to data stored in a computer system.

Furthermore, the power to extend a search to other computer systems should also be applicable when the system is located in a foreign jurisdiction, provided that immediate action is required. In order to avoid possible violations of state sovereignty or international law, an unambiguous legal basis for such extended search and seizure should be established. In this context, the measures must emphasize an urgent need, and how, when, and to what extent such search and seizure should be permitted. Adequate procedures, as well as a system of liaison, should be available to the investigating authorities so that they may request foreign authorities promptly to collect evidence. The requested authorities should be authorized to search a computer system and seize data with a view to its subsequent transfer. They should also be authorized to provide trafficking data related to a specific telecommunication, intercept a specific telecommunication, or identify its source.

The measures being taken for the protection of witnesses and collaborators against organized crime groups need to be strengthened. Given the types of serious criminality in which these groups are involved, they may pose a significant threat to public institutions as well, particularly if their economic wealth is combined with political influence. It is not surprising that since the fight against organized crime is likely to become the first priority of law enforcement throughout Europe, many countries seek to establish adequate counter strategies and measures, including the revision and adjustment of certain legal rules. Strongly recommended by law enforcement agencies, the use of informants, collaborators, and undercover agents for gathering evidence is very controversial in certain states and modifications of traditional guarantees of criminal procedure for the accused, such as the right to confrontation with witnesses at charge, raises serious reservations. Nevertheless, it seems that in the long run it is unavoidable that criminal procedural rules will be adapted to face the challenge posed by organized crime. It is obvious that any adaptation must not infringe upon the most fundamental principle of criminal procedure, the equality of arms, as guaranteed by the decisions of the European Convention of Human Rights (Harris, O'Boyle, and Wrabrick, 1995).

The extent to which witness protection measures are or will be employed is closely related to the extent of the problem faced by states. Large-scale witness protection programs, such as in Italy and the United States, are set up in countries confronted with serious problems of organized crime, whereas countries with lesser problems in this area are more reluctant to introduce special witness-protection measures. Often such measures apply to ordinary witnesses and "collaborators of justice." The latter category may, in general, refer to informants, "super-grasses," and also reformed criminals (also called *pentiti* in Italian). "Collaborators of justice" in a narrow sense are people who have knowledge of the structures and activities of criminal organizations, and the testimony of such persons is in most organized crime cases crucial in obtaining evidence concerning the offenses committed by the organization. The collaborating person requires strong protection measures in view of the collaboration. These measures, such as special penitentiary regime, admission to a witness-protection program, and material compensation must be spelled out and given concrete shape by the states.

Taking into account both the seriousness of the crimes and the power of intimidation of organized crime groups, it is necessary that states adopt specific rules of procedure to cope with problems of witness intimidation when devising measures against organized crime. States may, for example, consider the opportunity or necessity of keeping the personal data and whereabouts of witnesses secret from the defendant. Some states already have provisions on anonymous witnesses and/or provisions that allow technical measures to make the identification of witnesses more difficult. The use of the testimony of accomplices can be extremely helpful in prosecution of organized crime. Careful assessment and use of testimonies can enable the law enforcement process to penetrate the layers of secrecy characteristic of criminal organizations which would otherwise protect them from prosecution.

Some of these specific measures, such as concealing the identity of a witness, may be seen to be inconsistent with the right of the accused to be confronted with the witness. The rights of the defense must also be safeguarded throughout the proceedings. When the witness's statement is taken only in the presence of the defense counsel or is video-recorded in order to preserve the anonymity of the witness, procedural laws should ensure that the defense has proper opportunity to challenge the statement. Nevertheless, under certain circumstances, where criminal proceedings deal with very serious allegations in the field of organized crime and the witness is in danger, the rights of the defense must be weighed against the rights of the witness and the duty of the state to do justice. In accordance with the rulings of the European Court of Human Rights, the need for striking a balance between the interests of society and the rights of the defense still must be considered.

Witness-protection measures need to be supplemented with other kinds of special procedures that countries need to consider. The recording of statements made by witnesses during pre-trial examination may effectively discourage potentially harmful actions by the affected organized crime group against the witness. In cases of organized crime, procedural law should admit pre-trial statements as evidence in court. Furthermore, a limited use of pre-trial statements should, under certain conditions, be permitted in order to allow the cross-examination of a witness who withdrew previous assertions. In addition, the use of pre-trial statements as evidence should be permitted when the witness is excused from appearing at the trial due to threat of great danger to his or a third party's life. In such cases, the right of the defense to challenge the witness's testimony should be guaranteed at the pre-trial stage. In general, procedural laws should allow the witness's identity to be kept secret and only revealed at the latest possible stage of the proceedings. This still requires agreement among the participating countries, and without it, the protection program is unlikely to succeed.

Provisions for the protection of witnesses is of great importance in combating organized crime. It is therefore urgently required that national systems of criminal justice adopt legislative provisions and specific programs aimed at providing for the security of a witness. In particular, they should consider adopting measures for the protection of witnesses that allow for relocation and change of identity, along with their physical protection if there is a threat posed by a defendant and the defendant's associates. This may necessitate making arrangements to provide witnesses with documents enabling them (and any family) to establish a new identity and temporary housing, transportation of household furniture and other personal belongings to a new location, subsistence payments, assistance in obtaining employment, and other necessary services to assist the witnesses in leading a normal life. In considering the type of protection to be provided, the financial circumstances of a country must be taken into account. In addition, provisions should be made for the safe custody of incarcerated witnesses, including separate accommodations. Legislation may also be necessary to deal with the practical problems that may arise in connection with relocated witnesses, such as child custody disputes and crimes committed under their new identity.

The measures for controlling corruption in international dealings should go beyond punishing bribery in international business transactions: it should target both private and public corruption and should not only aim at a clean business/competition environment but, more important, make public administration more sound, transparent, and accountable for its decision making. Corruption may indeed be seen as a phenomenon of the society and in that sense one may speak of "systematic" corruption of legal systems, economic management, the delivery of public services, and policy-making. Such corruption can skew incentives disastrously, undermine voluntary compliance, deter investment, and render democracy ineffectual. It generates economic costs by distorting incentives, political costs by undermining institutions, and social costs by redistributing wealth and power toward the rich and privileged. When corruption undermines property rights, the rule of law, and incentives to invest, economic and political developments are crippled (Klitgaard, 1995). The concept of corruption is therefore wider than that of criminal corruption. This differentiation is important for the simple reason that no comprehensive and all-embracing strategy in the fight against corruption can ever be formulated, if one were to limit such measures to criminal corruption alone. Put differently, a corrupt practice or system might not as yet be considered by law an offense, but such an omission would not render it less corrupt in its character. It would only mean that under the current law or under a given system, no court action may as yet be taken to suppress it. It is not considered to be a crime and, of course, no punishment can ever be meted out.

Conclusion

The new century is here and the next generation will soon face the task of reacting to the new types of crime that will occur. Taking into account the time needed to develop appropriate instruments, it is advisable to start reflecting about this as soon as possible. It is important that countries achieve a common understanding of the fact that crimes committed by an organized crime group represent a larger threat than if the same crime is committed by an individual or a casual organization. A crime committed by an organized group may be considered an aggravated one. Criminal codes of many countries define the committing of a crime by an organized group as a qualifying feature. In some ways the existence of organized crime is a threat in itself because of the high probability of committing further offenses. The implication is that the offense of "participation in an organized criminal association," as provided by the Italian law (1982), or the offense of "participation in the affairs of an enterprise through a pattern of racketeering," as provided in the United States by the RICO statute (1970), should be considered as two ways of treating the same problem: the existence and the functioning of an organization devoted to committing crimes.

If such offenses are considered in substantive legislation this will enable criminal law to attack the organizational structure of the criminal groups more than the crime of conspiracy alone could do. The experience of the application of these two types of offenses has been very positive in combating organized crime in both Italy and the United States. In the Italian experience the offense of participation in an "organized crime association" has been decisive for the successful prosecution and conviction of many Mafia bosses in the first maxi-trial against the Mafia in Sicily. In the United States, the RICO statute is generally considered as the starting point of a new process of awareness of organized crime by the U.S. government and its law enforcement agencies. The effectiveness of RICO is shown in many indictments and convictions of members of organized crime groups since the legislation was passed. In order to deter organized crime, in addition to the traditional sanctions of incarceration and/or fines which may be imposed upon conviction, consideration should be given to other sanctions designed specifically for this purpose. In fact, some countries utilize judicially imposed limitations on property, residence, association, and daily activities of persons formally adjudged to be criminally dangerous. Corporate criminal liability should also be duly considered in most organized crime cases.

REFERENCES

Bernasconi, Paolo. 1995. Les Obstacles À La Coopération Judiciaire Contra La Criminalité Internationale. In *Nuovi Strumenti Giudiziari Contro La Criminalità Economica Internazionale*, Paolo Bernasconi, (ed.), 405–431. Napoli: La Città Del Sole.

Council of Europe. 1996a. *Economic Crime.* Reprint. Appendix, 11–12. Council of Europe Publishing.

Council of Europe. 1996b. Ministerial Conference organized within the framework of the "Octopus project." Reports of a joint initiative of the Council of Europe and the Commission of the European Communities. Sofia, December.

Council of Europe. 1996c. *Problems of Criminal Procedural Law Connected with Information Technology*, Recommendation N R (95) 13 and explanatory memorandum. Strasbourg: Council of Europe Publishing.

Csonka, Peter. 1996a. "Criminal Procedural Law and Information Technology: The Main Features of the Council of Europe Recommendation N R (95) 13." In *Computer Law and Security Report* 12, 37–42.

Csonka, Peter. 1996b. "Council of Europe Activities Related to Information Technology, Data Protection and Computer Crime." In *Information & Communications Technology Law* 5 (3): 177–196. Oxford.

De Ruyver, Brice and Tom Vander Beken. 1996. "Corruption and Organized Crime." Paper presented at the 14th Cambridge Symposium on Economic Crime, September.

European Committee on Crime Problems. 1990. *Computer-Related Crime*, Recommendation N R (89) 9, 69–94. Strasbourg: Council of Europe Publishing.

European Committee on Crime Problems. 1996. "Report on Responses to Developments in the Volume and Structure of Crime in Europe in a Time of Change" and the Addendum to the report on "Recent Crime Trends in Central and Eastern Europe." In *Europe In A Time of Change Crime Policy and Criminal Law*, Recommendation N R (96) 8, 26–82, unofficial publication.

European Conventions and Agreements. 1994. *European Treaty Series*. Vol. 6 (1990–1994), 114–136. Strasbourg: Council of Europe Publishing.

European Financial Services law. 1996. June, V 3, N 6, 181.

European Sourcebook. 1995. Crime and Criminal Justice Statistics, Draft Model, 34–46. Council of Europe Publishing.

Gully-Hart, Paul. 1992. "Loss of time through Formal and Procedural Requirements in International Co-Operation." In *Principles and Procedures for a New Transnational Criminal Law*, Albin Eser and Otto Lagodny (eds.), no. 33, 245–266. Freiburg im Breisgau: Max Planck Institute.

Harris, D.J., M. O'Boyle, and C. Wrabrick. 1995. *Law of the European Convention on Human Rights*, 202–273. London: Butterworths.

Klitgaard, R. 1995. "National and International Strategies for Reducing Corruption." Paper presented at the OECD Symposium on Corruption and Good Governance, Paris, March.

Lemonde, Marcel. 1996. "La Protection Des Témoins Devant Les Tribunaux Français." In *Revue De Science Criminelle Et De Droit Pénal Comparé*, N 4, 815–821.

Multidisciplinary Group on Corruption. 1996. *Selected Italian Criminal, Civil and Administrative Provisions Related to Corruption*. (Restricted) Document GMC (95) 81, 14.

Robert, Denis. 1996. "Appeal of Geneva." In *La Justice Ou Le Chaos*, editions stock, 331–334, Paris.

Savona, Ernesto and Sabrina Adamoli. 1996. "The Impact of Organized Crime in Central and Eastern Europe." Paper presented at the Council of Europe Multilateral Seminar on Organized Crime: Minsk, September. Published as Transcrime Working Papers N 7, 5–12, University of Trento.

Sieber, Ulrich. 1990. *General Report on Computer Crime: The Emergence of Criminal Information Law*. Montreal: International Academy of Comparative Law.

RUSSIA
KAZAKHSTAN
MONGOLIA
CHINA
INDIA
IRAN
AFGHANISTAN
PAKISTAN
TURKEY
SYRIA
IRAQ
SAUDI ARABIA
YEMEN
OMAN
U.A.E.
QATAR
BAHRAIN
KUWAIT
JORDAN
ISRAEL
LEB.
EGYPT
SUDAN
ERITREA
ETHIOPIA
DJIBOUTI
SOMALIA
KENYA
UGANDA
TANZANIA
MALAWI
MOZAMBIQUE
MADAGASCAR
COMOROS
SEYCHELLES
MAURITIUS
UKRAINE
GEORGIA
ARMENIA
AZER.
TURKMENISTAN
UZBEKISTAN
KYRGYZSTAN
TAJIKISTAN
NEPAL
BHUTAN
BANGLADESH
BURMA
THAILAND
LAOS
CAMB.
VIETNAM
MALAYSIA
SINGAPORE
BRUNEI
INDONESIA
PHILIPPINES
NORTH KOREA
SOUTH KOREA
JAPAN
Taiwan
PAPUA NEW GUINEA
AUSTRALIA
SRI LANKA
MALDIVES
Moscow
Ryazan'
Nizhniy Novgorod
Kazan'
Yekaterinburg
Chelyabinsk
Omsk
Novosibirsk
Krasnoyarsk
Irkutsk
Chita
Tynda
Komsomol'sk
Khabarovsk
Vladivostok
Samara
Kharkiv
Volgograd
Donets'k
Rostov
Atyraū
Aqmola (Tselinograd)
Qaraghandy
Semey
Almaty
Bishkek
Tashkent
Nukus
Dushanbe
Ashgabat
Kashi
Ürümqi
Dund-Us
Ulaanbaatar
Harbin
Shenyang
Beijing
Dalian
P'yŏngyang
Seoul
Pusan
Kitakyūshū
Ōsaka
Tokyo
Sapporo
Yinchuan
Golmud
Lanzhou
Xi'an
Jinan
Nanjing
Shanghai
Wuhan
Chengdu
Lhasa
Nanchang
Changsha
Fuzhou
Taipei
Guiyang
Kunming
Nanning
Guangzhou
Macau (PORT.)
Hong Kong (U.K.)
Hanoi
Haiphong
Vinh
Vientiane
Chiang Mai
Da Nang
Bangkok
Phnom Penh
Ho Chi Minh City
Cam Ranh
Songkhla
Kuala Lumpur
Singapore
Kuching
Bandar Seri Begawan
Manila
Legaspi
Cebu
Davao
Zamboanga
Manado
Palu
Samarinda
Pontianak
Ujungpandang
Surabaya
Jakarta
Palembang
Padang
Bengkulu
Medan
Banda Aceh
Sorong
Ambon
Jayapura
Wewak
Port Moresby
Kupang
Darwin
Wyndham
Cairns
Dampier
Ankara
Nicosia
Beirut
Damascus
Amman
Jerusalem
Tbilisi
Yerevan
Baku
Tabrīz
Tehrān
Mashhad
Baghdad
Al Basrah
Ābādān
Kuwait
Kermān
Bandar-e 'Abbās
Manama
Doha
Abu Dhabi
Muscat
Riyadh
Medina
Jiddah
Mecca
Herāt
Kabul
Islāmābād
Lahore
Karāchi
New Delhi
Āgra
Ahmadābād
Nāgpur
Bombay
Hyderābād
Bangalore
Madras
Jaffna
Colombo
Male
Vishākhapatnam
Calcutta
Dhaka
Kathmandu
Thimphu
Mandalay
Rangoon
Bassein
Moulmein
Phuket
Port Sudan
Khartoum
Asmara
Sanaa
Aden
Djibouti
Berbera
Addis Ababa
Baidoa
Mogadishu
Chisimayu
Kampala
Nairobi
Mombasa
Dar es Salaam
Mbeya
Mtwara
Moroni
Antsiranana
Lilongwe
Nacala
Antananarivo
Beira
Port Louis
Reunion
Victoria
Socotra (YEMEN)
Lakshadweep (INDIA)
Andaman Islands (INDIA)
Nicobar Islands (INDIA)
British Indian Ocean Territory (U.K.)
Cocos (Keeling) Islands (Austl.)
Christmas Island (Austl.)
Ashmore and Cartier Islands (Austl.)
Paracel Islands
Spratly Islands
Ryukyu Islands (JAPAN)
Okinawa (JAPAN)
Northern Mariana Islands (U.S.)
Guam (U.S.)
FEDERATED STATES OF MICRONESIA
Trust Territory of the Pacific Islands (U.S.)
Sea of Okhotsk
Sea of Japan
Yellow Sea
East China Sea
South China Sea
Philippine Sea
Sulu Sea
Celebes Sea
Java Sea
Banda Sea
Gulf of Thailand
Andaman Sea
Bay of Bengal
Arabian Sea
Persian Gulf
Red Sea
Black Sea
Caspian Sea
Aral Sea
Lake Baikal
Med. Sea
Indian Ocean
Tropic of Cancer
Equator
40
20
0
20
Scale 1:60,000,000
Miller Cylindrical Projection

PART 3

PERSPECTIVES FROM ASIA

Asia is the largest continent, covering about 30 percent of the land surface of the Earth. It is bounded by the Arctic Ocean on the north, the Pacific Ocean on the east, the Indian Ocean on the south, and on the west by the Red, the Mediterranean, and the Black Seas, and Europe. Asia is a diverse combination of about forty-two countries that comprises about 60 percent of the Earth's total population. It is a continent with striking differences in its population distribution. All of Eastern Russia, Central Asia, and parts of Southwest Asia are sparsely inhabited, but the Indian subcontinent and Eastern Asia are densely populated. Southeast Asia lies in the middle of these extremes. There are many different ethnic groups and languages that have descended from widely different traditions. Asia is the birthplace of the world's major religions, including Judaism, Christianity, Islam, and Hinduism. This incredible diversity within Asia has enriched its history, but it also has been the source of many conflicts among its people and nations that go back thousands of years.

Most Asian countries are developing nations without strong government or business infrastructures, and they have high levels of poverty. Notable exceptions are the developed nations of Asia that include Brunei, Cyprus, Israel, Japan, Singapore, South Korea, Taiwan, and Hong Kong (now a region of China). Therefore, in terms of organized crime Asia consists of a variety of "consumer" developed nations as well as "supplier" nations with fertile soil to grow opium and poppies. There is also a large number of people looking to leave their countries to find a better life—many of whom fall prey to human traffickers who transport them to developed nations, both within and outside Asia for purposes of prostitution and other illicit labor.

This section of the book considers organized crime in three of Asia's largest nations, and their problems are representative of some of their neighboring countries. Nevertheless, organized crime is pervasive and examples can be found in virtually every country. Many of the countries in Asia are small, so their problems sometimes do not attract the media attention that India, China, or Japan generate. For example, Thailand has been identified as a source country for prostitution, Hong Kong and Macau have organized crime groups heavily involved in drugs and vice activity, and Eastern Russia has reported many instances of political and business corruption and violence involving organized crime infiltration (Centre for Criminology, 1999; Richard, 2000; Chernyshova, 1998; Phongpaichit, 1999). Organized crime groups in Turkey have been found to operate as wholesalers, importing the vast majority of heroin reaching Europe (Galeotti, 2000). Students are encouraged to study Asia by looking at specific regions in order to gain an understanding of how organized crime exploits criminal opportunities by joining the resources of supply regions with consumer regions in order to make a profit and to gain influence. Single-country analysis sometimes can overlook the need for international connections in large-scale organized crime operations.

The presence of Asian ethnic gangs in the United States has grown with immigration, especially on the West Coast. The connections between these groups and their counterparts in their native countries is not well-defined, although specific instances have been documented of organized crime figures making their way into the United States to engage in criminal activities (Finckenauer, 2000). Following the activities of a well-defined criminal group, therefore, provides another perspective from which organized crime groups may be assessed in order to trace their activities and harm. Still another perspective involves following the flow of an illicit product within and among nations and regions. Some useful analyses of illegal drug flows, for example, provide clues for interdiction efforts (Rhodes, Layne, and Johnston, 1999). The recent research and periodical literature provide a good starting point for such an investigation in order to account for continually changing world events and criminal opportunities.

REFERENCES

Centre for Criminology. 1999. *Organized Crime and the 21st Century.* The University of Hong Kong. http://www.hku.hk/crime/organizecrime.htm

Chernyshova, V. 1998. *Organized Crime in the Maritime Province and the Far East.* http://www.american.edu/transcrime/centers/vladivostok/vlad1198.htm

Finckenauer, James O. 2000. *Chinese Transnational Organized Crime: The Fuk Ching.* Washington, D.C.: National Institute of Justice. http://www.ojp.usdoj.gov/nij/international/ctoc.html

Galeotti, Mark. 2000. "Turkish organized Crime: Where State, Crime and Rebellion Conspire." *Transnational Organized Crime*, vol, 4.

Phongpaichit, Pasuk. 1999. "Trafficking in People in Thailand." *Transnational Organized Crime*, vol. 3.

Rhodes, William, Mary Layne, Patrick Johnston. 1999. *Estimating Heroin Availability.* Cambridge, MA: Abt Associates. http://www.abtassociates.com/reports/criminal-justice/5351.pdf

Richard, Amy O'Neill. 2000. *International Trafficking in Women to the United States: A Contemporary Manifestation of Slavery and Organized Crime.* Center for the Study of Intelligence. http://www.cia.gov/csi/monograph/women/trafficking.pdf

CHAPTER 10

ORGANIZED CRIME: A PERSPECTIVE FROM INDIA

Arvind Verma and R.K. Tiwari

INTRODUCTION

India is the dominant nation in the galaxy of South Asian countries and is surrounded by Pakistan, Nepal, Bhutan, Bangladesh, and Myammar, with Sri Lanka and Maldives islands on its southern coast. As the second most populous country in the world after China, India's burgeoning population is reaching the billion mark, and is squeezed into an area about one third the size of the United States. There are 17 distinct officially recognized languages spoken in the country with more than 5,000 dialects. Every religion in the world has its followers in India, but Hindus constitute almost 80 percent of the population, followed by Muslims, Sikhs, Christians, Buddhists, and Parsis as some of the prominent groups. India's caste system has continued for more than 4,000 years, and the social conflict between different social groups as identified on the basis of religion, caste or class is endemic in the country. Although India's rural sector comprises almost 70 percent of the population, urbanization is increasing rapidly, with Bombay and Calcutta among the largest ten cities of the world and among seventeen cities with a population exceeding one million. India's economy is growing rapidly, too, with a GNP increasing by over 5.5 percent, and the estimated middle class is now equal to that of France.

  The large diverse population and a short turbulent history of political unity have made India a difficult country to govern and administer (Kohli, 1990). Unfortunately, after a remarkable non-violent freedom struggle led by Gandhi, India is now a land beset with terrorism, ethnic, religious and caste riots, and violent elections, and is a place where criminal activities are reaching dangerous proportions. As an established democratic constitutional polity, running an "open" government in a diverse and, in many ways, fragmented society has not been easy. The rising disparities between the rich and the poor, the threat of religious fundamentalism, and a growing inability to meet the burgeoning demands of the people are putting great strain on the democratic functioning of the government. It is also apparent that the criminalization of politics, wherein all the political parties have begun to bank upon criminal elements to win elections and confront opponents, creates law and order problems for the ruling party and encourages the growth of organized criminal activities in the country.

The police system in India has its roots in the 1861 Police Act that established the present form of policing in the Indian subcontinent. The police departments are organized provincially, with members of the elite Indian Police Service (IPS) holding all the senior positions from superintendent (district chief) to that of the director general, the chief of the provincial force. A police department also has a number of specialized units, like the criminal investigation branch, the special branch for intelligence gathering, the railway police, armed police battalions for law and order duties, and several others like the vigilance wing, the training academy, the traffic section, and so on. Except for the training of the IPS officers that takes place at the National Police Academy, the training of all the subordinate officers is conducted in the province. Despite the obvious differences between the provinces in the country, the police departments have largely maintained a similar structure and organizational ethos. The uniformity of the penal and procedural laws throughout the country has also implied that the India police function as a uniform force, although they are managed by the respective provincial governments.

THE NATURE AND EXTENT OF ORGANIZED CRIME

There is no formal legal definition of organized crime in India. The common perception of "crime syndicate or Mafia" made so popular by the Godfather series from Hollywood and emulated by the Bombay film industry does not really exist in any virulent form, nor is there a national crime syndicate. Media reports suggest the existence of organized Mafia in the coal fields of Dhanbad and in smuggling and in the real estate business of Bombay, but the organizational structure of any of these groups does not extend beyond a small, loosely connected structure.

Apart from the common forms of organized criminal activities there are also some that are peculiar to the country and to understand them we need to explore the literature to determine how such activities may be classified. Definitions of organized crime range from those that seek to describe its structure, composition, hierarchy, and membership to those that focus not upon its actions, but rather on the structure or nature of criminal and racketeering enterprises (Schatzberg and Kelly 1996: 16). Most researchers argue that several factors such as hierarchy, strict discipline, bonding rituals, violence, corruption, and links with legitimate businesses are essential features of organized crime (e.g., Albini, 1971; Bequai, 1979; Block, 1978; Caputo, 1974; Chalidize, 1977; Chambliss and Mankoff, 1976; Dorman, 1972; Fox, 1989; Kelley, 1989; Servadio, 1976; Yeager, 1973).

In the United States every state has defined organized crime in its own unique way and there is little consensus about what really constitutes organized criminal behavior. Different scholars have also used different definitions to describe the phenomenon. Maltz (1975: 76) suggests that "the objective of most organized crimes is power, either political or economic" and that " ...the two are not mutually exclusive." Shaw and McKay (1941) focus upon the organizational nature of such crimes, which " ...involves the cooperation of several different persons or groups for its successive execution."

Donald R. Cressey argued in his report to the Task Force on Organized Crime (1967) that organized crime groups in the United States are formed into monopolistic corporations that he called a family, headed by a boss assisted by *consigliere, caporegime,* and *soldati.* However, Francis Ianni argues that the Italian-American version of organized crime is a traditional social system "organized by action and by cultural values" (1972: 108). Abadinsky (1994: 20) suggests that organized crime is usually nonideological in character with a "willingness to use violence and/or bribery to achieve ends ...." Yet, reportedly organized crime in Japan is highly ideological and political (Kirk, 1976). Mack (1973: 103–104) has also argued that the U.S. model of organized crime is not to be found outside of North America, and in Europe, organized crime takes in all criminal operations, however small, that "cover anything other than spur-of-the-moment crimes." James Opolot (1981) reports that organized crime in Africa is usually engaged in smuggling activities where tribal loyalties transcend national boundaries and facilitate the crossing of borders for smuggling purposes. Chambliss and Mankoff (1976) also found that prostitution and gambling were professionally organized in Nigeria and operated with official protection. The main point appears to be that the criminality of persons involved in organized crime differs from that of conventional criminals because the organization allows them to commit crimes of a different variety or even conventional crimes on a *larger* scale than otherwise possible.

Based on this interpretation, organized crime in India may be defined as a group of criminals that are closely aligned with legitimate business, corrupt bureaucracy, and political leadership and are designed to make money or achieve power through violence, illegal means, bribery, and/or extortion. People that make up such organized groups include ordinary lumpen elements, businessmen, police and civil administrators and elected representatives. They all play a complementary role in the organization and execution of criminal activities. The lumpen elements, found both in urban and rural areas, usually act overtly, carrying out the physical task of violent threats, assaults, killings, collection and distribution of payments, and the disposal of property. They are organized, assisted, and maneuvered covertly by the combination of business, bureaucratic, and political shenanigans.

The businesspeople provide the capital, pay for the operating costs, and channel the profits into legitimate businesses. The bureaucrats participate by misusing their authority to give favorable decisions to the organized racketeers, by neutralizing or enfeebling the official agents that could pose threat to the criminal enterprise, and by taking a part of the profit in the form of bribes. The politicians, whose major motive remains the capture of power, act as godfathers, ensuring that attention is diverted from the criminal activities and that those who do get caught are treated leniently by the state. The results of such a powerful combination are deadly: the state stands compromised, the official agencies are demoralized and made ineffective, and the public exchequer is looted of huge sums of money.

Apart from this simple description, organized crime also exists in many other forms and over the years has steadily assumed dangerous dimensions. Some of these different forms could be categorized as "organized criminal activities," which we argue are of the same genre. Group criminal activities, like *dacoities* (armed robberies by groups), kidnapping, extortion, and even political corruption are also organized crimes since these are committed by a large group of people who are hierarchically organized, involved in illegal and violent activities, and whose main motive is money or power. Some of these are loosely organized, where the allegiance to the leader is transitory depending upon his/her power and influence, while some others have a formal corporatelike structure in which a small group collectively controls and directs the criminal activities of its members. Therefore, when we describe the extent and nature of organized crime in India we would also take into account those enterprises that operate through an organized group activity and are criminal by intent.

Interestingly, one such form of organized crime is even legally defined in India. *Dacoity* has been defined in law as armed robberies involving five or more perpetrators. Many other types that are a part of some organized crime activity like smuggling, drug offenses, prostitution, extortion, and political corruption are not so classified. Moreover, there is no single source to obtain statistics about organized criminal incidents.

Thus, the problem of determining the extent of organized crime in as a large a country as India is compounded by the fact that there is no official data on this form of crime. The National Crime Records Bureau (NCRB) annually collects all offenses reported to the police. However, in its "Crime in India," there is no single heading for organized crime and there is no format where two different crimes committed as part of an organized crime racket could be linked together. Sometimes at the police station level or even at the state level special reports are prepared by the criminal investigation departments about organized crimes, but these are for internal consumption only and not made public. Nevertheless, a broad picture could be constructed about these organized criminal activities from the incidents recorded by the different police agencies in the country. For instance, NCRB provides the information for Table 10.1 in its 1993 annual report about *dacoity*, which by definition is an organized form of group crime.

There is a good deal of minimization of these crimes, too (Verma, 1993), and it is perhaps more appropriate to believe that a fair number of *dacoities* have been registered as robberies to minimize the offense (Verma, 1994). Nevertheless, the previous figures do suggest that such forms of organized criminal activities are spread all over the country. Investigative journalist accounts (*India Today*, 1993) have shown how girls are procured from Nepal to be ultimately sold to brothels in Bombay and other major cities—data that is not found in police statistics. Obviously, the nature and extent of organized crime in kidnapping and abduction of women for prostitution purposes or other kinds of organized crimes cannot be gleaned from the figures provided by "Crime in India" alone.

Likewise, there are limited statistics that are provided by the NCRB about the seizure of drugs and number of people arrested for possession or trafficking within the country. Thus, we have the following limited information about drug related offenses:

Drug Type	Quantity Seized in Kg		
	1988	**1993**	**1997**
Opium	3,304	3,011	3,045
Heroin	3,039	1,088	1,122
Hashish	17,523	8,238	2,656
Methaqualone	1,649	15,004	1,740

TABLE 10.1

	Dacoity	Rate
States		
Andhra Pradesh	511	0.7
Arunachal Pradesh	41	3.8
Assam	798	3.2
Bihar	2,392	2.5
Goa	7	0.5
Gujrat	342	0.7
Haryana	58	0.3
Himanchal Pradesh	4	0.1
Jammu & Kashmir	43	0.5
Karnataka	288	0.6
Kerala	103	0.3
Madhya Pradesh	199	0.3
Maharastra	716	0.8
Manipur	14	0.6
Meghalaya	124	5.6
Mizoram	6	0.7
Nagaland	32	2.1
Orissa	263	0.8
Punjab	32	0.1
Rajasthan	149	0.3
Sikkim	0	0.0
Tamil Nadu	212	0.4
Tripura	61	1.8
Uttar Pradesh	1,010	0.6
West Bengal	409	0.5
TOTAL	7,814	0.8

Source: "Crime in India", 1999: NCRB

Crime in India—1999 also reports that in 1988, 2,350 persons were arrested for possession of drugs and in 1999 it went up to 13,281. The number of prosecutions for drug trafficking shows a similar rise. The NCRB does not provide a geographical breakdown of data nor other details like monthly disaggregated statistics that may be analyzed together with media reports for information on organized crime in drugs. Again little generalization can be made on the basis of this limited aggregated data, and at best one may conclude that organized crime in drug dealing obviously exists in the country, although its nature and extent remains unknown.

Smuggling of consumer goods, guns, drugs, and cattle (across the Bangladesh-Nepal border) is another crime that can function only as an organized enterprise. Yet little information is available about its extent in the country. NCRB does not separately inform about official statistics on smuggling and there is no other source that maintains such data. Only a rough estimate could be given about its nature from the limited information contained in the document "Crime in India." Thus, we learn that the Enforcement Directorate seized 45 million Indian rupees in foreign currency and the Narcotics Control Bureau arrested 144 foreigners and convicted 274 for drug-related smuggling offenses in 1993 (NCRB, 1995). However, this tells nothing about the nature or extent of organized smuggling going on in the country. Similarly, even though we learn that 38,240 murders were committed in the country and the number of currency counterfeiting cases was 3,728, there is no information to suggest how many of these formed part of any organized criminal activity.

The common perception of organized crime is that it cannot function without the involvement of corrupt politicians. Thus, political patronage for illegally organized activities is seen as an essential part of organized crime but is not seen as organized crime by itself. Nevertheless, we wish to argue that political corruption in India has taken on serious dimensions, whereby a large number of elected politicians have openly started operating illegal business enterprises, committing frauds, misusing office for personal gain, and are even charged with murder. The democratic functioning has turned violent and every political party without exception has encouraged an active role of known "mafia dons" or criminals with long police records in the elected offices of the state. This has necessarily blurred the distinction between organized crime and political corruption in the country. Elections for municipal bodies, legislative assemblies, and even for the national parliament are marked by "booth capturing" and intimidation of voters by every political party. The criminalization of politics is a term that has been used in the country to denote this phenomenon but none of this information gets officially recorded in any systematic manner. A Vohra committee report that has examined the deep nexus between the criminals and political parties has been tabled in the parliament, but the report has not yet been made public nor has any action been taken. At present a number of prominent politicians, including cabinet ministers and chief ministers of state, have been charge-sheeted for bribery, extortion, and corruption, and these cases have provided an extensive look into the nature of this political corruption. In every case it appears that prominent politicians have misused their power to favor certain parties, causing financial loss to the nation, and in these corrupt practices, violence and threats against those who attempted to prevent these transactions have been a common feature. Large-scale financial scams like the Hawala case, the animal husbandry case in Bihar, the telecom case, and the Jaya Lalita case have been exposed recently. They are expected to collectively involve a loss of $500 million U.S. dollars of public money. The "Crime in India" report provides information only about the cases registered under the Anti-corruption Act, which does not give information about the organizational nature of the crime. Accordingly, very few crime statistics can be cited that could provide realistic information about the nature and extent of politically organized crimes in the country.

Not only have crimes by the individuals increased drastically over the years, but crimes by gangs and interconnected groups have also risen sharply. Riots, especially caste and communal clashes that have led to large-scale killings and destruction of property, are also organized criminal activities. In some parts of the country like Bihar, Punjab, Uttar Pradesh, Andhra Pradesh, and even Assam these groups have targeted certain minority sections of the society and have even organized their own *senas*, or armed bands to subdue the other groups. The nature of such organized groups varies from state to state and within any state, as well. Since there is little official information about the nature and extent of such organized crimes in India, we will have to use different sources like media reports, journal articles, and books to construct what would naturally be a rough picture. Hopefully, it will still be informative and at least indicative of the serious dimensions organized crime has assumed in India.

As previously stated, the nature of organized crime in India overtly is no different from other places. The existence of organized crime in such well-known areas as prostitution, illicit liquor, drugs, arms, and other contraband smuggling is of the same pattern as any other country. However, the tentacles of organized crime have also spread in the political arena, which has perhaps assumed the most serious dimensions. We will also describe some other forms of organized criminal activities that have been a historical legacy. We will use the example of Bombay as a case study to describe the extent of organized crime. We will show how it has developed links with politics and is posing a serious threat to the country's integrity.

Dacoity

Of the several kinds of organized crimes, house and road *dacoity* organized and carried out by large groups was known to have existed during the period of Buddha, has its roots in social banditry, and is well defined in law. Long-distance travel, which is an essential part of religious traditions, was never safe in the Indian subcontinent, and a king's popularity rested upon his efforts to keep the main routes safe from the depredations of these *dacoits*. From the period of Ashok in 200 B.C. to the Mughal Empire, this form of organized criminal activity posed serious challenge to the state's authority. During the early days of English excursion in the country, the threat by such organized gangs led Gerald Aungier, the first governor of Bombay, to create in 1669 a militia of local people to combat these gangs. When the British began administering the country, special efforts were made to deal with this form of crime and the Criminal Investigation Department (CID) was largely concerned with the investigation and prosecution of these gangs. For example, the British law enforcement agencies found sufficient evidence for a countrywide organization that plundered pilgrims and travelers by winning their confidence and then, in most cases, murdered them. This group came to be known as "thugs" and their eradication by colonel Sleeman is one of the success stories of the Indian police. The Indian Penal Code enacted in 1861 recognized the existence of this form of organized crime, and sections 395–399 define its nature and punishments. *Dacoity* has been recognized as an organized crime and is defined as robbery committed by five or more people, usually with some form of violence or threat to life. The crime has been made punishable with severe penalty, including life imprisonment to its perpetrators.

Historically, most of the *dacoits* were recruited from the margins of the village economy, and documents from Bengal prisons in the early nineteenth century suggested that the largest occupational categories of these suspected offenders were laborers, fishermen, *palanquin* carriers, milkmen, and cowherds (McLane, 1985). The official view slowly hardened to associate lower castes with such crimes, and it became common to believe that most *dacoits* came from the lower castes.

Unable to contain *dacoities* through ordinary police operations and legislation, the British enacted some drastic legislation to deal with these forms of organized crimes. "When we speak of professional criminals we . . . [mean] a tribe whose ancestors were criminals from time immemorial, who are themselves destined by the usage of caste to commit crime, and whose descendants will be offenders against the law, until the whole tribe is exterminated or accounted for in the manner of thugs" (Yang, 1986: 109). This official British ideology formed the basis of the repressive Criminal Tribes Act (act 27 of 1871), providing for strong measures against almost 13 million people until its repeal in 1947 when India attained its freedom. The act empowered the police to register the members of these tribes, maintain surveillance, and keep control over their movement. The regulations also gave powers to the police to inspect an offender's house for any stolen property, and if any member was found outside the limits of his prescribed area of movement, to apprehend him without warrant. This act has been repealed, yet similarly organized criminal activities, many by members of these former criminal tribes, continue even today. The Bawarias and Santhi tribes of Rajasthan are notorious for their brutality and lust for gold ornaments. They are known to operate around towns well-connected with railways and travel long distances for their crimes.

Dacoity, with as many as thirty to forty members to a gang, is still a serious problem in several parts of the country. Despite sustained police efforts, large parts of Central India, particularly the states of Bihar, Bengal, Orissa, UP, MP, Rajasthan, and Andhra Pradesh, are plagued by such gangs of *dacoits*. Mostly these gangs commit house, road, or train robberies and occasionally kidnap for ransom. The Chambal ravines of UP, MP, and Rajasthan have been notorious for such crimes, since these ravines provide excellent shelter to the gangs that can operate with impunity from their hideouts. The gang of Man Singh, active during the 1960s, was at one period the largest criminal gang in Asia. Special police operations have been launched again and again, but the menace of *dacoits* in these areas has not diminished. In 1993, the province of Bihar recorded the highest number of *dacoities*, with 2,754 incidents and Uttar Pradesh was second with 1,778 (NCRB, 1995). Even large metropolitan centers are not safe from this form of organized criminal activity. Bombay recorded 117 incidents, followed by Calcutta with 38 and Kanpur with 34 incidents in 1993. *Dacoities* are committed in railways, as well, and the NCRB reported 132 such incidents all over India in 1993. *Dacoity* remains a serious menace and challenge to the Indian police.

Kidnapping and Abduction

Since disposal of property like jewelry and clothes is difficult, many of the gangs have shifted operations from *dacoity* to kidnapping for ransom. Kidnapping of businesspeople and even children has been reported in newspapers again and again, and this form of crime has been seen in Delhi, large cities of UP, Bihar, Gujrat, and even Bombay. In law, kidnapping has been defined as a serious crime and the Indian Penal Code prescribes punishment extending to life imprisonment for its perpetrators. Yet few offenders proportionately get the punishment, since most families, fearing for the safety of their beloved ones, rarely inform the police. NCRB reported 19,830 kidnappings in 1993, showing a rise of 43.3 percent over the decade and for which only 5,083 offenders were convicted. The kidnapping of industrialist Mukesh Jain from New Delhi (*India Today*, 1993) revealed how kidnapping has become a well-organized crime. In this case, the offenders had an organization running from Delhi to the states of UP and Bihar, and despite the publicity of the case, they could not be arrested.

However, most of the kidnappings and abductions are of women and minor girls for the purpose of prostitution. Flesh trade has been flourishing in India in various places and in different forms, from the red-light areas of cities like Bombay, Delhi, Madras, Hyderabad, and many more to the dancing Devadasis of temples. The notorious markets of Dholpur in Rajasthan, Jangalpet in Andhra Pradesh, and Muzaffarpur in Bihar are well-known places for the buying and selling of girls. Ashwini, a reporter from the *Indian Express*, exposed this shameful racket by buying a girl, Kamala, from these areas. Media reports suggest that there are over 100,000 prostitutes each in Bombay and Calcutta, while the Patita Udhar Samiti estimated the total number of prostitutes to be more than 25 hundred thousand in the country (Ghosh, 1991: 60). With the threat of AIDS, the criminals have begun turning to minor girls. Child prostitution is another major form of organized crime about which there is little statistical data to analyze. However, the media has exposed cases of young girls being sold as brides to the sheiks and young boys as camel jockeys in the Middle East, all of which does suggest the roots of organized crime in their kidnappings and abductions.

Illicit Liquor

The distillation and distribution of illicit liquor is a very profitable business, especially in states like Gujrat and Andhra Pradesh, where total prohibition has been imposed. Despite prohibition, liquor is, of course, freely available and generates huge profits for organized crime. It has been alleged that the total turnover of the bootleggers in Gujrat is not less than $250 million U.S. dollars (Ghosh, 1991: 46). The "liquor syndicate" has even become a powerful political lobby in the state and reportedly plays an important role in influencing governmental policies. An even more lucrative form of organized crime in liquor is the smuggling from one state to another. Excise taxes vary from state to state and the differences in prices provide profitable incomes to these interstate smugglers. The business is also profitable because the trade thrives on adulterated liquor on which there is no tax and over which little control is exercised by the excise departments. Every year several deaths from drinking such spurious liquor are reported from different parts of the country, but little action is ever taken since the crime is well-organized.

The so-called "spirits scandal" in Tamil Nadu and Kerala became widely known when excise authorities found documents showing the sale of liquor in one state without corroborating evidence of tax payments. It was revealed that thousands of gallons of spirits had been flown into Kerala from Tamil Nadu on fictitious permits to make country liquor. It was being sold at exorbitant rates and was depriving both the governments of hundreds of thousands of rupees in taxes. T.K. Ramakrishnan, Kerala's excise minister, was himself alleged to have played a prominent role in running this organized crime racket (Ghosh, 1991: 45).

Other forms of organized criminal activity now exist in virtually every part of the country, where it is seen in such crimes as gambling, illegal real estate transactions, smuggling, poaching, extortion, and even money laundering. The coal fields of Bihar, the ports of Calcutta, Madras, Cochin or Diu, the industrial belt of northern India, and the border with Nepal, Bangladesh, and Pakistan are of course well-known areas for these crimes. However, even in the sandalwood forests of Southern India, where organized crime exists on forest produce, or in the hills of Assam, where poaching is notorious, or in the little-known region of Mirzapur in Uttar Pradesh, where children are bought and forced to work in carpet factories, organized crime has taken deep roots in the country. However, among all these places, the case of Bombay for organized criminal enterprises is perhaps the most classic. Bombay also provides a good example of how widespread it really is and how its tentacles have reached even the higher echelons of Indian society.

Bombay is the economic engine of the country. Situated on a small island in the Arabian Sea, the metropolis is home to the corporate world of big Indian names like the Tatas, Mafatlals, Godrej, and Reliance industries, and virtually every large business organization has a branch office in the city. Bombay also produces virtually everything ranging from vehicles to chemicals to electrical appliances. The city is also home to the second-largest film industry in the world, has a large gold bullion and diamond market, and naturally attracts all who dream of making riches overnight. Accordingly, we will now describe different forms of organized crime in Bombay as a case study to suggest how serious the situation is in the country.

Organized Crime in Real Estate

Bombay has, of course, always been notorious for its gangs, which have found the crowded island a promising place to make quick profits. With a burgeoning population, rapid industrialization, and shortage of space,

Bombay became, from the early days of independence, a place where urban land was a prized possession and valuable property. In the last two decades, land prices, always the highest in the country, have risen still higher and have reached a stupendous level. Prime land in Bombay is perhaps costlier than in Hong Kong, and with the new economic policy, real estate has become a business running in the billions of dollars. Reportedly, more than $30 billion U.S. dollars of investment proposals have been made in Bombay because virtually every company doing business wants office space in the city. The Land Tenancy Act and the Bombay Rent Control Act, the two main laws on real estate and housing, are archival and it is extremely difficult to do property deals legally. The government remains reluctant to make rules that can give landlords the power to change tenants or change the nature of property, since this action goes against the socialist stance of the government. Consequently, there is little investment in new affordable housing, resulting in an acute shortage of residential space for people streaming into Bombay from all over the country. Considerable legal difficulties also exist in evicting tenants who have been living there for generations and who pay little more than a token in rent. The growth in slums, the rising costs of land space, and the absence of any governmental desire to deal with this issue have consequently made the real estate market appropriate and extremely lucrative for organized crime to step in and exploit. Several gangs have flourished in Bombay that specialize in forcing tenants to move out through threats, assaults, and even killings or through the capture of disputed properties. "Leading gangsters of Bombay's underworld such as Haji Mastan Mirza, Karim Lala Pathan, Yusuf Patel, [and] Vardarajan had done remarkably well in land and house property deals" (Ghosh, 1991: 40).

In this situation, Bombay's ailing textile mills, established during the British period, have further given impetus to these organized criminal activities. These mills occupy hundreds of acres in Central Bombay, land that is now worth millions of dollars. Consequently, most factory owners, unwilling to modernize, would rather sell the land that can fetch them more profits than their textile business. The government is unwilling to grant them permission to close the factories, since that would render thousands of workers jobless. The absence of legislation that can force workers to relocate or to terminate their services have further compounded the issue. The owners are not investing in their factories to make them competitive, since there is little economic incentive for them to do so and these units are slowly going into a loss.

Consequently, several of these business houses have been utilizing criminal gangs to terrorize the workers' unions and drive them out so that they may ultimately close the factories. Media reports suggest that the gangs of Gowli, Sudhir Naik, and that of Dawood Ibrahim have been active in supporting one mill owner or the other (Rahman, 1994a). The recent murder of textile mill owner Sunit Khaitan and JMP Biscuitwala have exposed the involvement of organized crime in real estate matters in Bombay. Bombay's municipal commissioner Khairnar (Rahman, 1994b) has also alleged the political involvement of Maharastra state's former chief minister, Sharad Pawar, by giving patronage to these gangs and industrialists. The powerful textile union leader Datta Samant has also leveled charges that mill owners undervalue their lands, keep the income tax authorities away, and use gangs to silence the workers. Money is paid as graft to the politicians, who grant licenses to convert property and who deny compensations to workers. Since the stakes are unusually high and there is little administrative initiative to tackle the matter, it appears that organized crime will continue to play an active role in the real estate dealings of Bombay.

Smuggling and Terrorism

Apart from the organized rackets in real estate, Bombay is also notorious for its organized crime in smuggling. Ever since India attempted to discourage consumption of foreign goods by levying heavy import duties, smuggling of electronic items, textiles, and toys became a remunerative enterprise. Similarly, there is a heavy demand for gold in the country, which produces barely 2 tons of gold per annum, while the consumption is estimated to be over 100 tons a year (Malhotra, 1995). This has created a profitable market for smugglers operating from the Middle East, especially from Dubai, where gold prices are much lower than in India. Rags-to-riches stories of people who profited from smuggling have become notorious in Bombay. Among all the smugglers, the name Haji Mastan stands out as one who attained notoriety by his phenomenal rise from a dock coolie to a person who started financing film productions and contributing to political parties. His name became synonymous with smuggling in the 1970s, and a few movies were even made of his life.

Dawood Ibrahim is another person who went from petty smuggling crimes to become perhaps the biggest don of Bombay's underworld today (*India Today*, 1994). His rise is reportedly based upon his gold-smuggling operations, which quickly established him as a powerful financier in several kinds of illegal enterprises. His links with real estate business, film finances, and *supari*, or contract killings, have made him a notorious personality in India. Ibrahim reportedly has not only cornered the smuggling racket, but has become the don who settles financial disputes outside the legal framework. He finances film productions and is courted by well-known film personalities. He is reportedly also muscling his way into the lucrative Bombay real estate market and has connections with the leading politicians of India (Rahman and Katiyan, 1993). Public outcry and pressure by the enforcement agencies have forced him to base his operations from Dubai, where he regularly hosts parties for world cricket and film personalities and continues his criminal operations brazenly. He created a stir when a contingent of Bombay film stars attended his son's birthday at Dubai recently (Ghosh, 1991: 42).

The reach of his organized criminal activities was recently seen when he organized attacks on Bombay's economy as retaliation against Bombay riots which hurt the Muslims. In March 1994, powerful bombs exploded at the Bombay Stock Exchange killing more than three hundred people. At the same time there were eleven other blasts that rocked different parts of Bombay, including famous hotels, Air India buildings, and many other important installations. The subsequent investigations revealed that Ibrahim supplied RDX explosives and arms through smuggling channels to the Memon brothers, who used criminal gangs to bomb these installations (*India Today*, 1994). The links with Ibrahim's organized crime syndicate were firmly established by the confessional statements of Yakub Memon, who was a participant in the bomb blast case in Bombay.

Moreover, the recovery of some of the arms from the house of Sanjay Dutt, the leading film star of Bombay, has further linked the association among smuggling, international terrorists, domestic mafia, money laundering, drug distribution networks, corrupt bureaucrats, politicians, and even film stars. Dutt assisted in hiding some of the deadly weapons used by these offenders in his house, and the investigation has further revealed how their money is being laundered to finance films (Rahman and Khatiyan, 1994). Bombay remains the conduit for smuggling goods into the country, and organized crime in this business is likely to remain well-entrenched.

Hawala Transactions—Organized Crime in Illegal Banking

The world's underground banking systems go by several different names like *chop, fei chi'ien, hundi,* and so on and account for anywhere from $100 billion to $300 billion in illegal money transfers (Malhotra, 1995). Most of these banks are based upon family or gang alliances and carry out their operations with an unspoken but unambiguous covenant of retributive violence. In India this system is known by the name of Hawala, or "reference" through which dollars are moved from Bombay to Hong Kong, gold from Singapore to Vancouver, or armaments from Karachi to Delhi, with all transactions based upon the word or reference of the trader without any paper receipts. All of these operations are intricate, and crime-laced, involving several people from a host of nations and even secret enforcement agencies like the Inter-Services Intelligence (ISI) of Pakistan. Reportedly, even small-time operators are estimated to transfer more than $60 million U.S. dollars illegally to India. In 1993, one Dinesh Goel, arrested by Delhi police, admitted to have transferred almost $1.45 billion U.S. dollars in Hawala payments to his clients in Dubai (Malhotra, 1995). The suspicion of Hawala operations led to the raid on the Jain brothers in 1991 in which $250,000 were recovered in cash. What is more significant is the recovery of two coded diaries and account books that contained more than one hundred names of India's who's-who to whom payments had allegedly been made by these brothers. The subsequent investigation has unearthed perhaps the biggest case of political corruption in the country in which more than fourteen cabinet-ranking ministers are involved, as well as politicians of virtually every party except the communists (Hindu, 1996).

It is not only a banking operation, for such huge amounts undoubtedly involve "enforcers," criminals who make the deliveries or do the recoveries from recalcitrant clients. Instances of Hawala-funded killings in the Indian subcontinent are not unknown and the links with terrorist groups operating in Punjab, Kashmir, Assam, and Tamil Nadu are openly admitted. Mohammed Aslam (alias Sheroo) reportedly killed custom's informer Amar Survana for a contract of $11,290, while Nagaland's Selim has been involved with the United Liberation Front of Assam (ULFA), extorting money from tea gardens to smuggle weapons (Asia Inc., 1995). Ibrahim's men carried out the aforementioned Bombay bomb blasts. The links of Hawala transactions with even large business houses and Indian industry have also been alleged by Delhi University's professor Gupta who suggests that most flourishing professionals, senior state officials, politicians, and others engaged in high positions have made ample use of Hawala operations.

Organized Crime in Share Market

Bombay is also the home of India's leading and Asia's oldest share market. Share markets in India have generally functioned outside the public scrutiny, since most of the brokerage has remained in the hands of specific castes that have used their own accounting systems to maneuver the markets. In the last five to six years, due to the economic liberation policies followed by the governments, these markets have suddenly been flooded with funds and have led to a much larger participation by new groups. The resultant speculations and illegal transactions have exposed several scams revealing the extent and nature of organized crimes in this sector. The case of Harshad Mehta is illustrative of the scale of profits and organization that extended to large business houses, banks, politicians, and international connections. Backed by several financial institutions Mehta started buying almost any share offered in the market and soon drove the share market index to dizzy heights. Overnight fortunes were being made without any economic activity to back the results. Ultimately, when the enforcement authorities started probing into the share transactions and sources of funding the dam burst open revealing the organization that stretched from Mehta to leading banks, both national and foreign, role of public financial institutions, and political bigwigs. Mehta's allegations that he paid the prime minister $2.5 million dollars (U.S.) shed light on the involvement of people at the very top of the society. Inquiry into the scam is still going on, and although Mehta is facing a large number of charges, little headway has been made into the role of bankers and politicians.

Drug-related Oranized Crime in India

India is an opium-producing country, as well as cannabis, which is available as an unwanted crop due to the tropical climate. Geographically, India is sandwiched between the golden crescent and the golden triangle and is thus a conduit for drug smugglers. The seizures since 1985 indicate that 80 percent of heroin and 50 percent of hashish is flowing from the golden crescent and almost all the states along the border have fallen victim to narcotic smuggling. These drugs are finally transported to the metropolitan cities of Bombay, Calcutta, Delhi, and Madras. The drug trade is also encouraged by the spurt in terrorism in the country, whereby the drug money has been used to finance acts of deadly violence in states like Punjab, Kashmir, and Maharashtra.

Statutory control over narcotics has been exercised through the Opium Act of 1857 and the Dangerous Drugs Act of 1930. In view of the changing nature of the narcotic substances and the increased threat to the country through drug smuggling, the Narcotic Drugs and Psychotropic Substance (NDPS) Act was passed in 1985. The act provided for the seizure of the property of a person convicted under NDPS and also an imprisonment of five years. The country and its enforcement agencies have also been pioneering efforts to trace the origins of the narcotics being brought into the country. In particular, chemical analyses through nuclear irradiation methods have been developed for this type of evidence collection. The assistance of the Atomic Energy Commission and nuclear reactors has been enlisted for this purpose. Comparison of chemical compositions and the concentration levels of trace elements and microconstituents has been of great help in establishing the geographical origin and in determining whether different drug samples seized could have come from the same source. This has assisted in tracking the gang affiliations and understanding the trafficking routes used by different couriers. Although drug-related organized crime has not become as formidable as in other countries, nevertheless, the threat to the nation is growing, causing concern to the government.

Oranized Political Crime

Perhaps the worst aspect of organized crime in India is the intrusion that it has made in the arena of politics of the country. Every political party uses criminals and antisocial elements for booth capturing, intimidating rivals, collecting funds, and exercising control over the electorate. Even as early as the 1970s a minister in Bihar, Kapil Deo Singh openly admitted on the floor of the assembly that, "I am honest enough to declare that I keep *goondas* [antisocial elements]. For, without them it is virtually impossible to win elections" (Ghosh, 1991: 13). The number of criminals who have been elected on party tickets in the last few elections is so staggering that "criminalization of politics" is now an accepted phenomenon in the country. Congress (I) Member of Parliament Prakash Yadav was arrested from a Calcutta brothel in 1987 and was involved in leading gangsters to attack teachers of a Patna college in Bihar. His father became a cabinet minister of Food and Supplies in the last government in 1992, where he used his connections and power to engage in a massive fraud of fake supplies in fertilizers. This fraud involving $330 million U.S. dollars is now under investigation. Suraj Deo Singh was a notorious muscleman and "don" of Dhanbad's coal belt, and yet he was openly patronized by the former Prime Minister Chandra Sekhar Singh. In the state of Uttar Pradesh, Virendra Pratap Sahi is a member of the legislative assembly and has more than sixty-three criminal cases, including murder pending against him in the courts. Sarju Prasad Singh is a member of the Janata Dal party and has been charge-sheeted for land grabbing, assaults, and kidnapping of a minor girl, a case that occurred when he was a member of the assembly. The former Chief Minister Veer Bahadur Singh shared the dais with Bhukkal Maharaj, against whom proceedings were going on under the National Security Act for forcibly preventing bidders from taking part in an auction of liquor shops. The former Defense Minister of India, Mulayam Singh Yadav, openly attended parties hosted by one Arun Shukla (alias Annaa), who has been involved in seventy-nine cases since 1973 and is facing murder charges in five cases. In the national elections of 1996, Annaa also campaigned for Yadav in the district of Etawah, moving around in jeeps with armed gangs. Annaa's brother Chotey and his brother-in-law S.C. Misra both were given party tickets and had won with comfortable margins. In the state of Madhya Pradesh, Minister Narsingh Rao Dixit allegedly entertained *dacoits* while Ashok Vir Singh, with thirty-two cases registered against him was made the Program Chairman for implementing Prime Minister's 20 point economic program. In Bombay, the notorious don Gowli, encouraged by the Congress party, has established his own political front and organized a large demonstration against the ruling party.

In Porbandar, the birth place of Mahatma Gandhi, of the one hundred eight candidates in the 1990 municipal elections, seventy had criminal antecedents (Ghosh, 1991). In the state of Gujrat, Babu Satyam Bhaiya, a gangster convicted for life in a murder case, still managed to obtain parole that was extended again and again on the recommendations of Congress (I) party's MLAs. While on parole he committed several cases of extortion and even kidnapping for ransom and managed to elude the police. In the remote state of Tripura, the Minister Surajit Dutta admits being a *mastan*, a don, and is known to have lost his right arm while making bombs. The case of Devendra Pandey and Bhola Pandey is, of course, notorious. They both hijacked an Indian Airlines plane on December 20, 1978, and yet their cases were withdrawn by the Congress (I) government, which also gave them tickets to be elected to UP Vidhan Sabha, the Upper House. Open use of these gangsters in capturing booths during elections and intimidating opponents was even shown on national television in a program entitled "Booth Capturing." In this program, professional booth capturers were interviewed, who admitted making a living by stamping the ballot papers for those who paid them. The show even displayed one such action where these criminals, while hiding their identities, still dared to demonstrate how booths are captured. In the recent national elections of 1996, violence and booth capturing were reported on a larger scale (Ramachandran, 1996; Indian Express, 1996; Singh, 1996).

Measures, Including Legislation to Combat Organized Crime

There are two measures visible in the country to combat organized crime. The first is the so called "executive measure" that forms the usual strategy of the enforcement agencies of different kinds that constitute the efforts by the state to fight organized crime. The other is what we call the non-executive forums that include different non-governmental groups (NGOs), people's movements, and victim groups that have emerged to combat the menace of organized crime.

Executive Measures

Although the executive measures are hampered by a lack of systematic effort by the law enforcement agencies, several measures have been taken to deal with organized crime. Every state has created an economic offenses wing in the police department and at the federal level, too, Government of India has established new specialized police agencies such as the Narcotics Control Bureau, the Directorate of Enforcement, and the Directorate of Revenue Intelligence. The government has also empowered the customs, excise, and border patrol units to combat the prowess of the smugglers and other organized crime syndicates. To provide an attractive incentive and encourage officers, the government has provided a certain percentage of seized goods as reward for their efforts, and consequently the number and value of seizures have gone up considerably, while at the same time controlling the corruption within the ranks of enforcement agencies. The Enforcement Directorate seized Rs. 451.93 hundred thousand in foreign currency, the Central Board of Direct Taxes seized Rs. 396460 hundred thousand worth of assets, while the Directorate of Revenue Intelligence seized Rs. 38896 hundred thousand in 1993. The Narcotics Control Bureau also arrested 13,723 persons for drug-related offenses, while 1,234 were arrested for smuggling-related offenses (NCRB, 1995).

The other forms of incentives like accelerated promotions, jobs to family members in case of accident or death of an officer on duty and training allowances have been provided. The government has also amended the Evidence Act, providing for admission of confession before senior police officers and providing for the seizure of property made from illegal means. A great deal of technological support from computers, communications, coast guard boats equipped with radar, and centralized data banks on criminals and their associates have also been introduced. The problem is that as compared to the state of regular police these specialized agencies are fairly sophisticated, but their numbers necessarily remain small. These also invite intraservice jealousies and hamper sharing of intelligence. Despite attractive emoluments, the working conditions remain dismal and most subordinate officers resent being sent to these special units. Consequently, the impact of such executive measures has at best been marginal. So long as the regular police forces remain at a dismal state, are unable to provide basic acceptable level of policing to the society, lack community support, and are influenced by corrupt politicians, a few specialized units are unlikely to be successful against organized crime.

Non-Executive Measures

On the other hand, India has seen a remarkable growth in non-executive measures taken at the initiative of NGOs, volunteer groups, and the unorganized sector. The fact that India is one of the few truly open societies and has a history of people's involvement and direct action taught by no less a person than Mahatma Gandhi, has encouraged a mushroom growth of NGOs, civil rights groups, and decline of dependence upon the state. The people's movements against small-time organized rackets such as plunder of forest products, illicit liquor trade, gambling, and extortion have seen remarkable success in the country. The "Chipko" movement in the Himalayas is a classic example, wherein women's groups literally hug the trees ("Chipko" means hugging) to prevent contractors from exploiting the forest products in connivance with corrupt officials. Similarly, the cooperative movement launched by a group called Anand, has successfully prevented price fixing in dairy and allied products. The human rights groups have empowered the people to resist extortion and abuse by organized syndicates and they have achieved remarkable success in fighting the scourge of bonded labor or slavery, especially of children, in the carpet industry.

Another form of people's initiative has emerged in the form of so called "Public Interest Litigation" (PIL). The judiciary in India has enjoyed considerable autonomy and under the leadership of Justice Bhagwati, it has evolved several innovative measures to combat vested criminal interests. The judiciary has accepted that a simple letter written by someone for a public cause can be treated as a writ petition, and it involves the interjection of the courts to inquire into the matter. This process evolved in the late 1970s and led to the release of prisoners awaiting trial, who were languishing in prisons due to delays. After this initial success, public interest litigations have been filed in literally thousands of cases and have assisted in demanding accountability in providing relief to the victims of crimes. Such PILs have in recent years led to the exposure of several organized crimes that involve prominent politicians. Following the example set by the Supreme Court several subordinate courts have also begun to entertain public interest petitions that make grave allegations and in which government agencies appear to be helpless in taking action due to the involvement of prominent people. Thus, the Patna High court entertained a public interest litigation and directed the police to investigate a multimillion-dollar scandal in the Animal Husbandry Department. The court severely indicted the Bihar government for failing to stop the ongoing fraud despite its public knowledge, giving patronage to officials who had been accused of corruption and even trying to preempt the court from giving positive orders in this regard (Indian Express, 1996: May 10).

This case has now led to the resignation of the powerful chief minister of Bihar and indictment of several senior officials apart from the business persons and other criminals involved in the case.

The surprise raid upon the premises of former Telecommunications Minister Sukh Ram led to the recovery of almost $15 million U.S. dollars in foreign currency, and opened the so called "telecom scam." The case has resulted in the arrest of a top official of the Telecom Ministry, Runu Ghosh, the arrest of the Minister Sukh Ram, and strengthened the allegations that large kickbacks have been taken from telephone companies seeking licenses to operate in India. Now, several more scams, the Jaya scam involving former Chief Minister JayaLalitha of the state of Tamil Nadu, the Himalayan corruption case involving the present Chief Minister Bhandari of the state of Sikkim, the ongoing securities scam, and the "shoe scam" involving Bombay shoe merchants have been similarly exposed. Recovery of gold, sarees, and expensive goods from the dreamlike house of JayaLalitha have perhaps been the most spectacular in Indian history. Illegal allotment of petrol pumps by Satish Sharma, former Petroleum Minister and once a powerful figure during Rajiv Gandhi's period, the Auyervedic scam in Uttar Pradesh, the fertilizer scandal involving the relatives of former Prime Minister Rao himself have all come out of the investigations and public pressure generated by the Hawala case. These cases have stirred the justice system as never before and perhaps for the first time exposed the deep links between politicians, businesses, and criminals.

Legislative Measures

The government has also empowered the enforcement agencies with several laws that provide for the seizure or forfeiture of property of those indulging in these dangerous criminal activities. The police departments have also been utilizing some other laws that were designed to deal with terrorist activities and threats to national security. Thus, Maintenance of Internal Security Act (MISA), National Security Act (NSA), or the Terrorist and Disruptive Act of 1984 (TADA) have been used to detain known smugglers like Haji Mastan or even film stars like Dutt, who aided Ibrahim's attack on Bombay's stock market. In addition, the government has sought to make smuggling less lucrative by reducing the import duties on a large number of consumer items. Further, new legislation permits individuals to import up to 5 kg of gold, a move that has suddenly brought the gold prices in India crashing down. Smuggling of gold has now lost its profit margin and with new liberalization policies, other consumer items have also began flooding the Indian markets. These moves are certainly going to dent the organized criminal activities in smuggling of gold and consumer items and thus reduce the power of such figures as Ibrahim and the like.

Comparative Evaluation of the Methods for Combating Organized Crime and Proposed Measures

Despite changes in the law, empowerment of the police agencies and providing incentives, the government has not been very successful in combating organized crime in the country. Traditional forms of organized crime like *dacoities*, kidnapping, and extortion remain a major concern. Smuggling, poaching, and organized plunder of Indian artifacts still go on. Rapid urbanization and inability of the government to meet the housing shortages have continued to make real estate transactions a major arena for organized crimes. Above all, political corruption despite well-publicized exposures like the Bofors, Harshad Mehta, Hawala, fodder scam, the telecom scam, and many others remains a serious threat. A large number of criminals continue to get elected to positions of power, and despite public outcry, the political parties have not been able to join hands in cleansing the politics of the country. Bribery and corrupt practices among the politicians are now virtually expected by the citizens and very little is being done to combat this form of organized crime that abets other forms.

The executive measures, like creation of special enforcement agencies, enhancing training of officers, and providing technological inputs in the form of computers and communication systems are much needed but have obvious limitations. These also present a contradiction in the fight against organized crime. The police and enforcement agencies cannot be good and effective in one field and poor in the others. Thus, it cannot be that police cannot do well against ordinary crime and yet are able to combat organized crime. For instance, to investigate money laundering, officers must first learn to investigate theft, burglary, and fraud in a competent manner. Similarly, to create a good intelligence system against organized crime, the police must first learn to work with the people, earn their trust, and become community oriented. When the police are unable to provide basic security and safety they can hardly be expected to be successful against organized crime syndicates. Unfortunately, the Indian police have a poor image, their officers are poorly trained and ill-equipped, generally corrupt, and have extraordinarily poor working conditions. Although the special agencies have had some success against terrorists groups in Punjab, have combated the drug smuggling efficiently, and have successfully acted against several "dons," the overall impact still leaves much to be desired. The Indian police need to improve their own house and learn to do simple policing effectively before they can combat organized crime successfully.

The legal reforms and measures against organized crime syndicates have also not been very effective. Since the system of law enforcement itself is flawed, the making of new laws hardly has any effect. Moreover, it has been seen that police are generally unable to implement ordinary laws and any special laws that are provided to facilitate state action against the criminals end up being misused by police. Extraordinary laws like MISA, TADA, and NSA have ended up being used against political opponents and civil rights groups rather than against criminals.

The success of people's movements has also not been very encouraging. The NGOs, victim rights groups, and those against organized crime have generally failed to extend their objectives. It has been easy to involve the people to combat organized crime, like drugs, slavery of children, extortion, illicit liquor and organize to drive away the front operators. However, this is generally insufficient, since the basic causes that encourage organized crime to set base, like poverty, inequality, consumerism, and lust for power have not been addressed. Moreover, successful movements, too, have foundered due to internal contradictions. Thus, the Chipko movement suffered a setback when the question of gender inequality cropped up after women fighting forest and liquor contractors began demanding more equality from their husbands, too. Ultimately, all such people's initiatives have to address questions of social relationships, inequality, power, greed, fascination with Western consumerism, and the basic democratic functioning of society.

Terrorism has taken a menacing posture in the country. TADA has become very controversial in view of its provision of two years' imprisonment without trial and limited legal access. A large number of human rights groups have been very vocal against its enforcement and it has also been challenged in the courts on grounds of its denial of fundamental rights. Recently, the government has allowed it to lapse in view of the strong objection to its misuse by the law enforcement agencies. Laws have also been introduced to remove financial constraints that encourage smuggling and money laundering. Import of 5 kg of gold has been legalized to discourage smuggling from the Middle East. Several banking reforms, too, have been introduced, especially in the share markets to regulate the speculation and illegal transactions. The Indian economy is being speedily liberalized to remove artificial bottlenecks and encourage more transparent transactions. This is expected to reduce the incentives in black-market economy and discourage laundering of ill-gotten wealth.

Citizen forums have been demanding new legislation to deal with political corruption and the criminalization of politics. In the national Parliament, too, these issues have figured again and again but all the political parties are reluctant to devise legislation and make honest attempts to keep away the criminal elements from the political arenas. Some electoral laws have been implemented that have made induction of money in fighting elections more difficult to conceal. Considering that all parties are equally affected and the courts have been active in pursuing a rule of the law, there is hope for laws to curb election expenses that encourage corrupt practices; however this is unlikely to come without more public pressure. A bill has also been filed in the Parliament that will reduce government control over the state-run television and radio stations. This Prasar Bharti bill is expected to empower the media and assist in opening up the society and thus facilitate free flow of information. The strengthening of media and the judicial system together with reforms in the administrative setup is likely to assist in combating organized crime that operates under the veil of secrecy.

International Cooperative Efforts

In the sphere of smuggling, terrorism, and money laundering, the government of India has been promoting international cooperative efforts to deal with these crimes that often have their roots outside the country. The successful extradition of Babloo Srivastava, a notorious killer and kidnapper, the arrest of the Memon family, involved in the Bombay blasts, the tracing of money laundered by Prakash Yadav in the fertilizer scam, the foreign links in the Bofors scandal, Hawala case, and fodder scam are pointers that international cooperation is necessary if any success is desired in combating organized crime. India has also been promoting regional cooperation amongst the South Asian Association for Regional Cooperation (SAARC) countries and enforcement agencies have seen an enhanced cooperation in combating the drug trade in South Asia.

CONCLUSION

Even though there is meager information about organized crime in the country, the picture that we have constructed from different sources is suggestive of the fact that the problem is alarming. Organized criminals have now penetrated the political sphere and their crimes are now threatening the very fabric of the society. Since all political parties have developed links with the underworld, violent lawlessness, brutality, terror, and assaults on the people have begun destroying the orderly nature of Indian society. Law enforcement agencies have been compromised, courts are clogged and ineffective, and the whole system of criminal justice in the country has lost its integrity. There is growing evidence of politically motivated criminality in the form of atrocities on weaker sections, murders of personal and political foes, smuggling, drug peddling, liquor trafficking, gun running, and prostitution that have assumed dangerous dimensions. Undoubtedly, all these criminal enterprises are becoming vast businesses organized by persons of power and influence. Since most of it is linked to political corruption and the criminalization of politics, the only way to deal with it will be through reform of the political process. The demand for more democratic polity, decentralization of decision making, participation of people in running their local governments, and village *panchayats* (council) are welcome signs. A code of conduct for the political parties may assist in keeping the criminal elements away, electoral reforms could ensure that such elements cannot seek political power, and the accountability of the politicians to the people and their commitment to the due process of law are measures that could prevent organized crime from destroying the country. There is a long way to go and strong measures need to be taken immediately.

REFERENCES

Abadinsky, Howard. 1994. *Organized Crime*. 4th ed. Chicago: Nelson-Hall.

Albini, Joseph L. 1971. *The American Mafia: Genesis of a Legend*. New York: Appleton Century Crofts.

Bequai, August. 1979. *Organized Crime: The Fifth State*. Lexington, MA: D.C. Heath.

Block, Alan A. 1978. "History and Study of Organized Crime." *Urban Life* 6: 455–474.

Caputo, David A. 1974. *Organized Crime and American Politics*. Morristown, N.J.: General Learning Press.

Chalidize, Vallery. 1977. *Criminal Russia: Crime in the Soviet Union*. New York: Random House.

Chambliss, William and Milton Mankoff (eds.). 1976. *Whose Law? What Order?* New York: John Wiley and Sons.

Cressey, Donald R. 1967. The Functions and Structure of Criminal Syndicates. *Task Force Report: Organized Crime*. President's Commission on Law Enforcement and Administration of Justice. Washington D.C. US Government Press. pp. 25–60.

Dorman, Michael. 1972. *Payoff: The Role of Organized Crime in American Politics*. New York: David McKay Co.

Express News Service. 1996. *Corruption charges against 17 Congress ministers: CPI*. New Delhi, September 22.

Fox, Stephen. 1989. *Blood and Power: Organized Crime in Twentieth Century America*. New York: William Morrow.

Ghosh, S.K. 1991. *The Indian Mafia*. New Delhi: Ashish Publishing House.

Hindu. 1996. *A Far Reaching Scandal*. January 18.

Ianni, Francis A.J. 1972. *A Family Business: Kinship and Social Control in Organized Crime*. New York: Russel Sage Foundation.

Inciardi, James A. 1975. *Careers in Crime*. Chicago: Rand McNally Publishing Co.

Indian Express. 1996. *EC Orders Repolls In 817 Bihar Booths*. Delhi, May 10.

India Today. 1993. *Kidnapping*. April 15.

India Today. 1994. *Terror in Bombay*. March 31, 31–41.

Kelley, R.J., R. Schatzberg, and K.L. Chin. 1989. "An Analysis of RICO and OCCA: Federal and State Legislature Instruments Against Crime." *International J Violence, Aggression and Terrorism* 9(3): 49–100.

Kirk, Donald. 1976. "Crime, Politics and Finger Chopping." *New York Times Magazine*, December 12, 60–61, 91–97.

Kohli, Atul. 1990. *Democracy and Discontent: India's Growing Crisis of Governability.* New York: Cambridge University Press.

Mack, John A. 1973. The Organized and Professional Labels Criticized. *International J Criminol. and Penology* 1: 103–116.

Maltz, Michael D. 1976. On Defining Organized Crime. *Crime and Delinquency* 22: 338–346.

Maltz, Michael D. 1975. "Policy Issues in Organized Crime and White Collar Crime." In *Crime and Criminal Justice.* John A. Gardiner and Michael A. Mulkey (eds.), 73–94. Lexington, MA: D.C. Heath.

McLane, John R. 1985. "Bengali Bandits, Police and Landlords after the Permanent Settlement." In *Crime and Criminality in British India.* Anand A. Yang, (ed.), 26–47. Tucson, AZ: Arizona University Press.

Malhotra, Angelina. 1995. "India's Underground Bankers." *Asia-Inc.*, February.

National Crime Records Bureau. 2000. *Crime in India 1993.* Faridabad: Government of India Press (published annually).

Opolot, James S.E. 1981. *Organized Crime in Africa.* Jonesboro, TN: Pilgrimage, Inc.

Rahman, M. 1994a. "Land Wars." *India Today*, June 30: 40–44.

Rahman, M. 1994b. "Striking a Chord." *India Today*, July 31, 18–24.

Rahman, M., and Arun Katiyan. 1993. "Bombay Film Industry: Underworld Connections." *India Today*, May 15, 66–73.

Rahman, M., And Rahul Pathak. 1994. "Bomb Blasts: The Conspiracy Unravels." *India Today*, June 30, 26–29.

Ramachandran, V. 1996. "Kurnool Lives Up To Its Violent Image." *Hindu*. April 20.

Schatzberg, Rufus, and Robert J. Kelley. 1996. *African American Organized Crime: A Social History.* New York: Garland Publishing, Inc.

Servadio, Gaia 1976. *Mafioso: A History of the Mafia from its Origins to the Present Day.* Briarcliff Manor, NY: Stein and Day.

Shaw, Clifford and Henry D. McKay. 1941. *Juvenile Delinquency and Urban Areas.* Chicago: Chicago University Press.

Singh, Ujjwal 1996. "The Killing Fields." *Business Standard*. May 4.

Verma, A. 1994. "The Phenomenon of Crime in India: Some Observations." *Indian Police Journal* 31 (1): 1–11.

Verma, A. 1993. The Problem of Measurement of Crime. *Indian J Criminol*. 21 (2): 51–58.

Yang, Anand A. (ed.). 1986. *Crime and Criminality in British India.* Tucson, AZ: Arizona University Press.

Yeager, Matthew G. 1973. The Gangster as White Collar Criminal: Organized Crime and Stolen Securities. *Issues in Criminol*. 8: 49–73.

Chapter 11

Organized Crime: A Perspective from Japan

Ayoka Uchiyama

Introduction

Japan is situated on the Eastern coast of Asia, and stretches in a narrow arc 2,375 miles long, ranging from 20°–30°N latitude. Japan's total area of 147,578.125 square miles is slightly larger than the United Kingdom. The archipelago consists of four main islands: Honshuu, Hokkaido, Kyushu, and Shikoku. Japanese is the main language, although many other dialects are also spoken. In 1995, Japan's population stood at 124.7 million according to the Ministry of Home Affairs. The life expectancy, among the highest in the world, is 76 years for men and 82 years for women (Asia: A World Data Book, 1996).

Modern Japan is a democratic society with a constitutional form of monarchy. Japan's Constitution, which was promulgated on 3 November 1946, upholds the high ideals of peace and democratic order. The prominent features of the Constitution are as follows:

1. The emperor is the symbol of the state and of the unity of the people. However, sovereign power rests with the people who exercise it through their elected representatives.

2. Japan renounces war as a sovereign right. It also renounces the threat of the use of force as means of settling disputes with other nations.

3. Fundamental human rights are guaranteed as eternal and inviolable to all citizens.

4. The Diet consist of two Houses, the House of Representatives and the House of Councilors, whose members are elected as representatives of

all the people. The House of Representatives has preeminence over the House of Councilors.

5. Executive power is vested in the cabinet, which is collectively responsible to the Diet.

6. The emperor has no powers related to government; he performs only those acts of state that are stipulated in the Constitution. Thus, for example, he appoints the prime minister and chief justice of the Supreme Court. The prime minister, however, is first designated by the Diet and chief justice, by the cabinet. The emperor also performs such acts on behalf of promulgating laws and treaties, convoking the Diet and awarding honors, all with the advice and approval of the Cabinet.

The economy of Japan is a thriving complex of industry, commerce, finance, agriculture, and all other elements of a modern economic structure. The nation's economy is an advanced stage of industrialization, served by a massive flow of information and highly developed transportation networks. One feature of Japan's economy is the major contribution of manufacturing and services such as transport, wholesale and retail commerce, and banking to the country's net domestic products in which such primary industries as agriculture and fisheries now have a minor share. Another feature is the relative importance of international trade to Japan's economy. Japan's economy continued to expand rapidly from the mid 1950s through 1980s. Although in the 1990s there was a slowing down of the Japanese economy, nevertheless, the GNP remains one of the highest in the world.

Compulsory schooling is nine years, six years for primary and three years for junior high education. However, most Japanese children also attend kindergarten before going to primary school, and most also complete three years of senior high school. College usually takes four years. At present the country has 100 percent compulsory education and 31.5 percent college education.

Japan enjoys a low crime rate as compared to other industrialized nations. Like other countries, property crimes form the bulk of the reported offenses, but violent crimes are comparatively rare. There were only 1,278 homicides reported in the entire country in the year 1994 while total violent crimes were 36,515. In 1994, Japan recorded a rate of 2,928 total offenses per 100,000 population. Most interestingly, official corruption and cases of breach of trust are unusually low, giving a glimpse into the nature of Japanese society.

The police law stipulates that the police should fulfill the following responsibilities: protecting the life and property of people and maintaining public peace and order. These are assigned to each prefecture, which is responsible for the enforcement of various police duties. The police law also prescribes that the national government set up a central police organization to control and supervise the prefectural police, to the extent of the specific national concerns. At both national and prefectural levels, public safety commissions have been established as administrative institutions of the police. With a strength of approximately 260,000 personnel, the Japanese police have an organizational structure consisting of the National Police Agency and 47 prefectural police headquarters (National Police Academy, 1996). The National Police Agency is responsible for planning the laws, regulations, and standards of police activities and for supporting and coordinating prefectural police activities. The execution of these activities, however, is solely the responsibility of each prefectural police organization, which performs such duties within its territorial jurisdiction. In order to ensure democratic control and political neutrality of the police, The National Public Safety Commission and Prefectural Public Safety Commission have been established.

The Japanese police have a system that utilizes a "koban" or police box, and has attracted much attention overseas. One characteristic of this system is that the police can maintain public peace and order through everyday contact with the people of the community. The Koban system consists mainly of the police boxes, where teams of local police officers keep an around-the clock watch by working in shifts and residential police boxes, where police officers reside and maintain the safety of the surrounding area. There are approximately 15,000 police boxes through the country. The Koban system contributes greatly to public safety because it makes the police a familiar presence in the community and enables a relatively small number of officers to maintain security. The people's trust in the police is essential for continuing this system. To further contribute to community safety under the Koban system, the police promote improved means of preventing crime and accidents, including the introduction and use of computers and patrol cars. The Japanese police excel in the use of scientific technologies, including satellite communications, mobile radios, patrol-car identification and command communications, fingerprint identification, analysis of crime modus operandi, and identification of minute objects. In addition, computers are extensively used in such areas as crime information, driver's license control, automatic fingerprint identification, and automatic license plate reading. The relationship between the community and the police is cordial and the essence of success for the Japanese society is to keep crime and social disorder at a very low level.

THE NATURE AND EXTENT OF ORGANIZED CRIME

Organized crime, unfortunately, is not unknown to Japan. The post-war chaos helped it establish deep roots within the society. Organizational loyalty of the Japanese, which has brought economic boom to the country, is also ironically helping the crime syndicates to extend and maintain their hold over their members (Hoshino, 1981). For instance, the organized group known as the Boryokudan has been a major threat to the Japanese society. The Boryokudan members are engaged in a large number of criminal enterprises and drug dealing, extortion, fraud, and prostitution are some of their more prominent criminal activities. The Boryokudan members are also known to be more cunning and daring in committing crime. The information provided here about the Boryokudan is based on empirical data collected by contacting and surveying a large number of Boryokudan members (Uchiyama and Enomoto, 1992).

There are three big organizations—Yamaguchigumi, Inagawakai, and Sumiyoshikai—listed as "the designated Boryokudan" under the Anti-Boryokudan Law. The total number of designated Boryokudan groups was counted at 24 by the end of 1995. Among designated Boryokudans, these three big groups included two-thirds of the total membership. At the end of 1995, including designated Boryokudan members, 79,300 Boryokudan members had been identified, showing a decrease of 1,700 from the previous year. The membership had reached almost 92,000, but steadily declined after the enactment of this law. The reduction also affected the number of full-time members, who were estimated to be about 46,000.

These Boryokudan are not homogeneous groups but may be classified in different categories. In particular, there are three prominent types of Boryokudan—Bakuto, Tekiya, and others—which are identified by the way they have been extorting their money for a long time. For example, the Bakuto are those groups who sponsor illegal gambling parties within their territories and earn profits from their gambling guests. Tekiya is an old name that was assigned to groups who peddled artifacts and were street performers or had a proclivity to do so. These groups have their own spheres of influence and do business on holidays on the premises of shrines and temples or on the streets. These group names still persist based on the classification relative to the modus operandi of extortion. However, they have become ambiguous in recent times, since these groups have ventured into several spheres of illegal activities.

In general, Boryokudan groups are formed by a quasi-blood relationship, which imitates the feudal paternal family structures. This is evident from the fact that the groups are often called so-and-so *ikka* (so-and-so family). The boss is called *oyabun* (literally parent's status), and the men under him are *kobun* (children's status). The groups are organized as a large pyramidal structure, with every subgroup being subordinate to the bigger organization. In many cases the bosses of these subgroups form a quasi-blood relationship with one another also. Boryokudan groups try to justify their relations and behaviors based on the previously mentioned feudal status system by such deceptive theories as unique "moral" codes (*jingi*) and a strong sense of duty, responsibility, and humanity (*giri-ninjo*). However, all these forms essentially cement the ties among the members and the whole group becomes a closely knit society (Uchiyama, 1987; 1989).

Internal Control

In the world of Boryokudan groups, the vertical relationship of oyabun and kobun is absolute and beyond any reason (Uchiyama and Hoshino, 1993). It is the duty and virtue of the men to follow the order of their boss without questioning whether the order of the boss is right or not, and whether it is good or bad. If a man disturbs the rule by questioning the boss and breaks the unity of the group by disobeying, failing to do the duty, and violating the rules of the underworld, he is severely punished. On the other hand, those who comply with the orders of the boss and other leaders and contribute to the group are given promotions and remuneration (Hoshino, Uchiyama, Harada, and Mugishima, 1987).

Punishment

In general, the gang members who disobey the orders of the boss and other leaders or break the group rules are subjected to strict punishment within the organization. The most severe penalties include lynching, finger-cutting, expulsion, and severance of relations. According to a survey in 1970, 39 percent of Boryokudan members (from 359 respondents) had cut their fingers and most of them cited the reason of finger-cutting as being a form of apology. The lighter punishments include confinement to the house, dismissal from the place of residence, and monetary fines. Those who are arrested or sent to prison because they did not observe the gang's rules are usually punished by withholding from them such assistance as sending food and other things while in prison. They are also ostracized and nobody goes to fetch them when they are released from prison, and no one celebrates their release, omissions that carry social stigma.

Purpose of Affiliating with the Boryokudan

The motives to join Boryokudan are shown in Table 11.1.

The most frequent motives to join the group were cited to be that "they were attracted to the smartness of the group members," and that "Boryokudan owns expensive material goods" (acquired materials symbolizing success). Second, the subculture of underworld *giri* (strong sense of duty or responsibility) and *ninjo* (humanities) also attracted many people. Third, many new members expected to lead a hedonistic lifestyle by

TABLE 11.1   REASONS FOR JOINING BORYOKUDAN

Under 19	20–29	30–39	40+	Total	New	Survey 1985	Survey 1967
Attracted by smartness of Boryokudan or its members							
47.1	40.4	32.8	11.8	36.5	36.7	49.3	26.4
Attracted by the world of giri-ninjo							
29.1	32.0	27.9	25.1	29.1	17.1	16.2	27.2
Given due respect as a man							
16.2	17.6	19.7	16.2	17.1	18.1	19.8	12.6
Wanted to spend hedonistic life							
17.9	17.0	19.7	11.8	16.7	13.1	23.0	20.2
To eke out a living							
10.1	9.6	17.5	17.3	12.2	12.1	19.5	14.2
Attracted to the rule of violence							
9.5	10.0	8.7	9.2	9.5	9.6	11.2	10.8
For convenience in carrying on business							
3.0	5.2	8.2	17.7	7.2	9.1	5.9	11.8
Wanted to be well off financially							
5.5	7.8	6.6	9.2	7.1	8.5	7.7	3.6
Expected the job would be easy							
4.4	2.8	5.5	3.7	3.9	3.5	5.9	5.2
Forced to join the underworld							
3.2	3.3	3.8	4.1	3.5	6.0	2.7	1.6
No special reason							
3.0	3.9	3.8	6.6	4.1	7.0	22.4	19.0

Note. Figures are in percentages.

affiliating with a powerful organization. Some of the members also joined the groups for the convenience accorded to their businesses. The survey results clearly showed that the Boryokudan organization had a strong attraction due to the lifestyle enjoyed or displayed by its members and for the business profits that accrued due to the support received from the large number of its members. The survey also showed that before joining the Boryokudan, some members had an experience of belonging to delinquent groups such as a hot rodders group (Bosozoku, 22.5%), drug abuse group (9.5%), or violent delinquent group (8.7%), suggesting that Boryokudan obviously attracted those who had criminal antecedents or inclinations

(Uchiyama, 1989). Table 11.2 displays the academic career of these members.

More than half of them had only a compulsory school education, suggesting that most Boryokudan members have attained only minimal education, which is even more evident from the fact that 95 percent of graduates from junior high school usually go to senior high school now in Japan. Moreover, these members were also seen to receive low marks in school achievement tests. Obviously, the Boryokudan attracts dropouts and those who have poor achievement in their lives (Hoshino, Mugishima, and Takashi, 1968).

MEASURES, INCLUDING LEGISLATION TO COMBAT ORGANIZED CRIME

The most prominent action taken by the government against the Boryokudan has been the enactment of a special law that not only acknowledged the existence of such organized crime in the country, but also made serious attempts to prevent its spread.

The law concerning prevention of unjust acts by Boryokudan Members was enacted in 1991 and is generally referred as the anti-Boryokudan law. The Boryokudan is defined by this law as an organization prone to perpetrate violent illegal acts, collectively or chronically using its organizational or collective power. The purpose of the law is to ensure security and peace in the life of the people by imposing strict restrictions upon the

TABLE 11.2 ACADEMIC CAREER OF BORYOKUDAN MEMBERS

	Under 19	20–29	30–39	40–49	>50	Total
Compulsory education	65.9	57.2	47.1	65.7	64.9	58.5
Drop out from Senior HS	34.1	30.7	34.8	21	17.5	27.6
Graduate from Senior HS	—	11	15.2	10	13.1	11.5
College education	—	1.2	2.2	3	3.6	2.2
Unknown	—	—	0.6	0.2	0.7	0.3

Note. Figures are in percentages.

organizational activities of this formidable group. In particular, the extortion and threatening acts carried out by Boryokudan members have been targeted under this act to prevent casualties or damage that result from the violent activities of Boryokudan members.

The outline of the anti-Boryokudan law is as follows: the groups coming under certain conditions are cited as "the designated Boryokudan" and the law is enforced on membership of those who are "the designated Boryokudan members." The law prohibits these designated Boryokudan members from unjustly demanding money, property services, and others by defining the influence of their group in the following fourteen criminal activities:

1. Exaction by taking advantage of person's weak point
2. Acts of unjustly demanding gifts
3. Acts of unreasonably demanding subcontract jobs
4. Acts of demanding *mikajime* (muscle-man's) fee
5. Acts of demanding protection money
6. Collection of high-interest-rate loans
7. Acts of unjustly demanding exemption from financial obligations
8. Acts of unreasonably demanding loans
9. Acts of illegally assembling on some land
10. Acts of unfairly intervening in out-of-court settlement arrangements
11. Acts of demanding money on falsified grounds
12. Acts of unjustly demanding money in return for evacuating plots of land and buildings subject to public auctions
13. Acts of unjustly demanding that companies and parties concerned buy up stocks of the companies
14. Acts of unjustly demanding that securities brokerages conduct credit transactions in securities

Laws and regulations have also been enacted to ensure that the confrontation or dispute arising between the designated Boryokudans and others could be controlled swiftly. When there is an apparent risk that the offices of the designated Boryokudan could be misused for purposes such as assembling their members, issuing commands and orders to take certain action, or coordinating activities of large numbers of the designated Boryokudan members to escalate the tension and precipitate confrontation, the law provides for preventive action against these designated Boryokudan members. Punishment of up to a period of three months' imprisonment could be stipulated to those who administer these Boryokudan offices. The designated Boryokudan members are further prohibited from coercing or enticing juveniles to enroll in the Boryokudan or obstructing their voluntary resignations from their group.

Centers have been established in Japan to encourage and promote movements for the elimination of violence in society. These centers carry out several kinds of operations to combat the influence of the Boryokudan. They design and conduct publicity through the media for the purpose of disseminating knowledge relating to the prevention of unjust acts by the Boryokudan members. They provide a consulting service to those victims who fall into distressful situations through unlawful acts by Boryokudan members. These groups also conduct activities to eliminate the influence of the Boryokudan on juveniles and carry out supportive activities for those desiring to resign from the group.

COMPARATIVE EVALUATION OF THE METHODS FOR COMBATING ORGANIZED CRIME AND PROPOSED MEASURES

The government's attempt to control this organized crime syndicate through a series of legislative and police measures has been fruitful. The anti-Boryokudan law has provided for strict police control and law enforcement forcing the Boryokudan to change in various ways.

A majority of Boryokudan members have been arrested more than twice during their criminal careers. The number of Boryokudan members arrested has ranged from 30,000 to 50,000 a year for the past two decades. The ratio of crimes committed by the Boryokudan members, especially in felonious offenses such as homicide and robbery and violent offenses such as assault and injury, also appear to be decreasing, but the ratios in extortion, fraud, and intimidation are still increasing.

Several changes have been further observed in the activities of the Boryokudan after the enforcement of the anti-Boryokudan law (Uchiyama, et al., 1993). The issuance of abeyance orders and orders to prevent repetition by the police during the last three years are clearly increasing. From this point of view, the new law appears effective to some degree. These figures of police orders (White Paper on Police, 1995) are shown in Table 11.3.

The effectiveness of the law may also be measured by the resignation of Boryokudan members. Boryokudan organizations that dissolved or disintegrated totaled 80 (involving 1,131 members) in 1990, 131 (1,430 members) in 1991, and 222 (2,604 members) in 1993.

There is also a marked change in the daily life of the Boryokudan groups. A major change brought on by enforcement of the new law was

TABLE 11.3 POLICE INJUNCTIONS BASED ON THE ANTI-BORYOKUDAN LAW (1992–1995)

Year	1992		1993		1994		1995	
Type	Abeyance	prevent	Abeyance	prevent	Abeyance	prevent	Abeyance	prevent
Total	241	7	610	35	1057	37	1321	33
art.9 Unjust demand for gifts	9	—	37	—	117	—	197	2
Demand for muscleman's fee	8	3	51	6	73	3	120	5
Demand for protection fee	52	2	136	25	175	25	256	22
Collection of loans	9	—	10	1	8	—	10	—
Exemption from debts, etc.	8	—	36	—	116	—	146	—
Demanding loans	—	—	14	—	20	—	19	—
Evacuating in auctions	—	—	4	—	2	—	1	—
Intervention in settlement	4	—	3	—	10	—	4	—
Demand for money, etc	17	—	34	—	65	—	34	—
Others	6	—	10	—	27	2	27	—
art.10 Criminal exaction	—	1	—	—	—	2	—	2
Helping criminal exaction	—	—	8	—	36	—	66	—
art. 16 Forcing membership	22	—	36	—	50	2	58	—
Forcing membership on adults	105	1	194	1	296	2	302	2
Forcing close people	—	—	33	—	59	—	77	—
art. 17 Forcing to become members	—	—	—	—	—	1	—	—
art. 20 Forcing finger cutting	—	—	1	—	1	—	2	—
art. 24 Forcing youths tattoo	—	—	—	—	—	—	1	—
art. 29 Illegal acts in offices	1	—	3	—	2	—	1	—

TABLE 11.4 REASONS WHY BORYOKUDAN ARE NOT ELIMINATED

	1989	1994
Some people utilize Boryokudan for settlement of problems	17.2	49.3
Many people do not report to police for fear of Boryokudan reprisal	23.9	49.1
There are people who succumb to Boryokudan's requests for money	31.0	47.9
Police control is lukewarm	40.3	26.8
There is no adequate legal system to control Boryokudan	39.9	25.3
Once a person joins Boryokudan, it is difficult to quit	30.0	24.0
People admire Boryokudan or are drawn into it because of their indecision	37.1	11.6
Penalties for Boryokudan members' crimes are not heavy enough	44.1	11.4
Others	7.05	.3

observed in the decrease of their income compared with previous years. These results were revealed through a survey conducted in 1985. In particular, the income of bosses and senior members from illegal sources had considerably decreased compared with that from legal sources.

There has also been an appreciable change in the attitude of citizens toward the Boryokudan. The enforcement of the law and surveillance carried out by the police has changed the ways in which the citizens view the Boryokudan. Generally speaking, there used to be an attitude that the Boryokudan are not so good, but that they are necessary to daily life. The big campaigns launched by the government and mass media against the Boryokudan have continued with the enactment and enforcement of the new law and have made the citizens' attitudes negative toward criminal elements. Table 11.4 shows the change in attitude toward the Boryokudan among citizens before and after the enforcement of the anti-Boryokudan law.

Conclusion

Despite the low crime rate, Japanese society has been known to be plagued by intense criminal activity that is organized and conducted differently than the more visible crimes. However, it took the Japanese government more than three decades to begin to appreciate the problem posed by organized criminal enterprises. Using the same organizational loyalty that made Japanese industry a household name all over the world, criminal groups became stronger and more widespread. Reacting to the gravity of the emerging situation, the Japanese government has taken tough measures, enacting a new law and empowering the police to control the activities of these organized crime groups. The results shown previously tell us that the enactment and enforcement of law to control the Boryokudan has been effective in suppressing their illegal and dangerous activities. Apart from the governmental measures, another important aspect could also be emphasized—the secondary effect of law enforcement on the citizens of Japan. Combined with the anti-Boryokudan law, a large campaign conducted among the citizens has also been successful in changing their attitude toward these groups. Although they used to be dependent on the Boryokudan to resolve civil affairs, since the enforcement of the anti-Boryokudan law they have changed their perception toward the Boryokudan. This is making a dent in the armor of the organized criminal enterprise that has been plaguing Japan for a long time.

REFERENCES

Uchiyama, A., and K. Hoshino. 1993. A Study on the Conformity of Boryokudan Members to the Boryokudan Sub-culture. *Reports of NRIPS* 34 (2): 27–35.

Uchiyama, A., K. Hoshino, M. Tamura, and S. Yonezato. 1993. The Changes in Way of Life of Boryokudan Members after Enforcement of the Anti-Organized Crime Law. *Reports of NRIPS* 34 (2): 13–26.

Uchiyama, A., and Y. Enomoto. 1992. An Analysis of Process to Contact the Boryokudan of Boryokudan Fringe Members. *Reports of NRIPS* 33 (1): 70–84.

Uchiyama, A. 1987. A Study on the Way of Life of Members of Organized Criminal Gangs. "Classification of Individuals' Life Patters." *Reports of NRIPS* 28 (1): 1–10.

Uchiyama, A. 1989. Economic Life of Members of Organized Criminal Gangs. *Reports of NRIPS* 30 (1): 89–100.

Hoshino, K., A. Uchiyama, Y. Harada, and F. Mugishima. 1987. A Study on the Way of Life of Members of Organized Criminal Gangs: Hour Assignment in Daily life. "Success-Goals and Social Relationships." *Reports of NRIPS* 28 (1): 1–14.

Hoshino, K., F. Mugishima, and Y. Takahashi. 1968. Social Background and Career of the Members of the Violent Gang. "Analysis of the Process of Affiliating with Gang." *Reports of NRIPS* 9 (2): 98–106.

Hoshino, K. 1981. A Study on the Newly Enlisted Members and the Fringe Members of Organized Criminal Gang. "Process of Their Affiliation with Gang." *Reports of NRIPS* 22 (1): 18–32.

National Police Academy. 1996. Police of Japan.

Asia: A World Data Book. 1996 Imidas: Shueisha.

White Paper on Police. 1995. Police Association. Tokyo.

Chapter 12

Organized Crime: A Perspective from China

He Bingsong

Introduction

China is the third largest country in the world after Russia and Canada and its area of 3,748,812.5 square miles is slightly larger than that of the United States. The country is rich in natural resources like coal, iron ore, and petroleum while it has the world's largest potential for hydropower. China is also the most populated country in the world, with an estimated 1,210,004,956 (July 1996 est.) people. Han Chinese are the major ethnic group followed by a small minority of Tibetan, Miao, Manchu, Mongol, Buyi, Korean, and other nationalities. China is a communist state with twenty-two provinces, five autonomous regions, and three municipalities. Recently, Hong Kong has also become part of China. A new constitution was promulgated in 1982 and its legal system is a complex amalgam of mostly criminal laws, both customary and statutory. A rudimentary civil code has been in effect since January 1987 and efforts are being made to improve civil, administrative, criminal, and commercial laws in resonance with the process of modernization and the opening up of the state.

The Communist Party is the only recognized political party and the National People's Congress is the supreme policy-making body. Although there is universal suffrage, all representatives are selected by the party. Beginning in late 1978, the Chinese leadership under the legendary Deng moved the economy from a sluggish Soviet-style centrally planned economy to one that was more market-oriented, but still within a rigid political framework of Communist Party control. The authorities permitted private agriculture in place of the old collectivization, increased the authority of local officials and plant managers in industry, permitted a wide variety of small-scale enterprises in services and light manufacturing, and opened the economy to increased foreign trade and investment. The result has been spectacular: agricultural output doubled in the 1980s, and coastal areas near Hong Kong in particular have experienced a boom in industrial production. The Chinese GDP is estimated to have more than tripled since 1978 and annual growth rates have surpassed 10 percent for many years. However, the hybrid system has spawned bureaucratic corruption and stepped-up inflation. The opening up of the system has also led to a surge in anti-governmental activities, one of which culminated in the famous Tiananmen Square massacre of student protesters. The government has been struggling to collect revenues due from provinces, businesses, and individuals and reduce extortion and other economic crimes. The problem of keeping afloat the large, inefficient, state-owned enterprises that are a heavy burden on the economy also has not yet been tackled. Rapid growth has made 60 to 100 million rural workers superfluous, and they are adrift between the villages and the cities, many contributing to increasing criminality in the country. The next few years are likely to witness increasing tensions between a highly centralized political system, in which a small coterie still controls most of the decision making, and an emerging decentralized economic system.

The People's Republic of China has undertaken several large-scale changes in its criminal justice system. After its establishment as a socialist country in 1949, several basic laws concerning criminal justice administration were enacted. However, it was in 1979, after the period of "Cultural Revolution," that the present criminal law and criminal procedure law were enacted. Thereafter, laws governing the organization and function of the courts and public prosecution, arrest and detention of suspects, civil suit procedures and marriages were established. Official Chinese records have suggested that the country has one of the lowest crime rates in the world. Of all the crimes reported, theft accounts for about 80 percent of the cases, but violent crimes like murder and robbery have been increasing. Crimes associated with gangs; trafficking in narcotics; smuggling of gold, endangered species, and human parts; counterfeiting of currency; prostitution; and credit card fraud have also been increasing steadily.

In the Chinese system, a fixed-term imprisonment is not less than six months and not more than fifteen years. An offender sentenced to a fixed-term imprisonment or life imprisonment is to have his sentence executed in prison or in another place for reformation. Reform through labor is to be carried out on any imprisoned offender, as long as he has the ability to labor. The death penalty is only to be applied to those offenders who commit the most heinous crimes. The criminal law also provides for supplementary punishments like fines, deprivation of political rights, and confiscation of property.

The number of police personnel in the whole country was 1.2 million in 1986. Chinese police have powers of inquiry, investigation, and surveillance. The police carry out supervision of offenders during both the suspension of execution of the sentence and after release on parole. Probationers and parolees are turned over by the public security organ to a work unit or a local organization. The policemen in charge of the community supervise their daily life, their work, and their ideological trend and keep in touch with their neighbors to check any law-breaking activities. The people's procuratorates (public prosecutors) are responsible for initiating public prosecution. These procuratorates also have the power to investigate criminal cases as well as the power to make decisions of prosecution, nonprosecution, or exemption from prosecution in each criminal case, considering the evidence of the case and the nature and circumstances of the crime. The people's courts are responsible for adjudication, and no other bodies are given the power to adjudicate criminal cases.

THE NATURE AND EXTENT OF ORGANIZED CRIME

Conditions of organized crime in the mainland of China are quite different from that of Taiwan, Hong Kong, and Macau because of the diversity of political institutions and social systems. As the mainland is the principal part of China, this essay will primarily discuss the situation of organized crime of the mainland. The nature of organized crime in Taiwan, Hong Kong, and Macau will be introduced very briefly.

Before China's Liberation, organized crimes were very serious. The most notorious underground criminal organizations—"Qing Gang" and "Hung Mun" and some regional gangs of hooligans—colluded with Kuo Min Tang's government and various regional reactionary forces, committing crimes of manufacturing and selling drugs, smuggling munitions, trading human beings, kidnapping, murder, robbery, gambling, and prostitution. Such organized gangs also penetrated into the enterprises of entertainment, movies, and real estate. Criminal organizations in some districts even controlled the banks and large-scale industries. Du Yuesheng, head of the underground organizations at that time in Shanghai, was the shareholder, manager, and chairman of the board of directors of many enterprises and corporations. This penetration of organized criminal forces into politics was shocking to say the least. Many heads of the underground organizations were the backers of the local political power and some were even holding power within the government.

The establishment of the communist government in 1949 and the great liberation war smashed the reactionary government of Kuo Min Tang, giving a heavy blow to the underground organizations in areas of the mainland. Yet, in spite of this change in government the underground powers were not totally destroyed. Some of these gang leaders fled to the districts of Taiwan, Hong Kong, and Macau and the rest continued to commit all kinds of crimes in the mainland.

Nevertheless, after the reform and "open-door" policy, the situation of Chinese politics and economy changed greatly. Under the effects of all kinds of negative factors, criminal organizations and organized crime have grown rapidly in China. According to statistics, from 1985 to 1986, when strong nationwide measures were taken against crime, 197,000 criminal groups and 876,000 group members were tracked down. In 1986, the number of criminal groups and members tracked down was 30,000 plus, and 114,000, respectively; in 1988, 57,000 and 210,000; in 1990, 100,000 plus and 368,000; in 1991, 134,000 and 507,000; and in 1994, 152,000 and 574,000, an increase of 306 percent and 403 percent, respectively, from 1986. The nature of criminal groups has also changed. Prior to 1986, most of them were loosely organized; only a very few were well-coordinated and planned. Since 1988, however, the rate with which these groups have transformed themselves into tightly structured and highly organized underground-type criminal groups has gathered speed. Although there is a lack of nationwide statistics to support the claim, the situation in many areas reflects the shocking speed at which they have grown. For instance, in the city of Shenyang, only two underground-type criminal groups were uncovered in 1990, but in 1993, the number had reached thirteen. In the first half of 1994, thirty-five such criminal groups in Chaoyang City of Guangdong province were tracked down. However, between September 1994 and March 1995, the number of underground-type criminal groups found in the smaller city of Shenyang alone was seventy-five.

These statistics reflect only the number of cases traced by the public security agencies. The actual number of such groups in existence is, of course, higher. Some scholars estimate that underground groups constitute approximately 20 percent to 30 percent of all criminal groups. These underground criminal groups usually have an established leader, some core members, a distinctly layered hierarchy, ingrained organizational discipline, rules for punishing violators, and a set of procedures or an initiation ceremony for joining the organization. Some underground criminal organizations also have their own code or organizational symbols.

Furthermore, a number of especially dangerous underground criminal groups have also emerged across the nation. Not only are they highly organized, they are also well-armed and possess considerable financial strength. They bribe government officials and law enforcement personnel to obtain protection and have effectively established their own turf in certain areas or industries that compete with the legitimate businesses in the society. To expand their turf, they either band together or engage in violent confrontations with one another. Although such groups are still extremely few in number and not very strong, they have already demonstrated certain common characteristics in their development.

As criminal groups associated with organized crime in China grow, they tend to expand in size and become centralized. Before 1986, criminal groups usually had only a few members. Today, large criminal groups have emerged across the nation, with memberships ranging from ten to over a hundred people. Additionally, these groups tend to merge and coalesce. These tendencies are more noticeable in some local gangs and in specialized criminal groups (e.g., those that abduct women for sale, manufacture drugs for sale, etc.). For example, some highly organized, specialized drug groups have emerged and formed integrated "companies" capable of masterminding all phases from purchasing to transporting, escorting, and selling the drugs. This operation is usually undertaken by multiple criminal organizations in joint efforts just like a well-organized business activity.

There is a distinct tendency toward modernization and use of technology in the development of organized crime, judging by the equipment used by criminal groups. Many underground-type criminal groups are armed with guns, hand grenades, explosives, and knives. They also have at their disposal various means of transportation such as automobiles and motorcycles, as well as sophisticated communications equipment. Some even have advanced weapons and equipment such as bulletproof vests, submachine guns, tear gas "guns," tear gas grenades, anti-tank grenades, cellular phones, and radio transmitters. This is a very serious trend that indicates China's organized crime groups are rapidly becoming violent. Weapons enhance the strength of these criminal groups, making them more dangerous and an even greater threat to society.

According to nationwide statistics, in 1994 serious criminal cases in which weapons were used increased by 85 percent from 1993. In 1995, there were 23,000 such cases, an increase of 13.5 percent from the year before. Many of these involved organized criminal groups. For instance, in 1994 cases involving armed criminals reported by local public security agencies to the Ministry of Public Security reached 604 in number, of which 236, or 39.1 percent, involved armed criminal groups. Along with the rapid development of criminal groups, the incidence of various kinds of organized crime is rising at a very rapid rate, too. The nature of their criminal activities has become increasingly diversified. Not only do they commit the usual crimes of murder, injury, rape, robbery, theft, fraud, extortion, and kidnapping, but they also provide illegal products and services such as smuggling, gambling, prostitution, pornography, manufacture and sale of drugs, guns, forged documents, trading human parts, organizing operations to smuggle people, loan sharking, extortion, and monopolizing construction contracts. Some underground criminal groups have begun infiltrating into legitimate enterprises to conduct money-laundering activities. They also bribe government officials and law enforcement personnel to recruit accomplices and patrons in party and government agencies as well as judicial departments. Some even participate directly in politics. These criminal groups conduct activities that seriously jeopardize the safety and property of the people, destroy law and order in the society, and damage the market economy and modernization projects. They have become a serious threat to the democratization and national security of China.

Criminal groups in China have also actively sought out underground organizations in Hong Kong, Macau, and Taiwan to work together to form alliances with underground organizations outside of China and/or to conduct joint criminal activities. The trend continues for Chinese criminal groups to collude with overseas underground organizations and jointly conduct transnational criminal activities. In recent years, many of the increasingly serious transnational drug trafficking and illegal gun trafficking operations have resulted from such joint ventures. For instance, in 1990 China solved the biggest drug case since the founding of the nation. In all, some fifty-one drug traffickers were arrested, both Chinese and foreign nationals. This was a huge drug ring spanning Burma, China, and Hong Kong. The emergence of transnational organized crime has signified that China's organized crime has gone international. Recently, a Hong Kong weekly called "The Windows" reported that the Russian Mafia had formed an alliance with Hong Kong's underground organization, the triad societies, and is now jointly conducting criminal activities in Hong Kong.

Nevertheless, as in other countries, organized crime in China has not developed in the same manner in all the regions. On the Chinese mainland, organized crime is more active in cities than in the rural areas and more aggressive in the coastal cities and provinces than inland. Nonetheless, the development of organized crime on the Chinese mainland is still at an early stage. Underground groups make up only a small percentage of the entire criminal community, and the especially dangerous underground groups are still few in number. They also lack organization and strength, and although they exhibit the basic characteristics of underground organizations, they are not highly developed criminal organizations. In China, the so called underground criminal groups have the following characteristics:

1. Involvement of an established, local, malevolent force that has a defined scope of influence;
2. Engagement in specialized criminal activities, conducting one or more crimes on a long-term basis;
3. A comparatively large, stable membership;
4. Strongly anti-society, doing all manner of harm to the people;
5. Economically secure, possibly controlling some economic entities and turf;
6. Seeking protection from corrupt government officials and judicial cadres through every possible means.

In contrast, organized criminal activities in Hong Kong, Taiwan, and Macau have attracted worldwide attention. Organized crime in Taiwan has a long history. As early as the Japanese occupation of Taiwan, organized crime in that region was known to exist and considered dangerous. Although there was a decrease in this type of crime for a short time after the surrender of Japan, Kuo-Min-Tang's escape to Taiwan, followed by a large number of immigrants, led to turbulent growth. The members of underground organizations who had immigrated to Taiwan from the mainland maintained contact, which gave rise to organized crime in both parts of the region. The acceleration of industrialization and modernization since 1960 has boosted the economy of Taiwan and also increased organized criminal activities. The development of different businesses and all kinds of recreational activities and traveling facilities provided the conditions for the growth and development of underground criminal organizations. More violent conflicts for spheres of influence among different factions of the organizations became one of the important characteristics of organized crime of this period. By 1970 organized crime was running enterprises on a commercial basis and changing from violent robberies to managing business enterprises. Nonetheless, violent activities of the underground organizations have not been reduced. Many large-scale underground factions established special armed forces for the purpose of protecting their economic interests and strengthening their power. By the end of the 1970s and at the beginning of the 1980s, smuggling of arms had spread rapidly to strengthen these forces. There were more and more violent crimes, and from 1975 to 1984, violent crimes increased by more than 100 percent.

After 1980, another major change of criminal organizations in Taiwan came to be known as the internationalization of organized crime. Relatively strong international criminal organizations, such as the Japanese Yakuza and others, penetrated into Taiwan and introduced transnational organized crime to the region. By the mid 1980s these underground criminal organizations had established themselves firmly in this region and their transnational criminal activities brought the attention of many countries to the dangers posed by these Chinese and East Asian criminal organizations.

Although from the beginning the police of Taiwan have pursued these underground groups, their efforts have not yielded notable results. According to the statistics revealed by Taiwan Criminal Police Bureau, there are at present around 1,236 underground criminal organizations with 10,582 members and it is feared that the actual number is much more. For instance, the Sha-Lian gang, which is the biggest underground organization in Taiwan, has an unwieldy and closed structure that makes it difficult to determine its exact membership and activities. In recent years the underground criminal organizations in Taiwan have also stepped up penetration into politics by manipulating elections or running for public office directly. By the end of 1994, 281 criminals in underground organizations were tracked down "supporting the elections" during the mayor's election in Taiwan Province. Among them, 37 people were prosecuted for election-related violence. In 1994, 150 members of the legislative assembly reportedly had various connections with underground organizations, or 17 percent of the 858 members elected to the counties and cities of Taiwan. Some criminals in underground organizations even managed to hold the post of president or vice president of the legislative body. Some have become the leaders of villages, towns, and counties, and, by misusing their positions, have provided economic benefits and power for their own factions.

These underground groups have reportedly penetrated the army, too. For instance, the official investigation of the murder of naval captain Shi Qingfeng revealed that 145 army personnel were members of criminal gangs; 41 naval officers were members of the Qing gang and among them were 6 high-ranking officers. At present in Taiwan, underground societies and businesses have jointly infiltrated politics, colluding with political entities to become a three-in-one power. This has been described by the people as "Black-Gold politics," alluding to the governmental corruption and the hidden power of underground societies.

The Triad of Hong Kong was originally called "Sam Hop Wui," which was, historically, a secret organization with the purpose of overthrowing the Manchu Ching Dynasty and restoring the Chinese Ming Dynasty. Although it has existed for quite a long time as an underground organization, continued to take the old name of the Triad and carried forward the pattern and rules of the organization, it has changed in character. The Triad rose in the early twentieth century and by 1940, Hong Kong had 130 underground organizations with some of their leaders holding important positions in the society. During the period of the Japanese occupation of Hong Kong, the underground organizations, with support from the Japanese Army, established themselves firmly in crimes of drugs, prostitution, gambling, and blackmail. Triad organizations grew into formidable groups; some with more than 500 members. The mainland Chinese underground criminal groups that moved to Hong Kong after the liberation of the mainland in 1949 further accelerated the development of Hong Kong Triad organizations. For instance, the Hong-Yee Association of Red Geet, formerly in Guangzhou moved away to Hong Kong, changing its name to "14k." In a short time of several years, it became the largest gang among Hong Kong underground societies, with thousands of members.

Although a working group was established by the Hong Kong Police Bureau to keep watch and combat organized criminal activities, it could not succeed in its endeavors. By the 1980s it was estimated that there were more than 40 large criminal organizations, and membership of criminal organizations had reached a staggering figure of 300,000. Today, around 50 Triad societies are believed to exist in Hong Kong, and only 15 have come to police attention. The San-Yee-On, which is thought to be the largest Triad society in Hong Kong, is estimated to have over 47,000 members. These Triad organizations are engaged in the crimes of drugs, blackmail, extortion, loansharking, gambling, prostitution and penetration of lawful businesses. Their criminal activities have expanded to the United States, United Kingdom, France, Holland, and Australia and they are committing transnational crimes of different types. Powerful organizations like 14k, San-Yee-On and He-Sheng-He, operating from Hong Kong, have firmly established their criminal activities around the globe, challenging the Italian Mafia, Colombian cartels, and Nigerian gangs.

Underground criminal organizations also have a long history of development in Macau. The rapid development of underground societies became prominent in the 1980s following the economic takeoff of Macau. Today, there are over 20 underground organizations with 14k, Shui-Fang, You-Lian, San-Yee-On amongst them, controlling most of the organized criminal activities in Macau. They have close connections with the Triads in Hong Kong, and it is understood that with the reversion of Hong Kong to China in 1997, these criminal organizations are spreading all across the vast region, from the Chinese mainland to Hong Kong, Macau, and Taiwan, controlling vast economic assets and enlarging their memberships.

Measures, Including Legislation, to Combat Organized Crime

After consolidating its powers in 1949, the government of the People's Republic of China dealt crushing blows to all the underground criminal organizations and their criminal activities. The process of the establishment of agrarian collectives and the strict suppression of counter-revolutionaries enabled the government to deal with organized criminal enterprises also. For instance, the Chinese government promulgated the Order Banning Opium and Drugs in February 1950, which led to the establishment of a committee for banning opium and drugs as an important part of controlling drug offenses. The work included strictly forbidding growing opium, forcing users to give up addictive drugs, and severely punishing the manufacture and sale of drugs. Within two years 1,223.5 tons of illegal drugs were seized, large numbers of opium dens were sealed, and thousands of opium offenders were severely punished. Some of the criminals involved in gang activities were also sentenced to death. In the southwest of China, plantations of opium covering 2,544,466 acres were destroyed. According to the statistics provided by three provinces with Shan Xi province included, the original estimate of 620,000 drug addicts dropped to 220,000 in the same year. In April 1952, the government issued "Instructions for Eliminating Drug Influence," arousing the masses to mop up drugs throughout China. As a result, 51,627 drug offenders were condemned and more than 169.5 tons of drugs were seized. Equipment and tools, which were used to manufacture and sell drugs, and weapons and ammunition covering drug crimes, were also confiscated. Furthermore, thousands of people were coerced to give up drug addiction. By 1956, China had eliminated drug crimes, becoming a virtually drug-free country. The entire success of the anti-drug struggle meant a complete collapse of criminal organizations engaged in drug trafficking. The organized crimes against which Chinese authorities were then fighting were, of course, more than drug crimes. As a result of the sweeping measures taken by the communist government, pornography, gambling, loan sharking, and smuggling were all drastically reduced. The struggle led to a signal victory and by the mid 1950s, the underground criminal organizations left by the old society were thoroughly destroyed. Years later, new criminal organizations and criminal gangs did emerge, but they were limited to a smaller scale with fewer members and did not pose a serious danger to public security.

Since 1980, the economic liberalization policies and loss of control by the communist regime has seen a reemergence of organized criminal activities. The Chinese authorities have focused on nationwide "crack down" programs against criminal groups, especially the underground groups. Efforts were made from a practical point of view, and outstanding results were achieved by launching special programs such as "Solve big cases, identify cohorts, track down fugitives, and punish criminals." Many criminal groups, especially the underground types, were broken up. A great number of cases involving organized crime were also solved.

In September 1993, in order to reinforce the battle against organized crime, the Ministry of Public Security decided to set up an anti-organized crime unit. At the same time, research on organized crime was enhanced and various discussion meetings were held. For instance, a regional meeting on group crimes for certain provinces, cities, and counties, and a similar meeting for the mid-southern regions were held to study the nature and characteristics of organized crime and the strategies to counter it. In May 1995, the Ministry of Public Security Bureau of Criminal Investigation initiated an "Organized Crime Theory-Study Group" for investigators, specialists, and theoreticians to promote the study of organized crime by uniting theory and actual practice and to enhance theoretical guidance on anti-organized crime work.

As a strategy against group crime, the Chinese government has attempted to prevent such crime by formulating a policy of "better early than late; better small than big; better offensive than defensive; better strict than lenient." In the battle against organized crime various levels of public security agencies have also attached importance to the enhancement of basic criminal investigative work. They have attempted to bring confidentiality to information gathering, use better investigative technology to greatly strengthen the work on information gathering, and use investigation through various channels. Importance has also been attached to reinforcing the surveillance of criminally active sites and gathering information from all directions and strata to find evidence against organized gangs. Technical investigative means and undercover operations have been employed to select an appropriate time to end the operation so that the whole lot could be caught in a dragnet.

Law has been seen as a powerful weapon in the battle against organized crime. The reorganization of the criminal laws has involved developing procedures for dealing with dangerous criminal activities. In some coastal cities and provinces local rules have been made to combat organized crime. For example, in 1989 the people's government of Shenzhen issued a "Notice on Banning Underground Societies and Underground-type Gang Organization." The first clause states that, "any underground society and underground-type gang organization are unlawful and must be banned from the day the notice is issued." The second clause stipulates that "underground societ[ies] or underground-type gang organizations and their members committing crimes such as affray, injury, extortion, forcing people to lend money, racketeering, stirring up trouble, and destroying public and personal property must be totally punished with severity according to law." Without stipulating the definition of organized crime, the rules have only enumerated the dangerous activities. Nevertheless, in judicial practice there has been a common understanding of the conception of underground organizations mentioned in the regulations. It has been generally held that the underground organization is not only a criminal organization that severely endangers the people's democratic dictatorship, harms the public security, and undermines the social public administrative order. It also has its own name, a rather closed organization, has relatively fixed places, areas and professions, and acts with feudal underground gang characteristics, reaction, and hooliganism. Such interpretations have strengthened the hands of the police authorities in dealing with organized gangs.

In 1993, the eighth conference of the Guangdong Standing Committee of the National People's Congress passed the "Issue for Punishing the Activities of Underground Criminal Organizations in Guangdong province." The second clause has clearly stipulated the concept of underground criminal organization, stating that the underground criminal organization mentioned in the issue is an illicit group that has a name, organized structure, group leader, and rules endangering social order in rather fixed areas, professions, and places. The regulation has also stipulated as unlawful various organized criminal activities such as fee-collection for safeguard, extortion, group gambling, kidnapping and selling women, manufacturing and selling drugs, and prostitution.

In Hong Kong, a different set of measures was taken by the then British colonial authorities. For example, legislation against unlawful societies has existed in one form or another since 1845. This legislation is found in Chapter 151 of the Laws of Hong Kong. Section 18 (3) of this Ordinance states, "Every society which uses any Triad ritual or which adopts or makes use of any Triad title or nomenclature shall be deemed to be a Triad society." Section 18 (2) states that "Every Triad society, whether or not such is a registered society or an exempted society and whether or not such society is a local society, shall be deemed to be an unlawful society." Sections 19-26 of the ordinance legislates penalties of up to 5 years' imprisonment and fines of up to $100,000 for various offences connected to a Triad society, such as "being an office bearer," "being a member," "claiming or professing membership," "attending a Triad meeting," or "inducing or inciting someone to join a Triad society."

On 20 October 1994, the governor of Hong Kong enacted the Organized and Serious Crimes Ordinance with the purpose of "creating new powers of investigation into organized crimes and certain other offences and into the proceeds of crime of certain offenders, providing for the confiscation of proceeds of crime; making provision in respect of the sentencing of certain offenders; creating an offence of assisting a person to retain proceeds of crime; and for ancillary and connected matters."

The Ordinance also gave a definition to the Triad Society in Hong Kong. "Triad society" includes any society which (a) uses any ritual commonly used by Triad societies, any ritual closely resembling any such ritual or any part of any such ritual or, (b) adopts or makes use of any Triad title or nomenclature. "Organized Crime" means a schedule 1 offense that (a) is connected with the activities of a particular Triad society; (b) is related to the activities of two or more persons associated together solely or partly for the purpose of committing two or more acts, each of which is a schedule 1 offense and involves substantial planning and organization; or (c) is committed by two or more persons, involves substantial planning and organization and involves the following:

1. loss of the life of any person, or a substantial risk of such a loss;
2. serious bodily or psychological harm to any person, or a substantial risk of such harm;
3. serious loss of liberty of any person.

Offenses listed in Schedule 1 include: Common Law offenses like murder, kidnapping, false imprisonment, and conspiracy to prevent the course of justice, and statutory offenses of smuggling, lending money at an excessive interest rate, drug trafficking, prostitution, forgery, theft, blackmail, and obtaining property by deception.

In 1978, Macau also enacted laws related to underground societies that especially focused on combating and punishing underground criminal organizations there. Clause 2 of this Ordinance states the definition of underground societies.

1. Any unlawful organization with stable structure and criminal purpose, which is known to commit one or more crimes in the following list through agreement or any other fact, is deemed to be an underground society:

   (1) drug trafficking;
   (2) theft, robbery, and breakdown of public property;

(3) false imprisonment;
(4) inducing prostitution of women and keeping a vice establishment;
(5) inveigling and corrupting juveniles;
(6) obtaining property by false protection or threats of violence;
(7) lending property unlawfully;
(8) abetting or helping unlawful immigrants and emigrants;
(9) managing an illicit lucky or mutual lottery;
(10) killing animals for mutual lottery;
(11) using, wearing, and keeping contraband weapons;
(12) speculating foreign exchange.

2. Any lawfully established organization that actually commits one or more of the crimes listed is deemed to be an underground society.

Section 2 of the article has further emphasized that an existing underground society does not have to:

1. have an address or appointed place for conference;
2. let the members know about each other and have meetings regularly;
3. have a headquarters or leader for exercising control and promoting members;
4. have a written agreement of its organization, activities, and distribution of interest and burden.

Article 3 of the Ordinance has also stipulated in explicit terms that 14k, He-On-Le, He-Siu-Yee, and You-Lian are underground criminal organizations.

Article 4 of the Ordinance has legislated penalties of two to eight years of imprisonment for any person belonging to an underground criminal organization and for any leader or director, a minimum sentence of five to eight years of imprisonment. The New Criminal Law of Macau has changed the aforementioned periods to three to ten years and five to twelve years, respectively, after promulgation of the ordinance. The rules have also stipulated that any person who is attempting to support or help the activities of underground societies and their members will be sentenced to two to eight years of imprisonment. The ordinance has prescribed penalties for the main criminal activities of prostitution, injury, using and carrying weapons, blackmail, and demanding the payment of debts unlawfully committed by underground criminal organizations.

Since the reform and open-door policy, China has further promulgated a series of significant criminal laws. These include "Severe Punishment for Criminal Elements Who Have Seriously Damaged Law and Order;" "Additional Regulations on the Punishment for Smuggling;" the "Decision to Ban Drugs;" the "Punishment for Criminal Elements for Smuggling, Manufacturing, Selling and Distributing Pornographic Products;" "Additional Regulations on the Punishment for Stealing Cultural Relics and Robbing Ancient Tombs;" the "Decision to Ban Prostitution;" "Severe Punishment for Criminal Elements Who Abduct and Trade Human Beings and Who Kidnap Women and Children;" "Additional Regulations on the Severe Punishment for Organizing and Transporting People Across the National Border;" and the "Decision on the Punishment for Sabotaging the Financial Order." These are all legal weapons to support the battle against organized crime in the country.

Further, to prevent and curb organized crime China has also promulgated new laws and executive rules, such as the "Gun Control Law," "Law on Forcibly Restraining the Taking of Drugs," "Regulations on the Use of Weapons and Police Equipment by the People's Police," and "Regulations on Border Inspections." The "Gun Control Law" clearly stipulates that guns are strictly controlled by the state and that criminal violations of it will be severely punished. Over twenty illegal behaviors have been identified as violations and severe punishment has been set forth for these behaviors. For instance, the death penalty has been prescribed as the maximum punishment for manufacturing, trading, or transporting guns without authorization; for an authorized enterprise to disobey regulations on manufacturing and distributing guns; for manufacturing guns without a serial number, or with identical numbers or false numbers; for a manufacturer to sell guns directly; or to sell guns intended for export for domestic use. Illegal possession of guns has been made into a violation, carrying a sentence of not more than two years of imprisonment even if there is no other crime. The maximum sentence for illegally carrying a gun across the national border could even be the death penalty. The maximum punishment for transporting guns without following regulations has also been prescribed to be a life sentence. For loss of guns by a government agency or an employee when the gun was officially issued and was for official use, the immediate supervisor or the person directly responsible may be sentenced to imprisonment for no more than five years. The aforementioned regulations have been intended to play an extremely important role in stopping organized crime from becoming armed and especially from committing violent crimes.

In fighting organized crime, the Chinese government has also taken measures to step up international cooperation. China has participated in international treaties such as the International Drug Treaty, joined Interpol, and has worked in concert with other countries in the battle against organized crime. China has also signed judicial-assistance treaties with many countries and has taken part in bilateral or multilateral cooperation in certain international programs. For instance, China, Burma, and the United Nations signed an anti-drug collaboration program and set up a plan to meet on a regular basis. Recently, China signed a joint anti-drug program with Vietnam and Laos. All have been designed to take the anti-drug cooperation program a step further.

Comparative Evaluation of the Methods for Combating Organized Crime and Proposed Measures

As previously described, Chinese organized crime has gained a new life after the reform and open-door policy initiated in the late 1970s. The penetration of the Triads from Hong Kong and their growth in the coastal regions of mainland China are indicators that the threat is growing rapidly. As of now the battle against organized crime has not yet reached a sophisticated level and several elements are lacking, including the following:

1. There is insufficient understanding of the nature, characteristics, and development of organized crime. The overall strategy against organized crime needs to be further improved.

2. Criminal law pertaining to organized crime needs to be perfected. There is no strict provision in the criminal law for dealing with underground criminal organizations, nor is there any stipulation for punishment. Some newly identified crimes such as money laundering have not been listed as violations that warrant investigation. In criminal litigation, the legislative body has not given sufficient consideration to legalizing special investigative techniques, emergency handling methods, and witness-protection procedures. There is an obvious need to further strengthen the monitoring mechanisms and prosecution procedures.

3. Supervisory and specialized anti-organized crime agencies need to be amplified. A national authoritative supervisory unit and a strong and effective command system are lacking. Local agencies that are specifically charged with anti-organized crime responsibilities lack resources and training. A strong and highly trained contingent to fight organized crime has yet to be formed.

4. Problems in training special personnel for the fight against organized crime and problems in updating technology and equipment have also not been solved. Lacking modern means and management methods,

intelligence-gathering mechanisms are weak. A data bank and information network to comprehensively control both domestic and foreign information and material regarding organized crime has yet to be established.

5. Having just begun to participate in international collaboration, the scope of collaborative work is rather narrow, and there are only a few collaborative programs. It is urgent that broader, more effective, multifaceted, and multiple-layered international collaborative programs be established that cover the areas of economics, law, training, technical support, information, and joint operations.

6. An interprovincial and interdepartmental coordination mechanism to pool efforts in the battle against organized crime is an urgent need that has yet to be established. The need to step up propaganda to educate the people about the importance of cooperation with the authorities in combating organized crime requires highest priority.

7. The industries' reaction to organized crime is still a very weak area in China in which much work still needs to be done. A sense of responsibility toward society needs to be strengthened. There is the need to reverse the notion that money is everything. Work ethics and business standards need to be enhanced and corruption curbed. The internal mechanism of corporations needs to be perfected to build up resistance to this disease and to decrease the corporations' vulnerability to the effects of crime. The requirements to heighten employee vigilance and awareness are important preventive measures against crime. Some of these efforts have yet to be tackled, and some have been started but are not doing well. Basically, the most important work is, of course, to continuously strengthen economic reforms to establish a socialist market economy. The triumphant completion of this endeavor will lay a strong foundation for the country to effectively prevent and contain organized crime in its economic domain.

The aforementioned elements are the weak points in the battle against organized crime and areas which need improvement, but there are also areas of strength and success. For instance, the already formulated and complete set of powerful policies, preventive measures, and guidelines to effectively contain the infiltration of underground societies from outside China has made it impossible for them to take root and spread their tentacles in China. This is something many countries, including the developed nations, have not been able to accomplish. Many years of experience in banning drugs by stipulating a three-prong policy to prohibit the selling, cultivation, and use of drugs have achieved excellent results in intercepting and blocking the inflow of drugs. These measures need to be strengthened by strictly implementing the laws and treating the problem by looking into both the root causes and the symptoms.

Conclusion

Chinese authorities have been reluctant to acknowledge criminal activities in their society. At present scholars have not blamed the economic reforms for the rampant increase in crime, especially organized crimes (Yu, 1993). However, most authors are beginning to recognize materialism and commercialism as major promoters of greed, conflicts, and crime in Chinese society (Yu, 1995). The rapid social changes, emergence of new values, foreign influences, increased mobility, and weakened community control are transforming Chinese society as never before. The economic boom has also attracted organized crime syndicates that had been kept away by the earlier communist regime. This economic development has also brought in increased inequality, and Dai (1996) has suggested that disparities of China's income distribution has become near or even greater than that of the United States. Zang and Zang (1996) have suggested that many low-income workers may be forced to commit crime in order to survive, as seen by the alarming increase in property crimes. All these factors are likely to promote the infiltration of organized crime into Chinese society.

While taking strong measures against organized crime, China needs to attach importance to preventive measures, as well. An important element in the fight against organized crime is the requirement to work with the people. The authorities have to rely on the people and mobilize them to join the battle against organized crime. This alone can encourage the people to take initiatives in reporting situations to the government in a timely manner and positively assisting and supporting government efforts to counter and prevent organized crime. The Chinese government has launched several schemes to promote morality in family and occupation as well as emphasizing social ethics as preventive measures against the rising tide of crime in the country (Shuliang, 1996). However, in a society where people's participation is not democratically structured and the communist party still controls most levers of decision making, the task of involving the people is difficult.

China is also handicapped by the lack of legal provisions in its administrative structures. For almost a generation the country was governed by the principles of communist ideology, and then, in a sudden turnabout, the nation has opened up. Lack of proper regulations and controls over economic activities have facilitated the entry and spread of organized syndicates in the country. There is still no special legal provision that focuses on punishing organized crime in the criminal law of the People's Republic and no clause defining organized crime. In judicial practice, the disposition of organized crime is according to stipulations concerning the criminal group and its accomplices. Similarly, in the general principles of the criminal law, conviction and penal discretion are based on the clauses in the special provisions of the law. These local statutes are incomplete in dealing with the different forms of organized crime. The problem is complicated by the fact that in the Chinese regions of Hong Kong, Macau, and Taiwan, the stipulations of organized crime in criminal law are quite different. For instance, there's no special stipulation on underground organization and organized crime in the criminal law of Taiwan. Thus, the need to analyze organized crime by scientific principles is an important task before Chinese criminal law scholars who are now doing research work on this subject.

At present, Chinese underground-type criminal groups, including the extremely dangerous ones, are not very strong either politically or economically, and their scope of influence is rather small. So far, there is little evidence of any county- or citywide or transprovincial underground organizations, not to mention any nationwide criminal organizations. That we do not have any now does not mean that there will not be any in the future. As long as the environment that creates organized crime exists, there is always the possibility for criminal groups to transform themselves into highly developed underground criminal organizations. Under certain circumstances it is almost inevitable. In view of the present situation in China, there is cause to worry about how organized crime may develop. The continued development and growth of organized crime is apparent, although the extent of this development depends on numerous variables that make it hard to predict its future growth.

REFERENCES

Dai, Yishen. 1996. "Haves vs Have Nots: One of the Factors Causing Crime in China." Paper presented at the International Symposium on Crime Control and Public Participation. Dalian, China.

Shuliang, Feng. 1996. "Confucian Moral against Crime: Crime and Moral Prevention." Paper presented at the Annual Meeting of the American Society of Criminologists. Chicago, 22 November.

Yu, Lie. (ed.). 1993. *The Study of Crime Problem in Modern China*. Beijing: Chinese Public Security University Press.

Yu, Olivia. 1995. "Crime in Modern China and Its Approach to Research and Control." Paper presented at the Annual Meeting of the American Society of Criminologists. Boston, 16 November.

Zang, Jian and Zang, Panshi. 1996. "The Crime Problem, Causes and Control Strategies in the Early Period of Social Transformation in China." Paper presented at the International Symposium on Crime Control and Public Participation. Dalian, China.

Caribbean Sea
North Atlantic Ocean
South Pacific Ocean
South Atlantic Ocean
HONDURAS
NICARAGUA
Managua
San José
COSTA RICA
Panama
PANAMA
Isla de San Andrés (COLOMBIA)
Aruba (NETH.)
Netherlands Antilles (NETH.)
Martinique (FRANCE)
ST. LUCIA
BARBADOS
ST. VINCENT AND THE GRENADINES
GRENADA
Port-of-Spain
TRINIDAD AND TOBAGO
Barranquilla
Cartagena
Maracaibo
Caracas
Barquisimeto
Valencia
San Cristóbal
Cúcuta
Ciudad Guayana
VENEZUELA
Georgetown
Paramaribo
Cayenne
GUYANA
SURINAME
French Guiana (FRANCE)
Medellín
Bogota
Cali
COLOMBIA
Isla de Malpelo (COLOMBIA)
Boa Vista
Macapá
Equator
Quito
ECUADOR
Guayaquil
Iquitos
Amazon
Manaus
Santarém
Belém
São Luís
Fortaleza
Teresina
Natal
Recife
Maceió
Piura
Trujillo
Huánuco
Rio Branco
Pôrto Velho
PERU
Lima
Cusco
BRAZIL
Trinidad
La Paz
BOLIVIA
Cochabamba
Santa Cruz
Sucre
Potosí
Arequipa
Arica
Cuiabá
Brasília
Goiânia
Salvador
Uberlândia
Belo Horizonte
Vitória
Campo Grande
Iquique
Antofagasta
Tropic of Capricorn
PARAGUAY
Asunción
Rio de Janeiro
São Paulo
Santos
Curitiba
Salta
San Miguel de Tucumán
Resistencia
Florianópolis
Isla San Félix (CHILE)
Isla San Ambrosio (CHILE)
CHILE
Córdoba
Santa Fe
Pôrto Alegre
Salto
URUGUAY
Rosario
Mendoza
Valparaíso
Santiago
ARCHIPIÉLAGO JUAN FERNÁNDEZ (CHILE)
Buenos Aires
La Plata
Montevideo
Concepción
ARGENTINA
Bahía Blanca
Mar del Plata
Puerto Montt
San Carlos de Bariloche
Comodoro Rivadavia
Scale 1:35,000,000
Azimuthal Equal-Area Projection
500 Kilometers
500 Miles
Boundary representation is not necessarily authoritative.
Strait of Magellan
Río Gallegos
Punta Arenas
Ushuaia
Stanley
Falkland Islands (Islas Malvinas) (administered by U.K., claimed by ARGENTINA)
South Georgia and the South Sandwich Islands (administered by U.K., claimed by ARGENTINA)

PART 4

PERSPECTIVES FROM SOUTH AMERICA

South America is the fourth largest continent in land area, bordered by the Caribbean Sea to the north, Atlantic Ocean to the east, and Pacific Ocean to the west. Drake Passage, south of Cape Horn, separates South America from Antarctica. The continent is joined to North America by the Isthmus of Panama, which forms a narrow land bridge to the countries of Central America. The present-day population of South America are descendants from four main groups: American Indians, Spanish and Portuguese Iberians, Africans, and European immigrants. The American Indians (Amerindians) were the inhabitants before Christopher Columbus. Iberians were the Spanish and Portuguese who conquered and dominated the continent until the early the nineteenth century. Africans were imported to the continent as slaves by the colonizers. Once the countries gained independence from colonial powers, many immigrants from overseas settled in South America, the largest groups coming from Italy and Germany.

The thirteen countries of South America lack the incredible diversity of cultures found in Europe and Asia, but they have formed several unique cultures derived from a blend of the four main population groups that inhabit the continent. This section includes detailed discussion of two countries from South America. Colombia has received the bulk of attention around the world due to its central role in growing and processing cocaine, and its continuing problems of large, well-armed criminal groups that have intimidated and in some cases controlled the government infrastructure of that country. Significant progress has been made in recent years in reducing the control of these criminal groups, but the country's strategic location, terrain, and climate make it a country to watch in its role in cocaine production and distribution.

Many countries in South America have documented problems with organized crime, and they differ only in the nature of the opportunities they present for organized crime groups. For example, Venezuelan groups have been linked to money laundering and to Russian organized crime figures (Webster and Cilluffo, 1998). In Peru and Colombia, drug money has been associated with funding of political campaigns, both for the government and for insurgents (Reuter and Petrie, 1999). Uruguay has requested a United Nations Conference on the illicit trade in light weapons (United Nations, 1999). A congressional commission in Brazil recommended that more than 800 persons, including a number of public officials, be charged with drug trafficking and money laundering in routes connecting Brazil to Bolivia, Colombia, and Paraguay (Associated Press, 2000). These examples provide an indication of the organized crime problems that exist in South America. More analyses of organized crime within countries, their connections to bordering countries, and illicit product flow routes within and outside nations will provide greater understanding of the changing nature of organized crime.

REFERENCES

Associated Press. 2000. "Brazilian Committee Accuses More than 800 with Involvement in Organized Crime. CNN.com, December 5. http://www.cnn.com/2000/WORLD/americas/12/05/brazil.organizedcrime.ap/

Reuter, Peter and Petrie, Carol. 1999. *Transnational Organized Crime: Summary of a Workshop*. National Research Council: National Academy Press. http://books.nap.edu/books/0309065755/html/index.html

United Nations. 1999. Statements Delivered during the General Debate in Plenary of General Assembly, New York. http://www.undcp.org/newyork/debate.html

Webster, William H. and Cilluffo, Frank J. 1998. *Russian Organized Crime*. Center for Strategic and International Studies Global Organized Crime Project. http://www.csis.org/goc/taskruss.html

CHAPTER 13

ORGANIZED CRIME: A PERSPECTIVE FROM COLOMBIA

Leonardo Jesus Ramirez Rivera, Jorge Cesar Quadro, and Roger Juan Marcelo Tomas Botto

INTRODUCTION

Colombia is sandwiched between Panama and Venezuela, and borders the North Pacific Ocean between Ecuador and Panama. With a land area of 649,188 square miles, the country is slightly less than three times the size of Montana. The nation is rich in petroleum, natural gas, coal, and iron ore and has large tracts of forest and woodland forming almost 49 percent of its land mass. Its population of 37 million is ethnically mixed, with Mestizo (58%) and White (20%) forming the majority groups. The country is largely Roman Catholic (95%) and Spanish is the common language. Colombia has a Republican form of government in which the executive branch dominates the government structure. The country has been divided into 32 administrative divisions and the legal system is based on Spanish law with universal and compulsory suffrage. A new criminal code modeled after U.S. procedures was enacted in 1992 and 1993.

In the judicial branch, the Supreme Court of Justice (*Corte Suprema de Justicia*) is the highest court of criminal law in which judges are selected from the nominees of the Higher Council of Justice for eight-year terms. The Constitutional Court guards integrity and supremacy of the constitution and emphasizes rule on constitutionality of laws.

Three insurgent groups are active in Colombia: Revolutionary Armed Forces of Colombia (FARC), National Liberation Army (ELN), and dissidents of the recently demobilized People's Liberation Army (EPL/D). These groups are now, reportedly, actively involved with drug trafficking operations also. Boasting a diversified and stable economy, Colombia has enjoyed Latin America's most consistent record of growth over the last several decades. Gross domestic product (GDP) has expanded every year for more than 25 years, and unlike many other South American countries, Colombia did not default on any of its official debts during the 1980s. Since 1990, when Bogota introduced a comprehensive reform program that opened the economy to foreign trade and investment, GDP growth has averaged more than 4 percent annually. Growth has been fueled in recent years by the expansion of the construction and financial service industries and an influx of foreign capital. Some foreign investors have been deterred by an inadequate energy and transportation infrastructure and the violence stemming from drug trafficking and persistent rural guerrilla warfare, but direct foreign investment, especially in the oil industry, is still rising at a rapid rate. Although oil consequently is overtaking coffee as the main legal export, earnings from illicit drugs probably exceed those from any other export. Business confidence also has been damaged by a political crisis stemming from allegations that senior government officials, including President Samper, solicited contributions from drug traffickers during the 1994 election campaign.

The Nature and Extent of Organized Crime

Colombia is known throughout the world for its illicit drug industry and is one of the largest producers of coca, opium poppies, and cannabis. About 50,900 hectares of coca was reportedly under cultivation in 1995, making it the world's largest processor of coca derivatives into cocaine. Colombia remains a significant supplier of cocaine to the United States and other international drug markets. At present, the active aerial eradication program seeks to eliminate coca and opium crops.

The improper use of narcotics produced by organized cartels in Colombia continues to cause tremendous damage to the addicts, their families, and the well-being of the world. The production and illegal trafficking also harm the economic development of the country and contribute to the spread of delinquency, violence, and corruption. The organized delinquency in Colombia is increasing, which poses additional dangers to the international community as well. The large multinational businesses of organized crime are actually a transitional network of branches in all the countries of the world. Their operations are extending constantly, becoming more sophisticated, resembling more legitimate multinational companies and earning more than a billion dollars annually. A study of organized crime by the Center of Investigations of Venezuela and the Mexican National University concludes that worldwide trafficking operates billions of dollars worth of business. The Intelligence Committee of the Drug Commission of the United States stated that 40 percent of the circulation of that amount was in the United States. It is also feared that with such a large amount of money and economic power, these organizations could even purchase nuclear weapons and threaten the world. It is no secret that Colombian and other drug cartels support terrorist groups and are also involved in arms smuggling. The cartels in some cases have even gained access to political levers of the state, although they prefer to work without getting involved in governance. Most organized groups prefer to work in the shadows and by means of figureheads. Infiltration and bribes are other means to obtain the benefits accruing from the political power. In Colombia, it is now not surprising to see judicial errors being made or executive measures being taken that openly benefit the organizations involved in drug trafficking.

Colombia has seen increasing problems accruing from organized crime that began in 1970 and continue today. The large scale of its drug-trafficking activities and the immense fallout on its people has also made it an important international concern. In no other country has this phenomenon become such a serious threat to the stability of democracy and the safety and rights of the people. At first, these were minor repercussions and organized crime did not appear to pose a major threat to the democratic institutions of the country. However, in a short span it has grown to an extreme point where it has entered into a complete war against the state, threatening its very existence. It is important to clarify that the objective of this study is not to make a strategic examination of Colombia, but instead to utilize this case as a model of study. We wish to show in a very synthesized manner the path that should be taken in an attempt to increase the degree of effectiveness in the fight against drug trafficking.

In the fight against drug trafficking it is fundamental to obtain political support. Without such support all efforts are useless. The main problem today is the failure of the law, which threatens the safety and integrity of the nations and the regions. If this seems exaggerated, think of the situation in Colombia a short time ago: There were open announcements about economic support to the political campaign of the current President by drug traffickers, which displayed their infiltration to the very top of the government hierarchy. Drug trafficking weakens governments by means of the corruption of the civil servants, intimidation of the people, and through economic destabilization. The irregular flow and circulation of a huge volume of drug money produces a destabilizing effect on the monetary system and the supply of foreign currency. In diverse regions of the world, drug trafficking groups also organize terrorist activities. During the cold war and even now, some governments avail themselves of the drug-trafficking routes to undermine opponents. Thus, drug trafficking ends up destroying societies all along the route from the producers to the consumers.

As already shown by the United Nations, the only way to end this problem is to eliminate the demand. However, the Colombian example suggests that this cannot be achieved by the prosecution of a drug addict or by infinite plans of preventive assistance, which the country has put into practice every year. It has also been difficult to pour massive resources into anti-drug campaigns or to support the development of social communications that could properly educate the people about the hidden dangers of drugs. It appears that policies which could convince the farmers growing drug plants to search for other alternatives to support their family are not even feasible in the context of Colombia.

The drug traffickers have usually managed to penetrate the economy with the assistance or connivance of some politicians. Sometimes, the cartels also invested in or even controlled a political party, such as in the case of the *Novimiento Civico Nacional* (National Civil Movement) in Colombia. Additionally, the drug barons corrupted the security forces and sometimes used it to pursue their opponents or rival groups. Finally, they attempted to influence the elite cultural circles (or circuits) with the purpose of spreading the drug culture in the society. Quite obviously, the drug cartels of Colombia have become very powerful and resourceful.

The attempt to combat them only through the police forces appears to have wasted these resources and submitted some of the police to the temptation to collaborate with the drug traffickers. By its nature and extension, drug trafficking has introduced a real conflict in the society. There is a conflict of interest between those who want to remove drugs from their borders and those who want to legalize them. This conflict, as with many others, has cultural characteristics that have been spread and popularized by the mass media. There has been a hidden economic aspect that is also equally important. Moreover, drug issues have involved a conflict between those people who desire the existence of moral laws and those who want a society empty of ethical content.

There are opposing positions among the countries of the world, some of which are principally producers and others that are centers of consumption. The former believe the most serious focus should be to end the demand. The latter believe the main effort should be to end production and eradicate the cultivation. Furthermore, it is a difficult situation, since the stage of drug trafficking is the entire world and profoundly affects the American continent. The main producers in the world are the countries on this continent: production of coca in Peru and Bolivia, poppies in Mexico, and cocaine in Colombia, while the central consumer is the United States.

The nature and extent of the drug-trafficking phenomenon has had a series of manifestations in Colombia since its first appearance. It began as a local conflict of a sociocultural nature; later it evolved to become a problem of worldwide consequence, affecting economics, society, politics, and the military. Its first target market was the United States and later, Europe, Japan, and the former Soviet Republics.

Drug trafficking in Colombia has had four large stages of action: marijuana, cocaine, poppy, and the drug trafficker's alliance with the rebel guerrillas fighting to overthrow the state. The cultivation of marijuana began in the 1970s and was the first narcotic activity for many Colombians associated with foreigners, especially Americans. At present, this problem is fairly well-controlled and only approximately 5,500 cultivated hectares remain. This phenomenon was practically replaced by cocaine, and those who continue to use the drug do so on an individual basis.

Colombia is the leading producer of cocaine and Colombian drug traffickers, the biggest traders of this alkaloid, covering most of the North American and European markets. The coca plant has historical ties to some of the cultures of the indigenous tribes who used the leaf for personal consumption. It was called *manbeo* and had no commercial value or intent. Since 1980, cultivated coca has been detected in non-indigenous areas and the purpose was to obtain the coca base and chlorohydrate of coca. Its cultivation has diminished as a result of the actions by the authorities, but there are an estimated 50,000 hectares still under plantation at the present time. It is important to note that a large part of the cocaine production is also supplied from prime materials from Peru and Bolivia.

Even with the actions taken by the government there is evidence of an alliance between the Colombian drug cartels and the Sicilian Mafia, by means of their descendants settled in Venezuela. The contacts for shipments to Italy and money laundering are done in in Venezuela, and they are largely responsible for supplying the drugs around the world. The appearance of processing labs for cocaine and heroin in Africa indicates other connections between Colombian drug traffickers and the Nigerian Mafia.

The first cultivation of poppy was detected in the 1980s, to which the authorities paid little attention because they were focused on the cocaine problem. At the beginning, the cultivated areas were in mountainous areas with altitudes between 2,000 and 3,000 meters. The plantations were from 3 to 30 hectares in areas where the government authority was sparse. Now, there are an estimated 14,000 to 18,000 hectares of cultivated poppies and their areas are growing as the demand and profits from heroin increase.

This is according to observations of the countryside, aerial detection, and information from police intelligence.

The production and business of heroin is an activity exclusively of the organizations of international character with good financial and distribution infrastructure. Despite the worldwide disrepute, several big Colombian organizations have actually diminished the shipment of large quantities of heroin due to the following reasons:

a. Heroin causes greater distribution and sales problems;
b. Its yield is good but very delayed; the situation generates inconveniences and affects commercial confidence;
c. Colombian heroin has not had the same reception as its cocaine;
d. The Asian competition is rather strong, due to their experience in this business;
e. Not all the heroin leaving Colombia is of good quality, which generates distrust in the market;
f. Not much is being produced in Colombia because the market is not well enough known for the larger Colombian organizations to be interested in participating.

In recent years the drug trafficking alliance with guerrilla organizations has also added to the problems. It is general knowledge that an alliance formed between the drug traffickers and the subversive groups, especially in the regions of the West Plains, was motivated by the need for protection of the laboratories and supplies by one side and by the rebels' need for financial support and supplies of weapons. It has appropriately been called Narcoguerrilla (drug guerrillas) (Quadro and Botto, 1995). Groups like these have taken over zones of the country by means of weapons, where political ideology was submerged for economic reasons and rebels did not hesitate to commit crimes of profit (Brooke, 1995). When the drug traffickers realized that they were being challenged and controlled by the authorities, they went to less accessible places, which coincided with the areas occupied by subversive activists.

At first, the agreement was that the guerrillas would provide the protection and the drug traffickers, the means and instruments. Later, the guerrillas opted to earn more money by using the skills they learned in order to aid the costs of their guerrilla movement. The guerrillas became more and more demanding until the agreement was broken. The two groups now fight between themselves, which adds insecurity to rural areas that already exists in urban areas.

Measures, Including Legislation to Combat Organized Crime

Colombia has experimented with different measures and laws to attempt to minimize the drug trafficking problem (Ramirez, 1996). Among the national governmental measures based on the Constitution, Decree number 1038 (1984), was very important. This provides the executive powers to the government to declare a state of siege nationwide if public order is disturbed. However, the government felt obligated to dictate exceptions, since drug trafficking became more dangerous and threatened the society, as well as endangering the institutional stability of the country. The steps taken were not sufficient to stop the harmful effects of drug trafficking and more measures were needed.

In response to the demands for more executive power, the legislative body introduced Decree number 1856 (1989), that provided for the "seizure and occupation of drug trafficking related properties." The norm was to seize and occupy all properties related directly or indirectly to drug trafficking. Decree 2390 (1989), in addition, extended the scope by providing for the seizure of property acquired through illegal enrichment. This is stated in Article 6 as: "Whoever lends his name in order to acquire goods with money coming from the drug trafficking crime will be summarily dealt with." These measures were intended against the so called figureheads who operated from behind the scenes.

Decree 1856, modified by Legislative Decree 2390, and which was also modified by Decree 42 on 3 January 1990, provided for the seizure of goods and all kinds of property directly or indirectly involved at the time of the drug-trafficking crimes and connected or resulting from them. The courts were also empowered to grant permission to administer and control the property to the government agents while observing civil rights of protection and maintenance of personal property. These measures were introduced, keeping in mind that the national economy had deteriorated as a consequence of drug trafficking. The government proposed the creation of *Consejo National de Estupefacientes* (National Council of Narcotics), an organization to provisionally designate the administrators, people, or entities who will be in charge of the seized elements (Quadro, 1996).

Several other measures taken include Decree number 494 of 27 February 1990, "Creation of the National Management of Narcotics," created as a special administrative unit under the minister of justice. Its main objective was to determine and execute the required administrative procedures for the following purposes:

1. Coordinate the development and execution of the national government's policies for the control, prevention, and repression of narcotics;
2. Process and maintain inventory of the seized goods for their direct or indirect use as evidence in drug-trafficking crimes;
3. Strengthen the process of seizing goods to ensure that drug traffickers do not get them back through threat or intimidation;
4. Complete necessary procedures so that the provisional storage of seized goods is effective;
5. Supervise the use of goods by the storage facilities;
6. Collaborate with judicial authorities in the disposal of these goods;
7. By means of power granted by the justice ministry, take part in the defense of the nation's interests.
8. Coordinate the functioning of the committee and technical advisers with narcotics officials located in the national territory.

Legislative Decree number 1857, "Rebellion and Sedition," replaces Article 125 of the Penal Code, which refers to the charge of rebellion. It also changes the maximum punishment from three to six years in prison and a minimum fine of $50 to $100 thousand dollars. It also replaces Article 126, which refers to sedition, which had a penalty of six months to four years and changes it from two to eight years in prison and a fine of $50 to $100 thousand dollars.

Legislative Decree number 1858, "Armed Proselytism," strengthens executive measures to maintain peace during elections. Armed groups and drug-trafficking organizations attempt to create instability during these times, so the government decided to take measures to punish them and to maintain peace. Article 1 states: "While public order is disturbed and there is a state of siege in the country, anyone using force or threats in an electoral campaign to obtain support or votes will receive 6 to 10 years in prison and a minimum fine of $10,000 to $50,000 monthly."

Legislative Decree 1859 (1989), is concerned with "retention and isolation by the judicial police." To combat criminal activities it was necessary to adequately equip the justice system and the investigative agencies. When Article 339 of the Penal Code Procedures [Decree Law 050, (1987)], was seen to provide insufficient authority, the national government executed Article 121 of the Magna Carta to achieve quick and sufficient administration of justice.

Legislative Decree number 1860 (1989), seeks to work with other nations in pursuing the traffickers. "Executive extradition for drug trafficking and related crimes," allows for Colombians to be extradited even if a public treaty does not exist in the requesting country, a measure that was earlier prohibited by law. The remainder of the decree reads: "The extradition will be requested, granted or offered in agreement with public treaties and if these are missing the requesting government will offer or grant the extradition in agreement with procedures established in the penal code." However, the measure has been limited to drug-trafficking offenses only and the decree adds, "In no case will Colombia offer the extradition of nationals, nor grant to indict nationals for political crimes." Nevertheless, the decree of extradition is not actually applicable since the Constitution of 1991 prohibits the extradition of native Colombians.

Legislative Decree number 678 and 858 (1990), was an administrative measure used to militarize the Antiochian townships of Envigado, Bello, and La Estrella for security purposes. Legislative Decree number 1861 (1989), is an attempt to strengthen the law. "Modifications of Penal Code," provides for judges to move throughout the country. It also authorizes the technical personnel of the judicial police to become more effective. Thus, the director can suspend an initial investigation after 180 days if the identity of a culprit has not been established. However, the case can be reopened if the identity is discovered later on. If the delinquent is outside Colombia, it further permits the judge to travel to other countries to guarantee evidence. If anyone challenges the violation of provisional liberty, the judge has been empowered to decide about such requests within three days.

Legislative Decree number 1863 (1989), is concerned with seized properties and provides for the "inspection of immovables by penal military judges." Article 1 authorizes the penal military judges to inspect sites presumed to contain evidence of illegal activities.

Legislative Decree number 1895 (1989), provides for punishment for the "illegal enrichment of individuals." It establishes prison penalties of five to ten years and there is an additional fine equal to the capital gained through the illicit activities.

Legislative Decree number 1896 (1989), provides for "control of runways." The government sanctioned the Department of Administration of Civil Aeronautics to disable unauthorized runways. This also includes authorized runways not used by the governors, managers, or commissioners of the region. The legislation also stipulated that the distributors of airplane fuel must present monthly reports of their sales on the fifteenth day of each month. It also established that the defense minister by means of the Colombian Air Force perfect the air-control systems using tridimensional radar equipment.

To combat the serious drug-trafficking problems, the governmental administration, through the National Council on Narcotics, also designed a national plan whose objective is to confront and reduce systematically the causes and manifestations of the problem. The following ten policies are aimed at reducing the problem:

1. Eradication of cultivation: Fourteen percent of the hectares seeded for drug production in the world are estimated to be located in Colombia. Between 1993 and 1994 the number of seeded hectares has been decreased to around 13 percent by destroying the fields. After the launch of "Operation Brilliance," it was estimated that within two years the illegal crops would be nonexistent. For 1994 the goal was to bring the cultivated area down to 44,000 hectares. The government promised to adopt special caution to avoid social impact of such a policy and not to produce any ecological damage. The fumigation does not cause ecological harm; rather it is the drug growers who clear forested areas to grow illegal drugs. For each hectare of illicit drug cultivation, they destroy 2.5 hectares of forest, approximately 180,000 hectares per year. The United Nations estimates that by the year 2000 Colombia will have lost one third of its tropical rain forests.

2. Alternative development plan: After destroying the illegal crops there is the need to find a legal way to assist the 300,000 small illegal crop growers to find alternative employment and earn their livelihood. There is also the need to improve conditions for their health, education, and work.

3. Industrial production of drugs: The plan envisages striking at the heart of the problem—the Colombian cartels. By means of radar and other technological devices the government agencies plan to prevent the extraction of coca pulp that forms the main ingredient in cocaine production.

4. Distributions: The destruction of the distribution systems of the drugs through different network organizations is a major scheme of the government. This is being done by improving the technical operations of the airports, maritime operations, and seaports. It is proposed to establish a coast guard base on San Andrés Island to control ocean and air traffic entering and leaving the archipelago. Further, it is planned to improve the system of airplane interception by means of sensors, aerial platforms, and other electronic intelligence-gathering equipment.

5. Money laundering: Drug trafficking is estimated to earn $500 billion per year, which is ten times the GNP of Colombia. Most of these funds are siphoned away from the country and laundered in the world's financial markets. Almost 75 percent of this money remains in the international financial centers and recycled into businesses invested with these funds. The government is working with the office of fiscal institu-

tions and superintendents of the stocks and banking sectors. The corresponding legal changes have already been made to curb money laundering by drug traffickers.

6. <u>Threat of consumption</u>: Additionally, there is a risk of Colombia becoming a leading consumer of drugs, with the availability of inexpensive drugs and traffickers concentrating on the domestic market as well. The government actions focus on the prevention of consumption, rehabilitation of drug addicts, special attention to vulnerable groups, and a mass action initiated by the vice minister of youth for education about the ill-effects of drugs.

7. <u>Repression and submission to justice</u>: Some of the problems have been attributed to certain judges and district attorneys who had adopted an open-door policy of immunity to the drug traffickers by imposing minimum penalties. Government and judicial measures have been taken to maintain pressure on criminals until they are finally convicted. A political strategy, with adequate international judicial cooperation is being sought to permit a successful fight against all the cartels that were previously beyond the purview of the law.

8. <u>Changes in the administration of justice</u>: All the previously listed changes require reform at the base of the system. However, with a weak judicial system and an ineffective criminal policy it is difficult to overcome the problem. The government has planned to activate its justice development plan with an approximately $3 billion investment. The change centers on the government's willingness, along with the higher organs of administrative justice, to create a new criminal policy directed at destroying complex forms of organized criminal groups like the cartels.

9. <u>Prosecution of the cartels</u>: The government is very willing to track down, judge, and incarcerate the drug traffickers. For these purposes, it is also improving the intelligence apparatus, which includes assistance from other countries, especially the United States.

10. <u>International Responsibilities</u>: Along with the aforementioned measures, Colombia is pressing for the following:

- Emphasis on decreasing the level of drug consumption in foreign countries;
- Intensifying the prohibition of ships illegally plying foreign waters;
- International control of money laundering through banking regulations;
- Reduction in the sale of preparatory chemicals by multinational companies.

COMPARATIVE EVALUATION OF THE METHODS FOR COMBATING ORGANIZED CRIME AND PROPOSED MEASURES

To evaluate the situation and impact of the policy measures it is useful to compare the punitive measures adopted by other South American countries. Argentina and Bolivia have illegalized possession even for personal use and have sanctioned punishments of up to two years in prison. Brazil and Colombia have also made it a violation. Venezuela has prescribed the most severe punishments on the continent. Even persons in the military, an institution once considered beyond reproach, are incriminated for possession. Paraguay considers drug use to be a crime against humanity and has illegalized drug-trafficking activities even though none occurs there. Peru has decriminalized and made legal the possession of a minimum amount of drugs for one's own use. They have also developed a system of quick seizure of goods related to drug trafficking. Brazil has incorporated a strong investigative branch into its legislative actions. It has been made a duty of every person to assist in drug-trafficking investigations.

Despite such stringent measures, unfortunately the statistics show an increase in consumption and more areas affected and contaminated by the drug problem. All these things are a clear indication that despite the enforcement measures and new policies against organized crime, drug trafficking and its related problems have continued unabated. Sadly, it has to be acknowledged that the measures have failed to keep a check on organized crime's involvement and its activities. Enforcement of the new legislation has not been very successful and the attempts by the anti-drug government agencies have hardly made any dent in the drug cartels' organization. They have remained as powerful as before despite the worldwide attention on their network and competition from new organized groups. Their geographical distribution and areas of control still remain as widespread as before.

Much is done to pursue drug distributors, but little is done to the people behind the scene who provide the capital or the chemical laboratories that clandestinely produce the illegal drugs. The problem affects all areas: political, economic, and social. There is a need to study the problems by strategic analysis in order to resolve them.

Thus, organized crime indicates a problem of police control, but the use of security forces is not enough to combat the problem. There is a lot of talk but little action. Political and financial leaders tolerate the informal economy, and it is even accepted by some inept economists as a salvation to the problems of underdeveloped countries. Generally, the military actions under the control of those people who are influenced by the cartels end up being the propaganda for public consumption.

Different Procedures

The direct strategy is based on placing a large physical force to confront the problem. However, unlike the powerful U.S. military, underdeveloped countries do not have such resources for a direct confrontation. The results of fighting the drug traffickers for the past thirty years also suggest the inadequacy of such an approach. Instead, the indirect strategy inverts the emphasis by placing moral factors at the forefront of the battle. Such a psychological ploy works by replacing the physical force with a well-constructed ideology. In this strategy the proposition to legalize drugs is unacceptable, since there will not be a moral force to substitute the physical one. Colombia faces this challenge, since the country is ethically and morally bankrupt from the point of view of politics, economics, military, and the society. The seriousness of drug trafficking has an economic implication, and in those countries not depending on drug money, the most serious focus should be to defend the morality of society. With morals there will be efficient justice, a productive economy, correct prevention, and impeccable repression.

We also have to examine the unwritten rules of the game that are followed in international relations. The imposition of the powerful countries on the integrity of the other countries is a classic example. The United States can enter Mexico and take away some people whom they accuse of drug trafficking. However, the underdeveloped countries cannot enter the United States or Switzerland to detain those bankers and businesspersons who encourage trafficking in these countries. The continuing hypocritical attitude toward agreed sanctions is another major rule in these relations. The different declarations carried out in the United Nations against drug trafficking remain simple decrees without any will to carry them out. Several countries also sanction the use of drugs on the specious argument that they are acceptable due to old habits. Thus, Argentinean legislation accepts cocaine intake as a mark of respect for the indigenous custom.

The characteristics of these rules of the game differ according to the level of conflict and narrow interests. Thus, it is serious not to repay a foreign debt, but financial institutions often ignore money laundering and thereby encourage it as payment for the international commitments. Such gross violations of international conventions and laws ultimately end up favoring the drug traffickers. Similarly, there is a fine distinction between the threat to security of the state and liberty of the citizens. If guarantees to the civil liberties are not reduced and drug trafficking increases, the police find it difficult to pursue them without violating the legal codes. However, if these rights are reduced, it produces an immediate rejection from the international community that sometimes designate the drug traffickers as victims of state brutality without appreciating the nature of the problems.

In conclusion, analyzing the Colombian situation makes it apparent that the drug traffickers are in a strong position, which makes the task of the state very difficult.

Interactive Measure

An interactive plan has been proposed by Russel L. Ackoff, a systems professor at the University of Pennsylvania. His proposal is to plan the business of the future that can be adapted to the fight against drug trafficking in Colombia or any other country. Ackoff states that the most important change occurs from the way one tries to understand the world. One cannot confront the change unless one understands its nature. Therefore, it is important to understand globally and not concentrate merely on some of its aspects. Based on his arguments, a systems perspective of combating the drug problem can be outlined. First of all, two perceptions of the drug-trafficking system are considered. One considers drug trafficking as an incorporated subsystem to the complete system of the society. The other considers it as an anti-system that injects chaos into the system.

We consider a system as a combination of two or more elements that satisfy three conditions:

1. The behavior of each element has an effect on the behavior of all elements;
2. The behavior of the elements and their effects on all are interdependent; and
3. Without assigning importance to the way subgroups of the elements are formed, each has an effect on the behavior of everything and no one element has an independent effect.

When the system is taken apart it loses its essential properties. Thus, not thinking systematically can lead us to ask for the death penalty or the participation of the armed forces in the repression of drug trafficking. The system method rejects this approach because it suggests that a single element cannot be effective in itself, all the systems together should respond to the anti-system.

The planned proposal is an active and democratic way to resolve a group of interrelated problems. This interactive plan contemplates an analysis of the existing sub-systems in the state system, the action of drug trafficking on those sub-systems, the obstructions that the criminal business generates impeding the normal state development, and so on. Once the formulation of the problem is completed, the projection of references is proposed based on the conflicts of the past and the present on the supposition that no significant change will occur. The planning is continuous; one can observe the effects on the implementation of the plans, the suppositions, and the expectations. If there are faulty explanations the plan can be suitably modified.

The Colombian government proposed the national plan for overcoming the drug problem based on this system. However, it left out an important principle regarding the participation of the people. The plan envisaged eradicating the cultivation of drug plants but without incorporating the alternate plans of providing other developmental avenues to the growers. Thus, the plan ended up being directed against the people rather than seeking their cooperation and building the community. Similarly, the need for coordination and integration are important ingredients of the system's approach. The holistic principle states that "when more parts and levels of a system plan simultaneously and interdependently, the results will be better." Unfortunately, in Colombia the security forces have been unable to establish coordination at the intelligence level and even less at the level of judiciary, between different armed forces and between public health and education organizations. They have also failed to develop good coordination on the continent with other national security agencies.

Conclusion

Drug-trafficking activities affect all the areas of the world and their economies and have social and political consequences. The problem began as one for the police and judiciary but has progressed into the political and social areas. The influence of the illicit business is increasing every day and is becoming an extremely serious problem. Drug trafficking is increasing in Colombia and the new participants are developing new styles that are more sophisticated and connected to international groups. There is a climate of uncertainty in the society due to constant accusations against the president of the country and his colleagues that link them to the drug cartels.

Analytical methods implemented by the government have caused a series of problems and made the government fall into disfavor with the people. This has hindered the efforts of the security forces and given advantage to the drug traffickers. The results are a sinking moral and ethical authority of the country's leaders and a growing despair among the people that has further benefited the cartels. The security forces have been focusing on short-term measures and have not addressed the fundamental reasons for the development of drug trafficking on Colombian soil. Their functional problems, lack of coordination, resources, and a proper operational plan or strategy have shown their ineffectiveness against the cartels. The reasons for drug trafficking, the demands, and easy acquisition of money through laundering have not been tackled due to the rules that benefit the cartels and place the governments of underdeveloped nations at a disadvantage.

The global and transnational drug business cannot be eradicated permanently. The most logical and viable option is to contain or limit the problem. The countries must act with the United Nations to control the expansion and consolidation of the cartels. This could be achieved by the proposed method of interactive planning as previously outlined. The need remains to encourage all countries to work together and energetically plan policies and strategies directed at the drug traffickers and at the companies participating in money laundering for the drug cartels. They also need to cooperate in raising ethical and moral values in the society, in curbing the culture of consumption and improving the means of social communication, and in concentrating on the whole system of supply and demand that promotes drug trafficking.

REFERENCES

Brooke, James. 1995. "Colombia's Rebels Grow Rich from Banditry." *New York Times.* July 2, 1, 4.

Quadro, Jorge and Botto, Roger. 1995. "Revista de la Escuela de Guerra Naval de la Rapublica Argentina." The Guerrillas of Narco-Traffic. July, n. 42.

Quadro, Jorge. 1996. "The Conflict against Narco-Traffic" (in Spanish). *Gaceta del Foro.* September.

Ramirez, Leonardo. 1996. "Destruction of the Drug Cartels" (in Spanish). *Catolica de Salta*, Argentina.

Chapter 14

Organized Crime : A Perspective from Argentina

Hugo Antolin Almiron

Introduction

Argentina is the second largest country in South America with a surface area of 2,350,796.25 square miles. Nevertheless, the population of roughly 35 million people is largely concentrated in small pockets and almost 88 percent of the people live in one or the other urban municipalities. The country shares boundaries with Bolivia and Paraguay in the North; Brazil and Uruguay in the Northeast; Chile in the West and has a large seaside front on the Atlantic Ocean. Except for the urban areas and highways linking them, the majority of the country is barren landscape of immense beauty and mountainous terrain. There are an estimated 7 million registered vehicles in the country, which is witnessing rapid economic growth in recent years. Argentina has been witnessing a rapid growth in its GNP, although unemployment remains high.

Argentina has a federal police with headquarters in Buenos Aires, the capital city of the country. The police force is controlled directly by the ministry of the interior, and it has jurisdiction not only in the federal capital, but over all other organizations and institutions that are administered by the national government (e.g., national universities). This organization also has jurisdiction over all federal crimes in the country and operates through a delegated unit in each province. The organization also handles important federal documentation, including passports.

In addition, each province has its own security police, with jurisdiction in its own territory and control over all crimes. This police force is administered by the provincial ministry of the government. A few provinces also have a judicial police whose function consists of criminal investigation of cases under the authority of the judiciary. This force is empowered to collect evidence and prepare a judicial summary concerning the case under investigation. Where there are no judicial police, the security police of the province are responsible for security and investigation.

Argentina, in its penal code (*Codigo Penal Argentino*) has not defined organized crime legally. The penal law in the country is "typical," which means, the criminal behavior must be exactly defined in the penal code. Juridical and legal analogy is forbidden in penal matters; only the law (as rule, penal figure), is considered a source of knowledge (jurisprudence, general principles, doctrine, among others cannot be used). In this sense the typical and appropriate phenomenon in the penal code defining organized crime is known by the doctrine of "illicit association," which can be shown to exist if certain characteristics are met. These are, for example, concurrence of three or more persons who are in agreement in a permanent and organized manner to commit offenses, through an organization, stable in character and that exists like a community with ownership links among its members.

Apart from the problem of a lack of clear definition of organized crime, extraordinary changes at economic and political levels in the world have further necessitated substantial modifications in the concept of organized crime. It is therefore necessary to elucidate what we understand by "organized crime." This is necessary, since different concepts are proposed according to the different points of view. The broad concept suggests that organized crime is characterized by a prior planning and uses a ruthless methodology involving coordination to reach criminal objectives. The legal concept on the other hand is formal—normative, varying from one country to another.

The Argentine Penal Code (art. 210) textually establishes:

> One who takes part in an association or gang of three or more persons with a view to committing crimes as a member of the association will be punished with imprisonment between three and ten years. For the chiefs or organizers of the association the minimum of the penalty will be of five years of imprisonment.

As one can see, the code is extremely general in scope and not useful to punish any form of organized crime. However, in view of the extraordinary nature of drug-related problems, the country has enacted a law to fight against drug trafficking:

Main considerations of Law Number 24.424 (in force)

- **Article number 26:** Suspends banking and financial privacy to facilitate the investigation;

- **Article number 26 Bis:** Allows pictures, films, and recordings as evidence, after checking its authenticity;
- **Article number 29 Ter:** Reduces sanctions for suspects who collaborate with information leading to the success of the investigation;
- **Article number 31:** All official and nonprofit organizations must send all information relating to drugs to the Argentine Federal Police (PFA), who operate a data bank for consultation among all concerned with drug trafficking;
- **Article number 32:** In urgent cases a judge may extend his territorial jurisdiction to avoid delay in the procedures;
- **Article number 33:** A judge can suspend the interception of drugs allowing the same to leave the country to determine the destination and connections in other countries;
- **Article number 33 Bis:** Establishes measures to protect witnesses assisting in the investigation.

The Argentine customs also have special code, which provides for penalties for various acts involving drug trafficking. The code covers officials and private individuals and takes into account the phenomenon of "illicit association" described previously. This code also deals with trafficking in firearms, but the legislation is only concerned with the responsibilities and powers of the customs department. However, many other forms of organized crime are not covered by the provisions in the penal code nor by special laws. Such crimes as trafficking in gold and children, money laundering, telephone line thefts, fraud, and other forms of economic crime, smuggling, diverse types of Mafias (principally Chinese), institutional and political corruption have been left out. The existence of organized crime in such diverse ways makes it imperative that this form of crime be treated conceptually at a broader level. The primary objective in this chapter will thus be to present a new perspective on organized crime and describe how it is being dealt with in Argentina.

THE NATURE AND EXTENT OF ORGANIZED CRIME

In Argentina, the principal problem of delinquency is in the urban areas and it is mostly directed against property. The etiology of such a behavior is located in the same social context in which delinquency takes place. This type of delinquency gives birth to a growing perception of insecurity, although the measured economic and social damage is no less than any other form of illicit activity. On the other hand, economic crime is constantly growing, and although it does not generate insecurity problems, it does give rise to the perception of immunity to the perpetrators who appear to have close connections with the establishment, including the police. This perception imparts a social damage whose dimensions cannot be estimated.

Presently there do not exist any concrete verifiable data on organized crime, but this does not mean that this form of criminality does not exist. Such a criminal activity constantly modifies its modus operandi and cases reminiscent of the Italian Mafia or of similar form seen in other parts of the world have been detected in this country, too. Nevertheless, organized crime in Argentina has a peculiar local character that thrives on the socioeconomic and political conditions prevalent in the country. Organized crime in Argentina is largely regional in nature and not international in scope. It consists largely of bands that commit offenses against property.

The only form of organized crime linked to international cartels is the one concerned with drug trafficking. Nevertheless, the objective of these criminally organized units is not only drug trafficking, but also trafficking of children, smuggling, marketing of stolen cars, tax evasion, and multiple other forms of offenses—especially of economic nature like embezzlement, fraud, insider trading, and financial swindles that affect both public and private spheres of national life. Corruption has penetrated deep within the public offices and has affected every stratum of the society and has further generated various types of misconduct. Corruption has not reached the dangerous stage as in some other countries, but its importance in Argentina cannot be underestimated.

Measures, Including Legislation to Combat Organized Crime

The measures that are being used to combat organized crime in the country include the institutional tools of law enforcement agencies and the legislative and organizational policies implemented through the criminal law. The police are commonly involved in the prevention and investigation of all offenses, and traditionally the fight against organized crime has been carried out by a special unit commissioned for such operations within the security police. The judicial police is also a kind of specialized elite unit in the struggle against crime. It professes to operate as the strong arm of the judicial organ and this association provides it strength that is not available to the other police forces. Criminal policy is another important tool in the fight against organized crime. The social control of a state is in fact manifested through its criminal policy. This involves legislative debates and general agreements on the nature of restrictive powers given to the enforcement authorities that are acceptable to the society.

The police institution in general terms, is intended to maintain public order and social tranquillity, provide for the stability of the institutions and safety of the citizens, screen the moral integrity of the population, and represent what is good and right in the society as described by Article 1 of Province Law number 6,791 (*Constitucion de la Provincia de Cordoba*, hereafter CPP). The role of the police in the country is to promote the material conditions favorable to the stability of the social order. Police are empowered to check attempts to alter these arrangements that constitute offenses against the state. In this "fight against crime," the police function acquires two differentiated aspects: the task prior to the crime and the one immediately subsequent to it.

Before the offense the police function consists in preserving public order and tranquillity, preventing offenses from taking place. This constitutes its crime-prevention role and this function is executed by the security police (art. 6 Province Law no. 6,701). However, the police have been constituted to work in close collaboration with the other state organizations also. For instance, some intermediate institutions, devoted to the prevention of alcoholism and drug addiction work with the police, are fundamentally in the task of crime prevention in accordance with the penal law.

After the offense, the function of the police is more complex and changes fundamentally. It is fulfilled by the judicial police (art. 7 Province Law no. 6,701; art. 187 Penal Procedural Code), and consists of the following:

- To impede the commission of the offense attempted to be committed (art. 289 CPP);
- To discover the perpetrators and to make possible the repression of the offense by judges (art. 321 CPP).

In this last phase, the police are an important accessory and auxiliary of the judiciary in the repression of the offense. Their powers are derived through the application of the penal law as defined by Article 18 of the National Constitution (*Constitucion de la Nacion Argentian*) and by Article 7 and 17 of the CPP. This aid is fundamental and intended to expedite the actions of penal law.

At the primary level, the policies to combat organized crime include all those actions that are concerned with the administration of criminal justice: prevention and investigation by the police, the slow-moving trial process, and culmination in the correctional system. Doctrinal discussions on the power of the public ministry have been extensive in the country. There have been extensive debates about the role of the executive, its relationship with the judiciary, the autonomy of the enforcement agencies, and the manner of exercising control over them. The CPP has established that the public ministry should integrate the judiciary and exercise its functions with regard to the legality of procedures and impartiality of its actions. Furthermore, it has been stipulated to operate through a hierarchical system in all the territory of the province (art. no. 171 Province Constitution).

This has been given shape by assigning several functions to the public ministry, for instance, to promote and to exercise the public actions before the competent courts (art. no. 172, Inc. 3, CPP). The General Prosecutor has been authorized to fix penal prosecution policies and empowered to instruct the subordinate prosecutors on the fulfillment of their functions with regard to the laws. He also manages the judicial police and this system has been thought fit to guarantee the efficiency of the preparatory penal investigation.

The new procedural code (Province Law no. 8123) has followed the accusatory principle and has put on the state the responsibility of the preparatory penal investigation to support the accusation. The judiciary strictly follows the procedures in determination of the guilt in accordance with the law. In this scheme, the public ministry plays the role of superintendent for formulating the criminal policy. The general prosecutor, assisted by the judicial police directorate, supervises the execution of this policy. This system warrants the efficiency of the penal investigation and the ministry remains responsible for gathering and preserving the useful and relevant evidence. It is possible to evaluate the credibility of the accusation as well as the failure to prosecute, and the association of prosecutors enables a fair assessment of the evidence. The political considerations that are represented here and which form the basis of all the policies and administrative rules, determine that the detection and prosecution of criminal behavior is being undertaken fairly. The justice administration has also been strengthened by adequate material and human resources while safeguards have been placed to ensure that the system operates within established parameters and in the fight against organized and ordinary crime, justice is not lost sight of.

COMPARATIVE EVALUATION OF THE METHODS FOR COMBATING ORGANIZED CRIME AND PROPOSED MEASURES

Although a strong police system has evolved, it is an organization that belongs to the executive section of the government, has a bureaucratic character, and fulfills delegated judicial functions. These organizational characteristics have introduced an element of inefficiency in all the enforcement agencies. The special unit's performance is similarly affected since it too carries the liabilities of the police department. The specific mission of the police role as a warrantor of public order causes the investigative task to be relegated to second place. This compounds the problem of combating organized crime, since these problems receive neither special incentives for the officers engaged in the uneven battle nor help in the growth of specialization to match the resources of the organized groups.

In addition to these performance areas there are problems about the nature of police activities. Thus, for example, in the prevention phase of the offense, it is evident that the task is fulfilled at different levels. Security police handle public order and safety, constituting or creating with this a material obstacle to the commission of crime. In this task there is clearly the existence of a discretionary framework that gives police performance some differential elements. On the other hand, in the field of "crime repression," police performance is completely regulated. As a rule, repression of crime is conceived by the state with due process and corresponding constitutional guarantees. The control of the crime requires the discovery of the offense, the identification of the offenders, the conservation of the evidence, and many other actions. All these tasks cannot be fulfilled by police agents because of their training and dependence on discretionary judgments. In effect, the fulfillment of these tasks requires the participation of police in an activity annotated by rules of procedural and substantive criminal law.

Security police forces face a dilemma in the prevention of crime. Repression of crime is a function that is accomplished by the police forces without the intervention of the judiciary. In this respect, police work is guided almost exclusively by a focus on conventional offenses. They do not count on predetermined structures to repress organized crime, unless it is drug trafficking. The essential function of the security police is to prevent the commission of the offense, but this obligation involves a multiplicity of functions like patrolling, solving petty problems of the citizens, maintaining order, and building contacts with the people. All these seek to deteriorate police performance as an auxiliary agent of justice, since order maintenance functions leave little time for any anti-crime work. This reality is seen in the inefficiency of penal investigation that has historically resulted in police solving about 6 to 8 percent of all crime.

The judicial police, as previously described, have a special and close relationship with the judiciary, which gives them added strength. However, their efficiency does not depend solely on its trigger but on its organizational characteristics, and the conflicting policies of the state intended to fight organized crime have further eroded its effectiveness. It is difficult to investigate and combat organized criminal structures if the policies discouraging or dissuading it are not adopted fully.

The judicial police are a direct consequence of our legal and political organization of the country. In this institution rests the constitutional principle of the division of powers. The repression of crime is properly an activity of the judiciary. Keeping this in mind, the judicial police were conceived as a necessary institution for the task of assisting the judiciary in its restrictive objectives. The nature of the judicial police's function consists in investigating the public crimes, to prevent their ulterior consequences, to identify the offenders, and to gather necessary evidence for the implementation of justice. In this form, it participates in the judicial function of the state as a pre-established organ to achieve the discovery of the truth about the presumed commission of crime and the performance of the penal law in the concrete case. The perspective is not *who* applies the law, but *what* facilitates its application. In this sense we can call its performance the "medium to finality."

As conceived, judicial police in Argentina are characterized as:

- Judicial: inasmuch as it is regulated by the Constitution and the Law.
- Auxiliary: of the commissioned courts in applying the substantive law.
- Contingent: since there is no intervention when the judiciary controls investigations from the beginning.
- Independent: in relation to other powers that may affect fair and determined investigation.
- Impartial: since it is not limited to gathering evidence, but acts to further the cause of justice.

For instance, Cordoba judicial police belong to the judiciary of the state and are an integral part of the public ministry. They were created by the legislature in 1939. In 1984, they were certified as the so called scientific police, and in May of 1996, their jurisdiction was gradually extended to cover the entire province. The judicial police operate under the administrative command of a directorate supplemented by a secretariat for ensuring the smooth operation of everything connected to judicial matters. The attempt has been to make it effective by suitable modifications of its organization, giving it an agile, dynamic, and flexible structure that will be able to accommodate the changes in the social, political, and economic institutions without affecting its efficiency.

In the capital city the judicial police receive assistance from the security police and also share the building and the organizational infrastructure.

Investigation is approached in methodical and multidisciplinary form coordinated by the director of judicial police. The principal operators of the system, the technical and investigative branches through an integrated policy, have begun to play their role in a reciprocal framework, avoiding operating as watertight compartments. Both police units work for achieving a common objective—to fight crime—and this realization has made them cooperate and become effective. Notwithstanding some of these recent attempts to improve the system, the role of the police, and judicial police in particular, has not been very effective in combating organized crime in Argentina. The most important reason for this failure is the nature of criminal policy being followed in the country.

The implementation of the new procedural laws demands a firm criminal policy that should establish what the criminal behaviors are that the enforcement agents will pursue on a priority basis. Without a selective weighing of these behaviors, the increasingly acute resource limitations make the whole operation a futile exercise. The system requires a credible criminal policy that can succeed in discouraging the impunity of the powerful people who are not deterred by the small-scale efforts launched by the police to combat their criminal activities. It is also necessary to use imagination to design criminal/political models that permit control of criminal behavior with greater effectiveness and, at the same time, encourage protection of the fundamental rights of those submitted to penal prosecution.

The system enacted through the new procedural code has linked the prosecutors as direct operators of the criminal policy. In this arrangement the need for operational independence for the police agencies has been lost because of the absence of clear administrative guidelines. There is also a lack of proper division of the responsibilities in the organization, both internally as well as externally. The absence of any criteria about the uniformity and accountability of performance has further complicated organizational problems. This deficiency in part has been overcome in the province of Cordoba with the passage of the new penal procedural code. The modified system has given evidence of its efficiency by virtue of Cordoba becoming the only province that has investigated and accomplished prosecution of public officials, including a former governor. The directors of two provincial banks have also been sentenced to prison after the introduction of this law. Second, the CPP lists as organs of administrative control the general accountancy of the province and thus serves to function as the ombudsman. The constitutional arrangement seeks to coordinate and keep a watchful eye on the fulfillment of the legal arrangements and the transparency of the acts of government. It is an effective tool for both prevention and investigation of organized crime.

Such examples do reveal the importance and leading role of the public ministry in combating organized criminal activities. Nevertheless, desired levels of effectiveness have not yet been achieved. The full implementation of the system with the new penal procedural code is an important step, but there are countless problems that we need to solve.

The judicial police in the fight against organized crime have not been very successful. The fight against organized crime can only come about with a body of highly competent and trained researchers, and this is a great challenge before the Argentinean authorities. The judicial police in this aspect need to improve the capabilities of their officers through a rigorous scientific training of their personnel. The training needs to target specific areas for specialization of the personnel, augmented by officers with experience in these fields. On the other hand, the security police need to devote a greater effort to their essential mission of prevention. They also need to encourage in some way the required specialization of personnel in the investigation of organized crime. To achieve the full impact of the system it must be accompanied by a controlling organ (the Public Ministry) that ensures the effective and coordinated integration of the operators committed to the investigation.

On the other hand, the judiciary needs to assume a real sense of mission, while at the same time ensuring its impartiality and providing the supreme guarantee of the just process. This kind of system will ensure the just balance of interests at stake and in the process, confer speed and efficiency on it. In this context, the effective investigation of organized criminal activities not only needs an accusing organ (for instance, the Public Ministry), but also a procedural and organizational system that ensures the compilation and conservation of evidence, the judicial police, and an effective procedural law.

The district prosecutor's office must also assume an effective and real commitment to penal prosecution. At the same time this office must also receive effective support from other powers of the state. Adjustments in the mechanisms for procedural efficiency must be accompanied by an authorization for wiretapping, witness protection, confiscation of assets purchased through illegal means, and so on. These provisions are imperative to ensure with certain optimism the success of the investigation and prosecution of organized crime.

There is an urgent need to give attention to organizational changes also. The struggle against organized crime cannot remain in the hands of traditional organizations. These should be made able and effective, and for this purpose we believe that the organization must be sufficiently agile and flexible to permit a rapid adjustment to the changes and operative modalities of delinquency. To illustrate these premises and principles the organization, administrative rules, and staffing patterns for the judicial police of Cordoba are a good example.

There is a fundamental appropriateness of the procedural and substantive legislation being proposed for Cordoba. Argentina does not have special laws to fight against organized crime, except those related to drug matters that are governed by the Law of Drugs number 23,737, Official Bulletin of 1 October 1989. The new criminal policy requires three elements:

1. A good administration of the commissioned services (police forces, justice, and penitentiary services) for making and executing the law;
2. A good penal legislation that promotes preventive acts and sanctions punitive measures as a way of dissuasion; and
3. A good procedural legislation that facilitates the investigation of offenses.

Organized criminal behavior that cannot be controlled by the aforementioned special legislation can still be repressed with the conventional tools contained in the procedural and penal code.

The Argentine Penal Code, in Article 210, establishes: "It (illicit association) will be repressed with imprisonment up to three years for the one which takes part in an association in a band of three or more persons intended to commit offenses, by the only fact of being a member of the association. For the chiefs or organizer of the association the minimum of the penalty will be five years or more."

Law number 23,077 incorporated as Article 210 of the Argentine Penal Code (illicit association opposed to the constitutional order), imposes imprisonment or prison penalties from five to twenty-five years on those who take part, collaborate, or help in the training or maintenance of an illicit association intended to commit offenses when the action contributes, or puts in danger the force of the National Constitution, as long as the association finds at least *two* of the following characteristics:

a. Be integrated by ten or more individuals;
b. To possess a military organization or is of military type;

c. To have cellular structure;
d. To have war weapons or explosives of great offensive power;
e. To operate in more than one of the political jurisdictions of the country;
f. Be composed by one or more sub-officers of the armed forces or of public safety;
g. To have notorious connections with other existing similar organizations in the country or abroad;
h. To receive some support, help, or direction from public officials.

The content in Article 210 is considered an autonomous offense. The critical analysis of the cited procedures suggests the insufficiency of the Argentine Penal Code to confront the new criminal modalities that are raising their heads at present. The illicit association produces a real cause for collective alarm. It is a breach against public tranquillity that threatens the safety of the citizens. The fight against organized crime requires a specific law that extends to the informer, the undercover agent, or the witness, a necessary and effective protection. A similar provision is contained in the Law of Drugs number 24,424. It is fundamental that procedural and substantive legislation shall contain the necessary tools to enable the enforcement agencies to successfully confront these types of offenses. This fight will not be won with criminal law and penal procedure. In the long run there is need of preventive actions that are more effective.

It is also imperative to realize that there is a limit to the ability of the criminal law to combat organized crime. The criminal law operates under certain limits and keeps close to the facts that could establish the actions said to have taken place in the commission of the offense. On the other hand, prevention avoids the alteration of the social order and is in this sense essential for citizen safety. The efficiency of the state lies in its ability to take preventive actions against corruption and organized crime. The full operation of the systems of control is one of the factors that can contribute effectively to the prevention of organized criminal activity such as corruption, tax evasion, trafficking in children, and so on.

As a corollary of what has been expressed, the best police or justice system in the world is useless without a penal law supported by the community it serves. It would not be useful at all that penal law promises penalties for given offenses if the penal procedural law is ineffective, fails to take action against certain individuals, and is difficult to carry to the stage of judgment. Finally, the best procedural and penal law loses if the judges do not apply the necessary tools, are compromised, or become corrupt.

CONCLUSION

Organized crime in Argentina exists in an incipient developmental stage, but at the same time it is becoming a major concern. The economic opening and the regional integration with other countries that form MERCOSUR (South Common Market) places the province of Cordoba and the entire country at risk. Repression mechanisms are insufficient and need to be strengthened.

CHINA
Wenzhou
Fuzhou
Xiamen
Shantou
Guangzhou
Hong Kong S.A.R.
Macau
(PORT.)
Taipei
Taiwan
Kao-hsiung
Luzon
Strait
Okinawa
Naha
RYUKYU ISLANDS
(JAPAN)
DAITŌ-SHOTŌ
(JAPAN)
NAMPŌ-SHOTŌ
BONIN
ISLANDS
(JAPAN)
VOLCANO
ISLANDS
(JAPAN)
Okino-tori-shima
(JAPAN)
Marcus Island
(JAPAN)
Tropic of Cancer
Philippine
Sea
Northern
Mariana
Islands
(U.S.)
Saipan
Wake Island
(U.S.)
South
China
Sea
Luzon
Manila
Guam
(U.S.)
Hagåtña (Agana)
PHILIPPINES
Panay
Samar
Palawan
Bacolod
Negros
Cagayan de Oro
Sulu Sea
Mindanao
Zamboanga
Davao
Enewetak
Kwajalein
MARSHALL
ISLANDS
Majuro
Yap
FEDERATED STATES OF MICRONESIA
Pohnpei
Palikir
Koror
PALAU
CAROLINE ISLANDS
Bandar Seri
Begawan
BRUNEI
MALAYSIA
Borneo
Celebes Sea
Manado
Halmahera
Tarawa
KIRIBATI
(GILBERT ISLANDS)
Equator
Samarinda
Palu
Molucca
Sea
Sorong
Yaren District
NAURU
Banaba
KIRIBATI
Banjarmasin
Celebes
Buru
Ceram
Ambon
Jayapura
Wewak
Bismarck Sea
New
Ireland
Ujungpandang
Banda Sea
PAPUA NEW GUINEA
Bougainville
SOLOMON
ISLANDS
Java Sea
INDONESIA
Madang
Lae
New Britain
Solomon Sea
Surabaya
Java
Bali
Sumbawa
Flores
New Guinea
TUVALU
Funafuti
Denpasar
Lombok
Sumba
Kupang
Timor
Arafura Sea
Torres
Strait
Port
Moresby
Guadalcanal
Honiara
SANTA CRUZ
ISLANDS
Timor Sea
Ashmore and
Cartier Islands
(AUSTRALIA)
Darwin
Gulf of
Carpentaria
Rotuma
Indian
Ocean
Coral Sea
Islands
(AUSTRALIA)
Coral Sea
Cairns
VANUATU
Port-vila
New
Caledonia
(FRANCE)
FIJI
Vanua
Levu
Viti
Levu
Suva
Townsville
Port Hedland
Mount Isa
Mackay
Noumea
Rockhampton
Alice Springs
Gladstone
AUSTRALIA
Brisbane
Gold Coast
Geraldton
Kingston
Norfolk Island
(AUSTRALIA)
Kalgoorlie
Broken
Hill
Darling
Lord Howe Island
(AUSTRALIA)
Perth
Bunbury
Esperance
Whyalla
Newcastle
Sydney
Adelaide
Murray
Canberra
Wollongong
Great Australian
Bight
Bendigo
Melbourne
Geelong
Tasman
Sea
Auckland
Hamilton
North
Island
NEW
ZEALAND
Hastings
Bass
Strait
Wellington
Indian
Ocean
Hobart
Tasmania
Christchurch
South Island
Invercargill
Dunedin
Stewart Island
120
140
160
180
20
40

PART 5

PERSPECTIVES FROM AUSTRALASIA

Australia is the smallest continent, but one of the largest countries on earth—slightly smaller than the United States. Together with New Zealand it forms the region known as Australasia. It is located south of Indonesia and Papua New Guinea and north of Antarctica, bordered by the Indian Ocean on the west and the Pacific Ocean on the east. Australia was the last continent (besides Antarctica) to be explored by Europeans. New Zealand is more than 1,000 miles southeast of Australia, and both countries are independent nations with no close neighbors.

Both Australia and New Zealand have comparatively homogenous populations of white European descent. Australia is 95 percent white, 2 percent aboriginal, and 1.5 percent Asian. In a similar way, New Zealand's population is about 80 percent of European decent, 15 percent Maori (descendants of original Polynesian settlers), and 5 percent Asian. Their isolated geographic locations have spared Australia and New Zealand the cross-border problems of many other nations. But the advent of rapid globalization of trade, travel, and communications in the late twentieth century made geographical distance less relevant to the distribution of illicit goods and services.

Asian gangs have been a problem in parts of Australia, but Internet crimes and money laundering are expected to be larger problems in the future (Ryrie, 1999). The traditional vices have been aggravated with the added feature of globalization. For example, one of the world's largest Internet child pornography networks was infiltrated in 2001, resulting in arrests of 107 men in 12 countries, including Australia (Police, 2001). Likewise, Internet gambling poses problems for enforcement of national laws in an international environment (Kelly, 2000). Australia also has implemented a revised visa system to separate conventional, low-risk travelers and visitors from others who require regular visa clearance for travel to the country (Christian, 1999).

Studies of organized crime in Australia and New Zealand must examine both the history and the current internal forces (social, economic, political, and legal) that influence the development of organized crime around supply and demand. In addition, the impact of immigration, technology, travel, and communications will shape the nature of organized crime in Australasia in the future.

References

Christian, Bryan Paul. 1999. "Visa Policy, Inspection, and Exit Controls: Transatlantic Perspectives on Migration Management." *Georgetown Immigration Law Journal* 14: 215, Fall.

Kelly, Joseph M. 2000. "Internet Gambling Law," *William Mitchell Law Review* 26: 117.

"Police Crack Global Child Porn Ring." 2001. *CNN.com*, 10 January.

Ryrie, Tasker. 1999. "Caught in the Net," *Charter* 70: 2, September.

CHAPTER 15

ORGANIZED CRIME: A PERSPECTIVE FROM AUSTRALIA

John Broome

INTRODUCTION

Australia's population of 18 million is concentrated mainly on its eastern seaboard, with more than 75 percent of its citizens living in the eastern states of New South Wales, Victoria, and Queensland. The largest population concentrations are in the provinces of New South Wales (34%) and Victoria (25%) (Australian Bureau of Statistics, 1995). Despite its rural or "outback" image, Australia is one of the most urbanized countries in the world, with over 85 percent of its population living in the major capital cities or smaller regional centers, particularly Sydney (4 million residents) and Melbourne (3.3 million).

From the first period of European settlement (1788) until the end of the Second World War, settlers from the United Kingdom dominated Australia's immigrant history. Since 1945, however, Australia has developed into a major multicultural nation, with significant (and growing) sectors of its population from non-English speaking and non-European backgrounds. (About 22% of Australia's population was born overseas.) In particular, there has been an increasing trend in immigration from Asia and South America and a decreasing one from the United Kingdom and Europe. This demographic shift presents challenges to law enforcement, not the least being maintaining adequate representation of the changing face of the nation within the ranks of the police services. The proportion of citizens born outside the country, too, has become very significant.

The Australian economy is a mixed one, with inputs from a range of sectors (agriculture, mining, manufacturing, construction, wholesale/retail, transport, and communication). While the performance of the Australian economy, as represented in the national income or gross domestic product (GDP), is important, there are significant aspects of the quality of life that cannot be captured in a system of economic accounts. Between 1981 and 1990 the degree of inequality in income distribution increased slightly. In 1981 the wealthiest 10 percent of the community accounted for almost 27 percent of all income, and in 1990 that percentage had increased to just over 29 percent. Households in the lowest 20 percent of income distribution can be characterized by a high level of dependence on government pensions and benefits, low levels of employment and educational attainment, and high proportions of young, aged, and one-person households (especially women). These income and social inequalities have significant implications for law enforcement in the country.

In Australia, the commonwealth, state, and territory governments each have law-enforcement responsibilities, and much of the crime occurring in Australia falls within the jurisdiction of the state and territory police forces. The Australian Constitution specifies areas of commonwealth responsibility, and the states and territories have responsibility for the remaining areas (including most personal and property crimes). In economic terms, Australia spends approximately $A4.8 billion on law enforcement, approximately 1.2 percent of the GDP, or $A278 per citizen, (Yearbook Australia, 1996).

Criminal activity in Australia varies considerably across jurisdictions, and poses unique problems to each of Australia's law enforcement agencies. Australia has eight police services, containing some 49,000 personnel. The great bulk of those, approximately 46,000, work for the state and territory police, and the remaining 3,000 are with the Australian Federal Police (AFP). While the state and territory police services are responsible for investigating the greater proportion of all crime, the commonwealth government directs its law enforcement effort toward upholding commonwealth laws, and investigating offenses such as drug trafficking (particularly at the customs barrier and internationally), and money laundering.

Other commonwealth regulatory and revenue agencies also have an investigative role, such as the Australian Customs Service (ACS), the Australian Taxation Office (ATO), and the Australian Securities Commission (ASC). In addition, specialized investigative units have also been established in some commonwealth government departments, such as the Department of Health, the Department of Social Security, and the Department of Employment, Education, and Training. Many of the states also have units performing similar functions, as well as special agencies like the Queensland Criminal Justice Commission (CJC), the New South Wales (NSW) Crime Commission, and NSW Independent Commission against Corruption (ICAC).

There are some who would argue that Australia has too many law enforcement agencies and that there is a real risk of lack of coordination, wasteful competition, and duplication. The number of law enforcement agencies in Australia is not large by international standards, however, even when compared on a population basis. In comparison with the eight major police forces in Australia, the United States has over 20,000 different police services while the United Kingdom has 45. The number of police officers in the Tasmanian Police Service (the smallest Australian state) is sufficient to class it within the thirty largest police forces in the United States.

In recent years there has been recognition by Australian law enforcement agencies that cooperation between jurisdictions at an operational and a strategic level is required to counteract organized crime. The benefits of cooperation are that:

- by sharing intelligence between law enforcement agencies, we are more likely to acquire a better picture of organized criminal structures, players, and activities;
- better intelligence is more likely to lead to better assessments of the vulnerabilities of criminal organizations; and
- cooperation ensures a much more effective and efficient use of resources.

Mechanisms for cooperation include a number of national or interjurisdictional forums for the identification of joint strategic or operational priorities and strategies. These include the Intergovernmental Committee (IGC), the National Crime Authority (NCA), or the Standing Committee on Organized Crime and Criminal Intelligence (SCOCCI), as well as the formation of national or interjurisdictional task forces under the NCA Act. Moreover, like all other elements of Australian society, the law enforcement community is now a part of the global community. As such, international cooperation is also essential to combat the activities of Australian and international organized crime groups.

Organized crime has been a particular focus of Australian law enforcement in recent decades. In the 1970s and 1980s, a number of inquiries were conducted that highlighted the difficulties faced by traditional law enforcement approaches in dealing with what was (then) seen to be a growing phenomenon of "organized crime." These inquiries established that there were groups of criminals engaged in serious criminal behavior in a variety of areas (in particular, robbery, extortion, protection rackets, illegal gambling, and prostitution). The inquiries also established that a variety of criminals conducted these activities, often with considerable impunity (due, in part, to corruption within some elements of Australian law enforcement). Drug importation, and the consequent growth of criminal behavior related to the distribution of illegal drugs, became a matter of significant community concern from the late 1960s onward. The significant profits to be made from the illicit drug markets not only attracted existing criminals, but also brought into the criminal environment many who had previously not been involved in criminal activity.

To a significant extent, Australia's experience in the latter part of the twentieth century has been similar to that of other jurisdictions. Crime has become more sophisticated and in many respects more complex. But Australia's experience of serious criminal activity is not necessarily the same as that of other countries: geography, demographics, and political and social structures have all contributed to creating an overall environment, which, in many ways, differs significantly from that overseas.

To understand the Australian experience requires some appreciation of the basic nature of the Australian society and the way in which Australian law enforcement is organized. In part, the small number of state police forces in Australia, dealing with the majority of criminal offenses, provides a different environment from that of many overseas jurisdictions, where there is often a multiplicity of police forces (even down to the level of the local city or town). On the other hand, a fairly rigid federal structure clearly delineates between the responsibilities of the Australian government and those of the states and territories. This provides some opportunity for criminals to escape detection by playing on these jurisdictional differences. For example, one might escape detection and subsequent capture by simply moving interstate. While there are not extensive procedures to provide for the extradition of suspects between Australian states, inevitably local law enforcement agencies place their primary emphasis on dealing with local priorities.

Although popular perception often sees organized crime as a series of formal, hierarchical criminal structures, the reality is somewhat different. (In Australia, as is no doubt the case elsewhere, many images of organized crime owe more to Hollywood than they do to reality.) In a definitional sense, the kind of criminal behavior generally regarded as falling within the description of "organized crime" is reasonably well-settled, at least within law enforcement circles in Australia. Organized crime in Australia is considered to involve the following elements:

1. Two or more participants
2. Use of sophisticated, complex techniques

3. Repeated engagement in criminal conduct, including major fraud, importation and distribution of prohibited drugs, corruption of public officials, tax evasion, currency violations, illegal gambling, obtaining financial benefit by vice, and violence.

Moreover, the NCA has a "working" definition of organized crime, that is, "a systematic and continuing conspiracy to commit serious offenses." Other commentators might wish to add additional characteristics, such as accumulation of profit, a structure to further the group's crimes, and the ability to corrupt government officials, police officials, and/or corporate officials.

THE NATURE AND EXTENT OF ORGANIZED CRIME IN AUSTRALIA

As part of a review of law enforcement commissioned by the Australian government in 1994, an analysis of the nature of organized crime was attempted. The approach adopted by the review was to identify groups of alleged criminals, based in part on ethnic origin, because of the significant evidence that criminal associations within various ethnic communities provided a framework within which serious criminal activity was organized. It needs to be emphasized, of course, that within the Australian community there is no evidence of any particular ethnic group being engaged in criminal activity to an extent that is disproportionate with the overall composition of the Australian society. Culture, language, and community associations do, however, provide a framework in which criminal organizations can be less obvious. To this extent Australia's experience mirrors overseas experience.

Further analysis indicated that organized crime (in Australia at least) tends to be far more entrepreneurial than was thought in the past. Its structures are far less rigid, and, although there are clear signs that significant criminal activity is engaged in by people with common ethnic origins, it is not correct to say that there is any link between ethnicity and criminal behavior.

Even in those communities in which there are tight social and community links, criminal activity often extends beyond these links, driven primarily by the profit motive. It is also important that stereotypes be avoided and that general assumptions about criminality within sectors of the Australian community do not cloud our understanding of the real nature of the problem. The level of criminality within identified ethnic groups is, in fact, less than the overall average for the Australian population.

Individual contact and networking between criminals appears to be expanding, both within Australia and internationally, reflecting the multicultural diversity of the Australian population, as well as the domestic and international nature of crime. Moreover, the entrepreneurial nature of organized criminality in Australia has meant that organized crime is both fluid and multidimensional, with many organized criminal groups involved in a range of criminal activities, as opportunities present themselves.

It has been possible to conclude that a number of areas of suspected organized criminal behavior have not developed in the way that had been predicted in the Commonwealth Law Enforcement Review Report (1994). The well-documented activities of criminal groups with their origins in the Soviet Union, but who have now engaged in activities in Central and Western Europe and in North America, do not appear to have yet reached Australia.

Subsequent national strategic intelligence assessments indicate that a new approach is required in the way we look at organized crime in Australia. Common ethnicity within organized crime syndicates is just one aspect of a series of far more complex (and interrelated) markets for illicit goods and services in Australia. Required is an understanding of how these various syndicates interact (either in competition or cooperation) within the illicit marketplace, and what strategies might be employed to disrupt or deter their engagement in these markets in the most cost-effective manner.

The NCA, in partnership with the AFP and the Australian Bureau of Criminal Intelligence, is developing a national overview of the criminal environment in Australia. This assessment is designed to provide an authoritative and comprehensive description of the current criminal environment in Australia, as well as providing a context for evaluating and formulating national law enforcement policies, priorities, and strategies. Based on this assessment, the NCA intends to map and analyze in far greater detail those areas of criminality that appear to have the greatest impact on Australia—the illicit drug markets. It is extremely difficult to estimate the extent of organized crime. Crime statistics that demonstrate a growth in offenses such as burglary, assaults, or theft do not in any sense measure the volume of organized crime, at least as that concept is used in Australia. The very nature of organized crime means that it is in large part undetected, although we often see its consequences. For example, the level of street dealing in narcotics obviously reflects undetected importation. It is the importers and high-level distributors who are regarded as those involved in organized crime rather than lower levels of distribution.

The entrepreneurial nature of organized crime, driven as it is by profits, means that the activities may well change. The shift in the popularity of various illegal drugs over time shows some evidence of the creation of markets by importers or manufacturers. There is a real risk that even if some drugs were legalized, the underlying social factors that create demand might merely see the creation of new markets. More important, there is the strong likelihood that development of global markets, new technologies, expanding financial systems, and reduced regulatory activities will create new opportunities not only for legitimate business, but for those who will seek to misuse these opportunities for criminal activities. The jurisdictional limitation of the nation state will ensure that our responses are restricted unless there is significantly greater international cooperation.

One possible estimate of the size of organized crime in Australia can be derived from the work of John Walker (1996), who estimated that the extent of money laundering in the Australian economy may be as high as $A3.5 billion per annum. A substantial proportion of this amount may well be derived from criminal activities that would not be regarded as organized crime, but the figure does demonstrate that the level of organized criminal activity is likely to be very significant. Moreover, it should be noted that there are few international estimates of the extent of money laundering. For example, the Financial Action Task Force on Money Laundering (FATF) has been unable to estimate the global nature of the problem. Many international estimates of the nature of the problem have significant defects in their methodology, and in many cases law enforcement agencies have an inclination to overstate the problem. As a result, it is not possible to provide any real assessment of the size of the problem in Australia, although there is widespread acceptance within law enforcement that significant organized crime problems exist, which require sophisticated techniques and resources if there is to be an effective counter-action of these activities.

MEASURES, INCLUDING LEGISLATION TO COMBAT ORGANIZED CRIME

In a federal system of government, there are particular problems that arise because the Federal Parliament jurisdiction and matters of state responsibility often leave loopholes. It requires a comprehensive and cooperative effort from all jurisdictions to satisfactorily address the issues. Criminals do not, of course, confine their activities within neat jurisdictional boundaries. The National Crime Authority (NCA) is the organization created to address these issues in Australia. The NCA's mission is to counter organized crime (particularly activities and structures extending beyond individual jurisdictions) and reduce its impact on the Australian community, working in cooperation and partnership with other agencies. In doing so, the NCA aims to effectively disrupt current organized criminal activity in Australia and to prevent and deter future organized criminal activity.

To achieve this, the NCA has adopted a number of strategies; one of the most effective is that of working in close partnership with other agencies to increase the effectiveness of *all* Australian law enforcement operations against organized crime. Importantly, the NCA has a strong commitment to contributing to national and international dialogue on organized crime issues.

The NCA is a unique organization within the law enforcement community in Australia. Under the National Crime Authority Act of 1984 it has a number of coercive powers, including the ability to compel people to produce documents and to appear before the Authority to give sworn evidence. Such powers are not available to traditional police forces. The NCA has a national as well as a multijurisdictional focus and can investigate offenses against federal, as well as state and territory laws. The NCA can, moreover, use facilities such as telephone interception and listening devices. These investigative tools are only available after a judicial warrant has been obtained under the relevant federal and state or territory legislation.

The NCA is not, however, a police service; rather, it is an investigative agency that utilizes multidisciplinary teams of police, financial investigators, lawyers, intelligence analysts, and support staff to investigate organized crime. The multijurisdictional focus and team structure, and the use of coercive powers, has enabled the NCA to conduct national operations in cooperation with other agencies against major areas of organized crime.

The NCA Act is a product of many compromises seeking to strike a balance between the liberties of the individual and the greater good of the community, especially in relation to the inherent difficulties in combating organized crime. In the twelve years since its enactment many lessons have been learned about traditional concepts of combating organized crime. For example, at the time the NCA was established it was generally accepted that one came across some form of criminal activity and then traced it to its perpetrators. This was, and still is, the traditional police model. Police forces investigate known criminality to identify offenders, arrest them, and bring them to trial. If the Authority discovered suspected criminal activity that was relevant criminal activity for the purposes of the Act, a reference could be obtained from the Inter-Governmental Committee and a special investigation could be commenced.

There was a general expectation that specific kinds of criminal activity or the suspected criminal activities of a particular criminal organization would be identified in a reference. However, many of the most significant successes were as a result of examining monetary transactions, which often identified the receiver of such monies but not the criminality involved.

It was only after painstaking investigation that is costly in terms of both time and resources that the relevant criminal activity was identified. This caused many problems with the drafting of appropriate references.

The formative years of the NCA were not easy and there was much jealousy and distrust among traditional law enforcement agencies toward the NCA. The NCA did not help itself by sometimes appearing in a "big brother" role to other police agencies in investigating certain types of criminal activity; but today cooperation between the heads of all relevant Commonwealth law enforcement agencies is extremely good. Unfortunately many of the old habits are taking a long time to wear off, and traditional jealousies still exist throughout all the organizations. There is now widespread acceptance that the best results can be achieved by assisting other traditional law enforcement agencies using the coercive powers and special skills of the NCA.

The NCA incorporates a scheme of statutory checks and balances. At all times the NCA can carry on general investigations into organized crime but it cannot use its coercive powers in relation to such investigations. As previously noted, the Act itself does not actually refer to "organized crime" but provides that one of the functions of the Authority is to investigate relevant "criminal activity." The NCA has other functions that include:

- The collection, analysis, and dissemination of information and intelligence relating to relevant criminal activities; and
- The establishment and coordination of a National/Commonwealth or State/Territory Task Force (where appropriate).

In carrying out its functions, the NCA can exercise wide-ranging powers, some of which are not available to other law enforcement agencies. There are, however, conditions under which these powers, particularly the coercive powers can be used. Legislative requirements specify that NCA's coercive powers may only be used in particular investigations known as *special investigations*. These investigations arise from matters referred to in the form of a reference (or specific mandate) from the Commonwealth and/or State and Territory governments. From time to time the NCA also conducts *general investigations*, which also relate to organized criminal activity, but are not conducted under a "reference." Under these circumstances, the NCA may establish task forces, but its coercive powers cannot be used.

If a relevant Minister of a State or Commonwealth considers that some relevant criminal activity is so serious that it requires the use of the NCA's coercive powers, they can approach the IGC. This committee consists of the federal attorney general and the police ministers for all states and territories. If the IGC considers it appropriate it will issue a reference to the NCA that empowers the Authority to carry out a special investigation in relation to the matters covered by that reference. Once the Authority is conducting a special investigation it can use its coercive powers, which include:

1. Summoning of witnesses to attend upon the Authority and give sworn evidence and produce documents referred to in the summons.
2. Obtaining by compulsion of documents from institutions, especially financial institutions, and requiring those institutions not to divulge the fact that the information has been obtained from them to any persons, including the person to whom the records relate.

A witness summoned to appear before the Authority can only refuse to answer questions if they have reasonable grounds to do so. The most common form of such reasonable grounds is the fact that their answers may incriminate them. Much valuable information can be obtained from people already convicted of offenses, especially drug couriers, who cannot refuse to answer questions on the grounds that it may incriminate them because they have already been convicted of such offenses. Of course they still enjoy the protection against self-incrimination in relation to conduct for which they have not been convicted. All hearings are held in secret and there are statutory prohibitions preventing the dissemination of information relating to the hearings or the fact that that particular witness has been summoned to appear before the NCA. The NCA has to report back to the IGC at regular intervals as to progress in relation to references; and the overall operation of the NCA is monitored by the Parliamentary Joint Committee (PJC), which is a committee consisting of members of both Houses of Federal Parliament from all parties.

At present the NCA's defined area of investigation includes:

1. The criminal milieu on Australia's East Coast;
2. Organized criminal activity originating in Southeast Asia, including Chinese-Australian and Vietnamese-Australian criminal groups;
3. Italo-Australian organized crime;
4. Lebanese-Australian organized crime;
5. Romanian-Australian organized crime;
6. Criminal groups originating in the former Eastern bloc;
7. Colombian cocaine syndicates;
8. The Yakuza;
9. Outlaw motorcycle groups; and
10. Organized pedophile networks.

That is not to say that each of these types of organized crime groups is seen as having similar importance or even to exist in significant measure in Australia. Rather, this is an identification of potential areas of criminal activity that need to be assessed and, if appropriate, investigated further. The current emphasis is in the area of major drug activity and, in particular, importations originating from Southeast Asia. In addition, entrenched criminality on the East Coast and the activities of some motorcycle gangs are important areas of investigation.

The NCA comprises "the Authority" (the chairperson and two members) and approximately 350 members of staff (deputized police, lawyers, and financial and intelligence analysts.). While the chairperson and the members have a corporate and collegiate responsibility for the NCA, neither the chairperson, nor the members actually exercise a direct management role over the particular regional office in which they are located. Instead, the senior management of the NCA consists of two general managers, who exercise functional responsibility for operations and corporate services. In addition regional directors are charged with responsibility for overseeing the day-to-day management of the NCA's five regional offices, located in Sydney, Melbourne, Brisbane, Adelaide, and Perth. The structure of the NCA requires both a flexible organizational approach and a high degree of contact and cohesion between staff and management to enable the ready deployment of staff among operational areas to satisfy common operational objectives.

The NCA examined 180 witnesses at hearings conducted during 1994 and 1995. When compared with the NCA's other powers and traditional information-collection techniques (including searches of public records and cultivating informants), hearings have proved to be an effective use of resources. They tend to be a highly focused technique for obtaining information that cannot often be obtained through alternative or conventional processes. Information obtained during the hearing process has assisted in prosecutions, contributed to determining the course of investigations, generated additional strategic and tactical intelligence, and has also been disseminated to other organizations (such as the Australian Taxation Office) for their own purposes. During the same period, the Authority issued over 700 notices to produce documents under section 29 of the Act, and these notices are proving valuable in the investigation of financial crime, particularly money laundering. Material obtained through hearings or by the notices to produce can only be passed on to other agencies in accordance with specific provisions in the NCA Act, which determine the extent that information can be disseminated to other agencies.

While the NCA has wide-ranging powers and responsibilities, it is only a small organization within a much broader law enforcement environment.

(For example, NCA staff represent less than 1% of Australia's total law enforcement resources.) The NCA recognizes, however, that it operates in a rapidly changing environment and if it is to remain responsive to current developments and meet the emerging challenges from an evolving criminal milieu, it must continue to promote strategic alliances with other agencies.

The NCA has cooperative arrangements with all the Australian police services, and with a range of Commonwealth and state/territory agencies, and the NCA relies on this cooperation to provide it with relevant information and documents. Cooperation takes many forms and may include meetings, dissemination of information, providing assistance to agencies, and working together on joint investigations. The NCA has also developed relationships with overseas agencies, into the maintenance of which it puts considerable effort, with the particular aim of promoting cooperation and liaison.

Cooperation and coordination between law enforcement agencies in areas like the investigation of major organized crime is complex and difficult. Knowledge, trust, and understanding are necessary for agencies to commit substantial resources to relatively long-term projects with uncertain outcomes. Different law enforcement agencies understandably have different priorities; resources are scarce and have to be balanced against public expectations and increased scrutiny of performance. Moreover, an increasing number of regulatory agencies are expanding their law enforcement role. The limited resources of such agencies means that organizations become increasingly reluctant to commit to projects they may not have much control over, or fear may compete with their own interests. Obviously, it is not an easy environment in which to operate, and the challenges that exist are unlikely to diminish.

Past experience has taught the NCA that, while cooperation is an effective strategy, the effectiveness of such an approach can be improved and must be relevant to individual police agencies. In doing so, the NCA and partner agencies have had to develop structures and procedures that enable all to participate in setting priorities for work undertaken collectively. Time must therefore be taken by each agency to consider the costs and difficulties and to ensure that these do not outweigh the expected outcomes and benefits. The NCA and partner agencies now realize that it is fundamental to reach a certain level of agreement and commitment at the outset of an investigation. These agreements must articulate the level of each agency's support, the priority attached to these cooperative ventures, and that the best chance of success is likely to come from a coordinated and cooperative effort. It is also critical that once a commitment to a joint project is in place, that all agencies are adequately informed about the progress and direction of all joint ventures.

Perhaps in the past it has been simply assumed that successful cooperation flows once a commitment is made. Experience has shown, however, that agencies need to work consistently at the processes of cooperation. Indeed, differences between and even within agencies in priorities, cultures, and personalities must be heeded. Cohesion and cooperation cannot be taken for granted, particularly in large national operations.

COMPARATIVE EVALUATION OF ANTI-ORGANIZED CRIME MEASURES

The NCA has enjoyed mixed success. In its early years it was successful in achieving large numbers of arrests and subsequent convictions. Its focus was primarily in the area of drugs, violence, extortion, fraud, and "gangland" activity. Largely as a result of major corporate collapses near the end of the 1980s there was a significant shift in the focus of Australian law enforcement toward corporate or "white collar" crime and the NCA undertook a number of investigations in this area. Out of necessity, these were long, complex, and expensive.

In more recent years the Authority has again directed its work toward more traditional areas of organized criminal activity. It has also built bridges to many other agencies in Australia and works in much closer partnership arrangements. Its results have reflected the benefits of these relationships.

The NCA's current focus is in areas of Asian organized crime, taxation fraud, and money-laundering activities involved with organized crime. The NCA's investigation of money laundering provides an example of how it has added significantly to the capacity of Australian law enforcement to tackle this problem. The increasing international dimension to organized crime is reflected in the growth of money laundering. The scale of the money-laundering problem is believed to be huge. For example, when FATF issued its first report in 1990, it estimated that as much as $85 billion (U.S.) a year in proceeds from drug trafficking in the United States and Europe was available for laundering and investment. If these estimates are accurate, money laundering has clearly reached such proportions that it is capable of affecting the economies and governments of some countries.

The NCA believes that targeting organized crime syndicates through the identification of large-scale money laundering activity is a highly effective strategy for counteracting and disrupting organized crime in Australia. Investigating the financial affairs of these groups in Australia (and around the world), sometimes leading to confiscation of their financial base, is one of the most effective tools that law enforcement agencies have in suppressing their activities. Nevertheless, law enforcement agencies alone cannot hope to stem the enormous surge in money-laundering schemes.

Australia is fortunate in having a highly advanced system of financial transaction reporting and analysis. Law enforcement agencies benefit from sophisticated commonwealth and state proceeds of crime and anti-money laundering legislation, bilateral international treaties providing mutual assistance in criminal matters, and a Commonwealth Evidence Act. Moreover, sophisticated taxation, customs, and corporate and securities industry regulators are in place, and effective overseas liaison is provided by the AFP's fifteen liaison offices in fourteen different countries. Nevertheless, money laundering remains a great concern. Australia's financial transaction reporting agency, AUSTRAC, published a report in 1995, estimating the extent of money laundering in Australia. Tentative conclusions indicated that a range of between $A1 and 4.5 billion is being laundered in and through Australia.

By using its coercive powers (under its generic money-laundering references) in a cooperative rather than an exclusive way, the NCA has sought to involve and work jointly with other agencies to identify and develop opportunities to target major organized criminal enterprises through their money laundering. In doing so, it uses suspect financial activity reported to AUSTRAC by banks and other cash dealers, as a key indicator of money-laundering schemes.

Under its national task force arrangements, the NCA combines these capabilities in a coordinated attack against major organized crime syndicates at their most vulnerable point—their financial base. Through the use of the coercive powers granted under NCA references, NCA has established strategic alliances with other agencies that have extended their own investigative capabilities. As a result, the investigation of any suspect financial activity is possible, particularly that which may be associated with the large-scale money laundering that underlies organized criminal enterprises. These task force arrangements have achieved significant successes through the cooperative efforts of participating agencies.

These successful cooperative arrangements are not restricted to Australia: The NCA and its Australian partners have worked with law enforcement agencies in international jurisdictions to combat organized criminal activities and money laundering. In *Operation Endure*, for example, an international heroin-trafficking syndicate laundered more than $A100 million through more than 300 false name accounts with the Bank of Credit and Commerce in Hong Kong, before investing it in various countries around the world, including Australia. The investigation of suspect real estate transactions in Australia led to the arrest of one of the key players, Tommy Law Kin-man in Hong Kong, and helped facilitate the confiscation of more than $40 million of the syndicate's funds in both Hong Kong and Australia. These investigations involved the cooperation of Australian, United States, and Hong Kong law enforcement agencies.

The experience gained in the last decade has revealed several limitations in the functioning and policies of the NCA. Many of the assumptions about the kind of criminality with which the Authority had to deal, the structure of those criminal organizations, the powers and functions that were appropriate to deal with them, and the legislative responses that were necessary, have changed. For instance, the legislation governing the proceeds of crime was based on an assumption that criminal proceeds were likely to be invested within Australia. This is not always the case. At the Commonwealth level, there was a view that such confiscation of assets should only occur after conviction for serious criminal conduct. Money laundering was identified as a major issue, but the offense itself was linked to a "predicate" offense. It was therefore necessary to establish the criminal behavior in relation to which the funds could be linked before those funds could be confiscated and a prosecution for money laundering undertaken. Today a different picture is emerging.

Often it is the movement of money itself that identifies possible criminal behavior. The proceeds of criminal activity are increasingly leaving Australia, often rather quickly. This emphasizes the need for international perception and cooperation and for the agency to reevaluate the kinds of offenses and legislative structures that are available to combat the crime.

There is a growing perception that the NCA should be changed. The need for a reference to delineate the criminal activities to be investigated before its special powers can be used is not a model that has been followed elsewhere in Australia. For example, there are major agencies with regulatory or law enforcement responsibilities in areas such as anti-trust, companies and securities regulation and banking and finance, which can exercise many of the powers of the NCA, but do so without the same constraints.

Another area where problems have emerged concerns the extent to which Authority staff can operate across Australia's various jurisdictions. It is essential in a federal system that a national law enforcement agency not be circumscribed by jurisdictional boundaries. The criminals are not so limited, and it is essential that national law enforcement be able to deal with offenses irrespective of the jurisdiction in which they take place.

A further area of limitation is in the release of information to other agencies. At the time the Authority was established there was great concern that information acquired through its special powers (i.e., hearings and notices to produce) should not be available to other agencies or even used in unrelated judicial proceedings unless stringent safeguards were met. This has meant that information of direct relevance to other proceedings may not be able to be used because of the secrecy provisions of the Act.

Proposed Measures, Including Legislation to Combat Organized Crime

While it is essential that adequate authority be conferred on any body established to deal with organized crime, that is by no means the end of the story. The experience over the last decade suggests that there are a number of factors that need to come together if there is to be an effective and efficient capacity to deal with organized crime. The need to develop new measures includes political commitment, adequate powers, funding, and coordination.

It is essential that the government support the work of law enforcement in dealing with organized crime. Real commitment rather than rhetoric is fundamental. The government's capacity to provide the necessary support exists far beyond its policy in relation to combating organized crime and also includes a preparedness to provide support facilities, such as the courts, to ensure that criminality is properly adjudicated. The need for adequate powers includes not only the powers to conduct hearings and obtain documents, but the capacity to legally intercept telephones and use listening devices and other electronic surveillance equipment. Similarly, adequate funding is essential to any large-scale and long-term operation. One simply cannot carry out investigative work into organized crime without adequate funding because it is extremely labor intensive and requires considerable capital outlay for equipment.

Moreover, it is essential that the public support the activities of those engaged in fighting organized crime. What tends to happen is that bodies are established with a flourish and soon become of less public interest (often because the media loses interest), and this is directly reflected in political interest and funding availability. The government must realize that cooperation is the key to any success against organized crime. Law enforcement agencies must work with the public, each other, and even with those agencies not directly involved in traditional law enforcement, such as Customs, taxation, and corporate regulatory agencies. The best way to engage in cooperative work is to have strong working partnerships, sanctioned by legislation, to enable the proper exchange of information. Furthermore, in federal systems such as Australia, one agency has to take a coordinating role. This does not mean that it dominates the relationships, or even that it directs them. Indeed, experience shows that shared management models work best.

The jurisdictional boundaries must be broken down. Again, this is a more significant problem within federal systems, but increasingly it is international jurisdictional constraints that assist the criminal. The best solutions are those that involve links between agencies in different countries, supported by effective legislative capacity to provide mutual assistance in criminal investigations.

There is also the urgent need for complementary legislation. Areas such as money laundering and corporate regulation need to be the subject of adequate laws. Lax company structures and open economies with no regulatory trails make it so much easier for criminals. Of course, a balance has to be struck with the demands of legitimate commerce, but law enforcement needs to ensure it has a place at the table in debating these issues.

Combating organized crime (and money laundering in particular) is not just a matter of fighting crime, but of preserving the integrity of institutions (especially financial institutions and, ultimately, of national and international financial systems as well). Impediments to that cooperation continue to exist, including a reluctance to report criminal activity because of the effect it may have on an institution's image (as a recent case with Sumitomo Bank indicates). It is also possible that by reporting criminal activity to law enforcement agencies, financial institutions fear that they may lose control of the matter while, at the same time, there is also the perception that law enforcement simply does not have the resources to deal with the problem. The law enforcement community has a responsibility to address these concerns and to dispel some of the myths. But the financial sector must also do more to ensure that financial institutions protect themselves from criminal penetration. This is particularly important because criminal organizations have drawn upon the expertise and knowledge of professionals to reinvest their funds in legitimate businesses or assets, when these professionals have not questioned the source of the funds in suspicious circumstances. If international financial institutions are to avoid national and international regulation, then a form of self-regulation is necessary.

In *Operation Endure*, for example, the syndicate was the bank's single depositor in Hong Kong—its best customer, and twelve operatives were able to generate about $50 million (U.S.) per year from this enterprise. Laundered funds were invested in the names of companies incorporated in Panama, Liberia, Hong Kong, and Australia. Solicitors, accountants, bankers, merchant bankers, and other financial and business advisers acted on behalf of the group in numerous countries.

In *Operation Flash*, representatives of the Mid Med Bank of Malta were convicted and sentenced after an NCA-led investigation uncovered schemes involving drug trafficking, money laundering, and tax avoidance. Three of the bank's representative offices were also suspended from trading by the Reserve Bank of Australia as a result of the involvement of senior banking staff in criminal activities. In this particular operation, information from AUSTRAC alerted the NCA to a series of structured deposits relating to offshore transfers of $2.5 million to Malta, that investigations eventually revealed were the proceeds of trafficking in cannabis. The investigation has also prompted the Maltese Government to conduct its own investigation. The extent to which these schemes are being carried out by other foreign offices in Australia is unknown. But the NCA has taken the steps to alert the treasury and the Reserve Bank of Australia to the need to closely monitor the operations of these banks.

Increasingly, the trend overseas has been for close working relationships between central banks, financial policy makers, and law enforcement in relation to dealing with the problem of money laundering. The British seem to have developed a very satisfactory "whole of government" approach to this problem, with close cooperation between bodies as different as the Bank of England, the Foreign and Commonwealth Office, the police, and the National Criminal Intelligence Service. There has also been a marked increase in the recognition by major international financial bodies such as the International Monetary Fund and the World Bank that money laundering is not just a major problem in combating organized crime, but also a significant threat to the integrity of financial markets.

A great deal of work is now being done in Australia to identify the extent to which the rapidly growing potential for electronic commerce is weakening the impact of central banks. Notions of controlling the money supply through devices such as interest rate policy may be seriously weakened if major financial transactions can take place outside the control of those national regulatory agencies. More important is the potential for electronic commerce to generate new ways for organized crime to operate. Not only do these systems provide the means by which the proceeds of crime can be moved around the world instantaneously, but the transactions can be anonymous and may be very vulnerable to fraud. It will require extensive international cooperation to develop appropriate systems to deal with this issue. There is now a global marketplace and our legal system is still based on traditional concepts of nation and sovereignty that may not be relevant in the twenty-first century.

Conclusion

Because organized criminal activity (particularly money laundering) is an international phenomenon, the response to it must embrace as many countries as possible. In recent years, both formal and informal cooperation between individual countries has increased significantly. Through mutual assistance treaties, Australia's efforts to combat money laundering and other organized crime activity has become better focused and more effective. (For example, the NCA has already made a mutual assistance request seeking the extradition of a person believed to be significantly involved in heroin importation and distribution and money laundering.)

While the NCA has benefited from the application of its special powers, experience has shown that national and international cooperation is one of the most important instruments in any successful attack on organized crime. While the NCA has worked hard to develop strategic alliances with its Australian partners in the law enforcement community, it recognizes that its most important challenges are yet to be faced. The NCA must now work toward creating a more comprehensive approach to combating organized crime by convincing an independent and rather conservative financial sector to become more active in the regulation and monitoring of crime and by developing stronger cooperative and mutually beneficial arrangements with its international partners.

We need legislative approaches to organized crime that are innovative, yet also reflect concerns about the basic rights of individuals and the key elements of our justice system. What we must do is to continually debate within the community the appropriate balances to be struck so that our legislative framework is consistent with the community's understanding of the problem and the appropriateness of measures to combat it.

As the area of electronic commerce continues to develop, there will be new areas of potential criminality and challenges we have not yet faced. Cooperation between law enforcement, financial regulators, and national legislators will be essential if we are to meet this challenge. Far too often our laws have failed to keep pace with social and technological change. The speed with which these funds are now moving makes it more difficult to trace criminal activity, but it is even more essential that we do it.

REFERENCES

Australian Bureau of Statistics. 1992. *Social Indicators 1992.* Canberra: Australian Government Publishing Service.

Australian Bureau of Statistics. 1995. *Year Book Australia 1995.* Canberra: Australian Government Publishing Service.

John Walker. 1996. http://www.ozemail.com.au/~born1820/index.html.

Nation's Commonwealth Law Enforcement Review Report. 1994. http://www.nla.gov.au/cleb/9596ann.html: Kingston ACT: Commonwealth Law Enforcement Board.

Year Book Australia. 1996. Attorney General's Department: Annual Report 1995–1996. Commonwealth of Australia, Sydney: National Capital Printing.

Chapter 16

Organized Crime: A Perspective from New Zealand

Greg Newbold

Introduction

New Zealand is a nation of 3.6 million people, located in the South Pacific Ocean. Comprising two main islands, known as the North and South Islands, it has a total area of about 17,000 square miles. Approximately three-fourths of the population live in the temperate and less mountainous North Island; 886,000 of them in the country's largest city, Auckland. The capital, Wellington, is the next largest, with 326,000. The third largest city, Christchurch (307,000), is the biggest urban area in the South Island.

An important feature of New Zealand's geography is its isolation. It has no contiguous borders with any other country and is approximately 1,200 miles from its nearest neighbor, Australia. There is only one fully international airport, in Auckland, and this remoteness makes smuggling into the country extremely difficult. Although the New Zealand coastline is large, the importance of the fishing industry and the threat imposed by poaching from foreign trawlers, requires extensive policing of territorial waters. In addition, New Zealand's inshore seas can be very rough and small boats often founder. In 1979, for example, an attempt to smuggle three kilograms of heroin ashore by yacht was foiled when the boat was wrecked on the South Island's rugged West Coast.

Systematic colonization of New Zealand did not commence until 1839, and in 1840 it became a British colony after a number of the chiefs of its native people, the Maori, ceded their sovereignty to the Crown. Since that time extensive intermarriage between Maori and Europeans has blurred racial divisions, but about 13 percent of the population now claims at least a degree of Maori ancestry. Other major ethnic subgroups include Pacific island Polynesian (5%), Chinese (almost 2%), and Indian (1%).

Although it has diversified considerably in the last decade or so, New Zealand is principally a farming nation, with one fourth of its export income deriving from meat and dairy products. Forestry and fishing are also major earners of foreign currency, and more than 10 percent of the workforce is employed in these areas. Deregulation of the economy in the 1980s resulted in soaring unemployment. However, since 1992, joblessness has dropped and now lies at about 8 percent. Maori and Pacific island Polynesians are disproportionately represented in unemployment statistics. The existence of a comprehensive system of benefits for the unemployed has allowed New Zealand to avoid the problem of long-term homelessness, which is evident in countries like the United States.

Although New Zealand has a reputation for being a peaceful nation, crime rates are quite high. In 1992 an international crime victimization survey of nine countries, including Australia, Canada, the United States, and several European nations found New Zealand to be highest in reported victimizations for burglary, theft of personal property, and assault or threat of assault. Comparatively high victimization rates were also reported in sexual assaults (along with Australia, the United States, and Canada). On the other hand, along with England and Wales, only one country, Sweden, had a lower rate of robbery and attempted robbery than New Zealand. Homicide rates in New Zealand are high relative to most other countries, but at around eighty a year, are still only about one fifth of the rate reported in the United States (Adler, Mueller, and Laufer, 1996). The disparity with the United States appears largely due to the fact that handguns in New Zealand are highly regulated and that New Zealand does not have a major hard drug problem. In 1996 there were 23,000 drug offenses reported to the New Zealand Police, but 93 percent of them involved marijuana.

Like the United States, New Zealand has experienced major escalation in levels of reported crime in the last few decades. This may be attributed largely to the end of the post-war boom in the 1960s, the oil shocks of the 1970s, and the share market crash of 1987 (see Newbold, 1992). During the 1990s, however, these levels dropped or have abated in most cases. In the absence of major changes in criminal justice or law enforcement policy, it is likely that the reasons for this decline lie in the nation's economic recovery, which commenced in 1992.

New Zealand operates as a unicameral parliamentary democracy. It has been self-governing since 1853 and has been fully independent since 1947. Nonetheless, the Queen of England remains the titular head of state, and no act of Parliament can become law without the signature of the governor general, who is the Queen's local representative. The nation has only one police force, which was established in 1886. Numbering about 7,000 sworn personnel, the New Zealand Police are well trained, professionally organized, and well paid. Recruits, who normally require at least four years of high school education, are schooled for six months at a residential college on a salary of NZ $27,164. Once sworn, the salary increases to NZ $37,803.

As with England and Wales, police in New Zealand do not normally carry firearms while on duty. The absence of weapons affects policing dynamics because it reduces the power differential between a policeman and the general public. Interpersonal skills are thus extremely important qualities in New Zealand policing, particularly in situations that are violent or potentially so. Armed suspects are normally dealt with by specially trained Armed Offenders squads. It is significant in this regard that at the time of writing (June 1997) only seventeen suspects had been shot dead by New Zealand police since 1941; six of them since 1990. Twenty-four policemen had been murdered in the line of duty since the force was formed in 1886. Three have been killed since 1990.

It is partly because of the small size of New Zealand, its unified police force, and good pay and high professional standards within the force that institutionalized corruption is virtually unknown in the modern New Zealand Police. The fact that policemen will break the law to enforce the law, but will not take bribes, is often lamented within the country's criminal fraternity. The incorruptibility of the New Zealand Police is an important factor in crime control because, as other chapters in this text demonstrate, organized crime cannot flourish without the protection of a crooked administration.

Nature and Extent of Organized Crime in New Zealand

Although sporadic instances of organized crime in New Zealand have been recorded as far back as the 1860s, as a specific and ongoing problem, organized crime did not appear there until the mid 1970s. However, not until 1987, as a result of concern that certain Asian immigrants may have criminal connections in their home countries, did the coordinated gathering of intelligence about organized crime begin. Three years later, a full-time organized criminal intelligence officer was established at Police National Headquarters. In 1991, as an extension of this measure, the first dedicated Asian crime units were created.

In New Zealand, the police definition of organized crime contains four essential elements:

1. The criminal activity must be continuing.
2. The activity must involve profit.

3. The activity must involve a group of persons.
4. The activity must be accompanied by the use of fear and violence (Fiso, 1996).

The New Zealand police definition thus restricts itself principally to the activities of the underworld. Ostensibly respectable organizations, such as commercial and governmental entities, although involved in crime that is organized through activities such as fraud, tax evasion, and misappropriation of funds, are excluded. In New Zealand, the prosecution of such white-collar offenses is normally conducted by a special agency known as the Serious Fraud Office (see Newbold and Ivory, 1993). Since parts of this paper rely heavily on intelligence supplied by the police, it is the police definition which will be used.

The commencement of organized crime in New Zealand coincides with the popularity of recreational drug use, which began in the late 1960s. The burgeoning demand for these drugs is demonstrated in cannabis-dealing offenses, which grew exponentially between 1972 and 1990. LSD seizures also became regular in the 1970s, and in the second half of the 1970s, a series of major heroin busts were made (Ministry of Health, 1995).

The Mr. Asia Gang

When organized crime appeared in New Zealand in the 1970s, it was drug-related. Semi-organized groups had been importing marijuana from Southeast Asia since the early 1970s, but the most active organized criminal gang in the 1970s became known as the "Mr. Asia" gang. The Mr. Asia gang is significant because it represents the only time in New Zealand history that an organized criminal enterprise has operated on a major scale. As we shall see, factors outlined earlier, relating to New Zealand's geographical and social context, frustrated the gang's attempts to control the country's drug trade for long.

In February 1974 Terry Clark, alias Sinclair, a 30 year old petty criminal serving a five-year sentence for burglary, was released from prison. Short of cash and wanting fast money, he organized a drug rip-off in Auckland and with the lucre thus obtained, he began the large-scale importation of marijuana and heroin from Thailand. By reinvesting most of his profits in further shipments, Clark soon became extremely wealthy. Shrewd and ambitious, by mid 1975 he was already developing plans to control the entire illicit drug trade in New Zealand and to franchise areas out to various distributors (Clark, 1995).

In 1975, due to police pressure in New Zealand, Clark shifted his operations to Australia. There his business boomed and the Mr. Asia gang became richer and more powerful than ever. By paying a retainer of $A22,000 a year to the Australian Federal Narcotics Bureau, Clark gained a degree of criminal immunity in Australia and was also able to buy information from the bureau at around $A10,000 a time (Kwitny, 1987). A ruthless operator, from 1977, Clark also began eliminating people who he perceived as a threat to his security. Thus, in late 1977, Clark ordered the murders of two of his workers, Greg Ollard and Julie Thielman (Hall, 1981). The following year, Clark shot in the head another of his workers, Harry Lewis. Further, in 1979, after police sold Clark tapes in which his workers Doug and Isobel Wilson could be heard informing on him, they, too, were shot.

By 1979, Clark was worth hundreds of millions of dollars and headed one of the biggest heroin syndicates in the world. Much of his money was laundered through the corrupt Nugan Hand Bank, which also had links with a number of retired senior American military officers (Kwitny, 1987). In May 1979, soon after the Wilsons' deaths, Clark flew to London. There he was joined by a number of his workers, including a former partner, Marty Johnstone. As a result of his own incompetence, Johnstone now had debts of $A2 million, much of it owed to Clark. Clark saw Johnstone as a security threat. Accordingly, in October 1979, Johnstone was taken north from London by two of Clark's men and shot in the head. His weighted body was then dumped in a disused, water-filled quarry in Lancashire.

It was this event that sealed the fate of the Mr. Asia gang. Soon after Clark had arrived in London, the Wilsons' bodies had been found in Melbourne, Australia. A number of the organization's members were already serving prison sentences, and police in New Zealand, Australia, the United Kingdom, Singapore, and Thailand now had extensive dossiers on the gang's activities. These countries eventually provided Britain's director of public prosecutions with 1,500 pages of evidence in the trial that followed (*Appendices to the Journals of the House of Representatives* G.6, 1980). Johnstone's death did not go unnoticed for long, either. Just a few days after the killing, recreational scuba divers chanced upon Johnstone's body in the quarry. In the panic that ensued, members of the gang began to talk, and as arrests began, more started to crack. Clark himself was apprehended in November 1979. In July 1981, after a 121-day trial, Clark and seven other gang members were sentenced to prison terms ranging from five years to life imprisonment. Two were acquitted. Clark received life with a 20-year minimum. He died of a heart attack in Parkhurst Prison in 1983.

The collapse of Clark's drug empire caused a dramatic drop in the availability of heroin in New Zealand. Clark was not the only operator, but his arrest, which had been preceded by the arrests of several other big importers in the mid to late 1970s, had a resounding impact on big-time heroin importation. Heroin seizures, which had peaked at nearly 2,000 grams in 1978, almost disappeared in the early 1980s. Imported cannabis also vanished and was replaced by hemp grown domestically. Although imported heroin remained comparatively rare, by 1984 it too had been replaced from another source: "homebaked" heroin and morphine manufactured in backyard laboratories from codeine-based analgesics (Committee on Drug Dependency and Drug Abuse, 1973).

Outlaw Gangs

The demise of the Mr. Asia gang did not result in the end of illegal drug use in New Zealand. All it did was alter the sources of such drugs, and, by the same token, the Mr. Asia arrests did not signal the end of organized crime, either. From the late 1970s onward, organized crime increasingly became the province of outlaw gangs.

Loose youth gangs had begun forming in New Zealand in the early 1950s (Howman, 1972; Yska, 1993). However, these disorganized groups lacked formal structure and only remained until 1961, when a chapter of the Hell's Angels Motorcycle Club (HAMC) was established in Auckland. The Hell's Angels had initially formed in San Bernardino, California, in 1948. HAMC (Auckland) was the fourth chapter of the Hell's Angels, and the first chapter to be established outside of California (Lavigne, 1987). It was not long before other patched gangs (gangs who wear identifying colors), such as Highway 61, the Road Knights, the Epitaph Riders, and the Mongrel Mob, also became a part of the New Zealand social scene.

Since the late 1960s, the Californian Hell's Angels had been dealing in LSD, PCP, and methamphetamine (Lavigne, 1987). Until the mid 1970s, however, HAMC (Auckland) was a gang of traditional type, with activities principally revolving around bikes, booze, women, and the odd turf war with other gangs. Then in 1976 a dozen Angels were imprisoned for manslaughter after a dispute with Highway 61. This was a significant milestone for the gang. Apart from the twelve on the manslaughter counts, several others were also in prison on different charges. With a membership of less than twenty-five, this meant that over one half of its complement was now locked up. The group's core was confined in New Zealand's maximum security prison at Paremoremo, near Auckland. Here, also, the country's most serious criminals were held, including a number of major drug traffickers. The population of Paremoremo was less than 200, so it was inevitable that close relationships among inmates would develop. At Paremoremo the Angels became involved in bookmaking and small-time drug distribution. By the time they started getting released in the late 1970s, many had formed friendships with members of New Zealand's criminal underworld. It is likely that the gang's involvement in organized commercial crime dates from about this time.

By the end of 1980 the Californian Angels had been dealing amphetamines, LSD, cocaine, and other drugs for well over a decade and had become a worldwide organization, with forty-seven chapters in ten different countries (Lavigne, 1987). The international brotherhood was strong, and when the Auckland group commenced dealing, its main supply source was in California. By 1980, members of the Auckland Hell's Angels had ready access to amphetamines and LSD. Early in the 1980s the gang was prosperous enough to afford a large piece of real estate and a spacious house in the expensive Auckland suburb of Mt. Eden, and a number of Angels were investigated for drug dealing. Further evidence of the Angels' international links came in 1986, when about one hundred members of chapters around the world attempted to enter New Zealand to celebrate the Auckland chapter's twenty-fifth anniversary (*New Zealand Herald*, 30 June 1986). A second international gathering was held for the group's thirtieth anniversary in 1991.

In 1981 a governmental Committee on Gangs reported that according to police, there were at least 80 different gangs or gang chapters in New Zealand, with approximately 2,300 members (Committee on Gangs, 1981). By this time the modern gang profile had been established, with three types of gangs identified: outlaw motorcycle gangs, numbering 20, with 630 members; Maori and Polynesian ethnic gangs, with 57 different chapters and 1,650 members; and an unknown number of white ethnic gangs. In 1988 the estimate reached 4,400, in 45 gangs. The largest gang was said to be the Mongrel Mob, with 670 members, followed by the Black Power with 413, the Devil's Henchmen with 108, and the Storm Troopers with 50 (*Press*, 26 September 1988). By 1989 the police gang estimate had increased to 5,356 members and associates, 3,041 of them fully patched (entitled to wear the gang's full colors). The Mob's strength was said to have increased to 1,630, of whom 741 were patched (*Christchurch Star*, 29 November 1989).

Like the Hell's Angels, there is good evidence that some of the larger New Zealand gangs became more organized in the 1980s as well. Perhaps the most successful was an Auckland chapter formed under the name "Sindis" in 1976 and that joined with Black Power two years later. In 1980 the chapter formed a charitable trust known as *Tatau Te Iwi* ("We, the People") (O'Reilly, 1986). By exploiting government employment-incentive handouts and gang labor, by 1986 the chapter had developed multimillion-dollar assets, including legitimate haulage, labor hire, security, and travel companies in Auckland. It owned a NZ $600,000 clubhouse in South Auckland and had purchased other properties for locating factories. It also had two limousines and a large number of Harley Davidson motorcycles imported from California (*Sunday Star*, 17 August 1986).

Until they were closed down in 1987, other gangs made use of these grants for contract work schemes also. In Christchurch, Black Power received NZ $483,000 in work-scheme payments in 1985 and 1986. The Christchurch chapter of Highway 61 received NZ $214,000, the Mongrel Mob's chapter, NZ $179,000. So in all, around NZ $800,000 a year in government money was being spent on gang-related schemes in Christchurch alone (*New Zealand Herald*, 1987).

The Mongrel Mob, which has existed since 1966, profited least from the tapping of public resources. Fragmented and still only semi-organized, it continued to commit principally low or zero-profit offenses such as rapes, beatings, intimidation, debt collecting, burglaries, robberies, and murders. Efforts to improve its tawdry image failed dismally. In December 1986 an attempt by the Mob to legitimize itself flopped when a highly publicized national gang convention ended in an even more highly publicized gang rape. Partly as a result of this, a scheme to arrange a NZ $2 million deal from the Middle East to finance job training schemes fell through (*New Zealand Herald*, 4 February 1987). In January 1987 and January 1989, government-funded work-skills vehicles owned by Mongrel Mob charitable trusts were used to commit armed holdups (*New Zealand Herald*, 8 January 1987; 6 January 1989). Later in 1989, an attempt to link up with outlaw gangs in Western Australia, ended with the Australian gangs denouncing the Mob as troublemakers and seeking to have them deported (*Christchurch Star*, 29 November 1989).

The failed criminal activity of these larger gangs is reflected in prison population figures. At the end of the 1980s, one fourth of all prison inmates were gang members or associates. Of these, one half belonged to the Mongrel Mob and almost one third to Black Power. Members of motorcycle gangs only accounted for about 11 percent of gang members in prison (Meek, 1992). In 1987, reflecting the high Mongrel Mob presence, 56.1 percent of all gang members were serving time for violence, as opposed to 38.5 percent of non-gang-affiliated inmates. On the other hand, gang members were only 3.3 percent of those doing time for drugs compared with 10.3 percent of the non-gang-affiliated (Braybrook and O'Neill, 1988). A later survey conducted in 1995 found that the percentage of gang affiliation in prison had dropped to 16 percent, but gang members were still more likely to be doing time for violence than the unaffiliated and were still less likely to be incarcerated for drugs (Lash, 1996).

These figures notwithstanding, certain gangs have continued to be involved in drug dealing. As the recession deepened in the 1980s, numerous individuals, not all of them gang members, resorted to drug dealing as a source of income. Reported cannabis trafficking offenses grew by 56 percent between 1980 and 1989. The amount of cannabis leaf seized more than doubled. Cash-cropping of marijuana became an important source of income in certain depressed rural areas such as the far North, the Coromandel Peninsula, and the East Coast of the North Island. Reflecting this, the number of plants seized annually escalated even more rapidly than seizures of cannabis leaf. There were more than five times as many plants seized in 1989 than there were in 1980. Official figures are not broken down into drug groups, but the number of non-cannabis dealing offenses reported in the 1980s also grew by 45 percent.

Exactly how much of these increases can be attributed to gangs, how much to other organized criminal groups, and how much to unorganized crime, we can only speculate about. But police believe that during the 1990s, the Hell's Angels continued to be a principal source of LSD and methamphetamine in New Zealand and that they distribute such drugs to other gangs. Gangs not linked with the Angels, such as Highway 61 and certain chapters of Black Power, sell marijuana through holes in the walls of their clubhouse enclosures. Many gangs are also a source of illegal firearms, often obtained through burglaries of the premises of known firearms owners. Another source, especially since the breakup of the Soviet Union, is sailors from Eastern Europe, who are able to purchase handguns relatively cheaply in their home countries and get a good price for them in New Zealand. Many of these weapons are sold to or end up in the hands of gang members. In addition to criminal activity, however, a number of gangs also have interests in legitimate tax-paying enterprises such as night clubs, massage parlors, and motorcycle parts outlets.

A feature of the 1990s has been a tendency for gangs to become corporate and to internationalize. In doing so, they have adopted the same globalization strategies that have been taken by legitimate businesses around the world. By 1987 the Hell's Angels had at least 1,000 members worldwide, distributed among 67 chapters in 13 countries on 4 continents (Lavigne, 1987). The Hell's Angels are now considered the wealthiest and most powerful of the motorcycle gangs in America, followed by the Outlaws, the Pagans, and the Bandidos. Together they number 3,000 members and represent the largest criminal organization in America. Of these "big four," only the Pagans do not have international connections (Kenney and Finckenauer, 1995).

In 1993 HAMC World, Outlaws MC World, and Bandidos MC World were reported to have set up a corporate global takeover plan. In Britain during the 1990s the Hell's Angels registered four companies bearing their name and established Hell's Angels (Europe) Ltd. to control the use of trademarks such as the death's head logo and to run concerts and bike shows (*New Zealand Herald*, 16 October 1996).

It appears that within New Zealand a similar process may be taking place. It has been reported that Highway 61 has frequent contact with Bandidos MC World in Australia (*Dominion*, 24 June 1996). But the best organized gang in New Zealand is still the HAMC. Numbering about twenty, the HAMC is tight and loyal and its public profile is low. It has international credibility and a long association with the most powerful gang in the United States. Seldom, nowadays, do its members appear in court. Rarely are they involved in the types of intergang strife that draw attention to other gangs such as the Mongrel Mob, Black Power, the Road Knights, and the Epitaph Riders. Sophisticated, unpretentious, well-attired, and polite to its neighbors, HAMC (Auckland) is a prototype of the successful gang of the future.

For some years, the Hell's Angels have sought to expand their sphere of influence from their base in Auckland. To some extent, this endeavor has been frustrated by a loose union of half a dozen or so gangs called "The Federation," which has resisted the Angels' advances. In 1992, however, the HAMC began prospecting in the small North Island town of Wanganui, forming a chapter there in 1994. Already having established business links with a number of North Island gangs, in 1995 it is believed that they began looking for a connection in the South Island. The group they chose to work with was the Road Knights MC. The Road Knights are a small motorcycle club that formed in the South Island town of Timaru in the late 1970s. The gang now has chapters in other South Island towns such as Christchurch, Dunedin, and Invercargill and interests in at least three registered companies. In Christchurch, where approximately fourteen Road Knights live, the gang is also closely associated with a small group of neofascist teenagers known as the Bandenkreig, who often contract themselves out to the Knights.

The most violent gang in the South Island, during the 1990s, the Knights, or their associates have been involved in beatings, drive-by shootings, arsons, robberies, and in 1991, the bombing of a police station. Given its high profile, the Angels' choice of partner in their South Island venture is surprising. According to police intelligence, initially the Knights were provided with cheap methamphetamine to allow them to cut out their opposition. This caused friction with other gangs, in particular with the Epitaph Riders, an old Christchurch gang formed in 1969. Conflict soon led to gunfire, with a number of drive-by shootings in Christchurch streets in the early part of 1996. Nobody was seriously injured in these incidents until April, when a female bystander was wounded in the chest by a .45 pistol shot fired by a Road Knights associate.

The result was a vigorous police crackdown on Road Knights activity, which resulted, for example, in gang members receiving NZ $13,000 in traffic offense notices in the months immediately following the April shooting. In 1996, twenty-three Road Knights members were sent to prison, including three jailed in relation to the shooting.

According to 1996 police estimates, there are around 45 different gangs in New Zealand, totaling approximately 5,500 members. The frequently violent criminal activity of the gangs is attested to by the fact that about 750 gang members and associates are currently in prison, most for crimes of violence (Lash, 1996). Between 1994 and 1996, Road Knights members alone were convicted of nearly 2,000 separate offenses (*Press*, 10 September 1996). Apart from a number of assaults, stabbings, shootings, robberies, rapes, and murders, in 1995 and 1996 New Zealand gang members were arrested for LSD and marijuana trafficking and for the manufacture of methamphetamine.

A very recent development has been the apparent linking of gangs with members of Asian crime syndicates. According to police intelligence, Black Power, the Mongrel Mob, the Headhunters, the King Cobras, and the Satan's Slaves have all liaised with Asian organized crime groups in recent years and may have been doing so for some time (Fiso, 1996). Perhaps the most disturbing of these associations has been that between the Mongrel Mob and the Hong Kong-based 14K Triad. In April 1996, police say, 14K offered the Mob NZ $140,000 to kill Detective Sergeant Api Fiso, the coordinator of the Asian Crime Unit in Wellington (*Press*, 19 November 1996). The implication of such developments for this country's law enforcement strategy will be addressed later in the chapter.

Organized Asian Crime

Immigrants of Asian extraction have been part of New Zealand's population since the early days of formal colonization. When gold was first discovered in New Zealand in 1861, large numbers of Chinese entered the country to work in the goldfields and many of them remained after the rushes had subsided. In 1881, out of a total population of 534,000, there were more than 5,000 Chinese residents in New Zealand (Department of Statistics, 1990).

Although discriminated against by a variety of legislation (see Department of Statistics 1990), the New Zealand Chinese have always been largely a law-abiding people whose principal vice until the end of the 1960s appeared to be the smoking, by some, of opium. With the 1970s and the pressure that came upon drug abuse generally, however, the opium habits of old Chinese were largely extinguished.

For most of the twentieth century, the number of ethnic Chinese grew only gradually, reaching 20,000, or .6 percent of the population, in 1986. After that, however, as a result of the opening up of the borders of mainland

China, and nervousness in Hong Kong and Taiwan over the impending transfer of Hong Kong to communist rule in 1997, a huge exodus of Chinese occurred to the nations of the West. A number of these emigrants came to New Zealand. Thus, the Chinese population in New Zealand doubled between 1986 and 1991, to 44,800 (1.3%). In the census of 1991, 30 percent of all immigrants living in New Zealand had been born in Asia. This made Asians (including Indians) New Zealand's largest immigrant group. At the time of this writing (February 1997), 1996 census data were not available, but between 1991 and 1995, the number of North Asians approved for residency in New Zealand grew from 10,564 to 24,519. This amounted to 44 percent of all residency approvals. In 1996, as a result of tighter residency rules, the number of North Asian permits dropped to 14,716, or 34.8 percent of all approvals. That year, the largest sources of Asian immigrants were China, South Korea, and Taiwan, in that order (Young, 1996). The bulk of Asians now live in the three major cities: Auckland (57.1%), Wellington (16.3%), and Christchurch (6.8%) (Statistics New Zealand, 1994; 1997).

With the idea of boosting local business with injections of capital, New Zealand's "Business Investment Policy" of 1987 welcomed immigrants who had sufficient business capital and investment skills to make a positive contribution to the New Zealand economy. Many Chinese, especially those from Hong Kong, Taiwan, and Malaysia, fell into this category. But a fraction of those who entered under the business provision had fortunes made through involvement with organized crime. They maintained links with such crime on arriving in New Zealand and thus, organized Asian crime became an issue for the country.

As noted, the existence of a specifically Asian component to organized crime was formally recognized in New Zealand in 1987. The country's first Asian Crime Units were established in Wellington and Auckland in 1991, and a third was set up in Christchurch in 1996. Wellington's facility now has two detectives assigned to it, Auckland has three detectives, and Christchurch has one (Fiso, 1997). The senior coordinating officer, Api Fiso, holds the rank of detective sergeant.

At first, the existence of organized Asian crime groups remained barely noticed by the New Zealand public. But by September 1991 the police were aware of the existence of Triad gangs, which were involved in drugs, prostitution, credit card fraud, and extortion (*Dominion*, 10 September 1996). By the end of 1991, the Customs Department knew that around twenty Triad members, six of them "highly ranked," were resident in New Zealand (*Dominion*, 27 January 1992).

As a result of this and other faults in immigration policy, in the 1990s the government passed a number of amendments to the Immigration Act 1987. In 1991 a "points" system was introduced, by which the suitability of residency applicants could be measured according to a range of criteria. At the same time, the Business Investment Policy was replaced with a "Business Investment" category. The purpose of these and other amendments was to tighten restrictions on immigration by closer scrutiny of the character of applicants and to be more prescriptive about financial and business requirements. The amendments sought to ensure that entrepreneurial immigrants were bona fide business people who would actively invest their money in New Zealand for a minimum period of time.

Whether the amendments did, in fact, prevent the entry of more syndicated criminals is a matter for debate. Certainly, Triad-associated persons have been in New Zealand for at least two decades. One of the earliest-known individuals with Triad connections is a person I will call Y, who entered New Zealand in 1973. Although he denies he is a member of a triad, Y admits he has known Ma Man-Chuen, a senior member of the 14K Triad in Hong Kong, for twenty years. Y once acted as foster father to Man-Chuen's son. In 1989, during friction with the Wo Triad in Wellington, a number of 14K members were recruited from Britain, and together with local members, they smashed up a Wellington restaurant owned by the Wo group and attacked the staff. As a result of this incident, Y was arrested for assault with a weapon and fined NZ $4,000.

14K, which had changed its name from Hong Yee upon moving to Hong Kong from Guangzhou after 1949 (Deputy Director, 1996), is currently the third largest Triad in Hong Kong (Harrington, 1997). This group is also one of the most powerful in New Zealand. First coming to police attention in 1987, when it was involved in the importation of heroin to Australia, 14K has since been associated with more drug trafficking, as well as with gambling, assaults, passport forgery, and illegal shellfish smuggling.

There are two other Triad-style groups in New Zealand: San-Yee-On and the Wo group. San-Yee-On, like 14K, has its origins in China. Currently the largest Triad in Hong Kong with 47,000 members (Deputy Director, 1996), the group is reputed to have forged alliances with corrupt officials in the People's Republic of China. Since the departure of its New Zealand leader in 1992, San-Yee-On is believed to be leaderless here, but remains in control of a gambling den in Auckland and retains contact with its counterparts in Hong Kong (Fiso, 1996).

The Wo group is in stronger condition, and one of its factional leaders is a retired Hong Kong policeman. The group is active in car theft, receiving, prostitution, drug smuggling, and shellfish smuggling. Since its confrontation with the 14K in 1989, the Wo group is believed to have declined in Wellington and now operates principally from Auckland (Fiso, 1996).

In addition to the Triads, a number of other Asian organized crime rings have links with New Zealand. Vietnamese immigrants, for example, many of whom came to New Zealand as refugees under a United Nations charter, have been involved in prostitution, gambling, and heroin importation. Young Asian immigrants, sent to New Zealand for education by their wealthy parents, have been associated with dealing in false passports and, as in Australia, are believed to be vulnerable to recruitment into organized crime groups (Fiso, 1996).

From Singapore and Malaysia are the Ah Kong group and its offshoot, Singma. Although of little influence in New Zealand so far, Ah Kong is highly active in drug smuggling in Europe, and both have been involved in heroin smuggling in Australia since at least 1990. Also since 1994, intelligence suggests that Ah Kong has had drug-smuggling links with New Zealand. In 1995, information was received by the police about the presence of a high-ranking Ah Kong member from Belgium (Fiso, 1996).

The final group, which has had a presence in New Zealand in recent years, is what Japanese officially call "Boryokudan" ("violent ones"), but who are known to themselves as "Yakuza," after a worthless hand in a card game (Abadinsky, 1990). Yakuza is actually a collective name for approximately 24 major groups operating in Japan and elsewhere. With a collective membership of 79,300 in 1995, the Boryokudan is the largest organized crime group in the world (Uchiyama, 1996).

Boryokudan groups have significant links with legitimate business in Japan and also have well-known connections in Japanese politics. Outside of Japan, Boryokudan are involved in a variety of activities such as violence, prostitution, gun smuggling, as well as a great deal of legitimate business. Although there is little evidence of major activity in New Zealand, several Boryokudan have entered or attempted to enter the country, one with $85,000 (U.S.) in his pocket. The principal activity of Boryokudan in New Zealand is thought to be money laundering, and there has been some evidence of prostitution as well (Fiso, 1996).

To date, Asian crime in New Zealand has had a number of manifestations. There were major heroin seizures in New Zealand in 1987, 1991, and 1993. Almost all of the significant heroin seizures since 1987, in fact, have involved Asians from identified criminal networks. A number of other Asian crime figures have been arrested overseas or been involved in trafficking heroin to Australia via New Zealand (Fiso, 1996).

Apart from drugs, organized Asian groups have been involved in gambling dens and the manufacture and importation of counterfeit gambling chips. Since 1993, such groups have also increasingly engaged in crimes of violence. Between 1991 and 1995 there was more than a 200 percent increase in the number of Asians apprehended for violence. Greatest areas of growth have occurred in the areas of assaults, robbery, and intimidation and threats. A number of cases of kidnapping for the purposes of extortion, and other forms of extortion, have been reported to the police since 1993. Throughout New Zealand, Asian criminal groups have become involved in organized burglary, shoplifting, and motor vehicle theft, and with the "fencing" of stolen goods. Police intelligence indicates that overseas criminal methods are being passed on to and adopted by local criminals (Fiso, 1996).

Since 1993, the counterfeiting of money and credit cards has been identified on a number of occasions and several arrests have been made. Passport fraud, too, has been detected, together with attempts to smuggle aliens into the country. Many such persons arrive with false or forged travel documents to work as prostitutes in urban massage parlors.

The impact of Asian organized crime is also being felt in juvenile offending. Youth gangs are forming along ethnic lines, principally: Hong Kong Chinese, mainland Chinese, Taiwanese, Vietnamese, Malaysian, Japanese, and Thai. In schools, tensions between different Asian groups, or between Asians and non-Asians, are being met by some students resorting to the use of offensive weapons such as nunchakas, softball bats, hatchets, knives, and firearms. In a number of cases, youths arrested as a result of confrontations have connections with known organized crime figures (Fiso, 1996). There is also evidence that schools are being used as recruiting grounds for Asian organized crime and that schoolboy gangsters are extorting "protection money" from the wealthy families of other students (*New Zealand Herald*, 17 October 1996).

As already noted, evidence of liaisons between organized Asian groups and established street gangs has recently emerged in New Zealand as well. Twice in 1996, Asians have attempted to contract local criminals to kill police officers. With only 24 law enforcement officers killed in the 110-year history of the New Zealand Police, these new developments are a cause for concern. Although many of these developments may sound alarming, it is important that Asian offenses be seen in terms of offending patterns nationwide. It is true that the growing presence of Asians in New Zealand has been reflected in greater representation in offending statistics. As a percentage of all apprehensions, for example, Asian apprehension grew fourfold between 1987 and 1996, from 0.3 percent to 1.2 percent. Greatest growth occurred in the areas of administrative offending, property abuse, violence and drugs, and anti-social offenses, in that order. But it is also true that in all areas of offending, Asian apprehension levels are still well below their overall representation within the New Zealand population.

Measures, Including Legislation to Combat Organized Crime

Over the past 30 years, a number of steps have been taken to control organized crime in New Zealand. We will describe them with reference to the specific type of crime that these measures are meant to target.

Drugs

To combat the drug threat of the 1970s, several legislative developments occurred. In 1975, controlled drugs were divided into three classes: A, B, and C, and in 1978 penalties were stiffened so that trafficking Class A drugs, which now include heroin, LSD, and cocaine, carries a maximum life penalty. That penalty has been awarded three times (and upheld twice) since the new law came into effect. Trafficking Class B drugs, such as hashish, morphine, opium, and amphetamines, retained the 14-year maximum, and trafficking Class C drugs, such as cannabis plant, codeine, and barbiturates, had its maximum cut to eight years.

In 1975 police were given the power to search for drugs without a search warrant and in 1978 the use of tracking and listening devices for detecting drug offenders was begun. Intelligence was also improved, with the establishment of a National Drug Intelligence Bureau in 1972 and the posting of a permanent drug liaison officer in Bangkok, Thailand, in 1978. A second liaison officer was appointed in Sydney in 1980. New Zealand drug liaison officers meet annually with their Asian counterparts for the purposes of exchanging intelligence and coordinating their activities.

New Zealand is signatory to a number of international agreements in relation to the control of crime internationally, particularly regarding drugs. New Zealand is a member of Interpol, which formalizes arrangements for international cooperation in criminal investigations and is a member of the Heads of Narcotics Law Enforcement Agencies (HONLEA), which is specifically aimed at international drug control. As a member of the United Nations, New Zealand is party to the World Health Organization's fight against international drug trafficking. For example, New Zealand liaises with the International Narcotics Control Board, and is a signatory to the 1988 Vienna Convention against Illicit Traffic in Narcotic Drugs and Psychotropic Substances.

A range of legislation exists that enhances New Zealand's ability to combat crime in a global way. The Fugitive Offenders Act 1881 and the Extradition Act 1965 formalize the processes of extradition of criminals between members of the British Commonwealth and other nations with which there is an extradition agreement, such as the United States. The

Mutual Assistance in Criminal Matters Act 1992 allows the Attorney General of New Zealand to seek the formal cooperation of foreign law enforcement agencies in criminal investigative matters, and section 10 of the Misuse of Drugs Act 1975 permits the prosecution of any person, who, while in New Zealand, conspires to commit any offense against the act in any other country.

More recently, and not just related to drug dealing, the Proceeds of Crime Act 1991 has been passed, allowing asset seizure when a person has been convicted of an offense punishable by more than five years' imprisonment and when a High Court judge believes the assets to have been accumulated as a result of crime. In 1995 an amendment to the Crimes Act made money laundering an offense in New Zealand, and the following year, the Financial Transactions Reporting Act made financial institutions responsible for reporting suspicious financial activity to the police. All of the aforementioned acts have international applications.

New Zealand thus has a wide range of agreements and laws in place that allow for global cooperation in policing and intelligence-gathering matters.

Gangs

Where outlaw street gangs are concerned, there has been little formal response. In 1972, the Leader of the Opposition's proposal for Parliament to "take the bikes off the bikies" as a controlling strategy was ignored on practical and human rights advice. The approach of police to the gangs has largely been one of tolerance within the boundaries of the law. Strategy has been to police gangs in the normal context of law enforcement, rather than to target them and try to wipe them out. The most likely consequence of a repression strategy would be to force the gangs underground and thus make their activities more difficult to monitor.

Where the illegal profile of a particular gang grows unacceptably high, however, or the gang is considered to be becoming a public menace in its own right, rigorous short-term harassment operations are common. In 1995, for example, a campaign against the Nomads in the North Island's Wairarapa district resulted in arrests of forty gang members or associates and the eventual imprisonment of the gang's leaders. It will be recalled that in Christchurch in 1996, an operation specifically targeting the Road Knights also resulted in dozens of arrests and thousands of dollars in traffic fines.

In 1989, amendments to the Criminal Justice Act and the Summary Offenses Act allowed the courts to impose non-association orders on convicted persons and empowered the police to disperse assemblies that threaten public order. The specific objective of the latter provision was to limit gang activity by giving the police greater powers to move gang members even though they had not committed an offense.

Asian crime is a recent phenomenon, with the existence of dedicated Asian intelligence units less than a decade old. Apart from the six detectives in Asian intelligence units, Asian crime portfolios are now held by detectives in four North Island and two South Island towns. By the beginning of 1997, the police still had no Asian or Chinese-speaking person attached to their units, due to the absence of any suitably qualified staff within the force. However, a specific attempt is being made to equip staff with skills in Mandarin, Japanese, and Thai languages. A number of bilingual Asian officers have been recruited, and there are officers working within their communities with the appropriate language skills. Training and information lectures are being given in a variety of police training courses, and since 1994, a number of New Zealand police officers have attended organized crime-related conferences overseas (Fiso, 1997).

At the same time, a systematic attempt is being made at coordinating training and intelligence at a national level, in particular with other departments such as Customs, Immigration, Inland Revenue, Security Intelligence, and Agriculture and Fisheries. An immigrant database has been created. English language entry requirements are being tightened and community group sponsorship has been abolished. Several government departments have officers working full time on intelligence and investigations relating to Asian organized crime. These and other agencies are coordinating their activities and knowledge in order to maximize the state's capacity to deal with the emerging problem of organized crime in New Zealand.

COMPARATIVE EVALUATION OF THE METHODS FOR COMBATING ORGANIZED CRIME AND PROPOSED MEASURES

The success of the measures has been variable depending on the type of crime and the actions taken to combat them.

Drugs

As noted, the steps taken in the 1970s to deal with drug importation were extremely effective. By the end of 1979 the Mr. Asia gang had been destroyed, with most of its members either dead or in prison. Certainly, the bulk of arrests took place in Australia or England, but prosecution cases were enhanced by multinational police cooperation, including input from New Zealand. In New Zealand itself, combined customs and police intelligence effected the apprehensions of a number of major importers of cannabis and heroin in the 1970s. Heavy sentences were imposed, even for relatively small amounts of drug. We have seen that as a result, the commercial viability of drug importation dropped to the point that by 1980, the ingress of heroin and marijuana to New Zealand had virtually ceased. For the same reason, cocaine has never featured as a significant problem.

But stopping the flow of foreign drugs into New Zealand did not stop the availability of all controlled substances. As noted, by the early 1980s backyard laboratories had begun manufacturing opiates from codeine, and a lively market for pharmaceutical analgesics such as palfium, pethidine, omnipon, and non-injectable morphine (MST) developed. MST is easily converted to injectable heroin by treating it with ascetic anhydride and bicarbonate of soda. Thus, a small drug addiction problem exists in New Zealand. Currently there are 2,500 opioid dependent patients on registered methadone treatment (Sellman et al., 1996) and every year, according to police reports, about 15 people die from drug overdoses. But few of these deaths are due to abuse of traditionally feared drugs such as heroin and morphine. In 1992, for example, a government report showed that in 1989 there were 25 deaths as a result of drug abuse. Only 5 of these were caused by opioids, none were caused by cannabis or hallucinogens, and none were caused by barbiturates. The remaining 20 deaths were attributed to unspecified "other" drugs (Adams et al., 1992).

The policing of borders did not reduce marijuana use either; it may even have stimulated it by creating a market for cheaper, domestically grown cannabis. Between 1980 and 1995, the number of cannabis plants seized in New Zealand rose steadily, from 37,000 to 352,000, an increase of over 900 percent. Neither have these massive seizures resulted in any apparent decline in cannabis use. The number of persons caught annually in possession of cannabis in New Zealand more than doubled in the same 15-year period, to 11,000. A recent report indicates that by age 19, at least 41 percent of New Zealanders will have used cannabis at least once, whereas only 9 percent will have tried hallucinogens, 3 percent, stimulants, and 1 percent, opiates (Adams, et al., 1992).

The market for cannabis in New Zealand is thus huge, and the growing and distribution of it is of considerable economic importance in some areas. This drug is a financial basis for many gang members who do not have access to more dangerous compounds such as methamphetamines. As mentioned, the police adopt a low-profile approach to the majority of gang activity. It is reasonable that this should be so. If marijuana was removed as a source of income to gangs and others whose livelihoods depend on it, other forms of perhaps more serious crime might result. Paradoxically, therefore, the existence of a certain amount of marijuana production in New Zealand may be seen as an unintended crime-control feature in itself.

Police operations in marijuana distribution have had some effect on the availability and price of the drug, but may be less effective in the future. In the past, undercover officers assigned to marijuana investigations have had to engage fully with the marijuana trafficking culture in order to make arrests. Inevitably, this has involved them in smoking the drug and has necessitated official training in smoking techniques (see Ansley, 1995). Consequently, however, by 1996 around thirty former officers were claiming a marijuana addiction and some were admitting to having perjured themselves in court when questioned about their drug-taking activities. This development has jeopardized the drug undercover program.

Gangs

According to police estimates cited earlier, gang numbers roughly trebled between 1981 and 1996. Such figures are only broad estimates, however, and do not take account of gang prospects and associates. Moreover, there is no way of assessing their accuracy. During the late 1980s, police gang estimates grew by roughly 28 percent but have remained stable since 1990. Numbers of patch members in prison have remained virtually unchanged, at about 400, since 1987. However, the prison population overall has increased so that the percentage of imprisoned gang members relative to non-gang members has almost halved during this time (Braybrook and O'Neill, 1988; Braybrook and Southey, 1992; Lash, 1996).

However, it is not the responsibility of police to reduce gang membership, since belonging to a gang is not itself an offense. Police are concerned, however, with the criminal activity gangs may be involved in. As seen in the cases of the Nomads in the Wairarapa and the Road Knights in Christchurch, vigorous repression campaigns against high-profiled gangs are successful, but such pressure cannot be maintained without compromising police effectiveness in other areas. The violent profile of gangs is high, and in terms of gang members incarcerated for violence, that profile is increasing. The ratio of gang members in prison serving time for a violent offense, relative to non-gang members, grew by 21 percent between 1987 and 1991 (Braybrook and O'Neill, 1988; Braybrook and Southey, 1992). Between 1988 and 1993, about 4 percent of all murders in New Zealand were gang-related (Miller, 1994). Homicides, however, have been declining since 1989 and robberies have stabilized since 1991. Conversely, grievous assaults have risen unremittingly, more than doubling since 1990.

Since 1990, police estimates of gang membership in New Zealand have remained stable, at about 5,500. Numbers of gangs identified have likewise remained constant, at about 45. There is no evidence that the profile of gang membership or gang activity has altered significantly so far this decade. However, 1996 was an election year and a number of politicians seized on the "gang problem" as part of their election platform. One politician called for the establishment of a national crime authority similar to that which exists in Australia. The proposal failed to get parliamentary support, however, and in May 1997 the relevant bill was thrown out.

Still under consideration is another piece of legislation, the Harassment and Criminal Associations Bill, which was introduced in 1996. Designed to provide police with greater powers to combat gangs, the bill makes it easier for police to use listening devices and search vehicles, it extends their powers to remove gang fortifications, and it seeks to make it illegal to associate with gang members who are known to engage in criminal activity. This last provision is highly contentious and the requirements of proof would make it almost impossible to enforce. The bill appears largely to be a sop to the public, and if it becomes law, it is unlikely to have any significant effect on gang activity.

The picture is thus far from simple, but it seems that the police do have the gang problem largely under control. Neither now nor ever before have the gangs presented a significant threat to the stability of the country or to the welfare of the average New Zealander. That comment aside, changing circumstances and recent intelligence about links between the gangs and Asian crime, will require close monitoring.

Asian Crime

The Asian crime problem has really only become significant in this country since 1993. To date, few police resources have been dedicated specifically to dealing with it. However, the coordination of interagency intelligence nationwide has so far proven effective in keeping police aware of major developments. Whether greater resources will be necessary in the future will depend largely on how the situation progresses in the next few years.

CONCLUSION

Police believe that in the future, unlike the gangs, Asian criminal groups may become more visible in their activities. Particular areas of potential growth include fraud, serious violence, illegal immigration, extortion, vice, dishonesty, drug trafficking, gaming, and the illegal exploitation of fisheries (Fiso, 1996). If this occurs, it is also likely that stronger links with outlaw gangs may emerge, with increases in their criminal effectiveness as a result. In a worst-case scenario, Asian groups could form functional alliances with large violent gangs such as the Mongrel Mob and develop a monopoly over criminal activities throughout the country. If gangs became organized at such a level, keeping control of serious crime could become extremely difficult.

There are several reasons why this is unlikely to happen. First, most gang members are highly visible. Maori gangs in particular, such as the Mongrel Mob and Black Power, advertise themselves through ostentatious forms of dress and extensive tattooing, particularly over the hands and face. Such men are unable to go anywhere in public without being noticed. Moreover, unlike Asians, gang members do not come from a subculture markedly distinct from that of the average New Zealander and they are normally well-known within their own neighborhoods. These factors severely limit the capacity of gangs to engage in covert activity.

Second, apart from a few exceptions such as the Hell's Angels, most gangs are disorganized and guileless, and much of their activity is incompetent. The lucrative job schemes of the 1970s, for example, were lost to the gangs as a result of conspicuous exploitation by some and the use of government-funded vehicles for armed robberies. Indeed, the high number of gang members in prison for rape, serious assault, robbery and murder is itself testimony to their bungling efforts to make a life out of crime. Sophisticated organizations such as the Triads would be unlikely to profit from relying on gangs for support. It seems probable that Asian crime leaders will realize this quite quickly.

Third, by themselves, Asian gangs are unlikely to gain a strong foothold in this country. The reasons principally have to do with those factors outlined at the beginning of this chapter: New Zealand's remote insularity, the small size of its population, and the nature of its police force. In the United States in 1968 the President's Commission on Law Enforcement and the Administration of Justice declared that without corrupt officials, organized crime cannot exist (Schweizer, 1996). One only has to look at areas in the world where organized crime has taken hold, such as Japan, Russia, and Latin America, to find testimony to this statement. In the current chapter we have seen that Terry Clark was only able to survive in Australia for so long because of his relationship with corrupt government officials.

A recent worldwide survey by the Berlin-based organization, Transparency International, has found New Zealand to be the least corrupt of all the countries studied (*Dominion*, 17 July 1995). I have argued earlier that systematic corruption is absent from the New Zealand Police. This situation will be significant in limiting the growth of organized crime in this country. The police are aware of the threat of corruption generally and specifically of that presented by organized crime (Fiso, 1996). They are also aware of the need to create confidence among law-abiding immigrant groups that reports about intimidation or attempted extortion by criminals will not compromise the complainants and will be dealt with quickly and effectively. As police confidence within the Asian community grows, the arena within which Asian organized crime operates will be reduced.

In the late 1970s, large-scale hard drug-running activities by organized groups were virtually eliminated from the New Zealand criminal scene. Today, the same factors that then restricted the viability of organized crime still apply. This does not mean that New Zealanders can be complacent about the re-emergence of organized crime in their country. What it does mean, however, is that with ongoing police vigilance, careful allocation of resources, and the continuation of interagency responses to developments in organized crime, the chances of major syndicated criminal groups taking root on New Zealand soil are slim.

REFERENCES

Abadinsky, Howard. 1990. *Organized Crime.* Chicago: Nelson-Hall.

Adams, Joanne, Judy Paulin, and Jacqui George. 1992. *Drug Statistics 1992.* Wellington: Department of Health.

Adler, Freda, Gerhard Mueller, and William Lawler. 1996. *Criminal Justice*, New York: McGraw Hill.

Albanese, Jay and Robert D. Pursley. 1993. *Crime in America: Some Existing and Emerging Issues.* Englewood Cliffs: Regents/Prentice Hall.

Ansley, Bruce. 1995. *Stoned on Duty.* Auckland: Penguin.

Braybrook, Beverley and Rose O'Neill. 1988. *A Census of Prison Inmates.* Wellington: Department of Justice.

Braybrook, Beverley and Pamela Southey. 1992. *Census of Prison Inmates 1991.* Wellington: Department of Justice.

Clark, Terry. Personal Conversation 1995.

Committee on Gangs. 1981. *Report.* Wellington: Government Printer.

Committee on Drug Dependency and Drug Abuse in New Zealand. 1973. *Second Report.* Wellington: Government Printer.

Department of Statistics. 1990. *New Zealand Official 1990 Yearbook.* Wellington: Department of Statistics.

Deputy Director of the Criminal law Research Center of China University of Political Science and Law. 1996. "Organized Crime and its Containment in China." Paper presented at the Third International Police Executive Symposium, University of Kanagawa, Yokohama, 28 November through 1 December.

Fiso, Api. 1997. "Asian Organized Crime in New Zealand." Report prepared for the Organized Crime Unit of the National Bureau of Criminal Intelligence, New Zealand Police, Wellington.

Hall, Richard. 1981. *Greed: The Mr Asia Connection.* Sydney: Pan.

Harrington, Paul. 1997. "Mixing Mystique and Murder." *Dominion*, 5 February.

Howman, J.D. 1972. "Polynesian Gangs in New Zealand." *Victoria University of Wellington Law Review* 6(3): 222–242.

Kelsey, Jane and Warren Young. 1982. *The Gangs: Moral Panic as Social Control*. Wellington: Institute of Criminology.

Kenney, Dennis J. and James O. Finckenauer. 1995. *Organized Crime in America*. Belmont: Wadsworth.

Kwitny, Jonathan. 1987. *The Crimes of Patriots: A True Tale of Dope, Dirty Money, and the CIA*. New York: Simon and Schuster.

Lash, Barb. 1996. *Census of Prison Inmates 1995*. Wellington, Ministry of Justice.

Lavigne, Yves. 1987. *Hell's Angels*. New York: Lyle Stuart.

Meek, John. 1992. "Gangs In New Zealand Prisons." *Australian and New Zealand J Criminol.* 25(3): 255–277.

Miller, Ian. 1994. "Murder in New Zealand 1988–1993: Patterns of Victim/Offender Relationships and Putative Motivational Influences." Paper presented at the New Zealand Psychological Society Annual Conference, Hamilton, 24 August 1994.

Ministry of Health. 1995. *Cannabis and Health in New Zealand*. Wellington: Ministry of Health.

Ministry of Health. 1996. *Cannabis: The Public Health Issues 1995–1996*. Wellington: Ministry of Health.

Newbold, Greg. 1992. *Crime and Deviance*. Auckland: Oxford University Press.

Newbold, Greg and Robert Ivory. 1993. "Policing Serious Fraud in New Zealand." *Crime, Law and Social Change* 20: 233–248.

O'Reilly, Denis. 1986. "Despite All Your Fears, People Have a Right to Be: The Evolution of Black Power." *Metro*, 133–135, December.

Schweizer, Otto. 1996. "Organized Crime: A World Perspective." Paper presented at the Third International Police Executive Symposium, Kanagawa University, Yokohama, 28 November through 1 December.

Sellman, J.D., J. Hannifin, D. Deering, and P. Borren. 1996. *Delivery of Treatment for People with Opioid Dependency in New Zealand*. Wellington: Ministry of Health.

Statistics New Zealand. 1994. *New Zealand Now: People and Places*. Wellington: Statistics New Zealand.

Statistics New Zealand. 1997. "Number of People Approved for Residence in New Zealand by Region and Nationality: 1982–1996." Spreadsheet supplied by Statistics New Zealand.

Uchiyama, Ayako. 1996. "Changes of Boryokudan after Enforcement of the Anti-Boryokudan Law." Paper presented at the Third International Police Executive Symposium, University of Kanagawa, Yokohama, 28 November through 1 December.

Young, Joanne. 1996. Immigration figures compiled from information supplied by the Client Services Division of Statistics New Zealand by the Department of Geography, Waikato University.

Yska, Redmer. 1993. *All Shook Up: The Flash Bodgie and the Rise of the New Zealand Teenager in the Fifties*. Auckland: Penguin.

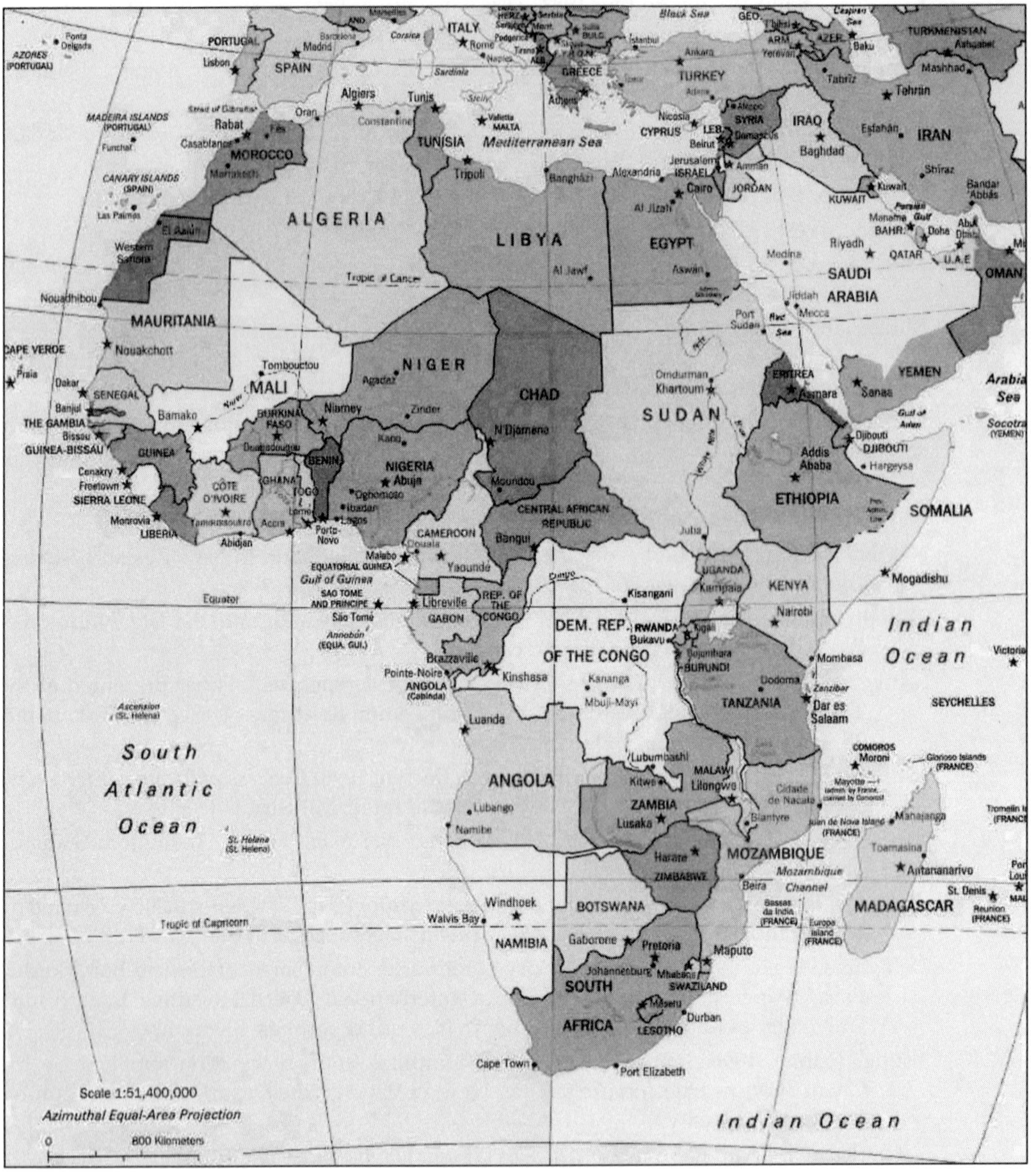

PORTUGAL
SPAIN
ITALY
GREECE
TURKEY
SYRIA
IRAQ
IRAN
TURKMENISTAN
CYPRUS
ISRAEL
JORDAN
KUWAIT
SAUDI ARABIA
QATAR
U.A.E.
OMAN
YEMEN
Black Sea
Mediterranean Sea
Red Sea
Arabian Sea
MOROCCO
ALGERIA
TUNISIA
LIBYA
EGYPT
Western Sahara
MAURITANIA
MALI
NIGER
CHAD
SUDAN
ERITREA
DJIBOUTI
ETHIOPIA
SOMALIA
SENEGAL
THE GAMBIA
GUINEA-BISSAU
GUINEA
SIERRA LEONE
LIBERIA
CÔTE D'IVOIRE
GHANA
TOGO
BENIN
BURKINA FASO
NIGERIA
CAMEROON
CENTRAL AFRICAN REPUBLIC
EQUATORIAL GUINEA
GABON
REP. OF THE CONGO
DEM. REP. OF THE CONGO
UGANDA
KENYA
RWANDA
BURUNDI
TANZANIA
ANGOLA
ZAMBIA
MALAWI
MOZAMBIQUE
ZIMBABWE
NAMIBIA
BOTSWANA
SOUTH AFRICA
SWAZILAND
LESOTHO
MADAGASCAR
COMOROS
SEYCHELLES
CAPE VERDE
AZORES (PORTUGAL)
MADEIRA ISLANDS (PORTUGAL)
CANARY ISLANDS (SPAIN)
Lisbon
Madrid
Rome
Algiers
Tunis
Rabat
Casablanca
Tripoli
Cairo
Khartoum
Addis Ababa
Mogadishu
Nairobi
Kinshasa
Luanda
Lusaka
Harare
Pretoria
Cape Town
Durban
Windhoek
Gaborone
Maputo
Antananarivo
Dakar
Bamako
Niamey
Abuja
Lagos
Accra
N'Djamena
Bangui
Libreville
Yaoundé
Kampala
Dar es Salaam
Dodoma
Tropic of Cancer
Equator
Tropic of Capricorn
Gulf of Guinea
Mozambique Channel
South Atlantic Ocean
Indian Ocean
Scale 1:51,400,000
Azimuthal Equal-Area Projection
0
800 Kilometers

Part 6

Perspectives from Africa

Africa is the second largest continent, which constitutes about one-fifth of the earth's land surface. Roughly triangular in shape, Africa is bounded by the Atlantic Ocean on the west, the Mediterranean Sea to the north, and the Indian Ocean and Red Sea to the east. Africa's tropical location, large deserts, and immigration and migration patterns have contributed significantly to its history and population. Despite its enormous size, Africa contains only 10 percent of the earth's population.

Africa's 43 countries are diverse in nature. Most are developing countries, and indigenous people are the majority in all African nations, but there are nearly 3,000 ethnic groups or tribes within Africa. These groups share a common identity but are not bound by national borders. African tribes often are identified by the language they speak, their cultural traditions, or by their religion, because nations do not signify ethnicity, as is the case in many European countries.

Organized crime in Africa has been defined in large part by corruption and the presence of its many developing nations. Political and government corruption has been an impediment to faster development in some countries, and there is likely a great deal of organized crime and corruption that exists in less accessible areas that has not been reported in the media (South African, 2001; Gottschalk and Flanagan, 2000). Political turmoil has resulted in weak state structures that do not provide an effective deterrent toward unlawful behavior (Striving, 2000). Likewise, rebellions in several countries across the continent have further uprooted people, worsened the economic situation, and caused unnatural migration within the continent. The result has been many vulnerable people and criminal opportunities that have been exploited by organized crime groups (Gastrow, 2000). For example, strict measures to prevent money laundering in developed nations have resulted in attempts to move illegal cash through the developing nations of Africa (Nevin, 2000).

Studies of organized crime in African nations are comparatively few. As the continent develops and government structures become stronger, greater efforts will be made to study and control organized crime there. Students who wish to pursue the study of organized crime in Africa might examine specific cities, illicit product and cash flows in and out of particular African locations, and the relationship between political corruption and organized crime in different jurisdictions.

References

Gastrow, Peter. 2000. "Organized Crime and the State's Response in South Africa." *Transnational Organized Crime* 4.

Gottschalk, Jack A. and Brian P. Flanagan. 2000. *Jolly Roger with an Uzi: The Rise and Threat of Modern Piracy.* Naval Institute Press.

Nevin, Tom. 2000. "Has Africa Become the World's Washroom for Dirty Money?" *African Business*, 20 March.

"South African Customs Investigation Nets Anti-Corruption Official." 2001. *The Independent*, Capetown, 1 February. http://www.wjin.net/html/news/7201/htm

"Striving amid Chaos: The Biggest Headache for Nigerian Business is Uncertainty." 2000. *The Economist*, 30, 15 January.

CHAPTER 17

ORGANIZED CRIME: A PERSPECTIVE FROM SOUTH AFRICA

C. J. D. Venter

INTRODUCTION

South Africa is one of the larger countries in the African continent and lies at the bottom, touching the Indian Ocean. The country is rich in mineral resources and precious metals and is an emerging economic powerhouse after the end of its infamous apartheid era. The new constitution has greatly transformed the country and has provided equality to its impoverished black population. The criminal justice system has also been reformed and reconstituted to make the police accountable to the elected civilian authority. Section 214 of the Constitution of the Republic of South Africa, 1993 (Act no. 200 of 1993), provided for the establishment and regulation of a South African Police Service (SAPS) structured at both national and provincial levels. The Police Act of 1995 upholds and safeguards the fundamental rights of every person as guaranteed by Chapter 3 of the Constitution and ensures effective civilian supervision over the service.

South Africa has a safety and security system in which the political and civilian leaders and the management of SAPS are aligned toward the same goal of effective and service-oriented policing within a framework of democratic values and accountability. This ministerial direction also reflects the priorities and objectives of various state departments, specific interest groups, non-governmental organizations, and the community who have contributed to the framing of the new Act. In the constitution, a post of the national commissioner has been established to exercise control and manage the service in accordance with national legislation and policing policy, to effectively fulfill the assigned responsibilities while taking into account the requirements of the provinces. The national commissioner's duty is to ensure that SAPS provides and maintains an effective, impartial, accountable, transparent, and efficient police service.

Organized crime has traditionally been seen as a domestic law and order problem affecting a relatively small number of countries. In the last few years, however, there has been recognition that the problem is no longer limited to only a few countries and can no longer be treated as something that falls within a single jurisdiction. The escalating global market for illicit narcotics, the end of the Cold War and the breakdown of the barriers between East and West, the deterioration of the criminal justice system in Russia and the other states of the former Soviet Union, the development of free trade areas in Western Europe and North America, the emergence of global financial and trade systems, and the emergence of cyber-technology have fundamentally changed the context in which criminal organizations operate (Cressey, 1971). All these have resulted in domestic groups linking and forming international criminal organizations. The persisting increase in the incidence of crime, especially organized crime, continues to threaten the stability and national security of an increasing number of states, including South Africa (Opolot, 1981).

The global threat of transnational organized crime has been recognized by governments, law enforcement, and intelligence institutions in countries affected by organized crime. The problem of transnational organized crime is a real one that demands proper/professional investigation and the devotion of greater resources. It is obvious that these criminal organizations/groups engage in extensive criminal activities on a regional and often global basis (Williams, 1995). Technological developments have provided these groups new opportunities to exploit. These have also enabled them to attain a level of prominence that threatens national and international security in a number of ways. Organized criminal groups can now:

- Violate national sovereignty
- Undermine democratic institutions
- Threaten the process of privatization
- Cause or endanger the devaluation of monetary value assets
- Corrupt the economic systems

Intensive analysis of the threat of such crimes is essential for effective action against these organizations, since part of the problem is a form of threat inflation. Dramatizing the challenge can galvanize public attention, mobilize support, and generate the resources necessary to deal with a problem that traditionally has had a relatively low profile. On the other hand, underestimating the threat also holds dire consequences for law enforcement (Jones and Steward, 1982).

The focus only on large organizations is also a simplistic approach that assumes that international organized crime will be eliminated if enough resources are devoted to the dismantling of these groups. The fluid network of these organizations, the diversity of these groups, their relationships with legitimate businesses, their capacity to exploit the market, and their ability to corrupt governments and law enforcement agencies make efforts to dismantle them extremely difficult.

THE NATURE AND EXTENT OF ORGANIZED CRIME

The extent of organized crime in South Africa is accentuated by the fact that 481 organized crime syndicates with a combined figure of 2,178 primary members, are currently known to be operating in South Africa. The majority of these syndicates specialize either in drug trafficking, vehicle theft, commercial crime, or any combination of these crimes. At least 187 of the 481 organized crime syndicates in South Africa operate internationally. The criminal activities of 125 of these syndicates are at present restricted to sub-Saharan countries in Africa. The syndicates, which have international connections, are involved in offenses such as:

- Specialization in either drug trafficking (136 syndicates), vehicle theft (112 syndicates), commercial crime (85 syndicates), or any combination of these crimes.

- Specialization in committing a specific crime, for instance, drug trafficking, vehicle theft or diamond smuggling (403 syndicates). The remainder (78 syndicates) specialize in committing more than one crime. For example, a syndicate can simultaneously be involved in drug trafficking, vehicle theft, and check fraud.

Crime networks are so well established that the same channels and networks are often used for the smuggling of firearms, drugs, vehicles, ivory, rhino horn, precious metals, and gemstones.

Organized crime groups in South Africa share some or all of the following characteristics:

- Interrelatedness of criminal activities: Drugs are linked to motor vehicles, motor vehicle theft/robbery to the illegal arms trade, and drugs and motor vehicles to money laundering and forgery.

- Organized crime groups supply contraband to criminal groups, which not only provide a ready market for these goods, but also form a vital link in the distribution.
- Forging of passports and other documents.
- Rigid hierarchical structures enforced by strict disciplinary sanctions.
- Restricted membership.
- Tight security and compartmentalization: Special care is taken to prevent police agents/informers from infiltrating organized crime groups.
- Ready access to weapons.
- Corrupt links with police and government officials.
- Laundering of funds through legitimate businesses: Proceeds of crime are concealed in such a way that it makes the tracing and seizure thereof very difficult, and in some cases impossible. Financial institutions are often used as a means of concealing the proceeds of crime, and the problem is further intensified by the fact that currently there are no obligations on financial institutions to report any suspected case of money laundering. There is at present a proposed legislation under discussion in the Parliament with regard to money laundering.
- International operations are noted in an increasing number of cases, but there is still no law for tackling such operations.

There are several contributing factors in the incidence of organized crime in South Africa. The increasing incidences of organized crime in South Africa can be attributed to factors such as:

- A renewed international investor interest in South Africa.
- South Africa's favorable geographical position on the major trafficking routes between the Far and Middle East, the Americas, and Europe.
- South Africa's accessibility via land, sea, and air routes, especially since its recent reentry into the international arena.
- A criminogenic market structure: Unsaturated demand for and ready availability of illegal goods (drugs, arms, vehicles, counterfeit money, endangered species products, etc.).
- The large-scale presence of illegal aliens, which has, apart from the alien role in crime (including organized crime), led to an increase in the already intense competition for scarce resources.

A number of social and technological developments have also combined to create opportunities for organized crime. Advanced computer and communications technology facilitate the electronic fund-transfer system through which vast amounts of money can be transferred around the globe within seconds, and faxes and cellular phones can be encrypted, making it all but impossible to trace calls made from them. Linkages between drug trafficking and weapon smuggling also exist, since many of the routes used are the same.

Cooperation between syndicates and criminal groups exists in South Africa, where they combine resources and personnel to create powerful criminal organizations. It is, thus, a safe assumption that many offenses that seem spontaneous are actually well planned. Many networks develop terminology of their own and specialize in their activities. Persons in control of such networks are often known to each other, cooperate in a symbiotic fashion, and even assist one another. Some gangs deliver stolen goods to the same syndicate and thus form part of a larger criminal network, which is often headed by an unknown syndicate leader. Some gangs do not even realize that they are part of such a network.

There is a direct link between the profitability of crime and the existing market for goods obtained through crime. There is an extensive market for stolen goods, motor vehicle parts, weapons, and drugs in South Africa. An international market around South Africa, especially for stolen vehicles and other commodities like ivory and gold, serves as a catalyst for syndicates to exploit these goods for big profits.

Measures, Including Legislation, to Combat Organized Crime

The anti-organized crime unit within the South African police establishment focuses on covert operations and infiltration of these criminal organizations. Policing in South Africa is undergoing a rebirth and the strategies, structures, and activities of the SAPS are in the process of being transformed in line with the principles and objectives of community policing. The adoption of this approach has created a number of enormous challenges to the South African society in general and police practitioners in particular.

South Africa is, for the first time in history, confronting crime in an organized, systematic, and coherent way. The first strategy to counter crime has been dubbed the National Crime Prevention Strategy, which seeks to coordinate the activities of a range of departments in order to maximize their crime prevention efforts (Government of South Africa, 1997a). The

National Crime Prevention Strategy was the result of extensive cooperation between all the government departments, which is a medium to long-term strategy. The second strategy, which is both linked to and separate from the first, was also developed to improve the effectiveness of the key departments in the criminal justice system.

The Police Plan, published in 1996, was an historic event for South Africa (Government of South Africa, 1997b). For the first time specific policing priorities and objectives were formulated in a participatory and consultative manner and placed in the public domain, and are therefore open to public debate. With regard to crime and violence, the categories of violent crime, narcotics, organized crime, commercial crime, and vehicle hijacking and other vehicle-related crimes have been prioritized.

Prioritization is necessary, because, in principle, there is no limit to the number of possible police activities. For instance, there are several kinds of potential preventive actions that can be undertaken, but the personnel and logistical resources needed for these actions are limited. The effect is that continuous choices must be made about where, when, and how policing activities should occur. Crime, and the causes thereof, are therefore being addressed in a three-tiered strategy in the following manner.

The strategy for the growth and development of the country has a focus on the socioeconomic framework with a long-term time frame of operations. The National Crime Prevention Strategy is a medium- to long-term supportive strategy, which seeks to desegregate the various crime-combating endeavors and to support operational endeavors by creating a favorable environment for combating crime. The National Crime Prevention Strategy is designed to produce short-term benefits and focuses on the criminal justice system, regional security, community values, and development of an environment conducive to crime prevention. Finally, a police plan has been developed that focuses on operational strategies and with a short-term goal in mind.

As has been indicated, the main purpose of prioritization is to increase the effectiveness of the police service. All priorities and objectives in this regard are therefore seen as laying the basis for the optimization of policing at the national, provincial, and local levels and at the same time working for the removal of related obstacles.

Subsequent to the adoption of such policing priorities, a process has been initiated to determine respective and/or mutually related national and provincial responsibilities with regard to specific priorities. This process goes together with a comprehensive operational plan to manage each priority. Detailed strategies in respect of each objective are being developed in partnership with all relevant role players. These plans will also assign responsibility, estimate required resources, and determine their costs as well as develop relevant performance indicators. The measurement of performance will not only promote accountability and transparency within the SAPS, but also provide benchmarks to determine the extent to which particular strategies contribute to the achievement of policing objectives.

In the assessment of these priorities and objectives, it should be noted that various key elements are transversal in the sense that they affect numerous other priorities and objectives. These elements should not be repeated for achieving each objective. For example, training programs must be comprehensive and seek to prepare the officers for all eventualities. The plan to target a particular crime syndicate must take into account that seemingly diverse activities such as the witness protection program, control and policing of ports of entry, strengthening of communications, and the gathering of crime intelligence all need to complement one another. In this regard the following key priorities and objectives were identified for the 1996/1997 financial year, in no particular order of importance or prominence:

1. To promote and ensure community involvement, participation, and co-responsibility through the operationalization of community policing;

2. To promote the efficiency and effectiveness of the criminal justice system through participating in multidimensional endeavors;

3. To enhance the operational effectiveness of the SAPS through prioritization and by making resources available to areas of greatest need and potential impact;

4. To utilize human resources in the most effective manner on the basis of individual potential, skills, and capabilities;

5. To implement and ensure the sustainability of community policing through pilot projects in selected areas, determine best practices, and identify potential obstacles;

6. To effect visible and qualitative improvement in service delivery in terms of results achieved (such as reaction times, public satisfaction, and reduced levels of crime and violence);

7. To increase the effectiveness of combating crime by supporting an integrated partnership approach, whereby all relevant endeavors are coordinated to maximum effect;

8. To ensure that policing is conducted in accordance with the fundamental rights of all persons involved in the criminal justice process, whether victims, perpetrators, or witnesses, without obstructing the

process itself. These rights should not be seen as a sign of operational weakness, and a balance must be achieved between the rightful use of policing powers and the limitation of such rights;

9. To promote adherence to national standards and enhanced control and supervision mechanisms;

10. To promote transparency and accountability in police operations.

Similarly, a number of key priorities have been identified to restrict organized crime in the country. Some of these are:

1. Compilation of crime-threat analysis;
2. To identify and neutralize organized crime syndicates involved in narcotics, stolen goods, and firearms;
3. To develop a national crime intelligence unit that collects and quickly communicates operational intelligence to the field agents;
4. To create a national integrated database that is comprehensive and open to the field agents;
5. To optimize crime information management system;
6. To implement new methods and techniques in the investigation of organized crime;
7. To reinforce the control and policing of borders and ports of entry in collaboration with SA Revenue Service, other services, and Home Affairs;
8. To optimize multidimensional, regional and international liaison, support and cooperation with concerned agencies;
9. To promote the blacklisting of stolen property;
10. To identify groups dealing in narcotics and identify their sources and financial transactions.

Since anti-narcotics operations form the major thrust of action against organized crime, the priorities exclusive to their control are also described here:

- To implement effective counter narcotic strategies in conjunction with enhanced investigative capacity and skills, supported by related intelligence, education, and awareness programs;
- To control and police the ports of entry effectively;
- To tackle all aspects of drug trafficking, whether the production, distribution, importation, exportation, or sale;
- To eradicate fields of cannabis by chemical destruction.

The annual plan forms the basis for the transformation of the police service into a more accountable and effective organization. After implementation, it will be capable of responding to the needs, not only of communities in South Africa, but of the Southern African region as a whole. A key principle of this plan is the importance of community policing, which entails partnership with the community for dealing with crime problems. Communities, their representatives, consumer and other interest groups, professional associations, and community-based organizations all need to be mobilized in the fight against crime. South Africa, in this sense, is part of the Southern African Global Village, with Southern African Regional Police Chiefs Cooperation Organization (SARPCCO) and the Inter-State Defense Security Conference as the vehicle for community policing in Southern Africa.

The Police Plan accentuates the fact that organized crime is one of the important issues that has to be addressed, not only in the country, but in the Southern African region, too. Organized crime primarily has to do with those crimes involving sophisticated distribution channels and/or a significant number of operatives. Areas of organized criminality causing the greatest concern to this region relate to vehicle theft (including hijacking), smuggling (of illegal weapons, narcotics, and other contraband), and serious economic offenses. Dealing with these crimes will need a degree of organizational flexibility and integration in South Africa, since many components with distinct skills, responsibilities, and areas of jurisdiction will have to participate in finding solutions to these problems.

During the SARPCCO workshop in November 1995 in South Africa, it was decided that an electronic mail (e-mail) facility was the only alternative to establish effective and immediate communication among SARPCCO members. A legal subcommittee was also appointed to harmonize the different laws of Southern African nations. Relevant recommendations will then be made to the respective governments. Another subgroup was formed to deal with police training and the relationship between SARPCCO, Interpol, and the Southern African Development Community (SADC) states. Some other subcommittees were created to examine the avenues for mutual assistance, joint strategy and operational planning, visa requirements, repatriation of exhibits, and extradition. A number of projects aimed at collecting information on organized crime, both domestically and internationally have also been initiated. One of the main role-players involved in these efforts is the newly created Regional Intelligence Liaison Office (RILO).

Apart from the important role that the Interpol plays in the exchange of information, numerous conferences are also held throughout the Southern African region to exchange ideas and information that lead to a better understanding of organized crime and to the establishment of mutual trust among all the role-players. The following arrangements also contribute to the effective combating of organized crime:

- Due to the democratization of South Africa, SAPS was re-admitted to the ICPO-Interpol in 1993 and, consequently, the SAPS gradually enjoyed increasing contact with other police services.
- Recently, SAPS has also placed SA Police officers at a number of South African missions to facilitate cooperation in regard to cross-border and international crime. These postings have been made at:

  Ghana
  Uganda
  Namibia
  Swaziland
  United Kingdom
  ICPO-Interpol General Secretariat in Lyons, France

Arrangements are under way to place SAPS officers in Harare (Zimbabwe) and Lesotho. Shortly, drug liaison officers will be placed in many countries such as Thailand, Kenya, Pakistan, India, Brazil, Argentina, and Nigeria. Much trust and goodwill have arisen from the exchange of crime information and the initiation of investigations have resulted through the establishment of these offices.

COMPARATIVE EVALUATION OF THE METHODS FOR COMBATING ORGANIZED CRIME AND PROPOSED MEASURES

In order to be specific it is necessary to address the issues in terms of practical experience and an operational approach. It is therefore useful to categorize the various approaches to give a meaningful understanding of the whole process. The two categories are: what works and what does not work.

a. What works: The restructuring of the SAPS and in particular, the detective service with specialized units to investigate specific crimes has been useful in several spheres of preventive actions:

- This has resulted in the establishment of the organized crime division with its own intelligence capacity;
- It has led to a fresh approach where the focus is on the group of perpetrators and their profits instead of the various commodities;

- The implementation of task teams to investigate multidimensional criminal activities;
- Technical surveillance and wiretapping;
- A proper remuneration system;
- Undercover operations;
- Integrated database;
- The establishment of an analytical and strategic office;
- International cooperation;
- A comprehensive crime-threat analysis.

b. What Does Not Work:

- The failures of the intelligence fraternity in collecting meaningful crime intelligence. The reason is that these intelligence agencies are not disciplined and experienced to gather intelligence that could be useful for prosecution and conviction.
- The department of Customs and Excise, which is not yet structured to address drug-related interdiction.

Some new measures that are being contemplated are:

a. **Legislation**

- Proceeds of Crime Bill;
- Money-Laundering Act;
- Revising extradition legislation;
- Legislation to repatriate exhibits;
- Protocols within the Southern African region;
- Mutual assistance agreements;
- Bail legislation;

b. **Measures**

- Southern African Regional Police Chiefs Committee;
- Anti-corruption Units;
- Deployment of electronic detection equipment at South African Borders;
- Witness protection program;
- National drug strategy;

- New passports;
- Reinforcement of borders.

Conclusion

There is no alternative but to pursue national and international initiatives as appear profitable. One can ask the question: "What can be done?"

1. There is a dire need for relevant agencies to be conditioned to see the whole scope from an international perspective and to have the necessary resources to achieve the tasks.
2. Communication channels and structures must be reliable to facilitate the exchange of intelligence on a national and international system. Informal communication lines are comprehensive and capable of fostering cooperation at different levels. Care must be taken that formal structures and communication lines do not smother the informal communication system.
3. Liaison officers in overseas countries need to be dedicated and experienced law enforcement personnel for the exchange and enhancement of intelligence.
4. Although joint operations are always approached with caution, and rightly, too, these must be enhanced to fight organized crime nationally and internationally.
5. International training needs to be pursued for field officers, since it is an excellent method of developing international cooperation.

Governments must empower their law enforcement agencies through effective legislation. Advanced technologies will continually have to be adopted to stay in touch with criminal organizations that vigorously pursue the use of sophisticated technology. The SAPS has adopted a number of strategies and plans in order to be more effective in combating crime. To some extent this represents a shift away from the functional division of ranks in the SAPS toward a more rational, integrated approach to the planning and implementing of strategies against crime. It also means that partnership, not only with other departments, but also with other police agencies and external role players, will be developed as required to foster greater safety and security within an environment of accountability. The SAPS, in partnership with all the sectors of the community, is emerging as an important mechanism to eradicate crime in order to ensure security for all the people, not only in South Africa, but in the whole region.

REFERENCES

Cressey, C.R. 1971. *Organized Crime and Criminal Organizations.* Cambridge: Heffer.

Government of South Africa. 1997a. *National Crime Prevention Strategy 1996–1997.* Pretoria.

Government of South Africa. 1997b. *Police Plan 1996/1997.* Pretoria.

Jones, C.C., and A. W. Steward. 1982. *Organized Crime: A Selective Checklist.* Monticello, IL: Vance Bibliographies.

Opolot, J.S.E. 1981. *Organized Crime in Africa.* Jonesboro, TN: Pilgrimage.

Williams, P. 1995. Transnational Criminal Organizations: Strategic Alliances. *Washington Quarterly* 18: 57–72, Winter.

Chapter 18

Organized Crime: A Perspective from Tunisia

Rekik Riadh

Introduction

Tunisia is located in Northern Africa, bordering the Mediterranean Sea, between Algeria and Libya. With a land area of 60,687.5 square miles, the country is slightly larger than Georgia. Tunisia is facing severe environment problems. Toxic and hazardous waste disposal is ineffective and presents human health risks, while water pollution from raw sewage, limited natural fresh water resources, deforestation, and overgrazing are leading to soil erosion and desertification. The population, estimated to be 9,019,687 in July 1996, with a growth rate of 1.81 percent, largely comprises Arab-Berber people (98%) with a few European (1%) and Jewish (1%) ethnic groups. Islam is the dominant religion and Islamic fundamentalist groups have been accused of waging terrorism to impose their ideology. The country gained independence from France in 1956 and adopted a constitution in 1959 that has ushered in a republican government based on adult franchise. The country has been administratively divided into 23 governorates and the legal system is based on French civil law system and Islamic law. The constitution permits some judicial review of legislative acts in the Supreme Court. Although five other political parties apart from the ruling party and the Communist Party are legal, an Islamic fundamentalist party, *An Nahda* ("rebirth"), has been outlawed.

Tunisia has a diverse economy, with important agricultural, mining, energy, tourism, and manufacturing sectors. Detailed governmental control of economic affairs has gradually lessened over the past decade, leading to increasing privatization of trade and commerce, simplification of the tax structure, and a cautious approach to debt. Real growth has averaged 4.2 percent in 1991 through 1995, and inflation has been moderate.

The police forces are responsible for maintaining public order and providing assistance, as well as judicial duties. The National Guard and the National Police come under the Ministry of the Interior, and their areas of operation include the whole country. The National Customs, a quasi police organization, functions under the treasury department. Their tasks include the control of drugs, foreign currency, antiques, and all illicit activities permeating through the boundaries in the form of contraband goods and smuggling. The Tunisian judicial police authority, which is considered the largest enforcement organization responsible for the repression of all types of criminality, is divided into four main departments:

1. A specialized anti-crime brigade investigates all kinds of crimes, within which units have been set up to combat serious crimes, terrorism, theft of antiques, and smuggling.
2. A brigade is responsible for investigating economic and financial offenses, crimes involving landed property, loan sharking, forgery of documents and checks, illegal duplication of records, and misappropriation of funds, either in banks or any other economic institutions.
3. A specialized anti-drug brigade is responsible for investigating all crimes related to narcotics trade and its consumption.
4. The social prevention brigade investigates all crimes related to child abuse, prostitution, and vices of similar nature.

The scope and area of operations of the aforementioned units constitute the whole of the country. More than twenty regional "criminal brigades" have also been appointed.

In order to examine the state of organized crime in Tunisia, we need to understand the concept of organized crime itself. The concept of organized crime, especially one having international links, is not a uniform one. Authors define it differently and there is little agreement about what kind of a criminal group could be labeled as an organized crime syndicate. Thus, one definition states that any enterprise or group of persons engaged in a continuing illegal activity, which has as its primary purpose the generation of profits irrespective of national boundaries, is organized crime. This definition was officially accepted by the Select Expert Working Group meeting on organized crime in Saint Cloud, France on 26 and 27 January 1988.

The European Union Group on Drug and Organized Crime, however, has defined it as "a collaboration between more than two persons . . . for a long unlimited term . . . suspected of committing grave and serious penal infractions . . . acting for benefit and/or power." Generally, organized criminal activity is marked by a conscious, willful, and long-term joint activity of several persons practicing a division of labor and intending to commit criminal offenses, often making use of modern infrastructures with the goal of realizing large financial profits as fast as possible.

Organized crime exists in several different forms. Each of these may be peculiar to the country or the region and is influenced by the socioeconomic and political nature of the society. On the one hand it takes advantage of the limitations in criminal laws of the country and on the other, it also steps in to fulfill certain demands of the people that are not met through ordinary market mechanisms or that are deliberately denied by the government. We will first outline the forms of this type of crime and then describe it more fully within Tunisia. The following could be said to be some of the main indicators of organized crime:

1. Preparation and planning of offenses that involve professional and meticulous planning of the crime as well as the disposal of the property. Furthermore, organized crime in the sphere of vice, prostitution, narcotics, and so on, operates by adjustment to market needs. This involves exploring the customer needs and making use of market gaps to find out where there is a large gap between demand and supply and the areas that could attract high investment of revenues from undisclosed sources.

2. The commission of offenses are done professionally through specialists and generally involve foreigners. The actions require a joint effort with proper division of labor, use of good resources that are comparatively expensive and difficult to obtain for ordinary groups.

3. Organized crime requires its perpetrators to adopt clandestine behavior, use of cover names, secret communication systems, and generally a low profile to avoid publicity.

4. The connection between offenders and offenses is usually supraregional, supranational, and even international in scope.

5. Organized crime groups are identifiable by a hierarchical structure, where there exists an unexplained relationship of dependence, a system of internal disciplinary measures, and a decision-making process that is highly centralized and regulated unquestionably by those on top of the hierarchy.

6. The leadership provides all kinds of assistance for group members, especially those on the run from authorities, like offers of bail, monetary support, and hiring of a prominent defense counsel. The organizers also ensure that the parties to the trial are threatened and intimidated or that the witnesses do not turn up for giving evidence. On the other hand, the appearances of witnesses for the defense is ensured and full care is taken of detainees while in prison, including the support given to their dependents.

They also play an important role in the rehabilitation of the member after release from prison. All these measures are carried out with the threat of maintaining total control and fearful silence on part of the persons involved.

7. Organized crime is highly profit oriented and involves such crimes as loan sharking, usury, sex, and illegal gambling. Organized crime syndicates usually monopolize and control gambling casinos and brothels, and demand a fee for "protection." The illegal proceeds typically involve money laundering, sometimes accompanied by forced business takeovers, and all these activities are carried out by corrupting others through bribery, inducements, and threats.

The true criminal organizations as illustrated by the aforementioned indicators, are active in all branches of crime, and seek to expand their activities by all avenues accessible to them. Perpetrators use all available means of communication (including international ones) for their activities and purposes. Thus, they reduce their personal risk of being discovered. They also make use of all means of transportation (including international ones), air traffic being particularly important.

Besides the firmly established hierarchically structured organization with strong leadership, there are persons instrumental to—but not members of—the organization and who are often unsuspecting of the role they are playing. For instance, migrant workers transporting goods and business people and bankers involved in money laundering operations may unknowingly work for organized crime groups. The improvements in technology and communications have further facilitated the spread and strengthening of organized crime syndicates. Criminals have found the opportunities to commit crime in various countries by easily passing through the frontiers, and they have evolved to a level sufficient to establish easier and better coordination among each other.

The organized crime phenomena, especially in the African context (Opolot, 1981), can be observed in particular in the following "subject areas" of crime:

- Narcotics trafficking and smuggling;
- Production and distribution of counterfeit currency;
- Arms trafficking and smuggling;
- Highly qualified property offenses, such as:

    Theft of expensive motor vehicles carrying high value loads;
    Theft of valuable property;

- Extortion of "protection money" (e.g., protection rackets);
- Economic crimes

    Fraudulent obtaining of goods on credit and disposing of them;
    Fraud involving credit and financing transactions;
    Smuggling illegal immigrants and procuring employment for them;
    Forgery of documents and checks;
    Illegal duplication of records (piracy);
    Illegal fraudulent gambling;

- Crime related to prostitution, pornography, and dealing in human parts.

The forms of organized crime in various areas of criminal activity can be highly diversified and are subject to constant change. International criminal groups have been illegally smuggling the citizens of underdeveloped or developing countries for supplying cheap labor or for avoiding the immigration authorities. These are large-scale, lucrative operations and involve a large number of members in the organization and financial support from businesses. The dimension of the human smuggling from countries throughout Europe and the increasing numbers of suspects of this type of crime suggest the existence of big organized crime groups. The desire to work and live in the developed countries also provides the organized groups large profits. These are desperate people willing to pay exorbitant fees to gain entry into the developed countries.

The prominent organized criminal groups operating internationally at the present period are the Italian organized crime organizations like La Costa Nostra, the Sicilian Mafia, Camorra, and 'Ndrangheta; the Asian criminal enterprises like Chinese Triads, Tongs, Japanese Boryokudon (Yakuza); the motorcycle gangs like the Hell's Angels and the Bandidos. These are only a few of the numerous prominent groups known internationally for their reach and organization.

THE NATURE AND EXTENT OF ORGANIZED CRIME

Except for some accidental criminal cases, and apart from the Islamic terrorism, we can confirm that there is *no* organized crime in Tunisia. What we find, generally, is a group of offenders who frequently know or have knowledge of each other and commit all types of crimes that seem to be perpetrated by criminal organizations. Certain indicators also apply to the activities of these groups, but in all cases, the intention to operate as a well-organized group is not present. These gangs have no intention to work with each other consciously on a long-term basis and with distributed responsibilities. They "organize" themselves for short-term operations in which there is little to suggest any form of hierarchical structure nor the meticulous planning for the crime and subsequent disposal of the property.

Some crimes such as holdups at banks and other financial institutions occur infrequently and are too small in number to suggest any kind of organization behind their actions. Mostly, these crimes have been attributed to the involvement of foreign criminal elements. In such crimes, offenders use stolen guns and cars, but no other sophisticated means as is the case in other developed countries. Firearms possession in Tunisia is strictly prohibited and this, too, has helped in preventing the spread of organized crime syndicates. It can be said authoritatively that there do not exist in Tunisia criminal organizations with hierarchical structure and international links practicing a division of labor. Thus, organized crime does not pose a major threat to the country at present.

However, Tunisia does experience a form of organized crime that is inspired by terrorism (Boulby, 1988). It is evident that the notion of organized crime cannot be separated from the sphere of terrorism, for there are many common points between the two phenomena. Even though it seems on the surface that terrorism is generally for a political purpose, usually terrorist activities take the form of organized crime such as murder, robbery, drug dealing, kidnapping, and threats committed in the name of some political cause. Tunisia is facing an onslaught of terrorist-inspired attacks on its people, installations, and foreign tourists by radical Islamic groups. Although the conflict with fundamental Islamic groups is fairly recent, the experience of the Tunisian government and people with Islamic terrorist groups has shown that under the cloak of religion and while claiming to be the bodyguard of Islam, these groups are really aiming for the overthrow of the legitimate government (Weitzman, 1996). Their leaders have conspired, abetted, and even carried out violent operations like setting fire to some governmental buildings with people still inside, exploding buses carrying innocent people, and selling drugs to ensure the investment of their programs. All these crimes have been done in the name of establishing an Islamic republic in Tunisia, but the objective of these terrorist groups has been the overthrow of the legitimate, duly elected government of the country.

As we are all aware, there is an inseparable relationship between terrorism, firearms, explosives, counterfeit currency, and drug trafficking. Right from the early 1980s when these terrorist activities began to emerge, sufficient evidence was available to suggest that several times on different occasions the Islamic groups smuggled firearms and explosives to finance their organization and carried out ferocious attacks on ordinary people and government agents. These terrorists groups have now been choosing the tourism industry as a target. They have been spreading false news about the country and using terror campaigns and threats before every tourist season to intimidate the visitors. This has harmed the nation, since tourism is an important means of contributing to the world's peace and trade through exchange of people. There were many specific cases in which terrorists who were arrested either before or after launching their operations confessed in their statements that they had a major objective to disrupt tourism. These groups have also recruited innocent poor students through indoctrination and by various inducements like paying their school fees to recruit them in their nefarious cause. The terrorist organizations have also been manipulating those people who have a strong belief in religion to support them by giving a call for supporting an Islamic movement.

Measures, Including Legislation to Combat Organized Crime

Tunisian authorities have been taking a number of forceful measures to combat the small-scale operations of organized criminal gangs. The security measures taken by the Tunisian police authorities against the high-value motor vehicles theft and trafficking in recent years has assisted the police in breaking up these vehicle traffickers. The modus operandi of these gangs had been to target expensive cars like the Mercedes, which command premium prices in the North African black markets. These vehicles were usually stolen in early morning from their parking places and immediately set on their way toward Libya and Algeria. Other involved members procured blank genuine registration licenses that contained the seal of the Libyan traffic authorities, on which they inscribed the characteristics of the stolen cars. Thus, once the borders were crossed the vehicles were given new identity and quickly disposed of. The perpetrators were mostly Tunisians, Libyans, and Algerians, a band comprising about twenty-five members. The success of the police authorities was marked by quick arrest of some of the leading perpetrators and the seizure of a limited number of vehicles in the Tunisian territory. Nevertheless, in spite of the considerable efforts made with the cooperation of Interpol, more than thirty vehicles have not been recovered. The police authorities have not been able to obtain correct information about the still absconding members who have presumably assumed different names to conceal themselves.

The Tunisian authorities (police and customs) have also been helping a great many of the European countries in this organized vehicle theft racket, which is spreading larger and larger in their regions. For instance, an important number of vehicles were seized by the Tunisian customs that were imported to Tunisia, especially from France and Italy, with either forged documents or genuine but stolen ones. The investigations revealed that the importers (or the drivers) of the vehicles did not belong to the gang apprehended by the Tunisian authorities, suggesting deeper roots of this criminal enterprise. The investigations are still going on with cooperation from Interpol.

There are many other instances of Tunisian authorities giving extensive cooperation to other police forces to curb the menace of organized crime rackets from spreading around. Recently, the criminal brigade arrested two Tunisian nationals in the country who were accused of perpetrating the murder of Belgian Vice-Prime Minister Andre Cool in 1991 in Brussels. This apprehension was a result of cooperation between the authorities of both the countries through Interpol. The two Tunisians were teenagers at the time of the homicide and were in a desperate situation because of their immigration status. The two perpetrators were misled by the organizers behind the crime and were given false information about the target. They were informed that the person against whom they were to commit their criminal act was only a high-ranking police officer who was causing too much annoyance to the activities of drug traffickers. The reward was a very negligible amount of money to these teenagers, a promise to be later recruited and involved in much more important illegal activities. These offenders have been prosecuted.

Such cooperation has ensured that criminals are not able to take advantage of the international barriers and are quickly brought to justice. Several measures have also been taken to safeguard the security and safety of those coming to the country. A large number of foreigners pass through the country's seaports and airports and are in need of strong security measures. The government has been making a constant effort at maintaining an alert vigil to ensure that organized crime syndicates find it difficult to carry out any illegal activity in the Tunisian unfortified territory. This is especially true about the activities of the radical terrorist groups that have been attempting to set up base on Tunisian soil.

As known, the objective of Interpol is to encourage and maximize cooperation among the police authorities of member nations to coordinate police action and exchange information. It has also a major task of encouraging the widest possible assistance amongst the member nations' police authorities and the establishment and development of all institutions able to contribute efficiently for prevention and repression of crime. In all member nations of Interpol, the tasks of cooperation are entrusted to a permanent body appointed by the government. In Tunisia, this body is known as the Central National Bureau (CNB). The Tunisian CNB has always maintained proper and prompt communication with organizations of other countries, keeping the General Secretariat informed. This has facilitated increased cooperation among member nations. Tunisian authorities have always acted promptly on the requests of foreign police organizations, providing assistance in all operations and police activities needed by member nations. There are routine requests for information on fugitives, verification of identities, seized materials asked for by judges for court proceedings, and execution of warrants against specific offenders.

Apart from the enforcement measures, many legislative measures have also been taken in Tunisia to combat organized criminal activities on a national basis. According to the Tunisian Penal Code (TPC):

1. (Article 131) Any formed band, whatever was its duration and the number of its members, which makes an agreement in order to prepare or to commit any offense against individuals or properties, will be considered violative of public security.

2. (Article 132) A six-year imprisonment penalty is inflicted on everyone affiliated in a band, or who participated in an agreement of the aforementioned kind. The penalty is twelve years for the ringleaders.

3. (Article 133) A six-year imprisonment penalty is inflicted on everyone who, on purpose, provided members of a criminal association a place for meeting, or made a pecuniary contribution, or helped them to benefit from the product of their misdeeds, or supplied them lodging or a locality for pension. The penalty is twelve years for ringleaders.

4. (Article 134) Those who are guilty of the mentioned infractions are exempt from penalties if, before any proceedings, they informed the authorities about the established agreements or the existence of the association.

5. (Article 260) Robbery perpetrated with presence of the five following elements is punishable with a perpetual imprisonment:

> Use of violence or threats against the victim or his close relatives;
> Scaling of a habitation or a dwelling place, forced entry or use of skeleton keys;
> Commission of the crime at night;
> Participation of several offenders;
> The offender or offenders holding apparent or hidden arms.

6. (Article 261) The penalty is twenty years' confinement when the robbery is committed with the presence of the two first elements.

7. (Article 262) The penalty is twelve years' imprisonment when the robbery is perpetrated with the presence of the last three elements.

The international situation with regard to drug abuse is becoming more and more disturbing. In spite of the efforts made by various states and international bodies, notably the United Nations' Program of International Drug Control (UNPIDC), drug consumption is increasing and drug trafficking still preserves its organized and international aspects. As far as the situation in Tunisia is concerned, drug addiction does not represent a veritable problem. Nevertheless, no one can deny that it may constitute a potential risk at a later stage. In fact, the large migratory population, the social and economic evolution, and the geographical position dangerously exposes Tunisia to drug trafficking and illicit narcotic abuses. For all these reasons, the Tunisian government ratified many laws and developed an adequate judicial arsenal to control the consumption of narcotics and combat illegal drug trafficking. The new promulgated laws aim at safeguarding Tunisian citizens against the misuse of intoxicants, especially unlawful drug use among youth. The laws also contain repressive measures to combat organized trafficking and money laundering. The penalties related to drugs, as mentioned in the Tunisian law of 1992, became very severe and differ according to the nature of the infraction. Drug holders with the intention of consumption are liable to imprisonment going from one to five years. Those who form, or join, or participate, even benevolently, in a band, either in Tunisia or abroad, with the intention of committing illicit drug activities are exposed to imprisonment penalties going from twenty years to perpetual detention. Nevertheless, the approach still favors the rehabilitative handling of drug addicts.

The organized criminal groups have considerable funds at their disposal, which they use for acquiring legitimate shares in companies and other businesses or for the establishment of new businesses. So, they create pseudo legal institutions to cover their criminal activities. That is why the common fight against organized crime comes from cooperation between the police and financial institutions at the operational level. The objectives are the repression of laundering of dirty money and other attempts by the syndicates to penetrate legitimate businesses. The following *operational* measures are used by Tunisian authorities:

- As a result of the offenders' increasing mobility, the exchange of information among police forces on the national and international levels has been intensified.

- International cooperation and communication in combating illicit trafficking of nuclear materials and other radioactive sources has been planned.

- The need for international cooperation to fight computer crimes has been emphasized.

- By destroying organized crime's ability to infiltrate economic life through the laundering of criminal proceeds, authorities have seriously targeted the breakdown of its social and economic power.

- Centralization of all information related to organized criminality has been undertaken.

- Harmonization of preventive policies and of fighting crime all over the world has been encouraged.

- The agreement on a unanimous opinion or definition of organized crime among criminal justice authorities, which can ease the determination of appropriate sanctions, has been advocated.

- Reduction of opportunities for profit through illicit activities and the minimization of governments and legal authorities' inability to prevent infiltration by organized crime have been given serious consideration.

Comparative Evaluation of the Methods for Combating Organized Crime and Proposed Measures

Despite the alertness shown by police and custom authorities and strong measures taken against criminal organizations attempting to build a base for themselves in the country, complete success has not been achieved. In spite of keeping strong vigilance against the use of forged passports and counterfeit currency, it has not been possible to keep a check on every new visitor. This has been especially difficult in the case of those Eastern European countries that underwent various political, social, and economic transitions recently and which have become vulnerable to drug trafficking, drug abuse, and organized crime. Citizens from these countries do not always possess adequate documentation, and it takes considerable time to obtain information from their employers. Observing these problems and learning about the legal loopholes provided by these newly emerging democracies, criminal organizations have attempted to take advantage of the situation to cross into Tunisia without undergoing proper verification. For these reasons, the Tunisian government has sought to further strengthen the cooperation with a view to exchanging information and expertise in order to maximize efforts in the common fight against organized crime.

Measures against the Islamic fundamentalist groups and terrorist organizations have met with considerable success. Although terrorist activities perpetrated by these groups in neighboring countries like Morocco, Algeria, and even Egypt have increased considerably, Tunisia has fortunately been peaceful to a large extent. The Tunisian government's political and educational efforts, supported by the media, have together successfully faced the challenge by Islamic fundamentalists. The authorities have proceeded with determination using all available means. Primarily persuasion and prevention have been tried, but repression, as the final step to maintain the authority of the legitimate government, has also been exercised. Some success has been achieved and many of these terrorists have been convicted at the national level. At present, about thirty members are absconding and are being pursued on an international level with assistance from Interpol. The Tunisian government is attempting to alert all countries to make them aware of the criminal activities of the persons who seek asylum on political grounds. Tunisia is requesting other governments to refuse entry to these people and assist in their detention.

The organized offenders benefit from a situation in which the principle of due process of law puts hurdles in the path of enforcement authorities. The need to closely follow and adhere to the legal provisions is one of the causes that immobilize the police and justice machinery, and this gives the offenders a considerable head start. As a consequence, police and justice authorities of Tunisia have not been able to prevent the criminals from taking advantage of the legal loopholes. The government has been devising ways to restructure the legal and operational measures so as to strengthen the actions taken against the criminals. The criminal intelligence units have been focusing mainly on established organized crime groups, rather than on specific criminal offenses at the street level. Attempts are also being made to weaken the criminal organizations through the severe condemnations of their members and the seizure of the unlawfully accumulated proceeds. A capability to ensure striking at their roots is perhaps the best deterrent possible against these organized groups.

Furthermore, the enforcement agencies have also been attempting to control those individuals who appear respectable in society but are otherwise engaged in antisocial activities. Such people are often integrated well into social and economic life but attempt to benefit from organized crime by becoming willing tools such as drug carriers or money launderers. Police surveillance over such people is helping to maintain control over their activities and is further preventing organized crime syndicates from developing roots in Tunisia.

Finally, the policy of correction and rehabilitation of detainees in prison has also been bearing fruit. The Tunisian authorities have been taking steps that aim at the reintegration of the offenders in the social life of their community. Such objectives, followed by a policy of providing assistance to those who were willing to give up a life of crime and work honestly for their living, have also been fairly successful. The number of repentants who have decided to cooperate with the police forces has been increasing in the past few years and gives hope that organized crime syndicates will not be able to establish themselves firmly in this country.

Conclusion

Organized crime is one of the dangers that threaten the international community. In order to face its challenges all member nations of Interpol should strengthen cooperation with a resolute, concerted, and audacious action, aiming at both prevention and repression. Organized criminality represents a parallel economic system, the turnovers and profits of which may in some countries exceed the gross national product. The financial profits originate from various forms of illicit activities: sale of firearms and contraband, trafficking in human beings (international prostitution, illegal immigration, trafficking in children, and trade in human organs), gambling, and most important, drug trafficking and distribution, as well as avoidance of taxation. The money is laundered through investment in companies with prosperous businesses and well-situated premises.

The effectiveness of these organized groups lies in their attempts to corrupt the government's enforcement machinery. Corruption has inevitable repercussions on public institutions, which constitute a supplementary burden for the state. The differences in the systems of rights and laws in the penal codes further give the organized criminal groups a considerable head start. Moreover, complexity of national legislation impedes international cooperation and hinders the tracking of criminals. It also obstructs legal proceedings.

The coordination for the fight against organized crime is challenging because various problems relate to the differences and incompatibility of juridical systems. The situation allows the organized criminal groups to act with flexibility, without worrying about frontiers. For instance, clandestine immigration has become a lucrative large-scale activity and yet the punishment for the offenders is not severe. It does not dissuade them from continuing their activities even after spending some time in prison. International cooperation is very essential for preventing these and other kinds of illegal activities. Tunisia is constantly cooperating and communicating with Interpol, which is the best source for fast, efficient, and accurate information. It helps in collecting extensive intelligence and ensures that the country does not become complacent. Although organized crime in

Tunisia has not assumed alarming dimensions, the authorities and the people cannot lower their guard and lose vigil over the activities of those likely to harm the society. Tunisia is also very interested in learning about the experiences of countries successful in pursuing organized crime activities. Tunisia needs to develop expertise for fighting organized crime.

REFERENCES

Boulby, Marion. 1988. "The Islamic Challenge: Tunisia Since independence." *Third World Quarterly* 10 (2): 590–614.

Opolot, James S. E. 1981. *Organized Crime in Africa.* Jonesboro, TN: Pilgrimage.

Weitzman, Bruce Maddy. 1996. "The Islamic Challenge in North Africa." *Terrorism and Political Violence* 8 (2): 171–188.

Chapter 19

Organized Crime: A Perspective from Zambia

Francis K. Ndhlovu

Introduction

The Sovereign Republic of Zambia, situated in Central Africa, is landlocked and surrounded by eight neighboring countries, namely, Angola, Namibia, Botswana, Zimbabwe, Mozambique, Malawi, Tanzania, and Congo. The country, with a land area of 290,586 square miles, has a long and open border and a population of about 9 million people. The country's population is multiracial and multilingual, but English is the official language. People are free to move about and traverse borders both in and out of the country under the new democratic dispensation without any undue interference. Naturally, crime has steadily increased, particularly in its sophistication. This crime wave is usually propelled through syndicates that are highly organized. Organized crime in Zambia is both national and international given that perpetrators usually plan the crime in one country and put the plan into effect in another without regard to national boundaries.

The administrative units have been grouped into eight provinces of which the copper belt with capital Ndola is significant. Zambian police, unlike most British-created colonial forces, have only limited paramilitary units. Most of the important crimes are investigated by the Criminal Investigation Department, and police forces are supplemented by a reserve unit, a traffic section, and an important protective unit for Lusaka. Additional forces in cases of emergency are provided by three police camps situated at Kabwe, Ndola, and Lusaka and a police paramilitary unit consisting of five hundred men. This unit is in charge of internal order and performs riot control duties. The units are also equipped with a few helicopters and assist the army if required.

The Supreme Court is the final court of appeal and the president appoints all its judges. The court, with twenty judges, has unlimited jurisdiction to hear and determine any civil or criminal proceedings under Zambian law. There are also resident magistrates' courts that sit at various centers. Local courts deal mainly with customary law, although they have limited statutory powers. The following table is a condensed summary of the general crime situation in the country. The figures have been obtained from the monthly crime returns as submitted by all police formations in the country.

CRIME TRENDS: ZAMBIA 1990–1995

Year	Reported	Cleared	Not Cleared	Convictions	Acquittals
1990	133,669	30,239	33,535	65,109	4,786
1991	132,717	22,355	46,955	59,186	4,221
1992	137,459	33,520	48,749	49,828	5,362
1993	117,567	30,873	48,021	34,411	4,262
1994	126,203	40,915	40,747	39,796	4,745
1995	129,187	34,725	57,176	32,464	4,822

THE NATURE AND EXTENT OF ORGANIZED CRIME

Organized crime in Zambia manifests itself in motor vehicle theft, drug trafficking, firearms smuggling, commercial poaching, bank fraud, and money laundering. All these are cross-border crimes whose syndicates have tentacles that have spread throughout the Southern African Region. This chapter attempts to highlight some of the major trends of organized crime in Zambia, the legislative as well as operational measures currently in place to counter the scourge, as well as a comparative evaluation of these measures. Further, it also attempts to show the proposed measures that the government is contemplating to deal with the problem of organized crime in order to effectively diminish, if not eradicate completely, its impact on the society. Organized crime has taken many forms in this country and has begun to pose a deadly threat to the security of its citizens and finances of the country. We will describe a few of these criminal enterprises by way of illustration of their nature and extent.

Motor Vehicle Theft

The vehicles, which are either stolen or grabbed at gunpoint, are either transported in broken-down components or are driven across borders to be exchanged for goods, cash, or drugs. In order to achieve easier movement of the motor vehicles and parts or components, erasures and alterations of chassis and engine numbers are commonly done by the offenders. Falsifications and forgeries of the documents relating to motor vehicle registration, movements, and driver's licenses are found frequently. Further, there is a marked tendency toward corruption in which public officials are involved with organized crime syndicates. Public officers from such departments as immigration, customs, and so on, as well as any other person in the way of organized syndicates, are either paid off or eliminated if they prove difficult to bribe.

Most vehicles stolen from Zambia find their way to Zimbabwe, Namibia, Botswana, Malawi, Mozambique, South Africa, Congo, and vice versa. Groups comprising foreign nationals living in Zambia, mostly Congolese, Zimbabweans, and West Africans are reportedly behind the thefts of motor vehicles. However, these foreigners work in collusion with the counterpart syndicates that comprise Zambians. During the last two years, thirty-seven motor vehicles stolen from other countries within the Southern African Region were recovered in Zambia. During the same period, fifteen motor vehicles stolen from Zambia have since been recovered in the neighboring countries. These figures refer to only those vehicles that have been positively traced to their legal owners by establishing a chain of ownership. A lot more motor vehicles without identification of owners are recovered by police across the country. In Zambia, and within the Southern African Region, Japanese-made motor vehicles, such as Toyota, Mitsubishi, Nissan, and Suzuki, attract greater interest from these syndicates.

An instance of motor vehicle theft that involved a well-organized crime syndicate in Zambia was fully demonstrated by the so called "Yedo" case. Winsome Yedo Kasoka is a Zambian national who is a gang leader of criminals involved in aggravated robberies of motor vehicles from Zambia to Zimbabwe and vice versa. His great interest has been in the latest models of Japanese cars that have a ready market in Zimbabwe. He established himself in this country, bought a mansion, and established a gang consisting of six Zambians and three Zimbabweans. The gang, armed with AK-47 assault rifles, was stealing motor vehicles in Zambia and driving through Mozambique to Harare in Zimbabwe. In Harare, the gang leader, Yedo, was receiving the contraband and delivering the same to prearranged buyers. The proceeds from the sale went to Zambia to be shared with other gang members.

Similarly, vehicles were being stolen from Zimbabwe and driven via Mozambique to Zambia, where they were sold. The Yedo gang had literally infiltrated the police, customs, and city council licensing staff in the revenue section. Yedo and his men would begin by obtaining signed original blue books from the Lusaka City Council's revenue section, facilitated by an employee working there. Armed with the "authenticated" blue books, the gang would then fill in the particulars of the stolen vehicle as legal owners and the culprits would go through the customs without difficulty. Wherever necessary, they would also pay off the officials, since they had developed a good capacity to bribe. Most of the motor vehicles were procured by way of aggravated robberies. It became difficult to arrest these criminals because public officers, including customs and immigration agents, were compromised through the gang's dirty money. It is, however, gratifying to note that today all nine members of the gang have been arrested and brought before the criminal justice system in both Zambia and Zimbabwe.

The syndicate (gang) leader Yedo was arrested in Zimbabwe for several of these offenses of theft of motor vehicles and for possession of stolen property. The rest of the gang members apprehended in Zambia, were charged with aggravated robbery, theft of motor vehicles, and forgery. It is interesting to observe here that a wife of a gang member was also involved in the whole scheme. During house searches police found her in bed with an AK-47 rifle hidden between her legs. She has since been arrested and charged with unlawful possession of a firearm.

Trafficking in Illicit Drugs

In Zambia the problem of illicit drugs, that is narcotic drugs and psychotropic substances, is becoming widespread and threatening to destroy the social fabric of the country. Illicit drugs surfaced on the Zambian scene in the early 1980s when few individuals were found dealing in the same. The drugs then were all foreign to Zambia, although cannabis sativa, or marijuana, grows wildly in the country and from ancient times has been used widely for medicinal purposes by the local people.

In 1985, the government responded to the emerging drug scourge by arresting and detaining a number of people, including some prominent personalities. A special tribunal called the Chaila Tribunal was set up. The tribunal, chaired by a High Court judge, found that the problem of trafficking in illicit drugs was real and a good number of those detained were deeply involved. This judicial revelation was considered only the tip of the iceberg. Presently, the country has seen a proliferation of all types of drugs. Whereas initially, Zambia was only a transit point of these drugs en route to Botswana, South Africa, and Southeast Asia, today most of these drugs are in fact consumed right in the country by all age groups.

The drugs peddled in Zambia mostly include cannabis, hashish, hashish oil, mandrax, opium, heroin, khat/miraa, cocaine, morphine amphetamines, LSD, diazepam, thiopental, scolm, and pemoline. Some of these drugs are even manufactured locally in clandestine laboratories using precursor chemicals. Furthermore, South Africa has become a major destination for a greater quantity of these drugs where they are exchanged for stolen motor vehicles. Thus, in Zambia today, one finds an increasing influx of posh cars largely acquired through drug money.

As a consequence of all these drug-related activities, the crime rate has soared to unprecedented heights. The drug syndicates in Zambia, involving local Zambians, Asians, West Africans, Greeks, and Lebanese, have direct contact with similar syndicates in South Africa and Asia. Most hard drugs like mandrax, heroin, and cocaine originate in Asia and are transited through Zambia. This country has become both a transit point and a consumption destination. From Zambia, the drugs are peddled to South Africa by couriers working for influential drug barons. The demand for these drugs, mainly by young people between the ages of fifteen and thirty years, is such that there is an increase in aggravated robberies, burglaries, hijacking of cars, and other violent crimes. The addicts commit these crimes in order to pay for the drugs to sustain their habits. Theft of money, expensive goods such as modern electronic equipment, jewelry, and motor vehicles are largely attributed to these drug users. These drug addicts have also been committing robberies and violent crimes and they are becoming most daring and violent criminals.

To show the nature and extent of drug trafficking in Zambia, the following statistics pertain to drug seizure, persons arrested and dealt with by law, and the type of drugs, as well as quantity involved from 1990 to 1996. It is apparent that there has been a marked progression in the number of criminals involved in the illicit drug trade. For instance, persons arrested for drug-related offenses were as follows:

Year	Number of Persons Arrested
1990	105
1991	127
1992	132
1993	206
1994	340
1995	1,032
1996 (Jan–Sep)	1,201

It is noteworthy that the preceding statistics reflect an upward spiral. Other details of drug-related crime statistics are as follows:

TABLE 19.1   RECOVERY OF DRUGS IN ZAMBIA

Drug Type	1990	1991	1992	1993	1994	1995
Mandrax (# tablets)	1,322,000	755,697	730,548	319,805	122,230	19,550
Cannabis (ton)		8	472.904	472.9	870	4.2
Heroin (kg)		3.84	50.003	75.79	2.44	0.152
Hashish (g)			74	2,028	47.1	258.2
Cocaine (kg)			2.2		3.77	1.76
Opium (g)				10.5	6,436	195.2
Morphine (g)				7,340	379	500
Khat/Miraa (kg)					30.99	39.88

DRUG ENFORCEMENT COMMISSION STATISTICS
DISPOSITION OF DRUG OFFENDERS

Status	1990	1991	1992	1993	1994	1995
Reported	85			184	240	906
Arrested	105	127	132	206	340	1,032
Prosecuted	36		108	206	340	964
Convicted	24		68	169	247	528
Acquitted	06		10	08	27	39
Discharged	00		10	16	29	66
Withdrawn	24		00	04	15	86
Pending	15		18	04	22	313

Illegal Trafficking in Firearms and Precious Stones

Zambia became independent in 1964, and the geopolitical situation at the time was such that neighboring countries such as Angola, Mozambique, Zimbabwe, Namibia, and South Africa were still under colonial bondage, or the apartheid system of government influenced these countries' foreign policy. Since Zambia is a landlocked country, it needs access through neighbors. So the country decided to support the liberation movements from the countries previously mentioned. The problem of armed banditry started when, at the onset of independence of these countries, firearms used by the various freedom movements could not be prevented from falling into undesirable hands. Some of these firearms were given to friends as the fighters left for their liberated countries. Assault rifles and pistols were soon found in hands of bandits through clandestine sale or through crimes. These arms caches have become the greatest source of the illegal firearms in the South African region. Related to the aforementioned scenario are armed conflicts continuing in regions such as Angola, Mozambique, Rwanda, and Burundi. In these countries, some dissatisfied combatants have taken up arms to fight in order to usurp power from elected governments that have been formed after driving the colonial masters away. Mostly, these bands have been formed and sustained on an ethnic basis, which has added another dimension to the complexity of the problems.

Ethnic conflicts are usually long drawn and seriously affect the economy of the rural areas. Because the people are immersed in war, food grain production has fallen rapidly. This has encouraged an exchange of firearms for food in the border areas of Zambia. In August 1996, the police recovered more than two hundred assault rifles of different makes and large quantities of ammunition from border areas with Angola. It was subsequently learned that the National Union for the Total Independence of Angola (UNITA), a rebel movement led by Jonas Savimbi, which controls a part of Angola, had run out of food and was responsible for the increasing cases of firearms transactions. It is important to observe that a number of illegal firearms, obtained cheaply and easily from rebel factions and villagers, are transported across Zambian boundaries to neighboring countries by different criminal groups. These guns find a ready market and are usually supplied to criminals in those countries. The large profits in gun smuggling have attracted organized crime syndicates that have made this into a big criminal enterprise.

This assertion is best exemplified by one known case of the Mabenga and Kunzley Syndicate. In this case, two Zambians and one Swiss national got into a loose partnership to mine emeralds in the copper belt province of Zambia. In the course of time, the three started an illegal trade in firearms. The Swiss national would leave the country, stay in South Africa for a while and dispatch a fax message to his Zambian partners informing them that he had obtained an export order and would provide a supplier or dealer's quotation for firearms to be shipped to Congo. He would then ask his Zambian friends to obtain and send over a tourist's import permit, which, according to the Act, could only be issued to a person who is visiting Zambia in the course of a journey to a destination outside the country and whose stay does not exceed six months. Incidentally, the Swiss had been in the country for some years and regularly engaged in business. Further, he was not a holder of a firearm dealer's license so he could not import any firearms and/or ammunition into the country.

Notwithstanding these provisions, his Zambian partners managed to get one copy each of the Firearms Provincial Certificate application form and a Tourist's Import Permit form and reproduce them liberally. They filled out each and forged the signature of the Firearms Registrar. Thereafter, the tourist import permit was faxed to South Africa on the basis of which the Swiss purchased the guns. These guns were never declared at customs entry points but found their way in. The licensing authorities were presented with forged Provisional Firearms Certificates and they, believing the same to be genuine, issued firearms licenses and blue books for legal ownership. Later, the guns were sold to unsuspecting purchasers together with the blue books, facilitating change of ownership.

Police investigations subsequently uncovered this racket and members of this syndicate have been arrested. About seventeen guns (rifles and handguns) were recovered from the suspects. The offenders were using a registered mining company called Mukumbe Mining Limited as a legal front for their illegal transactions. Proceeds from these criminal activities were laundered through the mining company. It is interesting to note that between 1995 and 1996 Zambian police recovered one hundred and twenty-six firearms, mostly pistols, shotguns, rifles, and handguns that involved such fraudulent firearms certificates.

As a result of the Mabenga case, Zambian police have intercepted several applications for change of ownership of firearms on finding that most of these firearms were fraudulently acquired. Since the bulk of these cases involve handguns, the Zambian Police Service have slapped a temporary ban on such change of ownership for two years by the Office of the Inspector General. This shall allow the police time to carry out thorough investigations into suspected illegal possession of and trade in firearms and ammunition, especially handguns.

Smuggling is not only confined to guns, but also to precious stones, animal parts, and electronic goods. Zambia loses in excess of $200 million U.S. dollars yearly through illicit emerald trade. Zambia is internationally acknowledged for the quality of its emeralds, which are considered second in the world only to Brazil's. Illegal mining and trafficking in emeralds and other precious stones continues to flourish to the detriment of the national economy. Some West African nationals, the majority of whom are Senegalese, Malians, and Congolese, have formed gemstone cartels, which are operating illegally. Some of these have influential Zambians to cover their tracks and consequently illegal profits in these enterprises are high. These gemstones are sold in Europe, Southeast Asia, and North America at high values. It is interesting that the trafficking routes for guns, vehicles, and precious stones are almost the same, suggesting the inter-linkages among these operations.

Bank Fraud

In recent years, the country has experienced a rise in fraud cases. These include bank fraud as well as insurance, credit card, and computer fraud. Bank fraud involving checks and other bills of exchange are more common. Available crime statistics show that over a period of five years, from 1991 to 1995, 15,054 cases of bank fraud were reported countrywide. Out of them, 2,381 convictions were secured and there were 721 acquittals. The following is a breakdown of cases for the years mentioned, showing the trend of bank fraud in the country.

BANK FRAUD CASES: 1991–1995

Year	Reported	Cleared	Not Cleared	Convictions	Acquittals
1991	2,696	735	1,307	528	126
1992	2,932	923	1,405	420	184
1993	3,136	1,007	1,457	530	142
1994	2,880	963	1,287	492	138
1995	3,410	813	2,055	411	131

Source: Annual Crime Returns, 1995

Commercial Poaching

The country is in danger of losing the entire stock of its fauna due to the indiscriminate killing of wild animals by commercial poachers. Rhinos, elephants, and some special species are now threatened with extinction. Poachers kill these animals for their valuable skins, horns, and ivory, as well as meat. Commercial poachers are affluent individuals or groups of individuals who carry on their illegal activities by hiring poor villagers who have few other avenues of income. They have modern, long-range communication devices. They carry very sophisticated, military firearms and ammunitions. They also have modern automobiles that make the transportation of the killed animals easier. In many cases, the logistical capacity of the poachers is better than that of law enforcement officers.

In the past 20 years, Zambia has lost more than 180,000 elephants worth over $10 million U.S. dollars. Out of a population of 200,000 elephants in 1972, only 20,000 now remain. The black rhino has become almost extinct in Zambia. Poachers have wiped them out for the horn, which is believed to contain aphrodisiac qualities. The demand for it is said to be high in Southeast Asia and the Arab world.

Money Laundering

Loosely defined, money laundering is a practice by which money earned from illicit business is systematically invested in legitimate businesses, thus concealing the real source of the funds. This prevents taxes from being paid and encourages the perpetuation of illicit businesses. In Zambia, there is ample evidence of money laundering. This is often done through commercial banks, which have proliferated in the midst of a declining national economy. In an economic environment where a lot of legitimate, long-established businesses are struggling to survive and a good number of them have already failed, one still finds a clique of local and foreign businessmen investing huge amounts of money in the banking, transport, food and beverage sectors, unaffected by the general downward trend of the economy. There are currently in Zambia many companies that are in effect legal fronts for money laundering. These are mostly trading companies like wholesale agencies, bakery and confectionery establishments, beer and liquor outlets, transport services, and commercial banks, but their real purpose is to channel the profits from corrupt business practices. It is also true to say that some foreign nationals living in Zambia are the moving force behind the legal fronts.

It is widely known that drug barons thrive on profits gained from illicit narcotics and psychotropic substances, which they supply to various parts of the world. The proceeds from these sources are often deposited in bank accounts or transferred to a different country and reinvested in some legal business. Similarly, criminal syndicates, which are behind the spate of motor vehicle thefts and aggravated robberies, intermingle proceeds from these activities with legitimate money in the banks and other investment portfolios. This system follows the same pattern as in other places where organized criminal syndicates accumulate substantive profits from their criminal activities and seek to legalize it through different means. Hence, every crime that has profit as a motive necessarily involves money laundering to such an extent that if the prospect for anticipated profits were removed from the criminal activity, most crimes would vanish.

The opening of Zambian economy to the outside world under the new democratic dispensation has brought in large foreign investments. However, a part of that investment is from laundered money and in most cases from proceeds of drug trafficking. As earlier observed, this dirty money is laundered through legitimate financial institutions and finally finds its way into the economy, thus fueling inflation and hiding much needed revenue for the government.

Measures, Including Legislation to Combat Organized Crime

The Zambian government has put in place several measures to combat organized crime. The Penal Code deals severely with thefts of moveable property, including motor vehicles. For instance, Section 265 of the Penal Code, Chapter 146 of the Laws of Zambia, makes it an offense for any person, who without the consent of the legal owner (or special owner), takes away moveable property with the intention of permanently depriving the owner of the same. Section 272 of the Penal Code prescribes the penalty for theft, namely five years' imprisonment. However, if the theft of a motor vehicle is committed using a firearm or any dangerous offensive weapon, or at the time of theft actual violence or threat of actual violence is used by multiple perpetrators, they commit aggravated robbery under Section 294 of the Penal Code. The penalty is a custodial term of imprisonment with a mandatory minimum sentence of fifteen years.

Under the same law the police can charge a person with the offense of failing to account for property reasonably suspected to have been stolen or illegally obtained. This particular offense gives the police officer wider powers to investigate the circumstances under which a person's property such as a motor car or spare parts thereof have come into that person's possession whenever reasonable suspicion of malpractice arises.

The Zambian Police Service has also established regional cooperation with other police forces as an ultimate alternative to effectively fight against organized crime in motor vehicle thefts. The establishment of the Southern African Regional Police Chiefs Cooperation Organization (SARPCCO), which groups together eleven countries in Southern Africa, has made it possible for Zambia to participate in joint operations. The SARPCCO members share criminal intelligence relating to the identification of thefts by motor vehicles syndicates, the names of persons involved, and their modus operandi, including the routes used. In addition, all eleven police chiefs are directly connected to the same database through an e-mail computer software system. So far a number of joint operations have been carried out between Zambia, South Africa, Mozambique, Malawi, and Zimbabwe. These operations shift or rotate from one country to the other, maintaining pressure against the transnational criminal syndicates.

In one such operation in July 1995, mounted right in Zambia jointly with South African police, forty vehicles were seized. It was discovered that they had been stolen in South Africa and illegally sold or transferred to individuals in Zambia. A similar joint operation was also organized in South Africa involving the rest of the SARPCCO members. A subregional Interpol Office (ICPO), was recently commissioned in Harare (Zimbabwe), which also serves as the SARPCCO Secretariat. This office established a common database in crime intelligence so as to identify stolen motor vehicles and to monitor their movements. Equally importantly, it gives personal profiles of criminals involved in motor vehicle thefts. Thus, we now have in place a practical and effective mechanism to break up criminal syndicates in thefts of motor vehicles in the region.

On the other hand, there are similar legislative and operational measures targeted at organized crime in drug trafficking. The Narcotic Drugs and Psychotropic Substances Act Number 37 of 1993, classifies illicit drugs and prescribes offenses and penalties for illegal possession, cultivation, manufacturing, trafficking, and consumption. The government of Zambia, having realized the effects of drug trafficking and money laundering, ratified the 1988 United Nations Convention against illicit traffic in narcotic drugs and psychotropic substances on 28 May 1993. This further gives the country the right platform and the right motive to continue efforts at liaison as well as cooperating with other countries in fighting the drug scourge.

Under the Zambian Narcotics and Psychotropic Substances Law, any person found with drugs in tablet or powder form, other than cannabis, with a minimum weight of 0.50 grams or with a minimum weight of 2.50 grams or milligrams in liquid/fluid form is taken to be a trafficker. Similarly cannabis solids or liquids with a minimum weight of 0.50 grams or 2.5 milligrams of Delta-9 Tetrahydrocannabinol raise a prima facie case of trafficking in drugs. The penalty is a maximum of twenty-five years of imprisonment.

The other measure that is now being employed to counter drug trafficking/drug abuse is public education campaign strategies. The National Education Campaign Division (NECDD), a unit of the Drug Enforcement Commission, plans and carries out radio and television broadcasts about the detrimental effects of drugs on the national economy. This message is also carried through to primary and secondary schools, colleges, and other higher institutions of learning. Pamphlets and magazines are produced in addition to mobile video shows. Open lectures and seminars are delivered to various target groups in urban and semi-urban communities. As of now, two-thirds of the country's primary and secondary schools have formed anti-drug clubs. As in the case of theft of motor vehicles, joint operations between Zambia, and the SARPCCO member countries against illegal trade in narcotics take place frequently. A recent operation incorporating Botswana, Namibia, Zambia, and Zimbabwe at the Kazungula border common to all four countries proved highly successful. A sizable quantity of drugs, mostly cannabis, was seized and many arrests made. Furthermore, realizing the need for special policing against drug traffickers, Zambia has established an independent police unit called the Drug Enforcement Commission that has been adequately empowered by an enabling act of Parliament.

The government is similarly addressing the problems of commercial poaching, illegal trade in precious stones, and fraud through legislative measures. As for commercial poaching, the law in place (namely the National Parks and Wildlife Act, Chapter 316 of the Laws of Zambia), makes it an offense for any person, in the absence of lawfully issued license by the Director of National Parks and Wildlife, to possess, buy, or sell game meat or any trophy. The penalty is seven years' imprisonment. Further, it is an offense for any person to hunt any wild animal in a game-management area without a valid license. Moreover, any person who is convicted of hunting, wounding, molesting, or reducing into possession any elephant or rhinoceros is liable to imprisonment for a term of five years.

On conviction of a person for an offense such as previously stated, the court, upon an application made by the prosecutor, orders any wild animal, meat of any wild animal, trophy, firearm, other weapons or materials or any vehicle, aircraft, or boat (with which the offense was committed or used in connection with the commission of the offense) to be forfeited to the state without any compensation. The wildlife police officer has also been empowered under the law to enter any area, search without a warrant, and to effect an arrest, if sufficient and reasonable suspicion exists that the provisions of the law have been infringed.

It is important to note that Zambia is a signatory to the "Lusaka Agreement on Cooperative Enforcement Operations Directed at Illegal Trade in Wild Fauna and Flora." This particular protocol was adopted on 8 September 1994. This protocol was a reaffirmation of the commitment to the principles and objectives expressed in the provisions of the African Convention on the Conservation of Nature and Natural Resources (Algiers, 1968), the Convention on International Trade in Endangered Species of Wild Fauna and Flora (Washington, D.C., 1973), and the Convention on Biological Diversity (Rio de Janeiro, 1992).

The Lusaka Agreement, read together with the other conventions as previously quoted, reiterates that intense poaching that has resulted in severe depletion of certain wildlife populations in African States is due to illegal trade and that commercial poaching will not be curtailed until such illegal trade is eliminated. Hence, there is a need for cooperation among states in law enforcement to reduce and ultimately eliminate illegal trade, particularly in wild fauna. As national governments are responsible for the conservation of their wild fauna, sharing of information, training, developing experience and expertise among these nations is vital for effective law enforcement against poaching. New laws have been passed that define "illegal trade in wildlife" as any cross-border transaction, or any action in furtherance thereof, in violation of national laws for the protection of wild animals. Such provisions have empowered the conservation efforts.

In Zambia, another special law enforcement unit called the "Species Protection Unit" has also been created as an appendage of the Anti-corruption Commission to investigate all cases of commercial poaching and/or illegal trade in wild fauna. The unit gets a lot of support from the World Wide Fund for Nature (WWF). Through WWF, the Species Protection Unit produces radio programs and publications for public education about the benefits of conservation and the dangers involved in poaching.

Perhaps the best measure is the one that involves the local rural communities residing in designated game-management areas. A non-governmental organization working to conserve nature has devised the Integrated Rural Resource Development Project (IRRDP) within the game-management areas. The organization called ADEMADE operates on the premise that any successful wildlife conservation program that seeks to root out poaching or illegal trade in wild fauna can only be achieved once the local people are fully involved. Thus, the rural communities are put in the forefront of these conservation efforts by making them share in the benefits from these areas. Game meat is periodically provided for consumption to villagers. Money is also distributed arising from the proceeds of different levies collected from tourists and hunters. It is spent to improve life through the provision of clean water, schools, health centers, and medical facilities, including basic infrastructure and necessities. Accordingly, each villager in a game-management area becomes a law enforcement officer ready and willing to fight off poaching. This way organized crime in illegal trade in wild fauna is effectively countered.

The problem of illegal dealing in precious stones has also been addressed in criminal laws. According to Section 321 of the Penal Code, possession of diamonds and emeralds without the written permission of the chief mining engineer, who is appointed under the Mines and Minerals Act, is an offense. In the same vein, it is an offense for any person to dispose of or sell any diamond or emerald to any person or organization without such permission. Since the offense is a misdemeanor, it is punishable in accordance with Section 38 of the Penal Code with imprisonment for a maximum term of two years or with a fine or both. Moreover, a person so convicted shall have his diamonds or emeralds forfeited to the state. Under this law a police officer of or above the rank of assistant inspector has the power to arrest without warrant any person reasonably suspected of having committed or attempting to commit an offense under the aforesaid section.

The government is also trying hard to frustrate illegal transactions in precious stones through the economic liberalization policy. The Ministry of Mines and Minerals Development has been encouraging prospective investors, both local and foreign, to apply for and obtain mining permits to enable them to legally explore and develop mineral resources, including precious stones. A lot of people now have these mining licenses. Further, the government through the Emerald Miners Association of Zambia (EMAZ) continues to sponsor and promote public auctioning of emeralds and other gemstones. The registered miners have an opportunity here to display their stones, have them commercially valued by experts, and offer them for sale to the highest bidders. This arrangement ensures that gemstone miners realize optimum value and at the same time, are shielded from raving con men. Also, it has considerably reduced the number and level of criminal syndicates in precious stones in Zambia. These syndicates used to control the entire emerald/gemstone industry in the country before 1991 but are now in decline.

Although Zambia does not have specific legislation tailored to address a particular form of economic crime, the existing laws are adequate to respond to crimes of an economic nature such as bank fraud, which is quite prevalent in the country. Thus, the crime of fraud is covered through the law on the basis of the concept of "false pretense". This concept says that any representation, made by words, writing, or conduct, of a matter of fact or of law, either past or present, where the person making it knows it to be false or does not believe it to be true is "false pretense," according to Section 308 of the Penal Code.

The gist of the matter lies in doing or saying something while realizing that it is based on falsehood and is detrimental to the other party. Such conduct is fraudulent. Bank frauds are no more than fraudulent conduct on the part of one individual or group of individuals or persons vis-à-vis economic or financial transactions and are so treated by the courts. Consequently, the acts of obtaining goods, pecuniary advantage, execution of a security, or credit by false pretenses; cheating to defraud a person of any money or goods; forging checks and other bills of exchange such as promissory notes, credit cards, letters of credit, or bills of lending; and dealing in counterfeit currency are considered frauds. The Penal Code describes these acts as offenses punishable with imprisonment for terms ranging from one to seven years.

In the area of bank fraud, financial institutions now hold seminars and workshops with law enforcement officers. The purpose is to share information, knowledge, experience, and trends regarding different financial accounting procedures or systems, methods employed by those practicing fraud (modus operandi), profiles of known criminals, and finally, to find better ways of defeating frauds. Some financial institutions have already developed a system of watermarks and other significant features on their official documents, including check leaves which are unique to that particular institution. Nevertheless, measures to curb money laundering in Zambia are presently inadequate. The Narcotic Drugs and Psychotropic Substances Act defines the offense of money laundering in a general sense. The Act does not show in what ways, by which practices, by whom, and at what stage this offense may be committed.

Further the Act does not contain any regulations pertaining to the investigative procedures, modalities of recovering laundered illegal proceeds, and related matters. The Act simply states that money laundering shall be an offense. This is plainly inadequate and legally unenforceable, since it is difficult to discern clean money from dirty money in any given business undertaking. Due to the weaknesses of the money laundering law in the country, a draft Money Laundering Prevention Bill is with the Ministry of Legal Affairs for formal preparation.

COMPARATIVE EVALUATION OF THE METHODS FOR COMBATING ORGANIZED CRIME AND PROPOSED MEASURES

We will evaluate the various measures, operational and legislative, previously described, for each of the forms of organized crime that we have mentioned. This will provide a better picture than evaluating the effectiveness in general terms only.

Thefts of Motor Vehicles

The law under the Penal Code relating to theft of motor vehicles is very weak. The general law of theft applies to motor vehicles in the same way as it relates to any other property or goods. The maximum penalty of five years' imprisonment has not done much to deter would-be offenders considering that there is always a tendency by the courts to suspend part of the imposed sentence. This technically sets criminals at liberty and frees them from punishment, creating an impression that crime pays. Hence, the measures under the present law have exacerbated crime rather than abated it.

On the other hand, the newly introduced operational measures under the umbrella of SARPCCO have so far proved highly successful. In particular, the joint operations with neighboring countries, which allow for the mounting of random roadblocks at selected points, both within territorial borders and at entry/exit points, have been very successful. More stolen vehicles have been identified and offenders arrested in this way. Further, the administrative practice of requiring the vehicle owner to obtain Interpol clearance from both the originating and the intended country of registration has been an effective measure. This check and verification has been facilitated with the standardization of import/export clearance documents among all the participating countries. All these measures have ensured continued success in breaking up criminal syndicates engaged in theft and the smuggling of motor vehicles.

Money Laundering

Organized crime, which operates in the areas of theft of motor vehicles, drug trafficking and illegal trade in wildlife (commercial poaching), precious stones, and firearms, is compounded by money laundering. The present law on money laundering is not adequate and is far from able to address the problem. The Narcotic Drugs and Psychotropic Substances Act states that money laundering is an offense. The Penal Code and the National Parks and Wildlife Act have provisions that empower the courts to forfeit to the state proceeds of crime which cannot be traced back to their lawful owners, such as recovered stolen motor vehicles, emeralds and diamonds, ivory, rhino horns and skins of endangered species, including game meat. In case of offensive or illegal firearms, the Firearms Act and the Penal Code provide for the forfeiture of the same to the state.

However, the law has not achieved much in this matter. In fact, criminals dispose of most of the illegally obtained goods long before the law enforcement agencies know about them. What the criminals endeavor to do is to transfer the property obtained through crime into money or other valuables through investment. That is why measures such as the inspection of bankers' books and requirements for financial institutions to disclose sources of deposits for questioned accounts are very important. These measures have been introduced in the new law on money laundering and aim at trapping all proceeds of crime irrespective of their form and shape. It is likely to be an effective way of fighting organized crime.

The government of the Republic of Zambia has taken a resolute stand regarding the steps to be followed in order to combat organized crime. This includes proposed legislation, especially for the most prevalent and dangerous crimes. Theft of motor vehicles and illegal trade in drugs are such crimes of greater concern. Money laundering is an inevitable fallout from these two crimes.

Given the high rate at which motor vehicles get stolen in Zambia and the fact that a greater number of motor vehicles, either stolen from neighboring countries or fraudulently acquired, are in circulation today, the Zambian Police Service has put forward legislative proposals to redress the situation. The new Motor Vehicle Theft bill contains offenses and penalties in connection with theft of motor vehicles. It seeks to regulate transactions in motor vehicles vis-à-vis motor dealers (i.e., manufacturers, agents, and other sellers) and prospective purchasers. The bill also provides for the police handling of stolen motor vehicles and matters connected with or incidental to these operations. Earlier, such matters were covered in different legislation, namely the Penal Code and the Roads and Road Traffic Act, which were inadequate to meet the new challenges of organized crime in this area. The new bill is a consolidated legislation on thefts of and/or fraudulent transactions in motor vehicles and is thus likely to be more successful.

According to new law, theft of a motor vehicle will carry a penalty of a mandatory imprisonment for two years without an option of fine. A minimum imprisonment up to ten years without an option of fine has been set for the second or subsequent offense. The bill also introduces the offenses of aggravated theft or the theft of a motor vehicle with violence. The former carries a penalty of death, as it involves use of a firearm. The latter carries a penalty of imprisonment up to twenty-five years without an option of fine.

This is a major shift in the law from the current situation, which enables most motor vehicle thieves to get away with a simple fine or a suspended sentence. Furthermore, the proposed law obliges motor vehicle dealers to report all suspected cases of tampering with motor vehicles such as erasures of the chassis and engine numbers and any obliteration and disfigurement of other identification marks. Failure to report to the police is an offense punishable by imprisonment for two years. The disclosure required of dealers in motor vehicles is meant to break the criminal syndicates, as it had become a common practice for some motor vehicle dealers to operate in league with the thieves. They would sell stolen vehicles on behalf of car thieves under the guise of their legitimate business. It is also proposed that vehicles bought within or imported into the country should not be registered by the Motor Vehicle Registration and Licensing Department before a police clearance has been received from the country of origin, as well as from the Interpol office's National Central Bureau, which keeps records of all vehicles in the region.

As a further step toward eradication of organized crime in the Southern African Region, SARPCCO member countries, comprising Angola,

Botswana, Lesotho, Malawi, Mozambique, Namibia, South Africa, Swaziland, Tanzania, Zambia, and Zimbabwe, have realized that different vehicle registration procedures and documents hinder effective responses to clearance requests. As a result, criminals were continually finding it easy to conceal stolen vehicles behind varying registration procedures and documentation in different countries. Accordingly, SARPCCO members have resolved to standardize registration procedures and import/export documentation as a long-term strategy. Equally important is the standardization procedure of police clearances within the Southern African region.

A Money Laundering Prevention Bill is to be introduced in Zambian Parliament for enactment into law. When it is passed by the Parliament, all proceeds of crime will be forfeited to the state. The advantage accruing from this law is that it covers all proceeds, whether monetary or material, from any kind of criminal activity. Financial institutions will be compelled to disclose such information as a client's bank statements, status of bank account, nature of client's business, investment portfolio, sources of deposits, and any other information held in confidence by the financial institution by virtue of the bank/client relationship. The whole object is to stop banks and other financial institutions from withholding information, which gives rise to money laundering.

The proposed law goes further by making money laundering an extraditable offense. This has the effect of purging the country of foreigners who are involved in criminal syndicates while hiding behind the facade of legal fronts or legitimate business enterprises for purposes of laundering proceeds of crime. It also ensures that offenders are not shielded from justice by other countries. The bill further seeks to promote international cooperation in the investigation of criminal activities, for criminals know no national boundary, especially in economic crimes. This is the main reason why the offense of money laundering has been rendered extraditable. Finally, the bill provides for the prosecution and forfeiture of proceedings of money-laundering offenses.

The measures for curbing illegal trafficking in and proliferation of firearms are already in place and quite adequate but only as far as legislation goes. The Firearms Act, Chapter 111 of the Laws of Zambia, regulates the issuance of firearms licenses and certificates, and provides for the control of the import, export, movement, storage, possession, sale, manufacture, and repair of firearms and ammunition. The legislative measure is by and large well conceived, but it is not backed by appropriate technical and operative enforcement measures. For instance, the act makes it an offense, punishable with a fine of K7,500 (kwacha, the local currency) or imprisonment for a term not exceeding fifteen years, or both, if any person is convicted of purchasing, acquiring, or having in his or her possession a firearm or ammunition without holding a proper license. Despite this provision one finds that people still have in their possession firearms and ammunition without the relevant legal authorization. Unfortunately, the law is enmeshed in bureaucracy and is ineffective.

This situation has resulted in a lot of illegal transfers of firearms from one person to another. It has incidentally also encouraged corruption and forgery among the concerned administrative machinery. Consequently, it has become apparent that this form of organized crime can best be circumvented by legislating to empower Zambian police through the Office of the Central Firearms Registrar to approve and issue all firearms certificates and the firearms licenses with blue books, which are used for first legal ownership and subsequent change or transfer of ownership. In view of the aforementioned, it is now being advocated that the solution lies in establishing a Central Firearms Registry for the whole region incorporating SARPCCO. This Central Firearms Registry must create a central data base with accurate up-to-date information about all registered firearms in the region, including profiles of licensed holders and their movements.

Conclusion

Organized crime in Zambia is a reality. It is a serious problem that transcends national boundaries today more than ever before and calls for concerted regional and international efforts. Criminal syndicates, perverse and pervasive, threaten to ruin the economic and social fabric of the society. The best approach is keeping organized crime at bay and to close ranks in the form of international cooperation. That is why Zambia values its membership of SARPCCO, created to counter the threat of organized crime in the Southern African Development Community (SADC) region. Several legislative and institutional measures have been taken to promote this cooperation and undertake joint operations against organized crime that transcends national boundaries. As already mentioned, bills mandated against gangs stealing motor vehicles, distributing drugs, and poaching animals have been successful. This result is further providing an impetus for more such joint operations and sharing of intelligence. It is expected that such regional cooperative efforts among the different criminal justice agencies will succeed in controlling the spread of organized crime in these areas.

Harmonization of legislation in criminal matters such as theft of motor vehicles, trafficking in firearms, narcotic drugs, and psychotropic substances, money laundering, fraud, illegal transfers of money, and commercial poaching (illegal trade in fauna) is a major necessity to deprive criminals of easy sanctuaries. Mutual legal assistance in criminal matters and the relaxation of national immigration procedures vis-à-vis international police organizations are the main basis of successfully combating organized crime. This subject is being examined deeply and the criminal justice agencies are pressing for an early implementation of new legislative measures that will strengthen the agencies and make the crimes of organized groups more difficult to commit.

REFERENCES

LEGISLATIVE

Copy Rights and Performance Rights Act no. 44 of 1994.

Customs and Excise Act Caption 662.

Firearms Act Caption 111.

Lusaka Agreement on Cooperative Enforcement Operations Directed at Illegal Trade in Wild Fauna and Flora: Adopted 8 September 1994.

Motor Vehicle Theft Bill (Proposed).

Mutual Legal Assistance in Criminal Matters Act no. 19 of 1993.

Narcotic Drugs and Psychotropic Substance Act no. 37 of 1993.

National Parks and Wildlife Act Caption 316 as amended by Act. no. 10 of 1991.

Penal Code Caption 146.

Prevention and Control of Money Laundering Bill (Proposed).

Zambia Drug Enforcement Commission. 1996. *Crime Statistics.*

Zambia Police Service. 1996. *Crime Returns.*

Chapter 20

Organized Crime: A Perspective from Zimbabwe

Augustine Chihuri

Introduction

Zimbabwe, formerly Southern Rhodesia, is located in the southern part of the African continent bordering South Africa, Zambia, Mozambique, and Botswana. With a total land area of 150,873 square miles, the country is slightly larger than Montana. The land is rich in natural resources, with important minerals and forests covering almost 49 percent of the land area. Nevertheless, deforestation, soil erosion, land degradation, and air and water pollution are major problems. The black rhinoceros herd, once the largest concentration of the species in the world, has been significantly reduced by poaching. The country's population has been estimated to be 11,271,314 by July 1996, and is growing annually by a rate of 1.41 percent. Zimbabwe, like other African countries has diverse population, with Shona (71%) forming the largest ethnic group. Caucasians (1%), along with Asians, still dominate economically.

The country has been divided administratively into eight provinces and two cities (Bulawayo and Harare), with provincial status. The country gained independence in 1980 from the United Kingdom and has adopted a legal system that is a mixture of the Roman-Dutch and the English common law, with variations due to local customs and statutes. The country has a republican form of government with universal suffrage. Those above the age of eighteen years are eligible to vote in the national and other elections. Agriculture employs 70 percent of the labor force of this landlocked nation and supplies almost 40 percent of exports. Mining accounts for only 5 percent of both GDP and employment, but minerals and metals account for about 40 percent of exports, a factor that plays a significant role in attracting organized crime syndicates to intruding in these activities.

Zimbabwe has a hierarchy of courts, namely the Community, the Magistrates, High and Supreme Courts. The Supreme Court is the highest court of appeal presided over by a chief justice. The High Court has jurisdiction in civil and criminal matters and any other such jurisdiction as may be conferred upon it by law. There are regional courts that have criminal jurisdiction and magistrates courts with criminal and civil powers, presided over by professional judges. A Customary Law and Primary Courts bill was passed in 1981 that has integrated the customary law courts of rural areas into the country's formal legal system. The president appoints the chief justice and judges upon consideration of recommendations made by the Judicial Services Commission. Judges may not be removed before retirement, except in cases of physical or mental incapacity or misconduct. The autonomy of the judiciary system is strictly maintained.

There is a general presumption worldwide that when one mentions the term *organized crime*, reference is often made only to the more established and world famous syndicates such as the Costa Nostra, the Mafia, or the Yakuza. Such a perception overlooks the fact that these syndicates developed from simple criminal activities by individuals. These individuals were either joined or they joined others after meeting in places of common experience such as prisons or while engaging in related activities on opposite sides such as in the illicit trafficking in narcotics, one being the seller and the other being the user or buyer. Such loose-knit gangs are initially localized, and if they exist for a considerable length of time, they strengthen themselves and establish regional relationships. The success of such organized criminal groups results in the mushrooming of other organized criminal groupings. The formation of such illicit groupings is precipitated by the lack of a concerted regional approach to police cross-border organized criminal activities and many other factors.

Organized crime is a serious threat to civilization, economic, and social development. It hinders effective government and has a debilitating impact on public health, safety, welfare, and morals. The whole world is aware of the dangers of organized crime and different strategies have been employed with varying degrees of success and failure in various parts of the world. Criminals have no respect for established national boundaries for their operations and therefore the law-abiding global village must come together and act in concert and common purpose to deliver a decisive blow to this vice.

While numerous attempts have been made to define organized crime, there appears to be no globally accepted definition of the term. However, there seems to be consensus that the key elements are first the perpetration of criminal acts by groups of individuals and second, the exhibition of coercion and violence in the commission of crime, whether it be by a group or a single person. The central issue therefore is that there should be a systematic marshaling of effort by individuals or groups of individuals designed to disturb or infringe on the social rights of others through aggression aimed at their person or property. It involves conscious or rational planning and ordering of human or other resources into a particular pattern to enable the achievement of a particular goal.

The goal of this chapter is to analyze the question of why and how criminals are able to organize themselves in such a way against the background of modern policing. The answer lies in that there still exist numerous factors in favor of criminality. Globalization in its entirety has enabled rapid exchange and interaction in culture, ideas, and technologies, which can be exploited for both lawful and unlawful ends. Proceeds of crime are not subject to any taxes and can be siphoned across borders without hindrance or bureaucratic procedures. The criminal is also able to move freely across borders, unlike law enforcement agents who face cumbersome procedures and are bound by international law and conventions. To make matters worse, effectiveness and efficiency of judicial machinery and law enforcement agencies vary from country to country. This therefore means that criminals are able to go into safe havens to enjoy their ill-gotten gains without fear of arrest and repatriation for trial. As if that is not enough, the criminals are even audacious enough to export their skills to their new domiciles.

It is important at this juncture to state that organized crime is not the existence of known crime syndicates with known names, structures, and resources. By the very nature of crime, organized crime cannot be allowed to formalize its existence in this way. What needs to be acknowledged is that individuals and groups regularly engage in well-planned and executed criminal acts. Once they have accomplished their mission, these individuals or groups tend to go underground while some may be brought to book. They may resurface or reorganize after a lull or following stints in prison. They exist alongside lawfully established corporations with legitimate objectives but indulge in illegal practices to enhance their profits. A third group also exists that may be driven by political or religious motives and engages in destabilizing activities of a very dangerous nature like bombings and other forms of terrorist attacks. These exist in various shades in many countries around the world and differ mainly in terms of level of organization, sophistication, motive, and mode of operation. Most countries have their fair share of these groupings.

The Nature and Extent of Organized Crime

Zimbabwe, together with other countries in the Southern African subregion, has not been spared the scourge of organized crime. From time to time new dimensions of and more sophisticated criminal activities have surfaced. A number of foreigners and locals have been apprehended while engaging in criminal activities showing signs of linkages with other local or foreign associates. Major areas of operation have been drug trafficking, motor vehicle theft, passport fraud, money laundering, and armed robbery, some of which will be described in this chapter.

Motor Vehicle Thefts

The crime of theft of motor vehicles was a relatively unknown phenomenon in Zimbabwe until independence in 1980. It has since mushroomed with the influx of people from various parts of the world who have developed expertise in theft and disposal of vehicles in the black market. The situation was exacerbated by a shortage of vehicles and spare parts in the early eighties, coupled with lack of exposure of the fledgling force under reconstruction to deal with this phenomenon. The situation was further compounded by the lenient sentences that were meted out by the courts for this crime. In general, the Zimbabwean society was literally taken by surprise by the wave of vehicle thefts. Now, a well-organized network has taken root that specializes in all kinds of vehicular theft. Motor vehicles are broken into, hot wired, driven away, resprayed, upholstered, identification numbers falsified, reregistered, and quickly disposed of to unsuspecting victims or accomplices. In some cases the vehicles are stripped of vital components and the bodies are dumped while parts are sold on a buoyant black market.

Drugs

Traditionally in certain parts of the country, Zimbabweans cultivated herbal cannabis, known in the country as "mbanje" for medicinal and personal consumption purposes. Prior to 1980 there was no drug problem in the country and the police had no interest in the area of organized drug trade. However, over the past decade the scenario has changed with an upsurge in drug consumption and trade as well as the introduction into the country and the region of hard drugs like cocaine, heroin, and mandrax. This has been largely due to external influences as evidenced by the arrest of several foreign nationals in connection with drug-related offenses.

Some form of organized drug network emerged in 1981 when about 100,000 tablets of a psychotropic substance commonly known as mandrax or methaqualone were seized at Harare International Airport. Ever since, numerous seizures of the drug have been made, mostly destined for South Africa, suggesting the existence of a well-beaten drug path from Bombay passing through Zimbabwe. The consistency of the route and the elaborate efforts to conceal the drugs show a clearly orchestrated plan to facilitate shipment of the drug. The country remains to this date largely a conduit of drugs to their places of consumption. The trend in illicit traffic in methaqualone has replicated itself in the cases involving cocaine and heroin. In these cases the involvement of some nationals of several West African countries is significant. Fortunately Zimbabwe is yet to become a significant consumer of these hard drugs.

A cause for serious concern to the police and other services in the region is the problem of large-scale trafficking in Indian hemp, or *dagga*. Herbal cannabis has regrettably developed to be a cash crop. Large quantities have been and continue to be seized while en route to markets in various parts of the world, including Zimbabwe. The drug is smuggled by boat, car, train, or commercial truck in large quantities. The recent arrest of two Mozambicans and a Zimbabwean led to the exposure of the existence of a drug ring based in Beira in Mozambique with a branch in Zimbabwe's capital.

The development of appropriate technologies for use in smoking, processing, packaging, and concealment of the drug shows clearly that the trade is well organized. In the 1995 and mid 1996, brick-molding equipment was found to have been converted for use in compressing *dagga* in Harare and the smaller town of Karoi. In both instances there was involvement of foreign nationals. In July 1995, a South African national was arrested at Harare International Airport with twenty-eight "bricks" or cubes of the drug strapped around his body while en route to London. The brand of the drug suggested that it had originated from the Middle East.

This lucrative illicit trade has grown in sophistication to the extent that in one case a haulage truck was escorted for about 200 kilometers while carrying 1,232 tons of drugs. The narcotics, which were from Malawi, were seized in Harare, and three people, a Dutch, a Malawian, and a Zimbabwean national were arrested in connection with the shipment. The major factors contributing to the continued trade are the big demand due to the high Tetra Hydro cannabis content and favorable growing climatic conditions in Malawi. This has tended to maintain the lucrative prices and high rewards in the trade. Measures put in place by the authorities to deal with the problem include strengthening the capacity of anti-drug units through training, use of sniffer dogs, stiffer penalties, tightening of border control checks, and public awareness programs.

Crimes of Violence

In the Zimbabwean context, organized crime of a violent nature has tended to be mainly in armed robberies targeting banks, vehicles conveying cash, public service vehicles, shops, and public institutions like schools and individuals known to be carrying large sums of cash or valuables (Opolot, 1980). Isolated cases of attempts to free arrested criminals have also been experienced. It is in this area where one usually sees the classic examples of occasional getting together of a small number of persons for the commission of offenses. The arrest of one member of the group has usually led to the total liquidation of the gang. In some cases, the plots are hatched by criminals who meet in prison. The presence of a lot of firearms in unauthorized hands in the aftermath of prolonged armed conflicts in the region has further contributed to the escalation of robbery cases involving lethal weapons. The advent of peace should usher in greater cooperation among police forces in the region leading to seizure of arms and arrest of the culprits.

Economic Crimes

The most harmful economic criminal is the one who exploits legal access and abuses his position of trust for personal gain. This usually manifests itself through fraudulent practices and corruption. Mushrooming of organized economic crime in Zimbabwe can be traced to the days of shortages of foreign currency at a time when the economy had not opened up. Various schemes to circumvent controls were devised, including abuse of export-retention scheme allowances. The chief culprits were bank officers who connived with businessmen to obtain and sell export-retention scheme rights.

The country also faced problems of illegal siphoning of funds outside the country. In this process, perpetrators arranged overvaluing of imports and undervaluing of exports, commonly referred to as transfer pricing, and siphoned valuable foreign currency in the transaction. However, the opening up of the economy has taken care of some of these problems, since several import restrictions have been removed. Still, such practices occur, although on a lesser scale because the repatriation rates are not always favorable due to market fluctuations. The government is attempting to reduce the remaining restrictions over import of consumption goods.

The exploitation of legal access to commit organized economic crimes has been most noticeable in financial institutions and public offices charged with procurement and processing of public payments. Prominent features in this regard include "ghost" purchases, forgery of checks, theft of checks, and other fraudulent bank transactions. In most cases, there is connivance with insiders who facilitate the activities using their positions in the targeted organization. Strategies to stem this problem have included greater cooperation between financial institutions and the police to tighten the security measures as well as regular updating of skills of police officers dealing with these cases.

Smuggling

Like other African countries, Zimbabwe has also been devastated by the poaching and smuggling of its endangered species. As mentioned before, black rhinoceros is almost on the verge of extinction while ivory smuggling has drastically reduced its elephant population (McIvor, 1991; 1992). The vast tracts of land make any meaningful supervision impossible and poverty drives people to encroach further into the protected reserve forests. Furthermore, the ethnic community links across the borders make it easy for smugglers to develop an informal market system on both sides of the border that facilitates transportation of goods, including animal parts from one country to another (Puffer, 1982). Smuggling of arms, especially those left over from the armed conflicts of independence wars, are also major problems for the country. These are dangerous, well-organized gangs that do not hesitate to attack even the enforcement officers, if cornered (New African, 1991).

Measures, Including Legislation, to Combat Organized Crime

Fighting organized crime should start with minimizing the opportunities and disturbing criminals' state of readiness to be involved in crime. Strategies should include the elimination of precipitating conditions, increasing the possibility of arrests and incarceration, as well as enhancing the capabilities of those involved in law enforcement. These can be broadly categorized as prevention, detection, investigation, and documentation.

Prevention

Increased police visibility creating an impression of omnipresence has always yielded tremendous success in combating crime. Such presence can be on point duty, road block, guard duty, foot patrol, cycle patrol, mounted patrol, vehicle patrol, or dog patrol. This gives the impression that police are everywhere and thus opportunities for successful commission of crime are minimized. In this respect, Zimbabwe has also mobilized the public to participate in policing in realization of the fact that for centuries members of society were closely involved in the policing process at the preventative and repressive level. This participation in our experience is in the form of starting neighborhood watch committees to join our police personnel, which augment patrol efforts of the regular members. This strategy leads to a great presence of the police on the streets and a good flow of criminal intelligence. Public participation in policing also ensures that there is no mutual suspicion, aloofness, apathy, or hostility, with public passivity converted to active participation.

In the area of prevention Zimbabwe has reaped immense benefits from public education programs on crime. Increased public awareness on crime issues makes citizens less vulnerable and the criminal's job more difficult. The programs, targeted at all sections of society, are firmly in place in Zimbabwe and interagency liaison has facilitated the exchange of useful crime information. An indirect but very effective tool in crime prevention is the imposition of stiff and thus deterrent penalties for any form of organized crime. This can be highly effective if coupled with an efficient detection system as it necessitates a thorough risk assessment prior to the commencement of any criminal action.

Detection

As a result of detection, strategies can be empirically assessed. Zimbabwe has put in place measures to assess such effectiveness and enhanced capacity to do so through regular training and review of methods. The introduction of hotlines and suggestion boxes, creation of specialist units, and development of effective intelligence networks have in our experience proved invaluable in fighting organized crime.

Investigation and Documentation

The use of a teamwork approach to deal with organized crime, with clearly set goals and standards, has kept criminal gangs on the run with barely any time to regroup. The teams have been able to gather information on suspects, wanted persons, and habitual criminals, while closely monitoring any patterns or peculiarities in modes of operation. The benefits of synergy are also reaped when mental resources are pooled toward a common objective. This has a positive impact on the quality of crime documentation.

Legislation

Enabling legislation has also assisted the cause against crime greatly. This legislation in Zimbabwe enables police to arrest suspects and seize articles used in commission of crime. In this regard authorities are also allowed to freeze bank accounts and proceeds associated with crime in order to facilitate investigation.

At one period, such was the sophistication of the operations conducted by the organized crime syndicates that it would take only a single day to steal the vehicles, change their identity, and drive them across the borders for disposal by the criminal associates. Such swift, well-orchestrated operations left the police completely baffled chasing shadows and not making any headway. Now authorities have revamped the vehicle registration system and introduced new measures to combat this growing menace. Legislation has been introduced that outlaws unauthorized possession of vehicle number plates, punching kits, and instruments suspected to be used to break into vehicles. Stiffer penalties for kindred offenses have further been introduced to deter offenders with jail terms of up to ten years, where previously a convicted criminal would have been jailed for only one year.

Other measures put in place to deal with the form of organized crime include computerization of motor vehicle registration records, training of police personnel, formation of specialized units, and making it compulsory for police clearance to be obtained prior to disposal of a vehicle. Tighter controls have also been instituted at border posts to monitor cross-border vehicle movement. On the other hand, the introduction of security devices on vehicles like central locks and alarms also assist in preventing the thefts. All these aforementioned measures have made the stealing and selling of stolen vehicles more difficult and risky, necessitating much more homework on the part of those contemplating it. Major successes in prevention and detection of theft of motor vehicles have thus been scored, although the crime is still with us.

COMPARATIVE EVALUATION OF THE METHODS FOR COMBATING ORGANIZED CRIME AND PROPOSED MEASURES

As can be discerned from the controls previously described, measures taken in Zimbabwe to combat organized crime have dealt mainly with prevention, detection, investigation, and documentation. These strategies have been augmented by initiatives aimed at dealing with the phenomenon in a regional context. They can be itemized as:

- Promoting policing by popular participation through public-awareness campaigns, hot lines, suggestion boxes, neighborhood watch committees, and a police voluntary constabulary;

- Strengthening of law enforcement agencies by empowerment through enabling legislation;
- Creation and development of specialized units to deal with various forms of organized crime;
- Promoting multiagency cooperation in dealing with various forms of organized crime;
- Developing a criminal records system that allows for monitoring of criminal activities of an organized and sophisticated nature;
- Imposition of stiffer penalties or sentences for convicted criminals involved in organized crime.

The promulgation of enabling legislation for law enforcement agencies is incumbent if the police are not to watch helplessly while organized crime prospers. There is, however, a need to ensure that individual human rights of innocent and law-abiding citizens are not unduly infringed. Also paramount is the need to guard against abuse of such legislation.

Public participation has always yielded immense benefits to all in policing. Care, however, should be taken to ensure that criminals do not derail the system. The use of specialized teams should be employed only as long as the need is justified. These can always be disbanded when their existence becomes irrelevant. A criminal records system that enables monitoring of organized crime is a very valuable planning tool in dealing with organized crime.

On punishment, the adage that it must fit the crime remains the best policy. However, when a criminal has indicated intent to perpetuate crime by being a member of an organized gang, this admission should be considered an aggravating factor.

It needs to be appreciated that while individual country initiatives are necessary, they may not suffice if there is no regional or global coordination. This is because of the transnational dimension of organized crime. An integrated approach is necessary to minimize criminal opportunities and eliminate precipitating conditions regionally or even globally.

The following measures are advocated:

- Establishment of formal regional police consultative structures to facilitate joint investigations and exchange of intelligence and information on organized crime;
- Establishment of regional centers or bureaus for the collection, collation, and dissemination of information on crime in general and organized crime in particular;

- Lobbying governments for harmonization of legislation for confiscation of proceeds of crime and mutual assistance in criminal matters;

- Recommending to governments the removal of legislative impediments to freer movement of law enforcement agents in pursuit of criminals across borders, extradition of wanted persons to places of trial, and repatriation of proceeds of crime;

- Simplification of procedures for conclusion of mutual assistance agreements;

- Simplification of procedures for obtaining and supplying of evidence on criminal proceedings across borders.

It is envisaged that these and any other initiatives will eliminate safe havens for criminals and remove hindrance to effective global cooperation in combating organized crime.

Conclusion

If we accept that second only to war, organized crime presents the greatest threat to human survival, it is imperative that cooperation of law enforcement agencies against this common enemy is enhanced. Concerted and integrated efforts to regain a comparative advantage over organized crime are not optional. In our subregion (Southern Africa), bold steps toward greater regional integration have been taken with the creation of an Interpol subregional bureau in Harare, as well as the setting up of consultative structures under the Southern African Regional Police Chief Cooperation Organization. It is expected to pay rich dividends in the near future, although the challenge remains formidable.

References

McIvor, Chris. 1991. "Ivory Ban Increases Zimbabwe Poaching." *New African*, 22: June.
McIvor, Chris. 1992. "Zimbabwe's Case on Elephants." *New African*, 35: December.
New African. 1991. *Zimbabwe Smugglers Kill Another Officer*, 26: November.
Opolot, James S. E. (1981). *Organized Crime in Africa.* Jonesboro, TN: Pilgrimage.
Puffer, Frank. 1982. *Informal Markets: Smuggling in East Africa: A Preliminary Discussion.* Worcester, MA: International Development Program, Clark University.

Conclusion

Challenges for the Future

Jay S. Albanese

Organized crime is tenacious in its ability to change its form, targets, and operations in ways that respond directly to shifts in public demand, prosecution successes, and new criminal opportunities. The perspectives in this volume from around the world illustrate this adaptability. An investigation of organized crime in the smuggling of exotic animals, for example, found that traffickers trading in tiger bones and skins for Chinese and Japanese buyers had developed a sideline in smuggling Russian women to work in sex clubs around the world (Pope, 1997). The Cali cartel in Colombia was said by U.S. officials to have supplied 80 percent of the cocaine smuggled into the United States. These drug profits were laundered through legitimate businesses run by close family members that included a supermarket chain and discount pharmacies (Schrieberg, 1996). After major arrests in Colombia, a shift toward increasing power of drug organizations in Mexico has been documented (Marshall, 1999). This entrepreneurial ability to exploit opportunities for organized crime enterprises makes them both dangerous and difficult to subvert. Organized crime has been found to exist to some extent in every country yet studied.

This chapter offers challenges for the control and prevention of organized crime that have not yet been overcome. These challenges are of two types:

1. What can governments do to control organized crime through a *criminal justice response*?

2. What *long-term prevention strategies* can be developed outside the criminal justice system that will reduce the incidence of organized crime in the future?

Satisfactory responses to these challenges lie at the foundation of a more successful and longer-term approach to the problem of organized crime.

THE CRIMINAL JUSTICE RESPONSE

A swift and certain response to organized crime has not yet occurred, although significant prosecutions in the United States, Italy, and many other countries suggest that inroads can be made in the operation of certain criminal organizations (Albanese, 1996; Jamieson, 1998). Five challenges for the future are paramount: internationalization, the immigration problem, political corruption, law enforcement cooperation, and imagination in sentencing.

INTERNATIONALIZATION

Drug trafficking in the late twentieth century will be remembered as the primary catalyst for the internationalization of organized crime. Similar to the way in which Prohibition in the United States during the 1920s created an opportunity to organize the illegal liquor market, worldwide demand for illicit drugs combined with economic conditions, technology, and political changes to create powerful criminal enterprises. Poor source countries found a new cash crop, new telecommunications capabilities were invented, and the fall of important long-standing political borders made international travel possible almost anywhere. These factors came together to create profitable opportunities for organized crime interests.

One example is the link between organized crime in Italy and the United States. Although there have been linkages between Italian and American organized crime in the past, it was never clear which country followed the example of the other. The Pizza Connection trial of the 1980s demonstrated for the first time a true Sicilian-American linkage in the heroin market, a linkage that included South American and Asian nations as well (Alexander, 1988; Blumenthal, 1988). Tommaso Buscetta, a Sicilian informer in the Pizza Connection case, claimed that he was told by U.S. crime boss Joe Bonanno in 1957 that it was advisable to set up a "commission" to resolve disputes among criminal groups (Lubash, 1985). This suggests that the organization of organized crime in Sicily may have been modeled after that in America, rather than the opposite as is commonly believed.

The Pizza Connection case is an illustration of how criminal groups have entered into "marriages of convenience" because of the huge profits to be made, and the need to transport narcotics from source countries, refine it into consumable form, and distribute it around the world. The scope of this task is simply too large for a single group to handle by itself. Hence, organized crime groups in different parts of the world now communicate with each other, a significant departure from the problem of "local crime groups," which characterized most organized crime until the latter part of the twentieth century.

It is estimated that 200 Russian organized crime groups have relationships with other groups in 50 countries, although the structure of these groups appears less formal than in traditional organized crime groups (Cilluffo and Burke, 1997; Finckenauer and Waring, 1998). Organized crime groups of the future will comprise criminals of many different nationalities and it is likely that none will dominate. Instead, it is probable that groups will work with each other to exploit criminal opportunities in the production, distribution, and enforcement of various criminal undertakings. Examples include predominately Italian groups that operate illegal gambling enterprises with Albanians and also with Cubans in New York (Kleinknecht, 1996; Ianni, 1998). Police from the United States, Canada, Jamaica, and the Bahamas arrested a smuggling ring that had transported cocaine and marijuana from Colombia by speedboat through the Caribbean islands to North America, where it was distributed by another group (Reuters, 2001).

International agreements among nations have begun to emerge in an effort to stem the development of worldwide alliances of organized crime groups. The FBI opened an office in Moscow in 1994 to pool intelligence about alleged Russian-American organized crime links. A police intelligence agency, called "Europol," also was established in 1994 to focus on drug trafficking and money laundering among Western European nations. The United Nations Convention against Transnational Organized Crime was adopted by the General Assembly in November 2000. It is the first legally binding United Nations instrument in the field of crime, but it must be signed and ratified by forty countries before it comes into force. When adopted, participating countries would be required to establish four criminal offenses: participation in an organized criminal group, money laundering, corruption, and obstruction of justice. The Convention identifies how countries can improve cooperation in extradition, mutual legal assistance, transfer proceedings, and joint investigations. It contains provisions for victim and witness protection and protecting markets from infiltration by organized criminal groups. Participating countries would also provide technical assistance to developing countries to help them take the necessary measures and upgrade their capacities for dealing with organized crime (United Nations, 2000).

Responding to the efforts of the international law enforcement community, organized crime groups are likely to make corresponding changes in their operations to remain successful. Sociologist Mary McIntosh has observed that criminal organizations must become increasingly sophisticated in order to maintain acceptable levels of success in their illicit activities (McIntosh, 1975). In response to the decline in the export of chemicals needed to manufacture illegal drugs, for example, domestic laboratories have been set up to produce the drugs within the consumer country. Laboratories can produce synthetic drugs, such as methamphetamine, PCP, and ecstasy. Illegal domestic laboratories are capable of producing a sufficient quantity of illicit drugs to satisfy the demand of U.S. users. Synthetic drugs are manufactured from chemicals that get diverted from their otherwise legitimate pharmaceutical purposes in small, illicit "kitchen labs" and thus do not require a "source country" (Beers, 2000; Green, 1993). The U.S. Chemical Diversion and Trafficking Act established federal recordkeeping, reporting, and transaction requirements for essential chemicals, but individual states and countries vary widely in the number and types of chemicals they track (Marshall, 1999; Sevick, 1993; U.S. Comptroller General, 1993). Law enforcement officials must stay abreast of these trends, while also formulating legislation and enforcement actions that affect the availability and tracking of chemicals that respond to changes in the criminal marketplace.

THE IMMIGRATION PROBLEM

It may be impossible to protect international borders from unwanted immigration, given their immense size, but perhaps the most pernicious role that organized crime plays in the immigration problem is alien smuggling. Groups from Latin America and China have been heavily involved in this effort due to economic and political oppression in those nations. Many illegal aliens are smuggled into developed nations by boat and pay fees of up to $30,000 for their passage. Sometimes they are dropped off in Canada or Mexico and then smuggled across the U.S. border by land. The exorbitant passage fee makes them slaves to their transporters once they reach their destination. Due to their illegal status, the aliens cannot work at legitimate jobs. As a result, they are exploited by unscrupulous employers or become active in prostitution, the drug trade, and other parts of the illegal economy. The Internet has made recruitment of unsuspecting victims easier (Hughes, 2000a).

In Asia, organized crime groups rely heavily on the sex trade for profits. The Yakuza in Japan work with Chinese Triads in Hong Kong to bring women to Tokyo. In similar fashion, Russia Mafia groups transport women from Eastern Europe to Macau. In many cases the women know they may be forced into sex, but they hope for a better future than what their home country offers them (Hughes, 2000; Vatikiotis, Sakamaki, and Silverman, 1995). U.S. authorities concede they probably interdict only 5 percent of the vessels carrying illegal immigrants, although the U.S. Immigration and Naturalization Service doubled the number of cases referred for prosecution from 1992 through 1998, making immigration cases the most common type of federal criminal prosecution. The majority of these cases involved illegal entry, transporting or harboring aliens, and passport or visa fraud (Kalfrin, 1999; U.S. Comptroller General, 1993a).

Given the immense size of international borders, it is clear that there must be greater effort to stop these smugglers before they set sail to foreign shores. This will require greater international trust and cooperation among nations, something that has been lacking in the past but that may develop quickly in the future due to the growing interdependent world economy. In Japan, for example, efforts are being made to open its markets to become a bigger player in the global financial system. Criminal groups there, notably the Yakuza and Sokaiya, have committed murder and other crimes to protect their interests. For many years racketeers in Japan have been used by legitimate businesses to help evict tenants, confiscate property, and exert pressure on competitors, customers, or clients (Hirsh and Takayama, 1997; Bremner and Thornton, 1997). This relationship between legitimate business and organized crime must be curtailed if Japan is to prosper in the wider world economy.

In Colombia, legislation has provided benefits for drug traffickers and other criminals who become informants for the government. Periodic crackdowns on smuggling of contraband (mostly drugs) between Lebanon and Syria and also between Pakistan and Afghanistan must be encouraged through international incentives (Builta, 1994; The New York Times, 1993a). Similar efforts in other countries, such as Mexico and Colombia, can make a substantial difference in international smuggling of people and contraband (Penhaul, 2001; Bailey and Godson, 2001 U.S. Comptroller General, 1994).

POLITICAL CORRUPTION

According to the National Strategy Information Center, "We are confronted with a world with increasingly weak states and governments" (Borsage, 1993). In the United States, for example, it is rare for organized crime groups to physically attack or kill a police officer or other government official. Crime figures in the United States know that an attack on a government official exacts the wrath of a very powerful government that will not stop until it finds the perpetrator. In many other nations, however, this is not the case. Governments are weak or corrupt, police forces are untrained and unprofessional, and retribution for strikes against the government is uncertain and often unsuccessful. In the Portuguese colony of Macau gangland war claimed more than thirty-five lives in 1997 and 1998, including the executions of police officers. The fighting took place between rival Chinese organized crime groups over control of casino gaming rooms, loan sharking, and extortion (Lague, 1998; Time International, 1998).

During the 1920s and 1930s in the United States, the so called "gangster" era, the situation was not too dissimilar. Most law enforcement officials were untrained, unprofessional, and easily corrupted. The same was true for local government officials. Eliot Ness and the "Untouchables" were so named because they could not be corrupted, something that was unusual at that time. The situation has changed dramatically in the United States since then, corresponding with police training, education, good salaries, and a general professionalization of law enforcement. This has served to promote loyalty to the profession and reduce the extent of corruption. Instances of political corruption and the influence of organized crime in government, emerge less often, although they have not disappeared. For example, an investigation found that New York State government paid $184 million in state contracts to firms that have been linked to organized crime, and drug-related police corruption continues to be a problem (U.S. Comptroller General, 1998; Lipman, 1993).

The fall of the former Soviet Union created a number of independent republics with a tradition of a black market in which bureaucrats would demand payments for services that actually were part of their official duties. Both high- and low-level government officials were investigated for corruption during the 1990s. One Russian publication found 15,000 investigations of malfeasance by officials in only two years; one third of these involved bribery (Cilluffo and Burke, 1997:47; Kelly, 1998). Indeed, it can be said that the economic and political infiltration of organized crime in Russia is due in large part to its inability to legislate and enforce laws effectively (Tomass, 1998).

In an effort to control international crime and corruption, the FBI's international law enforcement academies in Budapest, Hungary and Bangkok, Thailand, provide technical assistance (in law enforcement methods) and role models (for professional investigators) to show how law enforcement tasks can be carried out with proficiency and cooperatively (Meddis, 1994; Cutler, 1999). Many of the new republics in Eastern Europe are experiencing significant crime problems. In Russia, for example, armed bodyguards are necessary for many business owners to protect them from kidnapping, extortion, and murder. China has uncovered a series of major corruption cases involving illicit relationships between business and government officials (Rosenthal, 2001). In nations overrun with corruption and black-market profiteering, a more professionalized law enforcement presence will help police agencies to remain diligent and dedicated to their task.

Inter- and intranational pressure can work to advance organized crime control efforts. In 1994, for example, the United States stopped sharing evidence it had on Colombian drug dealers with Colombia because it believed the prosecutor general intended a "lenient prosecution of cartel members" (De Cordoba, 1994). Colombian police responded with the arrest of two leaders of the Cali cartel, brothers Miguel and Gilberto Rodriguez in 1995. In Italy, it took the assassinations of two leading judges, Giovanni Falcone and Paolo Borsellino, to move the Italian Parliament to finally pass laws enabling police to use undercover "sting" operations and wiretaps. These investigative tools are still unavailable to investigate political offenses, and it remains to be seen how far-reaching Italy's efforts to combat organized crime will be. In Mexico the election of a new president in 2000 brought about a major anti-corruption initiative, but it is too soon to know of its impact (Associated Press, 2001).

Law Enforcement Cooperation

Lack of interagency cooperation remains a fundamental stumbling block to more effective law enforcement, although there is evidence to suggest that law enforcement agencies are cooperating more now than ever before. The Europol agency established in Western Europe (previously described) is an example of a cooperative effort, as are a growing number of cases and initiatives involving law enforcement agencies of different governments (King and Ray, 2000). For example, more than 150 gangland-style attacks in Hungary helped forge a task force investigation with the FBI into possible links to Russian organized crime (Kaplar, 2000). Operation "Green Ice" ended with 201 arrests in five countries in an international cocaine ring operating between Italy and Colombia (Meddis, 1992). Operation "Dinero," an investigation involving British, Spanish, Italian, and American law enforcement agencies, resulted in the seizure of nine tons of cocaine, $52 million in cash, and the arrest of 88 people (Abbott, 1994). An international bank fraud case in Russia was defeated with the cooperation of Russian, British, German, Israeli, and Dutch officials (Cilluffo and Burke, 1997). The United States is at a peculiar disadvantage in coordinated enforcement efforts, because it is a nation of small police departments—nearly 20,000 of them. More must be done in standardizing police training, salaries, and the establishment of lateral entry for better career mobility. Moves like these will further professionalize law enforcement and make interagency communication and cooperation more common in the United States and abroad.

Corruption among police in organized crime cases is extremely serious because it feeds public fears regarding the potential misuse of investigation and prosecution tools. Unlawful police conduct in investigations generates controversy regarding the intrusive nature of some investigative methods. These scandals also serve to mobilize public opposition against future law enforcement tools designed for the public welfare. Leaks by police or other government officials to organized crime figures also do much to harm public confidence in the effort against organized crime. In San Jose, California, a judge was convicted of leaking wiretap information to an organized crime figure, and lying about it to the FBI (USA Today, 1990). A New York City Police detective was indicted for leaking secrets to John Gotti (Raab, 1991). It was alleged that Gotti learned the addresses of jurors in his trial from the detective. In New Jersey, a police detective unmasked an ongoing undercover operation of the Lucchese crime group by tipping off one of the suspects (Levy, 1994). In a more pernicious manner, eleven inspectors in the New York City Sanitation Department were indicted for extortion. They were charged with taking payoffs for promising to overlook violations or threatening to harass shopkeepers and vendors with summonses for nonexistent infractions (Raab, 1993). Cases like these make front-page news, damage the reputation of all law enforcement, reduce public confidence in the police, and work against citizen cooperation with police in the future.

IMAGINATION IN SENTENCING

For too long, fines, probation, and incarceration were the only penalties considered in criminal cases, including those involving organized crime. More imagination in recent years has helped break this mold, and other innovations are limited only by an unwillingness to try new ideas.

The most innovative method to defeat organized crime groups in the last decade has been asset forfeiture. Incarceration is viewed by career criminals as a cost of being part of the profession of crime. Being locked up for a few years is seen as an undesirable but necessary part of the job. Extending prison sentences under the racketeering and drug laws have raised the stakes, and certainly these changes have elicited the new breed of underworld informant. Asset forfeiture makes it possible to seize the proceeds of crime, leaving the jailed offender with nothing to return to on release. Forfeitures reduce the probability that a criminal enterprise can continue operating while a leader is in jail and makes it difficult to resume that enterprise after serving the sentence. The Kenmore Hotel in New York City, for example, was the subject of a forfeiture when the government established it had become a "supermarket" for drug users and dealers (Frankel, 1994). The deterrent effect of such an action is clear given the high cost of re-establishing such a base for criminal operations.

Forfeiture of foreign assets in the United States for violation of drug laws occurred for the first time in the 1990s, demonstrating America's willingness to support enforcement efforts within other nations (USA Today, 1992). On the other hand, the "zero-tolerance" drug enforcement program of the 1980s was dropped because it produced absurd results. For example, the seizure of a marijuana cigarette on a boat was used as a rationale to seize the entire boat. This betrays common sense and provoked a public outcry against the policy. It is important that penalties remain strongly linked to common-sense notions of proportionality. Otherwise, public support in the effort against organized crime rapidly turns into opposition. The United States revised its forfeiture laws in 2000 to better protect private property rights by placing the burden of proof of wrongdoing on the government in property seizure cases where convictions have not already occurred (Civil, 2000).

Perhaps the most interesting strategy to emerge in recent years has been direct government intervention in organized crime-controlled businesses. This has occurred most prominently in the case of the Teamster's Union and the Laborers International Union of North America. In these cases, the government obtained the authority to appoint trustees to run the labor unions, investigate and remove corrupt union officers, review union finances, and supervise union elections. This authority resulted from a showing that these labor unions have been unable to operate within the bounds of the law. Criminal prosecutions against a series of Teamster presidents, including Jimmy Hoffa, resulted in the convictions of those leaders, but no change in how the union was run (Herbeck and Beebe, 1995; U.S. Comptroller General, 1986). Court-approved agreements between the government and the unions that establish trustee control is an innovative way to deal with entrenched organized crime influence in a business. Its long-term effect remains to be proven, but it shows willingness on the part of the government to recognize that prior prosecutions have not accomplished their objective and that new methods are called for (Jacobs, Friel, and Radick, 1999).

A similar effort took place in New York City where management and inspection of the Fulton Fish Market, the largest wholesale seafood distribution center in the United States, was taken over by the city government. The city hired new managers and inspectors to rid the market of the influence of organized crime. Problems at the market were serious: vendor leases that had not changed in amount for twelve years and those who failed to pay rent were not evicted. In addition, the influence of the Genovese crime group allegedly resulted in "no-show" jobs at the market and the seafood "unloaders" who indirectly controlled market operations and priorities (Raab, 1994). In still another case of this kind, ten leaders of Local 2 of the Plumbers Union in New York were barred from participating in any union business while the judge considered a prosecution motion to appoint a trustee to oversee the union (Raab, 1993a). These direct interventions in organized crime-influenced businesses are a creative way to deal with the entrenched presence of organized crime in certain settings.

LONG-TERM PREVENTION

It is important to recognize initiatives that do not involve the criminal justice system, but that also can contribute to the reduction in the incidence of organized crime over the long term. These long-term prevention efforts include preventing infiltration of legitimate business, reducing violence, increasing citizen intolerance, and understanding the ethics that underlie organized crime.

INFILTRATION OF LEGITIMATE BUSINESS

Infiltration of business is the most serious form of organized crime. It directly impacts the legitimate economy, often involving extortion and an unwilling victim. These characteristics distinguish it from the provision of illicit goods and services, which involve a consensual exchange based on supply and demand. There are two ways that organized crime infiltrates business: skims and scams. The differences between the two methods are presented in Table 1.

As Table 1 indicates, the infiltration of legitimate business generally occurs in one of two ways: (1) using a legitimate business as a "front" for

TABLE 1 TYPOLOGY OF INFILTRATION OF LEGITIMATE BUSINESS

Type of Infiltration	Nature of Activity	Harm
Scam	Using a legitimate business primarily as a "front" for illegal activity (e.g., pizza parlors to launder drug money)	• To government in tax evasion • To other businesses in non-competitive practices • Use of coercion and/or co-optation
Corruption (or "skim")	"Bleeding" a legitimate business of its profits through illegal means (e.g., no-show jobs, creative bookkeeping)	• Legitimate profits siphoned • Business can be bankrupted • Use of coercion and/or co-optation

primarily illegal activity (a scam), or (2) "Bleeding" a legitimate business of its profits through illegal means without the use of force and (hopefully) without causing it to fail (corruption or skimming). A scam often involves a quiet change in ownership or management of a business, where a large bank deposit is used to establish a credit rating. Large orders are placed, goods are received and quickly liquidated, the management disappears, and the company is forced into bankruptcy by its competitors (DeFranco, 1973).

In the Pizza Connection case, pizza parlors were used as a front for illegal activity. Morphine was smuggled from Turkey to Sicily, where it was processed into heroin. The heroin was smuggled through U.S. airports and distributed through pizza parlors in the Northeast and Midwest. Then, illegal profits in excess of $40 million were funneled back to Sicily in a money-laundering scheme that involved banks in the Bahamas, Bermuda, New York, and Switzerland (Alexander, 1988; Blumenthal, 1988). This case illustrates how linkage is established between legitimate businesses (i.e., pizza parlors and banks) and their knowing misuse to engage in illegal acts (i.e., distribute heroin and accept and transfer large sums of cash in small denominations with no questions asked).

In many cases of organized crime infiltration, however, the purpose is *not* to steal from the business until it is bankrupt. Instead, it makes more sense to misuse the business in ways that it can provide a steady source of illegal income without endangering its survival. A massive investigation of corruption and racketeering in the New York City construction industry found that control of construction unions was the "base of power and influence in the industry" by organized crime, together with direct interests in contracting and construction supply companies. This hidden interest in construction companies was accomplished by using outsiders who "front" for the company on public records for purposes of certificates of incorporation, accounting, licensing, and permits. Anthony Salerno, later convicted as "boss" of the Genovese crime family in New York City, controlled Certified, one of the two major concrete suppliers in Manhattan. Paul Castellano, boss of the Gambino crime family until his murder in 1985, controlled Scara-Mix Concrete Company, which was owned by his son (Jacobs, 1999; New York State Organized Crime Task Force, 1990).

In other cases, it was discovered that known organized crime figures were openly listed as owners, managers, or principals of construction companies. Salvatore Gravano, counselor to John Gotti in New York City, was president of JJS Construction Company. John Gotti, Jr. is President of Sampson Trucking Company, and John Gotti, convicted boss of the Gambino crime family (and for the murder of Paul Castellano) held the position of salesman for ARC Plumbing Company. Even though these individuals were sometimes found to have very little to do with the business that employed them, such an "on-the-books" profession provided a legitimate position in the community and a reportable source of income (Jacobs, 1999; New York State Organized Crime Task Force, 1990).

In Russia, there has been serious involvement of organized crime elements in bank fraud. Criminals defeated electronic protection protocols at Citibank, for example, and withdrew large sums of money from the accounts of different customers and transferred the money to the accounts of their accomplices (who had previously opened accounts in different banks around the world). To avoid detection, the money was withdrawn in other countries, including Colombia, Hong Kong, and Indonesia (Cilluffo and Burke, 1997:37).

This combination of influences that involve opportunity, corruption, and co-optation can be combined to develop a model of predictive factors for businesses at high risk of organized crime involvement. A model to illustrate these high-risk factors has been formulated and is presented in Figure 1.

Opportunity factors consist of several distinct types, as Figure 1 illustrates. These include economic conditions, government regulation, enforcement effectiveness, demand for a product or service, and new product or service opportunities that are created by social or technological changes or by the criminal group itself. The criminal environment is assessed by the extent to which individual offenders and preexisting crime groups are available to exploit these opportunities. Third, technical, language, special access, or connections (with other criminals or crime groups) skills are needed to accomplish certain types of organized crime activity. For example, narcotics importation requires a manufacturing and distribution capability. This model quantifies the relationships among opportunity, criminals, and skills to predict the risk of organized crime in

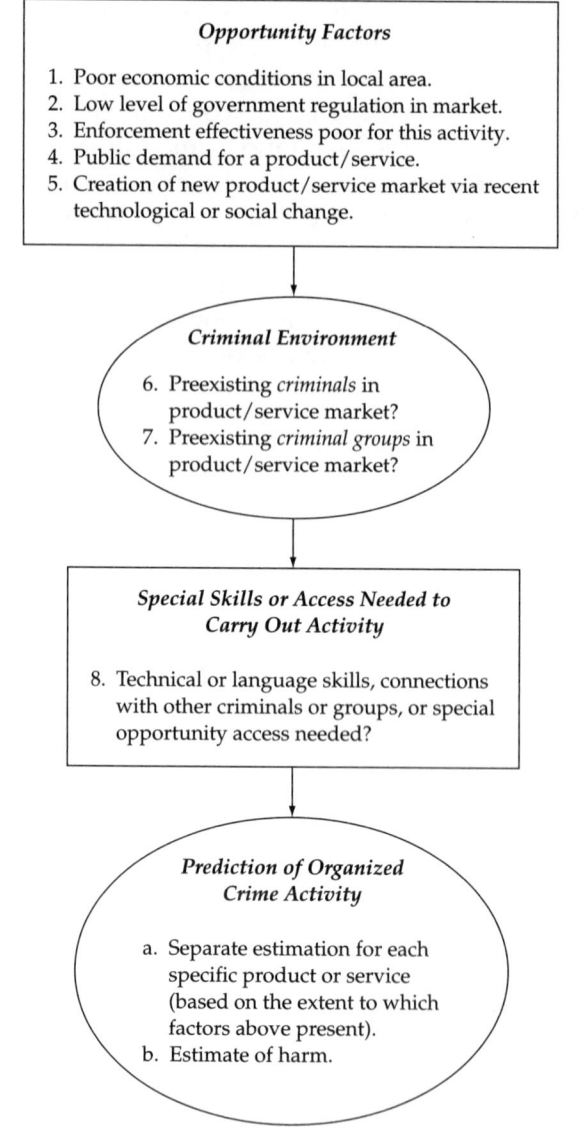

```
┌─────────────────────────────────────┐
│         Opportunity Factors         │
│                                     │
│  1. Poor economic conditions in local area.
│  2. Low level of government regulation in market.
│  3. Enforcement effectiveness poor for this activity.
│  4. Public demand for a product/service.
│  5. Creation of new product/service market via recent
│     technological or social change.
└─────────────────────────────────────┘
                    │
                    ▼
           ╭─────────────────╮
          ╱  Criminal Environment ╲
         │                          │
         │  6. Preexisting criminals in
         │     product/service market?
         │  7. Preexisting criminal groups in
         │     product/service market?
          ╲                        ╱
           ╰─────────────────╯
                    │
                    ▼
┌─────────────────────────────────────┐
│   Special Skills or Access Needed to
│        Carry Out Activity           │
│                                     │
│  8. Technical or language skills, connections
│     with other criminals or groups, or special
│     opportunity access needed?
└─────────────────────────────────────┘
                    │
                    ▼
           ╭─────────────────╮
          ╱ Prediction of Organized ╲
         │     Crime Activity         │
         │                            │
         │  a. Separate estimation for each
         │     specific product or service
         │     (based on the extent to which
         │     factors above present).
         │  b. Estimate of harm.
          ╲                          ╱
           ╰─────────────────╯
```

FIGURE 1   A MODEL TO ASSESS RISK OF ORGANIZED CRIME

various markets (Albanese, 2000). It is assumed that a separate version of this model would be needed for different types of criminal activity, because the opportunity, criminal environment, and skills required are likely different for various types of organized crime, such as narcotics distribution, human smuggling, money laundering, stolen cars, and so on.

An actual case illustrates how a model like this might be used in practice. In the New York City area it is easy for individuals in the solid waste collection industry to enter the market (little regulation). The industry is populated by numerous "small, frequently family-based, enterprises," with little difference in service among vendors (open competition in a market of nonprofessional managers). There is inelastic demand for the service (customers always available), and many firms were identified with "minimal capital and no reserve equipment" (supply for illicit patrons) (Reuter, Rubinstein, and Wynn, 1983). There is a history of organized crime involvement with the industry in the New York City area, and indictments of a number of New York City garbage haulers during the 1990s has led to larger, national haulers buying into the industry (Behar, 1996). The long-term impact on organized crime remains to be seen, but the model shows the structure of the industry and market of garbage-hauling in the New York City area place it at high risk for organized crime involvement.

Ko-lin Chin conducted a study of Chinese gangs in New York City's Chinatown. A significant focus of his study was on the extortion of Chinese-owned businesses. He found this to be a common and longstanding practice—nearly 70 percent of businesses in Chinatown had been approached by gangs for money, goods, or services (Chin, 1996:40). He found most victims were extorted three or four times per year. The businesses received a benefit from paying off gangs because this protected them from being shaken down by other individuals and gangs. Chin found that "most Chinese business owners comply with gang extortion demands because such practices are considered consistent with Chinese customs and not worth resisting. Businesspeople are generally willing to pay the gangs some money to avoid further, more significant problems" (1996:97). The gangs were exclusively Chinese (they spoke Cantonese 89% of the time), and their common heritage was central to the extortion efforts. For example, gangs often exploited the Chinese custom of "lucky money," where money is given away on holidays such as the Chinese New Year. These circumstances indicate that most of the factors in the organized crime risk model are present, suggesting a high probability of continued organized crime activity in New York City's Chinatown.

An analog to this procedure has already been attempted in case screening techniques developed for use by police. The Rochester, New York Police Department developed a system called "Early Case Closure" where information was gathered to assess the "solvability" of robberies and burglaries. By directing their resources toward crimes with the best chance of solution (and by spending less time on cases with little chance of solution), the department was able to significantly improve its clearance rates for those crimes (Bloch and Bell, 1976). A similar effort was undertaken by the Stanford Research Institute and Police Executive Research Forum, which developed a model for screening burglary cases, based on factors associated with the crime. Applying the system retrospectively, they were able to predict whether a burglary case would be solved 85 percent of the time (Greenberg, 1975). In an analogous way, law enforcement officials can reduce the amount of time spent on dead-end organized crime investigations, which invariably occur in proactive police work, with the use of a prediction model like the one proposed here. A law enforcement agency could use such a model as a screening device in its jurisdiction. Investigative resources could be focused on those markets identified as "high-risk" for infiltration, and perhaps less time would be wasted on investigations that do not lead to prosecution.

The Problem of Increasing Violence

There is debate over the long-term impact of organized crime prosecutions over the last two decades, but one outcome is certain: violence. Consider the case of the mob trials in New York. First there was the killing of Gambino boss Paul Castellano, ordered by John Gotti. Then, Bobby Boriello, John Gotti's driver was shot and killed while Gotti was in jail awaiting trial. Several killings also took place within the Columbo crime group in a struggle for power and loyalty to imprisoned boss Carmine Persico. Another struggle for power resulted in a violent death in the Lucchese group. The same occurred in the Philadelphia Cosa Nostra group. Similar violence occurs within Chinese gangs, a Harlem drug gang, and Vietnamese street gangs (Lubash, 1992; James, 1993; Raab, 1990; Hinds, 1994; Perez-Pena, 1993; Vietnamese, 1992). This is only a sampling of the organized crime-related violence that has occurred since the U.S. mob trials began in the mid 1980s.

In Russia, murders and arson against businesses whose owners refuse to pay extortion money are common. In 1996, the Russian ministry of the interior reported 580 homicides that appeared to be contract murders. Only 70 were solved. Targets of these murders included politicians, journalists, and business owners who challenged organized crime (Cilluffo and Burke, 1997:41; Arvedlund, 1997; Robinson, 2000). A similar situation exists in Colombia where organized crime violence has obstructed the ability of the judicial system to respond effectively to it (Rubio, 1998).

There is no doubt that many "turf," market, and gang leadership wars are being fought, but what will be the outcome, and why is so much violence tolerated by the public? The answers to these questions are not straightforward. One outcome of the violence has already been seen in the emergence of new organized crime groups around the world. There may also be a war for "non-leadership" of some of these crime groups. A significant error made by John Gotti is the same one made by Al Capone more than a half century ago. He enjoyed publicity. A primary reason why Al Capone was made "public enemy number one" was his high profile and the manner in which he taunted law enforcement. In a similar way, John Gotti's high profile made him a sought after prosecution target. It should be remembered that Gotti's predecessor, Paul Castellano, kept a very low profile and ran his crime group for a long time. Gotti and Capone, on the other hand, had very short tenures as organized crime leaders. They simply attracted too much attention to themselves.

This is why it is unlikely that the level of violence within organized crime groups will diminish significantly in the future. Organized crime groups are run largely by uneducated, egocentric people. Sometimes people are assaulted or killed just to "prove" that one should be feared. These feelings of superiority and hypermasculinity are outgrown by most boys in their teenage years. In the case of organized crime, it is likely that the unenlightened leadership of organized crime groups, with few exceptions, ultimately leads to their prosecution or undoing within their own criminal group. This is not a new phenomenon. A study of organized crime in the Netherlands during the seventeenth and eighteenth centuries had a similar conclusion: "The most striking characteristic of the chronology of Dutch rural organized crime is its lack of unity" (Egmond, 1993).

Despite the demise of many leaders of organized crime groups in recent years, the groups persist, not because of well-ordered structure in the organization, but because the criminal opportunities are multitudinous. If all it takes to obtain money is a bad reputation and occasional threats and violence, it is surprising there are not more people doing it. The reason for this level of violence and intimidation that is tolerated by the public is a more serious question.

CITIZEN INTOLERANCE

In Ebitsuka, Japan, citizens erected a small building across from a known Yakuza headquarters and videotaped everyone who frequented it. The citizens sent 1,500 postcards to, and filed a lawsuit against, Tetysuya Aono, a Yakuza Leader. Yakuza members fought back violently, but the town's police force of eight officers was supplemented by 300 from surrounding communities, and extensive publicity ensued. Ultimately, half the Yakuza group was arrested and Aono settled the lawsuit out of court, agreeing to abandon the building (Chua-Eoan, 1988). Why have actions like this not occurred in other nations? Is it fear, cynicism, or collusion?

Many citizens care little about organized crime "as long as they only kill each other." It is true that most criminal groups victimize their own members and neighborhoods, but occasionally this violence spills over into the community at large. The reckless "drive-by shootings" of drug gangs in recent years are the best example of this, and it is probably the one occurrence that helped mobilize public intolerance for drug trafficking more than any other single factor.

How is it possible to mobilize public opinion more effectively against organized crime, when most people are willing to buy "hot" property, gamble illegally, or engage in other illegal vices? Citizens' crime commissions provide a forum for public education and objective investigation of organized crime. Unfortunately, the abolition of the Pennsylvania Crime Commission in 1994, when it criticized the state attorney general, is not a hopeful sign of political will to support public opinion. Investigative grand juries have the authority to issue public reports on organized crime and corruption in their jurisdiction. Unfortunately, this powerful investigative authority rarely has been invoked. As a result, an important mechanism to educate the public and to mobilize public opinion in a community has been ignored. It is easy to forget that the effort against organized crime is made only in part by the prosecution of criminals. Without vocal public support, it is a lonely, and often futile, task.

> It is the dream of the visionary that some day an aroused public opinion will eliminate organized crime. The vision is Utopian. Organized crime will never be eliminated but it may be minimized and controlled whenever public sentiment is sufficiently aroused and stays aroused and wisely directed. To be directed properly there must be fact-finding and research. This is something the average citizen declines to support because it is neither spectacular nor interesting. Merely stirring public opinion to white heat because of some existing abuse or disorder is not sufficient. To be successful there must be devised a comprehensive plan which will provide the public with information concerning the efficiency and integrity of its law enforcing agencies in connection with the activities of criminals, (Chamberlin, 1932).

This statement by the director of the Chicago Crime Commission in 1932 still holds true today. Greater attention to fact-finding in a way that actively involves the citizens of the community is a way to develop strong public support for organized crime control initiatives.

THE ETHICS OF ORGANIZED CRIME

Ethics and morality lie at the root of all discussions of crime and justice, although they are rarely mentioned explicitly. Fundamentally, crime is a moral failure in decision-making. Numerous biographies of organized crime figures portray that it is not the likelihood of apprehension and punishment that keeps people from breaking the law. In fact, most career criminals understand the low odds of apprehension for most crimes and they act accordingly. An analysis of the memoirs of thirteen different American Mafia members found that the demise of the code of silence and the new era of informants is a "result of the erosion of traditional Mafia values" due to a new, younger generation of organized crime figures (Firestone, 1997).

Too often, organized crime groups merely play on our weaknesses—our weaknesses for gambling, drugs, prostitution, or our failure to stand up to extortion threats. Imagine a society where everyone refused to be victimized by drug traffickers or extortion threats. To whom would the organized crime groups turn? Our failure to stand up and be heard as a collective community is a victory for organized crime interests. As long as the public is divided, fearful, cynical, or unethical, there is no reason to expect organized crime to diminish. In one of the Gotti trials, for example, a juror was charged with soliciting a bribe from Gotti's friends to help bring an acquittal! The FBI arrested federal and state employees from Motor Vehicles Departments for selling fraudulent driver's licenses, social security cards, "green" cards, and passports (Gotti, 1992; The New York Times, 1993). Such crimes that also involve an abuse of one's citizenship are at least as shocking as many of the activities of organized crime groups.

Ethics are developed from an early age. It is hoped that ethics will become part of the educational process so that the accumulation of facts ceases to be equated with knowing what to do with them. Learning to live within the law because law violation fails to bring pleasure is the essence of ethical behavior. Apprehension and punishment are important social reinforcements to morality. But the law requires the minimum acceptable behavior, not the optimum level. During a drug raid in New York, some residents who were not targets of the raid, threw automatic weapons out the windows when the police pulled up (USA Today, 1989). A better quality of life will be achieved when fewer people are living so close to the line that separates the good from the bad.

REFERENCES

Abbott, Charles. 1994. "Two Year Probe Links Mafia, Colombian Drug Cartel," *The Buffalo News*, 20 December, p. 1.

Albanese, Jay S. 1995. "Where Organized and White Collar Crime Meet: Predicting the Infiltration of Legitimate Business." In *Contemporary Issues in Organized Crime*. J. Albanese, (ed.), Monsey, NY: Willow Tree Press. 35–60.

Albanese, Jay S. 1996. *Organized Crime in America*. 3d ed. Cincinnati: Anderson Publishing.

Albanese, Jay S. 2000. "The Causes of Organized Crime: Do Criminals Organize Around Opportunities for Crime or Do Criminal Opportunities Create New Offenders?" *J Contemporary Criminal Justice* 16: 409–423, November.

Alexander, Shana. 1988. *The Pizza Connection: Lawyers, Money, Drugs, Mafia*. New York: Weidenfeld and Nicolson.

Arvedlund, Erin. 1997. "Murder in Moscow," *Fortune*, 3 March, p. 128.

Associated Press. 2001. "Mexico Rids Corruption with Firings," the *New York Times*, 1 February, p. 1.

Bailey, John J. and Roy Godson, eds. 2001. *Organized Crime and Democratic Governability: Mexico and the U.S.* Pittsburgh: University of Pittsburgh Press.

Beers, Rand. 2000. "Statement before the Senate Caucus on International Narcotics Control." 25 July. http://www.state.gov/www/policy_remarks/2000/000725_beers_mdma.html.

Behar, Richard. 1996. "Carting Away New York City's Garbage Cartel," *Fortune*, 27 May, p. 28.

Bloch, Peter B., and James Bell. 1976. *Managing Investigations: The Rochester System*. Washington, DC: The Police Foundation.

Blumenthal, Ralph. 1988. *Last Days of the Sicilians: The FBI Assault on the Pizza Connection*. New York: Times Books.

Bosarge, Betty B. 1993. "International Organized Crime Poses New Threat to U.S. That Can't Be Met by Law Enforcement Alone." *Organized Crime Digest*, 14: 1, 25 August.

Bremner, Brian and Emily Thornton. 1997. "Blackmail!" *Business Week*, 21 July, p. 42.

Builta, Jeff. 1994. "Current Middle East Narcotics Activity," *Criminal Organizations* 9: 7–8, Summer.

Chamberlin, Henry Barrett. 1932. "Some Observations Concerning Organized Crime." *J Criminal Law and Criminology* 22 (5): 654.

Chin, Ko-lin. 1996. *Chinatown Gangs: Enterprise, Ethnicity, Extortion*. New York: Oxford University Press.

Chua-Eoan, Howard G. 1988. "Thugs Beware: Citizens Rout the Yakuza," the *New York Times*, 14 March, p. 42.

Cilluffo, Frank J. and Gerard P. Burke (eds.). 1997. *Russian Organized Crime*. Washington, DC: Center for Strategic and International Studies.

"Civil Asset Forfeiture is Law." 2000. *J Property Management* 65: 12, July.

Cutler, Stephen P. 1999. "Building International Cases," *The FBI Law Enforcement Bulletin*, vol. 68, December, p. 1.

De Cordoba, Jose. 1994. "Washington, Irked by Colombian Official, Ends Evidence Sharing on Drug Cartels," *Wall Street Journal*, 8 March, p. 10.

De Franco, Edward J. 1973. *Anatomy of a Scam: A Case Study of a Planned Bankruptcy by Organized Crime*. Washington, DC: U.S. Government Printing Office.

Egmond, Florike. 1993. *Underworlds: Organized Crime in the Netherlands, 1650–1800*, 179. Cambridge, MA: Polity Press.

Finckenauer, James O., and Elin J. Waring. 1998. *Russian Mafia in America: Immigration, Culture, and Crime*. Boston, MA: Northeastern University Press.

Firestone, Thomas A. 1997. "Mafia Memoirs: What They Tell Us about Organized Crime," in *Understanding Organized Crime in Global Perspective*, Patrick J. Ryan and George E. Rush, eds., 71–86. Thousand Oaks, CA: Sage Publications.

Frankel, Bruce. 1994. "Checkout Time for NYC Drug Dealers," *USA Today*, 10 June, p. 2.

Robinson, Jeffrey. 2000. *The Merger: The Conglomeration of International Organized Crime*. New York: Viking.

"Gotti Juror Charged with Soliciting Bribe," 1992. *USA Today*, 25 February, p. 3.

Green, Sherry. 1993. *Preventing Illegal Diversion of Chemicals: A Model Statute*, 1, Washington, DC: National Institute of Justice.

Greenberg, David. 1975. *Felony Investigation Decision Model: An Analysis of Investigative Elements of Information Menlo Park*, CA: Stanford Research Institute.

Herbeck, Dan and Michael Beebe. 1995. "Local 210 Told to Purge Mob Ties," *The Buffalo News*, 16 February, p. 1.

Hinds, Michael deCourcy. 1994. "FBI Arrests Reputed Leader of Philadelphia Mob and 20 Others," *The New York Times*, 18 March, p. 16.

Hirsh, Michael and Hideo Takayama. 1997. "Big Bang or Bust: Mobsters Slow Tokyo's Plan to Join World Markets," *Newsweek*, 1 September, p. 44.

Hughes, Donna M. 2000. "The "Natasha" Trade: The Transnational Shadow Market of Trafficking in Women," *J International Affairs*, Spring.

Hughes, Donna M. 2000a. "The Internet and Sex Industries: Partners in Global Sexual Exploitation," *Technology and Society Magazine*, Spring.

Ianni, Francis A.J. 1998. "New Mafia: Black, Hispanic and Italian Styles," *Society* 35: 115, January–February.

Jacobs, James B. with Colleen Friel and Robert Radick. 1999. *Gotham Unbound: How New York City was Liberated from the Grip of organized Crime*. New York: New York University Press.

James, George. 1993. "Man Tied to Crime Family is Shot to death in Queens," the *New York Times*, 22 October, p. B6.

Jamieson, Alison. 1998. "Antimafia Efforts in Italy, 1992–1997," *Studies in Conflict and Terrorism* 21: 233, July–September.

Kalfrin, Valerie. 1999. "Feds Top Prosecution: Immigration," http://www.APBnews.com, July 26.

Kaplar, Zsofia. 2000. "Crime Busters: With the Arrival of a New Task Force in Hungary, the FBI Steps Up Its Fight against Organized Crime," *Time International*, 8 May, p. 33.

Kelly, Jennifer A. 1998. "The Mafia Threat to Freedom in Russia," *J Social, Political and Economic Studies* 23: 121, Summer.

King, Leslie E., and Judson M. Ray 2000. "Developing Transnational Law Enforcement Cooperation: The FBI Training Initiatives," *J Contemporary Criminal Justice* 16: 386–408, November.

Kleinknecht, William. 1996. *The New Ethnic Mobs: The Changing Face of Organized Crime in America.* New York: Simon & Schuster.

Lague, David. 1998. "Murders in Macau," *World Press Review*, p. 46, August.

Levy, Clifford J. 1994. "Drive on Mob Sabotaged in New Jersey," the *New York Times*, 12 August, p. 8.

Lipman, Harvey. 1993. "State Contracts Linked to Mob," *The Buffalo News*, 11 November, p. 17.

Lubasch, Arnold H. 1985. "Mafia Member Testifies on Siciliy 'Commission'," the *New York Times*, 1 November, p. B3.

Lubasch, Arnold H. 1992. "Shot by Shot, An Ex-Aide to Gotti Describes the Killing of Castellano," the *New York Times*, 4 March, p. 1.

Marshall, Donnie R. 1999. "DEA Congressional Testimony," U.S. Senate Judiciary Committee, July 28. http://www.usdoj.gov/dea/pubs/cngrtest/ct072899.htm.

McIntosh, Mary. 1975. *The Organization of Crime* 29, London: Macmillan.

Meddis, Sam Vincent. 1992. "Cocaine Bust Links Mafia, Cali Cartel," *USA Today*, 29 September, p. 1.

Meddis, Sam Vincent. 1994. "Legendary FBI Director Sets up Shop in Moscow," *USA Today*, 5 July, p. 5.

New York State Organized Crime Task Force. 1990. *Corruption and Racketeering in the New York City Construction Industry.* New York: New York University Press.

Penhaul, Karl. 2001. "Colombia's Drug War," *U.S. News & World Report*, 12 February, p. 35.

Perez-Pena, Richard. 1993. "The Killings of Witnesses Cause Alarm," the *New York Times*, 22 November, p. B1.

Pope, Victoria. 1997. "Trafficking in Women," *U.S. News & World Report*, 7 April, p. 38.

Raab, Selwyn. 1990. "Ex-Unionist Shot to Death in 'Mob Hit'," the *New York Times*, 18 May, p. B1.

Raab, Selwyn. 1991. "Jury Indicts a Detective in Gotti Leaks," the *New York Times*, 12 December, p. B1.

Raab, Selwyn. 1993. "Inspectors are Accused of Extortion," the *New York Times*, 14 October, p. B1.

Raab, Selwyn. 1993a. "Judge Bars 10 from Plumbers Union Activity," the *New York Times*, 27 October, p. B4.

Raab, Selwyn. 1994. "Fish Market's Problems Revert to New York City," the *New York Times*, 27 March, p. 1.

Reuter, Peter, Jonathan Rubinstein, and Simon Wynn. 1983. *Racketeering in Legitimate Industries: Two Case Studies.* Washington, DC: National Institute of Justice.

Reuters. 20001. "U.S., Canada, Jamaica, Bahamas Smash Drug Ring," February 2. http://www.wjin.net/html/news/7197.htm

Robinson, Jeffrey. 2000. The Merger: *The Conglomeration of International Organized Crime.* Woodstock, New York: Overlook Press.

Rosenthal, Elisabeth. 2001. "Details of Corruption Emerge in China," the *New York Times*, 28 January, p. 1.

Rubio, Mauricio. 1998. "Violence, Organized Crime, and the Criminal Justice System in Colombia," *J Economic Issues* 32: 605, June.

Schrieberg, David. 1996. "Sins of the Fathers: The Children of the Cali Cartel Godfathers Can't Shake the Family's Past," *Newsweek*, 12 August, p. 50.

Sevick, James R. 1993. *Precursor and Essential Chemicals in Illicit Drug Production: Approaches to Enforcement*. Washington, DC: National Institute of Justice.

Simons, Marlies. 1994. "New European Police to Fight Regional Crime," the *New York Times*, 17 February.

The New York Times. 1993. "37 Arrested in the Selling of Documents," 4 November, p. B15.

The New York Times. 1993. "Colombia Offers Carrot to Cartel," 3 November, p. 9.

Time International. 1998. "Tales from the Dragonhead," 20 April, p. 22.

Tomass, Mark. 1998. "Mafianomics: How Did Mob Entrepreneurs Infiltrate and Dominate the Russian Economy?" *J Economic Issues* 32: 565, June.

United Nations. 2000. United Nations Convention Against transnational organized Crime http://www.undcp.org/palermo/convmain.html.

U.S. Comptroller General. 1986. *Labor Law: Criminal Investigations of Mr. Jackie Presser and Other Teamsters Officials*. Washington, DC: U.S. General Accounting Office.

U.S. Comptroller General. 1993. *Illicit Narcotics: Recent Efforts to Control Chemical Diversion and Money Laundering*. Washington, DC: U.S. General Accounting Office.

U.S. Comptroller General. 1993a. *Immigration Enforcement: Problems in Controlling the Flow of Illegal Aliens*. Washington, DC: U.S. General Accounting Office.

U.S. Comptroller General. 1994. *Drug Control: Interdiction Efforts in Central America Have Had Little Impact on the Flow of Drugs*. Washington, DC: U.S. General Accounting Office.

U.S. Comptroller General. 1998. *Law Enforcement: Information on Drug-Related Police Corruption*. Washington, D.C.: U.S. General Accounting Office.

USA Today. 1989. "Record Drug Seizure," 22 February, p. 3.

USA Today. 1990. "Judge Sentenced," 2 November, p. 3.

USA Today. 1991. "Police Wiretaps," 23 October, p. 3.

USA Today. 1992. "Property Seized," 7 October, p. 3.

Vatikiotis, Michael, Sachiko Sakamaki, and Gary Silverman. 1995. "On the Margin: Organized Crime Profits from the Flesh Trade," *Far Eastern Economic Review*, 14 December, p. 26.

"Vietnamese Street Gangs Make Mark Nationwide." 1992. *Organized Crime Digest* 13: 1, 23 December.

ADDITIONAL READINGS

AFRICA

African Events. 1993. *Zimbabwe: Land Justice* 9 (6):15.

Alao, Abiodun. 1996. "A Comparative Evaluation of Armed Struggle in Namibia, S. Africa and Zimbabwe." *Terrorism and political violence* 8 (4):58–77.

Ankomah, Baffom. 1991. Ivory poaching down after CITES ban. *New African*, July, p. 21.

Arthur, John A. 1997. Influences of Social and Economic Conditions on Crime in East Africa. *International Journal of Comparative and Applied Criminal Justice* 21 (1–2):51.

Ayittey, G.B.N. 1992. *Africa Betrayed*. New York: St. Martin's Press.

Bank, Leslie J. 1990. "The Making of the Qwaqwa 'Mafia': Patronage and Protection in the Migrant Taxi Business." *African Studies* 49 (1):71.

Cant, Charles Stewart. 1981. *Crime and deviance in heterogeneous societies: The impact of the imposition of Western norms on the aboriginal peoples of Canada and Zimbabwe*. Ottawa: National Library of Canada.

Cilliers, Jackie. 1996. The Evolving Security Architecture in Southern Africa. *Terrorism and political violence* 8 (4):124–155.

Cutshall, Charles R. 1982. Culprits, Culpability, and Crime: Stock theft and other cattle maneuvers among the Ila of Zambia. *African Studies Review* 25 (1):1–26.

Gastrow, Peter. 2000. "Organized Crime and the State's Response in South Africa." *Transnational Organized Crime*, 4.

Gottschalk, Jack A., and Brian P. Flanagan. 2000. *Jolly Roger with an Uzi: The Rise and Threat of Modern Piracy*. Naval Institute Press.

Hills, Alice 1996. "Towards A Critique of Policing and Development in Africa." *J Modern African Studies* 34 (2):271–291.

Ihonvbere, Julius Omozuanvbo. 1996. *Economic Crisis, Civil Society and Democratization: The Case of Zambia*. Trenton, NJ: Africa World Press.

Joubert, Pearlie. 1992. The Commuter. *New African*, February, p. 10.

Lan, David. 1985. *Guns and Rain: Guerrillas and Spirit Mediums in Zimbabwe*. London: James Curry.

Mbao, Melvin. 1992. "The Criminal Justice System on Trial in Zambia." *J African Law* 36 (2):175.

Mwalimu, Charles. 1991. Police, State Security Forces and Constitutionalism of Human Rights in Zambia. *The Georgia Journal of International and Comparative Law* 21 (2):217.

Nevin, Tom. 2000. "Has Africa Become the World's Washroom for Dirty Money?" *African Business*. March, p. 20.

New African. 1991. "Why Zimbabwe is against Ivory Trade Ban." August, p. 19.

New African. 1991. "Zambia Bank Comes under Attack." February, p. 28.

New African. 1991. "Zimbabwe: Ivory Ban Increases Poaching." June 01. N 285. p. 22.

New African. 1993. "Crime Wave Rocks Zambia." 01 July, N 310, p. 29.

Nkala, Collet. 1991. "Zimbabwe Bus Kidnapped in South Africa." *New African.* April, p. 28.

Nkala, Collet. 1992. "Ivory Trade Still flourishes." *New African.* March, p. 17.

Nkala, Collet. 1992. "Smuggling Revives Southern Economies." *New African.* March, p. 25.

Opolot, James S.E. 1995. *The Crime Problem in Africa: A Wake Up Call of the 1960s–1990s.* Houston: Univers de Press.

Ranger, Terence. 1992. "War, violence and healing in Zimbabwe." *Southern African Studies* 18 (3):698–707.

Sayila, Alfred. 1991. "Happy Days ahead for Zambia's Wildlife." *New African.* January, p. 39.

United Nations. Congress on Crime Prevention and the Treatment of Offenders. 1970. *A Review of Crime in Zambia over a six-year period (1964–1969): Its prevention and control; Social Defense in terms of National Development.* Kyoto.

Wildlife Trade Provides New Haven for Organized Crime. 1994. *The Animal Welfare Institute Quarterly* 43 (4):6.

ASIA

Basler, Barbara. 1988. "Hong Kong Gang Wields Vast Power," the *New York Times.* 12 December 12, p. 4.

Bolz, Jennifer. 1995. "Chinese Organized Crime and Illegal Alien Trafficking: Humans as a Commodity." *Asian Affairs: An American Review* 22 (3):147.

Booth, Martin. 1990. *The Triads: The Growing Threat from The Chinese Criminal Societies.* New York: St. Martin's Press.

Centre for Criminology. 1999. *Organized Crime and the 21st Century.* The University of Hong Kong. http://www.hku.hk/crime/organizecrime.htm

Chernychova, V. 1998. *Organized Crime in the Maritime Province and the Far East.* http://www.american.edu/transcrime/centers/vladivostok/vlad1198.htm

Che, Wai-Kin. 1990. "Mafia on Hong Kong—The Triad Society." *Police Studies* 13 (4):151.

Finckenauer, James O. 2000. *Chinese Transnational Organized Crime: The Fuk Ching.* Washington, DC: National Institute of Justice. http://www.ojp.usdoj.gov/nij/international/ctoc.html

Friman, H. Richard. 1994. "International Pressure and Domestic Bargains: Regulating Money Laundering in Japan." *Crime, Law and Social Change* 21 (3):253.

Galeotti, Mark. 2000. "Turkish Organized Crime: Where State, Crime and Rebellion Conspire," *Transnational Organized Crime*, 4.

India Today. 1992. "Domain of the Dons." 16 January 17 (2), p. 37.

Hamilton, V. Lee and Joseph, Sanders. 1996. "Corporate Crime through Citizens' Eyes: Stratification and Responsibility in the United States, Russia, and Japan." *Law & Society Review* 30 (3):513.

Hazarika, Sanjoy. 1993. "Indian Heroin Smugglers Turn to New Cargo," the *New York Times.* 21 February, 8.

Huang, Frank F.Y., and Michael S. Vaughan. 1992. "A Descriptive Analysis of Japanese Organized Crime: The Boryokudan from 1945 to 1988." *International Criminal Justice Review* 2:19.

Kakimi, Takashi. 1988. "Organized Crime in Japan: The Boryokudan Groups." *The Police Chief* 55 (10):161.

Kaplan, David E, and Alec. Dubro. 1986. *Yakuza: The Explosive Account of Japan's Criminal Underworld.* Reading, MA: Addison-Wesley.

Laufer, William S., and Alison J. Cohen. 1992. "Corporate Crime and Corporate Sanctions in Japan." *Business & The Contemporary World* 4 (3):106.

McKenna, James. 1996. "Organized Crime in Hong Kong." *J Contemporary Criminal Justice* 12 (4):316.

Overholt, Alison. 1995. "Vanishing Borders: The Expansion of Asian Organized Crime." *Harvard International Review* 17 (2):42.

Phongpaichit, Pasuk. 1999. "Trafficking in People in Thailand." *Transnational Organized Crime*, 3.

Rhodes, William, Mary Layne, and Patrick Johnston, 1999. *Estimating Heroin Availability.* Cambridge, MA: Abt Associates. http://www.abtassociates.com/reports/criminal-justice/5351.pdf

Richard, Amy O'Neill. 2000. *International Trafficking in Women to the United States: A Contemporary Manifestation of Slavery and Organized Crime.* Center for the Study of Intelligence. http://www.cia.gov/csi/monograph/women/trafficking.pdf

Rothacher, Albrecht. 1993. "Yakuza: The Socioeconomic Roles of Organized Crime in Japan." *Internationales Asian Forum: International Quarterly* 24 (1–2):111.

Sheu, Cheuen-Jim. 1991. "Nonsyndicated Organized Crime in Metropolitan Taipei, Taiwan." *Police Studies* 13 (4):145.

Song, John Huey-Long and John Dombrink. 1994. "Asian Emerging Crime Groups: Examining the Definition of Organized Crime." *Criminal Justice Review* 19 (2):228.

Takashahi, Sadahiko and Carl B. Becker. 1985. *Organized Crime in Japan.* Osaka, Japan: Kinki University.

Tsushima, Masahiro. 1996. "Economic Structure And Crime: The Case of Japan." *J of Socio-Economics* 25 (4):497.

Tokyo Business Today. 1994. "Yakuza Storming the Corporate Ship," V 62 (4), p. 46.

EUROPE

Albini, Joseph L., R. E. Rogers, and Julie Anderson. 1995. "Russian Organized Crime: Its History, Structure and Function." *J Contemporary Criminal Justice* 11 (4):213.

Arlacchi, Pino. 1993. *Men of Dishonor: Inside the Sicilian Mafia.* New York: William Morrow.

Boylan, Scott P. 1996. "Organized Crime and Corruption in Russia: Implications for U.S. and International Law." *Fordham International Law Journal* 19 (5):1999.

Carter, David L. 1992. "A Forecast of Growth in Organized Crime in Europe: New Challenges for Law Enforcement." *Police Studies* 15 (2):62.

Carter, David L. 1994. International Organized Crime: Emerging Trends in Entrepreneurial Crime." *J Contemporary Criminal Justice* 10 (4):239.

Catanzaro, Raimondo. 1994. "Violent Social Regulation: Organized Crime in the Italian South." *Social & Legal Studies* 3 (2):267.

ADDITIONAL READINGS

Chalidze, Vallery. 1977. *Criminal Russia: Crime in the Soviet Union.* New York: Random House.

Curzi, Candida. 1996. "Blood and Fear in Italy." *Media Studies Journal* 10 (4):121.

Fijnaut, Cyrelle and James Jacobs. (ed.). 1991. *Organized Crime and its Containment: A Transatlantic Initiative.* Deventer, Netherlands: Kluwer.

Fijnaut, Cyrille. 1990. "Organized Crime: A Comparison between the United States of America and Western Europe." *Brit J Criminology* 30 (3):321.

Half, Cameron. 1997. "The Russian Mafia: The Challenge of Reform." *Harvard International Review* 19 (3):52.

Handelman, Stephen. 1995. *Comrade Criminal: Russia's New Mafiya.* New Haven, CT: Yale University Press.

Hatton, Cindy. 1996. "The Organized Crime: Threat in Post-Cold War Europe." *Monterey Review* 16:44.

Holmes, Stephen 1997. "What Russia teaches us now: How weak states threaten freedom." *The American Prospect* 33:30.

Hughes, Donna M. 2000. "The 'Natasha' Trade: The Transnational Shadow Market of Trafficking in Women," *J International Affairs*, Spring.

Jankiewicz, Sara. 1995. "Glasnost and the Growth of Global Organized Crime." *Houston Journal of International Law* 18 (1):215.

Joutsen, M. 1996. "Recent Trends in Crime in Western Europe." Paper presented at V. European Colloquium on Criminology, Bled, Slovenia, September, pp. 25–28.

Kinzer, Stephen 1996b. "In Germany, Vietnamese Terrorize Vietnamese." The *New York Times*. 23 May, p. 4.

Modona, Guido Neppi. 1994. "Italian Criminal Justice against Political Corruption and the Mafia: The New Model for Relations between Judicial and Political Power." *Osgoode Hall Law Journal* 32 (2):393.

Moser, Michele. 1995. "Switzerland's New Exceptions to Bank Secrecy Laws Aimed at Money Laundering and Organized Crime." *Case Western Reserve Journal of International Law* 27 (2–3):321.

Nikiforov, Alexander S. 1993. "Organized Crime in the West and in the Former USSR: An Attempted Comparison." *Internat J Offender Therapy Comparative Criminol* 37 (1):5.

Oakley, Robin. 2001. "EU Acts on Illegal Immigrants," 8 February. http://www.CNN.com.

Executive Intelligence Review. 1993. "Organized Crime Makes Power Bid in Ukraine" 20 (20):32.

Paoli, L. 1994. "An Underestimated Criminal Phenomenon: The Calabrian Ndrangheta." *European Journal of Crime, Criminal Law and Criminal Justice* 2 (3):212–238.

Radio Free Europe. 2000. "Ukrainian Prosecutors Probe $4.6 Million Bribe Case," 7 November. http://www.wjin.net/html/news/6580.htm

Radio Free Europe. 2000a. "Russian Prosecutor Begins New Assault on Oligarchs," 2 November. http://www.wjin.net/html/news/6528.htm

Ruggiero, Vincenzo. 1993. "Organized Crime in Italy: Testing Alternative Definitions." *Social & Legal Studies* 2 (2):131.

Schmid, Ulrich. 1993. "Russia and the Plague of Organized Crime. *Swiss Review Of World Affairs* (9):6.

Serio, Joseph. 1992. "Organized Crime in the Soviet Union and Beyond." *Low Intensity Conflict and Law Enforcement* 1:127–151.

Shelley, Louise I. 1994. "Mafia and the Italian State: The Historical Roots of the Current Crisis." *Sociological Forum* 9 (4):661.

Shelley, Louise. 1995. "Post-Soviet Organized Crime and the Rule of Law." *The John Marshall Law Review* 28 (4):827.

Solomon, Joel S. 1995. "Forming a More Secure Union: Organized Crime in Europe as a Challenge to National Sovereignty." *Dickinson Journal of International Law* 13 (3):623.

Stille, Alexander. 1995. "Excellent Cadavers: The Mafia and the Death of the First Italian Republic." *Italian Journal* 9 (2):60.

Turbiville, Graham H. Jr. 1995. "Organized Crime and the Russian Armed Forces." *Transnational Organized Crime* 1:57–104.

Ueda, K. 1992. "Organized Crime in the Soviet Union" (in Japanese). *Gakujutsu Geppo. Japanese Scientific Monthly* 45 (8):17.

Van Duyne, and C. Petrus. 1993. "Organized Crime and Business Crime-Enterprises in The Netherlands." *Crime, Law and Social Change* 19 (2):103.

———. 1996. "Organized Crime, Corruption and Power." *Crime, Law and Social Change* 26 (3):201.

Van Duyne, C. Petrus, and A. Alan. 1994. "Organized Cross-Atlantic Crime." *Crime, Law and Social Change* 22 (2):127.

Vassalo, Peter J. 1996. "The New Ivan the Terrible: Problems in International Criminal Enforcement and the Specter of the Russian Mafia." *Case Western Reserve Journal of International Law* 28 (1):173.

Webster, William H., and Frank J. Cilluffo. 1998. *Russian Organized Crime.* Center for Strategic and International Studies Global Organized Crime Project. http://www.csis.org/goc/taskruss.html

Yugoslavian-Albanian Organized Crime. 1992. *Law And Order* 40 (7):93.

Zucchelli, Franco. 1994. "The Mafia and the Lega Nord in Italian Politics." *Mediterranean Quarterly: A Journal of Global Issues* 5 (2):84.

NORTH AMERICA

Abramovsky, Abraham. 1996. "Partners against Crime: Joint Prosecutions of Israeli Organized Crime Figures by U.S. and Israeli Authorities." *Fordham International Law Journal* 19 (5):1903.

Albanese, Jay S. 1996. *Organized Crime in America.* 3rd ed. Cincinnati, OH: Anderson.

Albanese, Jay, ed. 1995. *Contemporary Issues in Organized Crime.* Monsey, NY: Willow Tree Press.

Bailey, John J., and Roy, Godson, eds. 2001. *Organized Crime and Democratic Governability: Mexico and the U.S.* Pittsburgh: University of Pittsburgh Press.

Beaty, Jonathan and Sam Gwynne. 1993. *The Outlaw Bank: A Wild Ride into the Heart of BCCI.* New York: Random House.

Calavita, Kitty and Pontell, Henry N. 1993. "Savings and Loan Fraud as Organized Crime: Toward a Conceptual Typology of Corporate Illegality." *Criminol.* 31 (4):519.

Chambliss, William J. 1989. "State-Organized Crime." *Criminol.* 27 (2):183.

de Gennaro, G. 1995. "The Influence of Mafia Type Organizations on Government, Business and Industry." *Trends in Organized Crime* 1:36–42.

Dick, Andrew R. 1995. "When Does Organized Crime Pay? A Transaction Analysis." *International Review of Law and Economics* 15 (1):25.

Edelhertz, Herbert, ed. 1987. *Major Issues in Organized Crime Control.* Washington, DC: U.S. Government Printing Press.

Finckenauer, James O. and Elin Waring. 1998. *Russian Mafia in America.* Boston: Northeastern University Press.

Fiorentine, Gianluca and Sam Peltzman, eds. 1995. *The Economics of Organized Crime.* Cambridge: Cambridge University Press.

Firestone, Thomas A. 1993. "Mafia Memoirs What They Tell Us about Organized Crime." *J Contemporary Criminal Justice* 9 (3):197.

Godson, Roy and William J. Olson. 1995. "International Organized Crime." *Society* January–February, pp. 18–29.

Godson, Roy. 1994. "The Crisis of Governance: Devising Strategy to Counter International Organized Crime." *Terrorism and Political Violence* 6 (2):163.

Haller, Mark H. 1992. "Bureaucracy and the Mafia: An Alternative View." *J Contemporary Criminal Justice* 8 (1):1.

Ireland, Patricia. 1995. "The Rescue Racket: Organized Crime and Mob Violence against Women and Doctors." *Ohio Northern University Law Review* 21 (3):845.

Jones, Mark. 1993. Nigerian Crime Networks in the United States. *Internat J Offender Therapy and Comparative Criminol.* 37 (1):59–73.

Kelly, Robert J., ed. 1986. *Organized Crime: A Global Perspective.* Totowa, NJ: Rowman and Littlefield.

Kinzer, Stephen 1996a. "Biker's Wars in the Land of Vikings." The *New York Times.* 6 May, 5.

Klienknecht, William. 1996. *The New Ethnic Mobs: The Changing Face of Organized Crime in America.* New York: Free Press.

Lavigne, Yves. 1987. *Hells Angels: Taking Care of Business.* Toronto, Canada: Deneua and Wayne.

Martens, Frederick T. 1990. "African-American Organized Crime: An Ignored Phenomenon." *Federal Probation* 54 (4):43.

McCoy, Alfred W. 1991. *The Politics of Heroin: CIA Complicity in the Global Drug Trade.* Brooklyn, NY: Lawrence Hill Books.

Mieczkowski, Tom. 1990. "Drugs, Crime, and the Failure of American Organized Crime Models." *Internat J Comparative Applied Criminal Justice* 14 (1–2):97.

Mirsky, Wendy L. 1995. "The Link between Organized Crime and Nuclear-Weapons Proliferation: Fighting Crime and Ensuring International Security." *University of Pennsylvania Journal of International Business Law* 16 (4):749.

Moore, Richter H. 1995. "Twenty-First-Century Law to Meet the Challenge of Twenty-First-Century Organized Crime." *Futures Research Quarterly* 11 (1):23.

Myers, Willard H. III. 1995. "The Emerging Threat of Transnational Organized Crime from the East." *Crime, Law and Social Change* 24 (3):181.

Pearce, Frank and Michael Woodiwiss, eds. 1993. *Global Crime Connections: Dynamics and Control.* Toronto, Canada: University of Toronto Press.

Posner, Gerald L. 1988. *Warlords of Crime: Chinese Secret Societies-The New Mafia.* New York: McGraw Hill.

Punch, Maurice. 1993. "Bandit Banks Financial Services and Organized Crime." *J Contemporary Criminal Justice* 9 (3):175.

Reuters. 2001. "U.S., Canada, Jamaica, Bahamas Smash Drug Ring," 2 February. http://www.wjin.net/html/news/7197.htm

Shelley, Louise I. 1995. "Transnational Organized Crime an Imminent Threat to the Nation-State?" *J Internat Affairs* 48 (2):463.

Smith Jr., D.C. 1991. "Wickersham to Sutherland to Katzenbach: Evolving an 'Official' Definition for Organized Crime." *Crime, Law and Social Change* 16 (2):135.

Smith, John. 1990. "Organized Crime." *The Police Journal* 63 (4):306.

Southerland, Mittie D. 1993. "Applying Organization Theory to Organized Crime." *J Contemporary Criminal Justice* 9 (3):251.

Sterling, Claire. 1995. "Thieves' World: The Threat of the New Global Network of the growing problem of Organized Crime." Reviewed by Mariso L. Evriviades. *Mediterranean Quarterly: A Journal of Global Issues* 6 (2):163.

Tillman, Robert and Henry Pontell. 1995. "Organizations and Frauds in the Savings and Loan Industry." *Social Forces* 73:1439–1463.

Turbiville Jr., and H. Graham. 1996. "Weapons Proliferation and Organized Crime." *Airpower Journal* 10 (suppl.):17.

Walter, Ingo. 1990. *Secret Money: The World of International Financial Secrecy*. New York: Harper Business.

Williams, Phil. 1995. "The New Threat: Transnational Criminal Organizations and International Security." *Criminal Organizations* 9 (3):3–19.

AUSTRALASIA

Bersten, Michael. 1990. "Defining Organized Crime in Australia and the USA." *The Australian and New Zealand J Criminol* 23 (1):39.

Bowles, Allen. 1992. "Corporate Crime Group." *Criminol Australia* 3 (3):16.

Christian, Bryan Paul. 1999. "Visa Policy, Inspection, and Exit Controls: Transatlantic Perspectives on Migration Management." *Georgetown Immigration Law Journal* 14:215, Fall.

Doyle, Bernard John. 1988. "International Policing: Organized Crime in Australia." *The Police Chief* 55 (12):12.

Marks. 1990. "A Freer Market for Heroin in Australia: Alternatives to Subsidizing Organized Crime." *J Drug Issues* 20 (1):131.

"Police Crack Global Child Porn Ring." 2001. *CNN.com*, 10 January.

SOUTH AMERICA

Ambos, Kai. 1996. "Attempts at Drug Control in Colombia, Peru and Bolivia." *Crime, Law and Social Change* 26 (2):25.

Associated Press. 2000. "Brazilian Committee Accuses More than 800 with Involvement in Organized Crime. *CNN.com*, 5 December. http://www.cnn.com/2000/WORLD/americas/12/05/brazil.organizedcrime.ap/

United Nations. 1999. Statements Delivered during the General Debate in Plenary of General Assembly, New York. http://www.undcp.org/newyork/debate.html

Additional Readings

Bagley, Bruce M. 1989. "Colombia and the War on Drugs." *Foreign Affairs* 67:70.

Bouley Jr., Eugene E., and Michael S. Vaughn. 1995. "Violent Crime and Modernization in Colombia." *Crime, Law and Social Change* 23 (1):17.

De Lama. 1988. "For Colombian Officials Nowhere is Safe." *Chicago Tribune*. 2 November: 1, 12.

De Lama. 1989. "Most Anti Drug Aid for Columbia Used Against Rebels." *Chicago Tribune*. 31 October, p. 1, 8.

Dettmer, Jamie. 1997. "FARC's Formula for Chaos." *Insight on the News* 13 (43):42

Dietz, Mary Lorenz. 1993. "Master Of Paradise: Organized Crime and the Internal Revenue Service in the Bahamas." *Michigan J Internat Law* 14 (3):452.

Duzam, Maria Jmena. 1994. *Death Beat: A Colombian Journalist's Life Inside the Cocaine Wars*. New York: Harper-Collins.

Eddy, Paul, Hugo Sabogal, and Sara Walden. 1988. *The Cocaine Wars*. New York: Norton.

Ehrenfeld, Rachel. 1990. *Narco-Terrorism*. New York: Basic Books.

Florez, Carol P., and Bernadette Boyce. 1990. "Colombian Organized Crime." *Police Studies* 13 (2):81.

Gay, Bruce W., and James W. Marquart. 1993. "Jamaican Posses: A New Form of Organized Crime." *J Crime & Justice* 16 (2):139.

Gugliotta, Guy and Jeff Leen. 1989. *Kings of Cocaine: Inside the Medellin Cartel—An Astonishing True Story of Murder, Money and International Corruption*. New York: Simon and Schuster.

Executive Intelligence Review. 1990. "Have Bush and Colombia agreed to legalize drugs?" 17 (50):18.

Lee, Rensselaer W. III. 1992. "Colombia's Cocaine Syndicate." In *War on Drugs*. Alfred W. McCoy and Alan A. Block, eds., 93–124. Boulder: Westview.

Luft, Kerry. 1995. "Colombia's Vow: Eradicate the Drug Crop." *Chicago Tribune*. 15 January, p. 12.

Lupsha, Peter A. 1995. Transnational Narco-Corruption and Narco Investment: A Focus on Mexico. *Transnat Organized Crime* (1):41–58.

McRae, Patricia B. 1993. "The Illegal Narcotics Trade in Colombia: Power Contender to the State and National Security?" *Conflict Quarterly* 13 (2):7.

Morales, Edmundo. 1989. *Cocaine: White Gold Rush in Peru*. Tucson: University of Arizona Press.

Oppenheimer, Andres. 1996. *Bordering on Chaos: Guerrillas, Stockbrokers, Politicians, and Mexico's Road to Prosperity*. Boston: Little Brown.

Robert, Karen and Rodrigo G. Hermelo. Argentina. 1992. Where Youth Is a Crime. *Report on the Americas* 26 (3):12.

Saba, Roberto Pablo and Luigi Manzetti. 1996. "Privatization in Argentina: The Implications for Corruption." *Crime, Law and Social Change* 25 (4):353.

Shannon, Elaine. 1988. *Desperados: Latin Drug Lords, U.S. Lawmen and the War America Can't Win*. New York: Viking.

Sutlive, Vinson H., Nathan Althuser, Mario D. Zamora, and Virginia Kerns, eds. 1986. *Drugs in Latin America*. Williamsburg, VA: College of William and Mary.

Thoumi, Francisco E. 1992. "Why the Illegal Psychoactive Drugs Industry Grew in Colombia." *J Interamerican Studies and World Affairs* 34 (3):37.

Thoumi, Francisco E. 1997. "U.S., Colombia Struggle Over Drugs, Dirty Money." *Forum for Applied Research and Public Policy* 12 (1):91.

Tullis, LaMond. 1995. *Unintended Consequences: Illegal Drugs and Drug Policies in Nine Countries.* Boulder, CO: Lynne Reinner.

Turbiville Jr. and H. Graham. 1992. "Narcotrafficking: The Drug War Intensifies. Narcotics Trafficking in Central Asia: A New Colombia." *Military Review* 72 (12):54.

Uhlig, Mark A. 1990. "As Colombian Terror Grows, the Press Becomes the Prey." The *New York Times*. 22 May, pp. 1, 4.

Appendix

International Police Executive Symposium

The International Police Executive Symposium (IPES) was founded in 1994. The aims and objectives of the IPES are to bring police researchers and practitioners closer, to facilitate cross-cultural, international and interdisciplinary exchanges for the enrichment of the profession of policing, and to encourage discussions and writing on challenging topics of contemporary importance by those engaged in police practice and research.

One of the important activities of the IPES is the organization of an annual meeting under the auspices of a police or educational institution. To date, meetings have been hosted by the Canton Police of Geneva (Police Challenges and Strategies, 1994); the International Institute of the Sociology of Law in Onati, Spain (Challenges of Policing Democracies, 1995); Kanagawa University in Yokohama, Japan (Organized Crime, 1996); the Federal Police in Vienna, (International Police Cooperation, 1997); the Dutch Police and Europol in The Hague (Crime Prevention, 1998); the Andhra Pradesh Police in Hyderabad, India (Policing of Public Order, 1999); and the Center for Public Safely, Northwestern University, Evanston, Illinois, (Traffic Policing, 2000). The 2001 meeting was hosted by the Police Academy of Szcztyno, Poland, on 27–30 May 2001. (Corruption: A threat to World Order). The 2002 meeting was hosted by the Police of Turkey, 21–24 May 2002 (Police Education and Training)

The majority of those participating are directly professionally involved in police executive roles, but some of the participants are internationally well-known scholars and researchers in the field. These meetings have been fruitful as a way of disseminating information on all aspects of policing. During the four-day meeting, participants, researchers and practitioners from countries located on all continents interact in structured and informal ways. They exchange views and opinions, establish contacts and friendships, and find opportunities to engage in formal and informal dialogues on matters pertaining to policing. The executive summary of each meeting is distributed to those attending and to a wide range of interested police professionals and scholars. In addition, a book of selected papers for each meeting is published. These books are in various stages of publication preparation with Gordon and Breach Publishers and Prentice-Hall.

Closely connected with the IPES is *Police Practice and Research: An International Journal* (PPR). The journal is committed to highlighting current practices from all over the world; providing opportunities for exchanges between police practitioners and researchers; reporting the state of public safety and the resultant quality-of-life issues on global dimensions; analyzing practices that build around the world; and bridging the knowledge gap that exists regarding who the police are, what they do, and how they maintain order, administer laws, and serve their communities in different societies, including the regions beyond the frontiers of the developed nations.

The organization is directed by a board of directors representing various countries of the world (listed below). Registered Agent Douglas J. March; E-mail: mmdlaw@Macomb.com

IPES BOARD OF DIRECTORS

Dilip Das, President: E-mail: dilip.das@plattsuburgh.edu

Hofrat Maximilian Edelbacher, Vice President: E-mail: Edelmaz@magnet.at

Alexander Sam Aldrich: E-mail: aaldrich72@aol.com

H.J. Dora, DGP: E-mail: polchiefap@hotmail.com

Horace Judson: E-mail: Horace.judson@plattsburgh.edu

George Henry Millard: E-mail: cmtg@polmil.sp.gov.br

Snezana Mijovic-Das: E-mail: dilipkd@aol.com

Tonita Murray: E-mail: toni.murray@cpc.gc.ca

S.M. Ngangula: Fax: 260-125-3543.

Rick Sarre: E-mail: Rick.sarre@unisa.edu.au

Laurent Walpen: Fax: 41-22-301-3491

Dr. Jan Wiarda: Fax: 31-70-310-2009

Alexander Weiss: E-mail: alweiss@kellogg.northwestern.edu

INDEX

A

Aboriginal criminal enterprises in Canada, 54–55
Ackoff, Russel L., 314
Activities of organized crime. *See also specific activities,* such as Drug trafficking
   Africa, 395–396
   Argentina, 319, 320
   Australia, 332
   Austria, 195–199
   Baltic States, 135–137
   Canada, 50–52
   China, 281–282, 284
   Czech Republic, 134
   Europe, 217
   India, 243, 251
   international, 24
   Japan, 270
   New Zealand, 364, 365–366
   overview of, 7–8, 395
   Poland, 132–133
   Russia, 131, 154, 155–157
   Slovak Republic, 134–135
   Slovenia, 172–173
   South Africa, 381–382
   Triad societies, 287
   United States, 23–25
   Zambia, 407
Activity perspective of organized crime, 5
Adjacent country examination, 3
Africa. *See also* South Africa; Tunisia; Zambia; Zimbabwe
   activities of organized crime, 242, 395–396
   Algeria, 403
   Angola, 412

   Egypt, 403
   Morocco, 107–108, 403
   Namibia, 8, 11, 388
   Nigeria, 25, 110, 242, 305
   overview of, 377–378
Ah Kong (group), 365
Algeria, 403
Alien smuggling. *See* human smuggling
Andreotti, Giulio, 88, 97
Andropov, Yuri, 159
Angola, 412
Aono, Tetsuya, 453–454
Argentina
   acceptance of drugs, 313
   anti-crime methods comparison, 322–328
   "Illicit Association" doctrine, 318, 319, 327–328
   methods to combat crime, 320–322
   nature and extent of crime, 319–320
   overview of, 317–319, 329
   sanctions for drug use, 312
Art theft, 196–197
Asia, 237–239. *See also* China; India; Japan
Asian criminal enterprises. *See also* Chinese Triads
   Boryokudan, 270–277, 365
   in Canada, 52–53
   in New Zealand, 362–366, 369, 372–374
   in United States, 30–32
   Vietnamese, 31, 52–53, 365
   Yakuza, 28, 453–454
Asset forfeiture. *See also* Proceeds of Crime legislation
   Canada, 68–69
   Council of Europe, 219
   United States, 446

Index

Assistance to United States Law Enforcement Agencies statute, 40–41
Aungier, Gerald, 248
Australasia, 331–332. *See also* Australia; New Zealand
Australia
    anti-crime methods comparison, 204–209, 345–347
    criminality and ethnicity in, 337
    methods to combat crime, 339–345
    money laundering in, 8, 339, 345–347
    National Crime Authority, 11, 339–344, 345–347, 349–350, 351
    nature and extent of crime, 337–339
    Operation Flash, 349–350
    overview of, 333–337
    proposed methods, 348–350
Austria
    activities of organized crime, 195–199
    crime statistics, 193–196
    criminal groups in, 193, 195–196
    definitions of organized crime, 190–191
    long-term anti-crime strategies, 206
    medium-term anti-crime strategies, 207–208
    methods to combat crime, 200–203
    nature and extent of crime, 189–199
    overview of, 188–189, 209–210
    short-term anti-crime strategies, 208–209

B

Baltic States, 135–137
Bank fraud
    Russia, 449
    Zambia, 414, 420–421
Bank of Commerce and Credit International (BCCI), 74–75, 94
Basel Statement of Principles, 138–139, 202–203
Becker, G., 152
Biscuitwala, JMP, 253
Bolivia, 304, 305, 312
Bombay, India, 251–254
Bonanno, Joe, 439
Boriello, Bobby, 452
Borsellino, Paolo, 88, 91, 444
Boryokudan
    Japan, 270–277
    New Zealand, 365
Boutros-Ghali, Boutros, 142, 205
Brazil, 300, 312
Brodeur, Jean-Paul, 47, 48–49
Buscetta, Tommaso, 439
Business, prevention of infiltration of legitimate, 447–452
Business enterprise of criminal organizations, 152–153

C

Camorra, 89, 109, 193
Canada
    activities of organized crime, 50–52
    anti-crime methods comparison, 69–74
    civil forfeiture in, 68–69
    Controlled Drugs and Substances Act, 65
    Criminal Code, 61–65, 66–67
    Criminal Law Improvement Act, 65–66
    definition of organized crime, 48–49
    Forum on Organized Crime, 67–68
    integrated crime fighting units, 70–71
    nature and extent of crime, 19, 20, 48–55
    overview of, 46–47
    Proceeds of Crime legislation, 56–62, 70
    public involvement, 71–72
    recent developments in, 72–74
    task forces in, 10–11
Cannabis, 431. *See also* marijuana
Capone, Al, 453
Caribbean Financial Action Task Force, 139–140
Castellano, Paul, 449, 452, 453
Causes of organized crime
    China, 296–297
    Europe, 204–205
    Italy, 83–84
    overview of, 6–7, 98–99, 429
    Russia, 149–151, 162–163
    South Africa, 382–383
CDPC (European Committee of Crime Problems), 212–213, 215
CELAD (European Committee on the Fight Against Drug Abuse), 94, 140
Center for Strategic and International Studies, 38
Central European Police Academy (Austria), 200–201
Chechnya, 150
Chiesa, Dalla, 90, 92, 96
China. *See also* Chinese Triads; Hong Kong; Macau; Taiwan
    anti-crime methods comparison, 294–295
    anti-drug struggle in, 288
    corruption in, 444
    definition of organized crime, 6
    groups active in, 282–283
    increase of crime, 296–297
    methods to combat crime, 288–294
    nature and extent of crime, 281–287
    overview of, 279–281
    underground groups in, 284–285, 290
Chinese Triads
    Hong Kong, 286–287
    Netherlands, 109
    New Zealand, 363, 364
    United States, 26, 30–32
Chipko movement (India), 260, 263
Cigarette smuggling in Canada, 49–50, 52–53, 73, 74
Citizen intolerance, 453–455
Civil forfeiture in Canada, 68–69
Clark, Terry, 355–356, 373
Clifford, Clark, 75
Cocaine, 305
Colombia. *See also* Colombian criminal enterprises
    anti-crime methods comparison, 312–315
    cartels, 8, 26–27, 305
    corruption in, 444
    direct vs. indirect confrontation, 313
    interactive plan, 314–315
    methods to combat crime, 307–311, 442
    national plan of, 309–311, 315

Colombia, *(continued)*
  nature and extent of crime, 302–306
  overview of, 300, 301–302, 315–316
  violence in, 452
Colombian criminal enterprises
  Canada, 55
  Netherlands, 109
  United States, 29
Combating crime, comparison of methods for. *See also* combating crime, methods for
  Argentina, 322–328
  Australia, 345–347
  Austria, 204–209
  Canada, 69–74
  China, 294–295
  Colombia, 312–315
  Eastern Europe, 140–143
  India, 261–264
  Italy, 92–98
  Japan, 275–277
  Netherlands, 113–119
  New Zealand, 369–372
  overview, 13–14
  Russia, 160–161
  Slovenia, 179–185
  South Africa, 388–390
  Tunisia, 402–404
  United States, 40–42
  Zambia, 421–425
  Zimbabwe, 435–437
Combating crime, methods for. *See also* combating crime, comparison of methods for
  Argentina, 320–322
  Australia, 339–345
  Austria, 200–203
  China, 288–294
  Colombia, 307–311
  Council of Europe, 218–225, 233–234
  Eastern Europe, 137–140
  Italy, 90–92
  Japan, 273–275, 277–278
  Netherlands, 111–113
  New Zealand, 367–369
  overview of, 10–13, 99–100
  Russia, 157–159
  Slovenia, 174–179
  South Africa, 383–388
  Tunisia, 398–402
  United States, 32–35
  Zambia, 416–421
  Zimbabwe, 433–435
Commercial Crime Bureau, 39
Composition of organized crime groups
  Canada, 52–55
  United States, 28–32
Construction company corruption, 448–449
Contrada, Bruno, 97
Controlled Drugs and Substances Act (Canada), 65
Convention on Laundering, Search, Seizure, and Confiscation of the Proceeds of Crime (Council of Europe), 139, 215, 221–222, 228. *See also* Strasbourg Convention
Cooperation between criminal groups in South Africa, 383
Cooperative approach. *See* international approach to organized crime
Coordination of anti-crime measures. *See* international approach to organized crime
Corruption. *See also* government corruption
  Africa, 377–378
  Argentina, 320
  business, 447–452
  methods to deal with, 224–225, 232–233
  New Zealand, 354, 373–374
  overview of, 443–444
  police, 9, 445
  Russia, 163
  Slovenia, 174
  waste processing industry, 124–125, 450–451
  Zimbabwe, 432
Council of Europe
  anti-crime methods comparison, 225–233
  cooperation issues, 213–215
  on corruption, 224–225, 232–233
  criminal justice system, methods to improve, 226–227
  European Committee of Crime Problems (CDPC), 212–213, 215
  legislative initiatives, 227
  methods to combat crime, 218–225, 233–234
  on misuse of technology, 222–223, 226, 228–229
  on money laundering, 219–222, 225, 227–228
  Multidisciplinary Group on Corruption (GMC), 224–225
  nature and extent of crime, 215–217
  OCTOPUS, 180–181, 183
  research on organized crime, 218–219, 227–228
  role and principles of, 212
  search and surveillance issues, 223, 228–230
  Strasbourg Convention, 139, 203, 221
  treaties, 215
  witness intimidation and protection issues, 223–224, 225–226, 230–232
Counterfeiting in Canada, 51–52, 52, 65
Crime analysis, 118–119
Criminal Code (Canada), 66–67
Criminal Intelligence Service Canada (CISC), 47, 48, 52, 69
Criminal intelligence units (CIUs) in Netherlands, 102–103, 111, 117, 120
Criminal justice system
  methods to improve, 226–227
  response of, 439–447
Criminal Law Improvement Act (Canada), 65–66
Czech Republic, 134

D

Dacoity (India), 243–244, 245, 248–249
Dagga (Zimbabwe), 431
Data collection
  comparability and reliability of, 215–216
  India, 244
  Netherlands, 102–103, 111, 117

INDEX

Definitions of organized crime
  Argentina, 318
  Australia, 336–337
  Austria, 190–191
  Canada, 48–49
  conflicts between, 242
  European Union, 393–394
  FBI, 4, 190–191
  Hong Kong, 291
  India, 243
  Interpol, 4–5, 128, 190
  Netherlands, 103–104
  New Zealand, 354–355
  overview of, 4–6, 428–429
  Select Expert Working Group, 393
  Slovenia, 168–169
  United Nations, 128–129
Dick, Josef, 197, 198
Dismantling groups of offenders, 123
Drug trafficking
  Argentina, 318–319
  Austria, 198–199
  Baltic States, 135–136
  Canada, 20, 50, 52, 54, 55, 72
  Canadian legislative response to, 56–62, 65
  Colombia, 301, 302–306, 315–316
  Czech Republic, 134
  Europe, 216
  European Economic Community (EEC), 92–93
  India, 244, 246, 256–257
  internalization of organized crime and, 439–441
  Italy, 89, 90
  Netherlands, 107, 108, 109, 110–111
  New Zealand, 355–358, 359–360, 364, 367–368, 369–371
  overview of, 7–8
  Poland, 132
  prohibition and, 98
  Russia, 155–157
  Slovenia, 172
  South Africa, 386
  South America, 312
  Tunisia, 401
  United Nations Convention Against Traffic in Narcotic Drugs and Psychotropic Agents, 55–56, 137–138, 202
  United States, 20, 26–27, 28–32, 36–38, 75
  Zambia, 409–411, 417–418
  Zimbabwe, 430–431
Dubai, 253, 254
Dutt, Sanjay, 254, 261

E

Eastern Europe
  anti-crime methods comparison, 140–143
  Baltic States, 135–137
  criminal enterprises in Canada from, 53
  criminal enterprises in U.S. from, 35–36
  Czech Republic, 134
  expansion of crime, 216–217
  methods to combat crime, 137–140
  Poland, 8, 127–128, 130–137
  Slovak Republic, 134–135
  unemployment in, 188–189
Economic circumstances, 2
Economic crime. *See* financial crime; money laundering
Economic Espionage Act (1996), 42
EEC. *See* European Economic Community (EEC)
Egypt, 403
EMCDDA (European Monitoring Center for Drugs and Drug Addiction), 94
Estonia, 136
Ethics of organized crime, 455–456
Ethnicity trap, 7
Eurasian criminal enterprises, 30. *See also* Asian criminal enterprises
Europe. *See also* Council of Europe; Eastern Europe; *specific countries*
  criminal groups in, 93
  expansion of crime, 216
  long-term anti-crime strategies, 206
  medium-term anti-crime strategies, 207–208
  methods to combat crime, 92–98
  migration to, 188–189, 190
  organized crime in, 242
  overview of, 79–81, 209–210
  recognizing and addressing organized crime, 165–167
  short-term anti-crime strategies, 208–209
  sovereignty issues, 204, 214
European Committee of Crime Problems (CDPC), 212–213, 215
European Committee on the Fight Against Drug Abuse (CELAD), 94, 140
European Economic Community (EEC), 92–95, 204
European Union
  Austria and, 189
  Council of Europe and, 213–214
  Group on Drug and Organized Crime, 393–394
  PHARE program, 180
Europol, 24, 94, 140, 200, 440
Executive measures in India, 258–259, 262
Extortion
  Austria, 195
  Japan, 270
  New York City's Chinatown, 451
  Russia, 154

F

Falcone, Giovanni, 88, 91, 444
FATF. *See* Financial Action Task Force (FATF)
Federal Bureau of Investigation (FBI)
  definition of organized crime by, 4, 190–191
  international law enforcement academies, 444
  OC/DE National Strategy, 34
  Organized Crime and Racketeering (OCR) Section, 39–40
Fijnaut, Cyrille, 105, 167
Financial Action Task Force (FATF), 139, 203, 220, 339, 345
Financial crime. *See also* money laundering
  Austria, 197
  bank fraud, 414, 420–421, 449

Financial crime, *(continued)*
    definition of, 217
    electronic commerce and, 350
    Hawala transactions, 254–255
    Netherlands, 111–116
    overview of, 25, 98–99
    prevention of, 349
    share market, 255–256
    Slovenia, 174
    technology and, 383
    Zimbabwe, 432–433
Financial Crimes Enforcement Network (FinCEN), 37
Firearms in Zambia, 412–413, 424–425
Fiso, Api, 362, 363
Florida Department of Law Enforcement, 37
Forfeiture of assets. *See also* Proceeds of Crime legislation
    Canada, 68–69
    Council of Europe, 219
    United States, 446
14k (group), 287, 362, 364
Fulton Fish Market, 447

G

Gambling
    Austria, 199
    Canada, 50
Geographic location, 2
Germany
    criminal enterprises in Austria from, 195
    criminal groups in, 24
    definition of organized crime, 5
Ghosh, Runu, 260
Globalization, 429. *See also* transnational crime
Goel, Dinesh, 255
Gorbachev, Mikhail, 150, 159
Gotti, John, 445, 449, 452, 453, 455
Gotti, John, Jr., 449
Government corruption
    China, 281–282
    Colombia, 304, 311
    India, 246–247, 255, 257–258, 260–261, 264–265
    Italy, 86, 87
    overview of, 9
    Russia, 131
    Taiwan, 286
    as threat to United States, 27–28
    Zambia, 408–409, 425
Government intervention in crime-controlled business, 446–447
Gravano, Salvatore, 449
Gray, Herb, 67
Group migration studies, 4
Group perspective of organized crime, 5
Groups. *See also* Chinese Triads; Hell's Angels; Mafia; Russian criminal enterprises
    Ah Kong, 365
    analysis of, 118
    Asian, 30–32, 52–53, 362–366, 369, 372–374
    Boryokudan, 270–277, 365
    Camorra, 89
    in Canada, 52–55
    in China, 282–283, 284–285, 290
    in Colombia, 301, 306
    Colombian, 29, 55, 109
    cooperation between in South Africa, 383
    dismantling of, 123
    in Europe, 93
    14k, 287, 362, 364
    in Germany, 24
    Italian, 29, 53–54, 109, 193, 195
    Korean, 30–31
    La Cosa Nostra, 26, 28–29, 84–85
    Mongrel Mob, 359, 362
    Moroccan, 107–108
    Mr. Asia gang, 355–357, 369
    'Ndrangheta, 88–89
    in Netherlands, 103–111
    New Independent States, 35–36
    outlaw gangs, 52, 54, 357–362, 368–369, 371–373
    PKK, 195
    Road Knights, 361–362
    in Russia, 149, 152–155, 157
    San-Yee-On, 287, 364
    Sha-Lian gang, 286
    in Slovenia, 171–172
    sophistication of, 5
    transnational crime, 396
    in Tunisia, Islamic fundamentalist, 392, 396, 397–398, 399, 403
    Turkey, 107–108
    in United States, 28–32
    Vietnamese, 31, 52–53, 365
    Wo, 364
    Yakuza, 28, 453–454
    Yugoslav, 109, 195–196
Guerrilla groups in Colombia, 301, 306
Gun Control Law (China), 293

H

Hawala transactions (India), 254–255
Hell's Angels
    Canada, 52, 53, 54
    New Zealand, 357–358, 360, 361
Heroin, 305–306
History of nation, 2
Hoffa, Jimmy, 446
Hong Kong
    legislative initiatives in, 290–291
    organized crime in, 238, 284, 285, 286–287
Hoover, J. Edgar, 166
Human smuggling
    Austria, 199
    Europe, 80
    North America, 20
    overview of, 441–442
    Tunisia, 404
    United States, 25–26
Hungary, 219–220

INDEX

I

Ibrahim, Dawood, 252–254, 255, 261
Illicit liquor in India, 250–251
Immigration
    Austria, 188–189, 190, 206
    New Zealand, 363
    organized crime and, 441–442
    Tunisia, 402
India
    activities of organized crime, 243, 251
    anti-crime methods comparison, 261–264
    Bombay, 251–254
    dacoity, 243–244, 245, 248–249
    data collection, 244
    definition of organized crime, 243
    drug trafficking, 256–257
    executive measures, 258–259, 262
    government corruption, 246–247, 255, 257–258, 260–261, 264–265
    Hawala transactions, 254–255
    illicit liquor, 250–251
    kidnapping and abduction, 249–250
    legislative measures, 261, 262
    methods to combat crime, 258–261
    nature and extent of crime, 241–248
    non-executive measures, 259–261, 262–263
    overview of, 240–241
    political crime, 257–258
    real estate crime, 251–253
    share market crime, 255–256
    smuggling and terrorism, 253–254
Indian hemp, 431
Individual country trend analysis, 3
Infiltration of legitimate business, prevention of, 447–452
Information, sharing of
    Austria, 200–201
    importance of, 1–2
    Slovenia, 185
    United States, 39
Integral approach. *See* international approach to organized crime
Intercepted communications in Canada, 62, 63
Internalization of organized crime, 214, 439–441. *See also* transnational crime
International approach to organized crime. *See also* Europol; International Criminal Police Organization (Interpol)
    Australia, 335, 344–345, 346–347, 348–349, 350–351
    Austria, 202–203
    China, 293–294
    Colombia, 308–309, 311
    Council of Europe, 213–215
    India, 264
    international agreements, 440–441
    Lusaka Agreement on Cooperative Enforcement Operations Directed at Illegal Trade in Wild Fauna and Flora, 418–419
    money laundering, 228
    need for, 142–143, 185, 205–206, 207, 390

    Netherlands, 125–126
    New Zealand, 367–368
    overview of, 444–445
    South Africa, 387–388
    Tunisia, 398–400
    United States, 43–44
    Zambia, 416–417, 422
    Zimbabwe, 436–437
International Asian Organized Crime Conference, 39
International crime. *See* transnational crime
International Criminal Investigative Training Assistance Program, 43
International Criminal Police Organization (Interpol)
    definition of organized crime by, 4–5, 128, 190
    money laundering and, 140
    New Zealand and, 367
    objective of, 399–400
    South Africa and, 387–388
    Southern African Regional Police Chiefs Cooperation Organization and, 417
    Tunisia and, 399
International Police Executive Symposium, 469–471
Interpol. *See* International Criminal Police Organization (Interpol)
Islamic fundamentalist groups in Tunisia, 392, 396, 397–398, 399, 403
Italian criminal enterprises
    Austria, 193, 195
    Canada, 53–54
    Netherlands, 109
    United States, 29
Italy. *See also* Italian criminal enterprises
    anti-crime methods comparison, 92–98
    Camorra, 89
    corruption in, 444
    definition of Mafia-type associations, 84–85
    linkage between organized crime in U.S. and organized crime in, 439–440
    Mafia in, 8–9, 82–83, 85–88
    Mafia-type groups in, 89–90, 223–224
    measures to combat crime, 90–92
    movement against Mafia, 95–98
    'Ndrangheta, 88–89
    overview of, 82–84
    witness protection program in, 230–231

J

Jain, Mukesh, 250
Japan
    anti-crime methods comparison, 275–277
    Boryokudan, 270–277
    citizen involvement in, 453–454
    methods to combat crime, 273–275, 277–278
    nature and extent of crime, 270–271
    organized crime in, 242, 442
    overview of, 267–269
Johnstone, Marty, 356

K

Kasoka, Yedo, 408
Kefauver committee, 39
Kerry, John, 75
Khaitan, Sunit, 253
Kidnapping and abduction in India, 249–250
Koban system (Japan), 269
Korea, criminal enterprises in U.S. from, 30–31

L

La Cosa Nostra (LCN), 26, 28–29, 84–85
Lagana, Joseph, 69–70
La Torre, Pio, 90
Latvia, 136
Legislative initiatives. *See also* Racketeer Influenced and Corrupt Organizations Statute (RICO)
    Argentina, 318–319, 325–328
    Canada, 48, 54, 55–69
    China, 289–290, 293
    Colombia, 307–309, 442
    Council of Europe, 227
    harmonization of, 183–184
    Hong Kong, 290–291
    India, 261, 262
    Italy, 90–92
    Japan, 273–275
    Macau, 291–292
    need for, 208
    New Zealand, 367–369, 372
    overview of, 11
    Russia, 157–159, 161
    Slovenia, 174–178, 181–182
    South Africa, 389
    Tunisia, 400–401
    United States, 32, 41–42
    Zambia, 416, 417, 418, 423–426
    Zimbabwe, 434–435
LESAOC (Law Enforcement Systems Attack on Organized Crime), 34
Lima, Salvo, 88
Lithuania, 136
Logistics modeling, 125
Lusaka Agreement on Cooperative Enforcement Operations Directed at Illegal Trade in Wild Fauna and Flora, 418–419

M

Macau
    activities of organized crime, 238, 285
    corruption in, 443
    legislative initiatives, 291–292
    underground groups in, 284, 287
Mafia
    as enterprise, 85
    La Cosa Nostra, 26, 28–29, 84–85
    movement against in Italy, 95–98
    as political subject, 87
    Russian, 149, 153–155, 157
    Sicilian, 82–83, 86–87, 95–96, 305
    system aspects, 85–87
    use of term, 82
Man-Chuen, Ma, 364
Mannino, Calogero, 97
Marijuana
    Colombia, 305
    New Zealand, 370–371
    Zambia, 409
    Zimbabwe, 430
Mastan, Haji, 253, 261
Medellin cartel, 26–27
Meese, Edwin, 75
Mehta, Harshad, 255–256
Memon, Yakub, 254
Mexico
    anti-corruption initiative, 444
    drug trafficking enterprises in U.S., 29–30
    organized crime in, 19–20
Migration. *See* immigration
Misprision of felony, 69
Money laundering
    Africa, 378
    Australia, 8, 339, 345–347
    Austria, 197–198
    Bank of Commerce and Credit International and, 74–75
    Canada, 56–57, 60, 67–68
    Colombia, 310–311
    definition of, 222
    Eastern Europe, 137–140
    Europe, 94
    Italy, 91
    methods to combat, 201–203, 219–222, 225, 227–228
    Netherlands, 104–105, 107, 111–112
    overview of, 7, 8
    Poland, 133
    recognition of problem of, 350
    Slovenia, 173–174, 175–176
    Tunisia, 401
    United States, 25, 36–37
    Zambia, 415–416, 421, 422–425
Morocco, 107–108, 403
Morvillo, Francesca, 88
Motor vehicle theft. *See* vehicle theft
Mr. Asia gang (New Zealand), 355–357, 369
MST (non-injectable morphine), 370
Mutual Legal Assistance in Criminal Matters Act (Canada), 56

N

Namibia, 8, 11, 388
National Crime Prevention Strategy (South Africa), 383–387
National Crime Records Bureau (NCRB), 244–246
National Fraud Information Center (NFIC), 38–39
Naylor, R. T., 76
'Ndrangheta, 88–89
Ness, Eliot, 443
Netherlands
    anti-crime methods comparison, 113–119
    Coordinating Policy Council (CBO), 121

INDEX   479

core teams, 113, 120, 121
crime analysis, 118–119
criminal groups in, 103–111
criminal intelligence units (CIUs) in, 102–103, 111, 117, 120
domestic groups in, 106–107
foreign groups in, 108–111
methods to combat crime, 111–113
money laundering in, 8
naturalized groups in, 107–108
nature and extent of crime, 103–111
Office for the Disclosure of Unusual Transactions (ODUT), 111, 112, 113–114
overview of, 101–103
parliamentary inquiry in, 122–123
penal approach in, 119–122
prevention measures, 123–125
proceeds-based approach in, 115
Reporting Questionable Transactions (RQT) legislation, 111–112, 113, 115–116
waste processing industry, 124–125
New Independent States (NIS), criminal enterprises in U.S. from, 35–36
New York State Organized Crime Task Force, 142–143
New Zealand
  anti-crime methods comparison, 369–372
  criminal enterprises in, 362–366, 372–374
  definition of organized crime, 6, 354–355
  drug trafficking, 355–358, 359–360, 364, 367–368, 369–371
  Hell's Angels, 357–358, 360, 361
  methods to combat crime, 367–369
  Mongrel Mob, 359, 362
  Mr. Asia gang, 355–357, 369
  outlaw gangs, 357–362, 368–369, 371–373
  overview of, 352–354
Nigeria
  Colombian cartels and, 305
  criminal enterprises in Netherlands from, 110
  financial crime in, 25
  organized crime in, 242
"Nomenclatural" privatization, 151
Nongovernmental prevention initiatives
  Europe, 97
  India, 259–261, 262–263
  overview of, 12–13

O

OC/DE (Organized Crime/Drug Enterprise) National Strategy, 34
OCN (Organized Crime Narcotics) Trafficking Enforcement Program, 36
OCTOPUS (Council of Europe), 180–181, 183
Offender group analysis, 118
O'Loughlin, John, 27
Operational crime analysis, 118
Organizational approach in Slovenia, 178–179, 184
Organization for Economic Cooperation and Development, 224
Organized crime
  concept of, 4–6

control and prevention challenges, 438–439
criminal justice response to, 439–447
development of, 428
ethics of, 455–456
factors in, 191–193, 242, 394–395, 428–429
markets for, 14–15, 383
methods to combat, 10–13, 182–185
models of, 152
nature and extent of, 6–9
overview of, 380
recognizing and addressing problem of, 165–167, 186–187
tenacity of, 438
threat of, 1, 380–381, 428
Organized Crime/Drug Enterprise (OC/DE) National Strategy, 34
Organized Crime Narcotics (OCN) Trafficking Enforcement Program, 36
Outlaw gangs
  Canada, 52, 54
  New Zealand, 357–362, 368–369, 371–373

P

Paraguay, 312
Pawar, Sharad, 253
Pedagogical uses for text, 3–4
Penal approach
  Netherlands, 119–122
  Slovenia, 174–176
Perception of organized crime, 207
Perito, Robert, 25–26
Persico, Carmine, 452
Peru, 300, 304, 305, 312
PHARE program (European Union), 180
Phenomenon research, 124–125
Pizza Connection case, 439–440, 448
PKK (group), 195
Plumbers Union, 447
Poaching
  Zambia, 414–415, 418–419
  Zimbabwe, 433
Poland
  activities of organized crime, 8, 132–133
  nature and extent of crime, 130–137
  overview of, 127–128
  Russian criminal organizations in, 130–132
Police initiatives. *See also* Southern African Regional Police Chiefs Cooperation Organization (SARPCCO)
  Canada, 69, 70, 71
  China, 289
  overview of, 11–12
  screening techniques, 451–452
  South Africa, 384, 387
  technical equipment and, 184–185
Police Practice and Research: An International Journal, 470
Police system. *See also* police initiatives; Royal Canadian Mounted Police (RCMP)
  Argentina, 317–318, 320–321, 322–325, 326
  Australia, 334–335, 336, 339–344
  Canada, 47
  China, 281

Police system, *(continued)*
 corruption in, 9, 445
 India, 241
 Italy, 82
 Japan, 268–269
 Netherlands, 101
 New Zealand, 353–354, 369, 371
 Russia, 148
 South Africa, 379–380, 383, 384–385, 387–389, 390
 technical equipment for law enforcement, 184–185, 200, 269
 Tunisia, 393, 403
 United States, 23
 Zambia, 406–407, 416–417
 Zimbabwe, 433–434
Political and governmental situation. *See also* government corruption
 "cohabitation" with organized crime, 8–9, 84
 as factor in prevention efforts, 2, 182
Political corruption. *See* corruption; government corruption
Polygraph testing in Slovenia, 177–178
Pompidou Group, 93
Poppy cultivation, 305–306
Precious stones in Zambia, 413–414, 419–420
President's Commissions (U.S.), 40, 41, 43
Prevention strategies
 Austria, 207
 challenges of, 438–439
 China, 296
 financial crime, 349
 long-term, 447–456
 Netherlands, 123–125
 nongovernmental, 12–13, 97, 259–261, 262–263
 political and governmental situation and, 2, 182
 Slovenia, 182–183
 South Africa, 383–387
Private sector or nonprofit organizations in United States, 38
Procedural approach
 Europe, 201
 Slovenia, 176–178
Proceeds of Crime legislation
 Canada, 56–62, 70
 New Zealand, 368
Product-flow analysis, 3–4
Prostitution
 Austria, 199
 India, 250
 Netherlands, 102
 Slovenia, 173
 smuggling of women for, 26, 422
Public Interest Litigation (India), 260
Public involvement
 Canada, 71–72
 overview of, 453–455

R

Racketeer Influenced and Corrupt Organizations Statute (RICO)
 alien smuggling and, 42
 as model, 179
 prosecution under, 12, 13, 75–76, 233–234
 provisions of, 33–34
Ram, Sukh, 260
Ramakrishnan, T. K., 251
Real estate crime in India, 251–253
Repressive strategies, 182–183
RICO. *See* Racketeer Influenced and Corrupt Organizations Statute (RICO)
Risk modeling, 124–125
Risk of organized crime in business, 449–450
Rizzuto, Vito, 69
Road Knights, 361–362
Rock, Allan, 67
Rognoni, Virginio, 90
Rognoni-La Torre law (Italy), 90–91
Royal Canadian Mounted Police (RCMP), 47, 69, 70, 71
Russia
 activities of organized crime, 154, 155–157, 217
 anti-crime methods comparison, 160–161
 bank fraud, 449
 business criminalization in, 154–155, 157
 causes of organized crime, 149–151, 162–163
 corruption in, 443, 444
 crime statistics, 147
 criminal organizations in, 152–154
 drug trafficking, 155–157
 Eastern region of, 237, 238
 emigration from, 189
 Mafia in, 149, 153–155, 157
 methods to combat crime, 157–159
 nature and extent of crime, 149–157, 158, 161–162, 440
 overview of, 146–149
 penitentiary system, 149
 police in, 148
 politics and organized crime, 9
 reforms needed in, 162–163
 victims of crime, 147–148
 violence in, 452
Russian criminal enterprises
 Austria, 193, 197–198
 Canada, 53
 Netherlands, 109
 Poland, 130–132
 United States, 30, 35–36

S

Salerno, Anthony, 449
Salvo, Ignazio, 88
Samant, Datta, 253
San-Yee-On, 287, 364
Savimbi, Jonas, 412
Savings and loan insolvencies, 74, 75
Search and surveillance issues
 Canada, 61–64, 65, 66
 Council of Europe, 223, 228–230
Seizure of goods and property. *See also* Proceeds of Crime legislation
 Australia, 345–346, 347
 Canada, 68–69
 Colombia, 307–308

Index

Council of Europe, 219
　overview of, 446
　United States, 446
Senate Bill 735 (U.S.), 41–42
Sentencing issues, 445–447
Sex slavery trade, 26
Sha-Lian gang, 286
Sicilian Mafia, 82–83, 86–87, 95–96, 305
Skims and scams, 447–452
Slovak Republic, 134–135
Slovenia
　activities of organized crime, 172–173
　anti-crime methods comparison, 179–185
　criminal groups in, 171–172
　criminal offenses in, 169–171
　definition of organized crime, 168–169
　methods to combat crime, 174–179
　nature and extent of crime, 168–174
　organizational measures, 178–179
　overview of, 165, 167
　penal measures, 174–176
　procedural measures, 176–178
Smuggling. *See also* drug trafficking; human smuggling
　Canada, 49–50, 52–53, 73, 74
　India, 246, 250–251, 253–254
　Zimbabwe, 412–413, 424–425, 433
Social culture, beliefs, and traditions, 2–3
Sophistication of group, 5
South Africa. *See also* Southern African Regional Police Chiefs Cooperation Organization (SARPCCO)
　anti-crime methods comparison, 388–390
　methods of combating crime, 383–388
　National Crime Prevention Strategy, 383–387
　nature and extent of crime, 381–383
　overview of, 379–381
　Police Plan, 384, 387
South America. *See also* Argentina; Colombia
　Bolivia, 304, 305, 312
　Brazil, 300, 312
　criminal enterprises in Austria from, 196
　drug trafficking in, 312
　overview of, 299–300
　Paraguay, 312
　Peru, 300, 304, 305, 312
　Uruguay, 300
　Venezuela, 300, 305, 312
Southern African Regional Police Chiefs Cooperation Organization (SARPCCO)
　South Africa and, 387
　Zambia and, 416–417, 418, 422, 423–424, 425
Statewide Integrated Resources Model, 36
Strasbourg Convention, 139, 203, 221
Strategic crime analysis, 118, 119
Surinam, criminal enterprises in Netherlands from, 107–108

T

Taiwan, 284, 285–286, 297
Teamster's Union, 446–447
Technical equipment for law enforcement, 184–185, 200, 269
Technology
　financial crime and, 383
　methods to deal with misuse of, 222–223, 226, 228–229
　theft of, 27, 38
Telecommunication theft, 51
Terrorism
　Baltic States, 136
　India, 253–254, 263
　international crime and, 24–25
　legislative initiatives in U.S., 41–42
　Tunisia, 392, 396, 397–398, 399, 403
　United Nations definition of, 129
Thailand, 238
Thieves-in-law (Russia), 153, 159
Third International Police Executive Symposium, 1–2
Threat of organized crime, 1, 380–381, 428
Trafficking. *See also* smuggling
　in drugs. *See* drug trafficking
　in firearms and precious stones in Zambia, 412–414, 424–425
　in humans. *See* human smuggling
Training initiatives
　Austria, 208–209
　New Zealand, 369
　overview of, 10–11
Transaction (Netherlands), 101, 102, 113–114
Transnational crime. *See also* international approach to organized crime
　activities of, 24
　approach to, 140–143
　areas of operations for, 23–25
　China and, 284
　coordination of anti-crime measures for, 43–44, 404–405
　groups operating, 396
　growth in, 185–186
　overview of, 10, 380
　Taiwan and, 286
　unwritten rules of, 313–314
Treaty of the Union, 93
TREVI group, 93–94, 140
Triad societies. *See* Chinese Triads
Tunisia
　anti-crime methods comparison, 402–404
　Central National Bureau, 400
　methods to combat crime, 398–402, 404–405
　nature and extent of crime, 396–398
　overview of, 392–393
Turkey, 107–108, 238

U

Undercover operations
　Canada, 62, 63, 69
　New Zealand, 371
　Slovenia, 179–180
United Nations
　activities against organized crime, 95
　Convention Against Traffic in Narcotic Drugs and Psychotropic Substances, 55–56, 137–138, 202
　Convention Against Transnational Organized Crime, 440–441
　definition of organized crime, 128–129

United Nations, *(continued)*
  Program of International Drug Control, 401
  recommendations of, 141–142
United States. *See also* Racketeer Influenced and Corrupt Organizations Statute (RICO)
  alien smuggling into, 25–26
  anti-crime methods comparison, 40–42
  areas of operations for organized crime in, 23–25
  assets of criminal enterprises, 219
  corruption in, 443
  definition of organized crime, 4, 5, 190–191
  drug trafficking, 20, 26–27, 28–32, 36–38
  financial crime, 25
  forfeiture laws, 219, 446
  government corruption and, 27–28
  groups operating in, 28–32
  hidden agenda of, 74–76
  linkage between organized crime in Italy and organized crime in, 439–440
  methods of combating crime, 32–42
  organized crime in, 19, 20, 23, 43–44, 242
  overview of, 22–23
  police corruption in, 445
  private sector or nonprofit organizations in, 38–40
  technology theft in, 27
United States Department of Justice
  International Criminal Investigative Training Assistance Program, 43
  Organized Crime Narcotics (OCN) Trafficking Enforcement Program, 36
United States Department of Treasury, Financial Crimes Enforcement Network (FinCEN), 37
Uruguay, 300

V

Van Traa, Maarten, 122
Vehicle theft
  Baltic States, 136
  Canada, 51
  Europe, 196
  Tunisia, 398–399
  Zambia, 408–409, 416–417, 421–422, 423
  Zimbabwe, 430
Venezuela, 300, 305, 312
Vietnamese criminal enterprises
  Canada, 52–53
  New Zealand, 365

United States, 31
Violence, increase in, 452–453

W

Waste processing industry
  Netherlands, 124–125
  United States, 450–451
Winer, Jonathan, 28
Witness intimidation and protection, 223–224, 225–226, 230–232
Wo group, 364
World Business Organization, 39
World Ministerial Conference on Organized Transnational Crime, 140–141, 142, 205

Y

Yakuza, 28, 453–454. *See also* Boryokudan
Yugoslav criminal enterprises
  Austria, 195–196
  Netherlands, 109

Z

Zambia
  anti-crime methods comparison, 421–425
  bank fraud, 414
  commercial poaching, 414–415
  drug trafficking, 409–411
  Integrated Rural Resource Development Project, 419
  methods to combat crime, 416–421
  money laundering, 8, 415–416, 422–425
  nature and extent of crime, 407–416
  overview of, 406–407, 425–426
  Species Protection Unit, 419
  trafficking in firearms and precious stones, 412–414
  vehicle theft, 408–409, 421–422
Zimbabwe
  anti-crime methods comparison, 435–437
  drug trafficking, 430–431
  financial crime, 432–433
  methods to combat crime, 433–435
  money laundering, 8
  nature and extent of crime, 430–433
  overview of, 427–428
  vehicle theft, 430
  violent crime, 432